The
FIRESIDE
Book of
Pro Football

EDITED BY

Richard Whittingham

A Fireside Book
Published by Simon & Schuster Inc.
NEW YORK   LONDON   TORONTO   SYDNEY   TOKYO

FIRESIDE
Simon & Schuster Building
Rockefeller Center
1230 Avenue of the Americas
New York, New York 10020

FIRESIDE and colophon are registered trademarks
of Simon & Schuster Inc.

Designed by Irving Perkins Associates, Inc.
Manufactured in the United States of America

10 9 8 7 6 5 4 3 2 1

Library of Congress Cataloging in Publication Data
Whittingham, Richard, date
    The Fireside book of pro football / Richard Whittingham.
      p. cm.
    ''A Fireside book.''
    Includes index.
      1. Football—United States.   I. Title.
  GV954.W46 1988
  796.332′0973—dc19   89-18239
                                     CIP

  ISBN 0–671–65996–0

We have made every effort to trace the ownership of all copyrighted material and to secure permission from copyright holders. In the event of any question arising as to the use of any material, we will be pleased to make the necessary corrections in future printings. Thanks are due to the following authors, publishers, publications, and agents for permission to use the material indicated:

''Namath'' from *Sports of Our Times* by Dave Anderson. Copyright © 1969/1971/1972/1978 by The New York Times Company. Reprinted by permission.

''The N.F.L., 1984'' by Dave Anderson. Copyright © 1975 by The New York Times Company. Reprinted by permission.

''An Anthropologist Looks at the Rituals of Football'' by William Arens. Copyright © 1975 by The New York Times Company. Reprinted by permission.

''Emotional Pain Dooms Ex-Football Star'' by Ira Berkow. Copyright © 1984 by The New York Times Company. Reprinted by permission.

''At Play in Green Bay'' by Johnny Blood from *What a Game They Played* by Richard Whittingham. Copyright © 1984 by Richard Whittingham. Reprinted by permission.

''The Chief and Family'' by Roy Blount, Jr. from *About Three Bricks Shy of a Load* by Roy Blount, Jr. Copyright © 1974 by Roy Blount, Jr. Reprinted by permission.

(*Continued on page 327*)

This book is dedicated to all the great sportswriters who have addressed professional football, from Grantland Rice and Damon Runyon during the game's infancy in the 1920s to the myriad of creative and entertaining journalists who have chronicled it since that time—all the way through the 1980s.

To Richard Youhn whose devotion to and knowledge of the sport is approximately equivalent to that of all the contributors here combined.

And to the memory of Tim McGinnis, a wonderful editor and friend whose imprint is indelibly inscribed on this book.

Contents

Contents

Contents

PREFACE

PROFESSIONAL FOOTBALL is the prodigy of college football—prodigy defined, according to *Webster's Unabridged Dictionary*, as "a marvel . . . , a thing or act so extraordinary as to inspire wonder; as a child prodigy." It was indeed sired by the collegiate game, which if not in its dotage was at least over 50 years old when the formal birth took place in Canton, Ohio in 1920. The newborn pro game, however, was less than prodigious in the eyes of its imperious father, who, in fact, viewed the offspring as the most illegitimate of sons.

Amos Alonzo Stagg, coach of the University of Chicago 11, and one of the college game's most revered leaders, spoke for the athletic interests of the proverbial groves of academe when he announced to the press in the early 1920s:

> For years, the colleges have been waging a bitter warfare against the insidious forces of the gambling public and alumni and against overzealous and short-sighted friends, inside and out, and also not infrequently against crooked coaches and managers, who have been anxious to win at any cost. . . . And now comes along another serious menace, possibly greater than all others, *viz* Sunday professional football.

Hard to believe, isn't it, that the eminent Stagg was talking about the sport that would alternately mesmerize and ferociously animate tens of millions of people on practically every autumn and winter Sunday of the 1980s? Was the illustrious Amos merely in his anecdotage when he spoke so harshly of the sport that would eventually spawn the vaunted, hyperhyped, megadollar extravaganza known as the Super Bowl, which each year virtually brings the nation to a standstill for three-and-a-half hours on a Sunday in late January?

It is the same animal.

Born in disrepute, forced to weather its adolescence through a major depression and a world war, pro football had a truly trying youth. There was such disdain from the colleges and various sports fans over the idea of young men playing the game of football for (horrors!) money that in those early years the teams even took to calling their game "Post Graduate Football."

The press religiously followed college football, but as far as the pros were concerned, they might just as well have been playing sandlot soccer. As George Halas, end/coach/co-owner of the Chicago Bears remembered: "The newspaper people didn't even bother to come out to our games those first few years. The headline on the sports pages on a Sunday morning would be '50,000 see Illinois Beat Chicago' or 'Notre Dame Wins Again,' and then column after column about the colleges. We'd be lucky if we got a paragraph or two in the middle of the sports section. So I paid a press agent $10 a game to write it up and then my partner, Dutch Sternaman and I, after the game, would take copies of the story down to all the Chicago newspapers."

Is that the same sport that issues 2,000 sets of press credentials to members of the media and those others who produce the printed word for a *single* Super Bowl game?

Well, the change began in 1925. That was the year in which the already legendary Illinois halfback Harold "Red" Grange, aka the Galloping Ghost, finished his college career on a Saturday afternoon in November and began his pro career five days later on Thanksgiving Day, playing for the Chicago Bears against their then crosstown rivals, the Cardinals.

The redhead's decision to become a pro startled the sports world. His Illini coach, Bob Zuppke, had urged him against it. "Football isn't meant to be played for money. Stay away from professionalism." Grange countered: "You get paid for coaching, Zup. Why should it be wrong for me to get paid for playing?" With logic on his side, the Galloping Ghost joined the pros and Coach Zuppke did not speak to the greatest player he would ever coach for several years thereafter.

With Grange in the ranks, however, pro football suddenly became an entity to be reckoned with. When the Bears with their featured rookie traveled to New York to take on the Giants, the change in the game was forever evident. The fans flooded the stadium, and the press, the mightiest pens among them, were there as well. None other than Damon Runyon captured the historic moment for the *New York American*:

> I hear preach from the old familiar text,
> *It pays to advertise.*
> There gathered at the Polo Grounds in Harlem this afternoon the largest crowd that ever witnessed a football game on the island of Manhattan, drawn by

the publicity that has been given one individual—Red Harold Grange, late of the University of Illinois.

Seventy thousand men, women, and children were in the stands, blocking the aisles and runways. Twenty thousand more were perched on Coogan's Bluff and the roofs of apartment houses overlooking the baseball home of McGraw's club, content with just an occasional glimpse of the whirling mass of players on the field far below and wondering which was Red Grange. . . .

Listening in on the various discussions of the experts, one gathered a consensus that the professionals presented a nice line of football.

The gridiron savants agreed that the boys were in there fighting hard and that they played as well as college teams, which is not surprising, in view of the fact that most of the players have been at it from six to nine years.

When Grange and the Bears went on a barnstorming tour of the nation over the next two months, from Boston to Florida to the California coast, Runyon wrote about it, so did Grantland Rice and Westbrook Pegler, as well as scores of other lesser known scribes.

Suddenly the entire United States began to take notice of the phenomenon of men playing the game of football and getting paid for it. Well, not everybody. As Red Grange himself liked to tell the story: "There was the time we went to the White House. This was in December 1925, a couple of weeks after I joined the Bears. We were playing an exhibition game with a team called the Washington All-Stars, and it was the first time the Bears played in Washington, D. C. Senator McKinley of Illinois, called George [Halas] and me and asked if we wanted to meet President Coolidge. The senator sent his car to pick us up, and when we arrived he introduced me to the President as 'Red Grange, who plays with the Bears.' Coolidge shook hands and said, 'Young man, I always liked animal acts.' "

The barnstorming tour was a turning point in the time-line of professional football in America. A continuation in the trend toward recognition came in the 1930s with the showcasing of football stars of such exceptional magnitude as Bronko Nagurski, Don Hutson, and Sammy Baugh.

The era of T-formation quarterbacks and the passing game came of age in the postwar years with talented tossers like Sid Luckman, Bob Waterfield, Otto Graham, and, of course, Slingin' Sam himself, who made the difficult transition from single wing tailback to T-formation quarterback. Then came television, and after that, no one would ever again question either the quality of play or the popularity of the sport.

It has changed dramatically. The player who once toiled for $50 a game in the 1920s has been replaced by the player who has a multimillion dollar contract, a portfolio of annuities, an agent, and an accountant. The team that six or so decades ago performed for 5,000 spectators who sat on wooden bleachers has been transformed into one that plays in a domed stadium replete with skyboxes, heating, air conditioning, and artificial turf before a live gathering of 70,000 and television and radio audiences numbering in the millions.

And over the years, pro football has brought out the best in sportswriters. It has begged them to be creative in their analyses of the game and in the language they use to describe it. As an example, the fabled Red Smith writing about the Green Bay Packers the year before Vince Lombardi arrived, who had rung up a record of 1 win, 11 losses, and 1 tie: "The Packers were the most soft-bitten team in the league; they overwhelmed one, underwhelmed eleven, and whelmed one."

Then there was Larry Merchant, writer and wit *extraordinaire,* who loved to capture the downhome grit of those who played the game, describing the reason the Los Angeles Rams were victorious over the New York Giants, 31–3, in a 1970 game: "Some Giants advanced the Theory of Up and Down to explain the shellacking. The Rams were Up, the Giants were, by definition, Down. This is one of football's most popular and trickiest theories. (A euphemism for Down is flat, as in Joe Schmidt's classic postgame urinalysis, 'We were flat as a plate of piss.')"

It is the wonderful words, thoughts, and reminiscences of these wits and wags, serious scribes, and storytellers of varying ilks that comprise this anthology of some of the very best and most entertaining writing ever addressed to the sport of professional football. The stories tell of times past, of strange and raucous goings-on behind the scenes, of the vast array of characters who formed the game's inimitable and chaotic cast.

On the ensuing pages, the curious fan will find the humor of Merchant, Dan Jenkins, and Pete Gent; the uninhibited incantations of such roisterers as Johnny Blood, Shipwreck Kelly, and Kenny Stabler; the pathos of the demise of Big Daddy Lipscomb and Ira Berkow's moving tale of the terrible doom of another, lesser known football player; the poems of Ogden Nash and Grantland Rice; the insights of Vince Lombardi, John Madden, and George Halas; the acerbics of Shirley Povich; and the wonderful paeans to the game and its players by such gifted lyricists as George Plimpton, Red Smith, Roger Kahn, and Frank Deford. Among much else.

Amos Alonzo Stagg, with all due respect, we've got something here in the following few hundred pages we'd like you to read.

Richard Whittingham

The
FIRESIDE
Book of

Pro
Football

During his playing days, Joe Namath, among other things, brought the American Football League its first Super Bowl trophy, guest-hosted "The Tonight Show" in Johnny Carson's absence, introduced Bachelor's III to the Manhattan saloon scene, and modeled pantyhose on television. Despite awful knees and a frenetically burdensome social life, with his heaven-cast right arm he earned his way into the Pro Football Hall of Fame. During the journey to that Canton, Ohio edifice, Broadway Joe garnered more ink in the nation's newspapers and magazines than perhaps any football player in the second half of the twentieth century. This entertaining and insightful article devoted to the young man from Beaver Falls, Pennsylvania is from the pen of one of America's most respected sports columnists, Dave Anderson of the *New York Times*.

Namath

DAVE ANDERSON

THERE MUST be two Joe Namaths—the one some other sportswriters don't like and the one I do like. I've liked him from the first time I met him. He had come to New York for his first knee operation in 1965 shortly after having signed his $427,000 contract. Sonny Werblin, then the Jets' president, arranged a get-together with the New York writers in the upstairs room at Toots Shor's old restaurant. Not a news conference, just stop by, meet the rookie quarterback and have a drink. After a while, I was sitting at a small table with Lou Effrat, a *Times* sportswriter who had covered pro football for years, when Joe slouched over with a drink in his hand. Lou stared up at him.

"Joe," he said, "suppose you don't make it, Joe, what happens to the money?"

Joe never blinked. He looked at Lou and replied easily, "I'll make it."

I liked that. No false modesty. No hedging. No song and dance. No boasting either; just flat confidence. And the more I was around Joe Namath, the more I liked him. At his first training camp, I was talking to the Jets' two other quarterbacks—Mike Taliaferro, the holdover, and John Huarte, the Heisman Trophy rookie from Notre Dame who had a $200,000 contract. One of them mentioned that Joe had been classified 1-A in the military draft. I had stumbled on a big story but I didn't want to overreact. When Joe came by, I mentioned it casually and he confirmed it casually.

"Why don't you get married?" I suggested. "They're not taking married guys."

"I'd rather go to Vietnam," he answered with a grin, "than get married."

The next day I checked with his Beaver Falls, Pa., draft board. After the lady who answered the phone confirmed that he was 1-A, I thanked her and said, "Joe is big in New York."

"Joe," she said, "is big everywhere."

Bigger than even she and I thought, as it turned out.

The next day, to my surprise, my story was across the top of the *Journal-American*'s front page. All hell broke loose because the Jets had been trying to keep Joe's draft status quiet. He had to endure "one of those days," as he later called them, when newsmen were all around. That night I was in the Jets' press room at training camp when Joe strolled in, picked up a copy of the *Journal-American* and read my story. At one point he shook his head and said quietly, "I wish you hadn't used that line about Vietnam," but he knew he hadn't been misquoted. When he finished, he said, "I was a phys. ed. major at Alabama, not a business major."

"Sorry about that," I said. "I thought you took business."

He put the *Journal-American* down, said, "See you tomorrow," and strolled out of the press room as casually as he had entered. Other athletes of my acquaintance might have complained that the story had been "blown out of proportion," which perhaps it had been with the front-page treatment. Others might have griped that with so much publicity now, the Selective Service doctors would be tougher. But not Joe Namath; all he seemed concerned about was his quote about Vietnam and being incorrectly identified as a business major.

About a month later he was classified 4-F because of his wobbly right knee. He needed another operation on that knee following the 1967 season. That's when I liked Joe even more.

The week before Christmas that year, the Jets announced that Joe's surgery would be performed December 28, so I phoned him in Beaver Falls to get his reaction. As soon as I told him about the Jets' announcement, he snapped, "Damn it, I asked them not to announce anything until after Christmas because I didn't want my mother worrying over the holidays." We talked for a few more minutes, wished each other a Merry Christmas and I started writing. Half an hour later, Phil Pepe of the *Daily News* phoned me.

"I was just talking to Namath," said Phil, "and he told me to call you and say that he didn't realize it was going to be one of those days when everybody was calling him, that he thought he was quick with you and if you need anything else, he's still at that number."

I didn't need anything else, but I phoned Joe anyway. When he answered, I told him, "Now I know why all those broads think you're a helluva guy." I also told him that I had all the quotes I needed and that I didn't think he had been quick with me but that I appreciated his thoughtfulness.

"All right," he said. "I just wanted to make sure."

In my more than twenty-five years in the newspaper business, nobody else has ever done anything quite that thoughtful. Or quite that professional either. Joe Namath was a professional, on and off the field. It just took him

more time on the field. Rookie quarterbacks don't make it instantly, not even in the old American Football League, which the Jets belonged to then. But like most rookie quarterbacks, he believed his arm was enough. In those years the Jets' training camp was at the Peekskill (N.Y.) Military Academy, a decrepit prep school in its last years. In one of Joe's first workouts, wide receiver Don Maynard streaked downfield on a deep pattern. Joe let go a long pass that looked as if it might land in Vermont and it might as well have. He overthrew Maynard by at least ten yards. Coach Weeb Ewbank walked over to his rookie quarterback.

"You don't have to show me your arm," Weeb said softly. "If you couldn't throw, you wouldn't be here."

What the rookie quarterback had to learn was what Weeb always preached—it's one thing to throw a football, it's another to complete passes. But in his third season, Joe Namath completed 258 of 491 passes for 4,007 yards, the only quarterback ever to go over 4,000 yards in a season. Even so, those 4,007 yards did not change the skeptics' view that Joe Namath was merely a product of the A.F.L., that he wouldn't make it big in the N.F.L.—but the N.F.L.'s principal authority at the time, Vince Lombardi, was not among the skeptics.

"Joe Namath," the Green Bay Packers' coach told me early in 1968, "is an almost perfect passer."

In his 1968 opener, the almost perfect passer preserved a 20–19 victory in Kansas City by moving the Jets out from their own 4-yard line and controlling the ball for the last six minutes. But earlier in that game he was being dragged down by two Chiefs when he chose to throw anyway. Willie Lanier intercepted the short wobbly pass. Far down in my *Times* game story, I described it as a "foolish" pass. I soon forgot about that line but Joe didn't. Five weeks later in Houston he moved the Jets to the winning touchdown in the closing minutes for a 20–14 victory. On the Jets' charter home that night, Joe slid into a seat across the aisle and turned to me. "Well, David," he said with a grin, "did I throw any foolish passes today?"

Like most people, I usually think of a comeback about three days later. But for once, as I recalled that line about the "foolish" pass in Kansas City, I had an answer.

"I'm flattered, Joseph," I said. "I didn't think you read me that closely."

"That was a bad pass I threw," he insisted, "but it wasn't a foolish pass."

I laughed, he laughed, and that ended the semantics. About two months later, we had a much longer conversation on a Jets' charter, but this time we were going to Super Bowl III, where the Jets had been installed as 17-point underdogs. Much of what he said appeared in the *Times* the next Sunday, a week before the game:

FORT LAUDERDALE—Joe Namath had been lobbing passes on the practice field when Emerson Boozer appeared, the last of the New York Jets to emerge from the locker room.

"I told you, Weeb," yelled Namath, grinning. "I told you Emerson would practice this week."

"Well," said the coach, Weeb Ewbank, "it's nice of you to do us a favor today, Emerson."

The three of them laughed. The halfback had been delayed in the trainer's room, where his surgical knee required taping. Ironically, the true humor of the situation was that Namath, who is excused from the team calisthenics because of his surgical knees, usually is the last Jet out to practice. But not these days.

Joe Namath is preparing to challenge the superiority of the National Football League next Sunday in the Super Bowl game with the Baltimore Colts.

And when Joe Namath is confronted with a challenge, beware. As a $400,000 rookie he challenged the salary structure of pro football, but he proved to be a bargain. With his Fu Manchu mustache, he challenged the tonsorial tradition of American athletics, but he shaved it off for a $10,000 fee.

As the symbol of the American Football League, he is confronted with the challenge of penetrating the Colt defense.

His attitude is significant. Occasionally he presents a droopy appearance, but not now. He's alive and alert. When he saw the Jets' white uniforms, which they will wear in the Super Bowl, hanging in their lockers here, he reacted immediately.

"We're wearing the white uniforms," he shouted to his teammates. "That must mean we're the good guys."

He's anxious to face his moment of truth. But he's not awed by it or by the Colts.

"When the Colts lost to the Browns at midseason," he was saying on the Jets' chartered flight last Thursday night, "they didn't get beat by any powerhouse. I'm not going to take what I read about their defense. I'm going to go with what the one-eyed monster shows me."

The one-eyed monster is the projector that shows films of the Colts.

"The one-eyed monster doesn't lie," he said. "He shows it like it is."

In his blue turtleneck shirt and maroon corduroy slacks, he was sitting, as he usually does, on the left side of the aisle. That way he can extend his tender right leg into the aisle. But on this flight the seat in front of him was empty. He had folded the back rest and his right leg was stretched across it.

"When we won our title last Sunday, I said that Daryle Lamonica of the Raiders was a better quarterback than Earl Morrall, and now that's supposed to fire up the Colts.

"I said it and I meant it. Lamonica is better. If the Colts use newspaper clippings to get up for a game, they're in trouble. And if they're football players they know Lamonica can throw better than Morrall. I watch quarterbacks, I watch what they do.

"You put Babe Parilli with Baltimore," he continued, referring to the Jets' backup quarterback, "and Baltimore might have been better. Babe throws better than Morrall.

"There are more teams in the N.F.L. so they should have more good teams, but you put their good teams and our good teams together, or their bad teams and our bad teams together, and it's fifty-fifty, flip a coin. And we've got better quarterbacks in our league—John Hadl, Lamonica, myself and Bob Griese."

Hadl directs the San Diego Chargers, while Griese is with the Miami Dolphins.

"I read where some N.F.L. guy joked about Lamonica and me throwing one hundred passes last Sunday," he said. "We threw ninety-seven, but what's so terrible about that? How many N.F.L. teams have a quarterback who could complete as many passes to their wide receivers? In our league, we throw much more to our wide receivers.

"I completed forty-nine percent of my passes this season, but I could have completed eighty percent if I dropped the ball off to my backs like they do in their league. For wide receivers the Jets have the best. George Sauer has the best moves, nobody can cover him one on one, and Don Maynard is the smartest.

"The best thrower in the N.F.L. is Sonny Jurgensen of the Redskins. I've said that if Jurgensen had been with the Packers or the Colts or the Rams the last few years, he would have won the championship for any of them. But if you put any pro quarterback on our team, only a few would not be on third string.

"That's my opinion, and I don't care how people value my opinion. But I value it very highly, especially when I'm talking about football."

In his fourth season, Namath is considered to have matured as a quarterback, notably after two early-season games when the Buffalo Bills and the Denver Broncos each intercepted five of his passes to achieve upset victories. During his last ten games, including the title game, he had six interceptions.

"But after those games with the five interceptions," he acknowledged, "I disciplined myself as to throwing the ball. I was overcautious at times. I remembered an old rule: The only way to win is to keep from losing."

In the league title game an interception positioned the touchdown that put the Oakland Raiders ahead, 23–20, midway in the final quarter. But it did not deter Namath from connecting for three consecutive completions in moving the Jets 68 yards in 55 seconds for the winning touchdown of the 27–23 triumph.

"After that interception," he said, "I just told myself, 'you got eight minutes and you got to score.' That's all."

His arm has been his great gift, but he mentioned the luck factor for an athlete.

"Any player has to be lucky," he said. "Take our kicker, Jim Turner—suppose he had to have an operation on his right knee when he was playing quarterback at Utah State. If he did, he'd never be kicking now. I was lucky because I was trained good by my brothers, Bob and Frank, and I've had good coaches.

"Larry Bruno, my coach at Beaver Falls High School, he was terrific. We had thirteen guys go on scholarships to college, thirteen guys from one team. And to go from a coach like that to Coach Bear Bryant at Alabama, a kid has to be lucky. He made me feel proud to be a part of his team. I learned a lot from Coach Bryant.

"And then coming here, with Weeb, was lucky for me. Until this season, I don't think I really appreciated Weeb, but now I realize how hard he works.

"Something the trainer, Jeff Snedeker, said one day made me realize it. He told me that when he got to the locker room at eight o'clock one morning, Weeb already was there taking a whirlpool bath. I mean Weeb's an old man, he's about sixty, and he was in the locker room before eight o'clock in the morning.

"And the day we came back from San Diego after just about clinching our division, Weeb and the coaches got off the plane at seven in the morning and went straight to the stadium. They could have taken a break, but they didn't.

"I've had my disagreements with Weeb, I probably always will. I'm that kind. Like last Sunday, after we won the championship, there's a league rule that you're not supposed to have champagne in the clubhouse. But I told Weeb to break it out, and that all of us were three times seven and that I'd pay the fine out of my pocket.

"And later Mr. [Milt] Woodard, the league president, came over to talk to me about it and I told him that I thought it's a stupid rule, that all of us were three times seven and that it was the biggest day of our lives.

"Mr. Woodard tried to tell me that it was bad for the image of football, that it was bad for the kids to see it. You know what the real image of football is, it's brutality. Why don't they tell the kids like it is? Tell the kids that this guy is trying to hurt that guy and knock him out of the football game.

"Like the letters I get from people who hope some guy cripples me because of my mustache."

Namath swirled the ice in his plastic cup and glanced at his right knee across the folded seat.

"Some of those letters," he said, "I read for entertainment because those people are sick. Or maybe I'm the sick one, but I'm happy the way I'm sick."

(January 5, 1969)

On the Thursday night before the game, Joe was to be honored by the Miami Touchdown Club as pro football's outstanding player that season. That morning I asked him if he needed a ride. "No," he said, "they're sending somebody to pick me up. Ride with me." As it developed, I was the only other person in the turquoise Cadillac driven by Joe Facile, a used-car-lot manager who had been assigned to pick him up. Before leaving the Galt Ocean Mile in Fort Lauderdale, where the Jets were lodged, Joe stopped in the bar for a big paper cup of scotch and ice. As he sipped his drink all the way down Interstate 95 to the Miami Springs Villas, we talked of why we thought the Jets would win. It didn't surprise me when, during his acceptance speech, he said:

"And we're going to win Sunday, I'll guarantee you."

He didn't say it boastfully or loudly. He said it as casually as he had said "I'll make it" that first night I met him. He said it so casually, in fact, that I didn't react to it until his "guarantee" was in headlines in the Miami *Herald* the next morning. In big bold type his "guarantee" suddenly had much more impact than it had the night before, probably much more than Joe had intended. But when the headline appeared, he didn't back off. Neither did Weeb Ewbank.

"That's the way Joe feels about it," the coach said, "and I'm for him. I wouldn't give a darn for him if he didn't think we could win. I don't think Joe's whistling Dixie at all."

The psychology of the "guarantee" seemed to lift the Jets, but the Colts were annoyed. Their coach, Don Shula, agreed that Namath's prediction had created a "challenge" for the Colt players. Shula's use of that word was interesting. Originally, the challenge of Super Bowl III had confronted the Jets in challenging the N.F.L. establishment. But now the Colts were confronted with the challenge of Joe Namath's "guarantee." Coming down on the charter, remember, he had said, "It's going to be a challenge for us, but it's going to be a challenge for them too."

As it turned out, it was a challenge the Colts did not respond to in the Jets' 16–7 victory. Because of his "guarantee," Joe Namath has been thought of as a prophet, but he had not been trying to be a prophet—he just had been himself. Six months later he again was himself when he retired from football rather than obey Commissioner Pete Rozelle's edict that he sell his share in Bachelors III, an East Side bistro that was frequented by alleged "undesirable" customers. After a few weeks he capitulated to the commissioner and a news conference was hastily called in N.F.L. headquarters. When the reporters and cameramen had assembled, the commissioner and the quarterback sat together behind a table—the commissioner in an expensively tailored blue suit with a white shirt and a striped tie, the quarterback in a sport shirt, jeans and sneakers.

"Are we ready," the commissioner asked, looking around at the newsmen. "All set?"

"Hold it," Howard Cosell barked in his nasal voice as he stared at a cameraman who was fiddling with some wires. "My man's not ready."

"Fuck your man," Joe Namath said.

Howard sneered but the commissioner laughed, the newsmen laughed and Maxine Isenberg laughed. Mrs. Isenberg, one of the N.F.L. secretaries, was there to record the news conference. When somebody motioned to Joe that a lady was in a corner of the room, he glanced at her and winced.

"Excuse me, ma'am," he said softly.

She laughed again, and moments later, when the cameraman was ready, the news conference began. Joe's surrender was official. I've always thought that the Bachelors III episode drained him of some of his enthusiasm for football in 1969 and 1970. But in 1971, after having missed most of the previous season with a broken bone in his passing wrist, his enthusiasm returned. At training camp he even drew a "smile" symbol—a circle surrounding two dots for the eyes and a curved line for the mouth—on the left knee of his white football pants. That knee had required tendon surgery in 1968.

But in the Jets' first exhibition game, the smile was wiped off that left knee.

Against the Detroit Lions, he threw an interception. In trying to tackle Mike Lucci, the Lions' linebacker, he was blocked by Paul Naumoff, another linebacker. Ligaments in his left knee were torn. He needed his fourth knee operation. After the Jets returned to New York that night, I accompanied Dr. James Nicholas, the team orthopedist, to Lenox Hill Hospital where the operation would be performed:

Below, on Park Avenue, the only movement occurred when traffic lights changed in the morning darkness of the empty streets.

On the seventh floor of Lenox Hill Hospital early yesterday, Joe Namath, wearing a blue hospital gown, sat on his bed. His left leg extended, he winced as Dr. James A. Nicholas, the New York Jets' orthopedic surgeon, examined the knee with his fingers, probing the ligaments.

"Here?" the doctor asked.

"Yeah," Namath answered, grimacing sharply.

"Here?"

"Not bad."

"Here?"

"Yeah," said Namath, his voice rising. "Ow."

"There it is," the doctor said.

Namath's kneecap wobbled from side to side, like a door without hinges, as the doctor held it and nodded.

"The anterior cruciate," Nicholas said.

"You mean something's wrong with that?"

The quarterback knows the medical terms. Three surgical scars curved along his right knee, another on his left. He had been in Lenox Hill Hospital for three previous knee operations. Now, as Nicholas arranged for a "seven o'clock incision," Namath winced again at the rate for his private room, for which the Jets pay.

"It's a hundred and forty-eight dollars a day," he said. "It was sixty-five dollars a day the first time I was here, ninety-eight dollars a day the second and third times."

Soon the doctor departed for a couple of hours of sleep. It's his habit to operate as quickly as possible before the knee ligaments lose their elasticity. Namath had been injured about nine o'clock Saturday night in Tampa, Fla., but the operation would be completed here about twelve hours later.

"I feel more comfortable about this one," Namath was saying to Jimmy Walsh, his attorney. "Having been through it before."

Suddenly, the quarterback grabbed his left leg. He had a cramp in it, and he tightened his lips as he rolled onto his side.

"If it just wouldn't cramp," he said. "You can't do anything about it. And the worst is a cramp when it's in a cast. Cramp, cramp, go away, come back in about eight weeks."

By then, the cast will have been removed. But he talked of rejoining the Jets at their training camp while the cast remained.

"I don't know if it'll do me any good physically," he said, "but maybe it'll help them. I want to coach Al Woodall. I'm going to work with him as much as I can. After the way he played last year and with five more exhibitions, he might be able to do it."

Instead of pitying himself, the star quarterback had reacted stoically and fatalistically to his latest injury.

"What am I going to do?" he explained. "If it's supposed to happen, it's supposed to happen. The more you go through these things, the more you learn to adjust. With the exception of my leg, I feel pretty normal. I don't know if it's dawned on me yet."

He searched for the remote-control switch to operate the TV on a raised platform, but he couldn't find it.

"I'm going to get some movies for you," Walsh said. "We can close the blinds to make a screen. We'll charge three dollars a head, half a dozen people, that's eighteen dollars a night."

"It still won't be able to pay for the room," Namath said, grinning. "Damn, a hundred and forty-eight dollars a day, that's one thousand thirty-six dollars a week. But if you bring the films, bring my popcorn popper."

Soon an attendant arrived with a wheelchair to transport Namath to the X-ray room. He hobbled over and sat in it.

Two hours earlier, hobbling off the Jets' chartered airliner at LaGuardia Airport, he had noticed a gray canvas wheelchair in the rampway. He glanced at the skycap behind it and shook his head.

"No," he said firmly.

The left leg of his pink bell-bottom pants had been slit to the thigh in order to permit ice packs to be wrapped to the knee. Ignoring the wheelchair, he hobbled stiffly through the polished corridor of the terminal. Outside, a black limousine sped him across the Triborough Bridge to the hospital.

"He's proud," one of his teammates had said. "He didn't want any of us to see him in the wheelchair, or anybody else."

Now, after his return from the X-ray room, Namath rolled over as a nurse poised a hypodermic needle above his rump.

"Pick a soft spot," he said, smiling.

"Ain't no soft spot here," she said.

Not long after that, she returned with another needle. He glared at her and winked.

"If you hurt me again," he said, rolling over, "I'm going to slap your hand."

Outside, dawn filtered through the nearby apartment houses and office buildings. Pigeons soared across the rooftops. Below, a few cars moved along Park Avenue as the city began to stir with sun glittering on windows.

"It's a nice day," Walsh said.

Dozing now, his operation about an hour away, Joe Namath stirred, then grimaced as he turned his left leg. He glanced out the window at the daylight. Thinking of a phrase he remembered from *Little Big Man,* the movie, he smiled.

"It's a good day to die," he said.

(August 9, 1971)

But he was alive again late that season, returning to throw three touchdown passes against the San Francisco 49ers that almost pulled out a 24–21 loss. Early in the 1972 season at Baltimore he had his most productive game as a passer. I had stayed in New York that day to watch the Giants lose but I found Joe late that night.

In the dim light, Joe Namath swirled the ice in his glass. He was drinking vodka on the rocks with a splash of Kahlua, a Black Russian, and he was grinning.

"At the airport in Baltimore, waiting for the plane, Gerry Philbin came over to me," he said, referring to the New York Jets' defensive end. "He said, 'Damn it, we come out of the game after they score, but when you score on the first play, we have to go right back in. Damn it, give us a rest.' And he laughed. Everybody laughed."

On the jukebox at Bachelors III early yesterday morning, Tom Jones was singing "She's a Lady." At a table in the rear, Joe Namath had on a turtleneck shirt, jeans and sneakers. He was sitting with a few friends, and every so often he would sign an autograph for a stranger as he waited for a steak, French fries and salad.

"I'm hungry," he said. "I ain't eaten all day. I didn't have but two bites of steak at the pre-game meal down there."

With two bites of steak for nourishment, he had passed for six touchdowns and 496 yards as the Jets outscored the Colts, 44–34, in the most outstanding performance by a passer in National Football League history. Two other quarterbacks accumulated more yardage, but each did it against inferior teams. Norm Van Brocklin of the Los Angeles Rams totaled 554 yards in 1951 against the New York Yanks, who won one game that season. Y. A. Tittle of the New York Giants threw for 505 yards in 1962 against the Washington Redskins, who had a 5–7 won-lost record. But on Sunday, the Jets' quarterback dissected one of N.F.L.'s most respected defensive units.

"That's amazing, it really is," he was saying now. "I was lucky. Some days you got it and some days you don't, and some days you can spit in a swinging jug. But if a good quarterback has time, he can do well against a zone. If you have time, all you do is send one or two people deep in one area and another deep underneath, and that man underneath should be open. I had good time, but Bubba Smith not being in there for the Colts was a factor in me having time, a titantic factor. I'm not taking anything away from their defensive ends, they're outstanding players. But our interior line was giving me the time I needed to look at that zone."

In the final quarter he collaborated with Rich Caster, the tight end, for a 79-yard touchdown but then Johnny Unitas's second touchdown pass had narrowed the Jets' lead to 37–34 with about six minutes remaining.

"Waiting for the kickoff," he was saying now, "I was thinking about another long pass to Caster on the first play, but I wasn't sure if I should risk it, only three points ahead. But then I said to myself, 'If you ain't confident, you don't belong here,' so I decided to try to score again quick because I knew there ain't no way we're going to use up the clock running the ball in that situation. I knew the Colts would be storming the walls, and the first play, they were blitzing, but I had it picked up. I knew Caster had to be one-on-one so I just hustled the hell back there, set up, let it go and it was just right.''

He acknowledged that his new $500,000 contract over two years is his new motivation.

"I got paid for it, I'm supposed to do the job. It's cut and dried. I want to be convinced myself that I earned that money. I am so far, I always have been anyway. Comparatively speaking, wage-wise, it's way out of balance with the rest of the team. But situation-wise, it's not out of balance. Contract is business. Then after the business part comes the playing part. And that's still a business, but it's physical, it's a game, it's fun, it's emotional.''

His performance Sunday should convince the skeptics that he belongs with all the great quarterbacks—not that he had to be convinced.

"I'm convinced I'm better than anybody else," he said. "I've been convinced of that for quite a while. I haven't seen anything out there that I couldn't do and do well. When you go back to Sammy Baugh, guys like that, they were great, sure, but it wasn't the game it is now. Johnny Unitas is great, but I just like to believe I'm better. Out there playing, I get annoyed at myself for doing something wrong. Sometimes I tell myself, 'You ain't too good,' and that helps me play better because then I tell myself, 'You're the best, damn it, do it right.' ''

Another drink arrived. The quarterback mixed the Kahlua with the vodka, and smiled.

"You want to take a sauna with me out at Shea tomorrow?" he said to Mickey Kearney, one of the people with him. "By the time I'm finished tonight, I'll need a sauna.''

(September 26, 1972)

When he went to Baltimore the next season, he needed another hospital room. Stan White, the Colts' line-backer, had blitzed and pounced on him, slamming him into the hard brown dirt of Memorial Stadium's leveled pitcher's mound. His right shoulder was separated. But he didn't complain. He never did. Once he was talking with Bob Oates of the Los Angeles *Times* about whether the N.F.L. should create stricter rules to protect quarterbacks.

"I hope they don't do that," Joe said firmly.

"Why not?" Bob wondered. "It would help you.''

"Nothing should be done to detract from the essence of the game—the fight to get at the quarterback, the fight between the offensive line and the defensive line. If the defense wins, you've got to give them their trophy.''

"Their trophy?" Bob asked.

"Me," Joe Namath answered.

Sometimes he was a battered trophy. I was in Oakland the day in 1967 when Ben Davidson, the Raiders' huge defensive end, assaulted him with a taped right hand, spinning Joe's helmet across the sideline as if he had been beheaded. Joe's cheekbone had been fractured. That evening his face was swollen and he couldn't talk without wincing. But the Jets had a couple of days off before they were to regroup in San Diego for the final game of the season. In the lobby of their Oakland motel he appeared in a tuxedo with a glass of scotch in one hand.

"Where are you going?" somebody asked him.

"I'm catching a plane for Vegas," he said.

The next Sunday, with a protective mask over his cheekbone, he completed his 4,007-yard season, then celebrated with a few more glasses of scotch. But by 1973 he had switched to vodka, and in 1975, when he turned down an allegedly guaranteed $5 million offer from the Chicago Fire of the World Football League, he was drinking blackberry brandy.

"I wouldn't feel comfortable there," he said of the W.F.L. offer. "It was too big a chance.''

He realized that if the W.F.L. didn't succeed, much of his stature would be tarnished, no matter how successful he might have been personally. He realized that his stature affected his future as a commodity in business ventures and in his ambition to be an actor. And that indeed was too big a chance to take. But when his Jet contract expired after the 1976 season, he took a big chance. He joined the Los Angeles Rams for his last hurrah—to prove that Joe Namath was still Joe Namath.

"Some people don't think I can play anymore," he told me the day before the season opener in Atlanta, "but they're wrong and I'm going to prove them wrong.''

He didn't. After four games in 1977, the Rams were 2–2 and he had a bruised knee; also a bruised ego. On a rainy Monday night against the Chicago Bears in Soldier Field, he had completed only 16 of 40 passes, with four interceptions, in a 24–23 loss. Late in that game Pat Haden took over as the Rams' quarterback and Joe never played another down. I've always thought that the reason Joe threw so often that night in the rain was that he wanted to prove on prime-time national television that he was as good as ever. I mentioned my theory to Joe when he was at Super Bowl XII to do a TV show.

"No," he said. "Our game plan that night was to throw.''

During the rehearsal, I also asked him if he planned to retire. "I have a pretty good idea of what I'm going to do," he said, "but I don't want to talk about it until I talk to the Rams about it." Later that month I phoned him in Fort Lauderdale, Fla., to do a question-and-answer piece for our Sports Monday section. I wanted to get him to look back at his career and also to look ahead. I was sure he was going to retire, but I expected him to repeat that he didn't want to talk about it yet.

"Have you decided anything?" I asked him.

"I'm not going to play next year," he said.

"We can't hold that until Monday," I said.

He knew that as well as I did. His retirement story started on the *Times'* front page. He soon signed to do a movie and a TV situation comedy. I happened to be in Los Angeles when he went into rehearsal for the TV series:

BEVERLY HILLS—Out on the patio, palm trees filtered the glow of sunset. In the pastel elegance of the Polo Lounge at the Beverly Hills Hotel, the beautiful people paraded to their tables for a drink before dinner. Sitting near the door, Joe Namath was gazing at a blonde walking by when a gray-haired waiter leaned over and whispered, "I hear you're Joe now instead of Harry."

"Yeah," he said, "we've got to reshoot a couple of scenes that were in the pilot."

Joe Namath has begun rehearsing a TV situation comedy, *The Waverly Wonders,* in which he portrays a former pro basketball player hired to coach a high school team that has never won a game. In the original script, his name was Harry Casey but now he's Joe Casey.

"They decided," he explained, "that I'm a Joe, not a Harry."

He passed up a tray of dip and crackers as he sipped iced Sanka.

"I haven't had a drink in two months," he said. "I just decided to stop drinking, just like when I stopped smoking ten years ago."

Joe Namath had begun rehearsing *The Waverly Wonders* at a Sunset Boulevard studio on Thursday.

"It's a long day," he said. "It's like training camp with two-a-day workouts."

Training camp. For the first time since before he was in high school, Joe Namath is not in a football training camp. Instead, he is in a TV studio from 9 A.M. to 5 P.M. five days a week. Dick Martin, once a *Laugh-In* comic, is his director. The sitcom will be shown on the NBC-TV network on Friday evenings this fall.

"Doing those lines," Joe Namath asked during the rehearsal, "was I supposed to be sitting down?"

"No, no," Dick Martin said. "I like the way you were pacing up and down. That was fine."

Joe Namath rehearses his TV show as seriously as he rehearsed as a quarterback. He's no stranger to show business. He has been a guest host of the *Tonight Show* and appeared in several TV variety shows. And he's now made four movies, including *Avalanche Express* with Lee Marvin and Robert Shaw in which he's an intelligence agent. He was on location in West Germany

for three months for the espionage film that is scheduled to be released later this year.

"People tell me you're great, Joe," a Hollywood agent named Mike Greenfield had said to him earlier. "A natural."

Joe Namath never even smiled. He just stared at Mike Greenfield as if he had never heard him. In a way, he hadn't.

"All this talk about how good I am in the movie, how good I'm going to be in the TV show, all this talk doesn't mean a thing," he was saying now. "All this is before the race has started. I remember at Alabama when we were ranked number one before the season, Coach Bryant told us it didn't mean a thing. What counted was where we were at the end of the season. That's how I'm treating this. I don't care what other shows are in our time slot, I don't even know. But when the movie comes out and the TV series is over, then we'll find out how good it is, how good I am."

Suddenly a slim brunette was standing at his shoulder, whispering to him.

"Well, yes," Joe Namath said to her, "I'd like to see you again, too. Let's do that."

Over in Europe, hardly anybody had recognized him. Football players are not known there.

"It was wonderful," he was saying now. "I like to blend in, but I can't really accept blending in. I have to excel. And if you excel, you're known."

Joe Namath has been known ever since he excelled in Super Bowl III for the New York Jets.

"The only thing I really have been down on about the Jets," he said, annoyance in his voice, "is how they changed their letterhead. They took '1968 World Champions' off it. I know they wanted to change their image, but I'm disappointed they would go to that degree. I can understand they don't want to live in the past but that Super Bowl happened."

"Do you think the Jets will retire your number twelve this season?" he was asked.

"I don't know," he said. "In one respect, it would be a great honor. But in another respect, I don't give a damn one way or another."

Soon he was joined by Ray Abruzzese, once a Jet teammate, and Bobby Van, his longtime restaurant partner.

"I can't believe the hours you're working," Ray Abruzzese told him. "They're worse than football. But this place is better than living in those dorms at training camp."

"This is the only place," Joe Namath said.

"All that trouble Reggie Jackson is having," Ray Abruzzese said. "Doesn't that remind you of all the trouble you used to have. But at least Reggie got a candy bar named for him."

"In that case," Joe Namath said, "I'll stick with panty hose."

Much of Joe Namath's trouble involved his Bachelors III restaurant in New York and now those same three bachelors had gathered in the Polo Lounge before going out.

"You know," Joe Namath said, "that something's up."

(July 23, 1978)

But his TV show was a flop. After only four weeks, NBC canceled it because of bad ratings. Joe Namath had been cut as an actor, something he never had to worry about as a quarterback. I remember John Dockery, now a television sportscaster but then a Jets' corner-back out of Harvard, talking once about the emotion involved in anticipating the roster cut each week at training camp. "It's exciting," he said. "In a way, I feel sorry for somebody like Joe Namath who never knows what it's like—good or bad."

Joe knows now.

But whenever I write about Joe Namath now, I always wonder how good a quarterback he would have been if he had been blessed with even adequate mobility. I also wonder how arthritic his knees will be in a few years. I always remember the time we were caught in traffic near his East Side apartment. The traffic had backed up while an elderly man was being helped out of a double-parked car. Steadying himself on the fenders, the gray-haired man hobbled painfully to the sidewalk as Joe Namath watched patiently.

"Must be an old quarterback," he said.

George Orwell was not the only writer predicting what the world would be like in 1984. The pro football players' strikes of 1970 and 1974 prompted *New York Times* columnist Dave Anderson in 1975 to speculate about what the state of the labor-dispute-riddled NFL would be by that fateful year. Well, it didn't quite happen. But, with the unproductive and unappreciated strikes of 1982 and 1987, the article may only need to have its title updated to *1994*.

1984, Footballwise

DAVE ANDERSON

Cᴀʟʟ ʜɪᴍ Ishmael, call him the last of the pro-foot-ballniks. After nearly ten years in a coma, he awoke in 1984. He had gone into shock in 1975, when it appeared that the National Football League would not open its season because of a labor dispute. Throughout his coma, his body rejected nourishment except for a mysterious serum melted down from N.F.L. highlight films and fed to him intravenously. Offense for breakfast, defense for lunch, special teams for dinner. When he awoke with his doctor at his bedside, he didn't realize that he had been in a coma.

"Are they playing this Sunday?" he asked.

"Oh yes," his doctor said. "All six teams."

"You mean all twenty-six teams, not six teams."

"No, this is 1984, you've been in a coma a long time. There are only six teams now—Canton, Akron, Dayton, Rock Island, Hammond and Decatur."

"But they were charter teams back in 1920."

"Ashes to ashes, Rock Island to Rock Island."

"What happened to all the teams I knew?"

"The fans finally went on strike. They picketed the stadiums. They broke the TV cameras. They boycotted the TV sponsors. They burned all the products with the N.F.L. shield."

"But didn't Pete Rozelle do anything to prevent that?"

"Pete Rozelle is the mayor of New York now," his doctor explained. "He got elected after he arranged a one-hundred-billion-dollar deal for the TV rights to everything that happens in the city. All the citizens had to sign a contract that let the TV cameras go anyplace. It really got the city out of hock but it created some problems. With all that money around, most of the good teachers have agents now. The teachers also are complaining about being transferred from one school to another. They're threatening to take the Rozelle Reign to the courts. Even the cops and firemen have agents now. One detective just signed a one-year contract for four hundred and fifty thousand dollars and only a few years ago he had to sell his bar because alleged undesirables were frequenting it."

"Who won the Super Bowl last season?"

"Oh, the Super Bowl is a soccer game now."

"What about Ed Garvey, the union leader?"

"He's trying to organize the players in the National Handball League."

"What's happened to contact sports?"

"Too many injuries. What really turned the fans off was when the owners passed a rule to let Joe Namath pass from behind sandbags to keep him around as an attraction. Joe's back in Beaver Falls now. He's a gymnastics coach. He just got sued by three kids because he ordered them to get crew cuts."

"Did the Giants ever get to play in that New Jersey stadium?"

"One game. One quarter really. From the weight of

the sellout crowd, the stadium sank slowly into the swamp. Slowly enough that everybody got out alive. Wellington Mara wanted to go back to Yankee Stadium, but he couldn't get it Sunday afternoons. That's when they have the OTB bingo games.''

"Where's O. J. Simpson now?''

"Playing baseball. It only took him five seasons to break Henry Aaron's home-run record.''

"What about Mean Joe Greene?''

"He's the heavyweight champion. He knocked out Muhammad Ali with his first punch, a left slap. Hit him on the side of the head like he used to hit offensive linemen on the helmet and knocked Ali clear out of the ring. Any other place, Ali would've had time to get back, but Don King put the ring on top of Mount Everest because this was his first one-hundred-million-dollar promotion. Ali fell three thousand feet before he landed on a ledge. Landed on his feet doing the Ali Shuffle, but the referee had counted him out by then.''

"Who was the referee?''

"Don Shula,'' his doctor said. "He needs the money now. Most of the time he's a cook in a Hungarian restaurant. Larry Csonka owns it.''

"What about George Allen?''

"He owns nursing homes for old N.F.L. players, but he only lets in defensive players.''

"What about Al Davis?''

"He runs the C.I.A., but the agents don't like him. He makes them all wear black suits with silver ties.''

"What's on TV on Monday night now?''

"Monday Night Tennis, and it's on every Monday night.''

"Is Howard still on?''

"Howard and Frank and Jimmy Connors, the first player-announcer. He plays a different opponent every week for one million dollars, winner-take-all. But he has a hard time getting a word in because Howard keeps talking about how he wants to run for President again.''

"Again?''

"He ran against Frank last time, and Frank won.''

(September 21, 1975)

Football is a game filled with traditional rituals, from triumphal dances in the end zone to butt-patting on the sideline. It is, therefore, fair game for investigation by a variety of scientists, social as well as behavioral. Anthropologist William Arens thought so too and penned this scholarly treatise on the subject for the *New York Times* in 1975.

An Anthropologist Looks at the Rituals of Football

WILLIAM ARENS

THE ATTITUDE toward the football player has obviously changed since Shakespeare's time. Today the once "base football player," as Shakespeare described him in "King Lear," occupies the hearts, minds and television screens of millions. He is emulated and sought after, and the stratagems he uses in the game are often followed at the highest levels of government and business.

> Some concise but incisive views of the game:
>
> Vince Lombardi, legendary coach of the Green Bay Packers: "This is a game for madmen."
>
> Jack Kemp, peripatetic NFL quarterback before becoming a U.S. Congressman: "Pro football gave me a good sense of perspective to enter politics. I'd already been booed, cheered, cut, sold, traded, and hung in effigy."
>
> Fred Biletnikoff, perennial All Pro wide receiver for the Oakland Raiders: "Anybody who says they're not in it for the money is full of shit."

As an anthropologist I would contend that football, although only a game, tells us much about who and what we Americans are as a people.

If an anthropologist from another planet visited here, he would be struck by the American fixation on this game and would report on it with the glee and romantic intoxication anthropologists normally reserve for the exotic rituals of a newly discovered tribe. This assertion is based on the theory that certain significant symbols are the key to understanding a culture; football is such a symbol.

AMERICAN BRAND UNEXPORTABLE

Football has emerged as an item of our cultural inventory that we share with no other country except Canada, where it is of minor interest. We share our language, kinship system, religions, political and economic institutions and a variety of other traits with many nations, but our premier spectator sport remains ours alone. This is important when we consider that other societies have taken up baseball, which is derived from cricket, and basketball, a domestic product. Like English beer, the American brand of football is unexportable, even to the colonies.

Football, in contrast to our language and many of our values, was not forced upon us. We chose to accept it. Our society, like any other complex one, is divided by race, ethnicity, income, political affiliation and regionalism. Yet 79 percent of all the households in the country tuned in the first Super Bowl on television, implying that the event cut through many of these divisive factors.

The game does not represent Middle America, as is so often claimed, but rather the whole of America. A love of football is one of the few interests we share with few outside our borders, but with almost everyone within them.

The salient features of the game reflect some striking

similarities to the society that created and nourished it. More than any other sport, football combines the qualities of group coordination through a complex division of labor with highly developed specialization.

Violence is one of our society's most obvious traits, and its expression in football, where bodily contact and territorial incursion are essential, clearly accounts for part of the game's appeal.

To single out violence as the sole or even primary reason for the game's popularity is a tempting oversimplication. Boxing, for example, allows for an even greater display of legitimate blood spilling. Yet boxing's popularity has waned over the last few decades, an indication, perhaps, that reliance on naked individual force has less appeal for us than aggression acted out in a more tactical and sophisticated context. Football's violence is expressed within the framework of teamwork, specialization, mechanization and variation, and this combination accounts for its appeal. But we cannot explain football's popularity on the basis of violence alone because we are not unique in this respect. There have been many other violent nations, but they did not enshrine football as a national symbol.

Although baseball—the national pastime—has not suffered the same fate as boxing, interest in this game has also ebbed. Like boxing, baseball is not in step with the times. Its action does not entail the degree of complexity, coordination and specialization that now captures our fancy. The recent introduction of players who only bat or run bases, and who never field, are moves to inject specialization and heighten the game's appeal to modern America. Baseball, however, belongs to a past era when life was a bit less complicated.

GAME A MALE PRESERVE

While football, representing the typical American outlook, overshadows class, race and economic differences in our society, it emphasizes the division between the sexes. The game is a male preserve that manifests and symbolizes both the physical and cultural values of masculinity. Entrance into the arena of football competition depends upon muscle power and speed, which only a very few males and probably no females possess. Women can and do excel in a variety of other sports, but football totally excludes them from participation.

In an informal game between females in a Long Island community, the husbands responded by appearing on the sidelines in women's clothes and wigs. The message was clear. If the women were going to act like men, then the men were going to transform themselves into women. These "rituals of rebellion" involving an inversion of sex roles have often been recorded by anthropologists. It is not surprising that this symbolic rebellion in our culture involved a bastion of male supremacy.

If this argument seems farfetched, consider the extent to which football gear accents the male physique. The donning of the required items results in an enlarged head and shoulders and a narrowed waist, with the lower torso poured into skintight pants accented only by a metal codpiece. The result is not an expression but an exaggeration of maleness. Dressed in this manner, players can engage in hand holding, hugging and bottom patting that would be disapproved of in any other context, but which is accepted on the gridiron without a second thought.

Admittedly, there are good reasons for wearing the gear, but that does not mean that we should dismiss the symbolic significance of the visual impression. The game could just as easily be played without the major items such as the helmet, shoulder pads and cleats. They are as much offensive as defensive in function. Indeed, in comparison, Rugby players seem to manage quite well in the flimsiest of uniforms.

This stark, disturbing story is an overpowering human drama that just happens to be about a former football player. Ira Berkow composed it with a stunning combination of emotional depth and Hemingwayesque brevity to provide us with chilling evidence that football players, like anyone else, can be subject to life's cruel twists. The article first appeared in the *New York Times* and was later included in *The Sporting News* collection *Best Sports Stories 1985*.

Emotional Pain Dooms Ex-Football Star

IRA BERKOW

A SHOUT FROM below her window awakened Charlotte Smith. She had been sleeping in the bedroom of her second-floor apartment at 131 North 15th Street, a three-story red-brick building in Center City, here early Friday morning, October 26.

She heard, "Back against the wall! Back against the wall!"

It was still dark outside, around a quarter to three, and Charlotte Smith climbed out of bed. Her window was partly open because it was an unseasonably warm and humid night, and she pushed the window higher and leaned out.

On the sidewalk, she saw a large black man—she also is black—and the man was wearing a dark jacket or sweater and tan pants, she would recall. He was moving toward a policeman. The policeman, a white man and considerably smaller than the other, was hollering, "Back against the wall!" and slowly retreating from the advancing man.

She didn't notice a weapon or anything else in either one's hands. An empty police cruiser with a flashing blue light rotating on the roof was alongside the curb. The two men were now stepping into the yellow light on the sidewalk that spilled through the window from the night light in the closed luncheonette. Several yards away, at the corner of 15th and Cherry, two young black teenagers on mopeds watched. Otherwise, the street was deserted.

Charlotte Smith has on occasion been roused in the dead of night because, she told a reporter, "derelicts" come around that area—there are mostly office buildings, but the "derelicts" drift over from the bus terminal a few blocks away—and sometimes cause problems. Her immediate worry was that her boss, Murry Auspitz, might be in trouble. Murray Auspitz owns the luncheonette on the ground floor, where she works as a counter attendant. He arrives early to open the store.

When she saw it wasn't her boss, she said she "didn't pay it no attention," and got back into bed. A moment or so later, a loud crack rang out. "It was a gunshot," she recalled. "I've heard gunshots before."

She jumped up and looked out the window again and now saw the black man lying on the ground, bleeding. The policeman was at the squad car and, she recalled, "radioing in for help."

"I was hysterical in the window," she would say, "screamin' and crying."

She did not learn who the black man was until the following day, Saturday, when she saw the headline in the Philadelphia Daily News. It read:

"Cop's Bullet Kills '50s Grid Star."

The dead man was Charles Fletcher Janerette Jr., age 45, an English teacher at the Daniel Boone School in Philadelphia and a former All-American lineman at Penn State and one-time player in the early 1960s with both the New York Giants and the Jets. For the last 12 years, Janerette had suffered from what was described by his parents as manic depression.

His killing would raise numerous questions and inflame passions, particularly in the black community of Philadelphia. In the official police statement, the officer would say that Janerette had gotten into the marked squad car when the policeman stepped out to talk to the two youths on mopeds. Then, the policeman stated, he pulled Janerette from the car. He said that a scuffle ensued and his revolver went off. Janerette was shot in the back of the head. Janerette was taken to a hospital and died about 12 hours later.

Was Janerette, in fact, up against the wall? Was this a case of police brutality in extremis, or an accident, or did the policeman have no recourse in order to protect himself? How was it, if there was a scuffle, that he was shot in the back of the head? Had Janerette taken medication that helped control his mental problem? Toxicology reports, which should show whether he had been taking the medication, will not be available for several weeks.

The police officer, Kurt VonColin, age 33, who reportedly stands about 5 feet, 7 inches tall and weighs about 160 pounds, bears a well-known last name in Philadelphia. In 1970, his father, Police Sgt. Frank Von-Colin, age 43, was shot to death while alone at his desk in the Cobbs Creek Park guardhouse by a group of black men, members of a radical organization known as the Revolutionaries. The killing was considered by the police to be part of a conspiracy by the group to kill whites.

That crime touched off the largest manhunt in Philadelphia history. All but one of the assailants were caught. The only one still free is the one who is said to have pulled the trigger.

There are other questions that the story of Janerette raised. Some deal with the adjustments of life after football, some with racism in American society, and others with the problems of the manic-depressive, a psychosis from which, according to his family, Janerette had been suffering for the last 12 years.

Charlie Janerette grew up in Philadelphia, first in the Richard Allen projects, and later in a better neighborhood in West Oak Lane, and became an all-city and all-state high school lineman. He went on to Penn State, where he was chosen a second-team All-America by The Sporting News in his senior year, and he played seven years in professional football. He was with the Los Angeles Rams in 1960, the Giants in 1961 and 1962, the Jets in 1963, the Denver Broncos for the next two years, and finished his career in 1966 with the Hamilton Tiger-Cats in Ontario.

In 1956, Charlie Janerette became the first black president of Germantown High School. He was popular,

gregarious and exceedingly bright. By the time he was a senior, he had reached his full height, 6′ 3″, though, at about 240 pounds, not quite his full weight, which would go as high as 270 pounds with the Broncos. "Charlie," said a longtime friend, Garrett Bagley, "was a gentle bear."

Two of his boyhood friends were Harold Brown, now a North Carolina businessman, and the comedian Bill Cosby. Brown is believed to be the model for Cosby's comic invention, Weird Harold, and another Cosby character, Fat Albert, is believed to have been loosely based on Charlie Janerette.

Brown smiled when he recalled Janerette. "He was funny and he could take a joke," he said. "We said his shoe size kept up to his age."

Brown was asked if Janerette was in fact the inspiration for Fat Albert. "The guys have always thought he had a lot to do with it," said Brown. "He was rotund, robust, as a kid. Not fat sloppy, but robust sloppy."

The boyhood friends kept in touch through the years. Last year, said Charlie's sister, Hope Janerette, when Bill Cosby opened a show in Lake Tahoe, he sent Charlie Janerette a round-trip first-class ticket to Nevada. Cosby told Charlie he'd have a Rolls-Royce waiting for him to use there.

Charlie told Hope, "I can't drive that thing. What if I had an accident. I could never pay for the repairs."

One of the many bouquets of flowers sent to the Janerette home bore this note to the family: "I'll see you later." It was signed, "Bill Cosby." Several attempts to reach Cosby were unavailing.

Charlie Janerette was the oldest of five children, and the only male, born to Charles Janerette Sr., now a retired postal office supervisor, and his wife, Lillian Ernestine. The five children—the other four are named Carol, Faith, Hope and Charity—would all earn doctorates. Charlie had dreamed of becoming a physician, and he enrolled as a pre-med student at Penn State.

But, he would say, the requirements of football didn't give him enough time to pursue the rigorous discipline of medicine, and he instead earned a bachelor's degree in science, and later a master's in educational counseling.

When he first went to Penn State, Joe Paterno, now the head coach but then an assistant coach, recalls that they thought there might be a problem. "He was a sensitive, shy kid and we wondered whether he was aggressive enough to be a good football player," Paterno said. "But he was very committed, and he wanted to make something of himself. He was very quick and had a lot of explosiveness, and he got tougher and tougher."

Janerette was thrilled to receive a scholarship from Penn State, but, he said in a newspaper interview a few years ago: "They didn't tell me I'd be the only black on the team. I didn't worry about that, though. I saw all the huge freshmen, and I just wanted to survive.''

In the mid-1950's, blacks were just beginning to be recruited on a large scale for college athletic teams at major state universities around the country. It was no different at Penn State, the school tucked away in an area known as ''Happy Valley.'' Janerette, though, seemed to make adjustments.

Janerette was drafted in 1960 on the fifth round by the Los Angeles Rams. His contract called for $7,500, and he received a $500 signing bonus.

It was enough for Janerette to put a $3,000 down payment on a house for his parents and sisters, a brick, semi-detached four-bedroom house on a street lined with spruce and cedar trees in the quiet, East Mount Airy section of north Philadelphia.

He started some games for the Rams, but at the end of the season, was picked by the Minnesota Vikings in an expansion draft, and then traded to the Giants.

In two years with the Giants, he would recall to *The Philadelphia Tribune*, a black newspaper, he played ''a lot of defensive tackle when Rosey Grier was hurt, and I played on all the special teams. I even played with a broken hand. I had to.''

Andy Robustelli, a defensive end on the team, remembers him as a ''happy, jovial, always upbeat guy. But the Giant teams were so strong then and it was tough for anybody to break in.''

In 1963, Janerette was cut by the Giants and picked up by the Jets. Weeb Ewbank, then the Jets coach, remembers him as a ''nice person, never caused any problems, but we let him go because he was on the downside of his career, and we were building.''

Janerette went to the Broncos as part of a nine-player deal with the Jets. ''I remember Charlie getting up at a club we used to go to, called 23rd Street East, and doing great, funny imitations of James Brown,'' said Cookie Gilchrist, a teammate of Janerette in Denver. But there was another side. ''He didn't play enough, and he and I both thought he should have,'' said Gilchrist.

Denver, where Janerette earned his highest salary, $17,000, cut him and he played for a year in the Canadian Football League. He was 27 years old and finished as a professional football player.

He had married in 1965, and he and his wife, Joan, soon had a daughter, Dariel. There seemed no evidence of problems. He spent five years in the marketing department of General Electric in Syracuse, and it was in August of 1972, said Joan Janerette, when difficulties developed.

''He began acting strangely,'' she recalls. ''Very hyper. His movements were very quick at times, and he began to say strange things. Like he was going to solve all the problems of the world.''

He began to leave without telling her where he was going, and wouldn't return for days. She urged him to go to a psychiatrist, and he was eventually admitted to a Syracuse hospital and stayed there 10 days, she said.

She wondered about the source of his problems.

His wife believed he was suffering from manic-depression, in which there are sudden mood changes, surging from euphoria to deep depression.

The problems intensified. She went to a therapist, and she was told that he could be dangerous. ''He was a big man, and I found it hard to restrain him,'' she said. In October of 1972, she left him, taking their daughter to Pennsylvania.

On October 18, 1972, he was charged with driving while intoxicated when he was involved in a car accident in which a pedestrian was killed. He pleaded guilty to a reduced charge and as a result his driver's license was suspended for three months.

''Charlie was so broken up by that accident,'' said Hope Janerette, ''that every October 18 he would not go out of the house.''

Following the accident, there were days of unexplained absence from work, and he lost his job.

Paterno, who stayed close with Janerette and knew of his problems, hired him as a graduate assistant. Janerette stayed at Penn State for two years and earned his master's degree.

But Paterno saw times in which Janerette would not be ''acting right.'' And when Janerette next went to Cheyney State in Pennsylvania as an assistant coach under Billy Joe, there were more problems. ''He was a good assistant,'' said Billy Joe, ''and then on occasion he would do something completely out of character.'' At a football dinner, Janerette, the guest speaker, rose and soon, ''began yelling out and cursing,'' said Joe. Janerette had to be led away.

He moved to Washington, where he sold computer software to federal agencies. He told a friend that one day he had been picked up off the streets by the police for no reason and jailed for four days.

He returned home to Philadelphia, where he got teaching jobs.

After his death, a student whom he had taught, named Angela Hurts, wrote a letter to Janerette's parents: ''. . . I really do miss Mr. Janerette. He could joke with us, but he was also serious about his students getting to work, because he wanted us to learn. Even when I said, 'Mr. Janerette, I can't do this,' he would say, 'yes, you can. Try it.' ''

Although he took several jobs teaching in the Philadelphia public schools, he would continue to talk to friends about his dreams. ''He wanted some kind of entrepreneurship,'' said Garrett Bagley, a friend, ''or he wanted to get back into football. He missed football a lot, and he missed being a star. There were no more locker rooms, no planes to catch, no more autographs to sign.''

Janerette was aware, of course, of his mental problem. "He always thought that the last episode—he called them episodes—would be his last," said his sister, Charity. "He didn't really want to admit that he had a problem. And when he took his medication—lithium carbonate—he was fine. But when he didn't take it, and sometimes he didn't want to, he would be out of control. He was never violent, that we saw, but he'd be blinking his eyes and moving the furniture and talking fantasies.''

He lived for the last three years in the house he had bought at the corner of Boyer and Horttler. But Charity said he considered it "only temporary."

"We knew he was in pain because of the illness, and he suffered with it and we suffered to see him that way," his sister Carol said. "But it was pretty well hidden. Almost no one outside the family knew about it."

His parents worried, too. "I hoped he wouldn't be a street person," said Mrs. Janerette, "and when he was out late, we waited for him, and when I finally heard the key in the lock, I could go to sleep."

He was working then at Boone, a remedial disciplinary school for boys. "He really related well to the boys," said the principal, Willie J. Toles, "and we had absolutely no problem with his performance or his attendance. And he always looked nice—suit and tie."

On Thursday October 25 he did not report to school. The school called his house. He had not been home the previous night.

That afternoon, a student had seen Janerette in Center City, and the teacher gave him a few dollars, even though the boy hadn't even asked for it. Later, Janerette was reported to have asked a storekeeper he knew to lend him some money, and the storekeeper said Janerette berated him vulgarly for giving him so little.

At around midnight, Paul Jones, an old friend of Janerette's, and now a cab driver, saw him near the bus terminal.

"He didn't seem right," said Jones, who said he did not know of Janerette's mental problems. "He talked okay. We spoke about guys from 30 years back, but his movements seemed too quick, and his jacket and pants were disheveled.

"I said, 'Charlie, can I drive you home?'

"He said, 'No, but can you let me have a few bucks?' ''

Jones did, and told him he had to get a fare and would come back in a little while.

He never saw him again.

It was a couple of hours later that police officer Von-Colin was in his cruiser near 15th and Cherry.

He stopped two teenagers on mopeds for a possible traffic violation. During the ongoing investigation of the death, VonColin is not speaking publicly. According to the formal police statement, one of the teenagers told him that someone was trying to steal his squad car.

According to the statement, VonColin moved toward Charles Janerette.

"Charlie once told me," said Hope Janerette, "that he had heard that if you ever have trouble, or don't have money, and need help, then you should get into a police car. He said, 'They have to take you home.'

"When Charlie was in a bad state, he always had some presence of mind. He was never totally out of control. And I wonder if his getting into that police car wasn't a kind of plea for help." It was just about this time that Charlotte Smith heard shouts, and, soon after, the gunshot that killed Charlie Janerette.

Hundreds of people milled outside the gray-stone Beran Presbyterian Church on Broad and Diamond streets last Wednesday at noon, before the services for Charlie Janerette.

People were angry about the way he died.

Willie J. Toles thought that it was a "classic case of misunderstanding."

Inside, in a gray steel casket strewn with flowers, lay Charles Fletcher Janerette Jr.

"I'm glad for one thing," said Hope Janerette. "I'm glad that now Charlie is out of that little private hell he was living in."

Charlie Janerette was eulogized by the Rev. J. Jerome Cooper, and then Cookie Gilchrist read a poem he had written for the funeral. Next, Faith Janerette, a dramatic soprano, shook the church with a moving gospel, "Right On, King Jesus." Some of the congregants moaned and sobbed.

The mourners then filed out, and some of them sang along with the church choir accompanied by an organist to the "Hallelujah Chorus."

As the funeral procession was about to leave for Northwest Cemetery, Harold Brown spoke to someone beside him. "When Charlie and I used to sit in church, and they played the 'Hallelujah Chorus,' " he said, "and on the last 'Hallelujah,' Charlie, under his breath, would add a '50s rock group ending, a little doo-wop. And today it was there. Damned if I didn't hear it. He was speaking. And it made me think, 'Charlie's okay now. Even with all the tears here, he can still play jokes.' ''

Johnny Blood, *aka* McNally, seventy-nine years old in 1983, arrived at a brunch honoring the twentieth anniversary of the Pro Football Hall of Fame in Canton, Ohio, a coat-and-tie affair, wearing a T-shirt with the name Duluth Eskimos emblazoned across the front. He was an honored guest, having been inducted into the Hall as a charter member in 1963. He said he was wearing the T-shirt to honor his old pal Ernie Nevers, now deceased, with whom he had shared backfield duties at Duluth back in 1926 and 1927. Besides Duluth, Johnny Blood played for such NFL teams as the Milwaukee Badgers, Pottsville Maroons, Green Bay Packers, and the Pittsburgh Pirates and Steelers. A fleet runner and free spirit, he was enshrined in the Hall for his speed, elusiveness, and great pass-catching abilities. His reputation off the field was even larger, and if there were a rogue's Hall of Fame he surely would be a charter member of that, too. One writer of the time referred to the mercurial Blood as ''a Peter Pan who would never shed his eternal youth.'' Johnny Blood broke as many training rules as he did tackles, and ignored team curfews just as he did Prohibition.

At Play in Green Bay

JOHNNY BLOOD

M Y FIRST LESSON in playing football, my first experience was in an old child's game in Wisconsin called ''Run, Run, Forward.'' We played it in the town of New Richmond up there where I was raised. There was a lot of tackling, that sort of thing. This was back around 1910. I was very young when I got into it.

Starting when I got to kindergarten, I went around with boys who were always two or three years older than I was, played with them and tried to compete in their kinds of games. I wasn't as physically developed as they were and consequently got knocked around a lot. No one ever considered that I would wind up being an athlete back then.

I got out of high school at the age of fourteen, my mother had kind of pushed me through it fast, and I never played a game of any kind in high school, no sport at all. I'd graduated but then I spent another year, sort of postgraduate high school, that was a first up there. After that, I went to a teacher's college called River Falls Normal. I don't know why they sent *me* to a normal school. The truth of it, I suppose, was because my mother had gone there in the 1890s. Anyway, I went there but I didn't last too long, went AWOL from this River Falls Normal, a dropout. I think I went on a little spree of some sort and just forgot to go back there. My father then took me to his school, where he had gone in 1895, called St. John's University. It was in Minnesota and there were only a couple hundred of us there but they called it a university anyway. I was only 16 when I went up to Collegeville, where St. John's was, out west a ways of Minneapolis. It was both a monastery and a school, very strict school. I'm not sure it was ready for me, but still I stayed there for three years, somewhat amazing when you think about it.

My father hadn't lasted that long. He'd gotten thrown out in 1895. It had to do with him being a master spitter, tobacco, that is. You see, he had come from a small farm in Wisconsin, and they were all Irish immigrants around there and there wasn't much for them to do, no organized games or sports. So he mastered the art of spitting accurately, and this you know leads to a well-known sport. Well, one day my father was sitting inside a classroom, it must have been in the spring, and was spitting out a window. He and another student were having a little contest. This is a fact, I wouldn't kid you, they were trying to spit at flies that were going by. They both missed, he later told me, but he claimed that he came the closest. Some consolation anyway. Well, as it turned out, a prefect was walking along outside, just below the window, unknown to them, and a big splat of this tobacco juice landed on the prefect. So the next day at lunch, in the lunch hall, the abbott got up and said, "We know who did this dastardly act yesterday and if he'll stand up and admit to it, we will consider his case." Nobody stood up, of course. And they did in fact know it was my father, something like it had happened before, I think. So they kicked him out, but he still brought me there.

At St. John's I played basketball and was on the track team, and that's also where I played my first game of football. It happened this way. One day I was standing at the bulletin board, I guess I was seventeen by then, and a guy came up and said he drew me in the draft. At the time, I didn't know what the hell he was talking about. What they had were different football teams on the campus and that's how each got their material, a draft. It was really a kind of intramural league. So I said, "Is that so? How did you happen to pick me?" This guy said he had seen me running around the track one day, thought I was fast, and that maybe I might be pretty good at running with a football. So I said all right, and, well, I was pretty much an immediate success on a very small football team. As I recall, our team's name was the Cat's Pajamas.

As I said, I was a runt as a kid, but by the time I got into St. John's I'd grown up to be a spike. I suppose I never got to be any heavier than 165 pounds while I was there, but I'd been toughened up by working on the farm there in Wisconsin. I still worked there in the summers while I was going to St. John's. And also I was about the fastest guy around. Later, when I got playing for the pros, I was up around 185 or 190, just about right for a guy 6 feet 1 inch.

After three years there, I left of my own accord again. I guess I wanted the bigger time, so I went down to Notre Dame and enrolled there. But I didn't last the year, got in some trouble around St. Patrick's Day, some pretty good celebrating for the saintly Irishman, and then went AWOL. They didn't take to that well and, as I used to call it, I became a double-dipped dropout at Notre Dame. I'd tried out for the football team while I was there. Knute Rockne was coaching and they had the "Four Horsemen" on the varsity that year. I ended up on the freshman team because it was my first year of eligibility, but I didn't do anything there. I always like to say that my one contribution to Notre Dame football was that I used to write Harry Stuhldreyer's English poetry papers for him.

That kind of ended my career as a student. After it, I went to work for a newspaper in Minneapolis, and they put me in the printing end of it. It didn't pay very much and I was quick to find out it was not my kind of job. I'd also gotten one of my buddies from St. John's, Ralph Hanson, a job there. Around that time, I'd heard that there was a way to pick up some extra money by playing in a semipro city league in the Minneapolis/St. Paul area. Ralph had played football with me at St. John's and so we thought we might be able to pick up a little extra dough by playing football, something we both liked anyway.

At the time, I was thinking that maybe one of those days I might be going back to Notre Dame, in the unlikely event they'd have me, but still it was a possibility. And if I did, I'd want to play football there. I also knew we might play some games out of state with that Minneapolis team. So I said to Ralph, "I still have some eligibility left and I don't want to lose it. So when we go out for this team, let's use some fake names and that way we can protect our amateur standing." He agreed.

I used to get around town on my own motorcycle then, and so we both hopped on it and headed out to where this team practiced, some playground in back of a factory. On the way there, we passed a movie theater on Hennepin Avenue and up on the marquee I saw the name of the movie that was playing, *Blood and Sand* with Rudolph Valentino. Ralph was behind me on the motorcycle and I turned my head and shouted, "That's it. I'll be Blood and you be Sand." And so we went to the practice, tried out, and made the team, Johnny Blood and Ralph Sand. And, of course, I kept it as a football name from that time on.

I got a nickname too, "the Vagabond Halfback," which came about in a rather amusing way. In my childhood, back in New Richmond, Wisconsin, I was enchanted by railroads. In the town, two sets of tracks crossed, one going north and south and the other east and west, so there were trains going through both ways all the time. Freight trains and passenger trains, that was the way you moved most things in those days. And I would hear this loooong whistle, very plaintive and compelling; it was very romantic to a child. Far away places, dreams, new worlds, all that kind of thing. Maybe I'm still childish, but I'm still enchanted with the sounds of railroads.

Anyway, in those days, we used to play all kinds of games with the railroads. Hop a freight train and ride it down to Hudson or to other towns and then catch another train back. It was just part of growing up in a small town in Wisconsin back then. Hitching rides on these trains was a sport to all of us. We got to know the engineers, we knew a lot of the conductors on the passenger trains, and the workers on the freight trains.

Much later, when I was playing football at Green Bay, I decided to use the talents I'd gained with the railroads as a child. We had won the championship three years running: 1929, '30, and '31. Still, it was the Depression and we didn't get much money from playing football so most of us worked in the offseason at whatever jobs we could find. I was lucky because we were pretty well off, the family, that is, and as a result were pretty strong in New Richmond. Therefore, I was able to get a job there at a mill in the offseason. Well, when I got ready to go back to Green Bay for the 1932 season, I thought I'd save myself a little money, everybody worried about it in those days. To get there, I had to take the train and so I decided to do it the way I had as a kid. We might have been the NFL champs and I had a decent job in the offseason but I never had any money then. I spent it as fast as I got it.

Well, the Soo Line Railroad took you over to a junction where you could get another train that would take you to Green Bay. You see, New Richmond is on the western side of the state and Green Bay is just about as far east as you can get in Wisconsin. The first train was cheap, so I rode as a passenger on it. But before boarding it, I had the stationmaster wire ahead to hold the second train, the Green Bay & Western it was, for a passenger. The junction was in Chippewa Falls, as I recall, about thirty miles away. Anyway, the telegram was sent to hold the train for a passenger, which you could do in those days. When somebody needed to make a connection, they would hold a train if the wait wouldn't be too long.

So I rode the Soo to Chippewa Falls, got off, and sure enough there was the Green Bay & Western waiting for its passenger. I ran hippity-clippity down the siding and jumped on it, in the baggage car, that is. Well, they waited for their customer who'd sent the telegram but, of course, he never showed up, and so they finally went on. After a couple of stations, the door to the baggage car was slid open and a guy was staring at me, one of the railroad men. He did a kind of double take and then said, "Hey, aren't you Johnny Blood?" We were pretty well known in the state because practically everyone in all those towns were great Green Bay fans and we'd been the champs three years running.

"Yeah, sure am," I said.

"Well, come on down," he said. "Come on up front."

The upshot is that he took me up with the engineer and gave me a cup of coffee and a ham sandwich, shared his stuff with me. They treated me royally and I got to Green Bay for nothing.

I had a good friend down in Milwaukee, a writer for the newspaper there, who came up to Green Bay for all the ballgames. I told him the story and he said he wanted to write about it for his paper. "That's great," he said. "We'll call it 'The Hobo Halfback, Riding the Rails.' "

I said, "I don't know about that, 'hobo' is not really my style." I thought about it for a minute, then said, "Why don't we say 'The Vagabond Halfback.' It has a little more class." He agreed, and so he started referring to me in his columns as the Vagabond Halfback. Other writers picked it up and it stuck for a long time.

I didn't go directly to Green Bay as a pro, however. After that semi-pro team in Minneapolis, I'd built myself a little reputation as a good runner. One day, while I was working at the newspaper in Minneapolis, these two pro football players—I didn't know them—came in and asked for me. They said they were with a team in Ironwood, Michigan, which is up north on the border line between Wisconsin and the Michigan peninsula, way north. They said they'd pay me sixty dollars a game if I played halfback which sounded all right to me at the time. So I went. We played a few games up there. But one of the guys who had talked to me had played some games for the pro team in Milwaukee the year before. The team was named the Badgers and they were in the NFL, a big step above what we were playing in. Well, I did quite well up in Ironwood in those few games and the next thing I knew I got an offer to come down and play for Milwaukee, in fact the other two guys did, too. There was more money in it as well, so, of course, we went down there and played the 1925 season with the Badgers.

That was the same year that Red Grange came into the pros, at the end of it, that is. I played against him for the first time after the season, on that tour he and C. C. Pyle put together with the Chicago Bears. It was an exhibition game out in California. I got myself out there. It was the beginning of a lot of travel for me.

With the Milwaukee Badgers, we didn't travel all that much, not far anyway. I played five or six games that first year for them and I think we went to Steubenville, Ohio, Green Bay, Rock Island in Illinois, and that was about it. I played wingback that year and our team was pretty awful. We lost all the games that we played. There were twenty teams in the league that year, a lot of them from small towns like Hammond, Indiana and Duluth, Minnesota and Canton, Ohio. The big teams were from Chicago, the Bears and the Cardinals.

The next year, 1926, I was twenty-one years old and I signed with the Duluth Eskimos. It is one of my great memories because it was there that I got to play with Ernie Nevers, who was the star. No, he was the *team*. Ernie was a fine man, just out of college that year. He'd starred out at Stanford and he brought to Duluth the offense that Pop Warner had used so successfully out there, the double wingback with a blocking back and a fullback. The fullback was everything in that offense, and the fullback was Ernie Nevers. It was an offense especially designed for him. He received the ball from the center and he called the plays, and Ernie was also the coach. I admired and respected him. He was a fiery kind of guy, a different specimen really, and we had a pretty good football team up there, considering it was Duluth and not Chicago or New York. The "Iron Men from the North" is what Grantland Rice called us.

The Eskimos were actually run by a little Norwegian guy who had inherited the team from his father. I guess the guy had gone to high school with Ernie Nevers and looked on him as his hero. His father, who died, had a little money, too, and the guy inherited it which enabled him to sign up Ernie. The Duluth team he'd inherited had been a volunteer team prior to that, made up of guys who lived and worked in the iron range up there. Just like Pottsville, Pennsylvania, they had an iron industry and these guys who played worked there. They weren't necessarily very good football players, but they were rugged and strong, a different breed.

The Duluth club folded up after 1927 and a lot of us went over to the Pottsville Maroons, myself and Walt Kiesling among them. Walt was a great lineman. Nevers dropped out of football for a year. I think he went back to help Pop Warner coach out at Stanford. But then he came back to play with the Chicago Cardinals and was all-Pro, and, of course, scored that forty points all by himself in one game. No one has ever broken that record—single-handed he scored forty points in a game, that's hard to beat.

Johnny Blood was hired in 1937 by Art Rooney as the head coach of the then Pittsburgh Pirates. To his consternation, Rooney learned that the fleet halfback "wasn't always that dependable."

"Once we played a game out in Los Angeles, an exhibition of some kind, and Johnny missed the train home. We did not see him the whole week. Then the following Sunday I heard that he was in Chicago to watch the Packers, his old team, play the Bears. One of the players on Green Bay asked him why he wasn't with his own team.

"We're not playing this week," Johnny told him.

"No sooner did he get those words out of his mouth than over the loudspeaker came the score announcement: Philadelphia 14, Pittsburgh 7."

It was a game of running and tackling at that point, in the 1920s. In those days, the passing game hadn't been developed. I was a legitimate halfback, running back, and I played both right and left halfback, according to the way we shifted. We used alternating halfbacks most of the time. By that I mean the halfback would line up to the left on one play and the right the next. I played sixty minutes of every game and it was tough. You had to pace yourself. It was a primitive game, anybody who played it then will tell you that. The equipment, what there was of it, wasn't too good. The pay was worse. In Duluth I think I got $70 or $75 a game, less if we lost. Nevers, though, got $15,000 for the season, which was very big money in 1926. He and Red Grange were the big attractions then and they were the only two who got big money out of it.

I only played on the Pottsville team for one year, 1928. The great Pete Henry was our coach there and the mainstay of our line. He was just a huge butterball but, my, how he could play football. But as a team we were a pretty sorry group. Lost most of our games, but we did surprise Green Bay and clobbered them and they were one of the top teams in the league that year.

It was the next year that I went with the Packers. The Vagabond Halfback: it was my fourth team in five years. We had a wonderful team, though, won the title the first three years I was in Green Bay. We had Cal Hubbard and Mike Michalske in the line and Red Dunn and Verne Lewellen in the backfield with me. After them came Clarke Hinkle and Arnie Herber. Curly Lambeau, of course, was our coach, had been since they first got a pro team up there. I got along pretty well with Curly, for a while anyway. I was one of the only ones who did, most didn't like him at all. But for the first three or four years he put up with me and my antics. I think I was one of the few who could get the best of him, he had a hard time keeping up with me.

Actually, in the long run, I guess I didn't get along so well because he finally fired me. On paper I was sold to the Pittsburgh team but he really fired me. It came after several of us had been out one night, myself and a couple of other players. We were out all night as a matter of fact. Well, I went directly to practice in the morning, got all suited up. Lambeau was looking at me kind of funny as I remember. Anyway, I tried to punt the ball, missed it, and fell flat on my ass. Lambeau told me to get the hell off the field and after practice was over he told me he was getting rid of me.

I came back to Green Bay a year later and Lambeau took me back but we never got along very well after that.

There were a lot of good times in Green Bay, it was a swell town in those days. We were kind of riding on top of the world, champs, well-known. I have a lot of memories from up there. One in particular I'll always remember. I was known to kid around a lot, do the unexpected, so to speak. It was back around 1930, one of the years we won a championship. Well, we were all celebrating on the train on our way back to Green Bay. And I was a notorious celebrator.

After a while, we began horsing around and I started throwing some wet napkins at Lavie Dilweg. He was one of our ends, a big, tall, strong boy. He didn't like it a real lot and told me to stop. Of course, I didn't and he finally got up after me. Well, I took off down the aisle and he was chugging along trying to get his big hands on me. We'd been up near the front of the train, in the club car, and we just went racing through car after car, the people looking up wondering what the hell was going on.

I kept razzing him all the way. And he kept coming. Well, when we got to the last car, he thought he had me, but I went out onto the rear platform. He kind of yelled in triumph as he came through the door. But I stepped up on the back railing and pulled myself up onto the roof of the train. I looked back down and you should have seen the look on his face. He just stared up in disbelief. Then I said, "So long," and ran on back up the train, on the roof, jumping from car to car as I went.

Dilweg didn't follow me, of course. He had better sense than that. I went on past the club car, all the way to the engineer's cab. I surprised the hell out of him and the fireman when I climbed down from the roof—we were moving pretty fast at the time. I rode with them into town, it was only about another 15 miles, and they were nice, kind of got a kick out of it, I think. As I said, I've always had this thing for trains. They bring something out in me.

Another season in Green Bay I held out. That was kind of unheard of in those days. I was underpaid for the work I was doing, I felt. After all, I had made all-Pro and I was still making less than many of the other guys on our team. Lambeau, I knew, always felt that I was a soft touch, that money didn't mean all that much to me. He thought I wouldn't protest, maybe I was too easygoing. So this one year I decided to hold out. The Packers lost the first two games of the season and then they called me back. I went to the board of directors of the Packers, however, not Lambeau, and said, "I made all-Pro last year and I'm underpaid here." They knew all that, I found out, and so they told Curly to hire me back. Well, he had to, but I knew he'd be watching me all the time after that.

Lambeau had used me as a signal-caller before and he put me back in to do that after I held out. I got results for him. And he told somebody how much it surprised him because he could not believe that a character like me, who seemed to be so reckless, could call signals and get good results on the field for him.

In Don Hutson's second year with the Packers, 1936, he established himself as a fabulous receiver. We were now a good passing team, the best in the league. With Hutson and myself as receivers and Arnie Herber throwing, we were a real scoring threat. And, of course, we had Clarke Hinkle running, one of the very best in the game then. We came down to a very important game against the Detroit Lions late in the season, a truly crucial one. I was still calling the plays and signals then and Lambeau came up to me before the game. "We're going to surprise them," he said.

"Good," I said. I always believed in surprises on the football field. Trick plays, surprises, they can turn a game around.

But this wasn't that at all. Remember, we had the best passing attack in football at that time. It was our old ace in the hole. At the same time, the Lions had the best running attack. They had Dutch Clark and Ace Gutowsky and Glenn Presnell, all great threats. Dutch was one of the best ever. I remember one time when he was trying to run the ball out of the end zone and it looked for sure like we were going to tackle him for a safety. The entire left side of our line was surging in on him and he ran right at them, hooked his arm around the goalpost, swung himself around and headed off to the other side and made maybe 10 or 15 yards instead of being caught behind the goal line.

Lambeau's surprise wasn't anything tricky. "The surprise plan is," he said, "we're going to run the ball at them all day." I couldn't believe it. Before the game, he told the rest of the team. No one said anything; he was the coach, after all. But we all thought it was crazy. "Run it. Run them to death," he said. And that was that.

We had this play which worked well for us so often. It was a kind of option where we would fake a handoff to Hinkle and draw the defenders because he was such a threat, and then Herber would throw a pass to myself or

Hutson. I brought it up to Lambeau and he said, "Fine, but don't pass. Just give it to Hinkle and let him run it at them."

Well, we got out there and after about five minutes I knew we were not going to win that ballgame. There was no way we were going to beat Detroit by running the ball. So I called a pass, called two or three passes in a row. Lambeau pulled me out of the game and I sat on the bench. Meanwhile, Detroit was doing what they always could do so well against us: marching, marching, marching. Dutch Clark was having a fine day for himself. They'd move the ball and we couldn't. After a while, Lambeau came over to me on the bench and said, "If we lose this game, you are responsible."

I didn't say anything but I was burned up over it. We were actually leading by a point when he pulled me out even though they had been controlling the game. I said to myself, "How could I lose the ballgame sitting on the bench. We're ahead and I'm out of the game, but if we lose it's my fault. Crazy!"

When Curly finally put me back in the game we were losing by a couple of points. There was about five minutes to go and we had the ball. He looked at me on the bench and said, "Get in there." He didn't tell me not to pass, but he didn't rescind the no-passing order either. From his look I knew he still wanted to run the ball.

The ball was on our 40 yard line or thereabouts. Well, I ran out there, took a look at their defense and knew they were laying for a run. After all, that's what we'd been doing all afternoon. I said, "By God I'm going to try it." I called the option play but told Arnie Herber, our passer, to zoom it. That meant to fake it to Hinkle and let it fly to Hutson or myself. Arnie looked at me kind of funny, "Zoom it?" he said. I shook my head and when I did I knew my job was really on the line. Anyway, Hutson lined up on one flank and I was spread out on the other. When the ball was snapped we took off for the goal line like a pair of rabbits. I was well covered. That surprised me. There were two Detroit defenders hounding me. I thought, oh boy, this is it, especially when I saw the ball coming toward us. All three of us went up for it and somehow I got my hands on it and they bounced off each other and fell down. I scampered off for the end zone. I thought as I stepped across the goal line that if I didn't have the ball I wouldn't have had a job either. Well, it worked and we won the ballgame. That was in 1936 and we won the championship that year but if we hadn't won that game—it was the next to last of the season—we might not have won the title. After the game, Curly never mentioned the pass. I didn't mention it to him either.

I was reckless, they said, on the football field. Reckless in a lot of things, I guess. I liked to have a good time

back then: women, travel, a little drinking, loved to spend money. I had a lot of experiences. I was very uninhibited, that way all my life, even as a little kid. I was kind of split between my father and mother. They were a loving couple and treated me very well. But they were very different personalities, each had different goals. And I was usually caught in the middle. One time, when I was about three or four, and I got this from people who remembered it, my parents had a little game they played with me. They had three daughters who were older and now they had a son, which they had both wanted. I happened to be a responsive type of little kid, so they tell me. Anyway, they had this game. We had a pretty good size living room and parlor and one of my parents would get at one end and the other at the other end, maybe twenty-five or thirty feet apart. They would put me in the middle and say, "Which one do you love the most? Come to the one you love best." Well, I didn't know which one I loved the most. I had an aunt, who was older than my parents, and she was there watching this one day and she said to them, I learned later, "You ought not to play that game. You're shaking the kid up." I'd start toward one, you see, and then I'd start back toward the other. This was my fear. I had an emotional loyalty to both of them, but it was separate because each was different. My mother was a culture vulture, she believed in civilization and people and poetry. Whereas my father was a witty Irishman and interested in things more close to the earth. My mother would teach me Shakespeare and my father taught me sports. So all the time I was in the middle. Sometimes I would try to go with my mother, other times I would go with my father, and sometimes one would work on me and sometimes the other. I was a semisplit personality.

I guess we're all that way a little. Even Curly Lambeau. I remember back in 1963 when we were both elected to the Hall of Fame. I was out in California at the time, when we heard about it, down in Palm Springs, I believe it was. Curly had a home in California, too, and so I went up to see him in Los Angeles. I took him to a place for dinner and we wound up at the Palmer Hotel. Well, Curly was out with me and so I kind of guided things. In this place, in the Palmer, Chubby Checker was entertaining. He was there doing the twist, when it first came out. Chubby put on a demonstration and then the nightclubbers got to do it. I didn't get up, but out there on the floor was Curly, doing the twist. What a spectacle. Here was the guy who used to frown on me doing all that kind of stuff, and here I was watching him from the sideline.

I guess Curly was a human guy after all. He was not perfect, not an angel. But there weren't many angels in the pro league back then. I met a lot of good men there who had an angelic side and a devilish side. I'm sure a lot of them would say the same about me.

In 1973, Roy Blount, Jr., then a feature writer with *Sports Illustrated*, spent the entire football year, in his words, "loafing with (to use the old Pittsburgh term for hanging around with) a rich mixture of Steeler or Steeler-related persons." The experiences and observations were then fashioned into one of the most enjoyable and interesting books ever written about the sport of pro football, entitled *About Three Bricks Shy of a Load*. The excerpt here is an engaging, revealing profile of the preeminent Steeler of them all, The Chief, who is, of course, none other than founder/owner Art Rooney, one of the most revered and colorful figures ever associated with the game. The title of the book, incidentally, was contributed by a reserve defensive end, Craig Hanneman, who mentioned to Blount on the sidelines one Sunday afternoon when the Steelers were mauling the Oakland Raiders, "You picked the right team! Oh, a great bunch of guys! And a bunch of crazy fuckers! I'm crazy too! We're all about three bricks shy of a load!"

The Chief and Family

ROY BLOUNT, JR.

"TAKE A gas mask," said Noll, who hated cigar smoke.

"Take ten dollars," said Uncle Jim, who knew we were going to play the horses. "No more."

"You better take a can to pee in," said Richie Easton.

Richie, a chunky sanguine Syrian who drove a newspaper truck for a living and drove the Chief in his Imperial for recreation, and was one of the Chief's closest friends, was thinking of the Chief's disinclination to stop, for any reason, once he got rolling on the open road. The Chief, Richie and I were on a four-day trip to Liberty Bell Park in Philadelphia, Yonkers Raceway and Aqueduct in New York, Shamrock Farms in Maryland, and Shenandoah Downs in West Virginia. I kind of halfway hoped, professionally, to find out something disappointing about the Chief during this trip. It is a Jagov reporter who doesn't try to find out that people are different from the way they have been painted.

"Peezer Klingensmith," reminisced the Chief, after we had driven a ways. "Red Barr asked me to take Peezer up to St. Bonaventure, where the Steelers trained in those days. Peezer hadn't been feeling too well. He needed a rest. He was a friend of Red's. On the way to St. Bonny's, I thought we'd drive down to the farm. So we did, and spent the night there, and then we went to Delaware Park, and the next day to Garden State, then to New York, then back to Garden State for Saturday's racing. After the races we left for St. Bonaventure. We got as far as Scranton and went into a hotel, and here were these chicken fighters I knew from all over the country. So we went to the chicken fights. Right from the hotel. We didn't get nothing to eat. This is a Sunday now. We checked into the hotel finally at 4 in the morning. I said, "When is the first mass?" The man said '6:30.' 'Wake us at 6,' I said. So we went to mass and drove on and dropped down out of the mountains into St. Bonny's.

"When we got there Peezer said, 'I been gone for four days. All I ate was apples and peaches. We never slept. He drives a hundred miles an hour up and down mountains.' Peezer was in the hospital after that for a couple of weeks." The Chief curled his mouth in merriment and looked closely at his cigar. All through the trip the three of us smoked excellent cigars the size of Joe Greene's fingers steadily, from a big stock in the glove compartment, and sometimes it was hard to make out objects inside the car. The Chief called these cigars "Tobies."

We talked about Bradshaw's injury and the fans' reaction, which the Chief deplored.

"Sunday Bradshaw was down. Before the game he was telling me, there's a new study going on now. In your body, there are certain times you're at a low ebb. There's three waves in you, say. When these waves get below a certain level you're in danger. I was saying that's all the bunk. I hoped he didn't believe in that low wave. I said I'd been in that wave forty years. But then I met this provincial of the Holy Ghost Order. He understood these waves thoroughly. He said, 'Oh, that's a study they're taking in the human being.' The minute I saw Bradshaw come off that field with that shoulder I thought, there's no way to convince him those waves are the bunk. His wife's studying them at Pitt."

The news came over the radio that the Steelers were underdogs in the upcoming game with the Redskins. The Chief seemed pleased. "We ought to be," he said. "All our athletes got their bones broke."

His thoughts turned lightly to final things. "I put in my will that my funeral can't cost more than a thousand dollars. Did my wife start to squawk. I said what am I gonna know? Oh, she screamed. 'I'm going to have to be dead too,' she said, 'because you can't get anything for a thousand dollars.' She's a McNulty, they worry about being sick. She says all the Rooneys ever say about being sick is, if a person dies, 'Well, he musta been sick.' That's still in my will about the thousand dollars.

"I put people in her box, you know. She has a big box in the stadium, and I put people there. Tuffy Hacker, the trainer. Bobby Layne's going to be up there Monday night with six people. She says to Johnny, the usher, 'Who are these people in our box?' He says, 'Mrs.

Rooney, they've got tickets.' She says, 'I'm going to kill him.'

"I put a Greek archbishop in there once and she said, 'What am I going to say to him?' I said just the same as our bishop. They all believe in God. She liked him, though. Monday my cousin that's a nun will be in there and she don't wear her habit anymore. 'How can I tell?' my wife says. 'I don't know whether they're nuns or hoochie-coochie dancers.' Oh, she'll scream." The Chief shook in the front seat with pleasure and started a fresh Toby.

Just outside Liberty Bell, on a road lined with motels, the Chief said, "Dan Parrish told me to buy all this land in here. But I was never big on land. I don't know about anything, only horses. And football. Sports. I didn't know you could go to the bank and borrow money. I thought you had to have it in your pocket."

"What you have to realize," the Chief's son Pat told me once, "is that my father is a great man. None of his sons are."

But the Chief never borrowed a dime in his life, and his sons, without any capital to speak of except their name and the Steeler franchise, have borrowed over $60 million. With the Chief they constitute ten different corporations that own or control the Steelers, Yonkers Raceway, the William Penn Racing Association at Liberty Bell, Green Mountain Race Track in Vermont and Palm Beach Kennel Club, a greyhound track in Florida. The Chief is sole owner of Shamrock Farms. The Rooneys used to own a soccer team. They have made an offer to buy Garden State Park in New Jersey and they are building a thoroughbred track outside Philadelphia. If the boys are not great, they are certainly doing well, and they all reflect their father in various ways.

For one thing they will do what he tells them. "The old man is policy," says a man who has been close to the family, and the boys readily agree that they all talk to him every day, by phone or in person, and that if he rules against something they won't do it.

They also take pride in being down-to-earth like their father. They were all brought up in a poor neighborhood with other Irish kids, not feeling any different from anybody else. They knew, of course, that very rough kids refrained from swearing in the Rooney yard and that their father owned a football team. But they also knew that the family drove to the games in a car that sometimes had to be backed up steep hills.

They knew, too, that most of the time their father was off playing the horses, arranging some kind of athletic affair or swapping stories with Toots Shor or Billy Conn. But the Chief always came home on the weekends, and if at the end of a day he found himself as nearby as, say Cleveland, he would always drive home.

The Chief was not one for heart-to-heart talks with his

sons, but he kept their attention. When they put up a punching bag he would walk in and work out on it briefly in such a way as to leave the mouth of every kid present hanging open. He would also follow such unusual Christian procedures as bringing panhandlers in off the street for sandwiches. And when someone needed an authoritative opinion he would provide it, as when Artie complained that Timmy had just hit a kid over the head with a piece of sidewalk, which didn't seem fair. The Chief said, ''When you fight, you fight with whatever you need.''

The Rooney manse, an old Victorian house, had, and still has, white columns in front, 12 rooms inside, and a multipurpose backyard. The boys dug tunnels under it for war games, and in the winter they iced over the macadamized part for hockey, so they had plenty to do without hanging around pool halls. Their father told them never to hang around pool halls, and since he had hung around them enough as a boy to become a shark of some note, they figured he knew what he was talking about.

The Chief never had a harsh word for anybody else in the world, but he was inclined to call his sons ''chumps'' and ''newly made.'' The old man says, ''I always thought my coaches knew what they were doing. I *knew* the boys didn't.''

The boys remember calling his hand only twice. One day he went to watch Tim, John and Pat play sandlot ball. Tim singled to the outfield and when he reached first he turned to the right. The Chief went up to him and said, ''You're supposed to turn toward second.''

''That's the way you old guys did it,'' said Tim, who was then about twelve.

''Give me those balls and bats!'' shouted the Chief. ''I don't want people to know you're a Rooney.''

''I never watched them play ball again,'' he says today. ''You'll have to ask them about their athletic abilities. For this reason: I never thought much of 'em.''

The other moment of rebellion came more recently. Perhaps Tim was out of sorts after making the drive from Pittsburgh to Winfield, Maryland, the site of Shamrock Farms, the Rooney's thoroughbred stable. ''My father would sit there in the car saying his rosary,'' Tim says. ''He wouldn't talk to you, and he wouldn't let you turn on the radio, and he'd make you leave all the windows wide open in the middle of winter.''

At any rate, when the Chief told Tim to take off his boots inside the house at Shamrock, Tim complained. So his father gave him a good shot to the head. ''Then he turned to John, but John was on the track team, he ran,'' says Pat. At the time Tim was into his twenties, John was in college and the Chief was around sixty.

So if the resolution of the Oedipus complex requires the symbolic slaying of the father, the Rooneys will have

to count on the Oedipus complex not applying to the Irish. It was only in the last few years that the boys dared to drink in front of the Chief, or even to appear in public with him dressed in anything but a dark suit, white shirt and tie, such as he most always wears. But if they can't overthrow their father, they can expand upon him.

Each of the boys would have liked to take the helm of the Steelers. The family heirloom fell, however, to Dan, the oldest. The Chief had in mind Dan's becoming an electrician, since he didn't want to be a doctor or a lawyer; the Chief had an in with the union. ''But Danny just wanted to go up to the Steelers' training camp and work,'' he says, ''and there's no point in making a fella do what he isn't interested in''—anyway not when it is a matter of his life's work, as opposed to his waking up at six in the morning on vacation in Canada to go to early mass.

As for Artie, the scout, when someone suggests that he may have inherited his father's handicapping gifts, in terms of ballplayers rather than horses, Artie looks pleased as Punch. But what Artie wanted to be when he finished college was an actor. The Chief says he is always running into old friends from among ''Pittsburgh theatrical people,'' and he is proud enough that actress Anne Jackson is his cousin. But he was not eager to have an actor son. ''I knew Artie was wasting his time,'' he says, ''but I let him play the string out.''

So Artie went off to New York to try his fortune. ''Actually my type was pretty much in demand,'' he says. ''I made everybody around me on the stage look like fruits.'' But after a year or so on the boards Artie turned back toward a role more like his father's.

When racing was legalized in Pennsylvania and the family bought into William Penn Raceway, Artie worked there for a while, it being his turn to get a chance to prepare himself for a managerial job. If he had stayed on he would have become president and general manager instead of John, but Artie wanted to return to the Steelers. ''The other day after I got back from a trip to the coast,'' he says, ''my wife heard me telling somebody, 'I saw Fido out there, and he said he's seen Bow-wow.' '' Bow-wow and Fido are a couple of scouts. '' 'When are you going to get a real job?' my wife asked.'' Artie smiles.

Most observers, however, feel that of all the boys Tim, thirty-five, is most like the Chief. They think he has the most spark. But Tim couldn't cling to his Pittsburgh roots because there was no more room for Rooneys in the Steeler setup, and after he had worked for a few years as a stockbroker he went down to West Palm Beach to help run the dog track. Then the brothers took on their biggest challenge: the purchase of Yonkers Raceway for some $48 million.

When Artie came to New York to be an actor he was

warned by his brothers that if a man came up to speak to him on the subway it would be for the sake of making unnatural advances. So he nearly slugged the first man who asked him for directions. The Rooney boys are more sophisticated nowadays, but their venture into New York is a hazardous one. Off-track betting has cut into the attendance at Yonkers, the plant there is aged, Sonny Werblin is planning a big new harness track in New Jersey, and there are thirteen different unions to deal with.

The first night Yonkers opened under Rooney management there were pickets outside. Except for the 1968 NFL players strike, it was the only picket line the Rooneys had ever experienced. "If there was ever any trouble in Pittsburgh," Tim says, "there was no question whose side you were on; you were with the unions." But with Pittsburgh unions, he adds, "you were dealing with guys you grew up with."

There was no work for the twins, John and Pat, in sports when they finished college, so John taught high school for three years and Pat worked as a copper salesman. Then Liberty Bell opened and they worked their way up from punching tickets. Now John is president of William Penn, the nighttime harness operation, and Pat is president of Green Mountain.

At least one man who has been close to the family for some time thinks that Pat is the twin with the most spark. Certainly Pat comes closest of all the brothers to making a pointed remark about the Chief's view of life. "My father just doesn't understand that when some people wake up in the morning and look at their face in the mirror, it's not the greatest thing in the world," Pat says. "He thinks being a good Catholic takes care of all that."

None of the young Rooneys will ever enjoy the geographical unities of their father's life. But the boys have advanced beyond their father in necessary ways. "He's a brilliant man," says Dougherty. "But he's a man of the handshake. He finds transition to tax lawyers and comptrollers uncomfortable."

So far, with their father behind them and with the help of an expert Philadelphia lawyer-loan arranger named John T. Macartney, who is secretary-treasurer of the Yonkers corporation, the brothers are making the transition with a looseness that Johnny Blood might appreciate.

"They can be agonizing in their casualness in coming to meetings late or leaving early or not accepting what the meeting is for," says Dougherty. "Like the Yale band, they like to march out of step. But they do it in a way that's probably as disciplined as the Yale band."

There are people in Pittsburgh, and not just snobs or Protestants, who find fault with the Rooneys' original sources of power. "Senator Coyne was Andy Mellon's nigger; the Mellons kept him in power," says one such critic, who goes on to point out that for all the Chief's philanthropy, modesty and residential loyalty to the North Side, he has never had anything like the quality of civic bravery shown by Jack O'Malley—a local boy who played basketball with the Detroit Pistons, became a priest, could have been the bishop of Pittsburgh but went to live in the North Side and organize the poor blacks politically. Irish cops drive by the ground-floor window of O'Malley's apartment at night and yell obscenities at him, and he jumps out the window onto the sidewalk and offers to fight.

"The worst thing anybody can do is go into Art's office and say, 'I won a lot of money on that game,' " says an old friend of the Chief's, criticizing him from another angle. "He doesn't want to hear anything about gambling around him. All that money, he's got too much responsibility. He can have all that money. He's not the guy he used to be."

The guy he used to be must have had rough edges, in fact a rough center. They say the Rooneys could be cold-blooded about getting where they wanted to be, about avoiding being thought of as rubes or stiffs or yokels. Certainly, though he has given away a lot of money, he has never given away an edge in business dealings. The Chief is a teetotaler now, and he has always gone to mass every day when humanly possible, but he raised hell in the old days. He used to loaf in the saloon of Owney MacManus, who said before he died, "Naturally I had to drink with the boys and, as the day wore on, the effects began to show, I suppose. I've always been a great talker, but I never thought I was getting out of hand until my customers took it into their heads to throw me out one night. 'On what grounds?' I demanded to know. 'I own this place. On what grounds is the proprietor thrown out of his saloon?' They'd make some claim that I was guilty of monopolizing conversations. Pretty soon I was being thrown out of my own saloon every night. I even went to the extreme one day of refusing to drink anything at all. But did that stop Rooney and his gang? It did not. Cold sober, I was thrown out. That is man's final degradation—to be thrown out of his own place, sober."

That is the closest thing to a cold-blooded story about the Chief raising hell I have been able to turn up. Before he met his wife, Kathleen, a great woman in everyone's estimation, the Chief loafed with a lady who, according to an informed source, "was a rough one. When she got drunk she'd fight like a man." The Chief came up in politics at a time when North Side constituencies were poor and large sums of money came into political headquarters in cardboard boxes. Uncle Jim's advice to newly elected legislators is, "Get you an office with a high transom, so they can just throw the money in and you won't see 'em."

The Chief could be accused of dominating his brothers, except for Dan the priest, who probably could never have been dominated by anyone but God. The Chief was such a strong figure that it was perhaps easy for Jim and Vince to slip into drinking-uncle's roles, and for Jim to ruin the beer distributorship he and Vince went into, causing resentment on Vince's part. There is a family story that one afternoon while Jim, well into adulthood, was living with his mother, she said to him, "Jim, kill that fly for me," and he said, "I'll do it tonight." There is another story about Jim, that in his playboy days, when he was visiting New York frequently to patronize the Cotton Club in Harlem, he walked into his Follies girl's eighth-floor apartment and was confronted by a tiny dog that kept yapping and worrying at his feet. The Follies girl was in a back room, dressing. Jim picked up the little dog and dropped it out the window.

"Where's my little dog?" said the Follies girl, coming into the parlor.

"He's out taking a walk," said Jim. I guess that is a cold-blooded story.

I am trying to counteract some of the alleged saccharinity of my treatment of the Rooneys in *Sports Illustrated*. (I thought all that about his belting the boys was unsaccharine when it appeared in the story, but maybe not by Pittsburgh standards.) At the Super Bowl in Houston, when the Chief walked into a restaurant, a big table full of important TV people rose spontaneously and applauded. Norm Van Brocklin stopped his team's warm-ups before the Falcon-Steeler game to introduce all his players to the Chief. "There is no more beloved figure in the whole world of sports," says Edward Bennett Williams. It has been my experience that if you hang around a beloved figure long enough he will show a streak of meanness or fraudulence. Just like regular people. I was sincerely ready for such a streak to show up, hanging around with the Chief.

"My conscience is very elastic," said the Chief as we drove toward New York. "The way we came up . . . And some of this Watergate stuff has been going on since the beginning of time. Spies and that. But when you start forging telegrams and that, that's below the belt. And you use the security people you already have, legally. You don't go out and hire hoods.

"In this country, I don't think you would ever have the Nazis. The Jews, the Irish, Syrians, Italians, blacks. They wouldn't let them. It's not like there was all one kind of people, that could be fooled at once. But this here Erkleman, and Hardleman—it was like a fiction book. They had something on everybody. If someone hadn't got those guys, they would've been electing Presidents and senators for years.

"This Gray. I can see how a person can get involved in something. But the way he took those files, he hadda be either a rube or a weak sister. If anybody, I don't care if it's my brother, says 'Here, take these files and destroy 'em,' I'll say, 'You do it!' "

At Aqueduct the Chief apologized that he didn't know everybody the way he used to, but they recognized him right away at the gate, passed us all through, and people who looked like the tout on the Jack Benny radio show used to sound began to come up to him as soon as we got close to the windows. "Hello, Ott," they would say to him. "Were you in Florida? You know Ottie Siegel is very sick."

He played five races, using New York Racing Association vice-president Pat Lynch's "figures"—the kind of thing any serious horseplayer can work up, if he takes the time, from public information—and computed them out by his own formula, and he bet five or six hundred dollars altogether and came out close to $1000 ahead, hitting an exacta that paid $26.80. Not a bad day, but nothing like the killing he made in 1936 in two days at Empire City and Saratoga.

The Chief does not like to talk about the killing. I asked him about it in the car and he wouldn't say anything at all. It was probably the greatest individual performance in the history of American horseplaying. According to the story as it is usually printed, the Chief had $300 in his pockets and ran it to $21,000 one day at Empire City. He was planning to go back to Pittsburgh but he and a fighter named Buck Crouse dropped into a friend's sporting crowd restaurant and it wasn't long before the three of them were on their way to Saratoga. There the Chief bet $2000 eight-to-one on a horse named, portentously, Quel Jeu. The horse won, and so did several more during the day, by the end of which he had cleared $256,000.

Well, that is the kind of story which may well be inflated. In an attempt to get the truth of that story during my stay with the Steelers, I talked to six different people who were in a position to know, or to believe they knew. Here is what I found out.

Betting in those days was oral. You dealt personally, at the track, with established bookies, a class of people the Chief liked immensely. You could win bigger in those days because when you placed a bet at given odds it stayed at those odds, even if the bookie changed the price for subsequent bettors. When telephoning bets across state lines was made illegal, the Chief's large-scale betting days were over. He doesn't see much percentage in betting under the parimutuel system, whereby the odds are continually recomputed on the basis of the handle and the state and the track take healthy cuts. He enjoys it fairly often, but he doesn't see much percentage in it.

When the Chief went up to New York for the races that weekend in 1936, he owed bookies money, I was told, and the Steeler franchise was in bad shape. The Chief was by no means a rich man. The killing established the Rooney fortunes.

The Chief's bets were based on Tim Mara's information, which was, as they say, good. There may have been eleven winners in a row. The Chief had to hire an armored car to get the money back to Pittsburgh. A good piece of it was somehow lost along the way. The Chief walked into brother Vince's house with currency spilling out of his pockets and said, "You don't ever have to worry about money again." He gave a nice chunk to Father Dan in China. (Who later paid him back with information on the soybean crop in China which enabled the Chief to make a nice commodities score. The Chief has been known since it is said to peel off $10,000 and hand it to a priest with a worthy project whom he has just met after a good day at the track.) I am forced to conclude, however, that the total was not really $256,000.

"He told me," said Milton D. Taylor, the director of racing at Yonkers—whom the Chief called "the Babe Ruth, Hans Wagner and Ty Cobb of this business"— "that he went to Saratoga with $10,000 and ran it to $380,000. And he would've gone to $700,000 if Frank Erickson had been there. Frank Erickson was a bookie who never scratched his prices."

Every time I talked to a new informed source, the figure got more confidential and higher. All I am at liberty to say is that it may have been a good deal more than $380,000—1936 dollars—and it may have been a *lot* more. You can talk about Man o' War and Arcaro all you want. The Chief for my money is the biggest figure in horse racing history.

We spent the night in son Tim Rooney's eleven-room house in Scarsdale. Tim has what he believes to be virtually every book written by or about the Kennedys. The next day he gave us a tour of Yonkers, where he informed us that "the mushroom people" take all the track's manure away. Farmers used to pay for it, but then manure became unfashionable and the track had to pay to have it hauled away, but now it is somewhat back in style and the mushroom people remove it for free. The previous ownership of Yonkers would probably not have known such details about the operation.

We left Yonkers and headed toward the farm, which is in Winfield, Maryland, down the road from the place Whittaker Chambers used to have. On the way the Chief said, "I brought the first Brahmans into this part of the country. They all had humps on their backs. People used to come look at them, they looked like elephants. I used to have all exhorsepeople running the farm. Ex-grooms, ex-trainers, ex-jocks. They were all Irish. And they were all drunks. There'd be whiskey bottles under every tree. Seventy-seven cows died. I was on the train with this old guy and we got to talking, he said he was a farmer. I told

him about the cows dying. He said it was probably from eating out of galvanized tubs. Some of the galvanized got in their stomachs. Then we talked a while longer and he found out I was a horseman and all, and he said, 'Your cattle didn't die of those tubs. Your cattle starved to death.' I started to laugh. I said, 'You know, I think you're right.' My guys were all horse guys, not cattle guys. And they'd drunk too much to go out in the sun. So I had to get rid of the cattle." He laughed again.

The farm is now run by Arnold and Roberta Shaw, a sober couple. Arn Shaw used to work as a brakeman with the Bangor and Aroostook Railroad. We viewed a Black Angus bull named Timmy Rooney who had delighted the Chief by jumping around and causing himself and his cage to go end over end—"doing a Brodie"— before the Chief's eyes at the Gaithersburg Fair. The mailman had told Arn that the bull did it because a lady had walked by with a poodle. The Chief was delighted by the idea of his having been at the Gaithersburg Fair in the first place. "You know, for a guy like me. A fair. And animals." He had the air of a slum kid at a petting zoo. Smoking a Toby.

We looked at some cows, which looked at us the way cows always do, as if they were saying, "Say what?" or "Uhr, excuse me?" The Chief seemed to like the cows almost as much as he used to like bookies.

As we were getting ready to leave for Shenandoah Downs to watch the Chief's horse Christopher R. run, the big locust tree out in front of the farmhouse was discovered to be on fire. It was a strange sight: smoke pouring from the top of an old tree, no flames. It looked like a cigar, with branches, being puffed hard. The Winfield Volunteer Fire Department was represented within a few minutes by twelve men, two fire trucks, one pickup truck and a boy.

"A tree fire," one fireman said.

"I be dog."

They poked around in the hollow part at the bottom of the tree and found it to be glowing. Somebody said to a fireman named Howard, "Here's your far, Hard."

"An owl used to roost up there," said Arn. "Sit up there looking at the cat."

"We'll be all right," the Chief assured an inquisitive fireman, "if Hanratty doesn't get hurt."

"Where were you when they called?" one fireman asked another.

"Down over back behind the house somewhere."

Smoke was still pouring from the tree. "Who's got the ax?"

"I don't know. Who had it last?"

"Weiner had it."

"Where's Weiner then?"

"It's funny," said Roberta, "that tree *looked* like it was smoking an hour ago."

The firemen were filling the tree—which was now perceived to be hollow all the way up and down the trunk—with water from a hose directed down from the top by a man standing on a ladder leaning against the smoking tree. It smoked on. An ax was laid into the root of the tree and at the first cut black water rushed from it like blood.

The Chief looked as solemn as he had looked the whole trip. "You don't think it was the Toby I put in that hollow place at the bottom do you?" he asked.

The fireman took the ladder down and pulled the tree over with a rope. One fireman directed the hose all the way through the fallen carcass, which was still smoking and bleeding, and hit another fireman on the other end.

"Hey, Mr. Rooney," a fireman called as we left. "Them Redskins gonna burn out too."

"From the time I was a kid," the Chief said on the way to the track, "I was the manager of teams; running things, selling tickets. Kids don't have the opportunity to organize that I had then. I was like the coach of the Pittsburgh Collegians, the baseball team that traveled around. I was a kid, and they were young guys and old guys. We'd stay in places where you'd have to reach down with your hand and sweep the bedbugs out." This memory tickled him.

I asked him how he kept his teams together and under control. "Loafed with 'em. Never expected 'em to do anything I wouldn't do. If there were any fights I was right there. One time at a place called Cato, Ohio, at a Chautauqua, my brother that's a priest—he was a rough guy you know—he was the catcher and he took everybody on. That fight didn't end till the firemen came. All the clothes I had on at the end was my baseball pants."

At the track Christopher R. won the Tri-State Futurity—the biggest win for one of the Chief's horses in fifteen years. Tuffy Hacker, the horse's diminutive trainer, told the press in the winner's circle, "I'd rather not answer any questions. I just live from day to day and

I just train from day to day." He chased everybody he didn't know out of the picture. The Chief allowed it to be Tuffy's moment.

The Chief had been a bit querulous with Richie and me when we missed a highway exit or got bogged down in the wrong lane of traffic: "My wife says don't go unless somebody's driving you. But look at you guys drive. I wish the football team was as good as I drive." Richie told me that the Chief could be a lot more critical than that of a person's driving. But what his irritation seemed to stem from was just his eagerness to get on as directly as possible to the next glad place. "I like my life because it's pleasant," said Jimmy Cannon of a sportswriter's life. "I function in glad places."

In four days we had visited four racetracks and a farm, in four different states, talking everywhere to dozens of people of high and low estate who came up to the Chief as if they saw him every day, and he had won enough betting at Aqueduct to pay for the trip several times over, and the whole four days had been an easy recreative glide through the cigar smoke Noll hated. At 5 A.M., when we reached Pittsburgh after driving straight from the track, the Chief didn't look any tireder than he ever did, which is to say he didn't look tired at all, and I was worn out from looking for a mean or fraudulent streak. He hadn't shown me one, and he never did.

A remiss streak, yes. There were those seventy-seven cows. And it *was* the Chief's Toby butt that set fire to the tree. Joe Williams (Edward Bennett Williams's son, who was working on the farm) and I saw the long Toby-shaped ash there at the roots. Arn hushed Joe when he started to say something about it.

But if those ex-horsepeople were even less suited to running a farm than Johnny Blood was to coaching a pro football team, I'll bet they were good company in many ways. And I would have paid admission to see that tree fire.

It was Samuel Johnson, the great English poet, essayist, and lexicographer, who in the eighteenth century defined sport as "tumultuous merriment." Heywood Hale Broun borrowed the definition to title his own entertainingly merry romp through the subject in a book he wrote in 1979. A sportscaster, writer, and actor, Broun has observed, studied, and compellingly characterized some of the most famous sports figures of recent decades. Among the most interesting are those associated with the game of professional football to whom he addresses his pen in the excerpt that is reprinted here.

Tumultuous Merriment

HEYWOOD HALE BROUN

FOOTBALL HAS been rousing emotions for hundreds of years in a variety of forms, all having in common the idea of moving a ball from one place to another with varying degrees of violence as the means of propulsion.

When, in 1314, Edward II tried to ban the game "Forasmuch as there is a great noise in the city caused by hustling over large balls, from which many evils may arise," he was tilting at windmills as were Greek moralists who pulled their beards over the roughnesses of the game then called *episkyros*.

Football is, after all, a wonderful way to get rid of aggressions without going to jail for it. I thought of this while watching the game of street football the Florentines put on every year in the Piazza dei Signore to commemorate some civic triumph which now escapes me.

Teams from the four quarters of the city march into the square in gorgeous Renaissance costumes; referees flourish plumed hats at each other, and fifteen minutes later someone from the Western section has been kicked in the shin and has retaliated by tearing an East's ruffles and bloodying his nose. Within half an hour there have been quite a few scores and some of them are being settled in sanguinary fashion as the ball eddies from East to West.

Intellectual cynics think of modern American football as just a ruffianly way of making big money, but this is an oversimplification. I would agree with Bill Curry, the old Green Bay Packer, who said there wasn't enough money to pay for the pain of plunging at Dick Butkus late in a hard-fought match.

Curry said he kept getting up and bouncing off Butkus again because of the strong sense of fellowship that the joint shedding of blood and adrenalin engenders, the desire to throw one's arms around comrades at the end of a successful enterprise. The wish for this strong, if temporary, family feeling will make some men push through constant pain to play a game.

The intensity of the desire simply to play was brought home to me early in my stay with CBS News when a ramshackle minor league team called the Brooklyn Dodgers was assembling a roster. They had picked up a number of NFL old-timers and failed rookies, and as a last gasp held a one-day open tryout at the old Gaelic football field in the Bronx, a barren, bumpy stretch where grass dies under the blank-eyed stares of old subway cars lined up on an adjacent elevated structure.

More than seventy men showed up in varying states of dress and physical readiness, most with football shoes hung round their necks, shoes in which briefly they had felt the ground turn to fiery clouds beneath their feet in some high school or college triumph, a triumph that drives them to one more try for the feeling.

Coach Andy Robustelli was honest in his opening speech, pointing out that though this was a chance, it was a last chance and that those who did not make it here should put the dreams away with the shoes and find some earthbound occupation. It was not the expression of a high opinion of Andy's league, but he's always been a realist, and as a realist he warned the candidates that when they were doing something marvelous he might be looking the other way and that in an unjust world this would be a not unexpected addition to an endless list of injustices.

For two hours we watched, wondering at the self-deception that led most of the men to this minefield of humiliation, and marveling at the fierceness of desire and its tragic inability to overcome such handicaps as shortness of arm, heaviness of foot, and pervasive clumsiness. I saw men leap up for passes with the strained concentration on their faces that turns up in pictures of runners breasting an Olympic tape, and I saw the men miss the passes by as much as two feet.

One perfect football player turned up who passed a spiral as tight as a coil spring and spotted his passers with the ease and accuracy of a carnival shill knocking over wooden bottles. Unhappily, although he gave his height as five feet seven, he came only to my shoulder during our interview, and I am five feet eight. He would have fitted nicely into a pickup game of jockey room personnel.

When it was all over, one soccer kicker had been signed to a trial contract, and whether the unsuccessful took Robustelli's advice, I don't know. I suspect that those old football shoes had a few more futile steps in them.

Nobody, of course, epitomized the fanatical nature of competitive football more than Vince Lombardi, who made of the game a symbol of a life bearing the strange device Excelsior.

I first met Vince in December 1966, when, in search of a little warm weather in which to practice for a playoff game in Dallas, he brought his Packers to Tulsa, Oklahoma, and ran into the same frost that stopped Longfellow's young Excelsior bearer from getting across the Alps. The Swiss mountains, however, are accustomed to snowbanks, while Tulsa had no more snow removal equipment than has the city of Honolulu. The CBS Saturday News was there to do a feature on how the Packers were wrapped and braced for combat, and, with the leader's permission, we were all set up in the bowels of the stadium when the Packer bus arrived—and all the lights went out for five blocks around.

As the players stumbled down the dark stairs, our electrician, on Lamoreaux's instruction, shone a battery lamp on the light-colored ceiling, providing enough illumination for people to move about and enough for us to see Lombardi's face, which looked like the fright mask on a samurai helmet.

Seeing a group of strangers in his dressing room, Lombardi shouted—I interrupt here to set up some ground rules. In these permissive days I could reproduce all of Vince's words without fear of being arrested but they would have a shock value beyond what he intended. I could also use blanks but these take up space and start lurid guessing games. You must just accept that every other word on his side of our ensuing conversation (and of many of our later conversations) was what Penrod Schofield used to call "a vile oath," or in Penrod's spelling, "oth," although many of the words were oaths I hope Penrod had never heard—Anyway, with oaths stripped away, Vince shouted "Get out!" Bud pointed out that we had been given leave to be there by him and that anyway we were providing the only available light. Vince said he didn't care about the light, he just wanted us out of there.

He indicated that he wished we would leave Tulsa University Stadium, the city of Tulsa, and even the state of Oklahoma. He then turned on his heel and dashed into the office provided for him, or to put it more accurately, he dashed into the wall of the office provided for him. The subsequent sounds seemed to be vile oaths in purest form, if that's the right modifier, but at last a request for candles rang through the room, and a terrified janitor scurried off to fumble through a dark storeroom.

I pointed out to Bud that Lombardi's instructions to us were clear beyond the possibility of mistake and that we were still standing within range of the coach's formidable anger. Bud, a better psychologist than I, or perhaps more eager for the story, counseled patience and a waiting game, and in about three minutes Lombardi emerged from the office calm and smiling, told us that he knew he had behaved badly, thanked us for the light, hoped we would be able to supply it for a time even though filming would be impossible without full power, and asked us to join him and his coaches at the evening cocktail ritual where it was known that Lombardi—for a few minutes—actually relaxed.

The evening was an agreeable one, even though at rest Vince had that look of potential danger that one sees in a contented carnivore full of red meat—for the moment. The next day the lights had been restored, and we were able to guess the coach's dominance as we watched the walking wounded parade as the Packers entered the trainer's room. There, aluminum braces were fitted over knees purple with scars, swellings were pressed into an appearance of normalcy with little corsets of adhesive tape, and a group of men who had been shaken and battered into the rattling looseness of beloved old toys were tightened up for one more Sunday.

Quarterback Bart Starr stood before the trainer with his arm upraised so that a spongy rubber doughnut could be taped against his ribs to protect some torn cartilage. As the gentle fingers softly pressed the resilient rubber against the bruised skin, Starr gave a full-throated shout of pain. The Comanche code of stoicism that forbids groans on the field didn't apply here, but as I looked at Starr, biting his lip as the tape tightened the pressure, I realized that in a few days he would be prepared to stand with that arm upraised in a game, looking for his receiver and waiting, even as he was aware of the onrushing shoulder of a monster lineman, a shoulder armored like the ram of an Algerian pirate galley. If he didn't get the ball away soon that shoulder would hit the doughnut with the effect of a steam hammer on an egg, but one mustn't think about that. One must keep looking for the receiver. Vince wouldn't like it if you didn't keep looking for the receiver.

Victorious in the NFL Championship game—Vince wouldn't have liked it if they lost—the Packers moved on to the Super Bowl in Los Angeles and chose to practice away from the public eye on a field in Santa Barbara. Lombardi announced that no pictures would be allowed, so I was somewhat surprised when Lamoreaux told the crew to get ready for a trip to Packer practice. When I pointed out that for most people, the ukases of Lombardi had the force of the wishes of Genghis Khan, Lamoreaux said, "He owes us something for those lights in Tulsa and he's not the kind of person who forgets."

When we began unpacking beside the field Lombardi ran toward us with the gait and sound effects of a phobic rhinoceros. When he came close enough for recognition he rumbled to a stop and growled in a voice one would use to profaners of the inner temple, "Oh, it's you guys. Okay, but twenty minutes. Got that? Twenty minutes and OUT!" We assured him that this time would amply fill our needs and we were going to go into some further thanks when he turned on his heel and marched toward another cameraman whom he ordered off the field in a tide of scalding words.

"But Vince," protested the man, "I work for you. I'm the Packers' cameraman."

"One camera is enough," snarled Lombardi, "and right now, it's theirs. OFF, OFF, OFF!"

(Like a coloring book, the preceding conversation, like the one in Tulsa, comes ready for you to decorate from the depths of your vocabulary.)

We hurried through our work and on the stroke of the twentieth minute, Lombardi, like the late Zero Mostel, was again visibly turning into a rhinoceros, and only

subsided into his normal fury when he saw us pell-melling things into the car.

We met again from time to time and I always felt from him a certain cautious affability, a remembrance of a difficult day on which we had been helpful, and it became less cautious as it became obvious that Bud and I did not intend further to presume on the small obligation.

Our last meeting occurred on the day he took over the Washington Redskins at their Carlisle, Pennsylvania, training camp. The Skins had the reputation of being a rather jolly and sophisticated bunch who took winning and losing with the insouciance of oil sheiks at a roulette table, and the world was waiting to see how Lombardi, who regarded insouciance as something appropriate to games like lawn bowls, would do with his new charges.

His first words to me on arrival were, "No sound, Heywood. GOT THAT? I want you to shoot everything silent or get out. IS THAT CLEAR? No sound!"

I gave him the pleasant meaningless smile of a poker player looking at a raise, and Bud busied himself with some small task that would keep him away from the conversation. As soon as Vince had returned to his chores, planning began as to how we were going to achieve sound under the eyes of a man who can see a caterpillar yawn and hear a gnat belch.

One could easily see Vince's reasons for wishing to be presented as a vigorous Trappist. It was his obvious intention to use a volume of noise and abuse that would make the rhinoceros no more than a happy nightingale, and although he wished it to burn the Redskins' spiritual flab as Savonarola's sermons burned the hedonisms of Florence, he didn't want the whole nation to hear him in full cry.

Our methods were those of ingenuity rather than underhanded engineering. No ingenious bugs were taped inside helmets or gummed to the water bucket; all that was used in our subsequent piece were a few full-throated roars and such coachly advice as "Throw the ball here. That's where I want the ball thrown. I don't want the ball thrown way the hell up in here. I want you to throw—throw it in here." These admonitions accompanied by illustrative gestures. The vile oaths, although plentiful, were obviously not for the foreseeable future of television.

We knew that Vinnie was watching our soundman to see if he wore the headphones with which the levels are checked when sound is being recorded. The soundman in this case worked by guess, his ears proclaiming their innocence by their nakedness, and occasionally we withdrew from the equipment altogether for a conference, a moment after the cameraman had flicked with his toe the switch on the machine as it lay on the ground. The pictures of shoes were of little use but the sound was there. What we wanted was simply the cutting edge of a voice that could and did drive men to prodigies of physical effort.

I didn't think of myself as some sort of auditory paparazzo or sinister stealer of civil rights, but just as a man completing a portrait, a portrait which was, in fact, highly laudatory, since I always thought of Lombardi, given the philosophical framework in which he worked, as a great man. Setting great store by obedience, however, he never forgave me.

Months later, when Irv Drasnin, a CBS producer, wanted to do something about the Redskins, Vinnie cursed the bewildered Drasnin as if he were an underworld emissary with some unclean proposal about throwing games. It appeared that Irv's corporate connection with me made him unacceptable to Lombardi.

"What did you do to him," Drasnin asked me later, expecting to be told I had stolen a playbook or told dirty jokes in front of Marie Lombardi.

"I recorded his voice," I replied, and my colleague went away shaking his head in wonder.

Vince was iron-hard but basically fair, and when he became something of a conservative idol, I used to wonder what some of his admirers would think if they knew that the rooming lists at Green Bay were made alphabetically and entirely without respect to race. None of the euphemisms about compatibility, which other teams employ, would do for Lombardi. Any Packer should be proud to room with any other Packer.

In our last interview, when I asked whether fun and relaxation were not a necessary relief to the training grind, he said, "I think there's a place for laughter, but certainly not on the field. This is not a laughing business, and out here there's no—there's very little fun on the field. And I might add this: There's no laughter in losing, either."

That's vintage Vinnie, and whether you agree with it or not, you must admit that it marches with the iron tread that took Lombardi's ancestors, in their disciplined legions, to the corners of the known world.

We seemed, Bud and I, for people who were doing light, cheery features, to photograph a lot of tears. Some of the most copious came at the end of the Jets' 1969 Super Bowl triumph. The game will be knowledgeably discussed elsewhere in this book but suffice to say here that at the very end, as the Jets ran off the field, a security man, one of those people who say "Can I help you?" just before they hit you, threw me against the wall with what seemed to me unnecessary violence. Losing my head, I kicked him sharply in the calf and then, as he turned to do the job that brutality training had fitted him for, I recovered my head and ran into the Jets' dressing room. Bud and the camera crew followed, and suddenly

we were all alone in the middle of the celebration to which the press was not yet supposed to be admitted. Thus we were able to film one of the great scenes of our decade together. It was Joe Namath, one architect of victory, hugging a little old man in a funny straw hat while he and the little old man beamed love at each other and cascaded tears. The hat was on top of Namath's father and when the two Hungarians had finished laughing and crying, enough emotion had been expended to fuel two gypsy orchestras and a czardas competition.

It has always seemed odd to me that football players who bring high emotion and intense dedication to the game, and who recognize the need for constant sharpening of their skills, are so casual and so inept in their frequent forays into acting. Perhaps the arrogance that sustains them through the agonies of competition gives them the belief that they can do anything, but Joe Namath on the field had the fearful grace of a hunting leopard while on the screen he displays the nervous aimlessness of the leopard's trapped victim.

So, too, O. J. Simpson and Jim Brown, whose perfect timing on the field took them through opposing lines like mercury on a tilted table, do not show a concomitant deftness with the lines of a Hollywood script.

My firsthand look at football players as actors occurred a couple of years ago when a movie was being made from George Plimpton's book *Paper Lion*. Bud and I went to Boca Raton to make pictures of Alan Alda and the Detroit Lions making pictures.

The sequence being shot when we arrived entailed a good deal of movement as a group of Lions decide to take the young writer masquerading as a quarterback to dinner, and there were a number of crosses and recrosses that had to be done so as to reveal specific speakers at specific moments. The drill was not, however, any more complex than the average end sweep with pulling guards, and the amateur actors' inability to get it right was due largely to the fact that they were treating the whole thing like the first rehearsal of a fraternity musical and convulsing each other with primitive ad libs and physical improvisations that made hash of the necessary patterns.

The director, Alex March, was an old friend of mine. I had met him when he was an actor and I a sportswriter. I had been amazed that this sensitive young man was a sports fan at the uncritical level of the bubble gum card collector, and I was sorry to see that now the bubbles of those early worshipful dreams were bursting into a sticky mess and ruining take after take as the Lions continued throwing chaos at the choreography.

At last, by some miracle, everything went perfectly to the final line, which was spoken by Alex Karras. He was to say simply, "I've got the coat," and put it over Alda/Plimpton's shoulders. The cameras rolled, the players moved so that no line or action was covered,

Alex arrived and added an adverb of obscene and unlikely description to the coat.

Gray-faced, March got up from his director's chair and walked off the set, leaving the laughing Lions to pummel Alex in playful rebuke. I followed March and found him leaning his forehead against a cool metal sound truck. In my acting years I had worked under his direction and knew him to be a patient man but one who could be deeply angry when his patience broke. I didn't think it would help to be deeply angry with people like Karras and Roger Brown, who between them had about six hundred pounds of muscle and two ounces of common sense.

"I can't bench them," groaned Alex, "I can't fine them, and I can't trade them. What the hell can I do with them?"

All I could do was to suggest breaking for lunch, a suggestion which, for lack of a better one, he accepted. During the break I sought out John Gordy, a thoughtful man who was, at the time, the head of the NFL Players' Association, as well as a first-rate guard of ten years' experience. I pointed out that when Plimpton had joined the Lions there had been an undercurrent of resentment on the discovery of the masquerade. The players had been told that George was a legitimate candidate for the team, a quarterback from a college sufficiently obscure to have escaped sports page notice.

They felt that Plimpton's pretense was a put-down of their profession and they grumbled at his making a joke of a solemn calling.

Now the roles were reversed and I asked Gordy if Alda resented the fact that an art to which he had given his life, an art in which he was, in their terms, all-pro, was being treated like recess on the last day of school by a bunch of untrained Punchinellos.

Gordy gave it some thought and then came up with a complex but revealing answer.

"I don't think he resents us," he said, "because he would rather be a football player than we would want to be actors. Look at him out there, he's practicing his passes and skipping lunch."

Sure enough, Alda was patiently tossing footballs at a jacket on the ground, paying a respect to their skills which they denied to his. Later I asked him the same question I had asked Gordy and found him as tactful as Daniel or Androcles and for the same reason. He did wistfully admit, however, that he would like to bring off a few plays in first-class style before the movie was finished, and I hope that he did. They seem to have been called back in the cutting room.

The daydream of being a player, the thing . . . finally caught Alda by the arm, was illustrated, even further by an otherwise sane, successful family man, a forty-seven-en-year-old fashion photographer named Al Barrett, selected by Lamoreaux as a fan exemplar. He attended every Giant game and every football luncheon. When the Giants were unreachably on the road, he would set his children up in front of the TV screen in Giant sweat shirts to throw their unheard piping against the far-off cheers of the partisan crowd, while he and his friends hung tensely off the edge of the sofa and the wives lurked in the background ready to rush forward with the halftime cold cuts, as out there trainers would pass through the locker room with the halftime Gatorade.

Bud and I spent several days with Barrett contrasting his mingled lives of firsthand elegance in the high-fashion world and vicarious violence at the Stadium, and I still remember the light in his eyes when he said to me, "When a Giant runs down the field with the ball I sort of run with him, and somewhere inside I'm saying to myself, if I were a little bigger, a little faster, a little braver, it really would be me out there."

For the people who watch it, then, football is often the food of fantasy, and for those who play it there are a variety of fulfillments.

In 1971, after fourteen years of playing linebacker—in school, college, and in the pros—with a savagery that awed even his fellows in ferocity, Dave Meggysey had a change of heart, quit the St. Louis Cardinals in mid-career, and wrote a book called *Out of Their League.*

I had read portions of the then unfinished book before we sought out Meggysey in a Northern California hideaway where he was working on the final chapters and living the Berkeley life of natural foods and designedly noncompetitive exercise like jogging and a little free-form no-score soccer. The chapters on his childhood were bleak accounts of loveless, joyless years on a farm, years in which the anger built inside the boy like smoldering embers under the crust of a forest floor. Then one day in high school he made the great discovery that anger could be ritualized in football, a game which permitted you to do things on the field that you'd get arrested for off it.

In his years at Syracuse and with the Cardinals he earned such attractive nicknames as Mad Dog, and let loose the bottled flames of his rage until suddenly and oddly he was on the revival trail. It was with the highly self-conscious heaviness of the reformer that he opened our interview with "Football addresses itself, or talks about, or articulates—symbolically articulates—some of the worst values in American society. Certainly it is a militarist organization and the glorification of violence within that organization, and if we talk about athletics as a means of self-expression and a means to achieve competence, then it seems to me a little bit inhumane to achieve that notion of competence by defeating another person continually."

He seemed serenely sure that his volte-face was a

revelation and that he could leave behind him all that had driven him through the whole of his youth. Remembering that youth, I finally asked him the obvious question: "Dave, the conflicts of your childhood are still in you, stoking up the fire. If you quit playing football, how are you going to express that anger?"

The question was so obvious that he had, as all of us do, kept it just over the rim of consciousness. A troubled look ran over his newly mild features, and he sighed.

"I guess you're right," he said, "but I haven't given it any thought."

He was a kind of test-tube perfect example in the endless debate about whether brutal sport is a release of dangerous repressions, a substitute for war and violence on a larger and more dangerous scale, or a subtle corrupter that makes us view pain and its infliction as too commonplace to justify shock. I hope that Meggysey's new zealotry has been hot enough to keep the flue of his psyche in working order.

There is a phrase in psychiatric jargon. "Well compensated," which means that the cracks in a personality are being papered by some external circumstance such as fame, power, or money. Should these things be withdrawn the cracks may widen into splits, and the person would do well to seek help toward the goal of being "Well adjusted," a state that suggests that one can deal with anything except the basic unreasonableness of life.

Sport, with it fantasies and intensities, obviously is as useful as acting, with its opportunity to win the attention and even love of strangers, in arranging that the flawed are, for a time, well compensated. It should be pointed out, however, that the nature of the two occupations dictates that there are more old actors than old athletes, and that there's usually a lot of life to get through after the uniform has been turned in.

I once had a long talk with another troubled player, George Sauer, Jr., the brilliant pass catcher of the Jets who drifted out of football in search of fulfillment as a writer. I had warmed to him on a day when a couple of loud voices on their way to a hangover had stopped to watch practice. Burping out a disagreeable mixture of whiskey, steam, and venom, they kept shouting that he would never be the man his father, a great all-American,

had been, ringing a number of uninteresting changes on this theme.

Sauer ignored them and continued to run his pass patterns, but as he left the field he veered to run past me and murmur, "I've heard of your father, too."

During our subsequent talk I asked how a man of his considerable sensibilities got along in the aggressive world of football.

"You forget," said Sauer, "that I'm not expected to be aggressive. Just the opposite, in fact. As a wide receiver I'm always running for my life, learning that to be an outsider is the ultimate achievement."

In the end, this rationalization was not enough, and George, the loner who was not that well compensated by gladiatorial oneness, drifted out of the game while still at the peak of his athletic power.

It's true, of course, that when we speak of football in other than simple fan terms our approach is almost always a debate on the merits of its martial aspects. The fact that a dancer's sureness of foot and a cheetah's speed are also essentials tends to get lost.

Certainly the most unlikely looking football player that I ever interviewed was Noland Smith, who used to be a kick returner for the Kansas City Chiefs. Noland was about five feet six and weighed about 150 pounds. Despite this he was successful because, skittering downfield like a water bug, he escaped the behemoths as mosquitoes escape the ham-fisted slaps of weight lifters. When we took a picture of him feeding his tiny baby a bottle while his wife, who made him feel comfortably large, stood by, and it looked like a domestic scene in Lilliput, and when he sat next to big Buck Buchanan on the Kansas City bench I suddenly thought of a forgotten story from my childhood. It appears, according to this cautionary tale, that Richard the Lion-Heart, meeting Saladin the Saracen in a prebattle conference, endeavored to impress the Arab leader by cutting an iron bar in two with a blow of his broadsword. Saladin then took a silk handkerchief from a pocket, hung it over the blade of his scimitar, and with a flick of his wrist sent the blade upward to freedom as a pair of silk fragments fluttered down.

Maury Allen, a distinguished sports reporter in his own right, said of Jimmy Cannon, "He revolutionized sportswriting and made it noble. . . . He was the Joe DiMaggio of sportswriters." Maybe the Johnny Unitas of it as well. In this article he presents an interesting side to sportscaster-turned-team-owner, the often controversial Harry Wismer, who was awarded the charter AFL franchise for the New York Titans in 1960 but found making the payroll an insurmountable obstacle. Three years later, the Wismerless Titans, of course, became known as the Jets.

On Harry Wismer

JIMMY CANNON

THE LANDSCAPE of sports was changed by Harry Wismer. The American Football League was his idea. He put it together, and started it going. But trouble ruined him, and nothing worked after he got his team on the shabby grass of the old Polo Grounds. They were the Titans then, and on one Sunday they played to 1,100 buffs but Wismer claimed there were 11,000 in the ballpark. The club is now called the Jets, and 61,615 tickets were sold for the game with the Denver Broncos the Sunday before Wismer died at fifty-three.

Only the action seemed important to Wismer; it was being where it was happening and moving fast and traveling first class with famous people. He picked arguments as if he were waging a continuous fight against boredom. The angers always seemed spurious to me, and traced with a savage comedy.

The rage appeared to be sustained only as long as Wismer was entertained by the feud. The animosities would often end abruptly. The recollections elated Wismer who also dramatized the reunions. Excitement was the trophy. He went to great lengths to achieve it. Being conspicuous meant a lot to him, and he depended on controversy.

It began to break for Wismer when he became a sports broadcaster. He sounded like a drowning man hollering for help when he covered a football game. Even the timeouts were celebrated with a calculated hysteria. He dropped names during lulls, and would even mention the sportswriters covering the event. Years ago, imprisoned in my apartment by a virus, I listened to Wismer narrate a Notre Dame game.

"Sitting in the press box . . . Jimmy Cannon . . ." came that desperate voice.

He praised my style as a reporter, and I felt slightly ashamed that I didn't have the talent Wismer staked me to. Everyone was better than they were when Wismer noticed them on the radio. It was as though he wouldn't tolerate mediocrity being present at any game he was describing to a microphone.

Once Wismer held pieces of the Redskins and the Detroit Lions. But he couldn't stand the National League when he conceived the American. There was a strain of humor in the courageous stories he used to diminish the other league. But they were seldom funny in print. It was one of his gags to insinuate that some clubs in the National League were controlled by gangsters. It was all done to provoke a reply from the Nationals. They rebuked him with their silence. That hurt him. His nature demanded controversy.

There was a time when Wismer shilled for Joe Foss who was the first commissioner of the Americans. The name seemed a sacred ejaculation when Wismer uttered it because Foss had won a medal of honor.

Eventually, they quarreled. It was thought by many that Wismer was trying to get Foss bounced. But when he was married Foss was his best man.

Sports journalists were bawled out by Wismer if they didn't go along with him. The publicity was generally bad. But Wismer acted like a guy who enjoyed it. There was a series of press agents. They left or were fired for one reason or another. One of the last was Murray Goodman who understands the business of hustling newspaper space for sports promotions. He had been around a long while, and he laughs about the time he did with the old Titans.

It was 1962 and the Titans were training on the grounds of a school at East Stroudsburg, Pennsylvania. They had two coaches. Presumably, Bulldog Turner was running the squad because he had been recently hired by Wismer. But Sammy Baugh had a season left on his contract. He appeared on the field along with Turner and both of them seemed to be head coaches. It was Goodman's assignment to straighten out Baugh so that Turner could take over by himself.

"Sammy, what do you want?" Goodman remembered the other day as he reconstructed the conversation he had with Baugh.

"I want to get paid," Baugh said.

"How much would you take in cash?" Goodman asked.

"What do you offer?" Baugh wanted to know.

"Ten thousand," Goodman said.

The publicist called Wismer, and told him the sum and was told to make the deal. But Baugh was a proud man and money wasn't enough. They had stopped talking, Wismer and Baugh.

"I want Harry to say hello to me," said Baugh.

The proposition was relayed to Wismer. He turned it down.

"Harry insisted that Sammy speak to him first," Goodman said.

The league entered the negotiations. They gave Baugh $20,000 in installments, and it all seemed very bitter. But they shook hands in 1964 when Baugh coached the Houston team, and Wismer was out of football. It ended pleasantly because Wismer sat on the Houston bench that Sunday in Shea Stadium when the Jets beat the Oilers.

Near the finish the players on the Titans were worried about being paid, and the league guaranteed their salaries. College kids ducked the team because of its financial condition. But Wismer offered Ron Vander Kelen $125,000 and contended he would pay Sid Gilman $50,000 a year if he would come to New York.

It was Sonny Werblin, then one of the partners in the Music Corporation of America, who negotiated the original television contract for the A.F.L. The Titans are the Jets now. The Polo Grounds is leveled. The Jets are one of the most lucrative franchises in sports. The Americans and the Nationals have merged. Werblin runs the Jets, and Wismer is dead. And there wouldn't have been an American League without Harry Wismer.

What can one possibly write about a Roman-numeralized Super Bowl that several hundred other scribes attending the pageant are not already putting down on paper? It is always a dilemma. But Frank Deford found a novel way. As the editorial lead-in to his story explains: "Last January (1977) *Sports Illustrated* assigned Frank Deford to cover all the Super Bowl activities in Los Angeles. Unfortunately, he traded his press credentials to a stranger for a handful of seeds and spent the entire time visiting Santa Anita. Luckily, however, he was able to obtain wire-tap transcripts of phone calls that were made by several typical Super Bowl guests who were enjoying this great American sporting spectacle for the first time. Deford has assured us that these random impressions will provide a more accurate portrayal of the week-long Super Bowl scene than he could possibly have managed."

They do.

Sooper Dooper

FRANK DEFORD

HELLO, THIS is Cheryl, may I help you?"

"Yeah, Cheryl, I have a message to call Operator 6 in Amarillo, Texas."

"You can dial that direct, sir."

"No, Cheryl, I don' think you unnerstan' me. I'm in a motel."

"Yes, sir. I know. Just dial eight, and then zero, the call-back area code and number, and an operator will come on the line."

"Is that a fact? I didn't know you could do that in a motel. Thank you now, Cheryl. . . ."

"Hello, this is Jessie. May I help you?"

" 'Deed you can, Jessie. I'm tryin' to git ahold of Operator 6 in Amarillo."

"This is Operator 6."

"Son of a buck. Now ain't that a coincidence? All the operators in the Lone Star State, and I get right on through to you."

"Uh, yes, sir. And who is your call-back party?"

"Mah what-all?"

"Who are you trying to reach, sir?"

"Why, Herb Wiley. Mah boss over in Mesquite Creek. You unnerstan' now—it's him tryin' to git me."

"Yes, sir."

"Mesquite Creek *Globe-Express,* good afternoon."

"This is Los Angeles, and I have a WH on the line for Mr. Wiley. And your name, sir?"

"I'm Punch Zimmer."

"Hey, Punch! Hey, how's old Ellay? It's me, Doreen."

"Hey, Doreen, is Herb around?"

"Sir, ma'am, please. This call is for Mr. Herb Wiley."

"Well, operator, you tell Mr. Bigtime Punch, Mr. Super Bowl Hotshot, that Herb's in the little boys' room right now."

"Shoot, Doreen, he's rilly been tryin' to git aholt of me."

"Well, uh, ma'am, we can hold for one minute."

"Hang on, operator. I see him goin' over by Emil now. Herb! Herb! Punch is callin' from Ellay. . . . He's comin', Punch."

"Mr. Herb Wiley?"

"You bet."

"I have your call-back party from Los Angeles. Will you accept?"

"You bet."

"Hey, Punch, what's up? Here I go sendin' you off to the Super Bowl—the first reporter from the Panhandle ever to git within spittin' distance of the big time—and here it is Tuesday, two whole days later, and we ain't heard one word outta you."

"Herb, I was jes' now gonna phone in mah early prediction story to Emil."

"I ain't jes' talkin' 'bout your ole story, Punch. I mean, you could have called us—collect, o'course— jes' to let us know how-all it's a-goin'. God*dam,* it must be some excitin', right, ole buddy?"

"Well, Herb, I, uh. . . ."

"You bet. The greatest, most thrillin' single e-vent in the whole wide world of sports. Bar none! It must rilly be sumpin'. Right, Punch?"

"Fact is, Herb, uh, it's uh. . . ."

"What-all is this, Punch? You ain't tellin' me one word 'bout how tee-riffic it all is."

"Well, now, Herb, I don' know real well how to let on to this, but the truth is, Super Bowl Week's 'bout the most borin'est, the most blowed-up, the most stupid. . . ."

"Punch, Punch! Hush up! Doreen, are you still on this here line?"

"I'm jes' now hangin' up, Herb."

"Hold on there, boy. That's all we need—ole Doreen goin' round tellin' every soul in the county that mah sports staff don' like the Super Bowl. You plumb crazy, Punch? You been drinkin' too many of them sissy California drinks, where they stick Morton's salt up alongside the rim?"

"Well, it's a damn nothin', Herb. It's all hokey, it ain't got nothin' to do with sports, let alone the gridiron, and. . . ."

"Punch, Punch Zimmer! You gone be committed, you talkin' so foolish. Why, all the nationally known fellas I'm a-watchin' on NBC, they tell me the Super Bowl's 'bout the next best thing to heaven. And CBS allows that only heaven and last year's Super Bowl beats it. Now, Punch, who am I gonna b'lieve: ole Punch Zimmer from Mesquite Creek, or NBC and CBS? Hmmm?"

"Flat-out, Herb, I'd b'lieve me. 'Cause I ain't sellin' no commercials. And I ain't no regular NFL writer, shillin' for the league callin' it a 'showcase.' I give you a little hint, Herb: anytime you hear a fella say this here is a showcase, that is one sure sign you have got yourself a shill."

"But Punch, jes' ever'body says it's a showcase. If it ain't a showcase, what is it?"

"Well, I guarantee you it ain't no football game. You and me seen football games all over the Panhandle and as far away as Waco, and this sure ain't no game. This here is one big ole commercial that runs for a week, with a football game chucked in at the end. And excitin'? I seen more interest generated in a pinball game down at Skeeter's Starlight Lounge than for what-all Ellay cares. They might as well be playin' this game on the moon."

"Punch Zimmer, you stop with that subversive talk. Why, it says right here in the wire service that, quote, interest is at an all time high, unquote, and Vikki Carr herself gonna sing *America the Beautiful.* And then you come on the phone tellin' me stories that it ain't a showcase."

"You know, Herb, maybe I ain't on no first-name basis with the players, maybe I ain't never been to no Indonesia to see Muhammad Ali fight, maybe I only got the one off-cream leisure suit to mah name, but I can spot me a phony. This ain't no Super Bowl; this is a supermarket."

"Well, damn you, Punch, you keep these anti-'Merican thoughts to yourself, you hear me? And what do you know about traditional classic American e-vents, anyhow?"

"All right, I'll tell you one thing. When I was in the service up in Fort Knox, a spec-four in armor, I seen me two Kentucky Derbies, and also one year a bunch of us went up to Indy and seen that, too. And when I got released, 'fore I came back home, I went over to see mah cousin Ralph who lives in Greater Pittsburgh, P.A., and it was when the Pirates was playin' the O-ree-oles in the World Series; so no, I ain't no virgin in these exact matters. And lemme tell you, Herb Wiley, the Derby and Indy and the World Series is altogether diffrunt from this here showcase. Them other things was fun and there was real folks. And you know what-all, Herb? They had charm. And you're sayin' to yourself, what does ole Punch Zimmer know about charm from a carburetor, and I'll jes' tell you flat-out that if sumpin' ain't got no charm, then all of a sudden you know what charm is. And that's a fact, Herb."

"Well now, Punch, don't git me wrong. It's the 'Merican way to let a man holt a diffrunt opinion."

"Shoot, Herb. Ain't nobody even talks about the game here. All you hear is how much money it's a-goin' to pump into the local e-conomy, like it was some kind of new shoe factory comin' to town.

"I was down in the press room yestiddy, pickin' up the press releases they churn out ever' few minutes, and I started talkin' to this bigshot reporter from New York City, and he says, must be your first Super Bowl, and I says, yes, it sure is, and he says, it is sure one large slice of 'Mericana. And I says, well, this sure ain't no 'Mericana I ever seen. This here is only Hollywood and Madison Avenue thrown together.

"And he says, well it sure-all beats the World Series, don't it, 'cause, he says, he has to go to places like Cincinnati to see it. And he says, they are sure takin' the World Series away from Joe Fan, 'cause they play the games at night when it is a little cool and inconvenient for his deadline. And I says, it seems to me to play the games at Cincinnati at night is just about perfect for the workin' man in Cincinnati. And he says to me, what-all are you, son, some kind of Communist?

"He says, this here is the way sports should be playcd: someplace in the Sunbelt where there is plenty of nice hotels and restaurants for the press. He says, don't you unnerstan' what a showcase the Super Bowl is? They would never get the corporate biggies and the movers of Madison Avenue to come to the Super Bowl unless they played it for their convenience in the right resort areas. He says to me, I'm afraid you don't unnerstan' the bottom line a-tall, and I says, I always thought the bottom line in sports is the final score, and he says that jes' goes to show you you're jes' another naive country boy when it comes to this here showcase."

"Well, Punch, how is your 'commodations?"

"We are what is called 'centrally located,' which means that the press is 40 miles from the players in one direction and 'bout another 40 from the stadium in the other. And then, all the real important folks. . . ."

"The players?"

"No, the owners and advertisers. They're out in Beverly Hills. So all us press is stuck here, talkin' to ourselves. They have got more PR men than Heinz has pickles to take care of us, so I asked one of them why are we here, plumb in the middle of nowhere. I says, if I was coverin' the President, would you put me in Baltimore? And he says, this location is for your convenience, and I says, oh, thank you. I din't 'preciate that. He says, why sure, it is real convenient to the airport. I says, that would be nice if I was a 727, but I ain't goin' nowhere for another week. I says, I b'lieve I would rather be convenient to the football game.

"So we hang around the motel here, watchin' the airplanes overhead and speculatin' on the TV ratings, and, most important, talkin' 'bout this golf toonament they're havin' for us Thursday. I was a-wonderin' where all them cardigan sweaters came from, Herb. And another PR man says to me, do you know that Warner-Lambert is puttin' out nearly $100,000 for this golf toonament, and I says, sorry, I don' know the fella, and, besides, I'm a bowler.

"Well, he says, there is always a first time for ever' thin', but, he says, the NFL does have a free gift for you, which turns out to be this fruity little briefcase the color of spit-up that looked to me like it had been picked out by one of them faggots in Green-wich Village. Herb, if I was to tote this briefcase into the pressbox at West Texas, they would laugh me clear to Albukerk."

"Don't you ever get to see the players, Punch?"

"Sure. Herb. Ever' mornin' this bus picks us up and drives us off to Mexico or wherever it is they're at. The bus has a big ole sign up front that it also goes to Lion Country Safari, to Marineland, and to the picture studios at Universal, so the Super Bowl fits in right well with this bunch.

"First it takes us to the Vikin's, till this other PR man says, 'For your convenience, the buses will roll to the Raider camp at 9:45.' The players is all sorted out. At the Raider hotel, it is like a sock hop, with each table havin' a Raider's number on it, and the important ones like Stabler and Atkinson has tables full of writers, and some of the other fellas just sit all by their lonesome, like they was an ugly-type girl at a dance.

"O' course, nobody much-all talks about football. All the talk is 'bout the media theirselves and how-all will the media affect the game, so the more ever'body talks 'bout it, the more effect it has. I 'magine. This whole thing jes' turns in on itself so.

"I am over at the Vikin's, and I see this pretty blonde who is some kind of built, and I hear somebody say, lookee there, it is Chrystie Jenner, the wife of the world's greatest athalete, and a celebrity in her own right. And so I move up close to where she is talkin' to a bunch of hotshot writers from New York City, and they are sayin', remember me from Montreal and where is Bruce at and so forth, and one says, well, what are you doin' here anyway, Chrystie, and she says, well, I am coverin' the players' wives for ABC, and what brings you here yourself? And he says to her, well, I am coverin' all the hoopla at this showcase. Are you followin' me, Herb? Here we got a football championship, and we got a wives reporter and a hoopla reporter.

"But, for our convenience, it is time to see the Raiders. And their coach, the heavy-set guy, stands up. This is Madden, who they call Pinky, which is the part I like best 'cause that means the coaches at the Super Bowl is Bud and Pinky, jes' like they was over to Skeeter's. And a writer says that Tarkenton has let on that his team is obsessed, and what do you have to say to that? And Madden says, well, we will outobsess them, a remark which gets some kind of guffaw out of me. And then he starts gettin' all these questions about rhetoric, which, b'lieve me, Herb, if I didn't know any better, I would think was some kind of a formation, or a linebacker, maybe. Ever'body is askin' Pinky, will the rhetoric hurt the Raiders, and will they get used to the rhetoric and how will they dee-fense the rhetoric and what-all.

"Half the time, Herb. I don't know what anybody is talkin' 'bout. Bud Grant, he keeps referrin' to stature-type players. At first I thought he meant they were, you know, like statues that didn't move laterally real good, but later on I caught his drift. He means they have reputations. Ever'body talks funny at the Super Bowl, Herb. It's kinda a simulated language, the way the astronauts used to carry on.

"Well, I'm goin' to hang up now, 'cause it's your nickel. But I'll phone Emil mah early prediction story soon."

"O.K., Punch, and lissen up now: I'm gonna tell ever'one you're havin' one great ole time. I don' want folks to think you're no traitor to our 'Merica, Punch. I'm gonna do that for your own damn good, you hear?"

"O.K., Herb. And you tell Mary Beth I'm still scoutin' 'round for that simulated Vikin' corsage she asked for."

"You bet, Punch. Bye now."

"Operator, this is Los Angeles. Routes for Northfield, Ohio, please."

"Two-one-six, plus seven digits."

"Thank you. . . . There's your number ringing, Miss."

"Hello."

"Hello, Karen, it's me, Dianne!"

"Ooh, Dianne! Where are you, hon?"

"I'm calling direct from Beverly Hills!"

"Ooooohhhh. I won't keep you, but. . . ."

"Don't worry about the three minutes, Karen. Sandy told me—you want to call your girl friend, take as long as you want. He says he has a WATS line on his expense account!"

"Ooohhh, Dianne!"

"I can't begin to tell you, Karen. It's so fantastic, like. I saw Bob Newhart and Lorne Greene. . . ."

"Nooooo!"

"And Joe Namath was in the Polo Lounge, and last night was the official Super Bowl party, given by the National Football League itself! Oh Karen, if only you could have been there to share it with me. Up With People entertained!"

"Ooh! I've seen them on TV."

"And there was just nothing spared on the food and beverages, Karen! The canapes would not stop! And Sandy introduced me to this exotic foreign drink that has salt on the rim!"

"Oh Dianne, I'm so happy for you. How is . . . he?"

"Karen, he's just a doll. Some women . . . his wife doesn't understand him at all. He told me that confidentially. He's so sensitive, so concerned about my feelings. I told him back in Akron, in the cafeteria, oh Sandy, how could I come with you to the Super Bowl? Why, I would feel just like a common. . . . And you know what he said, Karen?"

"What?"

"He said, Dianne, don't ever say that about yourself. He said, I am the real hustler, I am the one forced by my company to go out to the Super Bowl and go to meetings and dumb parties, to drink with network people and football people, to try and keep our products in the corporate and video spotlight. Your going with me would give me the respectability I can't get from my job."

"Oh, Dianne, that is beautiful."

"He's just a beautiful-type person, Karen."

"Where is he now?"

"He had to play tennis today. His company makes him do that. It's one of his obligations, like. Sandy says if he doesn't play tennis with the right people, his company might not be allowed to buy football commercials next year. And Sandy says that is the upwardly mobile, high-demographics audience he seeks."

"Oh, I see."

"Sandy's so conscientious, Karen. He hates all these meetings he has to go to around the pool, but it is his nature, like, never to miss a one. And yesterday, he had to play golf all day. He was so tired, the poor thing, we were late getting to the party."

"But it was good?"

"Good? Karen, I saw Julie London there."

"Ooohhh, Dianne!"

"You see, like Sandy says, you really have to know someone to get in, Karen. Either that or you have to help make money for the NFL. They hold the guest list down to 2,500 VIPs. Some years they have had it on the *Queen Mary* or in the Astrodome. It's not for any Tom, Dick or Harry, like. This year they had it at the Pasadena Civic Center, and it was all decked out. Sandy said it was a south-of-the-border decor. He knew that because there was a mariachi band."

"Dianne, you said Up With People were there."

"They *both* were, Karen, Up With People *and* the mariachis."

"Oh, my Godddd, Dianne, two bands!"

"And two rooms, Karen! Two ballrooms! Adjacent, like."

"Oh, it's a fairyland, Dianne!"

"And not only that, but there was a special little section all fenced off where the people who own these football teams could stay all by themselves, like, and Sandy knew one of the owners, and we got right in there, right in the first-class section, and Sandy introduced me all around."

"What players did you meet there?"

"Who?"

"What players, Dianne?"

"No, there's none of them, Karen. I heard that the teams playing in the game are on the Coast, but nobody ever talks about them. Sandy says, maybe we should go down to Tijuana Sunday and see a bullfight instead. He says nobody cares about the football game. He says, this is the great American corporate game. Sandy says there's a veritable who's-who of the business world here. He says, this is the way business gets done in America. It's fascinating. Everybody has private planes and limousines. Sandy says an NFL man told him that the people here for the game will spend $50 million in Ellay. Sandy says the NFL man told him: 'Sandy, this is not your Disneyland, Knott's Berry Farm-type crowd. This is your sophisticated, drinking, betting, upwardly, mobile-type all-American sports crowd.' Why, everybody, just everybody, stopped off at Vegas. Sandy says, that's why Ellay is the ideal place to have the Super Bowl, because it is convenient to Vegas."

"Dianne . . . did you?"

"Did we! Nipsey Russell was in the lounge and Wayne Newton himself was the main attraction, like."

"Oh, Goddd, Dianne. I'm so happy for you, hon."

"That's why we had to leave Akron a day early. You see, Sandy's company made him go to Vegas first. They said he could make contacts there. Sandy says it is harder these days for a guy in the business to get the job done. Sandy says something called NFL Properties used to throw a special party for all the businessmen at the Super Bowl, but they found out they didn't have to anymore, because all the businessmen come anyway. So the businessmen have to find each other on their own. That's why Sandy has to spend so much time at bars, because as much as he hates the thought of it, a lot of business types hang around there."

"Oh, I see."

"But it's not all work for Sandy, Karen. He knows some TV types, too. Both NBC and CBS are putting on these terrific variety-type shows. With a football *motif*, like, Karen. Like we saw a rehearsal and the announcer says, 'Page sacks Stabler on the 19,' and Charo says, 'Who ees thees 19 in the sack?'"

"Oh, that's so comical, Dianne. Charo has such a funny accent."

"The casts are just star-studded, Karen. Besides Charo, there's Andy Williams, Don Rickles, Elliott Gould. . . ."

"And they'll be on TV?"

"Tonight. Live on tape from the Super Bowl. Oh, I just adore football so much, Karen. And you know, it's funny, but I never cared that much for it before, back in Akron. But I just adore the Super Bowl."

"I'm so jealous, Dianne."

"Well, I better hang up now. I have to get dressed. Sandy's going to try and take me to the theater."

"What are you going to see?"

"I really don't know. He just said he'd try to get away from the tennis long enough for us to get in a matinee."

"Oh, I hope you have good seats, Dianne!"

"Karen, believe me, Sandy's right. Every American should try and go to the Super Bowl, because it is so representative of Americana, like. I'll see you at work Monday, hon. Be good, now."

"Well, if I can't be good, I'll be careful."

"O.K., bye, Karen."

"Have a happy, Dianne."

"Hello, operator, would you be so kind as to get me a number in New York?"

"You can dial that direct, sir."

"Yes, I should like to very much, but I don't know the bloody number."

"Sir, dial one, plus 212, then 555-1212 and ask for the number."

"I see, yes. Thank you so much. . . ."

"Directory assistance."

"Oh, I'm so sorry, I was trying to reach information."

"Look, this is directory assistance, Mister. Do you want a number in Noo Yawk?"

"Indeed I do. I'm trying to secure the number of the Algonquin Hotel."

"Is it a new listing?"

"No, luv. I was there just the other day, and it was standing as straight as ever."

"What?"

"Madame Assistance, do you have the number?"

"All right, make a note of this: 687-4400."

"Thank you so much. . . ."

"Hello, this is Dale, may I help you?"

"I do hope so. I should like to reverse charges."

"Yeah, what's the name?"

"Just Room 407, please."

"Algonquin Hotel."

"Long distance for 407."

"Are you paid, operator?"

"No, it's collect to the room."

"Hello."

"Is this 407?"

"Yes it is."

"Ihaveacollectcallfromlosangeleswillyouaccept-charges?"

"I'm so sorry, what?"

"Darling, it's me, Michael."

"Sir, this is a station call!"

"Michael!"

"Lady, will you accept charges?"

"Yes, of course I will."

"All right, go ahead."

"Michael!"

"Sylvia, darling!"

"Where are you?"

"I'm in a bloody phone booth somewhere along Sunset Boulevard. I really don't know. I just had to get off this damned bus."

"Bus? What bus?"

"This awful chartered monstrosity that took me to the Super Bowl."

"Darling, the what?"

"The Super Bowl. Oh, Sylvia, you can't imagine. It's the American football championship, although as nearly as I could fathom, the journey to the bloody game, on this dreadful bus, was much more an attraction than the game itself."

"Darling, please back up. What in the world were you doing on this bus at this bowling alley?"

"No, no, football, Sylvia. And it's all so depressing. You remember Nick, that ghastly producer who belongs to the nude backgammon encounter group?"

"Oh, God, yes."

"Well, he called me up at a fever pitch last evening to say that an extra ticket to the Super Bowl football had come into his possession, and would I care to go. And of course I protested that it would be a terrible thing to waste the ticket on someone such as myself, who knows nothing about American football, but Nick insisted that this was the single most important cultural event in the United States, and for me to turn down such an opportunity would be—and I fear this is a direct quote, darling—the equivalent of turning down an invitation to have dinner with the Queen at Buckingham Palace."

"Oh, my God, Michael. I'm so sorry for you out there, poor thing."

"Well, if we're going to get the financing and a chance for McQueen, Nick is the fellow. Any port in a storm. So I accepted with gratitude. And then he informed me about the bus. This game, for reasons that still elude me, is between a team from Minnesota, which is somewhere amongst the Midwestern states, and Oakland, which is a rather shabby working-class suburb of San Francisco, but it is being played here in Los Angeles. Or rather, it is being played in some godforsaken place known as Pasadena, which is primarily fa-

mous for its smog. And it is, apparently, inaccessible by automobile, which is why everyone journeyed by bus. Well, I should not say everybody. The Midwest rooters all seem to have traveled in these awful conveyances known as vans—every last one of them boasting a CB radio—while the fans from San Francisco appeared to have arrived en masse on motorcycles. Most of these fellows even affected the early Brando."

"Poor Michael. Was it all so bad?"

"Worse, I'm afraid. These people who inhabit the Sunbelt take a rather perverse pride in the vulgar, you know. They absolutely lack taste in all things but the climate. They can discourse upon a partially sunny day as literate men and women once spoke of poetry or philosophy. And saddest of all, they try mightily to bring the rest of the nation down to their level. I was told that this utterly tasteless exhibition was a classic representation of America. One especially annoying buffoon on the bus, who was wearing an off-lime leisure suit and drinking another margarita. . . ."

"I'm sorry, dear, a what?"

"A margarita. It is this dreadful liquid concoction that was, alas, not stopped at the Mexican border by immigration authorities. As you know, Sylvia, Americans employ salt to excess on all foods. We should have known that before long they would find a drink they could also destroy in this way. Such is the margarita, which has become a sort of liquid French fry throughout the Sunbelt. In any event, this was the staple of our bus ride."

"Did you get to the match?"

"Oh, my God. I'm afraid we did. We had to leave at the crack of dawn to reach our assigned parking place, and to accommodate the television network, which schedules the game for the convenience of saloonkeepers in New Jersey, rather than for the poor devils, such as myself, who make the supreme effort to appear at the bloody thing in person.

"Then, when we emerged from our mobile vault, we were greeted by a scene, darling, the likes of which you would not attribute to Dante at his most vivid. A full landscape of CB vans and motorcycles, with matching people, all at their most outrageously harlequinesque, all consuming equal amounts of beer and bus exhaust and dodging Frisbees, which clattered about like hail. The lights of the stadium were already on, ready to penetrate the smog, I imagine, even though it was not yet midday. Everywhere, a profusion of vendors—of the quantity and persistence of beggars in Bombay—tried to foist upon us souvenir merchandise of such quality that it would all surely be rejected in Taiwan as beneath human standards. Here and there, as we drew closer to this antique arena, scalpers were trying desperately to sell tickets at face value."

"But Michael, I understood you to say this was the great championship that every American longed to see."

"Oh, indeed, there is a great deal of glib sociological talk about how it is the average fan who attends this spectacle, but the fact of the matter is that those present are either expense-account freeloaders, such as myself, or zealots who have traveled thousands of miles, and thus must be well-off—and further, they must also be rather asinine to do so.

"So basically, luv, what you have at a Super Bowl is not an average American at all. You don't even have an average American sports fan. Instead, you have a collection of the affluent foolish—The Affluish Americans."

"The worst of the lot."

"By and large."

"Well, I do hope that at least the game was exciting."

"No, not at all. It was perfectly dreadful. The team from San Francisco absolutely eviscerated the Midwest club."

"Oh, I'm so sorry."

"No matter. It didn't bother a soul, because they assured me that they were all quite resigned to this circumstance—that it was almost always a terrible game, and certainly always when the Minnesota club played."

"And this didn't upset the fans?"

"Oh, no. The league and the press have convinced the fans that the only important thing about the Super Bowl is that it be played in nice weather. I came to understand that the Super Bowl really was very representative of America—at least of the worst of modern America. It is all flash and no substance. A duel of transients passing by, played before transients. Of course the games are always going to be awful. Even the players must sense that they are the end result of a programmed, franchised society. The Super Bowl is the ultimate remove in this nation, luv."

"I do hope you kept these sentiments to yourself, dear."

"Oh, I was the perfect guest. Besides, we were kept busy in the stadium. Soon enough the public-address announcer advised us: 'You are sitting in the world's largest card-stunt section,' and for all of us to get ready our cards."

"Michael, what in the world?"

"Well, darling, we were programmed rather like those poor Chinese in Peking on Mao Tse-tung Day, holding up these cardboard sections to form rather infantile color patterns. I did ask why we were expected to perform these maneuvers, and Nick explained to me that it was for the convenience of the TV audience. It seemed to me that this was all rather backward, inasmuch as we had paid $20 a seat—a hard seat—while the people watching on the telly were enjoying the proceedings more comfortably and *gratis,* but since I was a guest myself, I agreed to quietly go along with this dreadful mass exercise."

"Oh, I'm so sorry for you, darling."

"Well, thereafter, like any drone, I merely followed the path of least resistance and tried valiantly to develop a taste for margaritas. And, at last, we were back on the bloody bus, and when I happened to glance out the window an hour or two later and saw a street sign indicating that we had returned to civilization—or at least to that second cousin of civilization that calls itself 'Ellay'—I made very hasty apologies, claiming that I was going to meet a dear old friend at the next corner, and exited precipitously from the bus as soon as it came to a stoplight. Darling, if I ever get a taxi back to the hotel, I'll be on the nine o'clock flight tomorrow morning. Till then, Sylvia."

"Good night, Michael. Oh, you poor dear."

Mike Ditka, head coach of a Super-Bowl-winning Chicago Bears team, Super Bowl XX to be exact, and as fierce a sideline stalker as the game has ever seen, is a catchment for adjectives: tempestuous, irreverent, bombastic, profane, hilarious, along with several hundred others cataloged by Webster. He is also the person who put the position of tight end in NFL playbooks, and played it well enough to be included in the Pro Football Hall of Fame's 1988 class of enshrinees. In his autobiography, *Ditka,* he tells of the last four years of his playing career, spent down in Dallas, playing for the Cowboys and trying to understand the likes of such personalities as diverse as Tom Landry and Duane Thomas. He was never known to hold back anything as a player—"the fiercest competitor I have ever met," according to CBS sports commentator Brent Musberger—and he has proven lately to be the same in regard to words, spoken and written.

We Hated the Cowboys

MIKE DITKA (WITH DON PIERSON)

THREE OR four days after I got home from Philadelphia, I got a phone call from Tom Landry. Out of the blue. He said, "We don't even know if you can play anymore, but we're going to bring you down and take a look at you and see if you can play a few years." He said they already had a tight end, Pettis Norman, and they were really happy with him. "We think you can complement him," he said.

I had been dead serious about retiring. I couldn't play a lick. But the Cowboys traded for me anyway. Sent Dave McDaniel, the burner, to the Eagles. He was the receiver who had such a fast time in the 40-yard dash until they found out the field was short. Anyway, I couldn't understand why they traded for me. Looking back, I was traded for a reason. The Good Lord put me

there. At that time, I couldn't really understand why it was the Cowboys or why it was Landry. But life is cycles and that was the start of a new cycle and it turned out to be an upbeat cycle.

It wasn't all roses in the beginning there, either. I really wasn't crazy about going there until I got there. I had never liked the Cowboys. When I played, if you played for the Bears or the Eagles, you didn't like the Cowboys, that's for sure. They were the good guys. They were the guys in white hats. They had the stars. They were good. When I was with the Eagles, I remember our running back, Timmy Brown, came across the middle and the Cowboys' middle linebacker, Lee Roy Jordan, gave him a shot and knocked out his uppers, lowers, everything. Timmy had about $2,500 worth of teeth in his mouth. When we had a beer after the game, he was drinking through cotton. He had to go right to the orthodontist. He was a mess. Lee Roy had hit him right across the chops with a good forearm. So I was trying to go after Lee Roy the rest of the game. I don't know that I ever got there, but I tried. Lee Roy became a good friend and I could understand why Lee Roy played the way he played. He played the way I played. He played tough and aggressive and went after people. That was O.K. with me, but when you were on the other side of the ball, then you had to go after that guy.

There was always bad blood between the Eagles and the Cowboys. We hated them and they hated us worse than anybody. Well, you don't hate anybody worse than the Redskins. There were some great rivalries in that division. Dallas and Washington. Dallas and St. Louis. Dallas and New York. It's a tough division for rivalries. Everybody enjoyed playing Dallas. They enjoyed playing against Dallas more than they enjoyed playing against Pittsburgh when the Steelers were winning. When people played Pittsburgh, they didn't know what they were getting into. But they always could understand a little about what they were getting into when they played Dallas. They always had the idea that beating Dallas would make them a star on America's flag or something.

But when I got to the Cowboys and met them and saw them, I realized they were just like anybody else. A great bunch of guys. That's a lot of the reason they were a good football team. They were good players on the field and good guys off the field. You could go out and have a beer with them and they had fun. I thought that was a lot of the reason they won. It wasn't that much different. They bitched about Tom just like the Packers bitched about Lombardi and the Bears bitched about Halas and the Browns bitched about Brown. It's never different. If they don't bitch about the coach, I guess something's got to be goofy.

My first season there, 1969, was kind of a funny year. Not much happened. I got in some fights when we scrimmaged the Rams and the Chargers. I didn't play much that first year except in short yardage and goal line. I couldn't ever understand that. In our sixth game that year, we were beating the hell out of the Giants and I wasn't playing very much. In the fourth quarter, Tom called me to go in and I just said, "No point in me going in now." And I wouldn't go in. Next day, he called me into the office and said, "If that ever happens again, just take off the uniform and go."

I said, "O.K." That's really the way I felt, because it didn't really matter to me the first year whether I stayed or left anyway. I wasn't that worried about it. Didn't bother me at all. But it never happened again. I started playing more. The other guy, Norman, was a good

blocker, but I was a good blocker, too. I wasn't in good shape my first year, so I wasn't going to beat him out the first year. But it didn't bother me because I really didn't give a damn.

After we got beat by Cleveland in the playoffs, I said to myself, "Hey, this is a good football team, as good as anybody." I made up my mind I was going to get in the best shape of my life or kill myself trying. And I did. I moved down there and lived down there and I worked out every day. I got into their offseason training program. Because of my bad foot, I started running barefoot. I'd run in the grass.

Alvin Roy, who was their strength coach, had a system. You lifted, then you ran a hundred down the field and a hundred back. Then you lifted another set and ran again. You could hardly move your legs. But this was how the Cowboys tested the players coming into camp. I think that year only Roger Staubach and Calvin Hill had better times than I did. I was in pretty good shape for a guy my age. That was in 1970, when I turned 31. I was in the best shape I ever got in my whole life regardless of the foot injury. Both 1970 and 1971 were Super Bowl years. The 1971 season was the best year I ever played.

That conditioning program enabled me to do it and I always thought the big edge the Cowboys had was so many guys lived in Dallas. Guys in Chicago and Philadelphia always had their cars packed and they were leaving. In Dallas, very few left. The climate was conducive for staying and the opportunities in the town were phenomenal. I think Landry's conditioning system was patterned after Lombardi's. He could tell the people who would pay the price during the offseason—Dan Reeves, Walt Garrison, that kind of player. Rayfield Wright was as good a tackle as I've seen. Dave Edwards. Whoever heard of Dave Edwards except the guys who played against him? A heck of a football player. Cornell Green switched from corner to safety and became the best safety in the league. He always had people like that. Those guys always paid the price. Any player today who doesn't understand the benefits of the offseason conditioning program is foolish. I had never really lifted weights before. There's a lot of ways to get in shape and as you get stronger physically, you get stronger mentally.

I thought Landry was going to be kind of a sterile guy. I had a preconceived idea he was going to be a very sterile person. Maybe that's not the right word. I just thought he would be a plain guy with a lot of authority and not much emotion. I was completely wrong. I think Tom has as much emotion and compassion as anybody. I saw it in meetings we had, but I saw it more when I became a coach. You really saw what made him work and what made him tick. You saw how bad he felt when he cut people.

People say he's cold. He's the furthest thing from cold. But what is he going to do? Sidle up to everybody buddy-buddy and go out and have a beer with them? You can't do that. The "plastic" image was something that came out to the public, but it certainly wasn't the truth. That bothered him. In staff meetings, we saw the personality, the friendship, the jokes and laughter. We played golf with him. Other people don't see that part of him. They just see the guy on the sideline calling the plays, wearing the hat, the guy who doesn't smile a lot.

We laughed at the way he murdered names. Pete Retzlaff was Rexlaff, Joe Scarpati was Scarpeter. He didn't call his own quarterback Gary Hogeboom. It came out Hogenboomer or Haagen-Dazs or whatever he happened to say. He does not do it on purpose. The Cowboys used to bring in over 100 rookies. Tom would call out the names and they'd have to stand up. Every once in a while, there would be a Wisniewski or a Kurzawski and it was just a holy terror to hear him say it. And he would say, "Correct me if I'm saying it wrong." The guy would say it right and Tom would say it again wrong. The guy would say it again right and Tom would say it again wrong. That was no reflection on how he felt about his players, though. You think coaches just cut people, that they enter into their lives and walk out of their lives. Coaches feel as bad as players in most cases.

We used to have to grade and evaluate our players every day. That way, we had a record so when it came time to cut, there was no question. The bottom guy had to go. It substantiated that you were cutting for no reason but lack of talent. And he tried to draw everything he could out of players. One time we cut a kid, Kenny Hutcherson, who was really a hitter, an inside linebacker who reminds me of Mike Singletary. He had been with us for one year and we had to cut him. It really shook Tom up. He broke down and he told the team, "I don't like this. But I have to do it because I think it's best for the team. That means I'll do it to anybody if I think they're a detriment to the team."

I knew when I saw that, boy, it had to be tough. Then when you go through it yourself, you know it's tough. People say after a couple of years it gets easy. I don't know what gets easy about it. I dread cutdown dates. Most kids know and accept it all right. Some don't accept it. I just try to tell them it's the decision of a lot of people. It's always a numbers game.

The four years I played in Dallas were difficult years for pro football. Think about what was coming out of college in 1969 and 1970. Think about what was going on then on college campuses. Everything was radical. Nobody wanted the Vietnam thing. Everybody had their own philosophies. Everybody was against the government. It was a different breed of person coming out. I had been playing pro ball for a while and seeing all kinds

of guys come in. Then all of a sudden we got that smell around the locker room. We would say, "What the hell's that smell?" Then we got to understand more about it. I never knew what marijuana was. I never heard of it. I don't know what it was called when I grew up. I guess it was called hemp or rope. I never knew what it was. But I knew what it was in 1970. I smelled it everywhere.

Duane Thomas was the Cowboys' first-round draft choice in 1970. We knew he had some problems, but we thought the problems could be worked out because we thought he was a catalyst and he could get us to the Super Bowl. I don't think people realized what the problems were. They just thought he was unusual. They didn't know drugs might be involved. Nobody wanted to talk about drugs back then. They understood there was marijuana around, but nobody really talked about it.

Duane Thomas was a mixed-up kid, but he was an intelligent mixed-up kid. He was no dummy. He perceived anybody who wasn't a flower child as being part of the establishment and the establishment was wrong. It was a different group coming up. Duane, Steve Kiner, Tody Smith, Billy Parks, guys with talent, but they were fighting the cause of who knows what they were fighting. They were arguing every day about Vietnam and this and that. Sure, it's fine to have an opinion, but they used to drive poor Roger Staubach nuts. He'd just spent four years in the Navy.

When they were told something, it was always, "Why? Show me this is the best way." They questioned everything. They even questioned what Tom told them. It became a very, very tough situation.

The worst anguish Tom ever went through was with Duane Thomas. I've never seen a man suffer in trying to do what he thought was best for a football team, for the individual, and for everybody concerned. It was very agonizing and tough for Tom, but he did it. We won a Super Bowl, but it was pure hell in dealing with the way Thomas treated everybody. He treated his teammates no differently than he treated the press or he treated Tom or he treated everybody. He was just a real insensitive person, but he was very mixed up at that time. When you're dealing with what he was dealing with, you've got problems. Duane is basically a good guy.

Landry never really bent the rules for Thomas, but I think he bent himself a little bit. He tried to keep the rules standard for everybody. Duane was on time for meetings, but he never talked. He never had conversations with anybody. I don't even know that he ever talked to the coaches, really. He never answered roll call. He would be in the room, but he never said, "Here." Things like that. I think Tom made some concessions in that area. He did it because he thought it was best for the football team. After he did it, I'm not sure he believed he could ever make those concessions again with anybody.

Duane Thomas was a big factor in us winning. He was a good football player. He was a good all-around receiver, runner, blocker. He was a fluid runner who never took a real hard hit. He was like Jim Brown. He knew how to give and go, slip and slide, and all that stuff. He was an excellent blocker, which people didn't know about. Dan Reeves worked with him and said, "That guy is really smart." He knew the fullback and the halfback spots. He had to know both because Walt Garrison got hurt and Duane had to go up to fullback with Calvin Hill at halfback. But it was just uncomfortable to be around him, no fun.

Once we were playing the Giants in Yankee Stadium. I always made a habit of going up and wishing everybody good luck before a game. I went up to him and just patted him on the back and said, "Good luck." He didn't acknowledge it. I went on my way. We played the game. The following Tuesday, I was sitting beside my locker reading the paper in Dallas before practice and he came up to me and said, "Hey man, don't ever hit me on the back before a game. It breaks my concentration."

I said, "Hey Duane. Go fuck yourself."

That was our conversation.

Thomas only played for two years with the Cowboys. Then he was traded to New England and they gave him back. Then he was traded to San Diego and Washington and ended up in the World Football League. It was a shame because he could have been a real excellent football player for a long time, because he had the body for it and he had the temperament for it. But he blew himself out.

You've got to keep everything in society in perspective, though. When I played, amphetamines were accepted because they were given out by the team doctor. Now, amphetamines are barred and I agree they should be barred. I agree that steroids should be barred, but people have used steroids for years not really knowing what the consequences are, just like people have used cortisone for years. What are the consequences of cortisone? Does anybody really know? Is that the reason I have an artificial hip now? Might be. From all the cortisone injections I've taken, it might be. You don't know, but it was injected into me with the idea of improving the healing process. Doctors told me that.

I disagree with all drugs and any form of them, although it amazes me that alcohol is legal and acceptable but drugs aren't. I took amphetamines when I played with the Bears. They were handed to me. I didn't know what the hell they were. They said they'd make you play better or run faster or jump higher. I'd take them and I never saw any difference. Well, a couple of times I did. The first thing I noticed was warming up I would get extremely tired. I would feel like I was drained. Then I would get my energy back. Then at the end of the game, you'd have two beers and you were up on top of the roof. I did it a couple of times and that was it. I quit doing it. I became exposed to marijuana in Dallas, but I'm not a smoker, I can't inhale. I smoke cigars, but I can't inhale. I could have more fun drinking a couple beers than anything else.

I came to Dallas just as Pete Gent was leaving. I played with the same guys he wrote about in *North Dallas Forty* and I never saw the things he described. Maybe I wasn't at the same parties. I had as much fun there as I've had anywhere. I thought Dallas was going to be completely different from what I pictured. I figured they would be a bunch of goody-goody guys, but they were super people, good football players who enjoyed themselves. They knew when to play, when to practice, and when to have fun. Gent wrote that a lot of football players in general don't particularly like each other. I find that hard to believe. To be a good team, the players have to like each other. They have to respect each other. They don't have to go out together and eat and drink together. Their wives don't have to socialize, but there has to be something there.

I didn't quite make the level of hell-raiser, but I was probably in tune with the guys who were. We didn't condone everything that was done, but we never said anything against it. We kind of went along with things. I think that's probably worse than being the guy who says, "Let's go do this." We'd say, "It doesn't make much sense to do it, but let's go ahead and do it anyway." So someone would say, "We're going to sit down and drink a shot of Wild Turkey for every year Walt Garrison had a birthday." And we'd start doing it. Garrison used to have a birthday party at training camp in Thousand Oaks every year. Used to get after that Wild Turkey. We would have a few shots and then start dancing. Dan Reeves had a staple in his knee. He started dancing and that staple came loose and we thought somebody shot him in the leg. We had to take him to the hospital. We had injuries dancing.

The first year I came to the Cowboys we were playing gin one night. Dan likes to tell this story on me. He said after I lost a few hands, I took a chair and threw it and it stuck in the wall. All four legs stuck in the wall. All Dan said was, "God, this guy must hate to lose." I'm not sure it happened exactly that way, but I'm not sure it didn't.

It was in Dallas where I got most of my nicknames. In college, they called me "Hammer" from my basketball days. I did bang people. In Dallas, Walt Garrison started calling me "Monk" and "Chip" because I had chubby cheeks like a chipmunk.

Playing on the Cowboys' first two Super Bowl teams

in 1970 and 1971 and scoring a touchdown in their first Super Bowl victory were highlights. I scored the final touchdown of our 24–3 win over Miami. Roger threw another touchdown pass to Duane Thomas, but I was wide open. I always told Roger if he had thrown the ball to me the first time, I would have won the car. When they honored all the MVP's at Super Bowl XX, I was going to tell him if he had thrown the ball to me, I would have been walking out there. I really should have scored three touchdowns. I ran a reverse and I really thought I had scored. I ran into my own lineman and misjudged the goal line.

You think it's going to last forever. You just figure the Good Lord gave you this body and it's going to keep working that way and it's not going to get hurt. You're going to wake up every day with enough enthusiasm to say, "Yeah, I'm going to play the game." All of a sudden, after you've been doing it for eight or nine years, even if you are healthy, then the mind starts playing tricks on you. It makes it tough. You start saying, "I don't know if I'm going to catch that one coming inside. I got hurt last time." You start to think, "If I can get through this year, maybe I can get through another year." It's the security you get in football. You get used to the good life, get used to the adulation, where people put you on a pedestal. The thing that's important is to be realistic about your talents. It's easy to say after 9, 10, 12 years, "Boy, I can still do it." Look at the film and you really can't still do it as good as you used to do it. And your enthusiasm isn't there as much.

I knew it was all over. I had lost a lot of weight and my back was killing me. I couldn't run at all and what had been my trademark, my strength and quickness, was gone. A lot of it was mental, because I had a lot on my mind. I was going through my divorce. The night before we beat San Francisco 30–28 in that comeback in the NFC playoff game, we were playing poker. When I got out of the chair, I couldn't straighten up to go back to my room. I knew that night that was the end. We played the Redskins in the championship game and got killed 26–3. I played at 208 pounds. I talked to Tom about it and I said, "I don't think I can play anymore." He said, "Well, that's something you have to evaluate on your own. You didn't have a great year and we're going to bring along the other guys." There was no question in my mind. It was a fair evaluation by all parties. The fallacy that you have is the parade is going to continue for you. But someday you can come to the end of the parade route and the parade's over. You're no longer in it.

Pro football comes to Texas, with verve and flair and a lot of down-home, Lone Star state theatrics. Bill Fay captured this historic event in September 1952 for *Colliers* magazine, just before the NFL's newest franchise, the Dallas Texans, took to the gridiron in the Cotton Bowl. The only problem was that Texas football fans neglected to show up to support the new-found toy. After four home games, with an average attendance of less than 15,000, the millionaire owners turned the franchise back to the league, and it was operated as a road-team with its home base in, of all places, Hershey, Pennsylvania. At the end of the season, the Dallas Texans were disbanded, their memory forever etched with the ignoble distinction of being the last NFL team to go out of business. The Texans, incidentally, lost 11 of their 12 games that year.

It's Hard-Ridin', Two-Gun Football, Pardner!

BILL FAY

"Cowgirls, that's what we need—about six of 'em in short skirts ridin' big white horses."

"Now, you're talkin'! When we hit Chicago, we'll parade 'em straight up Michigan Avenue, twirlin' their ropes and blazin' away with six-shooters."

"Why not make it a real parade? We could dig up a couple of fire engines—loud 'em up with players—and drive all over the Loop with the sirens wide open."

"Good idea. If we're goin' to outfit our boys in fancy boots and 10-gallon hats, we might as well show 'em off a little."

"You know, nothin' irritates me more at a football game than watchin' some tired old trainer runnin' out to the players with a water bucket durin' a time out. I figure we ought to fix up some kind of a water cart attached to a motorcycle. Then the trainer could go whizzin' out on the field—and we could plant a big Confederate flag on the front end of the cart to dress it up a little"

"Let's think about that flag idea some more, but gettin' back to those cowgirls, why not let 'em gallop up and down the side lines while our passers are warmin' up before the game? Then, when one of our players catches a long pass, a cowgirl, could swoom in and lasso him on the run—give the fans a look at some real Texas-style ropin'."

THIS CONVERSATIONAL prologue, transcribed from notes jotted down at a meeting of the Board of Directors of the Dallas Texans Football Club, Inc., clearly indicates that some strange and wonderful things are about to happen in professional gridiron circles. Fourteen Dallas businessmen, millionaires, all, have bought the first National Football League franchise ever granted to a city in the Southwest; and, during the last eight months, they have been happily engaged in making plans for a super deluxe gridiron organization, complete with cowgirls and mechanized water carts, which, coming from Texas, naturally will be the biggest and best pro football team in the United States.

Of course, all these electrifying developments may not come immediately. It must be remembered that Dallas' 14 millionaires acquired their franchise last January 24th by the bleak expedient of buying up the personnel of the now defunct New York Yanks for $300,000. In 1951, the Yanks won one game, lost nine and tied two, strictly on merit. So, the Texans are starting in where the Yanks left off—at the bottom of the league. With a little luck, however, the 14 millionaires hope to work their way to the top in a hurry.

The task of building the Texans into a title contender has been delegated to Jimmy Phelan, a resourceful and highly successful coach who's been in the business 33 years. Since last February 7th, when Phelan took up residence in Dallas, he has discovered that working for 14 football filberts, whose combined financial resources reportedly exceed $1,000,000,000 can be a unique and occasionally breath-taking experience. Example:

Several months ago, oil operator Jack S. Vaughn, the youngest of Phelan's millionaire bosses (he's 27), dropped into the Texans' office for a chat. When the conversation finally got around to halfbacks, Vaughn remarked:

"You know, Jimmy, it's a shame that a fine Dallas boy like Doak Walker—probably the greatest football player who ever lived—has to work for the Detroit Lions. Why, if we don't do something quick, Doak'll be down here playing *against* us in Dallas. Now, here's a starter"—Vaughn rummaged through his pants pockets and finally located a sheaf of $100 bills which he flipped onto Phelan's desk—"I'm opening the pot for $8,000. You get the other boys to match it. Then, you'll have about $100,000 and you can hop up to Detroit and buy Doak's contract."

Regretfully, Phelan swept up the currency littering his desk into a pile and slid the wad back to Vaughn. "No use going to Detroit," Jimmy declared. "The Lions wouldn't trade Walker unless we gave them the $100,000 and somebody to take his place. Right now, we don't have anybody who'd interest them."

After Vaughn had departed with the $8,000, Phelan glanced at backfield coach Cecil Isbell, who had heard the conversation. "Money," Phelan said. "What's money? It can't buy halfbacks."

TEAM TRADED FOR ONE PLAYER

Despite the reluctance of other N.F.L. clubs to ship their established stars to Dallas, C.O.D., Phelan managed to pull off one voluminous player transaction which not only strengthened his squad considerably but also demonstrated that he had become completely oriented to the Texas custom of doing things in a big way. That was the deal which dispatched Les Richter, the highly publicized line-backer from the University of California, who was Phelan's No. 1 draft pick, to the champion Los Angeles Rams in exchange for what virtually was a whole football team!

Phelan netted the following 11 players: ends Dick Wilkins and Tom Keane; center Aubrey Phillips; guards Jack Halliday and Vic Vasicek; center Joe Reid; quarterback Dave Anderson; halfbacks Gabby Sims and Bill Baggett; and fullbacks Dick Hoerner and Dick McKissack.

The deal backfired on the Rams in a dismaying way when Richter was later ordered to report to the Army on August 1st for a two-year hitch.

In Phelan's opinion, Hoerner and Keane were the key men in the 12-player deal which the Texans' publicity department proudly hailed as the biggest in National League history. "Hoerner's one of the best running fullbacks in the league," said Phelan, "and Keane is a versatile fellow who can do a good job at end or halfback on offense, then double as a pass defense back.

"You know," Phelan continued, "the Yanks were a pretty good *half-a-ball-team* last season. They had one good offensive unit, one fair defensive unit, including the great end Barney Poole, but no reserves at all. If you look at the '51 records, you'll notice they usually tired and blew their games in the second half. That's why this Rams deal is so important. In addition to first stringers like Hoerner and Keane, we picked some capable reserves who can spell our regulars and keep them gassed up for the second half. Actually, the Rams deal ought to lift us out of the *half-a-ball-club* category and give us a squad that can go 60 minutes at top speed. With a few breaks, we could come pretty close to winning half our games."

If the Texans play 50–50 football in their debut season, Phelan's entire roster of 14 bosses will be very happy, including Giles Miller and brother Connell, the textile mills tycoons; Harlan Ray, D. Harold Byrd, Jack C. Vaughn and Leonard Nichols, the big oil operators; J. Curtis Sanford, real-estate man and restaurateur; Harry and Don Stewart, the tractor firm executives; J. C. Thompson, Sr., president of the Southland Corporation; architect George Dahl; attorney Arthur Riggs; lumberman Fritz Hawn; and investment counselor John J. Coyle.

Club president Giles Miller, who negotiated the purchase of the Yanks' franchise for his associates, is thirty-two years old, stocky, dark, handsome and completely optimistic about the future of professional football in Texas. What's more, since young Giles can trace his ancestry back to a great grandfather named Sampson Connell (who was Sam Houston's wagon master at the battle of San Jacinto), he ought to know something about the gridiron tendencies of his Dallas neighbors.

"The average Texan," Miller frankly admits, "is a football nut. Take me, for example. I go to the Jesuit High School games here in Dallas on Thursday nights and the Highland Park High games on Friday nights. Incidentally, a big prep game here in Dallas will draw about 25,000 people. Then, of course, on Saturdays I watch Southern Methodist play in the Cotton Bowl which holds 75,000 and was packed every game last year even though Southern Methodist had a losing season.

"What some folks don't realize," Miller continues, "is that Dallas's population of 500,000 plus represents only about one sixth of the potential football fans in this area. You've got to remember that 20 miles used to be a fair day's journey in these parts, either by horse or oxcart, so trading posts sprang up at intervals on all the roads fanning out from Dallas. Nowadays, these trading posts have become fair-sized cities, so you'll find hundreds of small towns and about 3,000,000 people within a 200-mile radius of Dallas. Down here, folks don't think anything of driving 200 miles to see a good football game."

Fortunately, the Texans' organization numbers among its owners just the man to whip up a fine frenzy for pro football among the citizenry of the small towns around Dallas. That man is J. Curtis Sanford, the fabulous founder of Dallas's highly cherished Cotton Bowl football game.

To form an adequate estimate of Sanford's promotional potentialities, it is necessary to review a few highlights of his improbable career. In July, 1932, Sanford, then a twenty-five-year-old steel puddler, departed Birmingham, Alabama, in a $50 flivver and headed for the East Texas oil fields. Within a year, Sanford (a pleasantly persuasive, curly-headed six-footer) had bought and swapped enough oil leases to acquire title to a producing well which provided him with an income of $3,000 per day.

By 1936, Sanford had acquired several million dollars and a taste for football which prompted him to promote the first Cotton Bowl game between Marquette and Texas Christian. This sparsely attended affair cost Sanford $10,000.

"We didn't promote enough," Sanford confided to a friend. "Next year, I'm goin' to stir up some commotion—let the folks know we're in business."

To ensure that there would be ample commotion for the second Cotton Classic, Sanford wrote to the band directors of each of the several hundred high schools in Texas, Arkansas and Louisiana. In each letter, Sanford stated that he had been informed that the director had developed an organization whose musical presence would enhance the pageantry of the Cotton Bowl. Furthermore, if the director could find means of defraying his group's traveling expenses, Sanford would be looking forward to seeing the whole band in Dallas on January 1st.

Seventy band directors accepted Sanford's invitation. In a follow-up letter, Sanford advised each director to report with his band for pregame ceremonies in the lobby of the Adolphus Hotel at 10 A.M., on New Year's Day.

As might be expected, when an estimated 110 buses loaded with some 4,500 high-school musicians began to arrive in the vicinity of the Adolphus Hotel, a certain amount of commotion ensued. Nor did the situation improve approvably when the 4,500 bandsmen dismounted and attempted to reassemble in the lobby of the Adolphus Hotel.

"Happily," Sanford recalls, "a good many of the boys and girls brought their tubas and bass drums. For about two hours, we had the darndest traffic tie-up Dallas ever saw."

When the commotion finally subsided very few persons in Dallas were unaware of the fact that a Cotton Bowl football game was being promoted in their midst. However, Sanford reaped even more spectacular publicity triumphs during his successful campaign to build the Cotton Bowl into one of the nation's outstanding New Year's Day sports spectacles.

For example, shortly before the 1940 Cotton Classic, Sanford was extolling the merits of the opposing teams, Clemson and Boston College, at a routine press conference when a reporter objected, "Curtis, that's all pretty old stuff. How about giving us something with a fresh angle?"

"Well"—Sanford paused, reflecting just long enough to light a cigarette—"have I told you about my pigeons?"

"What pigeons?"

"Why," Sanford exclaimed, seemingly vexed with himself for neglecting to have mentioned such an important subject, "I mean the homing pigeons which are being shipped in here from all over the country. Now, here's the story, at the climax of our colorful half-time ceremonies, a huge flower-bedecked ball of cotton containing forty-seven pigeons will be carried to the center of the stadium.

"At a given signal"—Sanford paused again, thoughtfully—"I guess we'll fire off a cannon or something that makes a lot of noise, the huge ball of cotton will burst asunder and forty-seven pigeons will mount to the skies, each of them carrying a message of greetings and goodwill from the great and glorious commonwealth of Texas to the governors of every other state in the union.''

WHERE TO FIND THE PIGEONS?

Next morning, Sanford's pigeon pronouncements were front-paged in Dallas newspapers; and consequently, Sanford, who had plucked his goodwill-flight idea out of thin air, literally and figuratively, on the spur of the moment to accommodate the reporters, suddenly found himself confronted with the considerable task of locating some four-dozen pigeons in a hurry.

Sanford solved the problem rather neatly. Instead of going to the bother and expense of importing feathered messengers from such distant capitals as Salem, Oregon; Augusta, Maine; or Tallahassee, Florida, he called upon a man who raised pigeons in Oak Cliff, a suburb of Dallas, and rented forty-seven birds for the reasonable sum of $25.

Subsequently, on New Year's Day, a cannon boomed (precisely as Sanford had predicted), a huge ball of cotton burst asunder, and forty-seven startled pigeons took off from the Cotton Bowl in forty-seven different directions. The whole business was a tremendous success. Later, Sanford's enterprise and promotional genius were the subject of numerous editorials in Texas newspapers.

For several weeks after the game, reporters tried vainly to check the transcontinental progress of Sanford's goodwill fliers, but none of the forty-seven intrepid pigeons was ever seen or heard of again. Various theories purporting to explain their mysterious disappearance were advanced, including hailstorms, wanderlust, and unfriendly hawks. Sanford refrained from telling anybody that all forty-seven pigeons, upon regaining their cannon-shattered composure, had returned to their loft in Oak Cliff, about five miles by air from the Cotton Bowl, about the time Clemson and Boston College were going up for the second half kickoff.

In 1940, Sanford tendered the patent for a booming Cotton Bowl promotion to a Dallas civic committee. Since then, while serving as a consultant on Cotton Bowl affairs, Curtis has been busily and most sedately occupied with running at least three businesses simultaneously, including his real-estate firm, a string of restaurants and a furniture manufacturing plant. However, since joining up with the Texans, Sanford has been percolating with promotional ideas reminiscent of his earlier Cotton Bowl triumphs.

Currently he is urging that all the Texans dress up western style on road trips—a publicity stratagem which undoubtedly would pay off heavily with the news photographers. When one of the other owners suggested that some of the players—notably Art Donovan, a tackle from New York City—might object to appearing in public in such unfamiliar Texas trappings as fancy boots, cuffless pants, ten-gallon hats, silk shirts and string ties, Sanford roared:

''Object! Why, our boys ought to be proud to let folks know they're from Texas. If there's anybody in this club who feels that way, trade him to the Green Bay Packers!''

Despite whatever spectacular gimmicks Sanford dreams up to ballyhoo the Texans off the field, there is every reason to expect that Coach Phelan's footballers will stage an equally crowd-pleasing show on the field. Phelan has picked up quite a few fancy football tricks since he was graduated from Notre Dame back in 1917. During his consistently successful collegiate coaching stints at Missouri, Purdue, Washington (Seattle) and St. Mary's, and later during his first professional appointment (1948–9) as head coach of the departed Los Angeles Dons, Phelan was noted for his wide-open offensive tactics.

Last fall, when Phelan took over the hapless Yanks on short notice at the start of the season, Jimmy quickly developed an exceedingly effective spread formation which will be incorporated in the T-formation offenses of several other pro teams this fall. However, even with his fancy spreads, Phelan undoubtedly faces the toughest coaching assignment in pro football this season because his Texans are in the power-packed western division of the National League with the champion Rams, San Francisco 49ers, Detroit Lions, Chicago Bears, and the Green Bay Packers.

COACH OUTLINES PLAN OF ATTACK

Against this formidable opposition, Phelan proposes to spread his attacking forces all over the field. ''We're going to put our quarterback Bob Celeri, a mighty good passer, about five yards behind the center,'' says Phelan. ''Then, we'll split our ends out wide, close to either side line, and we'll spot our running backs—fellows like Buddy Young, a Negro star; Dick Hoerner and Zollie Toth—out in the flanks, inside and slightly to the rear of the ends. That'll give Celeri five wide-open and widely separated targets to throw at, and he ought to be able to hit somebody.

"Of course," Phelan adds, "there's no law against Celeri running with the ball, either, once we get the other team's defense loosened up to cover our spread ends and backs. Either way, whether Celeri throws or runs, he ought to stir up some excitement."

Phelan's predilection for wide-open football ought to fit in perfectly with Sanford's plans for a wide-open promotional campaign, including cowgirls, white horses, ten-gallon hats, fire engines, pregame rodeos, bells, sirens, whistles, and mechanized water carts.

"The big thing," Sanford recently confided to Coach Phelan, "is this: everywhere we go, we're going to make some noise and keep that football flyin'—let the folks know those crazy Texans are in town!"

Shinguards

BENNY FRIEDMAN

Benny Friedman (pro football's first true passing quarterback) remembered his introduction to shinguards and often told this story.

It seems in one game in 1930, he banged up a shin rather badly. Doc Alexander, who had coached the Giants a few years earlier and later was a kind of adviser in residence, told him afterwards that the best way to protect his shins was to wrap a copy of *Liberty* magazine over each and tape it tight. Friedman never did it but subsequently passed the advice on to a lady with whom he was talking at a cocktail party in New York. The woman had explained that she hated violent sports such as football but had agreed to let her son play soccer. Now she regretted it because he had been continually getting kicked in the shins.

"Don't worry," Friedman told her. "Tell him to do like the pro football players do. Tape copies of *Liberty* magazine over them to act as shinguards."

"All right," the woman said, then looked at him quizically. "Mr. Friedman," she said, "we don't subscribe to *Liberty*. Do you think *The New Yorker* would do?"

from *What a Game They Played*
by Richard Whittingham

Pete Gent's iconoclastic approach to football during his five-year career

with the Dallas Cowboys in the 1960's is somewhat legendary in the

National Football League. His quest during that trying (to him) and

turbulent (to the organization) time, was to bring a smile to coach Tom

Landry's stoneface, a pursuit perhaps as futile as it was well-publicized

in Texas. But he certainly got the attention of the Cowboys' coaching

staff and management when, out of football, he published his highly

successful novel *North Dallas Forty,* a piece of black humor that offers

a devastating look behind the scenes at a very icy, inhumane operation of

a professional football team—one whose cast of characters curiously

resembled many within the Cowboys' organization. Gent followed that

with an equally entertaining book touching on the same subject, *Texas*

Celebrity Turkey Trot, from which is taken this excerpt about the emo-

tional impact that comes all too dreadedly when a player's career comes

to its inevitable but unexpected end.

My Business Interests?

PETER GENT

SATURDAY AFTERNOON the two buses that would take us to the L.A. Coliseum to play the Rams were idling in the dormitory parking lot. We would leave in half an hour, but first Buck had scheduled a team meeting with the Everett Chemco artificial turf salesman. The coach felt we needed to renew our knowledge of the advantages of artificial turf versus the real ground. Besides, Everett Chemco was trying to sell the league on insisting on Everett Chemco artificial turf on all NFL fields. Jace Everett and the commisioner are old buddies. This was the only day the salesman could meet with us. We all hate artificial turf. It's like playing on carpeted concrete.

After a pitch designed to convince us that increased injuries on artificial turf were a "statistical quirk," the saleman in his red-and-yellow checked sport coat and white pants led us to the parking lot for a demonstration. He removed his coat and knelt down. He laid a foot-square swatch of "new, improved" Everett Chemco turf on the asphalt.

"Okay." He pressed the artificial turf down. "Somebody run up and cut on this and see how good it is. I'll hold it."

We all looked at each other.

"In our street shoes?" somebody asked.

"Doesn't anybody have game shoes around here?" Buck was angry. He liked artificial turf and felt a good sales demonstration would stop any complaining.

A rookie ran to the bus and returned with a pair of Adidas.

"LD," Buck said, "you try it."

"You kidding?" LD looked shocked. "I'll bust my ass cuttin' on that."

Buck turned pink and glared at the big tackle. The rookie was pulling on his Adidas.

The salesman was beginning to sweat through his shirt.

"I'm ready, Coach." The rookie bounced to his feet.

Buck nodded and the young man dashed at the tiny green swatch of plastic. He hit it with his right foot and cut hard. The plastic square ripped out of the salesman's fat hands and shot halfway across the lot. The rookie smashed to the asphalt with a sickening thud. He just moaned and lay still. He was hurt bad. Dobie Rank walked over to tend him.

The salesman looked sheepishly at Buck. "It must of slipped," he said. "Wanna try again?"

"That's okay." Buck looked at his watch. "Thanks anyway, but we got to get going. Saddle up, boys."

The players began drifting to the buses. Several stared back at the rookie writhing in the parking lot. Buck leaned over and patted the man's shoulder.

"Tough luck, son," Buck said and turned to the bus. The rookie grimaced bravely.

Dobie moved the injured man into the shade of Sonny's damaged Cadillac to await the ambulance.

The bus wound out of the tail end of the mountain range, ran a few miles along the coast, and then cut into Los Angeles County. The sun was low and orange when we pulled up to the Coliseum.

Hondo Higgins and Stormy, along with Farah and Jace Everett Junior, were waiting as the bus unloaded at the tunnel. Ezra Lyttle had tickets for them. As she took the tickets from her fiancé Stormy whispered something to Ezra. He jerked back, glared at LD, shook his head and walked quickly down the tunnel to the locker room. Stormy smiled and waved at LD, who looked at me and rolled his eyes in exasperation.

"She's taking the heat off Hondo by putting it on me."

"You've buttered your bread," I said, "now you have to sleep in it."

While getting taped I noticed Ezra pop a couple of Dexadrine hearts.

I hated to see my friends unhappy, but I had my own problems. The goddamn knee, my shoulder was sore and had kept me from sleeping well, and the last couple of days my little finger had gone numb.

"That collarbone is loose." Dobie Rank grabbed my clavicle and jerked. Pain shot through my shoulder and neck. "See. You oughta think about getting it fixed in the off-season. It'll be okay for now if we pad it."

I nodded. Nobody was cutting on me.

I went out with the kickers and practiced catching punts. Ezra and I were the return men. He was a flashier runner but I was smarter. Buck Binder wanted Ezra to field everything possible. I had had a twelve-yard average a couple of years ago. I was still good but I contented myself with good blocks and an occasional fielding opportunity on short kicks. I'm a team man.

I liked pregame warm-up in the Coliseum. Between punts I could scan the stands for movie stars and knock-out chicks. No wonder the Rams don't play well at home. Who can pay attention?

Skybuster Eaton, our punter, thumped a perfect spiral up above the lights. The ball hung in the twilight sky, then nosed over, came spinning down and smacked into my shoulder pads. It weighed a ton. Skybuster kicked a tall, heavy ball. He was a great kicker, although he cost us a game against the 49ers when a Kezar Stadium headwind got one of his towering boomers. Skybuster had looked forlorn standing there watching the football hang motionless high in the San Francisco sky. Then, as the Kezar wind took over, Skybuster had cried in horror, "My God—it's *coming back.*"

I saw Hondo Higgins, Stormy, Farah, and Jace Everett Junior in the stands. James Garner and John Wayne were sitting several rows behind them. Sonny Jeeter was behind our bench, leaning on his cane and talking to Burt Reynolds.

The Coliseum was slowly filling. The stadium lights came on as Alex Hart led the rest of the team out of the tunnel to join the kickers and receivers for pregame warm-ups. It would be the last time all night that the backup quarterback would smile.

We lost the toss and kicked off. I was second man on the right and was closing in on the L.A. return man when a yellow-and-blue flash knocked me out of bounds and into the photographers. Ezra helped me to my feet. He had a distant, angry look. His eyes were bright as we walked to the defensive huddle.

The Rams had the ball on their 28. We were in a flex 4-3 man-to-man. The Rams tried a draw-delay trap. LD slipped his block, filled the seam, and hit the ballcarrier a yard deep in the backfield.

Second and eleven. We were in a 4-3 roll strong. The tight end flanker set to my side. I inched up to cover the short side. At the snap I tried to bump the flanker. The pain in my knee made me stagger and I lost recovery. I left too big a zone and the Ram quarterback dropped the ball behind me to the flanker, who had hooked up. I was a step too slow. I dragged the flanker down from behind, but they had their first down.

Bob St. John, columnist for the *Dallas Morning News,* always enjoyed the wit of the Dallas Cowboys' restless receiver Pete Gent, and often told of this exchange: "Once Bob Hayes had been injured during a road game and on the return flight, Tom Landry decided he'd move Gent from flanker to the other side, split end, where he'd start against Philadelphia, instead of the injured Hayes. Landry walked to the back of the plane, the players' section, and found Gent.

" 'Pete,' said Landry, 'you'll be moving to the other side this week. So get ready.'

" 'You mean, coach,' said Pete, 'that I'm going to play for Philadelphia?' "

Buck Binder shook his fist at me. I can image what he was whispering. My knee ached as I leaned into the huddle.

The next play they swept right at me, leading with the onside guard. I tried to protect my knee, but the guard ducked under my outstretched hands. His helmet smashed into my kneecap. The pain burned up the front and back of my leg. I was hurt and went down like I had been shot. The runner cut inside, but LD closed fast along the line and cut him down. The L.A. guard lay next to me as I writhed on the ground. "Sorry, man," he said. "Didn't mean to hurt you."

As Dobie Rank helped me off the field, Buck sent a rookie from Arizona State in at my corner spot.

I sat on the bench with my knee packed in ice. A couple of plays later I got up and jogged. The pain was minimal and I was ready to return. Buck told me to take a rest. Sonny came and sat with me and we watched the Ram defense totally intimidate Hart. He threw three interceptions in the first half. But our defense played well, particularly Ezra, who played with a vengeance, making several unassisted tackles and a key interception in the end zone, and it was only 7-0 Rams at the half.

"I'm going to rest you," Buck told me in the locker room. "No sense getting really hurt this early in exhibition season."

I didn't mind. My knee was beginning to stiffen.

Hart couldn't generate any offense in the second half, but neither could the Rams. Our defense held them scoreless. Ezra was all over the field, making tackles and knocking down passes. The job was doubly tough because they had to call the zones to the rookie at my corner, leaving Ezra man-to-man most of the night.

In the last two minutes, with the score 7–7, Ezra fielded a punt on the six and took it back ninety-four yards for the winning touchdown.

In the locker room after the game Buck awarded Ezra the game ball and fined him a hundred dollars for fielding a punt inside the ten-yard line.

I was getting my knee wrapped when Ezra walked up, his face streaked with dirt. He was smiling and wired.

"You'd a won this if you hadn't gotten hurt." He tossed me the ball. "They did everything we were expecting. I knew everything that was coming."

"I sure didn't think you'd field that one on the six." I tossed back the ball.

"No guts, no glory." Ezra's eyes flashed.

LD Groover, still wet from the shower, stopped. He toweled off his chest. His tattoo of a black panther with red eyes scratched at his right nipple. The hole Ezra had punched in his chest with the dart was almost healed.

"How is he, Dobie?" LD asked the trainer, who was scowling as he swathed the damaged joint in sponge wrap.

"It ain't bad—a couple of days," Dobie said.

I immediately began to plan my rehabilitation and comeback. The rookie hadn't looked too good, but then he hadn't looked too bad. The films on Monday would tell.

Ezra started to head for the showers, then turned back and shook the game ball in LD's face. "What do you think about this? Sonofabitch." The defensive back laughed at LD and then disappeared in the steam of the shower room.

The Coliseum dressing area was broken up into individual stalls. As I passed the stall closest to the training room I heard Ezra's high-pitched giggle. I pushed open the door to investigate.

"Shut the door, turkey." Bobbyday Burke, the L.A. cornerback, decked out in suedes and platform shoes, was sitting next to Ezra. Ezra was snorting cocaine off the nail-file attachment to his fingernail clippers. I stepped in and quickly shut the door. The resulting breeze blew the cocaine off the nail file onto the floor.

"Oh, *man,*" Ezra cried. "You lame motherfucker."

Bobbyday Burke laughed. "I can afford it." He threw some more coke on the floor.

Ezra finally snorted and offered the cocaine bottle and fingernail clippers to me. I waved them off. Cocaine can make you bleed. Bobbyday slipped the bottle into his leather belt bag. Ezra put his fingernail clippers on the bench.

"This is sumthin', man." Bobbyday leaned back and put his feet on Ezra's equipment bag. "This is some life. I mean, look at this fine shit." Bobbyday held his arms as if to embrace the confines of the dressing stall. He picked up a towel and held it up. "I mean, this is some fine shit, man." He smiled and shook his head.

"Mabry, do you know what we used for shower towels in high school? Do you know?"

I indicated I didn't know.

"Our jockeys, man. That's right, our goddamn jockeys." Bobbyday got up and eased to the door. "But we didn't care, man. We was the niggers. Hell, when I went to SMU the freshman coach wanted me to get him a color TV. I was the only nigger he knew. And niggers know where to get hot TV's, right?" Bobbyday laughed. "I bought a used one in the want ads and charged the motherfucker twice what it cost. Everytime he sees me he winks and grins. Stupid sonofabitch."

The Ram defensive halfback laughed and pushed out of the dressing stall, heading for the tunnel. He stopped to hug Ryan O'Neal and Doug McClure, who were sitting and grinning on an equipment trunk. Their feet didn't reach the ground.

The tunnel was crowded with clusters of fans and family. Each group surrounded its player like piglets sucking a sow.

Los Angeles has the best-looking postgame tunnel show in the league—young men and women, tanned and beautiful. Pittsburgh and Cleveland always have the worst—everybody wears too many clothes and has a terminal head cold.

Ezra Lyttle moved quickly from one cluster to another, shaking hands and laughing, the game ball tucked under his arm.

I walked stiff-legged over to the crowd around LD, who was standing next to the giant motorized Ram helmet. LD had his arm around Farah Everett and was talking to her husband, Jace Junior. Hondo Higgins stood grinning in his cowboy drag. Farah formed the words "Are you all right?" silently on her soft red lips. I nodded.

"Listen, Junior," LD said, "I vote we go to the Luau and meet up with Sonny and Burt Reynolds."

"Well, I don't really care," Jace Junior responded, "but Ezra wanted to drop by the Daisy. He says Sinatra will be there. He wants him for our Celebrity Board of Directors."

Jace Junior paused, "Listen, man, don't call me Junior."

"Right." LD nodded, his mind on the benefits of the Luau's toy drinks versus the Daisy's chicks.

Farah Everett smiled and said something to LD, who looked at me and laughed. LD hugged her to him. Her black hair was tied back under a paisley scarf that knotted behind her right ear and flowed over her shoulders. Her breasts filled a fitted Neiman's glitter T-shirt. She wore tight jeans and deck shoes. A thick gold chain circled her neck.

Ezra walked up. "I think I got Merlin Olsen and Bobbyday Burke on the Celebrity Board of Directors." He grinned and shifted the game ball from hand to hand.

Then he spotted someone else in the crowd. "Klosterman. Hey, Don." The manic defensive back yelled at a man who had just left the Ram dressing room. "I wanna talk to you." Ezra strode toward the startled man.

LD watched Ezra go. "He still spends half his time coming and the other half going."

"Yeah," I said, my eyes on Farah Everett's face. "Let's hope he never gets there."

"Well, let's decide where *we're* going."

I wanted to go every place in town and end up with Farah Everett in a bungalow at the Beverly Hills Hotel, but instead I found myself alone on the bus heading back to camp. I had to elevate my leg and get some ice on it. Being injured is lonely business.

"How's it feel?" Buck Binder slid into the bus seat next to me and grabbed my thigh, giving it a hard squeeze. He smelled of Scotch. "You could always get good Scotch in New York," Binder often said wistfully. My coach was definitely sentimental about the Big Apple. It was a strange emotion to regard.

Buck patted my knee. "I'm sorry you got hurt."

"Thanks." I was embarrassed. He *was* sorry. I liked old, beat-up Buck Binder.

"I just want you to know you're still number one with me. We need older guys like you."

"What do you mean by that?" I asked.

"My God, Mabry." His Scotch breath reminded me Buck was a sentimental drinker. "I was just trying to cheer you up. What's gonna happen in this world when everybody's as paranoid as you?" He got up and staggered back to the front of the bus. The lights glared off the freeway.

The dormitory was strangely quiet. Those who hadn't stayed in Los Angeles were loose out in the Valley. A lot of them would be over at the Pub trying to screw Agnes while LD was in L.A. Curfew wasn't until two A.M.

"The lame and the strange, that's all that's here tonight." Jerome Beecher, the "root hog or die" rookie from the University of Michigan, talked to me from the doorway. I was on my bed, damaged leg elevated and packed in ice.

"The lame and the strange is all there is anywhere." I picked the ice bag off my knee and applied it to my head.

Jerome had an ugly gouge under his eye and both his knees were wrapped in Ace bandages. He was shaking slightly at the bottom end of thirty milligrams of Dexadrine. His eyes were big and dark. Jerome was an example of "the new young players" that the club was acquiring in what LD called "the android versus the animal dilemma."

"I'm just trying to get used to an organization," Jerome said. Jerome was an android.

LD and I were animals. We weren't trying to get used to anything.

"I hate this." Beecher lay down on LD's bed and clasped his hands behind his head, staring at the ceiling. "The coming down. It's really miserable. They tell me it has something to do with the going up but I can't keep it straight." There was no anger in his voice.

Jerome had spent the previous winter snowbound in the Bitterroot Mountains, doing yoga and reading Baba Ram Dass. Training camp in Southern California gave him cabin fever.

I returned the ice pack to my knee. "Jesus, I get lonely." Beecher shuddered and wrapped himself in LD's blanket. "I miss my kids."

Another *Texas Ranger* rerun flickered soundlessly on the television. Hondo Higgins was pistol-whipping another Mexican. I think Beecher started crying, but I didn't look to see. You'd think he'd take enough goddamn amphetamines to get him through the night.

The next afternoon Buck Binder was nailing the posterboard performance charts on the lobby wall. In blue and red ink the chart graded each player against the Rams. There were spaces remaining for the rest of the exhibition games. Good performances were recorded in blue ink, poor performances in red. A player was graded on every play: a zero if he did his job, a plus if he did more than his job, a minus if he failed. The charts were shot through with red lettering and players bunched around to learn the judgment on their last night's performance.

"Goddamn," someone growled. "How can they give me a minus? I pushed him all over the fucking field." Other players were making similar claims in the face of the red ink. Ezra Lyttle had gotten a plus 42, an unheard-of score. I looked for my name. It was followed with a red-ink −2 and the small notation "injured due to bad basic position." Because I was injured I had figured on getting a pass, not blame.

Buck Binder walked up. "Say, can I talk to you?" He clapped me on my sore shoulder.

I followed Buck to his room in the coaches' wing of the dormitory. The flapping of my sandals echoed down the empty hall. I figured he wanted to discuss some of the final details on my new contract. I wanted to get it signed this week. I needed the $15,000 front money. I had some paper due back in Dallas on a bad investment in a Willy Roy Rogers outdoor concert. Willy Roy got drunk and never showed.

"Listen, Mabry, we hate to do this . . ." Buck started talking as soon as I entered the room. ". . . it's just the way things worked out . . . I mean we have some real problems setting the roster, what with Sonny's injuries and now your knee"—Buck dug in his pocket for his Camels—"and today Bobbyday Burke was available.

We traded for him." Bobbyday Burke was the Ram cornerback.

"You traded me?" I was shocked.

"No." Buck frowned.

That was a relief. I could beat out Bobbyday Burke.

"We couldn't make deal for you . . . nobody was interested." Buck put his hand on my shoulder. "We're putting you on waivers. I'm sorry, you're a hell of a guy."

I lost my breath and my heart started pounding. Confusion, fear, and embarrassment crashed together in the back of my head. I lost my balance and quickly shifted my eyes to stare at a spot on the wall behind Buck's head. I concentrated hard to keep from coming apart. Discipline. Discipline. What the fuck was happening here?

"What do you mean nobody was interested?" I was suddenly mad.

"Nobody was interested," he repeated calmly, lighting up a Camel.

I was afraid that was what he meant. "Not even goddamn Tampa Bay?"

He shook his head. "Still . . . somebody might pick you up on waivers . . ." He tried to sound hopeful.

"Not even goddamn Tampa Bay . . ." I couldn't believe this was happening. It's not the kind of thing you think about a lot. "Those assholes . . . I'm better than anybody in that whole fucking secondary."

"I know you are, Mabry." Buck patted my shoulder. "Listen . . . I was wondering . . . we gotta make this move today." He looked at his watch. Smoke wafted off the cigarette in his hand. My mind raced, looking for a place to rest. I knew this would happen sometime, but not now. I was having my best camp ever. "Mabry, why don't you retire . . . you're thirty years old . . . it'll save the embarrassment of having to put you on waivers . . . you've had a great career . . . go out with your head up."

I had my head down, staring at the gray asphalt tile. One of the squares had been placed wrong and the pattern ran opposite to the rest of the tiles.

A long time passed.

"C'mon, buddy," Buck urged, checking his watch. "Make a decision."

"Me? Retire? I'm only thirty years old . . . I feel great. I'm having my best camp ever." My speeding brain searched for some explanation, some calming circumstance.

Buck shrugged. "It's up to you."

I needed to rest my mind; it was racing too fast. "Okay," I said suddenly. "You make the announcement . . ." I turned and walked away. It was like a dream . . . a nightmare.

"Okay, Mabry," Buck yelled and called after me, "I'll tell them you retired to spend more time with your business interests."

My business interests?

Frank Gifford is as familiar a face associated with pro football as any in the business, the handsome star of "Monday Night Football" and a respected spokesman for the game itself. He was, of course, an outstanding football player in his own right, earning a niche in the Pro Football Hall of Fame as a halfback for the New York Giants in the 1950s and early 60s. He is also a portrait in courage himself, making a remarkable comeback from a serious head injury suffered after a terrifyingly brutal tackle by fellow Hall of Famer Chuck Bednarik in a game against the Philadelphia Eagles. In his book, *On Courage,* Gifford writes about that virtue in other people; in the case presented here, about a teammate who rounded out his long and illustrious pro football career with Gifford as a Giant, the unforgettable Hall of Famer, Yelberton A. Tittle.

On Y. A. Tittle

FRANK GIFFORD

Y.A.'s COMING to New York took courage. Y.A. was highly respected by players but had never been considered a star in San Francisco. He had drawn boos there in recent years. He could easily fall on his face with the new club. There was enormous precedent for that. It was a gloomy-looking future for Colonel Slick, as I later affectionately referred to him. But I had meant what I said. I knew that the man I'd watched, admired, and played against for years had a lot of football left.

At that point, New York didn't have Del Shofner, who would join with Y.A. to form one of the outstanding pass-receiving teams in league history. Kyle Rote and I for several years had been New York's leading pass receivers. I had retired following a head injury in 1960 and Kyle was 34.

Why *did* Tittle go to the Giants? While he admits that I was persuasive, there was a lot to consider before he reversed his decision to give it all up. Quarterbacks who had started pro ball the same year as he—Johnny Lu-jack, Charlie Trippi, Harry Gilmer—all had retired. Why go to back up an established and popular quarterback and inflict again the mental and physical punishment and the severe asthma attacks that made special medication for him part of the team doctor's on-field equipment?

Knowing Y.A. as I do now, his decision probably hung on his pride and the fact that if he retired, his family's last memory of his football days would be the insult of the trade.

The next day, Y.A. flew to the Giant's training camp in Salem, Oregon. His fears of failure, his self-doubt didn't show, but he had to be concerned about his future in a game that for Tittle had begun nearly a quarter of a century earlier.

Y.A. walked into a difficult situation when he joined the Giants. Charlie Conerly was the quarterback and no one from the tightly knit offensive unit was going to become friendly with the man who might take his job. The defensive team, which was just as close, also went its own way and, typical of many great Giant teams, didn't want much to do with any of the offensive "pretty boys," much less an old, bald quarterback. With relatively few exceptions, the entire squad had been together at least since 1956.

Tittle was assigned to room with backfield coach Heinrich who would help him learn the Giant offense. Although Y.A. was older than Heinrich, players don't go out with coaches and Y.A. was left alone while the team went off after daily practice to the local friendly tavern. Like the new boy on the block, he kept his room door closed so no one would see him sitting alone.

When the Giants traveled to Los Angeles for an exhibition game against the Rams, Y.A. went down early to the hotel lobby, hoping for a spontaneous dinner invitation from the players passing through. Finally, he asked the doorman if he knew where the players had gone to eat. Then he walked to that restaurant and pretended he was looking for a nonexistent friend. Several Giants finally asked him to sit with them "while he waited."

During Tittle's first play the following night against the Rams, he bobbled the handoff and fell on the ball. A half ton of Rams fell on him—and cracked several bones in his back. Out for five weeks.

While he suffered, more from embarrassment and the return of nagging self-doubt than pain, Y.A. found himself beginning to root silently for Charlie. "I used to sit on the bench in San Francisco with Frankie Albert and, later, Brodie playing and clapping with my fingers crossed," he said, "hoping the SOB's next pass is intercepted because that was the only way I was going to get into the game.

"I couldn't do that with Charlie. He had so much class that although it was surely gnawing on his pride to see me there, he could come over in practice when I did something well and say, 'Well, you're looking pretty good, Y.A.'

"I knew what it was like to have someone else come in to play your position," Y.A. said. "We were both in the twilight of our careers." Y.A. broke off abruptly at this point, and I realized from his expression how strong an impact those events now 15 years old had had on him. For the first time, I understood with heightened clarity how painful that time had been for both Y.A. and Charlie. I would have been happy just sharing the work with Charlie. But when I got the starter's job, I knew how it must have hurt.

"Charlie was tough. He could cope, could handle physical punishment *and* mental punishment without letting either get to him. There was an extraordinary dignity about that man."

Sherman handled the situation well. He spoke with Charlie and Y.A. "Any split between you two old guys will crack this club right down the middle," he said. "It isn't going to be easy for any of us. Barring injury, there never will be a time when one of you isn't playing. You are both number one, no matter who starts."

"I was surprised when I came to the Giants," Y.A. told me. "The players didn't seem to have the physical ability of the men I had left behind on the 49ers. But they were far more successful. One reason was maturity. Their age and experience made them virtually unbeatable."

There was a second reason: The Giants *expected* to win. We based our end of season plans around the championship game. The 49ers hoped to win; the Giants expected to.

"I had never seen the spirit that club had," Y.A. said, "both the offensive and defensive players. The defense dubbed themselves, the DVW's, Defense vs. The World, and they were thoroughly confident they could handle any team."

Before the season began, the Giants traded for 26-year-old Del Shofner, a combination end and defensive back at Los Angeles, and tight end Joe Walton. The Shofner trade was a management error of major magnitude on the part of the Rams. They'd given up on one of the finest athletes I've ever seen because of a few nagging injuries that had bothered Del the previous season. Shofner could leave almost any defensive back in the league and instantly become Y.A.'s primary receiver. He broke my record for single-season receptions during his first year with the Giants; he caught 68 passes for 11 touchdowns. Del was the best end Y.A. had ever played with. Tittle had Billy Wilson in San Francisco. Billy had an extraordinary pair of hands, but he wasn't fast. Shofner had both the hands and the great speed.

Y.A. opened the 1961 season watching from the bench. Charlie started against St. Louis but the Giants did little offensively or defensively and lost, 21–10. New York was leading Pittsburgh in the second game, 10–7, when Conerly was shaken up. Tittle made his first appearance as a Giant. He hit his first six passes in succession and ended the day with 10 completions in 12 attempts. The Giants won, 17–14.

Feelings erupted only once. Early in the third game, against Washington, the Giants fell behind when one of Charlie's receivers missed his pass route and the pass was intercepted and run back for a touchdown. Tittle had been warming up on the sideline and Sherman chose that moment to send him in.

Charlie slammed the helmet to the ground, walked to the far end of the bench and sat down. Y.A. finished the game, bringing New York from behind in the last quarter to win, 24–21. Following the game, reporters in the locker room quizzed Tittle, Conerly and Sherman. All of them characteristically refused to comment on a situation that could have destroyed the ball club.

Y.A. started most of the games that followed but he needed help from Charlie twice, against Los Angeles and in the second game against Philadelphia, the defending league champion. The Washington game at midseason was the turning point. It followed a one-point loss to Dallas. I never saw the Giants play that year because I was always scouting their next week's opponent. I had felt Washington's new cornerbacks were vulnerable to deep passes, particularly since New York finally had a deep threat in Shofner.

The weapon was simple. The results were explosive. New York used a three-receiver pattern with Kyle and Joe Walton, the ends, breaking downfield just a few yards and then turning in to pull coverage from Washington's two deep men. Shofner, set as a flanker to the left, ran a "fly," a straight, allout sprint. The Redskins made an early mistake, single coverage on Shofner. Del got behind a cornerback, took Tittle's pass on the 10 and scored untouched. Tittle threw three touchdown passes as New York won, 53–0. The Giants went on to win four and tie one of the seven remaining games (scoring 170 points) to win the eastern division title.

Part of the credit for the first win over Philadelphia, which put the Giants in a tie for first place, went to Pete Previte, popular clubhouse man for the football Giants and baseball Yankees. He was forever making suggestions that we laughingly accepted in the locker room and forgot about on the field. But Pete was very knowledgeable about baseball and in this instance that knowledge paid off. "In baseball, fast men are put into the line-up in scoring situations," he reasoned, "why not football?"

He suggested using defensive backs Erich Barnes and Jim Patton, both of whom could run the 100 in under 10 seconds. The play worked well in practice so it was put into the Philadelphia ready list. With seconds remaining in the first half, Barnes and Patton replaced running backs Alex Webster and Bob Gaiters. Tittle shocked the Eagles' secondary with five receivers—Rote, Shofner and Walton were the additional three—and hit Barnes, who had beaten his man by a step, on the Eagle 26 for a 62-yard touchdown play. That put New York ahead to stay.

"Charlie pulling out the second Philadelphia game brought us into the final game against Cleveland needing only a tie, which we got, to take the eastern championship," Y.A. said. "He won two big games coming off the bench. That's the toughest way to win them. You're cold. You don't have the feel of the game. It takes time to gauge the speed of your receivers, the wind and the condition of the field. The defense knows you're cold

and they come at you like all hell. It's like pinch-hitting with two out in the ninth. The pressure is immense."

Charlie *was* hurting inside. Unless injured, he hadn't sat on a football bench since junior high school. Yet he was quick to compliment Tittle and do it sincerely.

After the first Pittsburgh win: "Y.A. made three or four big calls on third-down plays," Charlie told one writer. "Sometimes a quarterback can call a play that isn't worth a damn, but Y.A. didn't waste a single third-down situation."

After the second Pittsburgh game: "He was the master all the time he was out there." For our silent Mississippian, those are speeches, believe me; and far more than I had ever heard him say to a writer about himself.

> The Giff on the game: "Pro football is like nuclear warfare. There are no winners, only survivors."

The big-eared, big-nosed asthmatic who stuttered like a teenager when excited was a born leader. He radiated so much confidence that the Giants in those years were shocked when he—and they—didn't win.

His confidence sometimes got him into trouble. Y.A. insisted on running with the ball.

"I loved bootlegging. (The quarterback fakes a hand-off, hides the ball behind his hip and circles the end, a solitary figure running away from the flow of the action.) I fool everybody. I'm running full speed, but going so slow everyone says, 'Oh, he couldn't *possibly* have the ball.' "

Most of Tittle's injuries came when he kept the ball and ran. His cheekbone was shattered one day early in his career when he bootlegged for a touchdown against Detroit. A back grabbed his arm, Y.A. fell and rolled into the end zone as a safety dived to stop him and smashed his knee into Tittle's face. He suffered a concussion running into the end zone against Detroit with the Giants in 1962. His face was badly cut that same year when he ran against Pittsburgh. He suffered back injuries with the bootleg against Green Bay and Dallas. . . .

Against Pittsburgh, [Bob] Gaiters swept around end, saw Big Daddy Lipscomb, 285 pounds and one of the best defensive tackles in the history of pro football, leading the defenders coming at him and stepped outside to avoid being tackled. Tittle was there in an instant: "Don't you ever do that when I'm around. Put your head down and go."

During the same game, Tittle bootlegged around end, was shoved out of bounds and Lipscomb went after him and knocked him down. The Giants' Jim Katcavage went off the bench after Lipscomb but was pulled back. Tittle returned to the game with blood streaming from a cut over the eye, courtesy of Lipscomb.

In the second quarter, Y.A. ran again and, again, was shoved out of bounds and behind the players' bench when Lou Michaels, 235 pounds, leaped the bench and knocked Tittle down. Y.A. was shaken but responded by throwing an immediate pass to Alex Webster that put the Giants in front, 21–7.

Lipscomb and Michaels pounded Tittle so hard in that game that when Lipscomb came to the Giants' locker room after the game to congratulate the team, his good friend, Rosey Brown, stared coldly at him and said, "Big Daddy, sometimes I got to wonder about you."

Y.A. became sort of a captain-father confessor to our team. However, it didn't always work. New York's first draft choice in 1964 was a running back named Joe Don Looney. He had the potential to be an extraordinary player. But—there were problems.

He injured his leg early in training camp. So Sherman told him to see the trainer about it. To Allie's amazement, Looney refused.

His reason? "It's my leg. I know more about it than the trainer."

He wouldn't go to Detroit for an exhibition game. "I can't play: why should I go?" he asked me.

"You're part of the team," I said.

"I'm not part of the team if I can't play," he replied.

Joe Don came in an hour after curfew one night and was fined. "Not fair," he said, "I was in bed an hour early last night, so we should be even up."

He wouldn't throw his used socks into a marked bin because "I'm not going to do what any sign tells me to do."

Although I didn't see it, I understand that in scrimmages, he often ran one way when the play called for him to go another. His reason: "Anybody can run where the blockers are. A good football player makes his own holes."

As a last-ditch measure, Wellington Mara and Allie Sherman asked Y.A. and me to try to talk to the young man. Joe Don was 6'1", 224 pounds and ran the 100 in something like 9.7. They wanted to keep him.

We were still in training camp at Fairfield (Conn.) University. Joe Don was lying down in his room listening to music when we found him.

Y.A. flopped on the other bed and started to tell Joe Don about his trade to New York from San Francisco, which somehow Y.A. equated with Looney's problems: how difficult it was leaving the team where he had spent most of his career, his family, his business, being traded for a rookie lineman, coming to a team in a strange city with a popular quarterback ahead of him and how "alone" Y.A. had felt.

Clearly talking from his heart and, perhaps for the first time outside of his family discussing his gut feelings about the trade, Tittle went on for about 20 minutes with Joe Don and me listening intently.

Finally, Y.A. finished and stopped, serious, sad, thinking of what had happened just three years earlier.

Joe Don broke an embarrassing silence. He sat up, completely caught up in Tittle's reverie, and said sympathetically, "It must have been *really* tough, Y.A. Anything I can do for you?"

Joe Don didn't last much longer with New York and moved through a couple of teams. He paused briefly with the Detroit Lions. In a scene reminiscent of Y.A.'s "from the heart" advice, the Lions asked Joe Schmidt, the great middle linebacker, to see why Joe Don hadn't come to practice one day.

Schmidt walked into Joe Don's room and there was our errant ballplayer listening to music.

"Joe," Schmidt said, "we missed you at practice."

"I'm glad you did, Joe."

"You know, I've been with this club 12 years and I've never missed or been late to a practice. In all that time."

Looney blinked. "You never missed one practice in 12 years?"

"That's right."

"Boy, Joe, pull up a chair. If there was ever someone who needed a day off, it's you."

Before the 1962 and 1963 league-title games, Y.A. and our team were the focus of extraordinary attention. Fans at a hockey game in Madison Square Garden began to chant between periods, "Beat Green Bay (the 1962 opponent) . . . beat Green Bay." Disc jockeys and store owners in Manhattan picked up the line. Strangers stopped Y.A. on the street or in restaurants and cheered him on as they would an old friend.

It multiplied in 1963 when we were preparing for Chicago and the NFL championship. I was moonlighting on local television and I interviewed Y.A. a week before the game. Everyone looking in learned that he lived in Eastchester, a suburb of New York City. Y.A. didn't have an unlisted number so his phone rang until game time. Boys and girls knocked on his door to pledge their support.

He found a ticket for overtime parking on his car. Written across the back: "Forget the ticket, Y.A. Murder the Bears." A Christmas package was delivered with "Beat the Bears, Y.A." written on one side in crayon by men in the local post office. The teaching sisters in the parochial school Y.A.'s boys were attending sent word that they were saying the rosary for Y.A. every day until the game. And the Tittles weren't even Catholics.

"A lot of people were rooting for me, I guess, because they kind of figured I was getting close to the end of my career and that I would not have many more chances," he said. "I think all the people who were in their middle or late thirties were on our side. Not all of them were Giant fans. But this was an older ball club with a lot of guys who had been around for a long time. We were symbols to people in that age group for reasons I'm sure were not even related to football."

We should have beaten the Packers in 1962 and the Bears in 1963 for the league titles.

(I'll take Y.A.'s word for the 1961 championship game. I wasn't there. "We were hopelessly outclassed by the Packers. It was in Green Bay, the temperature as I recall was under 5°, there was a blizzard and we couldn't adjust. We were down about 37–0 with a minute or so left to go and I kept wanting to throw, to try to get something on the scoreboard while the guys in the huddle were thinking only of a hot shower and glared at me everytime I called a pass. They wanted runs up the middle, nothing that would stop the clock.")

In 1962, we had gale force winds and a temperature at about 9°. I was there for this one, at the end of my comeback year, and wished I hadn't been. Packer coach Vince Lombardi must have ordered the weather that day directly from Pope John. You can throw in rain; you can throw in snow; but you can't throw in gusty, high wind. I didn't get a pass all day. Y.A. threw one to me that went almost straight up in the air. He threw balls that landed behind him. It was quite simple. The Packers were a running team. We were a passing team. We lost, 16–7.

The following year, we knew we were in better shape than the Bears. We had a great offensive team and a good defensive team. We reached the Chicago 14 on our first series of plays in the game. I knew I could beat defensive back Bennie McRae on our favorite zig-out pass to the corner. I told Y.A. and we scored our touchdown.

But just as Y.A. released the ball, Chicago linebacker Larry Morris hit him across the left leg. The knee started to stiffen. Late in the second period, Chicago intercepted a pass and took it 61 yards for the tying score. Don Chandler kicked a field goal and we led, 10–7. Then Morris dove again into Tittle's left knee. "It was as if a knife had been stuck into the knee joint," Y.A. said. "The pain shot clear up my leg."

Before the second half started, Sherman asked Tittle if he thought he could play. The decision was Y.A.'s to make.

"I didn't know what to say," Y.A. told a writer years later. "Injuries are funny things. Football is an emotional game and sometimes you can do amazing things when you're hurt. I remember once I went into a game with two sprained ankles. I could barely walk into the huddle. But once I got under that center, I was cured on the spot. In 1953, I played a game with a shattered cheekbone and completed 29 passes. I went in for San Francisco once with a broken hand and won the game.

"I pulled a hamstring muscle with San Francisco in 1957 and was supposed to be out for three weeks, but John Brodie went bad in the first half the next week against Green Bay and Hickey asked, 'Can you play, Tittle?' What does a ballplayer say in a spot like that? I tried. I got out there and threw a couple of touchdown passes and we won 27–20."

For anyone who still had to know, the Bear game in 1963 was another one that proved Tittle's guts. He had no business playing the second half. His only backup was rookie Glynn Griffing. So Y.A. came in with his knee shot full of Novocaine and heavily taped. It was clear to all of us that he was playing in extreme pain. Yet he never complained about a missed assignment, a dropped ball or a knee that in spite of the pain killer must have felt as if it was held together by ligaments turned to spaghetti. Tittle was unable to set up to throw well. He couldn't drop straight back to pass. He had to back-pedal, which is far slower. He couldn't maneuver. The Bears' defensive coach George Allen knew this and Chicago kept coming at Y.A. with everyone but the ticket takers.

Another pass was intercepted and run back for a touchdown. That's how they won, 14–10, on two passes intercepted after Y.A. was put out of commission early in the first quarter.

Y.A. was on crutches for two weeks, but he still was criticized because New York lost. Many guys I played with and many I know today wouldn't have gone back into that game with a gun.

William Goldman, besides being an extraordinarily successful screen-writer (*Butch Cassidy and the Sundance Kid, All the President's Men,* etc.) and novelist (*The Marathon Man,* among many others), is an avid football fan—of both the present and the past. At one point in his novel *Magic,* he combined his knowledge of the sport and his unique writing style to tell the story of an aged but legendary Bronko Nagurski returning to the game to help the Chicago Bears when they sorely needed it in a personnel-depleted season during World War II.

The Bronko

WILLIAM GOLDMAN

"HE'S COMIN' in, The Bronko, The Bronko. And I sat there thinking omijesus, what a great spot for a legend to be in, coming back after so many years, one quarter to play, the title on the line, and ten points behind . . .

"And then the crowd started screaming like nothin' you ever heard because on the bench he stood up. Nagurski. And he reached for his helmet. And he come onto the field . . .

"Well, everybody knew they were going to give the ball to Bronko . . . and if you're smart and everybody knows what you're going to do, well you don't do it, you fake it and do something else and when they came out of the huddle and when they lined up with Nagurski at fullback and Luckman at quarterback well it had to be a decoy thing, they had to pretend to give him the ball and then Luckman could throw one of his long passes . . . Only it wasn't no decoy . . . They gave it to him and he put it under his arm and just kind of ran slow, straight into the Cardinal line. They were all waiting for him. And Nagurski tried, you could see that, but they just picked him up, the Cardinals did, and for one second they just held him on their shoulders."

"And then they threw him down?"

"Not exactly, they all fell backwards and he gained four yards . . . He kind of got up and shook himself off and went back into the huddle and out the Bears come again and this Luckman, he hands the ball to Nagurski and he lumbers up and they're waiting, only this time he falls forward for eight more. First down . . . But it was starting to get a little eerie on the field. You could see all

On the brutal, bruising Bronko Nagurski:

Dick Richards, Detroit Lions owner: "Here's a check for $10,000, Nagurski. Not for playing with the Lions, because you belong to the Bears, but just to quit and get the hell out of the league. You're ruining my team."

George Halas, his coach in Chicago: "I remember in one game, head down, charging like a bull, Nagurski blasted through two tacklers at the goal line as if they were a pair of old-time saloon doors, through the end zone, and full speed into the brick retaining wall behind it. The sickening thud reverberated throughout the stadium. 'That last guy really gave me a good lick,' he said to me when he got back to the sideline.'"

the Cardinal linemen slapping each other on the asses and the Bears come out again and this time they did fake and the pass was good for another first down and the next play was Nagurski kind of slipping down for six. He was like an ax hitting a tree. It doesn't matter how big the tree is, when the ax starts coming, you better look out.

"Now the Bears were inside the twenty. And there wasn't any doubt about what was gonna happen. It was gonna be the Bronko up the middle, and all these Cards, they bunched, waiting, and sure enough, here he comes, and they hit him and he hits them and for a second they did what they could but then he bursts through and he's doing five, six, eight, and then they knock him down and he's crawling—*crawling for the goal,* and every- body's screaming and there's a Cardinal on his back, trying to make him stop but he can't, he can't, and finally about six guys jump him at the one and stop him short of the TD. But they were scared now. They knew he was coming and they knew there wasn't anything they could do about it, and they waved their fists and tried to get steamed up but old Bronko, he just lined up behind the quarterback and the quarterback give him the ball and they're all waiting . . . and this old man starts forward and they're braced and he jumps sideways at them, the old man flies at them and they parted like water and he was through and the rest of the game was nothing, the Bears slaughter them behind the Bronko . . ."

Motion picture star Corinne Griffith was introduced to the game of football by her husband, George Preston Marshall, who happened to own a team, the Boston and later Washington Redskins. Her views of the subject were more concerned with what went on outside the actual field of play, focusing rather on the pageantry and personalities than the combat and competitors. In 1947, she wrote a book about the things she observed and experienced, and entitled it *My Life with the Redskins*. This chapter from it offers an entertaining insight into what life must have been like with George Preston Marshall and his beloved band.

I Love a Parade

CORINNE GRIFFITH

In 1937, the team played its first game in New York as the Washington Redskins. The fans drove from Washington to New York, a distance of 225 miles, in automobiles. They went by bus. They chartered railroad coaches. The Pennsylvania Railroad put on special trains, which arrived in New York at the Pennsylvania Station from ten in the morning until one in the afternoon. And the Baltimore & Ohio put on special trains.

The trains started leaving Washington at six in the morning. Some of the coaches had placards which read "Sammy Baugh Club," some "Cliff Battles Club," etc., etc. Some of the fans wore summer clothes and fall overcoats; some wore winter clothes and new winter overcoats; some wore men's hats, and some women's hats. But male or female, every hat had a red feather with 'Redskins' painted in gold stuck in the hatband.

The brass band was the last to arrive. It started to form lines in the middle of the Pennsylvania Station. The bandsmen wore their new costumes of burgundy and gold, with white feather head-dresses, imported straight from Hollywood. The leader and two drum-majors wore chief's war bonnets with streamers of white feathers that fell all the way to the ground.

It was Sunday, so the streets were fairly empty. It was fortunate that the men in blue were New York policemen. I have always contended that New York policemen are the finest and most understanding in the world.

As the bad marched out of the Pennsylvania's tunnel of dark shadows onto Seventh Avenue, the bright sunlight struck one hundred and fifty white feather head-dresses. The band was playing "Hail to the Redskins." The marching steps of the bandsmen gave an undulating movement to the white feather head-dresses as they spread like white foam their way toward Columbus Circle, twenty-five blocks away.

The fans with a "whither thou goest, will I go" expression, undulated right along with the band. Maybe they didn't undulate quite as steadily as the band, maybe their overcoats *were* falling off one shoulder to drag on the sidewalk, maybe the red feathers weren't standing as erect as when they had left Washington at six that morning, but just a year ago the Redskins had been homeless. Now they had a home and a large family and ten thousand of the family were there to prove their loyalty. In fact they were simply full of loyalty and red feathers and other things.

Bill Corum said: "At the head of a one hundred and fifty piece brass band, and ten thousand fans, George

Preston Marshall slipped unobtrusively into New York today.'' But in spite of what Bill Corum said, the first glimpse George had of the crowd from Washington was the one he got as we entered the gate down by the dressing-rooms at the Polo Grounds. Even with his new raccoon coat I could detect a decided sag at the shoulder line. In fact he seemed to sag all over. I was worried about his attitude. Then I began to worry about his longitude; I thought he was going to faint—all six feet two of him and in his brand new raccoon coat! I said, ''Let's sit here for a moment.''

He stumbled over to a vacant seat on the field, dropping his hands between his knees, his head hung forward. Tears rolled down his cheeks.

''I can't believe it—my home town—what a wonderful group of people.''

I didn't know what to do. It wasn't that I hadn't seen a man cry before, but this was different. After all, I had never had one six feet two weep into a brand new raccoon coat in front of sixty thousand people. So I wiped his eyes and blew his nose.

We reached our box just as the brass band came on the field. It was a thrilling sight. The bandsmen entered one at a time, and though there were one hundred and fifty of them, they looked like a million with their Burgundy and Gold costumes and white feather head-dresses in the bright sunlight. I was very proud.

Phyllis Haver, former bathing beauty, was in the box next to us. ''Corinne, they are *wonderful*,'' she enthused. ''Where did you get them all? Do they go *everywhere* with you?''

''Well, n-no,''—I stuttered, ''not *everywhere*, I like going to church alone!''

That day Cliff Battles had his greatest day, Baugh was perfection and the team ticked like a clock. There was one tense moment when the Giants came from 21 points behind up to a 21 to 14 score and scared us. That was at the beginning of the second half—but that was before Battles took off again. We won the Eastern Division Championship in our greatest victory over New York— 49 to 14.

Fifteen special trains had taken the fans, the team and the band to New York and fifteen special trains were bringing them back. We were on the train with the team, the last to leave New York. When we pulled into Washington around eleven o'clock, a crowd of ten thousand was waiting. A rousing good cheer practically lifted the roof off the Union Station, as the team pushed through and was greeted and kissed by the wives and sweethearts.

The white Indian head-dresses could be spotted here and there above the crowd, bobbing and nodding, in a peculiar, indignant, argumentative way, which I was

soon to learn would take place whenever a decision was against the Redskins.

Espey came shoving through. Above the noise and cheering of the fans, he explained the band and fans wanted to have a victory march, the cops wouldn't let them. They had no marching license and the cops were there to see they didn't march without one.

The bags and I were turned over to Welles. We were told to park across the concourse at the other side of the station. A clean rain-washed air, heavy with the thick odor of magnolia blossoms, greeted me. The oily-black wetness of the rain drenched streets, broken by the zig-zag reflections of the street lights, told of a very recent shower that had apparently stopped as suddenly as it had begun. Over the city fog hung low enough to catch the lights and hold them, then throw them back in a soft pinkish glow.

The Capitol dome, with its indirect lighting, stood out in calm relief against the sodden rain-soaked sky, lending a cool white serenity to the panorama. The Washington Monument, sentinel of simplicity, stabbed high into the night, disappearing in the softening edges of the fog. Heavy drops fell from the leaves of the trees in a slow rhythm to break the quietness. All was serene on my side of the station.

I sat there, accepting the slow rhythmic quietness on my side of the station as long as I could, then suggested we go over to the other side.

''We can park across the street and not disturb anyone,'' I told Welles.

The first thing that greeted my eyes on the other side was an old patrol-wagon, which looked as though it hadn't been painted since Betsy Ross formed her first sewing circle. Three or four policemen were there. I could see George arguing with them. Suddenly he started beating his chest. I waited for the wild jungle call of Tarzan, but instead one hundred and fifty white head-dresses were lifted high in the air and one hundred and fifty voices shouted,

''Hoorah!'' The head-dresses lowered, then raised again, and another,

''Hoorah!'' Then another lowering of the head-dresses and a third,

''Hoorah!''

I couldn't stand it any longer. I told Welles to go over and find out what was happening.

The hero of the hoorahs came over explaining that the cops wanted to arrest the band, because the band wanted to parade without a license. He was insisting that they take him instead. That explained the chest beating. I can imagine it was one of those, ''Do with me what you will, but touch not one feather of those old, white head-dresses.''

For once I agreed with him. I am not the type of

person who goes through life impugning the wisdom of cops, but I couldn't understand why they failed to see the practicability of his argument. I am sure that even with his extravagant gestures, George, sitting there in an argumentative mood and an old patrol-wagon, was much more practical than trying to cram one hundred and fifty members of the brass band, one hundred and fifty instruments, and one hundred and fifty white feather headdresses into one old patrol-wagon that needed a fresh coat of paint. I have never been on any police force, not even the police force of Beverly Hills and yet I could figure that out.

George got into the car and told Welles to drive up Pennsylvania Avenue. At a certain street we pulled up to the curb. The band and some fans arrived. The big secret was that they had lost the cops and if they could just march one block to one chorus of "Hail to the Redskins" everyone would be happy.

Just at that moment the old patrol-wagon arrived. It stopped long enough to let out the police sergeant, continuing on toward the band. The sergeant came over, leaned his elbows on the open window, and asked, "What's going on here?"

The Chief of all the Redskins explained that the band wanted to march just one block for one chorus of "Hail to the Redskins." They thought that if they marched far away from the stations and crowds, the cops would understand. ". . . like the New York cops."

Answered the sergeant, in no uncertain terms, "You're in the District of Columbia (as if we didn't know that) now, and not in New York. Let them foreigners run their country any way they want . . . Carter Glass lives in the next block—and Carter Glass has asked me to keep this district quiet—and Carter Glass is asleep now—and Carter Glass ain't gonna' be disturbed."

"But," explained the Big Chief very proudly, "Carter Glass is one of the Redskins' most loyal supporters and dearly loves to hear 'Hail to the Redskins.' "

"He ain't never told me that," said the sergeant in a way that proved he had a heart as hard as a cold lamb chop. The Chief of all the Washington Redskins resorted to his well-known salesmanship. Had the sergeant been anything but a sergeant, had he for instance, been a nice old-fashioned woodpecker, he would have been charmed right off the tree.

All the virtues of the forward-pass were extolled, all the virtues of Sammy Baugh and all the virtues of Pro-football. This went on for a long and interesting time, more long than interesting, but in spite of the Big Chief's great salesmanship and the Big Chief's great charm, the sergeant remained adamant.

"Carter Glass . . ." he started again. The Big Chief jumped out of the car. As he started toward the band, he smilingly tossed this one at me,

"You'll look out for the sergeant for me, won't you?" Had he added, "he's such a shy kid," I would have screamed.

"I see you've had some rain," I started.

"Yep."—

"Was it a very heavy rain?"

"Nope."—

"Awfully good for the farmers, though."

"Yep."—

The "Yeps" and the "Nopes" were coming thick, but not fast. Still I determined to win over this brilliant conversationalist, if it took the last calf in Dad's barn.

"Will Rogers once said, 'If you don't like the Washington weather, stick around awhile, it always changes.' " That may have been uproariously funny when Will Rogers said it, but the night I said it, it died a slow death, smothered in silence.

"Did you listen to the football game on the radio?" I asked very charmingly.

"Nope."—(My, my, we were at it again.)

"It was a very exciting football game. It's too bad you couldn't listen to it on the radio."

The sergeant took a deep breath, folded his arms and looked me squarely in the eye.

"Now you listen to me, young lady. I didn't listen to the football game on the radio for one reason and one reason *only*. . . . I don't like football!"

I sat there several separate seconds that rapidly froze together in the icy atmosphere. It was beginning to look like another staring contest, when the Chief of all the Washington Redskins appeared.

He had dropped his great charm, because his attitude was one that was far from "How to Make Friends, and Influence People." He brushed the sergeant aside in the most charmless way and hopped in the car.

"Drive on, quickly," he said and we started up Pennsylvania Avenue.

"No! No! Welles, not home. Precinct No. 1. We're going to jail."

It seems that at the first toot of "Hail to the Redskins," the cops had arrested the drum-major, the only man in the entire band who didn't play an instrument.

Precinct No. 1. There's really a pretty precinct, if ever I saw one!

We parked in front of it, and the Democrat I married jumped out, ran up the dimly lighted step, then called over his shoulder to Welles to bring whatever money he had; they might need it to bail out the drum-major.

Regardless of what was going on in other parts of Precinct No. 1, the station-house, like the Union Station, had its quiet side, too; so I began drinking in the quiet beauty of the area. The station-house was an old brick building of questionable Georgian architecture, that had been transformed into a jail. On the far side a driveway, deserted at this time of night, led to the rear of the jail. On the street side, four or five worn out steps led to the front entrance, whose double-doors stood open in a most inviting way, forming a square frame for a sluggish orange-colored light, that gradually crept as far as the doorway, got tired of it all, and stopped there. Hanging over the double-doors, a round frosted globe of the gas-light era gave the place a very bad name. Black letters painted on it read: "Precinct No. 1."

George came pouring out. "Did I have $5.00?" The Welles-Marshall wealth totaled only $20.00 and the bail was set at $25.00.

I looked in my bag, and thank Heaven, I had exactly $5.00, otherwise I might have been abandoned on the spot.

He ran back up the steps, saying he would be back as soon as he had posted bail and had the drum-major released. As always things seemed very quiet after he left.

Gradually my eyes became accustomed to the dim light, things began taking shape all around me. Buildings started peering out of the fog at me and a few angry looking trees pointed my way.

I noticed some printed letters along the curb where we were parked. They seemed familiar enough in the dim light, so I leaned forward, then suddenly they all ran together and spelled "NO PARKING." There I was parked in a NO PARKING area right slab-dab in front of a police station.

The only friendly sound in the close, black night was the distant sound of whistling. Then it stopped.

A slight metallic noise pulled my fear toward the driveway. From behind the jail two thin horizontal shafts of light stabbed the dark. A door slammed. For a few seconds there was nothing but silence, then the engine of a motor started. From somewhere that same someone began whistling again.

A car following its shafts of light, peeked from behind the jail, stealthily creeping forward. As it approached the curb, I could see a policeman at the wheel. I slid to my knees on the floor of the car, then pulled myself up just high enough to peek over the top of the front seat. Holy whiskers! Seated beside the policeman was a sergeant, the one with a heart as hard as a cold lamb chop. My hat was black and couldn't be seen. I was praying the sergeant wouldn't shoot even if he could see the whites of my eyes.

At the curb the car came to a full stop. The sergeant looked straight at me. He just stared, continued whistling, and I stared right back. After awhile I backed up onto the rear seat, and pushed my way over in the corner.

As soon as I was settled, the car turned in the opposite direction and drove away. The whistling hung in the air like the fade-out of a happy ending as the car and the sergeant were swallowed up by the fuzzy black night. He was whistling "Hail to the Redskins."

He was called "the grand old man of the game," and was known simply as "Papa Bear" by his associates in the NFL and the legion of football fans in Chicago whom his teams entertained for almost seven decades. George Halas was there at the meeting in the Hupmobile agency in Canton, Ohio at which the NFL was formed in 1920. He was with the Bears as player, coach, and owner over an association that lasted until his death in 1983. Papa Bear was also one of the more entertaining storytellers involved with the game, often digging out—and embellishing— tales of the embryonic and difficult days of the league. This story of the early Chicago Bears, sculpted and gilded over the 60 years from the time it happened, is a classic Halas tale, taken from his autobiography *Halas by Halas*.

Zuppke Was Right

GEORGE HALAS (WITH GWEN MORGAN AND ARTHUR VEYSEY)

OUR TEAM was ready for my first season. Our home-town sportswriter, Howard Millard, commented modestly: "It looks like the best bit of material ever gathered in Illinois. The fellows will meet some of the greatest football machines in the country. They are expected to hold their own with the best of them."

"Hold our own!" No, I thought when I read the article, we would win! We had the men, the skill, the daily practice and the desire. Blocking was the essential task. I was an eager blocker but I was too light. I tended to hold a bigger opponent whenever the umpire wasn't looking. In those days we had just three game officials—the referee, the umpire and the head linesman. Passing played little part in the game. We had a fat ball, hard to pass.

Fans bet heavily, but I forbade my players to gamble on any of our games. Betting on one's own team to win may not be harmful, because one player cannot make a team win.

One player can make a team lose, however, by fumbling or missing a pass or failing a tackle. Although players have a sixth sense for detecting when a teammate is not doing his best, there is a terrible temptation to bet against the team. No gambler has ever approached me. Perhaps the word got around that gamblers would, at best, be wasting their time.

We breezed past Moline Tractors, 20–0, and Kewanee Walworths 27–0. I quickly drafted to the Staleys an ex-Illinois linesman and kicker, Hubbard Shoemake, who had almost made a touchdown for Kewanee. The games drew a couple of thousand, too few to pay expenses.

We came against the Rock Island Independents, considered by everyone except Staley fans to have replaced Taylorville as the strongest team in the region. Staley fans chartered a train. The game drew more than 5,000, one of the biggest pro-football crowds up to that time.

Conzelman ran 40 yards for a touchdown. We won 10–0. Our starting eleven played the entire game and our betting fans cleaned up.

We beat the Chicago Tigers, 10–0, and massacred Rockford, 29–0. After Conzelman made the third of our four touchdowns, I suggested we go easy. I did not want to destroy all local pride in Rockford. We beat Champaign 20–0 and Hammond 28–0.

We returned to Rock Island. Local feelings were running high against us there because of the money Staley backers had made on the last game. Being cautious—off the field—I made our overnight headquarters at Hotel Davenport in Davenport, Iowa, across the Mississippi River from Rock Island. Several gamblers appeared in the hotel and offered substantial sums that the Independents would win. They boasted that George Trafton, our best defensive man, would be knocked out of the game in the first quarter. Some even mentioned the name of the Rock Island player, a Mr. Chicken, who would put Trafton on the bench, or worse.

Early in the game, the Rock Island hit man was carried from the field, knocked out by Trafton, accidentally, of course. The Rock Island doctor revived the unfortunate Mr. Chicken, put nineteen stitches in his scalp and a plaster cast around a broken wrist.

The Rock Island fans were extremely upset by the disappearance of Mr. Chicken and the continued aggressive tackling by our George. It was a tough game and neither side could score. Again, our starting eleven played every minute.

We foresaw trouble for our George. Fortunately, as the end neared we had the ball. We devised a play that had George running toward the exit. As the gun fired with the score still 0–0, George went out the gate. We threw him a sweatshirt to hide his numerals. He headed for the bridge and Iowa. A car stopped and carried him to safety across the river and the stateline.

Our share of the gate was $3,000, in cash. At the hotel I gave it to Trafton to bring to the train. I knew if we did encounter obstreperous Rock Island fans, I would run for the money but Trafton would run for his life. Trafton returned the money to me on the train.

Our next game was with Minneapolis. On the way there some of the older men gathered in the large Pullman washroom and started a dice game. Here was my first personnel problem. I was against gambling, even as a pastime among friends. And I favored early bed before a game.

What should I do? Had I gone in and said, "None of this, we've got a hard game tomorrow," they would have said, "This is a real jerk."

Or I could have said, "All right, get the books out.

Let's study strategy." That would not have earned me a gold star.

I joined the men. When midnight came, I said: "All right, let's go to bed."

I was down $12 so I was in a good position to propose a halt. Off to bed they went, those oldtimers. I didn't mind losing the $12. I think the lesson I learned that night in handling men was worth much more than $12.

We won the game, on a frozen field, 3–0. We had played nine games and no team had scored against us. Four days after that, on Thanksgiving Day, we were back in Chicago and again beat the Tigers, 6–0. The following Sunday, a very cold day, we lost to the Chicago Cardinals on a fumble, 7–6. The gate was encouraging—5,400. Capacity! Latecomers climbed trees and watched from nearby houses. I proposed a replay in the bigger Wrigley Field. The gate was 8,500. The Cardinals brought in some well-known college players. We won 10–0 although we were constantly put in trouble by the punting of Paddy Driscoll, my old Great Lakes friend. How I wished I could get him on my team!

We declared ourselves champions of the West. The Akron Indians, unbeaten, proclaimed themselves champions of the East. We arranged a match for the national championship.

Twelve thousand well-wrapped people came to Wrigley Field. Of these 10,800 actually bought tickets at 50 cents each. We won the toss but fumbled the kickoff. That's the kind of game it was. Neither side could move on the slippery, muddy ground, and the game became, as a sportswriter said, a duel of punters. Once I intercepted a pass. I was in the clear and should have scored, but slipped. Several times I managed to bring down the Akron star, a Black named Fritz Pollard who had been chosen by Walter Camp for his All-American team several years earlier. It was a hard, clean game—scoreless. We made just one substitution. The enthusiasm was so great I proposed a replay but Akron declined. I am certain 15,000 people would have come. What drew them? Fine players, tight teamwork and a great desire. We had won ten, lost one, and tied two. In all thirteen games our opponents had scored just once. We proclaimed ourselves World Champions.

The 1920 season confirmed my belief that professional football had a great future. It confirmed the correctness of Coach Zuppke's statement that college football players are only reaching their peak when they are graduated.

But professional football was expensive. The thirteen games we played brought in $38,762.49, an astronomical sum compared to the previous year's $1,950.41. Travel, park upkeep, insurance, equipment and other things cost $13,228. Had we been amateurs, the team would have earned $25,000. But we were professionals and Mr. A.E. Staley had agreed that gate earnings would be split among the players. The shareout averaged about $125 per man for each game played. Chamberlin got the most, $1,650; Sternaman and Trafton $1,618 each. I, as coach, player and manager, was voted an extra share. My take was $2,322.77. Our trainer, Andy Lotshaw, got $175 for the season and our praiseworthy sportswriter $100. In addition, each player received his full salary of $50 a week as a Staley employee. I had little trouble persuading them to stay.

The team gave a victory dinner for Mr. Staley. He said he was delighted with our performance; our success had spread the Staley name far and wide; he personally had enjoyed the season very much; he desired to have an even better team in 1921 and was already talking with the Cubs about our using Wrigley Field again the next year.

Mr. Staley was a good businessman. I assume he went over the accounts carefully. One glance must have shown him the way to the future did not lie in Decatur. The three games played there brought in $1,982.49 while our first game in Chicago brought $10 more than the three Decatur games together. Then, as word spread, the fans grew steadily until the fifth game in Chicago drew $6,594.14. The five Chicago games produced $20,162.06. The only good earner outside the big city was Rock Island.

Mr. Staley appointed me athletic director. Through the winter we all made starch. Then it was baseball time again.

The new man I sought most for the football team was Chic Harley, a 165-pound All-American back at Ohio State. He could pass, kick, run. His brother Bill offered to supply the team with Chic, Pete Stinchcomb, also an All-American, and John R. Taylor, an aggressive guard known as Tarzan, in return for a percentage of the profit.

I accepted. I had no idea of the problem I was creating for myself.

A 35–0 opener against a Waukegan American Legion team served as a workout for another meeting with the Rock Island Independents in Decatur. The American Legion was holding a state convention there. We doubled the stands to 3,000. Scalpers were busy.

Meanwhile something wonderful happened to me, although at the time I did not appreciate how it would change my life.

Mr. Staley asked me to come to his office. I had no idea of what he wanted. We had talked only on the field. But there was no question in my mind that the sports program would continue and I would make a good career in the engineering and chemistry departments of the company.

Mr. Staley greeted me warmly.

"George," he said, "I know you are more interested in football than starch. As you know, there is a slight recession in this country. Time lost practicing and playing costs a huge amount of money. I feel we can no longer underwrite the team's losses."

I was flabbergasted. I didn't know what to say.

After a very long half-minute or so, Mr. Staley said:

"George, why don't you take the team to Chicago? I think football will go over big there."

I was dumbfounded.

Mr. Staley continued talking. He said the previous season had indicated very clearly that towns the size of Decatur never could support a professional football team. The parks were too small; there would never be enough fans.

"Professional teams," he said, "need a big city base. Chicago is a good sports city. Look at the way the baseball games in Chicago draw profitable crowds."

I agreed with everything he said but there was still an immediate problem—ready cash.

Before I could ask, Mr. Staley went on:

"I'll give you $5,000 seed money to pay costs until the gate receipts start coming in. I ask only that you continue to call the team the Staleys for one season."

Five thousand dollars! Out of the goodness of his heart! A team of my own! Chicago! I could not believe such good fortune had come upon me. I was elated.

"I will do it," I said. "Thank you, thank you, thank you very much."

We shook hands.

A written agreement, presented to me by Mr. Staley some days later on October 6, filled in details. It said $3,000 was being given in return for two pages of advertising in our program, plus pictures and 100-word biographies of the chief Staley company officials. We would print 50,000 programs and any not sold would be given away. The other $2,000 would be paid at the rate of $25 a week per player up to a total of nineteen players.

I promised to obtain the "utmost publicity" for the Staley company. Of course, Mr. Staley made it clear that I could not incur any obligation on behalf of the company.

There was another provision that I liked very much. Mr. Staley demanded the team conduct itself, on and off the field, in a manner that would reflect credit upon the A.E. Staley Company.

From that day on, I have made it a team rule that my players behave as gentlemen and dress as gentlemen. I wanted to end a popular conception that professional athletes were a bunch of roughnecks.

I signed the letter of agreement. A whole new life opened to me.

* * *

Immediately after my conversation with Mr. Staley, I telephoned Mr. William Veeck, Senior, president of the Chicago Cubs Baseball Club, and asked if I could come to see him. He said yes. I hopped a train.

"I am bringing the Staley team to Chicago and I would like to use Cubs Park as our home, for practice as well as for our home games," I told Mr. Veeck.

He welcomed the idea. After the baseball season, the park was empty. With football it could have a second season of earnings.

"On what terms?" I asked.

"Fifteen percent of the gate and concessions," he said.

I considered that very fair. I rejoiced silently that he did not ask for a fixed rent, which might incur early obligations I could not meet, but I always had heard that in negotiations a person never should accept the first offer. So I said:

"All right, providing I can keep the program rights." Programs sold for 10 cents in those days.

"Done," he said.

I left the park a happy man.

This verbal agreement stood firm without change for fifty years. It is a pleasure to do business with people like the Veecks and the Wrigleys.

I rented ten rooms at Blackwood Apartment Hotel at 4414 Clarendon, for $2 a week a player. The hotel was cheap, clean, decent and within walking distance of the field.

When I returned to Decatur, and told the team we were moving to Chicago, only John Mintun declined to come. He explained that he had been born and reared in Decatur and intended to make a career at Staley's. He became night superintendent.

The essentials attended to, I telephoned Min. "Coming to Chicago! How wonderful," she said.

Our first task was to deal with Rock Island in Decatur. Staley people, Decatur fans and Rock Island supporters who came seeking revenge more than filled the doubled stadium. Never before did 3,600 people see a football game in Decatur. Nor did they ever again. We won 14–0.

I packed the Staley uniforms, orange and blue, the University of Illinois colors. Orange and blue are still the Bears' colors. Jerseys for carriers and receivers had broad vertical stripes of rough material to help players hold on to the ball.

The problems of running the team seemed endless. I decided to take a partner. I wanted Paddy Driscoll, but he wasn't available. So I looked around the team and settled on Dutch Sternaman. He was our most successful scorer. I offered him a 50–50 partnership. He would

have taken less. Had I made it 51–49, I would have saved myself a lot of heartaches and difficulties. He and I agreed to take $100 each a game, same as players—if any money were still in the bank.

I scheduled daily workouts at 9 A.M. and imposed fines on late players. The system made sure the players were in bed each night at a decent hour, although players were rarely distracted by the revelries of the big city. They were too interested in making good as professionals.

We beat Rock Island 14–0. The Jeffersons came from Rochester. George Trafton blocked a punt, the ball rolled behind the goal and Ralph Scott fell upon it, making his first score in all of his years as a tackle. We won 16–13. The 7,500 fans went home happy and I walked to the hotel very, very content.

The Dayton Triangles followed. Neither of us could score. In the final minutes we were on their 4-yard line. It was fourth down. We did a hide-and-seek play within the backfield. Sternaman tossed the ball to me across the goal. Dayton protested the play was illegal but the referee ruled for us. We won 7–0. The gate reported 7,239 paid admissions. I felt almost financially secure.

So it went.

Staley 20, Detroit Tigers 9; Chic out with injured ribs, gate 6,500.

Staley 3, Rock Island 0, played in snow; gate 3,000.

Staley 22, the great Jim Thorpe's Cleveland Tigers 7. Ten thousand fans howling as Stinchcomb ran 80 yards. Thorpe punted from behind his own goal line to our 10-yard line, the ball traveling more than 100 yards. Thorpe said in his eighteen years he never had met a team that hit harder. We had desire.

On Thanksgiving Day, the Buffalo All-Americans squeezed us out 7–6. Ten days later we met them again. Guy Chamberlin took a Buffalo pass on our 10-yard line and ran 90 yards to score. The Buffalo team got even by blocking a punt, recovering it and scoring. A Chamberlin placekick gave us a 10–7 victory.

Between the two Buffalo games, we met a new team formed by the Indian Meat Packing Company in Green Bay, Wisconsin. The manager was Curly Lambeau. We won 20–0 and began what was to be our longest rivalry and, for me, the happiest series of games.

We ran through the Canton Bulldogs 10–0. A week before Christmas with the temperatures near zero and fans fewer than 3,000, we played the Chicago Cardinals. We slid around scorelessly. There was just one substitute. Players were hardy. They loved to play. To take one out during a game was almost worth my life.

Our season ended with nine won, one lost, one tied. The League proclaimed us World Champions.

When the Hall of Fame was established at Canton, four Staley players were named—Chamberlin, Conzelman, Trafton and me.

Wonder of wonders, we paid all our bills and still had $7 in the bank. But the players had to seek jobs to carry them through to next fall, and Dutch and I had to find a way to finance the new season. Meanwhile, Min and I set our wedding for February 18, 1922.

My obligation to the A.E. Staley Company ceased. I considered naming the team the Chicago Cubs out of respect for Mr. William Veeck, Senior, and Mr. William Wrigley, who had been such a great help. But I noted football players are bigger than baseball players; so if baseball players are cubs, then certainly football players must be bears!

Sternaman and I established The Chicago Bears Football Club with capital stock of $15,000. Dutch and I put up $2,500 each and another $2,500 jointly. We locked the remainder of the stock in a safe. The $7,500 cash would see the new club through the winter and pay training costs in the autumn.

I asked the Association at our January meeting to transfer the franchise from the A.E. Staley Company to The Chicago Bears Football Club.

Unexpectedly Bill Harley produced a startling demand for one-third ownership because of our agreement the past year. He obtained a lawyer and went to court. He came to the Association meeting and asked that the Staley franchise be given to him.

The executive committee telephoned Mr. A.E. Staley. He said he had transferred the team to me the previous fall. The company, he said, was quitting all paid athletics.

The members debated all day and into the evening. In the end, they decided to vote on whether the franchise should be given to Sternaman and me or to Bill Harley. Eight voted for us, two for Harley.

The Chicago Bears were born!

Is it so awfully strange for a vicious defensive lineman to eat uncooked steak and raw liver? Probably not a big surprise to people who have more than casually observed those who play pro football. Human flesh, perhaps, might arch a few eyebrows; or maybe a dog, cat, or rodent—then again maybe it wouldn't. Bob St. Clair, a tackle with the San Francisco 49ers during the 1950s and early 60s is one, according to Arnold Hano, who was known for his savagery on the field and at the dinner table. Around the same time he mixed his careers by becoming a politician, elected to the City Council of Daly City, California. Maybe there is an analogy somewhere in all of this. Hano's fascinating profile of the carnivorous St. Clair was cited as one of the 25 *Grantland Rice Prize Sports Stories,* awarded in 1962.

The 49er Who Eats Raw Meat

ARNOLD HANO

ROBERT BRUCE St. Clair—"The Geek" to his San Francisco 49er teammates—stands six feet, nine inches tall, eats raw meat, wrestled a tornado, has toes bigger than his wife's fingers, and is so strong that he has graduated out of normal conversation and into a special frame of reverence.

When Sam Huff—generally conceded the toughest and best defensive linebacker in the business—speaks of professional football, he cites with hushed awe the one time in his career an opposing ballplayer ever really racked him up. The man was Bob St. Clair.

In his freshman year with the New York Giants, Huff was standing idly by a pileup, counting bodies, when St. Clair spotted him. Bob remembers the incident quite well, too. Like most pros, St. Clair gets a huge kick out of belting another man, especially one as good as Huff.

"Standing by a pileup is a typical rookie trick," St. Clair says with scorn. "You learn that in college. You know, never pile on, and all the rest of the Queensberry twaddle. So you stop short, say, 'Oops, sorry,' and there you are, all off balance, a fat target." St. Clair relishes the memory. "I saw Huff standing like that. Man, you can hit them so hard when they're off balance, they'll think their head was on a swivel. You can really pick 'em off that way."

Huff agrees. "Bob blindsided me and like to cut me in half." It was a sobering lesson for Huff. He no longer stands by while football players pile on. He jumps on, like the rest.

Bob St. Clair is the owner of a liquor store, the head of a family, the mayor of Daly City (a suburb of nearly 50,000, just outside San Francisco), but most of all, a professional football player. He is not mean or dirty. St. Clair's joy out of belting another man loose of his intelligence stems simply from the fact he can win recognition no other way. He is an offensive lineman, in an era where the cheers are for the quarterbacks, the halfbacks, the ends, and the whole defensive squad. Nobody loves the five men over the ball, from tackle to tackle.

"The fans will jump up and carry a guy on their shoulders because he's run 40 yards," St. Clair points out. "Meanwhile nobody comes out to the three or four linemen—who knocked themselves out to spring the back loose—to help them out of the mud."

St. Clair says this without rancor. It is a fact of his life, just as it is another fact that unless the defense is held off, the quarterback—who makes twice as much money as the average offensive lineman—will suddenly be playing up in Canada or selling insurance.

It is St. Clair's job to make the offense go, and he is a proud man who insists on doing his job as well as he can. He does it well enough, apparently. Four times voted to the Pro Bowl, and three times an All-Pro offensive tackle, there is a large body of footballers who think the 30-year-old St. Clair the very finest of all offensive tackles, a breed that includes, among others, the Colts' 275-pound Jim Parker and the Giants' Rosey Brown.

There is something about St. Clair that epitomizes professional football. This is the game Los Angeles Rams' line coach Don Paul says "is played for pay by huge, finely trained animals." It is the game of which San Francisco running back J. D. Smith once said: "I love to hit them. I like to see their faces when they get up." And the game St. Clair says "is built around roughness. There is a personal thrill out of knocking a man down, really hitting him. It is the only satisfaction a lineman has. It gets you up, hitting a man, it gives you a jolt of that old adrenalin."

It is a sport where power is still the touchstone. For all your wraithlike halfbacks, and all your dainty passing attacks, power makes them go. A passer is nothing, except dead, if nobody puts the blocks to Gino Marchetti, barreling in. A runner is nothing, except maimed, unless Joe Schmidt is swept out of the play by some mountainous tackle swinging into the secondary. Violence. Strength. Power. Bob St. Clair's trademarks.

A San Francisco writer suggested in 1960 that Bob St. Clair was "probably stronger" than any player in the NFL.

Nobody called him on it. And St. Clair, today, swears he's stronger now than he was then.

He is—shy three inches of seven feet—the tallest man in the NFL, and at a playing weight that varies from 255 to 260, one of the big boys.

Just to get his size down on record where mortals can comprehend it, all the doorways in St. Clair's house in Daly City have been made seven feet high. His bed, custom-built, is seven feet long and six and a half feet wide. On the road, St. Clair simply throws the hotel mattress on the floor, adds a couple of pillows to its length, and sleeps that way, saving a grateful hotel man-agement sudden obsolescence on box springs. He wears a size 15 shoe, and when he made his only appearance in a boxing ring in a Golden Gloves contest in Oklahoma, he had to go in barefoot, because there were no shoes to fit him. He is so tall that in 1956 he blocked ten field-goal attempts, surely a record in a category nobody bothers keeping statistics on. All Bob had to do was take two steps past the defense and stand his full height, and catch footballs in his mouth.

A few years back Bob blocked a Ram punt with his face, and in the process shattered a few teeth. He had the bloody shards extracted, and the next week in a game with the Giants, St. Clair demonstrated that he is more than just strong and big. He can run. The combination is terrifying. In an exhibition at Seattle before 49,000, Giant defensive back Em Tunnell picked off a Y. A. Tittle pass on his own 20 and headed upfield. The speedy Tunnell outran all defenders by midfield, and was on the 49er 30 when he decided to look behind him.

There was St. Clair, bearing down.

"Tunnell looked kind of funny," St. Clair recalls. "I guess he couldn't figure why I was gaining on him."

Funny, or a bit shaken. St. Clair caught Tunnell and rode him down on the 20. Catching Tunnell from behind remains the biggest personal thrill of St. Clair's pro career. It surely remains a nightmare in Tunnell's mind, a moving skyscraper getting ready to fall on him.

The reason St. Clair was gaining is that he is very fast—for a man his size, blinding fast. St. Clair ran the relays in high school, and with legs the length of redwoods, he eats up the ground. At the University of San Francisco, St. Clair was for a spell an offensive end, and one of the best on the West Coast. He is a graceful man, with a light, almost feathery touch. At high school, St. Clair once entered a ten-event agility test—situps, pushups, dashes and the rest—and won the contest, even though such courses are usually meat for wiry scatback types, not Cro-Magnon tackles.

But no matter how you try, you can't get around his strength. It is the key to St. Clair. On August 5, 1961, at the beginning of the practice session, coach Red Hickey asked St. Clair to show the rookie hopefuls at the 49er camp at Redwood City how to hit a tackling dummy. St. Clair obliged. (I know you've heard this before, but this time it's true.) He charged, snarling, and slammed into the mammoth dangling dummy they call Big Bertha. There was a sound like a thousand blownup paper sacks bursting. Down came Bertha, sawdust and all. It wasn't a case of breaking an old chain or rotting cable, mind you; the dummy itself split apart and broke in two. It was St. Clair hitting, and something having to give. That's the way it's been for nine pro years now.

It began that way. On a muggy July day in 1953 that marked the 49ers' first intra-squad scrimmage, St. Clair was just one of 13 rookies hoping to make the team. He took his place on the offensive line opposite Leo Nomellini. The ball was snapped, the men charged, and strong men blanched.

"It was," a Bay area poet later said, "like a couple of bull elephants trying to get out of a phone booth." More exactly, it was a quarter-ton of professional football tackles pasting each other, one a rangy broth of a lad, the other a whole bowl of minestrone.

What made the first contact so memorable is that St. Clair had never played a minute of offensive tackle since high school. This was his maiden outing with the pros. And Leo Nomellini was not only an All-Pro tackle, at 265 pounds, he was on his way to the greatest show of durability in any sport, 205 consecutive football games, through the opening of the '61 season.

They call Nomellini, naturally enough, Leo the Lion. It was against this beast that they threw young Bob St. Clair, a freshly handsome boy who was merely big and strong and growing, at 6-7 and 235 pounds, and greener than St. Patrick's Day.

With the odds stacked so high they resembled Pisa, Bob St. Clair held his own against the Lion on the 49er practice field. The divots that July day in 1953 were big enough to serve as family-sized bomb shelters. St. Clair made the team.

If there is a simple explanation for Bob St. Clair's strength, it is that he eats his meat raw. Literally. A conversation at a San Francisco restaurant dining table goes something like this. A waitress flounces up.

"What'll it be?"

"Steak."

"How?"

"Raw."

Pause. "You mean blood rare?"

"Raw."

Longer pause. "Sir, we—we're not allowed to. It's—against the law or something."

"Raw."

"Not—on the fire?"

"Take it out of the icebox and put in on a plate."

Later, while St. Clair is eating his raw filet, the cook will peep from behind his swinging door, and the management will try to keep nearby patrons from looking at St. Clair. For fear they'll get sick.

But raw it is, and raw it's been ever since Bob's grandmother gave the boy a dish of salted blood gravy from a roast. Whenever he can, St. Clair eats his meat completely uncooked: steak, unroast beef, hamburger. When St. Clair joined the 49ers, veteran guard Bruno Banducci tagged on the name "The Geek," and Bob's been "The Geek" ever since.

St. Clair also eats raw liver, the idea of which has been known to frighten Russians. He is not, by the way,

a big eater, for all his heft. It is the high-protein, energy-producing content that interests St. Clair, plus his insistence that raw meat is tastier than cooked. His diet also includes raw eggs, lots of salad, and little or no potatoes. He is addicted to wheat germ oil (which he does *not* consider tasty), gobbling it by the tablespoon with orange juice every morning because, he says, it is good for the heart. And he is especially fond of honey: "The only food that goes straight to the bloodstream without being digested through the stomach. It's a great energy food, a shot of pure glucose to the veins."

Honey and wheat-germ oil are not the only juices in St. Clair's life. He drinks good-sized amounts of beer, and after a ball game will stay up quite late with the boys and their wives at a San Francisco eatery, quaffing brew and later switching to vodka screwdrivers (which, with their orange juice, provide a pleasant path to vitamin sufficiency). St. Clair also chews tobacco during practice sessions, and smokes cigars.

At his Daly City home, where he lives with his wife Ann (who weighs in at a nifty 112 pounds) and their four kids, the obvious has transpired. Ann St. Clair one supper said to the children: "Come on, let's eat. Don't you want to be big like Daddy?" Now all four kids swear by raw meat. They don't, however, drink as yet, or chew, or smoke. Gary, the St. Clairs' older boy at nine, is shrewdly proud of his father. "I'm real glad Dad is a football player," he says. And adds: "Because he makes lots of money!" To which the older St. Clair, who earns around $13,000 in salary, says softly: "But not as much as a quarterback, son. Polish up that throwing arm."

St. Clair does not come from a family of outsized specimens. His mother is 5-3, and his father 5-10. Nor was St. Clair always bigger than average when he was a kid.

In his youth on the streets of the Mission district in San Francisco—St. Clair is the only native San Franciscan on the 49er roster the boy ran with a gang of chain-wielding, knife-flashing, trouble-making no-goods who spent their more sociable moments in mass war with other gangs. The rest of their activity was worse. Some of the boys ended up in jail. Straight-faced, St. Clair says his mates were picked up for "petty things. You know, like armed robbery. Or a little trouble with the interstate commerce commission—taking a stolen car across the state lines."

But all this time, Bob wasn't a big boy. One day while presumably a sophomore at high school, he stopped by and saw some boys belting each other with helmets and shoulder pads, and tossing an oval-shaped spheroid downfield. The 15-year-old St. Clair watched, fascinated, especially when the boys ran into each other, and bodies disintegrated under churning legs and swinging arms. The hope someday of being a fully-developed delinquent gave way before this new form of mayhem. He tried out for the football team. Coach Joe Verducci turned the boy away kindly. ''You're too small,'' Verducci murmured. And St. Clair was, at 5-9 and 150 pounds. Sadly, he rejoined his rock-throwing pals. But he also redoubled his health-food kick, poured the blood juices and honey into his veins, ate his steaks right out of the freezer, and by the time the 1947 football season rolled around, the boy was on his way: he reported to a bug-eyed Verducci at 6-4 and 210 pounds!

At Polytech High, where Bob became a big man, literally and figuratively, he met a pretty blonde, Ann Wickstrom, and the two went on a first date to Seals Stadium, to see a Pacific Coast League baseball game. Holding his girl's hand, St. Clair suddenly remarked that he thought his toes were longer than her fingers. Ann laughed, and told him not to be silly, and St. Clair promptly took off his shoes and socks and proved it on the spot. The two were married before high-school graduation.

St. Clair won a scholarship to the University of San Francisco where in his junior year in 1951 he played under Joe Kuharich. His teammates included Gino Marchetti and Ollie Matson and their USF squad was, as they say, undefeated, untied and uninvited. The team was so good that the university hastily dropped football after that 1951 season in a furor over athletic emphasis. So St. Clair accepted a scholarship to Tulsa for his 1952 season, and once again played with a big-time team, good enough to go into (and lose) the Gator Bowl.

It was at Tulsa that St. Clair met and defeated a Golden Glove boxer and a tornado.

The fight was by far the easier. The heavyweight division of a Golden Gloves tournament in northeastern Oklahoma was short of entrants, and the captain of Tulsa's football team suggested that St. Clair make an appearance. Bob agreed. They threw him into the ring with an amateur who'd won several Gloves matches. St. Clair had never even boxed oranges.

Despite his inexperience the sight of all those bare muscles rippling from a thin-aired altitude down to his huge bare feet set the crowd against St. Clair, and they began cheerfully to root for his smaller foe to take him apart.

With the bell, Bob moved out and tried a tentative left jab, because he'd read about such things. He stepped back, expecting his more knowing foe to unloose a barrage of punches.

''Then I saw he'd stepped back, too, and it dawned on me. Maybe the fellow was scared of me because of my size.''

So Bob waded in, throwing punches, and in a red haze of sudden fury, the boy in front of him went down, and the next thing St. Clair knew the referee was trying to

pull him off his unconscious foe. Bob shoved the referee to the canvas, and the crowd was in bedlam. The time was 20 seconds.

''I hated it,'' St. Clair has said since. ''I hated what it did to me. I hated what the fans called me. And I knew that no matter how experienced the other man might be, just because of my size, the crowd would always root against me. I never fought again.''

He has never faced a tornado more than that one time either. On a misty spring day in 1953, Bob and a friend drove off to a spot on the Grand River, a tributary of the Arkansas, where white bass are thick and hungry.

''We were having great luck, catching 'em like flies, when I looked downriver and saw a big black cloud on the ground, headed toward me. It looked like a black wall. My friend started to scream—we were a hundred yards apart—and began to wave at me. It was drizzling a little, and the wind had started to whip. Finally I realized he was saying: 'Tornado!' ''

St. Clair raced up the river bank, and the two boys piled in the car for protection just as the tornado struck full force.

''The car was bouncing up and down. All four wheels were off the ground at times. Finally the wind picked up the car and hurled it against some cement bulkheads. The car stood like that, leaning against the bulkheads, the wind banging it. The bulkheads probably saved our lives. Finally the wind passed on.'' St. Clair had lived through a tornado, and when you tell the anecdote to his 49er mates, they scoff. It had to be a pretty damn-fool tornado to tangle with St. Clair, even up.

Not that St. Clair can't be hurt. He takes his beating, and it is an awesome beating at times. After the opening game of the 1961 season (49ers 35, Redskins 3), St. Clair changed slowly into a blue shirt with a businessman's narrow blue tie and dark suit, and then casually asked trainer Henry Schmidt for a couple of codeine tablets. On a blocking play in the third quarter, St. Clair had badly bruised his left side, just below his rib cage and above the hip. ''It was a stupid play,'' St. Clair says. ''I tried to get fancy. I threw the block with the side of my body instead of running right up and over the guy, straight on.'' St. Clair played the whole game on offense, and nobody knew he'd been hurt until he asked for the pain killers.

Schmidt, the trainer, has ministered to football bodies for over 30 years, and he is still awed by St. Clair.

''It is remarkable the way Bob shakes off injuries. The only way you can get him out of the lineup is to hogtie him. During practice he had a bad kneecap, so swollen he couldn't close the knee. He kept playing. I fixed him a pad; he wouldn't wear the pad.''

Schmidt adds one note that is typical of St. Clair. ''Funny thing, whenever I'm working on Bob on the table, and I hit a tender spot, instead of crying out or whimpering the way everybody else does, he laughs. That's the only way I know it hurts.''

It isn't quite true you can't get St. Clair out of the lineup. In a game with the Rams in 1957, the 49ers missed a field-goal try, and the Rams ran out the ball. St. Clair made the tackle, and, in the ensuing pileup, felt a numbing twinge in his right shoulder. Despite the pain which grew so great he no longer could put his right hand to the ground on his charge, St. Clair played eight more minutes, or until a Ram plowed into his right shoulder. Bob nearly fainted, and he came out of the game. He had suffered a severe shoulder separation, and was operated on a few days later. Today he bears a three-inch scar across the top of his shoulder where it was opened up to insert a silver screw, and a second smaller scar where the screw was removed.

St. Clair missed seven weeks, and did not return until the 49ers were at Bear Mountain, New York, preparing to play the Giants. The 49ers had lost three in a row and were badly dispirited when the door to the lobby of the Bear Mountain Inn suddenly flung open, and St. Clair strode into the room. Never one to miss a dramatic moment, St. Clair announced in round, rich dark tones: "I am Moses, come to lead the 49ers out of the wilderness." The following Sunday, with snow on the ground, San Francisco upset the Giants, 27–17. St. Claire was back, his obliterating blocking once again providing running room and time to pass, and the 49ers closed out the season with wins over the Colts and the Packers, for an 8–4 record.

At the job upon which an offensive lineman's job pivots—blocking for the passer—he is the original immovable force. Monty Stickles says: "Bob's pass-blocking is invincible." It is only when St. Clair faces Gino Marchetti, his old buddy from USF, that the odds come down to dead-even, and in a game where head-on duels are becoming more than just spectacular side-shows, the St. Clair-Marchetti war is every bit as earth shaking as the Huff-Jim Brown love match.

St. Clair cannot stand up and let Marchetti close in on him. The defensive man, of course, is allowed to use his hands. "If Marchetti gets his hands on me in that first burst, he can control me. So I have to give ground slowly, chop at him, hold him off as long as I can." Sometimes it works; sometimes Marchetti pours through and smears the passer. Each time the duel is bone-crushing, a little frightening, and quite a bit majestic. St. Clair actually looks forward to games with the Colts, because, as he says with no trace of conceit: "Gino brings out the best in me, just as I bring out the best in him."

Someplace along the line these duels and the rest of battering contact will take some toll on St. Clair's seemingly limitless reservoir of strength. St. Clair was 31 years old February 18. On the 49er roster, only the ageless Nomellini, at 37, is older. But the big tackle has no set retirement date. He intends to play as long as he can.

"Hell," he said recently, "I couldn't quit now if I wanted to. I'm not playing football just to make money. My liquor store is real good. It's a matter of pride, of desire. I like the game. It has not become more painful. If anything, it is less painful. I am stronger now than I have ever been. I try to learn something every game. I play as well as I can because I don't want to look like a yokel out there, in front of 60,000 people."

So it seems that Bob St. Clair will step out as soon as he knows he is no longer enjoying the game. When he does quit, there is little doubt that St. Clair will always have it made. His liquor store, at 24th and Sanchez in the Twin Peaks section of 'Frisco, opened in January of 1961, and was swiftly a money-maker. Then there is St. Clair's political ambitions. Bob was elected in 1958 to the City Council of Daly City, where the St. Clairs have lived since 1954. The Council in turn recently selected St. Clair as Mayor. St. Clair intends to run for re-election to the Council in April of 1962, and he thinks, again without conceit, that he will be returned to office.

"I think the people here like what I've done so far," he says. "I helped push through a big new library. Other things, too."

Perhaps the flossiest addition to the town during St. Clair's term occurred when the city decided to rip out some old trolley tracks. It was St. Clair who suggested the planting of palm trees along a two-mile stretch of the new street divider. It dresses up an older section of town, and St. Clair often drives his Pontiac station wagon, or his Ford convertible along this stretch of palm, obviously proud of the new look.

St. Clair experienced just one touchy moment in his Council work. After John Kennedy's election in 1960, St. Clair—also a Democrat—decided to put up a large picture of the new president in the Council chambers at City Hall. Instantly there rose up a loud outcry; the Council is a nonpartisan body, and Californians take their non-partisan politics even more seriously than partisan elections.

So St. Clair went ahead and tacked up the photograph anyway, turned to his fellow Councilmen and townspeople, and said: "He's the president of *all* the people, isn't he?" and everybody quickly shut up.

The fact is, St. Clair has one tremendous advantage over other Mayors. Nobody—but nobody—ever dreams of fighting *his* City Hall.

The Big Extravaganza, of course, could only be the *Super Bowl,* the classic and hallowed pageant that ends each pro football season with much pomp and flourish. But never have football fans been treated to a more outrageous, more entertaining extravaganza than the mythical one between the Giants and the Jets that Dan Jenkins served to them in his best-selling novel *Semi-Tough.* Told by the now immortal Billy Clyde Puckett, "the humminest sumbitch that ever carried a football," as Jenkins allowed him to describe himself, it is a Super Bowl fans of all persuasions can attend and be royally rewarded without paying $75 for a ticket or having to put up with a couple of hours of commercials for various automobiles, beers, after-shave lotions, copying machines, computers, armed forces enlistment, and whatever else someone might want to shovel out for more than a half-million dollars for a minute of television time.

The Big Extravaganza

DAN JENKINS

I GUESS IT's time for me to settle down and talk about the big extravaganza, even though it's semi-painful in parts.

I still can't believe how nervous we were and how overeager we were at the start. Whatever the record was for tight ass holes, the Giants broke it.

Shake tried to make some jokes just before we came out of the dressing room for the opening kickoff but nobody laughed too hard.

"Remember this, gang," he said. "No matter what happens out there today, at least six hundred million Chinese don't give a shit."

The dog-ass Jets won the coin flip and got to kickoff, which is what we wanted to do. In a big game you'd rather kick than receive. That's to get in some licks on defense and let the other side know you've come to stack asses.

Everybody who was there or watching on television knows how fired up the Giants were just before the kickoff. That wasn't any act, the way we were jumping up and down and beating on each other.

The guys on our sideline said later that everybody on our bench was hollering, "Come get your dinners" at the dog-ass Jets and pointing down at their crotches. And those standing next to T. J. Lambert said that he was bent over and farting at the dog-ass Jets in tones they'd never come close to hearing before.

They said he timed his best one so that it exploded just as the Jets' kickoff man put his foot into the ball. They said T. J. cut one that was so loud and prolonged that a couple of dog-ass Jets going down on the kick turned their heads toward our bench in astonishment.

The last thing I said to our kick return unit as we huddled out there on the field was, "All right now. This is what we've been waitin' for. Let's get a cunt on a cunt."

Randy Juan Llanez and me are always the two deep backs on kick returns. I want to mention that in case you might have read some foolishness in *Sports Illustrated* about Shoat Cooper making a grievous mistake by using me on the opening kickoff.

I've only been returning kickoffs my whole life. Hell, I broke three all the way during the regular season. Against the Eagles and the Cowboys and the Cardinals.

It was unfortunate that the kick was a sorry one and scooted along on the ground, bouncing sort of goofy. Because Randy Juan Llanez never actually got hold of it before he was dough-popped by two or three green shirts on our ten-yard line.

I remember thinking instinctively, "Uh-oh, Jesus shit a nail." And I knew damn well I would get hit as soon as I retrieved the ball on our goal line.

Well, as you might know if you saw it, that lick Dreamer Tatum put on me from my blind side didn't feel so great. It's true, as *Sports Illustrated* wrote, that "the jolting blow momentarily separated Pucket from all that made intellectual sense—as well as the football."

Dreamer rang my hat when he busted me, all right, and then went on to recover the ball for a dog-ass touchdown on the very first play of the game. But I can't help laughing now at what he said to me after he came over and helped me up and patted me on the ass.

Old Dreamer said, "Stick *that* in your fucking book."

Throughout the whole first quarter, even the first half, I guess it would be fair to say that we were in some kind of a daze.

For a long time I didn't think Hose Manning would be able to draw back and hit the ground with the football if you held the turf up in front of his face-guard.

Shake got as open as Linda the Stew's wool three or four times but Hose only threw the ball about twenty feet over his head, as if Hose was afraid an interception would give him syphilis.

After Hose had missed on his first eight passes, Shake trotted back to the huddle and said, "It's sure nice out there today, Hose. Can I order you anything from room service?"

Old Hose ignored him. He just spit and said, "Let's go, bunch. Let's strike a match now. Here we go."

Hose wasn't getting very good protection, I've got to say.

Our line was trying to zone-block or scramble-block or some idiot thing that wasn't working. On situations

where I had to stay back and protect, it looked like a junior high school recess coming at me.

"Sumbitch," said Hose once, trying to get up after the whistle. "I thought you could only have eleven fuckers on a side."

What got us was, they were playing us normal, just like Shake and me felt they would. Dreamer played the wide part of the field, like any rover, even when Shake would split out toward the near sideline.

Obviously they were guessing that a good pass rush on Hose was the best defense against Shake Tiller.

Their defense jumped around a lot, trying to confuse us, when Hose would be up at the line calling signals. Dreamer would move up on the line of scrimmage, like he might be intending to come on a blitz, but he would back off.

It caused a couple of bad snaps and one or two delay penalties when Hose would try to call an audible. Once Hose called an audible for Booger Sanders to follow me through right guard, but Booger couldn't hear the play.

It was actually kind of funny.

Hose started his cadence at the line and then changed his play.

When he was calling out the new play, Booger hollered, "Check," meaning he couldn't hear the play.

Hose called out the signals again, and Booger shouted, "Check," again.

So old Hose raised up from behind the center and turned around to Booger Sanders and pointed at Puddin Patterson's butt and said, *"Right* fuckin' through here, you country cocksucker."

The dog-ass Jets broke up laughing, and so did the rest of us, and we got a five-yard penalty for delay of the game.

For a while, it was a bit unsettling to have Dreamer Tatum talking to us on the line of scrimmage.

Dreamer would say things like, "Hey, Billy Puckett, run at me, baby."

Or he would say to Hose Manning, "Watch it now, Mr. Quarterback. Dream Street comin' this time. Dream Street comin'."

You have to be a stud athlete that everybody expects miracles from to know what it's like to get as humiliated as we were in the early part of the game.

Especially in something like a Super Bowl before ninety-two thousand people and about a hundred million on television.

I'll grant you that we looked rotten, all of us, but I want to point out that it just isn't true what all of the newspapers and *Sports Illustrated* said about Shake Tiller—that he might have been suffering a slight case of overconfidence.

Some people have reasoned that this is why Shake dropped a couple of balls that Hose finally threw in his vicinity. And the reason why he fumbled the one ball he did catch in the first quarter. Which resulted in another touchdown for the dog-ass Jets.

The truth is, Shake dropped one ball because he was so wide open he was overeager to put some white stripes behind him. He knew there wasn't anything but six points in front of him if he could spin around and get going.

He just started too soon.

Shake unfastened his chin strap and walked slowly back to the huddle after the play. He winked at me and then looked at Hose and said, "Shit, it's no fun if you're gonna hit me in the hands."

Hose said, "Let's go, bunch. Let's pop the cork now and start pourin'."

I can testify also that Shake dropped the other ball because Hose threw it about five feet over his head and my buddy had to leap up, twist around, stretch out and grunt, and even then he only got one hand on it just as two dog-ass Jets high-lowed him.

But I guess the great sports writers think that if you're Shake Tiller you're supposed to be able to catch every flea that ever ran up a dog's ass.

When Shake fumbled that ball he caught in the first quarter, for what would have been our initial first down of the game, it was frankly because Dreamer Tatum knocked his eyelids off.

Shake grabbed it over his shoulder—it was just a little old quick-out—but just as he stopped to throw an inside fake, Dreamer, who was steaming up on him, caught him a lick that Barbara Jane said she could even hear.

The ball squirted straight up in the air, on our forty-five, and here came one of their dog-ass linebackers, Hoover Buford from Baylor of all places, to pick off the ball in mid-air and practically trot to the end zone.

The Baptist sumbitch could have stopped to take a leak and nobody could have caught him. I'd hit into the line and was too far away, and Hose, of course, is not exactly what you'd call your Metroliner.

Al (Abort) Goodwin would have had a chance, provided he knows how to tackle, but Al had sprinted his usual fifty yards down the sideline.

Barbara Jane says that up in the stands after we fell behind by fourteen—even though it was obviously the work of fate and not the dog-ass Jets—there were some fairly despondent souls among the Giant fans.

She said Big Ed couldn't decide who to cuss the most, Dreamer Tatum or Shoat Cooper.

She said Big Ed kept hollering: "Big toe! Big toe! Somebody kick that nigger in the big toe or he's gonna beat us by himself."

Barbara Jane said Burt Danby just kept shaking his head and saying: "We just want it too much, I guess.

You shouldn't want something as badly as this. You *really* shouldn't."

Barbara Jane said Elroy Blunt apparently hadn't been to bed at all—not for any sleep, at least—and that he was so tired and hung over and wool-whipped from his party that he couldn't even get excited about the game.

She said Elroy's eyes were the color of beets and he looked like he'd shrunk about two sizes.

She said that after the dog-ass Jets had us down by twenty-one in the middle of the second quarter—which was after Boyce Cayce had hit Jessie Luker on that seventy-yard bomb because Jimmy Keith Joy slipped down—that Elroy just looked up in the sky.

She said he just looked up at God and said:

"It's me again, ain't it? I got me ten large on it but you ain't gonna let me steal *nuthin'*, are you?"

She said Elroy turned to her with his floppy-brimmed suede hat halfway covering up his face and said quietly, "How come it's always my turn now instead of niggers?"

Well, of course, if anybody thinks it was semi-dreary up in the stands, they should have been down on the field.

Until T. J. Lambert smothered Boyce Cayce that time and got us a fumble on their thirty-five, we were on the brink of give-up because nothing would go right for us.

That fumble T. J. captured, which I think he got because he farted so viciously that no dog-ass Jet wanted to go near the ball, enabled us to get a field goal and at least get something on the scoreboard.

I didn't want us to take the three when we only had fourth-and-one on their two-yard line, especially when we were down by twenty-one, but Shoat Cooper wanted any points he could get.

That was Shoat's play and not Hose Manning's, so all of those Giant fans who threw all of those cushions and garbage at Hose when he came off the field ought to feel pretty apologetic about it.

I know it was Shoat's decision because Shake and me were in on the conversation when we called time out and went to the sideline to talk it over.

I wanted to try to stick in there myself, but Shoat said, "Stud hoss, if we was to line up tight, you'd get hit by ever-body in Queens."

Hose wanted to throw, but Shoat said we didn't have any passing room.

"If they stop us here without no points at all," said Shoat, "it'll give them piss ants too much of an emotional boost."

This was when Shake Tiller said, "Hell, they're tellin' jokes out there now."

I still think I could have stuck it in there for six, but

we did what Shoat ordered. Shake Tiller held the ball and Hose Manning kicked it through there and we got our three.

I was all set to block Dreamer when he rushed, but he didn't rush. He faked like he would, and then raised up and laughed. And before he jogged off the field, you may not have noticed how he patted Shake on top of the hat and shook Hose's hand to congratulate him. Would that piss you off at all?

Anyhow, that was the score, twenty-one to three, when we went in for the strangest halftime I've ever encountered.

I'm afraid that for about the first ten minutes we were in the dressing room we acted like a crowd of convicts who didn't like their fat meat. Just about everybody kicked something and slung his helmet against the wall or on the floor. It was T. J. Lambert of course who made the most noise.

"Tootie fruities!" he hollered. "We're all a bunch of goddamned tootie fruities."

T. J. snarled and puffed and built up to a roar and called out, *"We're through takin' shit!"*

There was general movement through the room, with guys going to get a Coke out of a drink box, or going to take a dump or a leak.

"Hose Manning!" T. J. yelled. "You know what your fuckin' old offense looks like out there? It looks like a barrel of hog shit!"

Hose was over opening his locker and getting out a clipboard with pages of plays in it. He sat down quietly on the bench and started looking through the plays, and smoking a cigar.

T. J. carried on.

"By God, my defense ain't give 'em nothin' but one diddywaddle pass and they don't get that if my nigger don't slip down back there," he said. "Jimmy Keith Joy, you Aferkin sumbitch, where are you?"

From across the room you could hear Jimmy Keith's voice.

"Yo, Daddy," Jimmy Keith hollered.

"Jimmy Keith, get your ass up here in front of everybody and take a fuckin' oath that there ain't no other tootie fruitie gonna get behind you the rest of the day," T. J. said.

Jimmy Keith Joy hobbled over into the center of the dressing room.

"I got 'em, Daddy, I got 'em," he said. "Everything's groovin'."

"We ain't takin' no more *shit!*" T. J. Lambert hollered, a lot louder than he can fart.

"Giants has got one more half to be *men,*" T. J. said. "Them fuckers ain't won nothin' *yet.*"

A group of us around Hose Manning's locker got a mite testy. I guess Shake Tiller started it.

"How much did you bet on the Jets?" Shake needled Hose.

Hose only looked up at him.

"Why don't you try throwin' balls in the same stadium the rest of us are in?" Shake asked.

Hose drew on his cigar and squinted and said, "And when did you forget how to run your routes, playboy?"

Shake said, "I can't run 'em in the stadium tunnels. They call that out of bounds, where the ball's been going."

Puddin Patterson interrupted.

"Let's stay together, babies," he said. "We can move it on them cats. I can feel it. We gonna sail like a big boat this half."

Shake said, "Bite my ass, Puddin. You haven't been off your belly all day. Sixty-four's all over you like the crabs."

Puddin said, "We're gonna move it this half. We gonna fly like a big balloon."

"Yeah, and I'm gonna be the first nigger on the moon," Shake said, spitting on the floor.

I said for everybody to cut the crap and let's talk about what might work.

"A runnin' back wouldn't hurt us any," Hose said, calmly. "You haven't showed me a lot of Jim Brown out there."

"Line gonna move them cats this half," said Puddin. "We gonna spin like a big record."

"Nothing wrong with us that a Namath or a Jurgensen couldn't fix," said Shake.

We had to get together, I said. "We got two quarters to play football and that's plenty. We only need three sixes if the defense can shut 'em down," I said.

Hose said, "I think the counter will give us something if Puddin and Euger can start gettin' a piece of somebody."

"Fuck Euger," said Shake. "Seventy-one's spittin' his ass out like watermelon seeds."

"We gonna stuff 'em like groceries," said Puddin.

It was from the other side of the room that we all heard T. J. cut one that sounded like a drum roll and then heard him call out: "Where the hell are the goddamn coaches? Shit, I wouldn't blame 'em for not wantin' to hang around this bunch of tootie fruities."

It must have occurred to all of us at the same time.

The coaches weren't there. Shoat Cooper wasn't there. The star-spangled Polack wasn't there. None of the coaches were in the dressing room at the halftime of the Super Bowl.

The only indication that a coach of some kind had even *been* there was on a big blackboard at the far end of the room.

Written in big chalk numbers was a message of encouragement, I think you could call it.

The blackboard said: 24 to 21.

None of us saw it when we first got to the dressing room because we were too busy throwing our hats and cussing each other. And who would have thought that the Giants' coaches would have sent us a simple message instead of their own selves?

We never did get around to discussing among ourselves what we ought to try to do. Speaking for myself, I think I just sort of thought I'd try to run harder. And I hoped Hose would discover something important on his clipboard.

Football studs, by the way, get a considerable laugh out of the things they read in the newspapers and magazines after a game.

We're always reading about our strategy and adjustments, and invariably it's wrong.

For instance, New York *Daily News* said that during the first half of the Super Bowl the big problem of the Giants was trying to ''shut off the concealed rush'' of the Jets.

Well, I'll read you what the *Daily News* says. I clipped it out and saved it for the book.

The halftime was devoted to a serious discussion of the options the Giants had. Shoat Cooper and his war counsel of Hose Manning, Billy Clyde Puckett and Shake Tiller calmly agreed to go with less deception in the last two periods.

In the first half, Manning had not been able to throw effectively into the seams of the Jets' sliding zone. Thus, the Jets had taken away Manning's favorite weapons—the double zig-out, the hitch-and-fly, and the post-and-go, all to Shake Tiller.

The different look of the Jet's defensive line, which shuffled in and out of a five-two, a four-three, four-four and a gap six, created disorder among the Giants' blockers.

''Our stutter rush, or what we call Foxtrot Green, gave 'em plenty of trouble,'' said Dreamer Tatum.

The rush not only stifled the Giants' passing game, it kept guessing exactly right on where Billy Clyde Puckett wanted to run. He had no room. He was virtually shut down, and you could see the frustration written on his square jaw as he came to the sideline, time after time.

Wisely, however, Shoat Cooper went to Plan B. After halftime consultation with his war counsel—Manning, Puckett and Tiller—the Giants switched to Man blocking from their linemen and decided to employ basic muscle.

Although their lucky white jerseys with the blue and red trim were now soiled and tattered, and their proud blue helmets were dented and smudged by the relentless thudding of the Jets' defense, the Giant attack came alive in the second half and prevented no less than an outrageous embarrassment.

Now is that some cheap crap or isn't it?

Do you know when we finally saw Shoat Cooper?

The halftime festivities were practically over and we were getting ready to take the field when Shoat stuck his head in our door.

The door opened incidentally just as we all were yelling and rushing toward it. The door hit Al (Abort) Goodwin in the head and knocked him cold. That's the real story of why he never played the last two quarters.

''Awright, quiet down,'' Shoat said. ''Al will be O.K. You can't hurt a sprinter unless you tweak him on the tendon. If Al ain't O.K., we'll go with Randy Juan, and that's that. Now I only got one thing to say to you pine knots. You got thirty more minutes of football to play and you can do one of two things. You can play football the way you're capable of playin' football, or you can go back out there and keep on lookin' like a bunch of turds what dropped out of a tall cow's ass.''

And Shoat Cooper spit and left.

There's no point in me trying to argue that we weren't lucking right after the second half started. They kicked off out of our end zone and we got the ball on our twenty, and it was important for us to show the Jets that we had come back with some spunk.

What we needed to do was get a good drive going, and more than anything we needed to get us six.

In the huddle on first down at our twenty, Hose said:

''O.K., ladies, let's tend to our knittin'. Lots of time now. Plenty of time. Let's block now, bunch. Everybody blocks. Ain't that right? O.K., bunch. Here we go. Gotta be smooth now, bunch.''

Shake Tiller finally said, ''Why don't you call a fuckin' play so we can get on with it?''

Hose called an inside belly and I got four yards. It was the longest run I'd made. And Puddin got a block.

''They all mine now, babies,'' said Puddin, back in the huddle. ''We gonna stick like a big knife.''

As everybody knows, the drive was not exactly semi-perfection.

An interference call on Shake Tiller didn't hurt us any, and neither did another one on Thacker Hubbard. Something else that didn't hurt was the quick whistle which saved us the ball at midfield after Booger Sanders fumbled.

''We got a little luck goin','' said Hose. ''A little luck, bunch. A little luck's out here with us now. O.K., bunch. It's all there to be had. It's all there waitin' for us. Just a stroll in the country, bunch. That's all it is. Just pickin' up flowers.''

Shake said, "Hose, you want to can the shit and call the game? We know why we're here."

That was a hell of a catch Shake made on a wobbly pass that Hose threw which got us down to their thirty-one. Just a typical one-hander from the repertoire of old Eighty-eight.

I guess this was the first time that we felt like we had moved the ball, and we were sure in sniffing distance.

I made a little yardage on a sweep, thanks to Euger Franklin's blocking, and Hose scrambled for about ten, and now we were down on their seven, and Hose called time out.

Me and Hose went to the sidelines to chat with Shoat, and this was the first time that I actually think I heard the crowd. It was almost as if I had just woke up. Say what you want to, but a big old thing like the Super Bowl causes nerves and numbness.

"What's workin'?" Shoat asked Hose.

"That interference play ain't bad," Hose said, winded but grinning slightly.

Shoat looked down at his feet.

He said, "One way or another, we got to get in that end zone. I'd sure like to stick that sumbitch right up their neck."

He said, "They's men down in the trenches and if we could score down in there it would let 'em know if they's men on both sides."

Shoat took the toothpick out of his mouth and said, "Try old stud hoss here and see if you get anything. You may have to throw. We ain't goin' for no more threes."

I got two yards on a slant and I got four more on a wide pitch, and we had third down at the one. Actually, Dreamer tackled me on the three but I crawled to the one and the zebras let me have it.

"Good lick," I told Dreamer, getting up.

He patted me on the butt.

Hose called me on a quick hitter on third down, and I knew when I took the handoff that I wasn't going anywhere. It was like trying to run over the Davis Mountains. I just hugged the ball and hit in there, and it was fourth down at the one-foot line.

Shoat called time out again, the dumb-ass, wasting one we might have needed. And over on the sideline, he chose to recite some coaching wisdom for us.

"They's one thing you always do when you're down to the nut-cuttin'. I never knowed anybody from Bryant to Royal to Lombardi who didn't say to go with your best back on his best play. Let's stick stud hoss here in there behind Puddin and see if we can get just enough of a crease. Is the Pope blockin' anybody? Tell that toothless Catholic sumbitch to give you a good snap. We got to have this sumbitch, Hose. You hear what I'm sayin'?"

Some people will probably always look back on this play as the biggest of the game, but there were a lot of those. This one was sure the play which caused the most fuss, of course.

It's always a close call when a back tries to leap up and dive over the line, and then gets shoved back. Was he over or wasn't he? I climbed right up Puddin's ass, and I remember hearing a lot of grunts, and I surely remember the lick that Dreamer and Hoover Buford put on me, up there in the air, on top of the heap.

The question that the head linesman had to decide was whether I had crossed over the goal before the ball jarred loose, and I was thrown back, and here was that scramble and fist fight for the football.

One zebra signaled a touchdown. Another one signaled a fumble and a Jet recovery. Another one signaled time out. And, meanwhile, six or eight Giants and six or eight Jets got into what you call your melee.

Both benches emptied out onto the field, and whistles were blowing, and guys were cussing, but the one thing I could hear above all of it was guess what? You got it. T. J. Lambert cut some that really and truly belonged in a zoo.

As much as anything, I think, it was the odor that broke it all up.

I didn't get into the fisticuffs because all you do in something like that is get injured. Neither did Dreamer. What we actually did was sink to our knees, off to one side, and laugh.

When the fight stopped, the zebras talked a long time and finally decided to give us a touchdown. I don't like to think that their decision was swayed by the fact that T. J. stood right in the midst of them, snarling and cutting some short sweet ones. But it might have been.

I understand that even on slow motion instant replay nobody could tell whether I scored or not before the fumble, but we got to count it, anyhow. That's the main thing.

It was twenty-one to ten, after Hose made the conversion, and we were back in the ball game.

Barbara Jane said that up in the stands, some of our friends, for the first time, had started to sense a glimmer of hope for a miracle.

She said Big Ed was furious at Shoat Cooper's goal-line calls but the touchdown calmed him down.

Barb said that Big Ed said, "We're almost back in the goddamned contest. I just don't know how much character our niggers have got."

I know there'll probably always be an argument about whether I scored on fourth down at their one-foot line but I truly believe I got over before Dreamer and the others knocked me and Puddin back to the five, and the ball back to the ten.

It was surely that drive to start the second half which made us a lot more eager to do battle. In pro football, being down by twenty-one to ten is not nearly so bad as it seems, particularly when there's still a quarter and a half to go and you've suddenly got some momentum.

Of course, it took a little of the juice out of us when they came right back and drove eighty yards to our one-inch line and had a first down. And I'll never know how T. J. Lambert got back there and took the ball away from Boyce Cayce just as he was handing it to Gruver Allgood without being called for offsides.

That was certainly one of the biggest plays of the game, even though *Sports Illustrated* failed to mention it. If the dog-ass Jets had scored then, it would have been twenty-eight to ten and we might have been deader than a Jew at River Crest.

When T. J. came off the field you might have noticed that he brought the football with him and refused to give it back to the referee because he wanted it as a keepsake.

"I sucked this sumbitch up from them tootie fruities and I'm gone keep it," he sneered.

Of course, in so far as the big plays go, you can't say enough about Jimmy Keith Joy redeeming himself by recovering the punt they fumbled on the following play. Hose Manning really got into a good punt and it didn't hurt any that the ball took a crazy bounce past their twin safeties and rolled damn near the length of the field, or all the way to their twelve-yard line.

Old Jimmy Keith Joy was chasing that sumbitch all the way, you might remember, as if a carload of red necks were after him. And even though Jimmy Keith and Jessie Luker sort of wound up in a tie for the ball, I think the referee made a good decision when he awarded it to us on their fifteen.

I knew with two successive breaks like that we would score quick.

In the huddle Hose Manning called for Shake Tiller to split out by Dreamer Tatum, fake a hook and then beat him to the flag.

"Drill it on the break," said Shake, "and my numbers'll be there."

It was really a pretty play. Shake put his move on Dreamer and left him hollering, "Aaaaah shit!" and Hose blew it right in there at Shake's numbers and we had us another six.

When the fourth quarter started and it was some kind of a ball game, twenty-one to seventeen, Barbara Jane said that some of our Giant fans were bordering on insanity.

She said Burt Danby had run over a couple of box seats away and was hugging Strooby McMackin and slapping people on the back and shaking his fist at the whole stadium behind him.

She said Burt was shouting, "Guts! Courage! Class! Never say die! Giants forever! *God,* I love our city!"

Barbara Jane said that Big Ed said, "We've got 'em now. They're on the ropes. You can see it. It's all over. The moment of stress has come and their goddamn niggers'll quit. Watch what I'm telling you."

She said it was just about then that Dreamer Tatum intercepted Hose's screen pass and went fifty-five yards for his second touchdown of the game.

I don't mind saying that this gave us a sick feeling, to be on the verge of catching up, and then to have something like that happen. To pull up to within four points of somebody and then suddenly to have something terrible like that occur and fall back by eleven was almost enough to make us want to vomit.

We probably would have, too. We probably would have just sat down and thrown up and cried pretty soon if Randy Juan Llanez hadn't taken that kickoff and run it right up their ears.

Some things I've read say television clearly showed he stepped out of bounds twice, at our forty and at their twenty-two, but all I know is that Randy Juan Llanez got credit for going ninety-eight steps to their alumni stripe, and it was six more for our side.

And if he's not the greatest little spook-spick I've ever known then you can go browse through your taco huts and find one to top him.

I'm embarrassed that I made such a spectacle of myself when Randy crossed the goal line. I was running right behind him all the way. And I was so happy when he scored that I guess I must have looked like a dress designer the way I wrestled him down to the ground and hugged on him, celebrating.

All I remember is that I was overcome with joy and Randy Juan was squirming and squealing underneath me. He said his ankle was pinching.

Barbara Jane said that Big Ed was in some kind of shock by what Randy Juan Llanez had done.

She said Big Ed just shook his head and said, "Goddamn if you'd asked me about it, I'd have said the little spick isn't good at anything but driving the team bus."

Barb said that Elroy Blunt looked at the scoreboard and then looked up at God and said:

"Twenty-eight to twenty-four, Skipper, and you know I'm a sinner. What kind of fuckin' is it gonna be?"

Barb said Burt Danby was screaming tears, standing up on his seat, purple in the face, shouting back at the stadium behind him:

"It's *class!* It's *guts!* It's *courage!* It's *Manhattan,* by Christ!"

I really wish I could tell you that we knew what we were doing there at the last.

I'd like to be able to divulge that we said a lot of dramatic things to each other in the huddle. I wish I could say that every time we went in the huddle on that eighty-five yard drive, which was against both the dog-ass Jets and the dog-ass clock, that we were fresh enough to be witty or clear-thinking or exceptionally heroic in one way or another.

I've thought about it a lot over here on Lihililo Beach, where I can look out at the old Pacific or up at the rain clouds and the high waterfalls on the mountains, or at the fairly distracting sight of Barbara Jane in a bikini over on the lava rocks.

All I can truthfully remember is that I was so whip-dog tired and bruised up that I was just going along on what you call your instinct.

Over and over in the huddles, Hose Manning would be panting and jabbering things like, "Gotta have it, bunch, gotta have it. Let's get it, let's get it. Guts up time now. This is a gut check. Gotta have it."

I recall hearing Hose calling an audible at the line, now and then, like, "Blue, curfew, eighty-three," and at the same time I recall hearing Dreamer Tatum yelling defensive signals like, "Brown, bruin, foxtrot," and then the Pope would snap the ball and I'd run somewhere and take another lick.

I guess I ran where I was supposed to run.

Somewhere along the way, Shake asked me, "You tired, Billy C.?" I remember that. And I remember Hose saying, "I'll tell him when he's tired."

That was a hell of a call Hose came up with when we had fourth fucking down on our own thirty-seven and two to go. I knew we had to go for it, because of the clock. If we punted, we might never see the ball again.

I didn't know what Hose would do. Run me, maybe. Try to hit Shake on a quick sideline, maybe. Just something to get the first down. I didn't expect what he invented and obviously the dog-ass Jets didn't either.

In the huddle Hose said, "Bunch, I got to suck it up and pick a number. This might be the ball game so everybody give me their best shot."

Hose didn't make up a play so much as he made up a change of positions. He put Shake Tiller at tight end and he put Thacker Hubbard into a full-house backfield with me and Booger Sanders. The only guy he split out wide was Randy Juan.

Then he called tight end deep, only man down. This meant that it was going to be a deep pass for Shake Tiller, out of a run formation. It was going to be that or nothing.

"I got to have good boards on this one," Hose told Shake.

"Just throw that sumbitch. I'll get there," said Shake.

If Hose had thrown a real good pass, of course, it would have been a touchdown because the play had everybody fooled, including Shoat Cooper. Nobody was within ten yards of Shake.

As it was, we only got thirty-five yards after Shake jumped up and caught the ball over his head and came down off-balance and toppled out of bounds. Instead of semi-dead, we were down on their twenty-eight.

He caught the ball near our bench, and you would have thought he had just been elected Roman emperor, the way our bunch mobbed him.

I want everybody to know that I was fairly astounded later on when I found out that I carried the ball six straight times from there.

I don't at all remember the ten-yard sweep where they tell me I flat ran over Dreamer Tatum, cunt on cunt. And he had to be helped off the field for the first time in his career.

That last carry wasn't Twenty-three Blast, by the way, like *Sports Illustrated* said. It was what we call Student Body Left, which is a play where everybody pulls left and I run a slant or a sweep, depending on how the blockers clear a path.

We called time out before the last play but I didn't go to the sideline. I just sat down and tried to breathe. I did look up at the clock on the scoreboard behind the goal post and saw that there were only four seconds left in the game.

I sat there and looked all around the stadium at those ninety-two thousand people and although there must have been a lot of roaring, I couldn't hear anything. It was weird. Really eerie. It was like I was swallowed up by this great movie, all around me, but it was a silent movie.

They say I cut inside on the play and pretty much ran over Puddin Patterson's big ass again. All I can say is that I was so tired and numb that those three yards were the longest I ever tried to make.

They say I climbed right up Puddin's big ass and then dived, headfirst like a silly damn swan, over the alumni stripe, and came down on my face-guard to win the game.

What happened for the next few minutes is also pretty much of a blur. Let's see now. They carried me off the field, of course, and I damn near got stripped naked from little kids clawing at me.

I can still hear Elroy Blunt rapping on my helmet and saying, "We done fucked 'em. We done fucked 'em."

T. J. Lambert lifted me up in the air and said, "Remind me to buy you a sody pop."

Burt Danby had tears streaming down his face and went so far as to kiss me on the goddamn lips.

Shoat Cooper managed the one and only grin of his whole lifetime and said, "What I call what you done out there is *football*."

Big Ed Bookman shook my hand and put ten one hundred dollar bills in it and said, "Spread this around among some of your blockers and tell 'em I don't just appreciate it by myself but the whole goddamned country does."

It was pretty much after all the celebrating had died down in the dressing room—after everybody had stuck their heads under bottles of Scotch and champagne—that Shake Tiller came over and quietly shook my hand.

"Ate up their ass is all you did, Billy C.," he said.

From the man who gave us the semi-sacrilegious *Semi-Tough,* here is an equally irreverent look at the 1976 state of affairs and semantics in the National Football League. This is vintage Dan Jenkins, who saw the game through his very own kaleidoscope eyes, and reported it so uniquely on the pages of *Sports Illustrated.* I mean if it weren't for Jenkins and his guidance through the parlance of football, an ordinary football fan would probably have difficulty understanding this assessment of the Oakland Raiders' chances behind the quarterbacking of Kenny Stabler: "If Snake can hit the Pop, the Hitch, and the Shake, particularly against the Orange Three, and if he can read the El Paso as good as he reads the Tango, there's no reason why we can't Double Sponge anybody, especially if we're using George and their Jill is cheating."

Cracking the Language Barrier

DAN JENKINS

THAT THING all those dock workers, meat packers, icemen and railroad brakemen started almost 60 years ago, and which came to be known as professional football, is about to lead us once again on a thundering off-tackle 29 Oley Bob P-Series Power Ride into the grinding teeth of a 56 Stub-I Rex Change defense, if not a 43 Purple Sloop. It is going to happen whether O. J. Simpson likes it or not. Momentarily. Just as soon as the sport's newest glamour-boy-quarterback-hero, Baltimore's Bert Jones, gets his hair combed and his autographing hand taped.

But four long months from now, after the last set of linebackers has run the last "Bazooka" at the last "Calypso" formation, the chances are excellent that the same two teams—Pittsburgh and Dallas—will return to the Super Bowl, this one to be played at the Woody Hayes Memorial Funeral Parlor in Pasadena, Calif., otherwise known as the Rose Bowl.

During the intervening months of soaring incomple-tions and commercial pauses, however, it is altogether possible that America will not discover very much new about the game it has taken to wearing on its head like a VFW cap. More than likely, in fact, America will only be reminded that:

- After all these years 14 of the NFL's 28 teams still play in stadiums made for baseball.
- There are only eight certified, guaranteed NFL head coaches: Chuck Noll, Tom Landry, Don Shula, George Allen, Hank Stram, Bud Grant, John Madden and Lou Saban. The number of college dropouts has swollen to eight, and now includes USC's John McKay at Tampa Bay, UCLA's Dick Vermeil at Philadelphia and North Carolina State's Lou Holtz with the New York Jets. But the pro coaches are predominantly a cluster of escalated assistants who have yet to prove themselves. Plus one car dealer, Bart Starr.
- It is easier to place a bet illegally over a New York telephone than legally with the Delaware lottery.

- ABC-TV should be up for a community-service award for keeping Cleveland, Denver, San Diego, Tampa Bay, Atlanta, Seattle, Chicago, Detroit, Green Bay, New Orleans and the New York Giants off Monday Night Football.
- "Limbo" and "Cha-Cha" are signals for the Dallas defense.
- The quarterback breakdown remains the same. The once and future stars: Bert Jones and Atlanta's Steve Bartkowski. The reliables: Terry Bradshaw, Roger Staubach, Ken Stabler, Fran Tarkenton, Bob Griese, Ken Anderson, Jim Hart and Bill Kilmer. And the jury is still out on: Steve Ramsey, Dan Pastorini, Manning-Scott-Douglass, Harris-Jaworski, Joe Reed, Craig Morton, Jim Plunkett, Lynn Dickey, Steve Spurrier, Mike Phipps, Ferguson-Marangi, Steve Grogan, Mike Boryla, Jim Zorn, Bob Avellini, Mike Livingston, Longley-Fouts and what is left of Joe Namath.
- Lynn Swann may get to Mars before Viking III.
- Joe Namath has reached the point where he ought to consider peddling Mr. Coffee instead of Brut.
- In a "Cyclone," the "Banjo" chops down a "Rocket" with an "Ax" as long as the "Outlaw" remembers to "Skunk." Got it, Howard?
- Minnesota and Los Angeles should win their divisions by Sept. 26.
- Ohio State's Archie Griffin heard a pass play called in the Cincinnati huddle and didn't know what it was.
- And, finally, the Buffalo Bills have put in a running play inspired by O. J. Simpson and called "The 32 Retainer and a Share of Increased Sales Over Present Dollar Volume."

Although the season lies ahead, many of the big stories of Pro Football '76 are already behind us. So, for those who may have missed them, they are re-created here as accurately as possible:

NEW YORK—Larry Csonka, who twice led the Miami Dolphins to Super Bowl glory and once led the World Football League to dissolution, signed a contract today with the New Jersey Dwarfs. Terms of the contract were not revealed but it is known that Csonka has agreed to carry the ball at least 12 times during the 1976 season. In exchange, Csonka has reportedly received from the Dwarfs:

1. $4 million spread over the next six months.
2. A helicopter.
3. A penthouse duplex.
4. 300 tickets to each game.
5. $5,000 a month to entertain clients.
6. A Bloomingdale's charge-a-plate.
7. Notification well in advance of any "Waco Hammer" rotation on the part of an opposing team's defense.
8. Six dozen first-class round-trip plane tickets for friends.
9. A 20-year loan of $10 million at minimum legal interest rates.
10. A makeup artist for road games.

SAN FRANCISCO—Columnist Herb Caen, speaking for the City by the Bay, said it was unfortunate that San Francisco had to give up the Golden Gate Bridge and Union Square but it may have been worth it to obtain Quarterback Jim Plunkett for the 49ers. Plunkett said his five years' experience without pass receivers in New England would prove invaluable to him in his new role.

"All I have to do is learn what a 60 Basic Split Post is," he said.

KANSAS CITY—The All-Fellowship of Christian Athletes Team was announced today with several repeaters, including the Steelers' Ernie Holmes and free agents Joe Gilliam and Mack Herron. The 11-member all-star team, selected on arrests rather than actual convictions:

- Possession: Ernie Holmes, Steelers; Darryl Carlton, Dolphins; Ken Payne, Packers; Shelby Jordan, Patriots; and Gilliam.
- Firecrackers on airplane: Terry Metcalf, Cardinals.
- Holding Vitamin C: Mack Herron, cut by Rams.
- Herb in car: John Matuszak, Redskins.
- Accident-scene leaving: Jeff Winans, Raiders.
- Disturbing peace: Scott Anderson, Vikings.
- Punching bicycle rider: Mark Koncar, Packers.

Each member of the all-star team will receive galley proofs of Lance Rentzel's new book and life-size posters of W. K. Hicks, Warren Wells, Paul Hornung and Alex Karras.

EAST RUTHERFORD, N.J.—Quarterback Craig Morton of the New Jersey Dwarfs said today he is contemplating legal action against a clothing manufacturer he represents for using his picture in a magazine ad. Morton said the photograph, which showed the veteran passer in bikini briefs, had forced him to change his phone number 27 times since it appeared.

WASHINGTON, D.C.—After visiting 12 different training camps and interviewing as many coaches, owners, and players as possible, Running Back John Riggins selected the Washington Redskins today as his new NFL team. Riggins said money was no consideration. "I wanted the club with the most colorful terms," Riggins said. "Things like Log, Smack, Adios, King, Queen, Jack, Ace, Pic, Poc and Double Poc."

Riggins explained that it had been very dull playing

for the Jets where they only used such expressions as "Bubble" to describe an area covered by a linebacker.

"Coach Allen says if our Do Dads and Tares and Obies work the way they're supposed to, I can make some yardage off the Witch, provided the tight end isn't tailored," Riggins said.

A spokesman for George Allen said this was not necessarily true if the Redskins were playing Dallas, which might be in a "Rifle," "Pistol," or "Mombo" coverage.

Observers at the Redskin's training camp say it probably doesn't matter. Bill Kilmer has been running the "Woolworth" to perfection without risking a "Bingo," and the "Sally Rand" has not come up against a single "Orvil," "Zelda" or "Ruby Doo."

WILMINGTON, DEL.—All 187 residents of this state apparently favor legalized betting on NFL games, but just how popular the lottery cards will be with tourists remains to be seen.

Typical of fan reactions was that of Angelo (Hit the Middle) Rossoff, a longtime NFL enthusiast who says he has frequently flown over Delaware. Rossoff was in town from Rochester to inspect the computer cards on which a fan must pick all seven winners to share in the lottery pool prize each week.

"It don't do much for the guy who wants a dime on the Colts take 7½ and a dime on Miami give 6½," he said. "I'm stayin' home."

THOUSAND OAKS, CALIF.—Dallas Cowboy Quarterbacks Roger Staubach and Clint Longley got into a pinching contest today during lunch break at training camp. It started when Staubach accused Longley of stealing a milk carton off his food tray. The scuffle between Staubach and Longley was not the first. Earlier in the week they had been seen tugging at each other's chinstraps and untaping each other's socks. It was during the first episode that Longley clearly frogged Staubach on the arm, an act Staubach described as "gutless," inasmuch as he was throwing a pass to Drew Pearson at the time.

"Staubach shouldn't use a word like gutless," Longley said. "It is not part of the Cowboys' terminology. He should have said Wanda or Sarah."

Observers said the scene during lunch was one of near pandemonium. After Longley allegedly stole Staubach's carton of milk, Staubach hollered, "Liz!" indicating a left-side pass rush. When Longley looked away, Staubach took a helping of navy beans off the backup quarterback's plate.

The pinching contest began when Staubach told Longley, "I'm going to catch you in a Skeezix and run a 60 Dig across your Easter Bunny teeth."

PETE ROZELLE'S DICTIONARY

BAZOOKA: Blitz by three linebackers.

BUBBLE: Area covered by a linebacker.

BINGO: What a player yells when he intercepts a pass.

CHA-CHA: Pass rush with one tackle looping behind the other.

DO-DAD: Double-team block by the guard and center.

EL PASO: Stunt between the defensive end and tackle.

FLARE CONTROL: Defense keeping an eye on a back going into the flat.

FIRE PROTECTION: Blocking on a quick pass pattern.

GEORGE: Tight end and tackle block in, guard blocks out.

LIMBO: Pass rush with an end looping behind a tackle or vice versa.

MEG, MAC, MARY: The middle linebacker.

MOMBO: Pass coverage rotation to the strong side.

ORANGE 3: Three-man defensive line.

ORVIL: A defensive formation.

RED HOT: Call after a fumble.

SARAH or SAM: Strongside linebacker.

SALLY RAND: Naked reverse, what else?

WACO HAMMER: Defensive rotation to the weak side.

WANDA: Weakside linebacker.

ZELDA: Prevent defense.

29 OLEY BOB: The two-back through the nine hole with a double guard pull and the other back blocking a linebacker.

43 PURPLE SLOOP: Fake blitz.

56 STUB-I REX CHANGE: Combination defense with a linebacker blitz and a stunt on defensive line.

60 BASIC SPLIT POST: Deep pass pattern in which the flanker and the tight end cross, with the flanker heading for the goalpost.

60 DIG: Two wide receivers cutting across the field on a two route.

Longley countered with, "Hey, Tunnel Vision. Get off my case."

The more experienced members of the press corps who witnessed the incident said it reminded them of the time two other quarterbacks competing for the same job—Washington's Bill Kilmer and Sonny Jurgensen—retreated behind a hedge to have it out but went to get a couple of six-packs first and never returned.

STUDIO CITY, CALIF.—O. J. Simpson announced today that unless Commissioner Pete Rozelle put an NFL expansion team in St. Tropez he would not play football in 1976.

"I've enjoyed my years in Buffalo, but now it's time for me to think about becoming closer to my family and the Cannes Film Festival," Simpson said.

As Simpson spoke, he tried to conceal the fact that his right arm was bandaged, the result of a fall he took recently while filming a Hertz commercial.

Simpson said his decision to play only in St. Tropez or retire was based partly on a new contract he had signed with TreeSweet Products.

"Participating in marketing activities can be fun," Simpson said. "Also, TreeSweet doesn't play exhibition games."

It had been rumored that Simpson was willing to be traded from Buffalo to the Los Angeles Rams if the Rams' owner, Carroll Rosenbloom, would assure him that he would not have to play all four backfield positions at the same time.

"That's absurd," Rosenbloom said. "O.J. would be asked to do nothing more than play running back, fullback and wide receiver, just as he did at Buffalo."

Simpson said he expected his Hollywood career to blossom more rapidly now that he was free of his football obligations.

"If I can avoid being typecast as a security guard or an elevator operator in TV movies of the week, I think I can make it," he said.

Buffalo Owner Ralph Wilson wished Simpson well.

"I don't see why O.J. can't succeed as an actor," Wilson said. "For seven years he did a good job of acting like he didn't hate Buffalo."

OAKLAND, CALIF.—The Oakland Raiders, a team noted for coming up with innovations, have developed yet another novelty for the 1976 NFL season. Specifically, Coach John Madden said his team was going to eliminate confusion by adopting a new terminology. "You won't hear any more 'Mississippi Gambler Open Decks' around here." Madden said. "And we're not going to call a deep pattern a 'Fly' either. We're going to call it an 'Up.' A lot of teams use the word 'Stunt.' I think that has a circus connotation. We'll say 'Twist Right' or 'Twist Left.' The same goes for lateral. Too many syllables. We'll use 'Flip.' "

Madden said the idea occurred to him last week in a Raider scrimmage.

"In our lexicon, a fumble has been known as a fumble, and we've had a lot of injuries to guys going after the ball," said Madden. "Now we call a fumble a 'Red Hot' and you don't see as many people banging into each other."

Al Davis, Oakland's managing general partner, was asked what he thought privately about Oakland's chances. "I'll say this much," said Davis. "If Snake can hit the Pop, the Hitch and the Shake, particularly against the Orange Three, and if he can read the El Paso as good as he reads the Tango, there's no reason why we can't Double Sponge anybody, especially if we're using George and their Jill is cheating."

As Terry Bradshaw strums idly on his guitar and Jack Lambert sips from a thermos of warm blood, both awaiting Pasadena, so begins another season.

Perhaps he is more famous for chronicling the golden age of the Brooklyn

Dodgers and the mystique of Ebbets Field as he did in *Boys of Summer,*

but Roger Kahn also covered the football front from time to time. In this

1976 piece for *Time* magazine, he offers a glimpse of the newly enfran-

chised Tampa Bay Buccaneers, who were playing in the American Foot-

ball Conference that maiden year, and their coach John McKay, just after

losing their ninth consecutive game on the way to an 0–14 season.

Aboard the Lusitania in Tampa Bay

ROGER KAHN

THE ENTRY of John McKay into professional football, riding a swan boat across the glinting waters of Tampa Bay, was converted into a financial report by certain elements of the press. There is a lingering Neanderthal quality in some of our new sports journalism. If you can't find a sex angle, write money.

According to a glut of stories, McKay was leaving the University of Southern California—where he had won four national championships—for a salary of $175,000 a year, a $350,000 home, complete with furniture, maid, gardener and pool service, plus five new cars and a variety of land deals that could have seduced the Shah of Iran.

McKay's response was characteristic and brief. "Nonsense," he said. "The figures are wildly out of line. Actually, I'm going to Tampa for the cigars."

The Contract. In becoming midwife to the Tampa Bay Buccaneers, currently staggering through their first season in the National Football League, John McKay won instant independence. At 53 he will not again have to worry about economic indicators. But by concentrating on the man's capital rather than his style, one misses the point. McKay was a great college coach who never publicly confused his success with the state of humanity. Football, he has suggested, is only a game. "You draw Xs and Os on a blackboard and that's not so difficult. I can even do it with my left hand."

Among the governors of the N.F.L., such talk is heresy. They insist that football is America, manliness, work ethic, integration and Vince Lombardi saying for the thousandth time, "Winning isn't everything. It's the only thing." This, if it means anything at all, means that Lombardi saw a movie called *Trouble Along the Way* in 1953. Playing a football coach in that film, John Wayne mouthed the lines that everyone now attributes to Lombardi.

But like McKay, Lombardi had a style. It was ferocity. That, plus his victories at Green Bay, made him the focus for a generation of football writing. Presently, we heard from the right that Lombardi was the noblest Roman since Octavius. (Not Brutus. Brutus lost.) The left suggested that he would have made a perfect fascist. In the cacophony people forgot that Lombardi was only a football coach who put Xs and Os on a board—right-handed.

The Tampa Bay Buccaneers were formed from a pool of pro freshmen—"rooks" in the argot—and a group of veterans other teams considered expendable. Approaching Tampa, McKay said that it would take three years to assemble a competitive team. Meanwhile, he would do the best he could.

After three losses in exhibition games, the Buccaneers defeated the Atlanta Falcons, 17 to 3. "Ho-hum," McKay said, in controlled delight. "Another dynasty." Then came this championship season. Tampa lost con-

— 115 —

secutively to Houston, San Diego, Buffalo, Baltimore, Cincinnati, Seattle (another expansion team), Miami and Kansas City. When I caught up with them in Denver their record was 0 and 8, but their spirits were stained with hope. The Denver Broncos had been playing poorly, and a Denver physician who played football told me, "We need a new quarterback and a new coach." That complaint classically signifies trouble, and trouble—somebody else's trouble—was what the Buccaneers needed most.

The Game. The afternoon offered a brilliant Colorado sky. Denver scored ten points in the first quarter and McKay lost Lee Roy Selmon, his best defensive lineman, with a knee injury. But the Buccaneers resisted collapse. Helped by three penalties, Steve Spurrier put together a reasonable touchdown drive in the second quarter. Later Dave Green kicked a field goal and tied the game.

After the half, Tampa, sensing the possibility of victory, drove to the Denver 9. They stalled. The Buccaneers drove again, reached the 18 and got a field goal. Two good drives. Ball possession for most of a quarter. And a total of only three points. Then that brilliant sky fell on McKay and his urchins.

The Broncos scored on a 71-yd. pass play. Within a minute they intercepted and scored again. Soon the Broncos led by 48–13 and were trying for more.

Afterward McKay refused to congratulate his conqueror, Coach John Ralston, who came to Denver out of Stanford. Instead, he called Ralston a ten-letter word, "for stacking on the points." When Ralston was mentioned in a press conference, McKay chomped a cigar. "He's a prick. He always was a prick. I hope he gets fired," said this devoutly civilized man. From another world Lombardi smiled ferociously.

In his office at Tampa the next afternoon, McKay had regained his poise. "I shouldn't have said those things. Bear Bryant, my best friend in coaching, says that after a bad loss you ought to stay in the closet for a week. I know Denver needed a win and maybe Ralston was saving his job by winning big."

The Loser. Bob Moore, Tampa's starting tight end, played under Ralston at Stanford. "I'm not getting in between the two coaches," he said. "I'm used to winning. I won in college and I won with the Oakland Raiders and this is just awful for me. We lose every week and the group experience is negative. Sometimes I feel as though I were on the aft deck of the *Lusitania*."

Moore, who is black-haired and disciplined and handsome, shows how a pro can lose with the shadow of a smile. In three years I hope McKay shows the country how to win at professional football without presenting the game as a metaphor for life.

Winning is neither everything nor the only thing. It is simply better than losing on a Sunday under a high Denver sky. Then Monday comes and everybody, except the football players, has to go back to reality and work.

Before acting and appearing in a myriad of television commercials and on various talk shows, Alex Karras was a football player and a very good one with the Detroit Lions through the 1960s. A defensive tackle, he was inappropriately nicknamed ''Tippy Toes'' and appropriately known as one of the most obstreperously funny men who engaged in NFL combat. In this excerpt from the book he wrote about his pro football career, *Even Big Guys Cry,* he remembers one of the most memorable of all NFL players, teammate Bobby Layne.

Remembering Bobby Layne

———— ALEX KARRAS (WITH HERB GLUCK) ————

WHAT GOES into the memory of a pro football career? How much do I remember of that time? Those players? Those coaches? What happened to the rush of stadium scenes, training-camp incidents, and long hours spent in hotel lobbies and airport terminals and cocktail bars? And in cars that bumped along on roads no longer traveled by me? There's so much to remember, and an image is already formed of some faraway place called Cranbrook, where I see myself singing the Iowa fight song on top of counters, in the bathrooms, in the showers. Cranbrook is where I shined shoes, and fetched towels, and ran all kinds of errands. Cranbrook. Where I stare in wonder at a legend called Bobby Layne. And feel the iron in his voice as he roars with laughter and pounds the dining-room table so hard that plates jump and the toughest rookies flinch in their seats. I see him now and remember the scene:

''Hey, rookie,'' he says. ''Y'all think you're something? Hell, you're nothing but a rookie who don't know enethang. You understand?''

''Yes, sir, Mr. Layne.''

''From now on, rookie, you just follow me around like a puppy dawg. You understand?''

''Yes, sir.''

He liked me. He called me Puppy for a few days. Then he changed it to Tippy. Pretty soon all the vet-erans called me Tippy Toes, because Layne thought it fit.

Now I think of him at practice and remember the way he'd grind his jaws, then spit, clap his hands, and bring the guys into a huddle. ''Awraht, men,'' he'd yell in that back-country Texas twang of his. ''Let's git it going, heah? Snap. Snap. Make it count.'' Then he'd go to work, and never break a sweat. And I'd reel around under the sun and wonder what I was doing on the same field with him.

He was the baddest-best pro football player of my time. He feared nobody. Sooner or later he'd find a weakness in a player and capitalize on it. Invariably. It might take him two periods, or three, or into the final seconds to get his points when he absolutely had to. He would often throw short decoy passes, just to see the defensive reaction. When the victim—a cornerback, tackle, linebacker, somebody—broke down once too often, Layne knew exactly where to strike. Bam! It was as though he was riding on the pulse of unnatural movement, propelled by an invisible force.

That was Bobby Layne, the player. I didn't know him too well as a man. Maybe nobody did. Not altogether. But once, while I was chauffeuring him around and he was in a drunken stupor, he told me a story. When he was a kid, about nine or so, he and his father were driving down a country road, and the car turned over. His father was killed instantly. He spent the whole night sitting by that upside-down car with his father inside, until they were found.

I waited a few minutes before Layne spoke again. Then he suddenly said he didn't like the dark. He was too scared to sleep, he said. We were headed for some bar in Pontiac at the time. It must've been two in the morning. Layne's eyes were wide open. And wild.

I was his personal chauffeur. Following the afternoon practices he'd holler for me in the dormitory. "Hey, Tippy! Let's git some Cutty!" He'd drink nothing but Cutty Sark Scotch. We'd drive to bars like the Bar-B-Que, or the Town and Country in Pontiac, and Layne would drink five or six Cutty Sarks and then I'd drive him back to Cranbrook for the evening meal. After that, we'd go right back to Pontiac again and he'd drink Cutty Sark all night. He made me drink with him. I never drank Scotch in my life until I started to run around with Bobby Layne.

One night, after the Cutty turned me into a sick drunk, Layne drove back to camp, singing at the top of his lungs while I held my head in my hands. He was singing "Ida Red." That was his favorite song. He sang it over and over. Pretty soon I looked up and saw that he had his right foot up on the dashboard, the left one stuck out the window. And while he was singing, I noticed that the accelerator had jammed. I checked the speedometer. The needle shivered at one hundred miles per hour, and we're roaring down the expressway with things shaking and bouncing inside the car. All the while Layne's singing "Ida Red, Ida Red." So I finally got down off the seat, and on my knees I begged him to stop the car. But we kept moving down the expressway with his feet still in the same position and a look of contentment all over his face.

By some miracle we made it back to camp. A few nights later I woke up shaking like an epileptic. From then on, I drove the car—no matter how much Cutty I had in me. Even if I had to rest my chin on the steering wheel and drive six miles an hour. We'd come home with the sun sliding up over the horizon and climb through a window into our beds. I'd get an hour's sleep before breakfast. And Layne would be in the shower, singing. I couldn't imagine how he did it.

* * *

I wasn't aware that the coaches were unhappy with Layne. When he got on the field, it was *his* field. He owned it. The coaches would work out precise diagrams on the blackboard, which were copied into the playbooks for study, and then Layne would come out for practice, spit into the wind, and tell the coaches,

"Y'all advise that end over theah to break it off about two more yards. Heah?" Or he'd say, "Now, George, when that boy makes an outside cut, y'all tell him to take it fahv more yards deep." The coaches went along, because they knew Layne was the best quarterback in the game.

Wilson was using as many young players as possible in the exhibition games. It was hard to tell what the final makeup of the club would be, but I could sense there was a rebuilding program going on. That came by just looking into the eyes of the veterans. On a thirty-five-man squad, twelve rookies remained after the fifth and last game of the exhibition season. The defensive team was more or less as it was the year before, with me filling in behind Gil Mains. The offense, with Layne as our leader, seemed solid enough. We had good outside receivers, strong backs, and a powerful line. So the 1958 Lions were set to make another run for the championship.

We played our opening game in Baltimore. Bobby Layne missed an important field goal when he scuffed the pitcher's mound. After that we gave up. The next week we tied Green Bay in a game filled with lost opportunities. The next day the Lions *traded* Bobby Layne and fullback Tom the Bomb Tracy to the Pittsburgh Steelers for quarterback Earl Morrall and two draft choices.

The whole team went into shock. It just didn't make sense. Bobby Layne was gone. And for me, a security blanket had been ripped away. Funny thing, though. I really didn't know why.

In utter disarray, we staggered around for a few days, then played the Rams at home. They shellacked us. Then Baltimore beat us at home. We flew to Los Angeles after that, and won. But we lost in San Francisco. In San Francisco, Gil Mains picked up a slight injury, so I played more than usual, and didn't disgrace myself. At least, George Wilson thought so. He started me when we faced the Browns in Cleveland. The Browns. It was Paul Brown's club, then. They had Jimmy Brown, Lou Groza, Willie Davis, Chuck Noll, Bobby Mitchell, Ed Modzelewski, Milt Plum, Ray Renfro; those were some of the names on the 1958 roster.

Before the game, Gil Mains said, "The only thing you don't have to worry about is the trap play. The Browns never trap." What I should've known is that the Browns ran ninety-percent traps. They trapped me all afternoon. And Gil told me after the game, "I think I should have my job back." But I played the rest of the season as starting tackle.

We had a dismal 4–7–1 record that year. Still, George Wilson was just wonderful to me. He brought me along diligently, without applying much pressure. Good games and bad, his attitude didn't change. He kept cool—

rough and gruff as he was—as long as I gave my best. I got to love that man.

Meanwhile, my brother Teddy had finished his first pro season with Pittsburgh. He was traded to the Steelers shortly after George Halas of the Chicago Bears signed him as a free agent. Halas masterminded the deal. An illegal deal. But he got away with it. This is how it happened: Halas thought Teddy needed additional seasoning at the guard position, so he purchased Abe Gibron, a veteran guard, from the Philadelphia Eagles and made a handshake arrangement with Steeler owner Art Rooney to have Teddy play in Pittsburgh for two years, then return to Chicago *if* the Bears wanted him. Teddy was dismayed, but there was nothing he could do about it. He went to Pittsburgh. Not long after that we sent Bobby Layne there.

During a Christmas family reunion in Gary, I asked Teddy a lot of questions about the Steelers. He seemed depressed, unwilling to say very much about the team. When I asked him about Bobby Layne, his eyes narrowed. "I can't handle that man," he said. "Every time I turned around he yelled and screamed at me."

John Sims "Shipwreck" Kelly arrived in New York City in 1932 and soon after engraved a truly inimitable imprint everywhere from Ebbets Field to the Stork Club. He came from the rolling hills of central Kentucky, from a wealthy family, owners of a 3,000-acre dairy farm among other things, and he was unawed by Manhattan and its sophistications.

An all-American halfback at the University of Kentucky who was dubbed in his college yearbook as "the fastest man in the South" because he ran the hundred-yard dash in 9:8, Shipwreck was equally adroit, he quickly proved, at moving through New York's cafe society. Shipwreck signed first with the New York Giants and played a season with them. The following year, in partnership with Chris Cagle, the all-American from Army who had also played in the Giants backfield in 1932, Shipwreck, at age twenty-three, bought the Brooklyn Dodgers NFL franchise. When Shipwreck was not in a locker room or on a football field, he could usually be found in places like El Morocco or "21" or perhaps out in the Hamptons or up in Newport. His closest friends included people like Dan Topping, Jock Whitney, and Bing Crosby. He dated Tallulah Bankhead and various Broadway starlets, and he married New York's most glamorous debutante, Brenda Frazier.

So I Bought the Brooklyn Dodgers

SHIPWRECK KELLY

MY FOOTBALL career started at Springfield High School in Kentucky. After that I went to St. Mary's College, a little Catholic college, for a year and then came back to Springfield. From there I went to the University of Kentucky, and I thought I was hot shit, but they didn't. I knew I could play football, and that I could run like hell. But the coaches there hardly ever let me play.

Finally they put me in during the last freshman game of the season against Centre, which was a smaller school in Kentucky. Centre was beating us, 21–0, at the time. I made three touchdowns after they let me in the game that day, and from that time on they knew I could play.

It was while I was at Kentucky that I got the nickname "Shipwreck." Around that time there was a man who was known as Shipwreck Kelly, an old sailor, who went around sitting on flagpoles. He came to Lexington one day and climbed up and stood on a flagpole and people thought he was very funny. I guess I was a junior or senior then and a pretty big hot shot. Well, after we won a big game, somebody said something like, "You sure can play football, but you can't sit on a flagpole like Shipwreck Kelly."

I said, "Bullshit." And I climbed up on a flagpole and stood there on top for a few minutes. Then I started down and somebody yelled, "What are you coming down for?"

"I have to piss," I said.

By the time I got to New York, after I graduated, I was known mostly as Shipwreck because I climbed that flagpole. The nickname just stuck.

It was Percy Johnson who wanted me to move to New York. He was from Kentucky and was like a father to me. He was chairman of the board of the Chemical Bank, a guy like J. P. Morgan, wealthy as hell. When I was in school he used to come down to Kentucky and watch me play football. He had a son who was my age and in the same class and we were great friends. I used to go up to New York every summer and stay with them. Then, after I graduated from Kentucky, Percy Johnson said, "Come on to New York."

So, in the summer of 1932, I came and he gave me a job at the Chemical Bank. I worked there two weeks, I think it was. I saw what it was like and decided I wanted to play pro football. I went to see the people at the Giants and they offered me a contract, a shitty contract like they all were in those days, but I played. Tim Mara was the man I talked to there, the owner. There was also Jack Mara, his son, and a little kid called Wellington Mara, but Tim Mara was the whole thing. Steve Owen was the coach, a nice friendly sort of guy, too friendly in fact and a lot of the players used to bullshit him a lot because he was too nice sometimes. His brother Bill played on the team and was pretty good.

I didn't get to play until the second game of the season. It was against Green Bay, and we weren't doing a thing. The Giants hadn't scored a single point in their first game that year, and against Green Bay we hadn't scored one either. So Owen sent me in. I broke a couple of runs, one was about 30 yards, and I caught six or seven passes that day, but we still didn't score a point. But I became a starter after that.

I played about six or seven games with the Giants that year, but then I quit because the doctor told me I wasn't in shape for it. I had a small touch of rheumatic fever and I didn't feel very good and they weren't paying me very much money anyway. I had some money myself and so I went back to Kentucky.

After the season, Chris Cagle, who had been the Giants' best back that year, called me up on the phone and told me there was a football franchise for sale, the Brooklyn Dodgers. Bill Dwyer owned them and he wanted to sell out, Cagle told me. So I called up Percy Johnson and asked him what he thought about it. I told him I might want to buy the team. He said, "Well, if you think you can make it go, come on up and I'll help you."

So I went back to New York and I bought the Brooklyn Dodgers with Cagle. We turned out a pretty good team that first year, won more than we lost. We had some pretty good players. Of course, Cagle, and we had big old Herman Hickman in the line. He was all-Pro. And I'd gone out and hired Benny Friedman, supposed to be the best passer in pro football then.

I paid Friedman a helluva lot of money to play for us. He was a nice fellow. But let me tell you what happened to him the first game he played for us that year. We were playing against the Bears and on the first play Friedman went back to pass. Well, they had this end who used to play without a helmet, Bill Hewitt. Tough son of a bitch. If you could have seen what he did to Friedman. Knocked him on his ass and Friedman left the game. He sat on the bench and after a while I went over and asked, "What the hell are you doing?"

Friedman said, "I'm tired. I'm weak today."

I was paying him thirty-two hundred dollars a game, and this was his first game. I said, "What's the matter with you. I'm paying you to play, not to rest your ass on the bench."

"I took a laxative last night," he said.

I said, "You took a thirty-two hundred dollar shit on us, that's what you did."

I didn't talk to him anymore that day and he stayed out of the game and the Bears beat us, 10–0. But he did play after that, and he was there for the Giants game, that was the big draw in New York back then when Brooklyn played the Giants. He was a great passer though and with he and Cagle throwing the ball I caught the most passes in the league that year, twenty-two I think it was.

We didn't do as well in 1934. Early in the season Cagle wanted out. He needed the money, I guess. And Friedman left, too. I think he went to coach some college team. Anyway, in the meantime, I had gotten to be friends with Dan Topping, who was a playboy and big shot around New York. On account of my playing football and he liking sports I got to know him pretty well. So Dan and I got together and talked about it and Dan bought Cagle out. Dan and I owned the Dodgers for a number of years. I moved in with Dan, we shared an apartment in New York for a number of years, until he got married. Then I got my own apartment. Then he divorced that first wife and married Sonja Henie, the famous ice skater. When he married Sonja Henie, she decided that she wanted to get into sports, besides the skating. So she bought half of Dan's ownership in the Dodgers.

It was around that time that I got Ralph Kercheval to come to Brooklyn. He'd played at Kentucky just like I had. He was a halfback, but his real greatness was in kicking the football. He could punt, he could placekick. He was the best kicker ever to play the game. Hell, he could fart the football farther than these guys can kick it today.

New York was a great place to be back then. I had a helluva life. I really was a protégé of Percy Johnson when I came up to New York and if you're a protégé of someone like that you can tell everybody to kiss your ass, and everybody's nice to you because he was so powerful and had so many influential friends. I met all kinds of people through him, the socialites, the big people on Wall Street, a lot of very important people. I would be invited out to Southhampton and East Hampton and the place where I met most of the hot shit was Newport, up in Rhode Island. I nearly married Bill Woodworth's daughter around then. Bill Woodworth, he was one of the biggest bankers in the world then, had houses in three or four places.

I was having a great time around then. Topping and I were all over Broadway and shit like that. He loved the showgirls. There was another guy, another multimillionaire, that I was good friends with, too; Ed Madden. He bought me a LaSalle so I could get around New York easier. After a while I shit him around. I said, "You mean you want me driving around in a car like this?" So he took it back and got me a Cadillac instead. Madden also got me to run for the New York Athletic Club. I ran the 100 and the 220 in a lot of those big relays, in New York, Philadelphia, Pittsburgh, quite a few places. I ran the 100 in 9:8 then and I tried out for the 1936 Olympics, but I lost out to Jesse Owens and Ralph Metcalf in the sprints.

We used to go to the nightclubs around New York all the time, too, but not during the times I was playing football, at least not a lot. I was serious about football. The one that was my favorite was the Stork Club because Sherman Billingsley liked me. He owned it and he had piles of money. I used to go in there and if I wanted any money he'd give it to me and say, "Pay me back when you get ready." He was a wonderful guy. He did the same thing for Walter Winchell and a lot of people that went in there. He'd give it to you and you'd pay him back when you wanted to.

The hot shit of them all, though, was El Morocco. I knew John Perona, the owner there, and he was very nice to me. The big thing was to get into the nightclub and even then only if you were a hot shit would you be sitting where the hot shits were. If you were not, they'd put you in the back or in a corner somewhere out of the way.

I remember one night in the El Morocco when I was with four or five people at one table. In walked a big guy with a beard—there weren't many beards in those days—and John Perona came over and said to me, "Do you know who that guy is?"

I said I didn't. "It's Orson Welles, the actor." On second thought, I said, I thought I'd seen a picture of him somewhere. So Perona brought Orson Welles over to the table and introduced me to him. I tried to be a smart aleck, like I did a lot of times in those days, I said, "Gee, Mr. Welles, it's nice meeting someone like you." He didn't know who I was or that I played football or anything about me. But he was very pleasant. Then I said something like, "Why do you cultivate something on your face that grows wild on your ass?"

"Mr. Kelly," he said, "you are fresh in New York, and if I were you I wouldn't tell my friends how much you know about my ass."

I felt like shit and got up and left.

Another time I remember was at the Stork Club. I took Tallulah Bankhead there. I used to date her a lot around that time. In walked this beautiful young girl, Brenda Frazier, one of the richest, most famous debutantes of the time, with three young men and they sat down on the floor near the table Bankhead and I were at.

Well, the waiters were giving out balloons and one of them was supposed to have a hundred-dollar bill inside it. It was something Billingsley used to do every once in awhile. I think this time it had probably been fixed because Bankhead got the balloon with the hundred dollars in it. She got up and walked over to where Brenda Frazier was sitting on the floor and handed it to her. "Here, my dear," she said. "I think you'll need it. I've been reading in the papers lately how broke you are all the time."

"Thank you, I can use it," Brenda said. "I don't get my money until I'm twenty-one."

I didn't let that crap interfere with my football playing, however. I kept the two apart. You had to because it was a rugged game, much tougher than college ball. The sons of bitches in the pros were bigger and stronger, and all of them were pretty damn good, whereas in college only two or three players on a team might be worth a shit.

Two of the toughest I remember were Bill Hewitt of the Bears and Father Lumpkin, who played for Portsmouth and Detroit and then came with the Dodgers. They both played without headgear. Harry Newman of the Giants was a helluva ballplayer, too. He was very small but tough and good. Probably the greatest was Dutch Clark. I played against him. The greatest I saw after I left the sport was Sid Luckman. I ran into him on the street one day in New York and he came up to me and we talked a little and he told me I had been his hero when he was a kid growing up in Brooklyn. That was very nice. I really appreciated it, him remembering me for playing football. I get tired of all those people remembering me because I married a rich girl and was in the café society thing all the time. Football was important to me. One thing I'm especially proud of is that I never made a fair catch of a punt. Never. I'd take it on the run no matter what.

I quit playing after the 1934 season. But then the coaches asked me to come back in 1937. One of their backs got hurt or something and the team was doing shitty. I guess they thought I could run like I used to be able to. Potsy Clark was the coach that year. Anyway, they had to persuade me to come back, but I wasn't the player I was before. I wasn't in shape. I couldn't help them on the field. But I did help them in another way. I got them to go after Ace Parker. I had read about him and seen him play for Duke. I thought he would be just what they needed, and, of course, he turned into a fantastic pro back.

After that I got out of football for good. Then I married Brenda Frazier. And after that I did that work for the FBI. Not many people know about that, but I did it all the way through the war, and then when it was over J. Edgar Hoover wrote me this letter, thanking me for what I'd done. I traveled everywhere for them. You see, I could because of the society that I hung around in. I mean I went to Europe, to Cuba, then to Mexico, to Peru, to Chile, and when we got in the war I spent a lot of time in Argentina. I could meet people at parties and things, the big shots there because of my connections. An ordinary person didn't have access to them. But I did. There were loads of rich Germans in Argentina and high-ranking officers, all in that same international society. I would try to find out about the ships, the submarines, things like that, that were off our coasts. And there were a lot of them. A lot of these people knew where they were, when they were around, that kind of thing. I kissed everybody's ass in Argentina to find out things like that, and I found out a lot. I also found out who the others who were sympathetic to the Germans were, others in that society. I worked at it all the way through the war for Hoover. Then I got out of that part of it and he and I were good friends, did things together many times in the years after the war.

But football was great. It helped me in a lot of ways. And I tried to do my job right in the years I played. And it's nice to be remembered for that part of my life.

Tony Kornheiser, writing for the *Washington Post* in 1981, provides a marvelous behind-the-scenes view of the festivities before and at the Super Bowl spectacle through the peregrinations and personalities of Pete and Carrie Rozelle. The NFL commissioner and his wife took in the entire scene in New Orleans, from the French Quarter to his box at the Louisiana Superdome. And in the process Kornheiser provides a revealing profile of the gentleman who has guided the NFL for nearly three decades. The article was also included in *Best Sports Stories 1982*, selected by the editors of *The Sporting News*.

The Rozelles: PR and Pizzazz at the Super Bowl

TONY KORNHEISER

HE IS in a deep-blue suit, and his skin tone, which has always been Pete Rozelle's finest feature, is copper. Against it, his teeth are pearls.

She is in a gold-sequined blouse above a long, black skirt, and on the replays from all the different angles, from the front, the back, the sides, Carrie Rozelle sparkles.

They don't just walk; they glide.

They don't just smile; they beam.

They don't just greet people; they embrace them.

It goes on for hours here in New Orleans at the National Football League party that provides 4,000 pounds of food for 3,000 invited guests at a cost said to be $400,000. "Super Bowl XVI . . . And All That Jazz." Oysters, crab fingers, creole-stuffed peppers and strawberries served XV, count 'em, XV different ways, jazz bands, Dixieland bands, dancing waterfalls and two young, beautiful women swinging gently in perches made to look like musical notes, tossing miniature football helmets to the crowd.

His league. Her Theme. Their night.

The people never stop coming at them and for each there is a special clasp, a personal question, a warmth in the Rozelle manner that suggests cashmere. It is one

thing to know your role; it is quite another to be perfectly natural at it, to never be gratuitous, to be sincere. To believe in it.

It may well be that it is hollow at the core of Super Bowl Week, that when you get there, there is no there there. But first, last, and always Pete and Carrie Rozelle thank you for coming.

The Job This Week:

"The first thing Pete does when he gets to the Super Bowl city is he makes sure the league people have done what they've supposed to," says Jim Kensil, who was executive director of the NFL before becoming president of the New York Jets. "Then, he shakes hands with everybody who wants to shake his hand."

And then?

Kensil laughs.

"That's it."

Be visible. Be available. Be accessible.

Pass among the people. Thank them for coming.

From the Governor's Suite on the 27th floor of the New Orleans Hilton, there is a view of the Mississippi River that belongs on a travel brochure. This is where Pete and Carrie live this week, and Pete has just come from his annual Super Bowl tour-de-force press conference where once again (''that's XV in a row'') he struck just the right tone and said just the right things to leave 1,300 accredited journalists marveling at his skill. Having taken off his tie and put on slippers, he is sitting with his feet upon an oak table, and in his left hand is his ever-present Carlton cigarette. As always, he seems perfectly calm. Nothing to hide. Nothing to get hung about. He wouldn't spill his drink in an earthquake.

''To a great extent I accept what Jim says as valid,'' he says. ''It's probably the most superficial week of the year because of the ceremonial responsibilities.''

Parties. All over, parties. Musts.

Three on Thursday, including a black-tie dinner given by Mayor Ernest ''Dutch'' Morial, two more on Friday including the big one; no less than six on Saturday including a reception hosted by the Rozelles' close friends, the Kemps, as in Joanne and Jack, the former quarterback turned All-Pro Republican in Congress; three more on Sunday. Public relations. Classic case.

They're tiring, but Pete and Carrie have made a separate peace with that; in fact, Carrie says, they rather like them now that they've learned how to do them well.

''Look,'' she says, ''I like people. I love to talk to people. I'm lucky to have been that way all my life. Cocktail parties can be dreadful; I'd much prefer having dinner with six or eight people. But if I couldn't make small talk at these things, I'd be a total loss to Pete. I'd stand there looking like a jerk. I know I'm on stage this week, and I see myself as a hostess. For this week especially I'm the commissioner's wife and I want to look good. It's kind of frivolous, and at times, it's excessive, like the Mad Hatter's Ball. And it's a good time. It's like having a magic wand. I can help make a lot of people feel really good for a few days, and Pete, well, this week it's as if Pete were an orchestra leader.''

Rozelle shrugs.

''Carrie's better at it than I am,'' he says.

The Swarm:

The game was sold out; the hotels were filled, the joint was jumping.

All week long the French Quarter swelled to become the French Half. In a city built on food and music, restaurants on Bourbon Street routinely told eager gourmets that the wait was no less than 90 minutes and jazz joints were so jammed that people had to do their toe tapping on the streets. Must-go bars like The Old Absinthe House were so crowded that reaching for your wallet was a delicate surgical procedure. If you drank enough—and a lot of people made that their mission—it could take all night to realize that the topless dancers with the large, bare breasts in the honky-tonk weren't women at all. Mondo Bizarro . . . And All That Jazz.

New Orleans officials estimated that The Swarm deposited $40 million on the city last week in anticipation and celebration of America's Game, and that doesn't count the profit made by ticket scalpers who got as much as $500 a pop for one of the 75,500 tickets clearly marked with a face value of $40.

After XV years surely mere ''hype'' can be discarded as an explanation for all this. The Super Bowl has gone far beyond the hype stage, far beyond the ''ultimate game'' stage. For most of the people who went riding on the city of New Orleans, the game was just the last event in a siege party. Last call, if you will. Super Bowl is now a holiday week, an American celebration. It moves of its own pace.

''I had no idea it would get like this,'' Rozelle says. ''That it would become such a total package. People are coming for a full week and the game is played on only one day.''

It may be that the ''how'' and the ''why'' are beyond us, that the snowball has become a glacier, frozen and fixed in the mid-winter conscious.

Still, you can try.

Why are we here?

''Hmmm, that's so strange,'' Carrie says. ''I've never been asked that before . . . You don't think, in part, that it's a media event? . . . It's funny, but I hear so many people say the game is meaningless compared to the parties. I know a lot of people say the game is a letdown when it finally comes. People seem to talk about where they went and who they saw. You know, celebrities, athletes, movie stars. Isn't that very American, though?''

She pauses to consider all of it.

''Maybe it's no longer a sports event,'' the wife of the commissioner says. ''Maybe it's part of the American scene.''

The Hostages:

The NFL executives started talking about the hostages two weeks ago, when it appeared they might be released before the inauguration. Rozelle knew from last year that the hostages were particularly interested in the Super Bowl and he made available 100 copies of the Super Bowl program for Air Force One to carry to West Germany, enclosing a personal note he'd written to all 52.

Had they been released earlier, the NFL might well have invited them to the game (NBC actually did), but coming when it did—just five days before the game—Rozelle chose not to push it.

''To me,'' he says, ''it just didn't make sense for them. We'd never bring them here just as a showcase for the NFL—only if they wanted it.''

Still, there was concern as to ''how do we commemorate the release without being corny? How do we do it tastefully so it isn't viewed as taking advantage of the media and the hostages and deifying the Super Bowl? You try to strike a fine line in what's tasteful or appropriate as opposed to overkill.''

The solution was to make a brief, commemorative announcement of the release before the singing of the national anthem. And to give each ticket holder a yellow bow as they entered the Superdome.

And to fasten a massive yellow bow—80 feet by 30 feet with 180-foot streamers—to the face of the Superdome.

So you could see it from Mars.

Pete and Carrie:

He is 54. She is 43. They have been married almost eight years, the second marriage for both. He had one child. She had four. She was married to Ralph Cooke, son of Jack Kent Cooke, the owner of the Washington Redskins. The commissioner of the NFL is hired by the owners.

"So Pete was an employee of my father-in-law, if you will," Carrie says. "The circle is very curious."

Carrie says she was in the process of divorcing when she and Pete, both avid tennis players, were paired as doubles partners after Super Bowl VII in Los Angeles.

"I thought Pete was terrific," Carrie says. "It was instant on my part. I ran right after him."

She was born in Canada to a banking family. (She is still a Canadian citizen, though she promised Jack Kemp that if Ronald Reagan became president she would file for American citizenship.) The family had money and her father opted for becoming a college professor and told Carrie—the oldest of his three daughters—that it was important she have a profession. She spent a year in medical school, but dropped out and became a nurse instead. "I was never going to hack it," she says. "It wasn't the time to pioneer." She modeled off and on— she has the classic up-turned nose and slight overbite that produces a clean, wholesome look in magazines like Seventeen—then married.

He was born in California to the working class. He went to high school with Duke Snider, and they became close friends. What he really wanted to be was a sportswriter. But when he was a student at junior college, he began hanging around the L.A. Rams' training camp as a gofer for the team's publicity man and discovered he was a natural at P.R.

He did sports PR for the University of San Francisco while an undergraduate there, then PR for a brewery, then PR for the Rams and later became general manager of the Rams. In 1960, when he was just 33, the NFL, apparently in desperation on its 23rd ballot, named Rozelle as its commissioner. He was in the men's room washing his hands when Carroll Rosenbloom, who then owned the Baltimore Colts, came in to give him the news.

To say the league has prospered under his leadership is to say you can get wet under Niagara Falls. The league has grown from 12 to 28 teams, each of which makes $5.8 million a year from a television package worth $650 million over four years. In 1961, the Cleveland Browns were sold for $3.8 million. Today a franchise in the NFL—any franchise—is worth $35 million.

The league pays Rozelle $430,000 a year. There are some who say it's crumbs given his record.

They seem very much in love. They often hold hands when they walk, and one never leaves or enters their home in Harrison, N.Y., without a kiss from the other.

The day they married they vowed never to spend a night apart, and they never have. In fact, it is written into Pete's contract that Carrie goes wherever he goes. She drives him whenever he needs a car, and she does all his secretarial work on the road.

"My payoff," she says, "is that I'm married to him."

The Food Tasting:

Because she knows that people are looking at her and because she wants to look "as feminine and as stylish" as she can, Carrie Rozelle has brought different outfits for each of her public appearances. Today, for the ceremonial food-tasting of what will be served at the big NFL party, she is in a deep purple dress with thin gold earrings, a gold necklace, and gold bracelet. Gold becomes her, she wears it well. Some women don't. Some women wear so much of it they look like a branch office of an import-export firm.

"Carrie has great style, grace and personality," says Don Hewitt, producer of "60 Minutes." If you went to central casting for a commissioner's wife you'd come up with Carrie."

Accompanying her to the food-tasting—thinking all the while it would be an informal lunch—are some of her best friends: Joanne Kemp, Edie Wasserman and her husband, Lew, head of Universal and MCA, and Joan Tisch and her husband, Bob, head of the Loews Corporation. Notables.

As it turns out, more than 30 people including camera crews and reporters are waiting for them. Now *this* qualifies as hype, especially when the NFL man takes five full minutes to introduce the chef and all but invokes the memories of Washington and Lincoln in singing the praises of American cuisine.

Through it all, Carrie is cool.

She doesn't miss a name.

"Total recall," Joan Tisch says. "She's good at it, and she likes it."

As the chef leads her from course to course to course to course, explaining each one, she asks questions.

"How many avocados will you use?

"Is this a traditional New Orleans dish?

"Are the recipes available?

"What happens to leftovers?"

It is a small touch, but a nice touch. Rather than make the chef act like a trained seal, she has involved him in conversation and eliminated whatever tension he might have felt. It does not go unnoticed by Joanne Kemp, a politician's wife.

"She's a pro," Joanne Kemp says.

When it is all over, Carrie has taken just one bite of a main dish and one spoonful of a strawberry and whipped cream dessert, yet she has paid such attention to the contents in each of the 11 chafing dishes that it seems she surely tasted enough food to feed Bulgaria.

"I've known her for almost eight years now," says a friend of Rozelle, "and I've never seen her make a wrong move."

On her way out, Carrie Rozelle thanks everyone for coming.

The Reputation:

"He has no conscience, no point of view, no philosophy," says Ed Garvey, head of the NFL Players' Association. "His whole effort is public relations. If you ask about contractual negotiations with the players, he tells you to take it up with the management council, a body he created so he could stay above the real issues. If you ask him why there aren't more blacks in coaching or management, he says, 'Well, gee, golly, gosh, it's not because of anything I've done.' He's a disaster on the social issues, but when it comes to asking the press, 'How's the lobster Newburg?' he's terrific."

"He's a great salesman," says a writer and social friend of Rozelle. "You can't lay a glove on him. Each time you think you've got him, he comes up with another film, another angle you haven't seen."

"The world's greatest PR man," Al Davis has called him. Al Davis owns the Oakland Raiders and is, by the way, suing the NFL and Rozelle to move his team to Los Angeles.

P.R.

They're even his initials, thanks to an uncle who called him Pete rather than his given name, Alvin.

Good old Pete, slicker than Teflon.

"He's slick," Carrie says. "Of course, he's slick. He does his homework. He knows what he's talking about. That's slick. He is a PR man. That's how he started. And he's very good at it. And that's why, in part, the league has been so successful."

And courting the press? Providing millions of releases, mountains of worthless information, arranging tennis and golf tournaments, a 24-hour free bar, enough free food to fill the Taj Majal during Super Bowl week?

"He doesn't try to buy the press," Carrie says. "He

respects the press. He likes the press. Remember, he wanted to be a sportswriter."

P.R.

"I imagine it's my long suit," Rozelle says. Nothing to hide, nothing to get hung about. "Life, to a great extent, is public relations . . . my reaction to being classified as a PR man depends on how it's written. In defense of the inference, in 21 years on the job I've learned more than just public relations . . . I come to the floor on controversial issues, and I'm constantly in the role of authority. The general public could have no awareness that I'm really a sensitive person."

What it comes down to is the tone.

Do we mean "slick" as in "calculating and conniving?" Or "slick" as in "smooth, confident and without deceit?"

Given the choice, Rozelle chooses "smooth."

After you shake his hand, you don't have to count your fingers.

The Press Conference.

The Rozelles normally find Super Bowl Week tiring, but exhilarating and satisfying; this year Carrie was apprehensive.

The Davis Business.

Al Davis had not only become partner to a lawsuit threatening the NFL constitution and socialistic revenue-sharing that is the legacy of the Rozelle Era, but Davis has gone so far as to accuse Rozelle of personally scalping tickets, a low, common crime.

"It's been a long, tough year," Carrie was saying. "The business with Pete and the Raiders has been hanging over our heads and making us uncomfortable. Neither one of us has been sleeping well; Pete's getting up in the middle of the night, chain-smoking, pacing. I worry about his health. He's tired. You can see it in his face. He has deep circles under his eyes."

People who hadn't seen him in a year were saying the boyish commissioner was finally looking his age. The press conference, they said, would be a real test. Surely Rozelle would look out at so many Indians that if he wasn't 100 percent he might pull a Custer. The press conference is legendary among those who cover Super Bowls. It is conceded to be Rozelle's finest hour. "He's absolutely in command," said a writer who'd seen VIII of them. "He manages to be witty, charming and substantive. Watch him with the cigarettes, watch how he'll light one whenever he wants to buy time."

For almost two hours before, Rozelle huddles with his aides and attorneys, preparing for what will surely come. They fire questions, suggest responses.

When he takes the podium, he has his game face on.

He is in a light blue suit, and his eyes are crystal.

"Visine," Carrie says.

He lights a cigarette, puts it in an ashtray and looks out at more than 1,500 people.

O.K., shoot, he says.

As reporters raise their hands with questions, Rozelle often calls on them by name, as in, "Okay, Brent?" For years it has been part of his game plan to cultivate familiarity, and the first-name identification is a metaphoric arm around the shoulder of an old friend. It always scores points.

The first eight questions and 16 of the first 20 questions are about Davis, and Rozelle's answers are in effect a public deposition. His voice is strong, his manner authoritative, but his tone is nonthreatening. He never wavers, never ducks. He looks each questioner in the eye for the whole of the answer.

Somehow he manages to call the proposed move of the Raiders from Oakland "unconscionable" and Davis "an outlaw" without making a personal attack. And Rozelle's famed wit shows through when he is asked, "Where will Oakland be in eight months?" and he answers, "Across the bay from San Francisco unless the San Andreas fault interferes."

It goes on for 80 minutes.

He's breezing. Never lights a cigarette.

Then, probably from habit, he lights one before taking a question, and that question—not about Davis—is the last one.

"Anybody else?" Rozelle says.

No one.

"Thanks very much. I hope you had a good time."

Carrie has watched and listened attentively to all of it, and now she is smiling as her friends come up with their reviews.

"Marvelous," Lew Wasserman says.

"Super job," Joanne Kemp says.

"Politicians should be so candid," Jack Kemp says. Then, noticing a reporter scribbling, Kemp adds, "Well, some of us are."

Later, Rozelle will review his performance with the attorneys, but for now, he is pleased. "I think I hit the tone I wanted to project," he says, "one of candor and honesty. It's not just a slick hype. I knew I'd have to spend most of the time on the Raiders' situation, but I didn't want to take on Al. It's not between Al and me; it's between 27 owners and one owner."

It is pointed out that he lit only two cigarettes, took a total of three puffs.

"Don't tell Carrie," he says. "My God, she'll be all over me, insisting I can quit."

Laughing, he lights another.

The Game:

The commissioner's box is stocked with food and drink and good friends—the Kemps, the Tischs, the Wassermans, among others. There is a TV set inside and another outside, so you can see replays while facing the field. There are headsets with TV or radio feeds, and two telephones, one for the commissioner to call NFL control, the other for him to call NBC control. As command posts go, it is a little bit of Park Avenue.

Pete and Carrie arrive early, some two hours before game time; they take seats in the second row, immediately behind Jack and Joanne Kemp. It may be impossible for Pete Rozelle to root, but he can still talk football and who better to talk it with than Kemp?

Fifteen minutes to kickoff and Rozelle is on the phone. It's Don Weiss, the NFL executive director, calling.

Rozelle is beaming.

"The hostages are watching," he says. "'We just got word."

He looks up at the monitor.

The face he sees is his own.

He had taped an interview with NBC two days before, and he listens to the audio feed through the headset. "I'm mainly interested in how it appears I'm answering," he says. "I want to come across as candid and honest."

What surprises him is that his appearance is not followed by Davis. Instead, there is only a commentary piece on Davis by NBC's Pete Axthelm.

Though he shows no emotion while listening to the commentary—not even when it is reported that Davis had called him "corrupt"—he places a call to Weiss as soon as the segment ends.

"The only reason I agreed to the interview is because they said Davis was going on, too," Rozelle says. "I'd have preferred not to go on, but I'd have looked bad if I didn't."

Rozelle feels used.

"That burns me," he says.

As the game goes on, Rozelle continues to watch the field and listen to the feed. Carrie just watches. "I prefer the visuals," she says. It is especially hard on her not being able to root. "Awful, just awful," she says, "I like to yell and scream." She opens her hands to reveal two gold ear rings. "I sit there holding these like Captain Queeg," she says. "Sometimes I actually even sit on my hands."

By the middle of the third quarter it becomes obvious that Oakland is by far the superior team today and that Rozelle will have to present the Super Bowl trophy personally to Davis. The friends in the box—and they are good friends—say nothing about it, but it is clear they feel for him.

"He's prepared for it," Bob Tisch says. "He's set for it. I'm sure he'll handle it well."

Pete and Carrie watch the game quietly.

Often they look at each other and smile. If they share a joke, it is a private one.

With 5:30 left in Super Bowl XV Rozelle leaves his seat to confront the inevitable. "I'll point out that it's a tremendous organization," he says. "They did it the hard way," coming in as a wild-card team and having to win four games. "I'll credit Al for putting it together and Tom Flores for a great coaching job."

Nothing to get hung about.

"There might be some reaction from the players," Rozelle says. "But not from Al." On his way out the door he says, "The one thing I'm sure he won't say is that he's happy to win this one for the fans."

Then, cigarette in hand, he is gone.

Carrie watches it on TV. While the others crowd around the set inside the box, she sits facing the field, watching the monitor, listening through the headset.

She sees Pete graciously give the trophy.

She sees Davis graciously accept it.

And now, her Super Bowl done, Carrie Rozelle is alone with her thoughts and smiling.

Jerry Kramer is perhaps best remembered for the pile-driving block he laid on Jethro Pugh of the Cowboys to enable Bart Starr to sneak in for the touchdown that gave the Packers the NFL title for 1967 in the famous 13°-below-zero Ice Bowl in Green Bay. He is also known for writing one of the most popular books ever penned on the subject of pro football, in particular the Green Bay Packers of the dynastic years under Vince Lombardi, *Instant Replay,* from which this anecdotal excerpt is taken.

Summering in Wisconsin

—————— JERRY KRAMER (WITH DICK SCHAAP) ——————

JULY 15

I went to jail today, I started an eight-week sentence in Sensenbrenner Hall, which is a student dormitory at St. Norbert College in West De Pere, Wisconsin, a ten-minute drive from Lambeau Field in Green Bay. Eight weeks a year, since 1958, I've lived in this dormitory; I deserve an honorary degree from St. Norbert.

The whole thing is a pain in the ass. The worst part is that you're completely a captive of Lombardi and of football. It's not like you put in two hours in the morning, two in the afternoon, and two in the evening. You're required to attend breakfast at 7 A.M., ride in the bus over to the stadium, ride back in the bus, eat lunch, go over to the stadium and back again, dinner, meeting, curfew. If you're lucky, you get an hour and a half or two hours a day to do whatever you want.

I'm in Room 207, the same room I've had for five or six years, and now that Jimmy Taylor's gone, I'm rooming with Donny Chandler, a place-kicker for six months a year and an Oklahoma businessman for six months a year. Our room is neither spacious nor gracious. It is exactly like every other room, perfect for college sophomores, but adequate, barely adequate, for pro football players. Our beds are about six feet long and three feet wide. My head hangs over one end, my feet hang over the other, and my arms hang over both sides.

We each have a closet, a dresser and a desk, and everything is jammed. I've moved in a modest wardrobe, fifteen or twenty pairs of slacks, a dozen Bermuda shorts, two dozen sports shirts, and several pairs of shoes and sandals. I'm a little more clothes-conscious than most of the players, although the guys do care about clothes. We're in the public eye a lot, and we have to dress well.

The room is wired completely for sound. Donny brought in a portable television set and I brought in a stereo system and a dozen records. I've also got a handful of books and, most important, my cribbage board. Cribbage is the national pastime here; I usually support myself in the game.

For obvious reasons, we try not to spend too much time in the rooms, except for playing cribbage and sleeping. We do get our share of sleep. Curfew, which means in bed with lights out, is 11 P.M. six nights a week and midnight on Saturday. The married players whose families are in town are allowed to sleep at home Saturday nights, but my wife and our three children are out in Idaho, visiting relatives, so I have to sleep in the dorm every night. The curfews are strictly enforced; Lombardi runs this place like a penal institution.

I still remember Lombardi's first year, 1959, which was also the first year I roomed with Taylor. At eleven on the dot one night, Vince came by our room and Jimmy was sitting on the edge of his bed, with his socks and his shorts on.

Coach said, "Jimmy what time you got?"

Jimmy whipped out his watch and said, "I've got eleven o'clock, sir."

"Jimmy, you're supposed to be in bed at eleven, aren't you?" Coach said.

"Yes, sir," said Jimmy.

Coach said, "Jimmy, that'll cost you twenty-five dollars."

Jimmy looked at me open-mouthed and I raised my eyebrows a little bit and I said, "Ooh, this guy's pretty serious."

The next day, Ray Nitschke was in the phone booth two or three minutes after eleven and it cost him $50. (Our fines, incidentally, usually go to charities, like the St. Norbert building fund.) We began to believe right then that Lombardi was very, very serious about everything he said.

After about three weeks, a few of us decided we had to test Lombardi. Paul Hornung asked me if I wanted to sneak out of the dorm after curfew. It was very difficult talk me into it; it took Paul about three seconds. At 11:30 we began our big getaway. Paul's roommate, Max Mc-Gee, said he was going with us, and the three of us started sneaking down the hall.

"Wait," said Max, "Let's get Ringo."

Jim Ringo was our captain then, and we figured if he was with us and we got caught, we wouldn't get fined as much.

I said, "Great, get Ringo."

Ringo happened to be rooming with Dave Hanner, who is one of our coaches now, and Dave said that he had a psychological problem, that he couldn't sleep alone, so he joined us.

When the five of us passed Bill Quinlan's room, Quinlan woke up and said, "I'm going with you." Quinlan's roommate, Dan Currie, told us he was afraid of the dark; he came along, too.

Then there were seven of us crazy little creatures, running up to 280 pounds apiece, sneaking down the hall, tippy-toeing, our shoes in our hands. We made it outside, and, of course, we had no plans. We just wanted to sneak out to see if we could get away with it. We went to the local pizza parlor, and naturally

everyone in the town knows every Packer by sight and knows what time we're supposed to be in bed. We sat around eating pizza and giggling like schoolgirls till two or three in the morning. Then we snuck back in the dorm, and we thought everything was beautiful. No repercussions, no fines, nothing. Later, we discovered that Vince knew everything, knew exactly who had gone out and where we had gone and how late we had stayed; he was just holding back his fire until he could catch us in the act.

"People have been phoning me saying that they've seen some of you guys out after curfew," he announced, "but I don't pay any attention to those crank calls."

A few weeks later, Max McGee tried to sneak out alone, and Lombardi caught him, and the following day, at a team meeting, where we try to bring everything out in the open, Lombardi said, "Max, that'll cost you $125. If I catch you again, it'll cost $250."

Perhaps a year or two went by before Max got caught again. And again we had a meeting, and again the emotion, the wrath, the screaming, the hollering, a typical Lombardi production. "Max," Vince shouted, "that'll cost you $250. If you go again, it'll cost you $500."

Max doesn't scare easily.

Another year passed, and Max, a shrewd Texan who loves life, got away with a few. Then one night he snuck out and the Wisconsin state police, who are strict around here, caught him speeding. Max promised them the world if they would keep the ticket out of the newspapers, but they didn't. When the item appeared, Max could hear Coach Lombardi screaming from the training room clear to the dorm: "MAX! MAX!"

The inevitable meeting followed. "MAX!" Vince said. "That's $500." Coach was really shaking; he was very, very upset. He seemed to be fighting a losing battle, and Lombardi does not like to lose at anything. "MAX!" he yelled, "I said that'll cost you $500 and—" Vince turned purple "—If you go again, it'll cost you a thousand." The room was totally silent, hushed. Lombardi stopped shaking and actually managed to grin a little. "Max," he said, softly, "if you can find anything worth sneaking out for, for $1,000, hell, call me and I'll go with you."

Big Daddy Lipscomb, the monstrous tackle for the Rams, Colts and Steelers in the 1950s and early 60s, died at the age of 32 in 1963, the result of acute heroin poisoning, a case that remains highly controversial to this day. This sensitive, penetrating tale of the tragedy of a young man from the slums of Detroit, feared on the field and doomed off it, written by Ed Linn, orginally appeared in the *Saturday Evening Post* in 1963. It was also honored in the book *Thirty Years of Best Sports Stories.*

The Sad End of Big Daddy

ED LINN

John Henry told the Captain,
"A man ain't nothin' but a man
And if I don't beat your steam drill down,
I'll die with a hammer in my hand.
Lawd, Lawd,
I'll die with a hammer in my hand."

John Henry, as any folk singer worthy of his union card can tell you, was a legendary Negro giant who hammered himself into the grave, gloriously, because he was unwilling to live in a world where the machine took the place of nature's muscle and sweat.

Eugene (Big Daddy) Lipscomb was a fun-loving Negro giant who really lived. He was so great and so colorful a football player that he had become almost legendary himself before he died, ingloriously, on May 10, 1963, at the age of 32. According to official records he died of acute heroin poisoning, accidentally, but by his own hand. Daddy lived grandly, but he died bad. Which proves again, one way or another, the world has its ways for grinding down the man of muscle and sweat.

I tell you something true as life,
And, Big Daddy, you better be believin';
You lay that needle down right now,
Or your friends will all be grievin';
You lay that needle down, boy,
Or your women will be grievin'.

What the official report omits is that none of Big Daddy's friends, none of the thousands who mobbed his funeral, is willing to believe that he could have stuck a needle into his vein of his own free will, even though the alternative is, if not unthinkable, certainly improbable and unprovable. "Whiskey and women, yes," they say to a man, "but drugs, never."

"I'm a B and B man," Daddy liked to boast. "Booze and broads." And his capacity to handle both was one of the wonders of the civilized world.

Big Daddy worked hard on a football field, and when the game was done, it was time to get around some and have a little fun. "Let's go out and get me a jug," he'd say. "Let's have a taste." A jug to Gene Lipscomb was a fifth of whiskey and he could throw down the fifth the way you or I would throw down a beer.

To no small extent, Gene made himself up. He got his nickname during his early years with the Los Angeles Rams when he was better known for rough, dirty playing than for ability. He took to calling everybody "Little Daddy," which—since he stood 6-feet-6 and weighed 285—was a sly way of inviting them to call him "Big Daddy" in return.

It wasn't until Baltimore bought him in 1956 for $100 on waivers that Eugene Lipscomb became "Big Daddy" for real. On the field he wore his uniform sloppily, his pants drooping, his shirttail flapping. He had tremendous speed for a man his size. He was so fast that he could beat almost any halfback in a 50-yard dash. Generally two or three rival linemen were given the assignment of keeping Big Daddy off the passer. The Cleveland Browns usually set four men to harass him. In Baltimore Big Daddy led the Colts to two successive championships.

One of Lipscomb's favorite tricks was to let a blocker make contact with him so that the ball carrier would be encouraged to skirt him. Then he'd flip the blocker away and run down the ball carrier. "Where you going, little man?" he'd say, as he clubbed his arms around him. "This is Big Daddy, and once Big D puts the clamps on you, you're dead."

His real delight, though, was to burst in, his shirttail flying, and flatten a passer.

> *Little passer, you better be nimble,*
> *Little passer, you better pray,*
> *'Cause if you get in Big Daddy's way,*
> *Tomorrow will be yo' burying day.*
> *Lawd, Lawd,*
> *Tomorrow will be yo' burying day.*

In case he hadn't made his presence known to everybody in the park, he'd linger for another moment to pick up the passer and carefully brush him off. And the smaller the passer, the longer Daddy would linger. With that sure instinct for the dramatic, he was the first professional lineman to take the play away from the backs and become a personality himself.

Off the field he dressed for effect, except here he was dressed not to maim but to kill. Well, when Big Daddy came swinging into a bar with that easy, dancing step of his, you could hardly keep from noticing him, what with a diamond ring on his little finger, a white silk shirt like a rock 'n' roll singer, a tie so red that it threw off heat, and alligator shoes that crawled right on his feet. And didn't Big D always look pretty grand in that small-brimmed hat with a feather in the band?

> *And Daddy would twist to that driving beat*
> *Till he danced those chicks right off their feet.*

"Gene didn't need to take drugs for kicks," his cousin Walt Chattman, himself a pro football player with the Philadelphia Eagles, says. "Being Big Daddy was all the kicks he ever needed."

His appetites were gargantuan and insatiable. A typical breakfast consisted of a dozen eggs and a pound of bacon, washed down by a pint of booze. Having learned to cook in the Marine Corps, he would make huge meals, run to the bathroom and throw up halfway through, then come back and finish off the food.

His fondness for variety in women cost him three marriages, as he freely admitted. His favorite story was about the time he passed underneath the room of one of his teammates, just before they were to play an exhibi-

tion game in Texas, and caught the echo of a soft and sibilant sigh. Daddy shot up the stairs with a mighty roar, while his teammate, showing quick reflexes, slammed shut the door and tossed the girl into the closet.

Well, now, Daddy went poking around, sniffing at the air until his eyes reached the keyhole and stopped right there. As he always said, and he didn't lie, "All I seen looking back at me was one big eye."

Big Daddy stepped back and Big Daddy was smiling. "Big Daddy is here," Big Daddy cried.

Well, Daddy had a lot of women chasing after him, a lot of the time, and he was never known to run the other way.

Drugs take away a man's appetite for liquor and women both, and that's one reason, his friends tell you, the official story of his death just can't be true.

What makes it even more ridiculous, they tell you, is that Gene had escaped from the streets of Detroit, at the age of 16, by joining the Marines. He never knew his father, who died in a CCC camp. When Gene was 11, a plain clothesman came to the house, put his arm around his shoulder, and told him his mother had been stabbed 47 times by a boy friend while she was waiting on a street corner for a bus. Gene was reared in Detroit by his maternal grandfather, who tried to keep him from running wild. Gene rarely talked about those early days, but he would occasionally tell how his grandfather had once tied him to a bedpost and whipped him as punishment for stealing the old man's whiskey. Even here, though, he would tell the story with affection, as if he were trying to show that someone had cared enough about him to go to all that trouble.

Signed out of the Marines by the Los Angeles Rams, he was one of the few pro football players without a college education, a condition that always bothered him. Still, he had a quick, if profane, wit, and after he became so famous and popular, under his magic "Big Daddy" cloak, he would grin and say, "When we're on a football field, man, I got a degree, too."

He knew what he had escaped from, and he had a peculiar, all-encompassing phrase for it: "the scum." The phrase, for him, covered the whole condition of the ghettoized Negro; the slum itself with its dirt and its crime, plus all of its human oozings—the junkies, the hustlers, the pimps, and the bums. He would walk through the worst sections of the cities with his closer friends and he would say, "Doesn't it make you feel great to be able to walk through here like a king, with your head held high?"

Buddy Young, the old Illinois All-American, who became Gene's tutor and conscience, says: "If somebody told me Lipscomb died in an automobile accident or in a fight over a woman, I'd believe it. If it had happened when he first came to Baltimore, a hoodlum and a thug, I'd have believed it. But Gene had grown out of hiding and had come face to face with reality. A man doesn't take away from himself the one thing he has to offer, his ability to play football. Football was his past, present, and future, and nobody knew that more than Gene. He knew what his image was, because he had made it himself. He wouldn't destroy that with drugs."

Gene was so jealous of that image that he quit the wrestling circuit when he was asked to become a villain. "That ain't Big Daddy," he said.

It has fallen to Buddy Young to protect that image and to protect it, curiously enough, against a man he has never seen, a man as different from himself as any other man could possible be.

Young, who is now a Baltimore radio executive, exudes good will and sincerity and, if the word isn't too embarrassing, goodness. He has the solidity and conservatism of the self-made man. He can use words and expressions which would sound unbearably pretentious coming from someone else. ("I was often reminding him of his responsibility as a professional football player to be conscious of his actions, of refraining from expressing himself with vituperativeness.")

Buddy Young made himself a sort of den father for a group of Baltimore players, including Daddy, tackle Jim Parker, wingback Lenny Moore, and defensive back Sherman Plunkett. Daddy lived with Plunkett in the tree-shaded, middle class Hanlon Park section of Ashburton, not far from Buddy Young's own home, although Daddy had been traded to Pittsburgh and Plunkett to San Diego of the American Football League.

But still, the Baltimore writers who were closest to Daddy knew he would grow uneasy around the businessmen Young tried to surround him with, and that, from time to time, he would feel the need to cut out to the "back of town" district where he felt more at home. It was at the Uptown Bar in the "back of town" that he first ran into Timothy Black, the man who saw Big Daddy die.

Timmy Black, 27, is a slim, sparrowy man who came to Baltimore from the South 17 years ago, his left leg withered from a boyhood attack of polio. Even more than Lipscomb and Young, he is a man of his time and his place. His place is in the slums Daddy escaped from. His time stretches back a hundred years.

He is, admittedly, a man who would do his best to get you liquor, women, or drugs according to your taste— the functions, he says, he served for Big Daddy. He has, he admits, been in jail, although he balks at revealing the charges. At first glance he seems to be a shy, mumbling, naïve man, soft of voice, quick with deference, apologies, and respect. He has a delicacy of language that leads him to refer to the women he has dealings with as "young ladies" and "lady friends."

"Daddy and I weren't friends," he says, correcting you quietly, as if he is a man who has accepted his curious uses in life. But people close to Timmy Black called him "Hap," and every now and then you see the features shift a little under the slight tilt of his summer straw hat, and you catch a fleeting glimpse of another man underneath, the man who has committed himself to whatever he has to be to survive in his jungle. He is, too, a man with a sick and pregnant wife. Four months ago he got himself on the assembly line of a bottling company, a job he still holds.

When Black tells the story of Big Daddy's death, he leaves the impression that it was Daddy who wouldn't let him alone. According to Black, Lipscomb first asked him to get him a "deck" of heroin about six months ago, right after the end of the football season. "No," Black says, not volunteering the information but only answering the question, "he didn't act like it was the first time."

From then on, says Black, Daddy was taking heroin on the average of three times a week, the last time only two or three days before his death. Once, Black says, Daddy even "shot" himself in his car. "All it takes is a whiskey cap to put the stuff in, and a match to boil it up."

Impossible, say Daddy's friends. "He would come to the house never less than three times a week," Young says. "Walk through the door—I can see him now bending his head to get through—and he'd always call out to my wife, 'Hello Sweetiecakes. Here's the Daddy.' He couldn't have walked in here and faced me, because I would have known it. He couldn't have lived with Plunkett, day in and day out, and not have him know."

Big Daddy's third wife, Cecilia, who lived only a block away from him, is equally incredulous. "He could never have put a needle in himself," she says. "He was terrified of pain. He got a splinter in the bottom of his foot one time, and the way he carried on you'd have thought he'd lost the leg. He wouldn't even let the dentist pull a tooth without my sitting in his lap. I saw him three or four times a week, and he never could hide too much from me. I could read him like a book.

Young last saw Lipscomb on Wednesday, May 8, a burning-hot morning two days before Daddy died.

Baltimore Colts coach Weeb Ewbank was once asked how his enormous defensive tackle, 290-pound Big Daddy Lipscomb, managed to be so successful in stopping the opponent's running game. "He tackles everybody," Ewbank replied, "and then throws them away until he comes to the one with the ball."

Daddy had come to see him at station WEBB and waited outside until Young got off the air. "He was in brown khaki pants and blue *sleeveless* sport shirt. It was one in which he had torn the sleeves off. His shirttail was out, and he was wearing a pair of—what would you call them?—shower shoes?"

Daddy wanted to tell Young he was going to drive to Pittsburgh on Friday morning to sign his contract. Daddy had never made more than $14,000 a year, and he intended to ask for a two-year contract at $15,000 a year, the figure he had always looked upon as the ultimate goal. He had called Buddy Parker, the Steelers' coach, to ask if he'd have trouble getting the raise. He also asked Dan Rooney, a Steelers publicity man, to send him $500 "to meet an insurance payment on my car," the first time he had ever asked the Steelers for an advance.

On Thursday morning he cashed the $500 check at the Union Trust Bank. "Besides the money from Pittsburgh," Buddy Young says, "he had $400 that I know of. He put $200 in his checking account and paid two small bills that came to $40. That means he went out on Thursday with more than $600 in his pocket. Find what happened to that and you'll know why Daddy is dead."

If there was one thing Gene liked as much as football it was pitching softball. He played in a doubleheader that evening, and, after the games were over, took a couple of the boys from his team to have some drinks. "When Daddy had a lot of money on him, he'd take his wallet and lock it in the trunk of his car. I talked to the players he was with that night, and before he went into the bar, he locked the wallet in the trunk."

Daddy had another odd habit. Before he was to go on a motor trip, he would always stay up all night. When they were leaving the bar, around 11 o'clock, he asked one of the softball players to double-date with him, but the man already had a date. "If only that guy had been free," Young says, "Daddy would be alive today."

Timmy Black, the sparrow, worked late that night at the bottling plant and didn't get home until eight. After dinner, as was his custom, he went to the Uptown Bar. "I was outside on the corner of Monroe and Edmondson most of the time," Black says. "A guy came by who lived on the next street to me, and I asked if he could drive me home. But he wasn't going home; he was going the other way. If I'd only went home like I asked to, I wouldn't be in the trouble I'm in today."

Around midnight, Black says, Daddy came by in his big yellow Cadillac convertible—there was another fellow with him—and called him over. "I had an idea he wanted heroin, figuring I might know where to get it, but he didn't say anything about it then, because he didn't want everybody to know."

As soon as Daddy dropped his passenger, presumably one of the softball players, he and Black headed out in search of heroin. Instead, Black says, they ran into two young ladies. Then they bought a six-pack of Country Club, a malt beverage, and took the girls to Black's apartment. At 3 A.M. the young ladies asked to be taken home. At some time after three o'clock, then, Daddy, according to Black, asked, "You still think you can get down?"

Black could try. "Daddy drove to Pennsylvania Avenue on 'The Block' [Baltimore's large strip-joint center]. We parked near the corner where we could be seen. There was a fellow right up the street in front of a restaurant, just a few yards away. Daddy gave me the money to get down for him and I bought a $12 bag." A "$12 bag" contains enough heroin for two or three users.

And now Daddy drove back to Black's apartment, at 434 North Brice Street, and from this point on all his movements take on that heavy finality that comes when you know in advance that all of the thoughtless, everyday actions are the last he will ever make.

North Brice Street is small and narrow, little wider than an alley, really, and less than 100 yards long. On either side of the street there is one low, flat continuous row of connected apartment houses, constructed of light brown brick. It is a neighborhood with a reputation second to none for teen-age addicts.

Black's apartment was on the second floor. Daddy walked up a single flight of stairs, so narrow that he must have filled it completely, like a big ship squeezed into a small berth. When he reached the top of the staircase, he was also in the apartment, the bathroom a step ahead, the kitchen ahead to the right.

It was a small kitchen, painted yellow, dominated by a large table against the near wall. Across from the table were a refrigerator and a small stove. At the head of the room, alongside the door leading to the back porch, was an old-fashioned radiator. Overhead hung a bare bulb. A man Daddy's size would have difficulty moving through the open space without bumping something.

It was in such an apartment that Gene Lipscomb lived out his early days in Detroit. It was as if, at the end, the "scum" had reached out to bring Daddy home.

The heroin was cooked up in a wine cap and sucked into a homemade syringe, with a piece of paper providing the neck where the needle and the syringe joined. Daddy, says Black, "shot" himself first and then handed the needle over to him so he could "shoot" himself, too.

Heroin is not a stimulant but a depressant. After the first shock it sends the user into a "nod," a sort of semiconscious daydream in which the user sees himself living out the life he would like to be leading. Black's first warning that something had gone wrong, he says, came when Daddy's lips began to vibrate rapidly. Little rivers of foam formed at the sides of his mouth. Black, roused by fear, went to the refrigerator for some ice to press on top of Daddy's head and underneath his testicles.

At this point, says Black, a third man, Robert Waters, came into the apartment, put a solution of salt water into the syringe, and shot it into Daddy's arm, an old-wives' antidote which possibly has some value, though not very much.

When Daddy still failed to come around, Black says, he told Waters to go out and phone for an ambulance. The call was made at about 7:15 A.M.

After Waters left, Black tried to revive Daddy by slapping him across the face. That only served to bring about the final indignity, as Daddy toppled off the chair and fell to the floor, face down upon the worn linoleum.

The police arrived first, followed shortly by an ambulance. Black handed the police Daddy's car keys and $73. "I knew the ambulance would take him away," Black explains, "and, you know, I took it out of his wallet to protect it."

Big Daddy Lipscomb was still breathing when he was carried out to the ambulance to be rushed to Lutheran Hospital. He was DOA—dead on arrival.

"We split the bag in half," Black insists. "I took the same half he did and it didn't kill me. But he was drinking in the bedroom with the young lady and I didn't know it. If I had known . . ."

It is true that alcohol "potentiates" the effect of drugs. But Daddy had not been drinking that much. The autopsy showed the alcoholic content of his blood to be .09 percent. Daddy's drinking through the years did have its effect, though. The autopsy showed that his liver was somewhat damaged. Since detoxification takes place in the liver, the heroin remained in his system longer than normal.

The autopsy was performed by the assistant medical examiner of Baltimore, Dr. Rudiger Breitnecker. As he explains, it is not the heroin itself that does the damage, because heroin breaks down immediately upon injection. One of the main degradation products is morphine, and morphine is the killer. Daddy had about 10 milligrams of morphine per 100 cubic centimeters of bile, which would correspond to 11.3 milligrams of heroin.

When morphine is used therapeutically, it would be rare for more than a two-milligram dosage to be prescribed. In other words, Daddy's body contained *more than five times* what might normally be considered a safe dosage. "Any dose would have a serious effect on a beginner," Dr. Breitnecker says, "but, speaking generally, 10 percent is a lethal amount. It would take a hardened addict to survive 10 percent."

The question that arises, of course, is whether there is any medical evidence that Daddy had ever taken drugs before. There isn't. A needle mark, as anyone who has ever taken a simple blood test knows, heals completely within a couple of days.

Doctor Breitnecker did find "at least" four needle marks that were only two to four hours old. ("If that's true," Black says, "then three of them would have to be the salt-water injections. He only took one shot of heroin.")

In the course of the autopsy, Dr. Breitnecker also took one very small, very thick slice of skin from the inside of the elbow and, by the use of dyes and high magnification, came across an old needle mark, which was still identifiable only because a small fiber, which seemed to be cotton, was lodged in the puncture. Most addicts filter the cooked solution through cotton or bread as they suck it up into the syringe. Still, one needle mark is just like any other, and no man would be foolish enough to state that a piece of fiber couldn't have become lodged in any hypodermic needle, used for any kind of shot.

And so, while nothing Black says is inconsistent with the findings of the autopsy, it is also true that nothing Daddy's friends say is inconsistent, either. "There is hardly evidence to call him an addict," Dr. Breitnecker says. "We cannot, as a matter of fact, say positively that he ever took more than one shot of heroin in his life." The diagnosis, for the record, is that he died of acute heroin poisoning.

The key question, in the fight to save Daddy's reputation, is whether he could have been knocked out before the heroin was put into his system. To this, at least, Dr. Breitnecker can give a flat reply. "My answer to these attempts by a loyal public to explain away the fact that Big Daddy did take heroin, at this time, of his own free will, is that our tests showed he was not under any sedative, that he was not intoxicated, and that there was not a scratch on him of any kind."

But Daddy's defenders still make out their case. Robby Waters is hardly the passing stranger Black tried, at first, to make him out to be. In their statement to the police, the two young ladies had Waters getting into Lipscomb's car, taking the wheel to drive them to the apartment, and then returning from time to time while they were still there.

What gripes Daddy's friends is that there is only Black's story of the last hours. "Who is this man Black?" Buddy Young asks. "None of Daddy's friends ever saw him or heard of him."

Black was held, at first, on a charge of involuntary homicide, but it was quickly changed to mere possession of narcotics paraphernalia. The original bail of $10,000 was reduced to $3,000.

Black is not an addict. He has not used any narcotics, he insists, since the night of Daddy's death. He is a married man and he has a job. There seems little doubt that when his case comes to court he will be placed on probation.

Black faces the unasked question in his own indirect way. "I was the one who told Robby Waters to call the ambulance," he says. "I didn't want to take Daddy out and throw him in an alley. Right today you pick up the paper and find they die on steps or in an alley. I was frightened. Seeing that happen to Daddy was the worst thing that ever happened to me. I liked Big Daddy."

To which Buddy Young replies, "Nobody knows what happened in that room before the police were called. Nobody knows who was in the room or how long it took to call the police.

"Gene Lipscomb had a soul, he had a faith, and I'd walk with him all the rest of my life without believing that he was an addict. I know you can never tell what a person will do, but Daddy wasn't Marilyn Monroe out to commit suicide. He was at the summit of his career, he had come to the place he wanted to be. He knew how big he was."

And then, Buddy Young smiled, and the legend of Big Daddy had taken over again. "He'd have liked to have seen the crowd he drew at his funeral. I could hear him saying, 'See, Young, See, Little Man. You never knew how big Big Daddy really was, did you?' "

> *Don't weep for me, Little Daddy,*
> *Don't bother with no prayer;*
> *I don't want to go to heaven*
> *Unless they swing up there.*
> *Don't take me up to heaven, please, Lawd,*
> *'Less there's kicks and chicks up there.*

Vince Lombardi got his first head coaching job in the NFL in 1959 when he moved from the staff of the New York Giants to Green Bay. In two seasons, he transformed a team that had not had a winning season in 11 years and who were 1–10–1 the year before into an instant winner. In nine years he brought the Packers five NFL titles and nine winning seasons, and forged a legend for himself in the coaching ranks of the NFL. A taskmaster of monumental proportion, Lombardi *ruled* the Packers up in Wisconsin; as end Max McGee once put it: "When he says sit down, I don't even bother to look for a chair." In 1963, he drafted a diary of a book called *Run to Daylight*. The following chronicle of a Monday morning in his life after a crucial game is taken from that book.

Thoughts on a Monday Morning

———— VINCE LOMBARDI (WITH W. C. HEINZ) ————

MONDAY

3:15 A.M.

I have been asleep for three hours and, suddenly, I am awake. I am wide awake, and that's the trouble with this game. Just twelve hours ago I walked off that field, and we had beaten the Bears 49 to 0. Now I should be sleeping the satisfied sleep of the contented but I am lying here awake, wide awake, seeing myself walking across that field, seeing myself searching in the crowd for George Halas but really hoping that I would not find him.

All week long there builds up inside of you a competitive animosity toward that other man, that counterpart across the field. All week long he is the symbol, the epitome, of what you must defeat and then, when it is over, when you have looked up to that man for as long as I have looked up to George Halas, you cannot help but be disturbed by a score like this. You know he brought a team in here hurt by key injuries and that this

was just one of those days, but you can't apologize. You can't apologize for a score. It is up there on that board and nothing can change it now. I can just hope, lying here awake in the middle of the night, that after all those years he has had in this league—and he has had forty-two of them—these things no longer affect him as they still affect me. I can just hope that I am making more of this than he is, and now I see myself, unable to find him in the crowd and walking up that ramp and into our dressing room, now searching instead for something that will bring my own team back to earth.

"All right!" I said. "Let me have your attention. That was a good effort, a fine effort. That's the way to play this game, but remember this. You beat the Bears, but you know as well as I do that they weren't ready. They had key personnel hurt and they weren't up for this game. Those people who are coming in here next week will be up. They won again today, so they're just as undefeated as we are. They'll be coming in here to knock your teeth down your throats, so remember that. Have your fun tonight and tomorrow, but remember that."

"Right, coach!" someone behind me, maybe Fuzzy Thurston or Jerry Kramer or Ray Nitschke, shouted. "Way to talk, coach!"

Am I right and is that the way to talk, or has this become a game for madmen and am I one of them? Any day that you score seven touchdowns in this league and turn in a shutout should be a day of celebration. Even when the Bears are without Bill George, who is the key to their defense, and Willie Galimore, who is their speed, this is a major accomplishment. But where is the elation?

Once there was elation. In 1959, in the first game I ever coached here, that I ever head-coached anywhere in pro ball, we beat these Bears 9 to 6 and I can remember it clearly. I can remember them leading us into the last period and then Jimmy Taylor going in from the 5 on our 28-Weak, and Paul Hornung kicking the point, and then Dave Hanner breaking through on the blitz and nailing Ed Brown in the end zone for the safety. The year before, this team had won only one game and tied one out of twelve, so now they were carrying me off the field because a single league victory was once cause enough for celebration.

What success does to you. It is like a habit-forming drug that, in victory, saps your elation and, in defeat, deepens your despair. Once you have sampled it you are hooked, and now I lie in bed, not sleeping the sleep of the victor but wide awake, seeing the other people who are coming in next Sunday with the best defensive line in the league, with that great middle linebacker, that left defensive halfback who is as quick and agile as a cat and a quarterback who, although he is not as daring as Johnny Unitas or Y. A. Tittle or Bobby Layne, can kill you with his consistency.

I don't see them as I do from the sideline, but as I have seen them over and over in the films. I see them beating us 17–13 in our opener in Milwaukee in 1961. I see them beating us 23–10 in their own park the year before, and that's what I mean about success. My mind does not dwell on the two games we beat them in 1959, or the single games we took from them in 1960 and again in 1961. For the most part you remember only your losses, and it reminds me again of Earl Blaik and West Point after Navy beat our undefeated Army team 14–2 in 1950.

"All right," the Colonel would say whenever there was a lull. "Let's get out that Navy film."

You could see the other coaches sneak looks at one another, and although you couldn't hear the groans you could feel them in the room. Then we'd all file out and into the projection room once more.

"Look at that," the Colonel would say. "The fullback missed the block on that end."

How many times we had seen that fullback miss that block on that end I do not know. I do know that every time we saw that film Navy beat Army again, 14–2, and that was one of the ways Earl Blaik, the greatest coach I have ever known, paid for what he was.

So what I see now is that opener in '61, the last time they beat us. I see them stopping us twice inside their 5-yard line. I see us running their quarterback out of his pocket, the rhythm of that pass play broken, and both their split end and Jesse Whittenton relax. I see that end start up and Whittenton slip and that end catch it and run it to the 1, and on the next play their fullback takes it in. Then I see them on our 13-yard line and their fullback misses his block and falls. As he gets up, their quarterback, in desperation, flips the ball to him and he walks the 13 yards for the score.

Lying there like this, in the stillness of my house and conscious of any sound and every sensation. I am aware now of the soreness of my gums. It is this way every Monday, because for those two hours on the sideline every Sunday I have been grinding my teeth, and when I get up at eight o'clock and put in my bridge I'll be aware of it again. That, come to think of it, is only fitting and proper because that bridge had its beginnings in the St. Mary's game my junior year at Fordham. Early in that game I must have caught an elbow or forearm or fist, because I remember sitting in that Polo Grounds dressing room during halftime and it felt like every tooth in my head was loose.

8:52 A.M.

I'm in the line of traffic now, and I guess what it comes down to is that success demands singleness of purpose. In this game we're always looking for catch-phrases, especially with a connotation of masculinity, so I call it mental toughness. They have written about the mental toughness with which I supposedly have instilled this team and, when they ask me what it is, I have difficulty explaining it. I think it is singleness of purpose and, once you have agreed upon the price that you and your family must pay for success, it enables you to forget that price. It enables you to ignore the minor hurts, the opponent's pressure and the temporary failures, and I remember my first year here. I remember that first day of full practice in training camp, and when I walked back to the dressing room I wanted to cry. [The lackadaisical ineptitude, almost passive resistance, was like an insidious disease that had infected almost a whole squad.] The next morning, when I walked into the trainer's room, there must have been fifteen or twenty of them waiting for the whirlpool bath or the diathermy or for rubdowns.

"What is this?" I said. "An emergency casualty ward? Now get this straight. When you're hurt you have every right to be in here. When you're hurt you'll get the best medical attention we can provide. We've got too much money invested in you to think otherwise, but this has got to stop. This is disgraceful. I have no patience with the small hurts that are bothering most of you. You're going to have to learn to live with small hurts and play with small hurts if you're going to play for me. Now I don't want to see anything like this again.''

Then I walked out. The next day when I walked into that room there weren't fifteen or twenty in there. There were two, so maybe that's how you do it.

8:56 A.M.

There is a traffic light at the corner of Monroe and Mason and I stop behind a line of cars in the left lane. When that left-turn arrow turns green, and if everyone moves promptly, six cars can make that turn. Six days a week this traffic light is the one thing that invades my consciousness as I drive to work, that consistently interrupts that single purpose of winning next Sunday's game.

I tried to plant that seed of single purpose in the first squad letter I wrote before training camp that first year. I must have rewritten it ten or twelve times, trying to tell them what I hoped to do and how I hoped to do it without making it sound like I was setting up a slave labor camp.

That summer, as every summer, the first-year men, which is what I call the rookies because I think it implies more respect, came into camp at St. Norbert College, just up the Fox River from here. They arrived three days before the veterans were due, but a half dozen of the veterans came with them. Then two of these veterans, two of my stars, took off on a frolic and I didn't see them again until I collared them in the hall on the third day.

"What do you think we're running here?" I hollered at them. "Just a home base where you can pick up your mail between social engagements? When you came into this camp, no matter how early, it was expected that you came here to work. . . ."

I've got all the emotions in excess and a hair-trigger controls them. I anger and I laugh and I cry quickly, and so I couldn't have told you five minutes later what else I said or just what I did. I have heard it told that I had one of them by his lapels and that it looked like I was going to bang his head against the wall. They say you could hear it all over Sensenbrenner Hall, and that after it was over the two of them walked into somebody's room and one of them said, "I'm not gonna play for this—. He's a madman."

An hour later I was leaving the dormitory to walk across the campus to the science building for the first full squad meeting. They say I caught up with one of the two

and slapped him on the back and said, "C'mon, let's go to that meeting.'' It's possible, because as fast as I heat up I cool off.

"And there's nothing personal about any of this," I was telling them all a few minutes later. "Any criticism I make of anyone, I make only because he's a ballplayer not playing up to his potential. Any fine I levy on anyone, I levy because he's hurting not only himself but thirty-five other men."

They were big men wedged into those varnished oak classroom chairs with the writing arms on the right. They were wearing shorts and slacks and short-sleeved sport shirts, and I went into the regulations and my system of fines because big as they are, sports-page heroes though they may be, there is an almost adolescent impulsiveness in many of them.

Paul Hornung, Golden Boy of Notre Dame and Green Bay and Vince Lombardi's Hall of Fame halfback, often told this story about his coach: "One night, after a long, cold, difficult day, Lombardi came home late and tumbled into bed.

" 'God,' his wife said, 'your feet are cold.'

"And he answered, 'Around the house, dear, you can call me Vince.' "

This is something that the abandon with which football must be played encourages. Beyond that, and for as long as most of them can remember, which would be back to their first days in grade school, they have been subject to regulation. As their athletic ability turned them into privileged high school and college celebrities, many of them became masters at the art of circumvention.

I remember the two at the Giant camp at Winooski, Vermont, who climbed the fire escape after curfew but picked the wrong window and became entangled in the venetian blinds in the room of Doc Sweeny, the Giant trainer. I remember the defensive end who was tiptoeing down the hall one night, his shoes in his hand, when Jim Lee Howell, who was coaching the Giants then, surprised him.

"You going somewhere?" Jim said.

"Why, yes," the end said, and you had to grade him high on his speed of reaction. "I lost my wallet, so I thought I'd go out and try to find it."

"I see," Jim said, looking at the shoes. "You planning to sneak up on it?"

So in that first meeting I gave them the camp curfew: in bed and lights out by eleven o'clock, midnight on Saturdays. Any breaking of that curfew would cost the player $500. Any player late for a meeting or practice would be fined $10 a minute, and any of them caught standing at a bar would be knicked for $150. Then I took a little off it by telling them to appoint an Executive Committee, empowered to discuss any fines or any grievances with me, and I said that all money collected would go into a team fund. With it the team could throw a party, at a proper time, or put it to any other use that they preferred, with the restriction that none of it was to be returned to any fined player.

"Now I've already told you," I said, "the names of the places that are off-limits in town. When we travel you'll be given the names of all off-limits spots in every city. If you're found in one of those places you won't be fined. You'll be off the ball club."

I was reaching them where I knew I could hurt them—in their pocketbooks—but a week later I caught the first one. I hit him for $500, and when the Executive Committee came to me, protesting that it was too stiff. I told them that if we didn't set an example none of our regulations would be worth anything, and I told them to talk it over again.

"We've talked it over," they said when they came back, "and we agree the fine should stand."

But the game goes on. I would be naive to believe that we can keep every one of thirty-six healthy, adventuresome males confined for eight weeks with only an hour and a half off six days a week and five hours off on Saturdays. Every year there are three or four who try me, and every year there are three or four who get knicked, and I can tell you beforehand who they'll be and just about when they'll make their tries.

So our five coaches and our personnel director pair off and stand the watches. The first week of camp the heroes are muscle sore and body weary, but a half hour after curfew on the second Saturday one of them walks down the hall from his room and stands in the open doorway of the office. He is wearing undershorts and shower clogs and he waits, like a small boy, for the coaches to look up.

"You want something?" one of them says.

"Yes," he says. "May I get a drink of water?"

"Why not?" the coach says.

"Thank you," he says.

They listen to the sound of the shower clogs on the hard floor of the hall. They hear the clink of the coin in the pay phone.

"He just dropped a dime in the water fountain," one of them says. "He's going tonight."

"And I know who's going with him," the other coach says.

They hear the shower clogs coming back and they watch him pass the door. They go to bed and one of them gets up at 2 A.M. and checks the room, and our

parched hero, who stood there like that small boy and asked for that drink of water, and his roommate are both gone.

"I've got to go tonight," another finally announces to his associates every year. "I've just got to try him."

So he tries me, some of his clothes and some towels rolled up to bulk like his body under the covers of the bed, and I knick him. It's a game, and in my struggle to understand it I am reminded of something Lou Little once said about his Columbia football players to Frank Graham, the New York sports columnist.

"When I see them on the field they look like gladiators," Lou said, "but when I see them off the field they're just kids."

9:15 A.M.

I have looked through the sports pages and I see that Paul Dudley, who was a fourth draft pick for us and one of our first-year men this year, scored his first touchdown for the Giants. He couldn't break into our backfield but he's got good speed and fine moves and he's rugged enough and he's a good one, and every time you trade off one of those, because you happen to be deep at the moment, you wonder if you're not making a mistake, if he might be even better than you think and you'll be haunted by him for years. This year they're haunting Paul Brown for having traded Bobby Mitchell, but it could happen to me.

In the stories about our game with the Bears the papers all say the same thing, each in their own words. We're "power-packed" and "precision-timed" or "all-powerful" or "indestructible." They don't overlook that the Bears were hurt coming in, but that 49–0 score in the big black numbers in the headlines makes us look better than we are and I wish we had a couple of those touchdowns in the bank for this week.

9:20 A.M.

Bud Lea of the *Milwaukee Sentinel* and Gene Hintz of United Press International come in, and I have been told that any time a sportswriter asks me a question I almost visibly flinch. . . .

"Tom Moore has a muscle pull in his shoulder," I say, "and Hornung pulled a groin muscle. I think they'll be in shape, but I don't know."

It's an odd thing about that Moore. He was the first ballplayer I ever drafted for the Packers. He was our number one draft choice in 1960 and I've never regretted it. He's got good size and speed and power, and in his first year scored five touchdowns and caught five passes and led the league in kickoff returns. I have had to play him behind Jim Taylor at fullback, or Hornung at halfback, and the odd thing is that, when one or the other is hurt and I send in Moore, he gets banged up, too. He is an upright runner, and I wouldn't change that for a minute because it's his way of going, but I've got to get him to button up as he gets hit, which is something that Taylor does instinctively and Hornung has mastered. You can't go in there upright in this league without getting racked.

"If I know Paul Hornung," Bud Lea says, "he'll be ready, if it's possible."

If I, too, know Paul Hornung he'll be ready because this is one of those great money ballplayers, but he was in the army for nine months, seven of them after the season ended. From June into the third week in July the newspapers were carrying rumors of when he would get out, and finally, one evening of our second week in camp he showed up and I saw him getting out of his car in front of Sensenbrenner Hall.

It was dark by then and he walked over into the light from the doorway. You have to know what Paul Hornung means to this team to read all the meaning into the searching inspection I was giving him. I have heard and read that Paul Hornung is not a great runner or a great passer or a great field-goal kicker, although no one can fault him as a great blocker, but he led the league in scoring for three seasons; in 1960 he broke Don Hutson's all-time league seasonal scoring record with 176 points and he was twice voted the league's outstanding player. What it comes down to is that in the middle of the field he may be only slightly better than an average ballplayer, but inside that 20-yard line he is one of the greatest I've ever seen. He smells that goal line. Henry Jordan, our defensive right tackle expressed what Hornung means to our team when he said, "Before our 1961 championship game I was under the impression that Moore could run as well as Hornung and that Ben Agajanian could kick as well or better, but the week before the game, when Paul got that leave from the army and walked into that locker room, you could just feel the confidence grow in that room."

We were shaking hands now in the light from that doorway, and he had on dark gray slacks and a T-shirt. He is not a Spartan liver and there were those months in the army and I was looking for fat.

"What do you weigh?" I said.

"Oh, about 222," he said. "I'm only about seven pounds over."

"Good," I said, and that's what I thought. He checked in then and for four or five days on that practice field I watched him building himself back in shape. Late in practice on the fifth or sixth day just before sending them in, we lined up our kickoff team against our receiving team. They were all in shorts and T-shirts, just to run through it and to reacquaint them with their as-

signments after seven months, and Paul, in a sweatsuit, was the deep man to the right in the end zone.

"Watch this," someone on the sideline said. "Aggie will kick it to Hornung to make him run."

Agajanian was in camp to work with our kickers, and he booted it to Paul, who took it about 5 yards deep in the end zone. He tucked it in and started out and was great for the first 15 yards. At the 20-yard line he was absolutely coming apart. He was trying to get his knees up and the effort was almost bending him over backward and he looked like he was a participant in a potato race at an Elks picnic.

"All the way!" I was shouting at him. "Run it all the way to that goal line!"

On the sideline now some of the other players were cat-calling and whistling at Paul Hornung. Watching him, barely able to run, all I could think was: Can this be the famous "Golden Boy"? Can this be the most valuable player in the National Football League, the most publicized ballplayer in pro football, that runner, blocker, kicker and great competitor on whom so much depends if we are going to hold on to that title? And I closed practice.

"Well," I said to him, walking off the field, "I guess you got the news."

"I got it," he said, trying to get his breath, the sweat running off his face.

"That was ludicrous," I said. "That was absurd. What the blast have you been doing with yourself?"

"I don't know," he said. "I don't know."

This is a man with great pride, I knew, and he loves this game, and that would have to be the saver. When the Packers drafted him in 1957 he was All-America at Notre Dame for two years and the Heisman Trophy winner his last year and he came here preceded by all that publicity. They tried him at quarterback and then fullback, and like many a great college star who does not make it big with the pros he fell into that what's-it-to-you attitude that they erect as a defensive perimeter around their egos.

When I joined this club in 1959 Paul Hornung was more celebrated for his reputed exploits off the field than on, but after the months I had spent studying the movies of Packer games I knew that one of the ballplayers I needed was Paul Hornung. With those I could take into my confidence I investigated meticulously that reputation and I found that, although Paul Hornung had given the gossips cause, their malicious imaginations had taken it the rest of the way, and the first talk I ever had with him was right here in this office and it was about that reputation.

"If that's the way they want to think," he said, "that's the way they'll think."

I liked the way he looked me right smack in the eye

and I found that, while you have to whip him a little, he is no malingerer. This is a good-looking, intelligent and charming celebrity whom I can't expect to lead the life of a monk, but he is also a dedicated ballplayer who, pre-season, will run up and down those steep steps of City Stadium to get his legs in shape—and we'll need him this Sunday.

10:12 A.M.

I drive one block out South Washington Street and turn right over the Mason Street Bridge. The weather is still good, but there is a slight haze over everything now. Yesterday it was so clear that the sky was like a blue bowl over the stadium. It will not surprise me if we get rain for this next one, and I doubt that anyone in this league ever wants rain. We all draw our plays on dry paper and we count on the ability of our backs and our receivers to make their cuts on a dry field. I don't think that there is a mud-thinker among us, because we all have to conceive of this game as it should be played.

As I turn onto Oneida Avenue, the two practice fields, the camera tower between them, are on the left, the low green bleachers, empty now, along the avenue, and the stadium are on the right atop the rise of the vacant parking fields. For every hour of game play that we put in at that stadium and at the others around the league, we put in fourteen on those fields. That is pre-season and during the season, and then there are those equal hours spent in those meetings, and all of this does not include the time we coaches spend in preparation for those practice sessions and those meetings, and that time seems to me to be almost incalculable.

I see my coaches' cars and maybe a half dozen others parked outside now, and I walk through the empty dressing room and into the trainer's room. Tom Moore is sitting on one of the rubbing tables, stripped to the waist, and Bud Jorgensen, our trainer, is using the diathermy on Moore's shoulder.

"How does it feel?" I say.

"Not so good," Moore says. "It's pretty sore right now."

"Will he be all right?" I say to Jorgensen.

"I think so," he says.

"How about Hornung?" I say. "Is he in yet?"

"No," Jorgensen says. "He'll be in later. The pull isn't in the groin, it's inside the thigh."

Every week there are the injuries. It is foolish to think that, the way this game is played, you can escape them, but every week I feel that same annoyance, and I need Hornung and I need Moore if we are going to beat these people. . . .

He's not big for a fullback [Jim Taylor]—6 feet and 212 pounds—but he is so sincere in that all-year muscle-building program of his that when you bump against him it's like bumping into a cast-iron statue. Nothing gives, and he has developed those neck muscles to the point where, when he wants to turn his head, he has to turn his whole upper body.

"What's the matter with you?" I said to him on the practice field the other day when he couldn't turn for the ball on that very play. "Can't you twist your head?"

"You just can't make a greyhound out of a bulldog, coach," he said.

And he is a bulldog. Your fullback must be big enough to make the tough yardage, have enough speed to go the distance when you break him into the clear and he should, as should all backs, have that real quick start. He should be a great blocker, because he is that remaining back on passes, when the center and the fullback pick up the red-doggers. He must have good enough hands to go out on pass routes, too, because if he hasn't it won't be long before the other defenses learn to ignore him as they do some fullbacks.

In an open field our James is something else again. I think that when he sees a clear field ahead he hunts down somebody to run into, and while you have to enjoy body contact to play this game, Jimmy exults in it. After one of our 1960 games with the Bears I made him watch himself on the film going out of the way to run over Charlie Sumner, who was then their weak-side safety.

"What were you trying to do out there?" I said.

"You gotta sting 'em a little, coach," Jimmy said. "You know you've gotta make those tacklers respect you."

They respect him. In fact, every time he carries the ball there are eleven of them, all of whom want to pay their respects to him personally, and in our game with the Rams in 1961 in Los Angeles I remember four of them nailing him right in front of the Rams' bench.

"How to go, you guys!" they tell me Jimmy said when he jumped up. "That's the way to play this game!"

Now, if I could just get him to block with the same abandon, he might be the best in the business. He is not a bad blocker, but he would be a great one with his ruggedness, his quickness and his agility, if they would just change the rules to let him carry a football while he's blocking. . . .

Bart's too tense, I'm thinking. I noticed it last week and the week before, and I can understand it because there is no one on this team who is more conscientious and dedicated than Bart Starr. By the nature of his position your quarterback is your number one man, and we are the champions and I know that Bart feels that he has the whole burden of our offense on his shoulders and I will have to try to relax him.

When I joined this team the opinion around here and in the league was that Starr would never make it. They said he couldn't throw well enough and wasn't tough enough, that he had no confidence in himself and that no one had confidence in him. He was a top student at Alabama so they said he was smart enough, and after looking at the movies that first pre-season I came to the conclusion that he did have the ability—the arm, the ball-handling techniques and the intelligence—but what he needed was confidence.

He is the son of a regular army master sergeant and he grew up on army posts and air force bases and he still calls me "sir." When I first met him he struck me as so polite and so self-effacing that I wondered if maybe he wasn't too nice a boy to be the authoritarian leader that your quarterback must be.

He impressed me getting ready for our first pre-season game in 1959. At our quarterback meetings, even though he was not first-string, he could repeat almost verbatim everything we had discussed the previous three days, and that meant he had a great memory, dedication and desire. He is also a great student of the game, always borrowing movies from our film library during the sea-

son and between seasons, to take them home and study them over and over, and with our success and his own success I have seen his confidence grow.

"A couple of years ago," he said to me the day last summer when he brought his contract into the office, "I'd have signed anything you gave me, but now you've taught me to be more aggressive and self-assertive and you've given me more confidence, and this is what I want."

"So that's it," I said. "Like Frankenstein, I've created a monster."

He's tough enough on that field, too. In 1961 he played the first half of the season with a torn stomach muscle, and for three games he kept it from me. He was throwing so poorly to one side that I was trying to change his feet and do anything else I could think of until the trainer told me. He has licked himself and he has licked public opinion. It's just that when you combine sincerity with sensitivity and intelligence the individual tends to be tense, and I'll have to find the right time this week to try somehow to relax him.

In the modern world of professional football, agents are as ubiquitous as waterboys were in the fledgling years of the NFL. The reasons: big dollars, big deals, annuities, incentive clauses, signing bonuses, and deferred income. Each player is today a big business unto himself and, of course, his agent. Who are these artful negotiators, crafty manipulators of money, friends to the players, foes to management? Douglas S. Looney, a senior writer for *Sports Illustrated,* sought out one of them, Jack Mills (whose business address is not, as one might think, in the canyon of Wall Street, but in the shadow of the Colorado Rockies), in order to find out just what kind of a 1987 day an agent puts in at the old office.

Jack Be Nimble: A Day in the Life of an Agent

——— DOUGLAS S. LOONEY ———

A DAY IN the life of sports agent Jack Mills, 49, of Boulder, Colo., is one of ringing telephones and negotiations that are at once high-powered and low-keyed. Mills deals mostly with football players and their teams, and he's always polite, always at ease.

He walks into his third-floor office in the morning and looks out on the glories of the front range of the Rockies. The pigeons on the balcony coo, and he likes that. He throws his coat over a chair. This is a casual man not given to flashiness. In a recent family portrait he and everyone else wore brown.

Mills passes the autographed pictures of clients past and present—Randy Gradishar, George Rogers, Eric Dickerson, Dean Steinkuhler, Irving Fryar—and sits at his desk, which is awash in pink phone messages. The phone is ringing. He leans back and takes his first call of the day, from Kansas City Chiefs general manager Jim Schaaf. It's 9:02, and Schaaf wants to talk about Christian Okoye, the Chiefs' second-round draft pick, from Nigeria via Azusa Pacific University. Okoye, a 253-pound running back, fumbled 26 times in 28 games, but

Mills is quick to point out to Schaaf that "only nine were in his senior year.

"He's another Earl Campbell, only faster," says Mills, who is not above hyperbole. He and Schaaf spar. "You got anyone signed yet?" Mills asks. They spar some more. Schaaf finally makes an offer that averages $200,000 a year for four years. He tells Mills, "This is low, and I know you're going to think it's low."

Mills says politely, "It's O.K." Not O.K., as in "I accept," but O.K., as in "Fine, negotiations have to start somewhere. . . ." Schaaf thinks he's making more headway than he is and suggests a meeting. "I'll get back to you when I can," Mills says. He is thinking of a deal averaging $300,000 per year.

He calls Okoye and says, "It's a start." Okoye repeatedly says he just wants to play. "Don't be nervous," Mills responds. "*I'll* be nervous."

Mills's understated ways work, he says, "because I tend to be easy on people and hard on the problem." After all, what would have been gained by giving Schaaf a piece of his mind? Okoye is feeling better. "Call me if you need anything," Mills says, signing off.

At 9:42 he's on the phone with Mike Chernoff, a Colts vice-president. They spar. Mills asks, "Any new and different ideas on Chris Gambol?" Gambol, another Mills client (since 1967 Mills has represented 414 football players, including 31 first-rounders), is an offensive lineman from Iowa and the Colts' third-round selection. Chernoff is interrupted by a call from his team's owner, Robert Irsay. Chernoff calls back four minutes later, and Mills says innocently, "I bet Bob Irsay said to give Jack Mills everything he asks for." Chernoff, less jovial, says he hopes there won't be any problems. Mills assures him there won't "if y'all will do my deal." Chernoff makes an offer, and Mills says, "O.K., right,I hear you, O.K." In fact, the offer is nonsense. They'll talk later.

It is 9:50, and Okoye is back on the phone. He wants to leave Kansas City and go home to Sacramento. Mills plans a meeting with him when he changes planes in Denver.

At 10:05 somebody calls who wants Mark Bavaro of the New York Giants to put in a day's work at a football camp. For $6,000. "That might get his attention," says Mills. He calls Bavaro, who has family plans scheduled for the day. Bavaro decides to turn it down. "Call me if you need anything," Mills says.

At 10:14 Victor Scott, a cornerback for the Cowboys, calls to discuss buying a house. Mills tries to steer him toward something a little cheaper. "Sure, you know you can call me at home, anytime," says Mills. At 10:26 Mike Gann, a defensive end for the Falcons, calls to get figures on investments he has made with and through Mills. "Call me anytime," says Mills. "I'll help you fill in the blanks."

Another call. It's from Bronco linebacker Jim Ryan. "What can I do for you?" asks Mills. Play golf, that's what. They arrange a date.

Gambol calls. He wants to play football. Mills soothes him. "Don't worry. It's just a waiting proposition," he says.

At 11:30 a turkey-and-cheese sandwich arrives at his desk, and the phone keeps ringing and Mills keeps talking. Nearly an hour later the sandwich is half-eaten. Meanwhile, Ron Brown, a wide receiver cut last year by the Giants, comes in to sign papers. He will get a look from St. Louis, thanks to Mills. While Brown is there, Mills says with a sigh, "This is a business of trust and honor, and there's not much of either. Most agents are not trustworthy. This is a business that has developed a bad reputation. There is this big opportunity to steal and be dishonest because people are trusting you. And if you are out to fool 'em, you can fool 'em. It doesn't take much." Brown laughs—a little nervously.

The day grinds on. It's 1:31, and Okoye calls again. "Anything I can do to help?" Mills asks. "I'm a little short of cash," Okoye answers. Okoye is reluctant to say how short, but Mills, who views himself as something of a father figure, says, "I'll bring a couple of hundred to the airport."

At 1:42 a call comes from Brown's wife, Tracy. She's anxious. Mills knows that Brown's chances are slim (indeed, Brown will be cut after a month in camp), and he looks for the silver lining: "And if they don't keep him, they'll pay to send him home," says Mills. Tracy laughs.

Exactly at 3:00 there's another call from Schaaf. He's obviously feeling local media heat and is concerned about a comment that Mills made to the press. Mills had been quoted as saying Schaaf hadn't made an offer. That had been true when Mills last talked to anyone from the Kansas City media. But now it makes Schaaf look bad. Mills is conciliatory: "You're in a real precarious position."

At 3:21 an Indianapolis reporter calls. First Mills says gently that there are "significant differences" between how much the Colts think they should pay Gambol and how much Mills thinks they should pay Gambol. Sounds bad, says the reporter. Mills shifts gears and says of the latest offer, "It's respectable, not a lowball." Ultimately, Gambol will get a signing bonus of $129,500 and a three-year deal for $110,000 the first year, plus $15,000 more for making the roster; $135,000 the second year, plus a $10,000 roster bonus; and $180,000 the third, plus a $10,000 roster bonus. Mills will evaluate the deal as "excellent."

A few minutes later he strides past his LeRoy Neiman print of running back Larry Brown and leaves the office to get his '87 Cadillac, which he drives the 30 miles to Denver to meet Okoye. Mostly he goes to assure him that everything will be O.K. He also does another small favor, negotiating a first-class-seat at coach price for Okoye. "He's a big man," Mills explains to a very small gate agent. "You'll get used to this," Mills says jokingly to Okoye.

A couple of days later Mills will get Okoye a contract that pays a $250,000 signing bonus plus $125,000 the first year, $150,000 the second and $200,000 for an option year. Mills wanted a deal shorter than the four years originally offered by the Chiefs, because he thinks his client will be a big star and soon will command more money.

Now it's back to the office and the phones. Messages have piled up, and Mills keeps phoning. At 5:45 he talks hurriedly with the Rams, making a deal for 12th-round pick Alonzo Williams, a running back. The Rams' general counsel, Jay Zygmunt, says he has never spent so much time on a 12th-rounder. They share a laugh, adversaries in arms. The bottom line for Williams: an $8,000 signing bonus. At 5:52 Mills has Williams on the phone and is talking optimistically. But when he hangs up, he looks a little sad: "Twenty-eight teams passed on him 11 times, but they could be wrong." They weren't. Six weeks later Williams was cut. He gets to keep the $8,000; Mills's fee—it varies from 3% to 5%—brings the agent $400.

The calls are really beginning to back up now. Mills's secretary, Vicki Spanswick, takes more messages. A relative of free agent quarterback Loren Snyder—he played at Northern Colorado—calls and asks Mills and his family to attend a going-away barbecue for the young athlete, who will get a look-see by the Dallas Cowboys. Mills accepts the invitation. By now it's 6:00, and Mills

is, as is his custom, quitting for the day. The phone is ringing as he walks out.

It's a 12-minute drive to his house in the shadow of Devil's Thumb. His front door opens to the foothills of the Rockies, and his rear door overlooks city lights; deer play near the hot tub. On this spectacular evening the whole family is home. There's his wife, Cirrelda; Tom, 19, a University of Kansas sophomore; Deborah, a 24-year-old University of Oklahoma graduate (Jack's alma mater, where he also got his law degree); and Mary, 22, who helps coordinate Elizabeth Dole's activities on behalf of presidential candidate Robert Dole. The shish kebab is on the grill, and the sun is setting behind Flagstaff mountain. All is peaceful—for a while.

It's 8 P.M. The phone rings.

From the man who has grabbed the attention of millions of American sports fans with the simple admonishment, ''Hey, wait a minute,'' came a 1984 tome appropriately enough entitled *Hey, Wait a Minute, I Wrote a Book*. Certainly one of the most entertaining and knowledgeable commentators on the game of professional football, the former Oakland Raider head coach, spokesman for Miller Lite beer and a horde of other products, and world's foremost fear-of-flying personality, offers a glimpse here of his life while on the sideline instead of the more familiar broadcast booth of today, taken from his first book.

My Fair Advantage

JOHN MADDEN (WITH DAVE ANDERSON)

PART OF the fun of coaching is the other coaches. At an NFL meeting once, we were trying to come up with a precise definition for legal pass protection, as opposed to holding. After a while, Weeb Ewbank, who was coaching the Jets then, put on his best sincere look. His offensive linemen were some of the most notorious holders in the NFL, but Weeb was all innocence.

''We have to get this defined so we can coach it,'' Weeb said. ''I just want my fair advantage.''

That *fair advantage* is all any coach ever wants, physically or psychologically. One Saturday before a big game with the Kansas City Chiefs, I noticed some workmen at the Oakland Coliseum going in and out of the visiting team's locker room.

''What are you guys doing?'' I asked.

''We're exterminators,'' the boss said. ''We were told a couple of rats have been seen in the visitors' locker room.''

''You serious?'' I asked.

''Dead serious,'' he said.

''Come back Monday and get rid of them,'' I said. ''Monday is plenty of time.''

''We're supposed to do it today.''

''No, no you have my permission to leave now and come back Monday morning,'' I said. ''Leave the rats in there. Throw some food in there for 'em. Just wait until Monday to get rid of 'em.''

''If you say so, coach,'' the boss said.

Even without rats in the locker room, Oakland was a hard place to play for a visiting team. Coming in, they had to walk through a dingy, damp, gray hallway and then go down some gray stairs into the bowels of the stadium. The visiting team's locker room was partitioned into a series of small rooms, so they never had the feeling of being together. They also knew that as soon as they emerged out of another dingy tunnel onto the field, they would be booed unmercifully. Oakland was not a fun place to play, especially for Hank Stram and the Chiefs, one of our biggest rivals then. As soon as the Chiefs were settled in their locker room Sunday morning, I knocked on the door. One of their equipment men answered.

''I have to talk to Hank,'' I said.

Hank appeared, dapper as always, a red vest under his black blazer. Behind him, the locker room was hushed as it always is before a game, but I didn't invite Hank out into the hallway to talk. I wanted him to stand there with the door open so some of his players could hear me.

''We've got a problem,'' I said loudly. ''Some *rats* have been seen in this locker room. We've got exterminators working on it but some *rats* might still be around. Just to be safe, Hank, you better warn your players about the *rats*.''

Every time I used the words rats, I could see some players looking around. I had established my fair advantage. I don't know if it helped, but it didn't hurt. We won the game.

At the Pro Bowl after that season, Willie Lanier of the Chiefs told me how his teammates had been squirming around in the locker room, checking their shoes and their shoulder pads. Some even peered into their helmets before putting them on. I always liked to put something in Hank's mind. Before another game in Oakland we were out on the field, which was actually below sea level. If there was any rain at all, the water table would rise and the grass would be slick. That week it had rained enough for me to give Hank something to think about.

''You won't believe this, Hank,'' I said. ''Yesterday I told the groundskeeper to put two hours of water on the field. But after he turned the water on, he took a lunch break and fell asleep. The water was on for eight hours. I'm really sorry about this, Hank, but your receivers can work around where it's really wet.''

Hank stormed off, but not before I had wished him good luck, which he hated to hear. Most coaches don't want the opposing coach to wish them good luck, because then they have to wish the opposing coach good luck, which they don't want to do. Most coaches think that if they have to wish you good luck, then you *will* have good luck and win. I didn't care. I knew that wishing the other coach good luck had nothing to do with winning or losing the game. But if you wish most coaches good luck, they grudgingly wish you the same.

''Yeah, good luck,'' Hank would always say quickly, his voice dropping. ''Yeah, yeah, good luck.''

Anything to get the other coach thinking negatively. But there were times when Hank got me too. Hank had a team chaplain, Monsignor Vincent Mackey from Boston, who showed up for almost all the Chiefs' games, home and away. Hank called him ''Blackbird,'' after his priest's black suit. Back in 1969 we beat the Chiefs twice during the season even though the Monsignor was there. But when we played for the AFL championship in Oakland that year, we lost. Virginia and I are Catholics, but she blamed the Monsignor.

''What's he doing at football games on Sunday?'' she said. ''I'm going to write to the Pope about him.''

She never did, but Hank had gotten to her. And to me. Hank got to a lot of coaches, but some probably never knew it. Not long ago Hank told me a story about Kansas City's old Municipal Stadium where both benches were on the same side of the field. One of his assistant coach's friends always had a photographer's credentials and a camera. But he never had any film in his camera. He just wanted to watch the game as he walked between the benches. One time he was near the other team's bench when he overheard the coaches talking about throwing a long pass, an ''up,'' to the wide receiver being covered by Jim Marsalis, a Chief cornerback. He hurried over to the Chiefs' bench.

''Watch for the up against Marsalis,'' he told Hank. ''They're gonna throw an up against Marsalis.''

Hank and his coaches alerted Marsalis, who knocked down the pass. Whenever he talked about it, Hank would puff with pride at the memory of discovering what the other team was planning. After the Chiefs moved to Arrowhead Stadium, the 1974 Pro Bowl was scheduled there. As the AFC coach that year, I was in a little meeting room going over the game plan with my quarterbacks, Ken Stabler and Bob Griese, when I heard a voice.

''The comeback pass will never work,'' the voice said.

I realized it was Hank's voice. I don't know where he was, but somehow he could hear me and I could hear him. I talked some more and he kept answering. He obviously had some sort of intercom plugged into that room. He still laughs about that. Hank was always up to something. But that was all right with me. That's the way he was. I could count on Hank being up to something, just like I was every so often. And because Hank was consistent, I enjoyed him just as much as I enjoyed Don Shula for being straightforward.

To me, Don Shula is the best coach of my time. Tom Landry, Chuck Noll, and Bud Grant also have won over a long period—which is the test—but Don has done it with different teams in different cities in different eras.

He won in Baltimore with Johnny Unitas at quarterback, he won there with Earl Morrall at quarterback when Unitas was hurt. He took over a team in Miami that had Larry Csonka and Bob Griese and he won the Super Bowl twice, the first time with a perfect 17–0 season. Then he put together another team that got to Super Bowl XVII with David Woodley at quarterback. Now he's developing Dan Marino at quarterback. He's won with offense, he's won with defense. He's won with Bill Arnsparger as his defensive coordinator, he's won without Arnsparger, who left the Dolphins in 1974 to be the Giants' coach and who left the Dolphins again in 1984 to be the Louisiana State coach.

Against a Shula team, you have to play your best to win. You have to be the better team that day to have a chance.

The most frustrated I ever was as the Raiders' coach was in our 1973 AFC championship game in Miami, a 27–10 loss. The Dolphins would run Larry Csonka inside and we would adjust our defense, but then they would run Mercury Morris outside. Bob Griese even ran a quarterback draw against us. No matter where the Dolphins ran, they never left a Raider unblocked. It seemed like we were never in the right defense. We never got our compass fixed on anything. That game was an example of why Don Shula is such a good game coach, meaning a coach you can seldom get an advantage on. In preparing for some teams you can watch their game films and know that you can do almost anything you want to do almost any time you want to do it. You can keep doing the same thing over and over. But against a team with a good game coach, once you do something, they adjust and you can't do it again. You might find something else that's open but not what was open before.

As good as the Dolphins were in winning their two consecutive Super Bowl rings, I thought my Raiders were just as good. But the Dolphins were better on artificial turf (the Orange Bowl had Poly-Turf then) and we were better on real grass—if only because that's what our home fields were made of.

Early in the 1973 season, remember, we stopped the Dolphins' 18-game winning streak, 12–7, on grass at the University of California's stadium in Berkeley (the A's were using the Oakland Coliseum for baseball at the time). And in the 1974 playoffs, when the Dolphins were hoping to be the first team to win three consecutive Super Bowls, we beat them on grass at the Coliseum, 28–26. They went ahead, 26–21, with only about two minutes left, but then Kenny Stabler put together the best drive I've ever seen. After a kickoff return by Ron Smith put us at our 32, he completed 6 consecutive passes, throwing off-balance to Clarence Davis for 14 yards and the winning touchdown with 26 seconds left.

After a few plays in that drive, I had expected the Dolphins to blitz us, but they didn't. I never asked Don why, but through the years I often phoned him to talk football. He never tried to con me. If he didn't want to tell me something, he always said, "I don't want to tell you." As simple and as straightforward as that. But usually he shared his knowledge. One year at training camp my players were lethargic, so I phoned Don to ask if he had ever had that problem.

"If you want to rest your team," he told me, "you don't have to give 'em time off—just cut down on the physical activity."

I believe Don was the first to use what are known now as walk-throughs, where in practice the players just walk through the plays instead of running hard. But until I talked to him, I knew only one way to coach—go hell-bent. He taught me another way.

In all our years as rivals, I only had one misunderstanding with Don, over a 1969 exhibition game before we really got to know each other. He was still with the

Colts and I was a rookie head coach. Before coming to Oakland, the Colts worked out at Cal Poly in San Luis Obispo where one of our part-time coaches, Morrie Schleicher, happened to be attending a teachers' seminar. One day Morrie went over to watch the Colts practice and somebody spotted him. Don phoned me.

"Get your spy out of here," he said.

"Believe me, he's not spying on you," I said. "He's down there as a teacher, he's not there for us."

"He better not be," Don said.

We lost that game, 34–30. Maybe we should have had Morrie spying, but I've always considered spying to be overrated. I never felt anyone spied on my team, and I never spied on anybody else's team. I've heard that spying existed in the AFL's early years. Every time we saw a helicopter near our practice field, we joked that Weeb Ewbank or Sid Gillman had a spy up there, just as Weeb or Sid thought Al Davis had a spy in every helicopter or high-rise building near their practice fields.

But when the film-exchange became dependable, there was no reason for spying. Those game films are all you need—if you get them.

Back in my early years with the Raiders, the AFL didn't enforce the film-exchange rule the way the NFL office does now. My two years as an assistant coach, one of my duties was our film-exchange. When we got our game films on Monday morning, I drove over to the Oakland Airport and air-expressed a copy of the films to our upcoming opponent. I also telexed the receipt number to the opposing team so it would know the films had been sent. Later that day or early the next day I drove back to the airport to pick up our opponent's game-films after they arrived. Nothing annoys a coach more than not receiving an opponent's film on time. I learned that if I wanted to delay a film sent to an Eastern team like the Jets or the Bills, all I had to do was air-express it through Chicago where it always seemed to get lost for a day or two.

"Whatever you do," I always told Eastern teams, "don't send your films to us through Chicago."

Some teams you could depend on. One of the nicest guys I dealt with was Jesse Richardson, the Patriots' defensive line coach who also handled their film-exchange. Back when I was a rookie with the Eagles in 1959, he was a good defensive tackle who played on their NFL championship team the next year. During the 1968 season the Patriots played a game in Denver, then stayed at our training-camp base in Santa Rosa the week before coming down to Oakland to play us. I phoned Jesse to find out when I could expect their Denver film.

"I don't know what to tell you, John," he said. "We only have one film made up."

Most teams had two or three copies made of a game film, but the Patriots were trying to save some money.

Jesse checked with Mike Holovak, their coach at the time, and called me back.

"Mike told me to send you our film first," Jesse said. "When you're through with it, send it up to Santa Rosa."

That's cooperation. But with some teams, I learned not to send our film until we got theirs, especially the Chargers. Any film exchange between Oakland and San Diego should be easy. Put the film on one of Pacific Southwest Airlines' non-stop flights between the two California cities and it's there in an hour and a half. But it never quite worked out that way. Sid Gillman didn't trust Al Davis, so Sid wouldn't send the Chargers' films until he got our films. Meanwhile, we weren't about to send our films until we got the Chargers' films. After a day or two, one of us would weaken. But by then the Chargers were blaming Al Davis.

"We know it's not you, John," one of their coaches would say on the phone. "We know Al is trying to screw us."

The funny thing is, Al usually wasn't aware of it. I was the one handling the films.

Then there was the time, my fourth season as head coach, before our first playoff game with the Steelers in 1972, that we never got their films and they never got ours. Both teams just got too stubborn to send them.

Looking back now, maybe that was an omen for one of the roughest rivalries in NFL history.

I like rivalries, the NFL needs more rivalries. I think two weeks in the schedule should be set aside for games featuring rivalries—one week for geographic rivalries (Raiders–Rams, Jets–Giants, Cowboys–Oilers), another week for long-standing or current rivalries outside the usual divisional rivalries. But the best rivalries involve top teams playing for something big, like we were with the Steelers for the 1974, 1975, and 1976 AFC championships. Our rivalry had flared in the 1972 playoffs when the Steelers beat us, 13–7, on Franco Harris's "immaculate reception" for a 60-yard touchdown with 5 seconds left. But as controversial as that play will always be, I think the tone of the rivalry was set the night before. We were staying downtown at the Pittsburgh Hilton. After dinner, I was in the lobby when a screaming, surging crowd of several hundred Steeler fans appeared outside the big glass windows.

"Go upstairs to your rooms," a Pittsburgh policeman was instructing everybody in the lobby. "If you're staying here, go up to your rooms."

The people outside had attended a downtown rally celebrating the Steelers being in the playoffs for the first time in the forty years of the franchise. Now they had decided to come over to our hotel to hoot us, but the police were guarding the doors to the lobby. I was about to take an elevator up to my room when my tight end, Bob Moore, wobbled into the lobby with blood all over

him. He had gone out for a walk and when he tried to return to the hotel, the police had mistaken him for a Steeler fan trying to get into the lobby. Bob had to go to a nearby hospital for stitches in his head. With his bandage, he couldn't put his helmet on the next day. We had lost our tight end, and when we lost the game on that "immaculate reception," a rivalry burst into flame. Several weeks later I had a decision to make. I had been invited to speak at the Dapper Dan dinner in Pittsburgh, and I had accepted.

"But with everything that's happened since then," I said to Virginia one night, "I don't know if I should go."

Mike was sitting with us. Mike was nine then and when I didn't seem to know what to do about the dinner in Pittsburgh, he spoke up.

"You have to go," he said.

"What do you mean I *have* to go," I said. "I don't *have* to go."

"Yes, you do."

"Why?" I said.

"You told the people in Pittsburgh that you were going," he said, "so now you have to go."

"You're right."

From the mouths of babes. If you say you're going to do something, you do it. You don't back out because you lost a football game on a controversial play, or because your tight end got roughed up. I liked the Steelers, especially Art Rooney, their owner and one of the all-time great guys. He liked me too. Every so often I'd get a letter or a postcard from him. Nothing to do with football, just out of thoughtfulness. If you don't like Art Rooney, you don't like people.

Even so, I wondered what sort of reception I'd get. But everybody in Pittsburgh was nice to me. At the dinner, I was applauded. No boos. When it was my turn to speak, I had some fun with Chuck Noll being honored as Pittsburgh's "man of the year" for getting the Steelers to the AFC championship game.

"God let the Steelers win that game with us," I said, thinking of Franco's touchdown. "The committee wanted to give the award to God but since God couldn't be here, they had to give it to a human being—Chuck."

In later years, our rivalry with the Steelers got so intense, it separated Chuck and me as friends. We say hello now, but that's about it. Back when we were assistant coaches, Chuck with the Colts and me with the Raiders, we arranged our college-scouting trips so that we could drive together. In our early years as head coaches, we remained friends. But when the Raider–Steeler rivalry erupted into George Atkinson suing Chuck for slander for talking about a "criminal element" in the NFL, the competition got the best of our friendship. It's a shame it had to come to that, but in our case it did. I think it's happened with other coaches. Hank Stram and Sid Gillman, to name two. And probably a few others who won't admit it.

That doesn't diminish my admiration for Chuck as a coach. He doesn't get the respect he deserves. When people talk about the best coaches, they mention Shula and Landry and whichever coach has a hot team, but they don't mention Chuck and it seems like they never mentioned Bud Grant of the Vikings.

Bud had different players, different personalities, different styles. But he always adjusted to putting everything together for a winning season. He's the best coach nobody ever talked about. To me, he was up there with Shula, Landry, and Noll. If I were an NFL club owner, I'd like to have any of those four coaches running my team.

I never really got to know Tom Landry until after I stopped coaching. The way the schedule fell, when I was the Raiders' coach, we only played the Cowboys once in the regular season. But in my talks with him for CBS the day before Cowboy games, I've realized that he's truly an amazing man.

Tom is totally different from his image. He's not the robot he appears to be on your TV screen. He's an interesting guy with a great sense of humor. One time the Cowboys were about to play the Eagles after one of the Cowboys' running backs, Ron Springs, had popped off about the Eagles' defense. In one of his meetings, Tom looked over at Tony Dorsett.

"Tony, when you line up for the first play," Tom said, "I want you to point to Ron and tell the Eagles' defense, 'Hey, that's Ron Springs, that's the guy who's been saying all those things about you.' "

Knowing him now, I can understand why, in 1984, Tom will be in his twenty-fifth consecutive season as the Cowboys' coach. I thought ten years was long but Tom has been coaching the Cowboys for a *quarter of a century*. The reason is, Tom doesn't worry about things he can't control. Tony Dorsett once had a chest problem. If my best running back had been questionable, I would've been a basket case. But when I asked Tom if Tony would play, he shrugged.

"We'll see how he is in the warmup," he said.

I'm sure Paul Brown was a great coach, but I never knew him back in the 50's when he had those great teams in Cleveland every year. I knew him mostly for putting together the Cincinnati Bengals as an expansion team. In those years with a young team, he did the best job of losing of any coach I've ever seen. He never let the Bengals get blown out, never let them be embarrassed. If you got ahead of the Bengals, he would pull in his horns and play conservatively. He kept the score tight. If the Bengals got a touchdown on a blocked punt or an interception, they suddenly were back in the game.

Sometimes they even stole the game. And if the Bengals lost, it seldom was by a big score. He always could tell his players that they weren't there yet, but they were only one touchdown away from the Raiders.

In the seven seasons I coached against Paul Brown, we always had a much better team than the Bengals, but in eight games, they beat us three times. In our five victories, we won once by 20 points, but the other margins were 7, 4, and 3 twice (once in a 1975 playoff, 31–28, his last game as the Bengals' coach).

I've always heard about how intense Paul Brown was, but Don Coryell is the most intense coach I've ever been around. Long before he took over the Chargers, I was his defensive coordinator at San Diego State for three years. His intensity carried over into everything he did. In my years with him, the staff always went out to dinner once a week. But whenever one of us opened the door to get into his little Pinto station wagon, it always stunk.

"Damn it," Don would say, "I forgot to leave the garbage at the corner."

Once or twice we could understand. But this happened almost every week. Don's house was on top of a hill, up from where the garbage truck stopped. On garbage days, he would put the garbage cans in the back of the station wagon to drop off at the corner. But then he would start thinking about football and forget the garbage—until we opened the station wagon that night. Sometimes he even forgot his daughter Mindy was in the car. When she was little, she liked to ride down to the corner at the bottom of the hill, then get out and run back home. But if Don forgot about her being in the back seat, Mindy would never say a word. She loved the ride. Don wouldn't remember he had forgotten to drop her off until he got to the office and noticed her. He'd bring her in and phone his wife.

"I'm sorry, honey," he'd say, "but I forgot Mindy again. Can you please come down and get her?"

One time I was driving Don around California on a recruiting trip. He was dressed up in a tie and jacket, which maybe accounted for the headache he had that morning.

"I'll stop at the drugstore for some aspirin," I said.

"No," he said, "just let me out. I'll run it off."

I drove along slowly while he ran a couple of miles like he had when he was a young boxer. But this time he was running in his good shoes. When he got back in the car, his headache was gone.

On the sidelines, Don glowers in concentration so much, he looks like he's modeling for a headache remedy. But he's not always that intense. One year we were having trouble getting summer jobs for our players in the San Diego area. Suddenly an opening developed at the Pepsi-Cola plant.

"Give that job to Dowhower," he said.

Rod Dowhower had been Don's quarterback at San Diego State, but then he had been cut by the 49ers and now he had returned to San Diego, recently married and without a job.

"He needs that job more than any of our kids," Don said.

Don never forgot his players, even after they couldn't play for him—and that's the test. Don later hired Rod as an assistant coach. From there Rod went to the Bronco and the Cardinal staffs.

My three years at San Diego State, one of our assistant coaches was Joe Gibbs, now the Washington Redskins' coach. My first year there, Joe was a graduate assistant. Don assigned him to defense under me. But when it came time for the Varsity-Alumni game at the end of spring practice, Don put Joe in charge of the alumni team.

"I need your plays, Joe," I said.

"You're not getting our plays."

"You've got to give me your plays," I said. "I've got to draw them up on cards so we can practice against them."

"No," he said.

"Hey, listen, when we play another team, we get their plays off the films. Give me your plays. There's nothing wrong with that."

"No," he said.

"We work together. If you don't give me your plays, you'll never coach another down with me."

"I guess I'll never coach another down," Joe said.

He never gave me the plays, but we remained good friends. We were just two hard-headed guys. As it turned out, he never did coach another down with me. The next season, Don Coryell assigned Joe to offense.

"The only time I ever got fired," Joe says now with a laugh, "John Madden fired me."

Don Coryell went on to coach the Cardinals and the Chargers (where Joe Gibbs was on his staff), so I wound up coaching against the coach who gave me one of my big breaks when he put me on his San Diego State staff. In my ten seasons, I coached against all the best coaches of that era.

One of my biggest dissappointments was that I never got to coach against Vince Lombardi. My first year as the Raiders' head coach in 1969 was his first as the Redskins' coach. But before the 1970 season started, Vince Lombardi died of cancer.

My only personal contact with him occurred at the coaches' meeting where we were discussing pass-protection as opposed to holding. Out of respect for the older coaches, I hung back, listening to Weeb Ewbank talk about wanting his fair advantage and then watching the great Lombardi stand up to speak.

"Gentlemen," he began, "I'll tell you what pass-

protection is. This is pass-protection. The hands are in here."

He was holding his hands tight against his chest, with both fists clenched, then the textbook way to block for the passer. Holding his hands there, he continued to expound for a few minutes on his theories of pass-blocking, then he sat down. Silence. The other coaches looked around at each other, as if nobody dared to follow him. Except me, who didn't know any better. I had been waiting to talk anyway and now I stood up.

"That may be what pass-protection is to you, Coach Lombardi," I said respectfully, "but that's not what it is to me and that's not what's going on in this game. If you look closely at game-films now, you won't see many pass-blockers doing what you're talking about."

I went on about how an offensive lineman couldn't keep his hands in close to his chest when pass-blocking, that he had to keep his hands out in front of him and use his hands to fight off the pass-rusher. Under the rules then, the pass-blocker couldn't move his hands outside the plane of the pass-rusher, but the pass-blocker had to keep his hands out in front of him if he hoped to be effective, not close to his chest. More and more pass-blockers were using this technique in order to cope with the bigger and quicker pass-rushers. All around me, I could see the other coaches nodding in agreement. When the meeting ended, Vince Lombardi looked over at me.

"John, you're right," he said. "That's what the pass-blockers *are* doing now."

We started to talk football. For the only time in my life as it turned out, I was talking football with Vince Lombardi, just as if I were back in Daly City talking football with John Robinson outside the pool hall. The more we talked, the more I knew I had to ask him a question that had always intrigued me.

"What is there," I said, "that separates a good coach from a bad coach?"

"Knowing what the end result looks like," Vince said. "The best coaches know what the end result looks like, whether it's an offensive play, a defensive coverage, or just some area of the organization. If you don't know what the end result is supposed to look like, you can't get there. All the teams basically do the same things. We all have a draft, we all have a training camp, we all have practices. But the bad coaches don't know what the hell they want. The good coaches do."

After that, whenever I put something new in the Raider playbook, I always tried to picture what the end result should look like. And then I worked to create that end result.

Even though I didn't know Vince Lombardi very well or very long, I treasure my memories of being around him, listening to him. Those older coaches were fun to listen to, even Weeb Ewbank, who was always trying to con everybody. Cherubic little Weeb, you had to trust Weeb—except nobody did. Late in the 1972 season we had already clinched the AFC West when the Jets arrived in Oakland for a Monday night game with a 7–5 record. They had to win to stay in contention for a wild-card playoff berth. Out on the field before the game, Weeb wandered over to talk to me.

"You know, Johnny," he said, "you'd really be better off if we won this game."

I've forgotten Weeb's reasoning, but I remember that we won, 24–16, even though Joe Namath passed for 403 yards. Weeb was always trying to slip something past you. One time before a game at Shea Stadium, where the wind off Flushing Bay would swirl in gusts, we were out warming up when Weeb took me aside.

"Johnny," he said, "I've never told another coach this, but I'm going to tell you because you're my friend."

Weeb pointed to what looked like a long gray rag fluttering from the mezzanine deck behind the goal posts at the closed end where home plate is for baseball.

"The wind is treacherous here," he said, "but the way you tell which way it's blowing is by that gray thing there."

Weeb might as well have bored a hole in my head and put that gray rag in it. I didn't dare tell any of my players, especially my kicker George Blanda, about that gray rag. I didn't want to psyche him the way Weeb had psyched me. But whenever we were moving toward the closed end that day and I started wondering if we might have to settle for a field goal, I thought about that gray rag—but I refused to look at it. For all I knew, Weeb had somebody up there with an electric fan blowing that flag every which way. I just knew that if I looked at it, I'd get taken somehow.

We won that game too, but Weeb had me. And he had what every coach wants—his fair advantage.

If there was a single honor for the MVP of pro football writers, it would have to be awarded to Tex Maule for his long and distinguished career reporting and philosophizing on the many nuances of the game and the varying personae associated with it. Appearing season after season on the pages of *Sports Illustrated,* his words and insights entertained and educated legions of football fans. He covered the 1958 NFL title game between the Baltimore Colts and New York Giants for *SI,* wrote the obligatory wrap-up of the festivities, then came back to illustrate for us why this contest of "high drama, nerve-twanging tension, and great athletes performing at their best, created a classic of sports history."

Here's Why It Was the Best Football Game Ever

TEX MAULE

No one who saw the Baltimore Colts win the world professional football championship from the New York Giants by 23–17 on Dec. 28 (SI, Jan. 5) will ever forget the game—and some 50 million people did watch, in person or on television. The classics of the pre-television era have been perpetuated only in the minds of the spectators on hand and by the newspaper accounts; this, for the first time, was a truly epic game which inflamed the imagination of a national audience.

The principal architect of excitement was a lanky, crew-cut castoff quarterback named John Unitas, who operated the wonderfully proficient Baltimore team with the cool *sangfroid* of a card-sharp. Of course, he was far from the whole show. A magnificent Baltimore offensive line blocked savagely all afternoon; a myopic end named Ray Berry, who wears contact lenses, caught 12 passes, most of them unbelievably; and a thick-set fullback named Alan Ameche thundered into the good Giant defense with an impact often audible over the continuing roar of the crowd. Later, reflecting on the biggest day in his life, Unitas said, "You have to gamble or die in this league. I don't know if you can call something con-

trolled gambling, but that's how I look at my play-calling. I'm a little guy, comparatively, that's why I gamble. It doesn't give those giants a chance to bury me."

No one buried Unitas in this very nearly perfect game, and his controlled gambling brought victory. Here are details of how and why the Colts won.

FIRST QUARTER

In the early testing and probing the Colts failed to score, but two developments affected their eventual victory. First, a long pass to Halfback Lenny Moore established him as the Colts' most dangerous receiver, so the Giants assigned two men to him, sometimes covering Berry with only one man, a fatal mistake. Second, a Colt field goal was blocked when Spinney turned out instead of in, leaving Linebacker Sam Huff a clear route. This was corrected when they kicked the game-tying last-seconds field goal. Late in the quarter a 36-yard field goal by Pat Summerall gave the Giants a 3–0 lead.

The great pass-protection blocking of the Colt line became clearly apparent now, and it became apparent, too, that two players who had been keys to the Giant success were off form. Frank Gifford, carrying the ball like a loaf of bread, fumbled twice, and the Colts recovered both; Roosevelt Grier, the anchor of the Giant defensive line, was too crippled to be effective. Unitas' canny play-selection kept the Giant defense scrambling and, with the line unable to break through the Colt blockers, the Giant secondary could not cope with the varied Baltimore pass patterns. Two Colt touchdowns now brought them a 14–3 lead.

THIRD QUARTER

The Giant defense, which had leaked in the first half, changed the complexion of the game with a great effort which denied the Colts a touchdown in four tries from the Giant three-yard line. Later, when the Colts lost the toss in the overtime period, Coach Weeb Ewbank, given his choice of goals to defend, decided to defend this same goal, taking the wind in the face of his team in order to make sure the footing would be good should Baltimore penetrate inside the Giant 20. Ewbank felt that the poor footing at the west end of the field had helped the Giants stop the Colts; in the overtime period, Ameche had no trouble getting traction at the east end of the field. Now, early in the third period, the stand ignited a strong Giant rally good for two touchdowns. The first of these at the end of the quarter cut the Colts' lead to 14–10.

FOURTH QUARTER

The trend set by the Giants' defensive effort in the third period lasted until only two minutes were left. The Colts had played technically perfect football before, but now, with time running out, they looked to be confused and nearly helpless. The Giants scored easily as the quarter began, Quarterback Charley Conerly (42) throwing off a fake reverse which broke End Bob Schnelker loose for a 46-yard pass to the Colt 15. Wellington Mara, Giants' secretary, had taken some Polaroid camera pictures of the first half, which showed that the Colts overshifted their secondary to the right when the Giants were strong right, and Conerly threw on the next play to Gifford to the left and the Giants were ahead 17–14. For a long time it looked like enough—but the Colts rallied.

Inches From Victory

It was third and four with the clock running out. The Giants lined up in a balanced T and Conerly called a sweep to the right. A first down here would almost surely have meant victory. Gifford swung to his right, trying to go around the mighty Colt End Gino Marchetti (89). Marchetti fought off Schnelker, moving to the sideline; then, when Gifford cut in, Marchetti lunged awkwardly away from Schnelker's block, got his hands on Gifford and slowed him. Tackle Gene Lipscomb (76) piled on and the impact broke Marchetti's ankle, but it stopped Gifford inches away from the vital first down.

Time and Tied

With some two minutes to go, Unitas calmly marched 73 yards to field-goal range. The Giants, worried about a long bomb to Moore, gave away the short pass, and Unitas threw three times to the best end in the league, the three passes good for 62 yards. Ray Berry (82) on each catch made the play count for more yardage by superb running. His second completion, made on a spectacular flying catch, was good for first down on the Giant 35, and his third carried to the Giant 13 with only seconds to play. No offensive end in history ever made three more important plays; they won a championship.

Quick, Straight Kick

With only seconds left, the Colts did not huddle before this tying field goal by Myhra. The field-goal team hustled in; Guard Spinney, who had turned the wrong way on the blocked field goal in the first quarter, remembered and cut off the route up the middle, and Myhra rather calmly kicked the 20-yard field goal which sent the game into a sudden-death overtime. The clock showed seven seconds to play when the referee raised his hands, but time had run out for New York.

SUDDEN DEATH

Now, for the first time in the history of football, a game would be decided in a sudden-death overtime. Unitas made his only bad call of the day on the flip of the coin with Giant co-captains Kyle Rote and Linebacker Bill Svoboda. So the Giants chose to receive the kickoff. And now the gallant, season-long effort of this courageous team finally foundered. You felt, watching the Giants' last three offensive plays following the kickoff return, that this wonderful team had run out of gas. Gifford gained four yards, and then, with Schnelker breaking away deep enough for a first-down pass, Conerly missed him. With third down and six yards to go, Conerly tried to pass again, but the Colt secondary blanketed his receivers and the 37-year-old quarterback ran for it. He came close, too, running hard outside the Colt right end, but he was hit first by Linebacker Bill Pellington as he neared a first down and then by Middle Guard Don Shinnick, the second tackle coming in from the side and slewing his body suddenly sidewise, killing his forward momentum and bringing him to a stop only a foot short of the first down. The rest of the overtime belonged to the Colts; they were now the better, fresher team, and their winning drive had an inexorable quality.

Seventh Play

The great Colt blocking and a Giant slip kept Baltimore moving. With third and 15, Unitas (19) called for a pass to the right to Moore, but Lenny was covered. Robustelli had spun inside, trying to get away from Parker, but the big Colt tackle bottled him up. When Unitas looked to his left, the Giant line had been swung away from him so that he had time to wave Berry (82) deep when he saw that Carl Karilivacz (21), covering Berry, had slipped. Berry caught the pass, whirled away from Karilivacz, and carried to a very important first down for the Colts. The play was called from a formation used for the first time in the game—a slot right, with Moore the slot back.

Eighth Play

Unitas here took advantage of the hard-charging Modzelewski (77). "He was blowing in too fast to suit me." Art Spinney (63) cut across behind center, felled Moe with a great trap block; George Preas (60) cut off Huff (70), who was playing too deep, and Ameche was away for 23 yards.

11th Play

Unitas (19) calls for a fullback slant off right tackle. Ameche (35) took a step toward right tackle but saw

daylight in the middle and cut in, but Huff (70) slipped away from Buzz Nutter (50), the Colt center, and Modzelewski (77) cut in from the side to close the hole for one-yard gain.

12th Play

Unitas catches the Giants off-balance with a completely unorthodox call—a dangerous pass to Mutscheller (84), which, had it been intercepted, might have meant a Giant touchdown. Unitas lofted the ball high over Cliff Livingston (89), a perfectly thrown pass which carried to the New York one.

13th Play

The same play as in 11th, but the Giants are in a goal-line defense, closing the middle. Two great blocks, by Mutscheller on Livingston, the corner linebacker, and by Moore (24) on Halfback Emlen Tunnell (45), coming up from secondary, opened a gaping hole outside tackle for Ameche.

Summary

Unitas' play selection and execution in his drive to victory was nearly perfect; his icy calm let him direct his team as steadily as if he were on the practice field. The drive itself was a blend of the ingredients which make pro football such a heart-wrenching drama for the spectator: some luck and the precise implementation by a great team of the inspirational leadership of a quarterback who ranks with the best in the history of the pro game. It was just the right climax for the best game of football ever played.

THE 13 CALLS OF JOHNNY UNITAS

1. Unitas chose his plays deliberately. "I wanted to move on the ground to minimize loss of the ball. I

didn't give a damn about the clock. It was our pace to set.''

2. ''This could have busted up the overtime real quick. Crow barely tipped the ball and Moore was going so fast he couldn't recover to handle it.''

3. This was a special play for this game. ''Huff followed Ameche everywhere. This draw to Dupre took advantage of that. An inch or two and he might have broken.''

4. ''Just a flare to Ameche. Svare forgot to pick up the flare man, staying with Berry, so I just hit The Horse.''

5. This was a good first-down call. ''They hadn't adjusted too well to our running stuff. So we stuck with it.''

6. Modzelewski slipped block, ran by Moore to dump Unitas. ''I had a pass play called but Moe just wrapped me up.''

7. This was one of the game-turning plays, giving the Colts a tough first down. ''This was a new formation for this game. Our steady slamming into the line had helped set things up, and when Ray shook loose I unloaded.''

8. This 23-yard gain by Ameche on a trap play really sealed the Giant doom. ''We'd run this once or twice in the game. It's not a long gainer. Usually we figure it four or five yards. But Huff had been playing to his left and back. This made an easy blocking assignment for our tackle. Huff was playing for a pass, and the way Moe had been crashing I figured they were right for a trap. I hit it right.''

9. ''No recollection of this play at all.''

10. ''Just a plain old slant pass is all.''

11. This was the same play as the one which Ameche scored on later, but Ameche turned into the center. ''Huff was waiting and just closed Alan off.''

12. This call had been criticized as an unnecessary gamble here. ''They were playing for the run, one on one on Moore, the linebacker head-up on Mutscheller. I told Jimmy to get out there real quick. All I had to do was flip it up in the air and have him catch it.''

13. ''Our only call, a power play. We got the halfback blocking ahead of Ameche with a double team on the tackle. When I slapped the ball in Al's belly and saw him take off I knew nobody was going to stop him with one yard. They couldn't have done it if we'd needed 10 yards.''

Bill McGrane, a onetime reporter for the *Des Moines Register* and the *Minneapolis Tribune*, is presently the Director of Administration for the Chicago Bears and is a regular contributor to *Pro* and *GameDay* football magazines. These tales from the trenches of training camp where rookies are absorbed into the flesh of a team or discarded and forgotten are from a collection of his columns entitled *Insight*, which was published by National Football League Properties, Inc. It provides a unique, behind-the-scenes view of the fraternity of players and pledges by a man who has watched the hazing ceremonies year after grueling year.

Rookies

BILL MCGRANE

JULY

It is your standard small town. The divided highway says goodbye at the off-ramp in front of the Holiday Inn. You bump across the railroad tracks on Front Street, then go over the bridge and past three downtown streets.

The residential streets are old, which means they also are wide, quiet, and made of brick, although marred here and there by blacktop resurfacing. There's elm and oak, old enough and tall enough to form a shady cathedral nave over the old, red bricks.

You go south, a block past the Presbyterian church, left to the bookstore, then you take a right at the fork and up the hill.

The hill road winds up and around with the box elder growing almost out to the curbings. You come out of the last curve abruptly, onto the top, surprised at the sudden absence of trees and shade; however, trees and shade come in second when a hilltop gets bulldozed to build a college campus.

It is July, and just past one in the afternoon and the streets are deserted because the first summer session is over. It's also deserted because afternoon practice is still two hours off.

At the east end of the campus, past the library and the administration building and the fieldhouse, the twin-towered dorm shimmers in the heat. Fire doors are propped open in violation of codes and in search of a breeze. Windows are open on the three floors where the players live and an occasional curtain—institutional green—flaps half-heartedly.

On the uppermost of the player floors, a rookie running back lies on his bunk and attempts to look comfortable, which he isn't. He is wearing red shorts, a Grossinger's T-shirt, blue tennis shoes, and a forced smile. The latter is attributable to the verbal brickbats being left at his doorsill by every passerby.

A national television crew is filming the rookie for a segment to run in a preseason telecast. They've laid enough cable that the floor of his room looks as if it's covered with spaghetti. The lights have raised the temperature 10 degrees. The director, out from New York, is wearing a new safari jacket, jeans with clever stitching at the pockets, desert boots, and a beard.

"Hey, Eddie . . . tell 'em about that five-flat forty you run yestiddy mornin'."

The forced grin stretches as he hollers at his antagonist: "But it was rainin'!"

"Rained on ole Murphy, too, 'n' he done four-seven!" comes the retort.

The director mops his brow and the back of his neck with a new red farmer handkerchief.

"Just relax, guy . . . won't be a minute, here." The director turns to a member of the crew and rages in a controlled whisper: "Let's get the damned thing running! Can you do that?"

The camera purrs agreeably, and lights are refocused to correct for movement.

"We're rolling. Now, the first question will be, are you still disappointed that you weren't a number-one draft choice?"

There is loud cackle in the hallway, and the rookie shakes his head.

"Aw . . . hey, do you know what's goin' on here? I mean, I'm tryin' to make this football team! Man, the draft was a long time ago . . . and this is now! I'm hangin' by my fingernails, 'n' you come on with worrying about where I got drafted!"

The director's beard is the color of dirty straw. The grin parts it.

"Not what we were going for, but I like it . . . you like it, Ralphie?"

Ralphie is the size of somebody's kid brother, but identifiable as corporate because of his sweat-dampened corduroy suit, dusty Guccis, and wire-rimmed glasses. Ralphie stabs his Cross pen through a script line on a blue flimsy and nods:

"I like it."

They wrap it up just before two o'clock and the rookie walks down three flights, out through the fire door and into an ambush of 11-year-olds brandishing ballpoints and autograph books. He keeps walking as he signs, the key to survival.

By three o'clock it's leveled off at 90 and the sun is an unblinking adversary. Three guys faint during practice and the rookie survives a similar fate only by biting his lip until it bleeds.

After 90 minutes of practice he gets extra grass drills—a hideous blend of running in place, flopping onto belly or back, then back on your feet. He gets extra grass drills a couple times a week because he had a big reputation in college and doesn't mind standing up to veterans. He has to fight hard during grass drills to keep from throwing up.

After practice he wades back into the autograph guerrillas, sings his school song three times at the evening meal, and fights the drowsies during meeting.

He goes down the hill with two other rookies after meetings for beer at Bruiser's. Back at the dorm, he has 20 minutes before lights out.

His handwriting is tight and disciplined, childlike, on the ruled tablet. He is not a letter writer, but his mother is alone now, living over the restaurant in the Bronx, and he knows she worries:

"Dear Ma: Things are okay here but pretty different from college. It's hard, here. It's hot, like home, during the day, but there's generally a breeze at night. . . ."

A defensive back wearing bib overalls and no shirt surveys the prospects while balancing his tray on one hand and scratching his chest with the other. He approaches a table where two rookies are staring into their roast beef with the same total involvement microbiologists might give to their slide plates.

There is a smile behind the defensive back's moustache, and his voice is so soft as to be almost inaudible against the background noises of the dining hall:

"Good evening. I wonder if one of you gentlemen might be good enough to give us a song?"

The farther rookie shifts his X-ray gaze from the roast beef to the mashed potatoes, but has the good sense not to look up.

The near rookie—a lean end from the Dakotas with red hair and a sunburn—is less fortunate. He looks up . . . and says, "Pardon me?"

Before the defensive back can repeat his question, a veteran tackle, who grew up in the Texas Panhandle, comes up behind the rookie. The Texas tackle has a voice like a rockslide:

"SING, Rook!"

The Dakota rookie scrambles up to stand on his chair in less time than it took the Texas tackle to make his request. Due to the abruptness of the journey, there is now a large splotch of roast beef *jus* on the rookie's shirt front.

The rookie begins his school song in a reedy tenor:
"Oh. . . ."

"Rook!"

The call is from a bespectacled flanker, peering over the afternoon newspaper. His face shows no emotion . . . unless viewed from an angle that catches the gleam in the eyes behind the thick lenses.

The rookie turns, teetering, toward his questioner:
"Yes, sir?"

"Rookie . . . do you have a heart?"

"Yessir," the boy answers, clapping his right hand up high against his chest.

Now the flanker is standing, hands on hips: "Do you know where it is, rookie? You have your hand on your Adam's apple!"

The boy shifts his hand and begins anew:
"Oh. . . ."

A running back in the chow line shouts:
"Louder! I can't hear you!"

Louder: "Oh. . . ."

A guard, seated near the wretch, looks up, his face rich with indignation:

"Sing . . . don't shout! You're ruining my dinner."

The bespectacled flanker has moved from his table to the coffee urns. He fills a cup and turns to stare at the rookie:

"You have a dreadful voice," he says. "This is a bad camp for singing and you are the worst of a bad lot."

The defensive back in bib overalls—the one who started it all—stands in front of the stricken singer. His hands are crossed on his chest and his head is bent as if in meditation.

Shakily, now: "Ooooh. . . ."

Suddenly, the defensive back holds up a hand.

"Wait! I think I've got it!"

The smile behind the moustache is equal parts tolerance and comradeship. Probably, it is not unlike the smile the wolf reserves for the deer it has run to ground.

"You're not singing with emotion!"

The defensive back turns toward a vast defensive end seated nearby:

"John . . . do you think this man is singing with emotion?"

The defensive end's brow puckers in concentration before he answers:

"No . . . no way. Karl, I think that man is a very unemotional singer."

The defensive back looks up at the rookie.

"You're from the Dakotas, aren't you?"

"Yessir."

The defensive back turns toward the vast defensive end:

"He's from the Dakotas, Moose."

The vast defensive end smiles and shakes his head in pleasant reflection.

"The Dakotas are beautiful, Karl," he replies. "The Dakotas have rolling wheat fields . . . those monuments carved on the mountain . . . the Black Hills."

The defensive back nods in agreement. Through it all, the rookie singer has the look of a man in need of one of those tidy little bags labeled "For Motion Discomfort" by the airlines.

The defensive back shouts to the rear of the room, where the bespectacled flanker is finishing his coffee and kidding a defensive coach.

"Flakey, do you think this man should sing with more emotion?"

"I think it is wrong for him to sing about such a beautiful area . . . an area with such proud traditions . . . in such a horrible voice. I think we are doing a disservice to the Dakotas."

The bespectacled flanker studies the rookie for a long moment. "Sing 'Jingle Bells' instead," he says.

The rookie does . . . poorly and haltingly, because by now he can not remember his middle name, to say nothing of "Jingle Bells."

The bespectacled flanker regards him for a long moment.

"Merry Christmas," he says with a smile.

The Dakota rookie has fair hands and he'll block but he doesn't have even good speed, let alone big speed. So he won't make it.

But this fall, in a Dakota beer joint, he will be in great conversational demand, envied for his insights into the personalities that make up one of the pro teams all of them watch so faithfully on television.

He will chuckle and shake his head in pleasant reflection and he will say:

"Listen, that's a great bunch of guys."

A lady catching the prop-job back to Billings stopped to stare.

She was sixtyish and small, but she clamped her son-in-law's arm in a no-nonsense grip. She peered over her spectacles with a proper scowl.

What on earth, she wondered, were all of those big fellows doing, loafing at that unposted gate? She sniffed in mild reproof and yanked the son-in-law back into the stream of concourse traffic.

A veteran running back entered the waiting area. The rookies had been bused up from camp and now the veterans straggled in. Some brought wives and children.

The veteran running back had dressed only to a level that might be classified as "standard" cool . . . no sense going too heavy on a preseason trip. He wore a machine-faded denim jacket-and-pants outfit; a figured shirt with enough collar and cuff showing to let you know it was a designer original; lizard boots that should have cost $300 but didn't; and a cream-colored rancher's straw hat, sized just a shade too small, so as to fit properly.

The veteran running back's luggage was at sharp odds with his outfit. He carried only a slim, cowhide briefcase.

He click-clacked across the marble waiting area and planted a dutiful kiss on the cheek of a linebacker's wife just arrived from "down home." Then he slumped into a chair to await the boarding call. In the process of tilting the rancher's straw down even further over his eyes, the running back glanced at a rawboned rookie flanker from Huron.

The training camp sun had left the rookie flanker's nose and neck the same deep and angry shade of red once popular in roofing shingles. The rookie flanker wore his hair short enough so it wouldn't show under his helmet. He also wore a heavy plaid suit, a patterned tie, and a white shirt with a stiff collar. And, under the veteran's steady gaze, he wore an expression of vague discomfort.

The running back thumbed up his rancher's straw in a manner previously unique to Marshall Dillon . . .

the more remarkable, because never in his life had the running back lived south or west of Royal Oak, Michigan. He stared at the rookie flanker and whistled softly:

"My God . . . is that a real suitcase?"

The rookie flanker fluttered briefly in his chair and jammed his plaid knees together . . . as if that could hide the elderly two-suiter. The suitcase was the color of coffee with not enough cream. It had a dent on one side and a travel sticker from St. Louis on the other.

The running back glanced down at his own sleek attaché case and shook his head in wonder.

"Rook . . . are we goin' on the same trip? I thought this was overnight . . . not a month!" The running back inserted a gentle nudge into a large section of ribs in the next chair. The ribs belonged to a vast defensive tackle who appeared to be sleeping.

"Growler," asked the running back, "you own a suitcase . . . a honest-to-God suitcase?"

The vast defensive tackle did not move, nor did he open his eyes, but his voice rumbled up from some depth; a similar sound announces new oil wells.

"Mah daddy had one once . . . when Ah was in high school. That was when Daddy was travelin'."

The rookie flanker swallowed against his stiff collar and stared at the toes of his brown shoes.

Now the huge defensive tackle's eyes were open. His face wrinkled as he studied the rookie and the suitcase. He looked as if he suddenly had become aware of an unpleasant odor.

"Rook. . . ." He sounded like the front end of a summer thunderstorm in Kansas. "You fixin' to brang that?"

The rookie now stared through the toes of his brown shoes and into the marble floor. Silently, he asked God to make either himself or the suitcase vanish. God refused.

"Damned shame," growled the defensive tackle, "for a man to mar a fine trip like this with a ugly old suitcase."

The running back stroked his chin in reflection.

"What's in it?"

"Just clothes and my playbook." The rookie recognized the voice as his own . . . barely.

The running back returned to stroking his chin. The defensive tackle went back to dozing.

"Growler," said the running back, "how much Coors you figure that old suitcase could hold?" The running back's eyes gleamed softly.

The defensive tackle belched spectacularly; mine shafts have collapsed with less provocation.

"Best part of two cases, Ah'd reckon."

The running back nodded his assent: " 'Bout a case apiece," he mused.

The rookie flanker stared through his brown shoes and through the marble floor and into that nether region reserved for the damned . . . and the rookies.

The defensive tackle opened his eyes again and impaled the rookie flanker on a steely smile . . . quite a bit of it terrifying.

"Why," he croaked, "don't I bring some back in my suitcase?"

The enigmatic Bud Grant, Iceman of the North, the rockfaced Viking chief who strode the Minnesota sideline for 18 years, brought the franchise to four Super Bowls and earned for it 11 divisional crowns, is the subject of Bill McGrane's artful biography *Bud, The Other Side of the Glacier,* from which this chapter is drawn. Grant, an extraordinary athlete himself who won varsity letters in football, baseball, and basketball at the University of Minnesota and later played for the Philadelphia Eagles in the NFL and the Minneapolis Lakers in the NBA, is a man of many facets masked by the most unrevealing of facades. But here the man and coach come to life with a special vibrancy.

Eskimos, Sweat Pants, and So Forth

BILL MCGRANE

THE MAN is many-sided.

It was very quiet in the locker room after that first Super Bowl loss against Kansas City. There was just the distant hum of the heating system and every now and then a deep-throated grunt of pain or a curse from Joe Kapp as the doctor worked on his shoulder.

"Goddamned redwood trees," Kapp kept repeating, his face contorted. "They kept fallin' on me, they were like goddamned redwood trees!"

Bud Grant stood in the center of the room, his face as hard and cold as Vatican marble. He was waiting for their fury to subside to where they'd listen.

When he spoke, his voice wasn't loud, but it filled the room.

"I know what you're thinking . . . if only we could play them again, we could do better."

His eyes swept the dirty, shattered faces.

"Well, we can't. It might be different next time, but we just had this time. All we can do is learn from it." His voice took on a cutting edge. "We will learn from it," he said. "We will be a better team for what happened here today."

They opened the season against Kansas City the next year . . . and beat them 27-10. At the team meeting the night before the game, Grant walked in and turned on the Chiefs' Super Bowl highlight film. It didn't have much to say about the Vikings that was good. When the film was over, Bud just got up and walked out.

The Vikings played out of doors until 1981. How cold did it get at the Met?

Following a December win over Chicago . . . the Bears bowed to conditions by enhancing the halftime bouillon with a pint of brandy . . . defensive end Carl Eller faced a band of reporters.

"I knew I wasn't cold," said Eller, "because Bud told me I wasn't." He stared down at his large feet then and shook his head wistfully. "But I sure wish someone would have told my feet!"

Grant puts cold weather and its influence on the same shelf with death, taxes, and officiating . . . fates over which the individual holds no sway.

"What can happen is that you don't know what's

going to happen,'' Grant explained in good Casey Stengelese.

"If the cold weather was an advantage for us, it was because we didn't want our players to be concerned about it. We couldn't do anything about it, so why waste time worrying?''

Must have worked . . . the Vikings, from 1967 through 1981, played twenty-five games at the Met after December 1. They won nineteen of them.

Visiting teams mushed into the Met in the manner of Arctic expeditions, done up in thermal underwear, electric socks, and mittens that reached almost to their ears. The Vikings greeted the change of seasons with shirtsleeves, equanimity, and the warmth of Grant's annual storytelling.

He told two stories every year, one about a dog and the other about Eskimos.

"I told the dog story because it had to do with practicing outside in cold weather,'' Grant explained. "A game's one thing, but practice isn't nearly as attractive. I told them we were like a dog when we went out to practice in bad weather. As it gets colder, a dog's coat grows longer . . . I told them, by going outside, regardless of the weather, our skin would grow thicker and our tolerance for the cold would increase. If we didn't do anything else, we'd get outside for a while.''

Grant still enjoyed telling the stories, and claims the teams enjoyed hearing them. "Veterans would tell the new fellows, 'With the weather getting colder, he'll tell the Eskimo story pretty soon.' ''

And what was the Eskimo story?

"After World War II,'' said Grant, "our country built a radar network across the Arctic because there was concern about the Russians attacking us. It was called the DEW line.

"Because of the permafrost, the ground never really thaws out up there, so putting in those big radar installations was a hard job, and it required heavy equipment. The army guys assigned to run the bulldozers would bundle up in all the clothing they could find in order to stay warm. But regardless of what they wore, they could only sit up on those bulldozers for thirty minutes at a time, and then they had to get down and go warm up. As a result, the job fell behind schedule.

"There were Eskimos around the work site,'' said Grant, "so eventually the army people taught a couple of the Eskimos how to run a bulldozer. The Eskimo would get up on the bulldozer and sit there all day. Before long, they had the job back on schedule.

"The army couldn't figure out why the Eskimo could work in the Arctic while our soldiers couldn't. So they brought the Eskimos down to the States and put them through all sorts of tests. They measured body fat and blood chemistry and hair . . . everything they could

think of. They spent half a million dollars on the project.

"And they came up with one conclusion.

"The Eskimo got up on the bulldozer, and he knew he was going to be cold, but he still could run the bulldozer. The army guy got up there and wanted to be warm while he ran the bulldozer . . . as soon as he got cold, he had to get down.

"The moral of the story, as it applied to our team, was that we might be cold, but we could still play football.''

There are students of Bud Grant who will tell you that his finest prank may well have been removing all of the commode lids in the Viking office restrooms one April Fool's Day.

There was another, involving a pair of sweatpants, when Grant had the tables turned on him and still won out.

One April Fool's Day his wife, Pat, decided to beat her husband to the punch. He never misses an April Fool's.

Pat got up at the crack of dawn, bundled up the kids, took every last pair of pants Bud owned, and went to a friend's house to hide out.

Grant was to speak at noon at a downtown civic luncheon.

Bud got up when the alarm went off, showered, and surveyed his looted closet. Then he got dressed, had breakfast, and went to work.

Pat called the office right after nine.

"What's he wearing?'' she demanded.

"A sport coat, shirt and tie, and sweatpants,'' came the reply.

She called again, a little after eleven.

"What's he doing?'' she asked.

"Getting ready to go downtown, he's speaking at a luncheon.''

"And he's still wearing sweatpants?'' she wailed.

"Sure . . . he said they're the only pants he's got. But he doesn't seem upset about it.''

Pat roared into the parking lot a few minutes later with a pair of pants.

He's part Indian, but he laughs at suggestions of blood having anything to do with his love for the outdoors.

"My dad wasn't an outdoorsman,'' he points out. He is of French, Scottish, and Indian descent. "My uncle used to tell me I was the only blue-eyed Indian in Wisconsin.''

Pro football officiating does not bring out Grant's best side. He is troubled by the fact that games and seasons and careers are influenced mightily by the decisions of men who are not as wholly immersed in the sport as are its players and coaches. Unlike baseball, professional football officials don't work full-time, but leave their regular jobs as salesmen and school administrators and real estate appraisers and so forth to officiate on weekends.

When the Vikings acquired a player from another team, or hired a new coach, Grant debriefed the acquisition and did it with enthusiasm.

"I'm interested," he said. "Another team might have a technique or a training camp drill or a philosophy . . . some aspect of their operation . . . that is better than the way we do a thing. If you take the time, you can learn a lot from new people. It might just be what they eat or when they eat. It helps . . . if nothing new is coming in, you can get inbred."

He will take the time to draw out a shy youngster, but he can be calculatingly cold to a star type.

In 1967, we had Grant and his coaches over for dinner . . . their families had not yet moved to Minnesota.

Pete, our oldest son, was just a toddler then and quite shy.

What with barbecuing out in the backyard and visiting with assistant coaches, I forgot all about Grant. I went inside to look for him . . . he was on the porch, seated, with his back to me. I thought at first glance he'd dozed off because he had his head down. But when I got closer, I saw Pete, sitting in front of Bud, on the floor. They were having a talk. Kids know . . . they can pick out the adults who will talk with them, as opposed to the adults who only talk at them. Pete was smiling and chattering away . . . he'd forgotten all about being shy.

Maybe, he's just an imposing presence to all of us normal, hung up adults.

On a Sunday night, in the old Cadillac hotel in Detroit, he stood in the lobby, waiting for Frank Gifford, who had called to request an interview. The Vikings would play the Lions the next night in a game televised by ABC TV.

As Bud stood waiting, the most-identifiable voice of Monday Night Football rang out across the lobby:

"Harry Peter Grant . . ."

There was quite a bit more, but it was a long time ago. Howard Cosell kept talking as he walked, and he walked right up to Grant. There were a lot of people in the lobby, they recognized Howard, and Howard recognized the fact that he was being recognized. He executed one of those wind-depleting, wonderfully complex yet grammatically perfect sentences that seem to last for two or three minutes. You had to admire Howard's lung capacity, especially in view of the fact that he was a steady smoker.

He ended up his sentence with something like " . . . and what do you say to that, Coach Bud Grant?"

Gifford was approaching by then, looking vaguely uneasy.

What Bud said was nothing . . . for what seemed like about six weeks. He stared at Cosell. After a while, Howard's smile took on a quality to suggest it had been painted into place. Bud just stood there, staring . . . silent.

Finally, he made a tiny nod and said, "Howard."

Then he turned to Gifford and said, "Let's go up to my room, where we can talk."

It was, at least to one witness, a devastating thing to do . . . Howard was left in their wake, cigar drooping.

The thing is, Grant doesn't appreciate people who trundle their own spotlight around with them.

He is comfortable around people he knows . . . although the reverse of that theory isn't always true.

He had all the Viking staff members and their wives over to his house for dinner the night before a training camp. It was the cocktail hour, before the lake trout dinner, and Bud was being the perfect host. There were ice-cold Leinenkugels from the basement bar, and everyone was having a good time.

My wife was seated on a couch, visiting with Susan Patera, whose husband Jack was the defensive line coach. Neither one of those ladies is a conversational slouch . . . they started out lamenting a mouse discovered in one of their basements and promptly expanded the topic to spell out, quite clearly, their mutual discomfort with wild creatures in general.

Grant stood behind the bar, watching and listening. After a time, he just sort of ambled away, presumably for more Leinenkugel, which is a Chippewa Falls, Wisconsin beer and Bud's favorite. Bud's not really a beer authority, but it is good.

He returned, but not with more Leinenkugel . . . what he had was a fat, full-grown raccoon tucked under his arm. The ladies were still visiting at a gallop, so Grant just eased the raccoon down on the edge of the couch, right behind my wife. The ladies didn't notice at first, and the raccoon just sat there, looking sleepy. But it must have moved against her, because my wife turned and saw it.

She's got a good yell under normal conditions, but this one was special. Both ladies more or less jumped into each other's laps.

Grant, behind the bar again by then, looked surprised.

"I thought you knew we had a pet raccoon," he said.

Part of being the coach is dealing with the media. Is it a hard part?

"I can't say that it is," said Grant. "It's an important

part of the job, and it's also a tool. You either take the time, or you take the consequences. I prefer to take the time. Some writers don't want to hear what you have to say, because it might not jibe with what they want to write. But it's important to take the time, to keep the record clean, and to be in a position where the reporters will come to you with their questions.''

Grant ignores articles or reports that are either inaccurate or caustic.

You mean, if someone writes a piece and takes a strip off you, you ignore it?

"That's what I mean.''

Will you still talk to that reporter?

"Sure, and I hope he wouldn't be able to notice any reaction on my part to what he wrote or said.''

What would be wrong with saying you thought the piece was unfair?

"It would be wrong,'' Grant said, "because then I would have to enter into a dialogue over it, and I would prefer just to ignore it.''

What if someone writes a piece that you like?

"I'll let him know,'' Grant answered.

Football seasons, like new trousers, seem awfully long. Instant reaction . . . elation over a win, despair over a loss . . . can prompt a very dangerous fatigue. The coaches who seem to prosper are those who view the season in long form, realizing there will be ups and downs, rather than give in to those jarring, weekly vignettes of emotion.

"There is an advantage,'' said Grant, "to having coached for a long period of time. I would imagine that Bill Walsh, for example, finds it easier to coach now than he did early on. I think you become more comfortable with yourself . . . you come to know yourself, really, your strengths and your limitations. And you realize the emotions you are feeling aren't any different from those someone else is experiencing. You learn that you don't have all the answers . . . you still look for them, but you admit to yourself that you're never going to have all of them.''

Bart Starr, the former Green Bay coach, asked a question of Grant a few years back.

"He asked if we had a secret for coming back,'' said Bud. "He wanted to know how we could look so bad one week and then bounce back, and play well the next. Bart said he thought our trademark was that we didn't stay bad . . . we might play poorly one week, but we'd bounce back. He wanted to know what we did that was different.

"The only answer I could come up with was that we didn't do anything different,'' said Grant, "whether we won big or lost big. Maybe that's the answer.''

He was not a "method'' or "system''-oriented coach. He was no more bound to one philosophy of football than he would be to one hunting tactic . . . he took advantage of cover and terrain in both.

His early Viking teams were strongest on defense, because that's where the team's best athletes were. Yet, they weren't all great athletes. Page certainly and Eller and Marshall were up front, and their rush was a thing of fury. But the secondary was modest in ability. The thing the secondary did was play with discipline. The hinge between the two groups was that freebooting corp of linebackers, Winston, Warwick, and Hilgenberg. The mesh of the entire unit was marvelous.

Yet, when Tarkenton came back, the emphasis went to offense because the circle had run on . . . the better athletes were on offense. Tarkenton, and later Kramer, gave Grant and Burns full range of offensive motion . . . and receivers like Gilliam and Rashad and Sammy White and Foreman made a sophisticated passing attack a necessity, rather than a luxury.

He once had the mayor of Winnipeg don a Blue Bomber uniform and, unannounced, run the opening kickoff back in an intrasquad game. "We had it blocked beautifully,'' said Grant, "but he ran out of gas at the 20 and fell down.''

He has been criticized for his low-key approach to the challenge of preparing players emotionally for a game. He ignores the criticism.

"They're professionals, and this is their job,'' said Grant. "It's up to each man to prepare himself . . . I can't do that for him. We don't pretend that what we do is the best way,'' said Grant, "but we try to deal in facts. We try to look at people and situations as they really are.''

His normal office uniform during the season is a flannel shirt, corduroy trousers, and scuffed moccasins. If he must wear a tie, he wears a clip-on.

The times have changed. Nowadays, athletes have joined their peers within the entertainment industry as millionaires.

Can a million-dollar halfback still get down . . . grab grass and growl . . . when the need arises?

"There is no easy solution,'' said Grant. "Just because a team pays the most money doesn't give it a guarantee on winning. You placate people with money, but you don't buy them unless they are willing to join the effort. It's hard to buy winning.''

The Tigers Are Still Champions

JUST BEEN EATING 'EM ALIVE

One of the Hardest Fought Bat=tles in Foot Ball History.

Tigers 13, Bull Dogs 6.

Massillon Scored Five Points in the First Half, and in the Second Half Ripped Canton's Line to Pieces--Made Great Gains Around Ends and Toyed With the Bull Dogs Generally.

The first of the great pro football rivalries, an intra-state affair in Ohio between the Massilon Tigers and the Canton Bull Dogs. To come would be such enduring, thoroughly hate-filled intercity hostilities as those waged between the Green Bay Packers and the Chicago Bears, the Washington Redskins and the Dallas Cowboys, the Pittsburgh Steelers and the Cleveland Browns, the New York Giants and the Philadelphia Eagles, and the Los Angeles Rams and the San Francisco 49ers.

PRICE 10 CENTS

NEW YORK FOOTBALL GIANTS
vs.
PORTSMOUTH SPARTANS

KEN STRONG (Giant Back)

POLO GROUNDS   NOVEMBER 5, 1933

When programs were a dime, and stars like Ken Strong were known as triple threats (run, pass, and kick) and played both offense and defense.

HE CAN REALLY THROW PASSES

GEO. HALAS CHICAGO

PREVIOUS TO THIS SEASON SID HAD BEEN NO FARTHER WEST THAN ITHACA, N.Y.

AMONG THE TOP FIVE IN THE TRIBUNE 1939 ALL-STAR VOTING CONTEST

OUTSTANDING PASSER OF THE 1938 SEASON WITH 132 ATTEMPTED, 66 COMPLETED FOR 866 YARDS AND 9 TOUCH-DOWNS WITH A COLUMBIA TEAM THAT LOST 6 OUT OF 9

YES SIR, HE'S 6 FEET TALL 197 POUNDS AND MARRIED

Sid LUCKMAN

COLUMBIA UNIVERSITY TRIPLE THREAT BACK AND UNANIMOUS CHOICE FOR ALL-AMERICAN HONORS ▪ AVERAGED 4.6 YARDS IN 92 ATTEMPTS BEHIND MEDI-OCRE LINE.

WON 3 LETTERS AT SHORT STOP AS WELL AS 3 IN FOOTBALL

STUART MERRELL

DETROIT·1935

LIONS·14
BEARS·2

STACY   5 HEWITT   27-MORSE   G-BONZANI   MUSS

Helmets were not always considered indispensable—witness Bill Hewitt, Chicago Bears end and future Hall-of-Famer, zeroing in on Detroit Lion end Butch Morse (27). Also helmetless at the far right is another future Hall-of-Famer, Bear tackle George Musso. Maybe the helmets helped that day in 1935, because the Lions won, 14–2.

DAVE BOSS
HOF/NFL PHOTOS

— 175 —

The immortal Jim Thorpe, playing in this 1926 game for the Canton Bulldogs, lunges for Chicago Bears halfback Dutch Sternaman. Apparently about to throw a classic clip behind Thorpe is another football immortal, George Halas. Thorpe was 38 years old when this picture was taken and played only one more year in the NFL; Halas, on the other hand, maintained his association with the Bears until his death in 1983. Both are charter members of the Pro Football Hall of Fame.

1941 SEASON TICKET PRICES

PRICE No. 1

$13.20

One choice seat for the 6 Chicago Bears' home games at Wrigley Field. Either the lower deck, close to the field of play, or the upper deck, from where you can see the intricate plays open up.

PRICE No. 2

$10.80

One reserved grand stand seat for the 6 Chicago Bears' home games at Wrigley Field. All grand stand seats are between the 30 yard lines. Your choice of upper or lower deck.

**CHICAGO BEARS
1941 Schedule**

Sept. 7 - N. Y. Giants Here
(NOT INCLUDED IN SEASON TICKET)

Sept. 28 - - at Green Bay

Oct. 5 - - at Cleveland

Oct. 12 - Cardinals Here

Oct. 19 - Detroit Here

Oct. 26 - Pittsburgh Here

Nov. 2 - Green Bay Here

Nov. 9 - Cleveland Here

Nov. 16 - Washington Here

Nov. 23 - - at Detroit

Nov. 30 - at Philadelphia

Dec. 7 - at Cardinals

**Home Games Played at
Wrigley Field**

**CHICAGO BEARS
CHOICE SEAT
INSURANCE**

Loyal Bears' Fans are entitled to special consideration. Therefore the management has inaugurated this "Choice Seat Insurance" which guarantees special privileges.

Approximately a 15% saving of the regular purchase price is merely one of the many advantages which this plan offers.

More important, however, the fan who wishes to avoid that last minute ticket rush is assured of receiving the same choice seat for each and every home game of the 1941 season.

Making it a policy to order your season ticket requirements now will pay a yearly dividend in enjoyment and thrills. Your order places your name on a permanent list entitling you to the privileges of retaining the same good seat each year . . . a life-time insurance.

CHICAGO BEARS FOOTBALL CLUB

Geo. Halas
PRESIDENT

37 SOUTH WABASH AVENUE

Season tickets weren't all that pricey in 1941. But then, there weren't any skyboxes in those days either.

JUST A HELMET LINER NOW

BOBBY MITCHELL

PAUL HORNUNG

SERVICE CALLS

MURRAY OLDERMAN
HOF/NFL PHOTOS

They grappled just as ferociously in 1946 as they do in the 1980s. Here halfback Steve Bagarus of the Washington Redskins is corralled by Chuck Cherundolo (21) of the Pittsburgh Steelers.

One of the game's most powerful fullbacks ever, Marion Motley (76) puts a shoulder to a Los Angeles Rams defender. Motley was a member of the Cleveland Browns team that won four consecutive AAFC championships, 1946–1949, and played in four NFL title games, 1950–1953. He was enshrined in the Pro Football Hall of Fame in 1968.

Who said the face mask brought about face-masking? In this 1948 grapple, Chicago Bears end Joe Abbey tries to make a bowling ball out of the face of quarterback Fred Enke of the Detroit Lions.

Talk about stiff arms! Hall-of-Famer George Connor, one of the game's greatest 60-minute men (offensive tackle, defensive linebacker), lays one on fellow Hall-of-Famer Tom Fears of the Los Angeles Rams after intercepting a pass in the L.A. Coliseum in the 1950s.

PHIL BISSELL
HOF/NFL PHOTOS

LOU DARVAS
HOF/NFL PHOTOS

Obscured somewhat by Dallas Cowboy defender George Andrie (66) is Pittsburgh Steeler quarterback Bobby Layne looking for a receiver downfield. Number 51 on the Steelers is Buzz Nutter, 42 is Dick Hoak, and 88 is John Powers. For the Cowboys, number 44 is Don Bishop, and chasing Hoak is All-Pro linebacker Chuck Howley. Layne, who left his biggest impression when he quarterbacked the Detroit Lions from 1950 through 1958, was elected to the Pro Football Hall of Fame in 1967.

OLLIE
MATSON
CONSIDERED TOP
RUNNING BACK
IN PRO GAME

Fred Reinert
PLAIN DEALER

FRED REINERT
HOF/NFL PHOTOS

Frank Gifford, whose face may be more familiar today to Monday Night Football audiences, finds a gaping hole in the Philadelphia defense in this 1955 game. It was the next-to-last game Gifford and the Giants played at the Polo Grounds before moving across the Harlem River to Yankee Stadium. Helping keep the way clear is Jack Stroud (66), and apparently about to block somebody is quarterback Charlie Conerly. Number 73 on the Eagles is Lum Snyder. Gifford played for the Giants from 1952 through 1964 and was inducted into the Pro Football Hall of Fame in 1977.

Certainly one of the greatest passers of all time, Johnny Unitas (19) of the Baltimore Colts prepares to practice his specialty here. Pressure is being applied by Detroit Lions tackle Alex Karras.

BILL LANFIELD

FRED REINERT
HOF/NFL PHOTOS

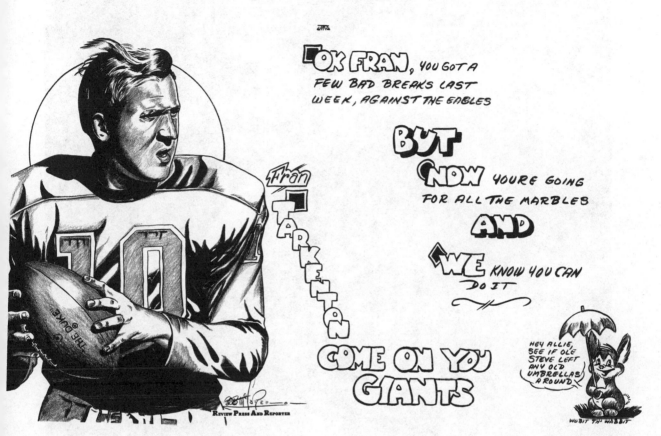

HOF/NFL PHOTOS

The Dallas Cowboys' great quarterback Roger Staubach cannot scramble away here from big John Mendenhall of the New York Giants. Coming in to add a lick of his own is Giant George Martin (75). Staubach's 11-year career with Dallas earned him a berth in the Pro Football Hall of Fame, inducted in 1985.

THE DIVIDING LINE

GREEN BAY

PRO

PROS LEAD STARS, 18-8, (2 TIES)

COLLEGE ALL-STARS

COLLEGE

MURRAY OLDERMAN

HOF/NFL PHOTOS

HOF/NFL PHOTOS

Perhaps the most dazzling open-field runner of all time, Gale Sayers (40) of the Chicago Bears displays here what he did best. In Sayers' first year in the NFL, 1965, he set two league records for a rookie by scoring 22 touchdowns, 6 of them in one game against the San Francisco 49ers—both still standing today. Sayers was inducted into the Pro Football Hall of Fame in 1977.

One of the most famous portraits of pain, frustration, exhaustion, and dejection is this one of Y. A. Tittle. The bloodied, 37-year-old New York Giants quarterback kneels in quiet desperation in the end zone after a savage hit in a 1964 game against the Pittsburgh Steelers. Tittle, who had also quarterbacked for the Baltimore Colts and the San Francisco 49ers, was enshrined in the Pro Football Hall of Fame in 1971.

In one of the greatest rivalries in NFL history, fullback Pat Harder (34) of the then Chicago Cardinals looks for an opening in the defense of the Chicago Bears. Running interference for him is George Petrovich (18), and the other Cardinal behind him is quarterback Jim Hardy, who had just pitched the ball to Harder. In this 1950 game, the Bears demolished the Cardinals 27–6.

FRED REINERT
HOF/NFL PHOTOS

— 199 —

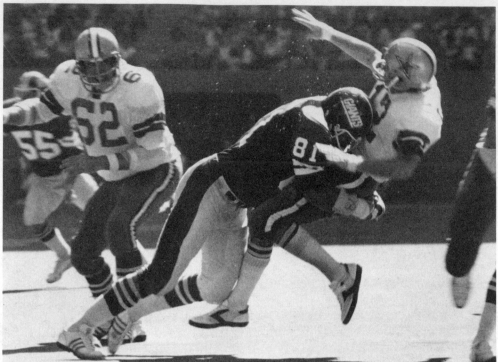

NEW YORK GIANTS

Quarterback perils. At least Roger Staubach got this pass off for the Dallas Cowboys in the mid-1970s just before New York Giants defensive end Jack Gregory (81) applied some 260 pounds of flesh and padding to Staubach's very vulnerable midsection. Number 62 on the Cowboys is John Fitzgerald.

A matchup in the snow. Fullback Larry Csonka of the New York Giants (39), but better known for his play in sunny Florida with the Miami Dolphins, charges across the ice to meet Chicago Bears linebacker Doug Buffone in 1977. The Bears, by the way, squeezed out a 12–9 win on that wintry afternoon at Giants Stadium in East Rutherford, New Jersey, the Giants' second year out of New York City.

NEW YORK GIANTS

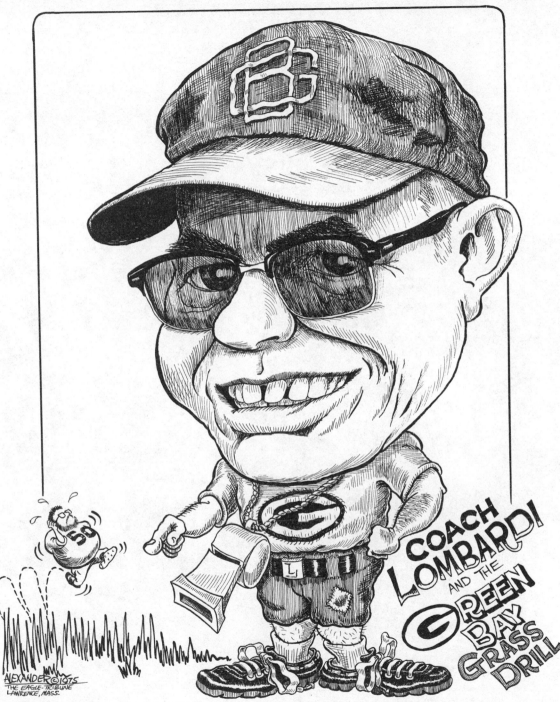

COACH LOMBARDI! AND THE GREEN BAY GRASS DRILL

ALEXANDER ©1975
THE EAGLE-TRIBUNE
LAWRENCE, MASS.

ALEXANDER
HOF/NFL PHOTOS

A vaulting Jim McMahon (9) heads into the end zone for one of the Chicago Bears touchdowns in Super Bowl XX. In that January 1986 game, the Bears rolled up the largest win margin in Super Bowl history when they drubbed the New England Patriots 46–10.

Joe Morris (20) takes off around end during the New York Giants Super Bowl championship season of 1986. In the background is Giant quarterback Phil Simms (11), and on the ground is Morris' tandem running back Maurice Carthon (44). Morris, incidentally, gained 1,516 yards rushing that year, the most in the Giants' more than 60-year history. (Fred Roe)

TANK McNAMARA®   by Jeff Millar & Bill Hinds

The two cities under study here are an ocean away from those that Charles Dickens addressed. They are Philadelphia, in which the Eagles reside, and New York, where the Giants could be found, at least in 1971 when this tale appeared in Larry Merchant's book . . . *And Everyday You Take Another Bite*. Always amusing, often barbed, ever entertaining, the writings of Larry Merchant on professional football are among the best in America. The title for his book, incidentally, was contributed by Detroit's most famous linebacker, Hall of Famer Joe Schmidt, who once made the memorable observation: "Life is a shit sandwich, and everyday you take another bite."

Tale of Two Cities

LARRY MERCHANT

Under a gray October sky on the Plains of Troy yesterday the mighty defense of the Trojans made their last goal-line stand. A trick play by the Greeks pushed over the winning score in the dying minutes.

Odysseus, the quarterback for the invaders, said that after slamming into a stone wall for ten years he decided to use the old Wooden Horse play. "They have the best front four in the league," Odysseus said. "We felt we could distract them by spreading our ends and halfbacks. I just galloped alone up the middle. Normally I run only from sheer fright."

The victory of the Greeks stilled rumors of dissension and an impending coaching change because they hadn't scored in such a long time. It had been reported that Achilles, the great defensive end, was feuding with Agamemnon, the head coach. Agamemnon admitted that some players were unhappy, but he said it was a healthy sign.

He was more concerned with the crippling heel injury suffered by Achilles. It may end his career. Achilles said he was hit from behind by Paris. "It was a cheap shot," he said.

WITH APOLOGIES to that great English scribe, Charles Dickens, this is a tale of two cities that have known the best and the worst of times in professional football, Philadelphia and New York. In the decade of the NFL's greatest growth, the '60s, the Philadelphia Eagles and the New York Giants had the best of times immediately followed by the worst, bringing to the surface the supreme nuttiness that is one of homo sap's enduring charms.

First some background music.

The Eagles and the Giants are two of the seven pioneer franchises in the modern NFL dating from 1933. The others are the Pittsburgh Steelers, the Green Bay Packers, the Washington (nee Boston) Redskins, the Chicago Bears and the St. Louis (nee Chicago) Cardinals.

Four pioneer families still run their teams; the Maras of the Giants, the Bidwells of the Cardinals, the Rooneys of the Steelers, the Halases of the Bears. George Preston Marshall founded the Redskins, Bert Bell the Eagles, Curley Lambeau the Packers. Tim Mara, Charles Bidwell and Art Rooney were self-made sportsmen about town associated with horse racing. George Halas, Bell and Lambeau were player-coach-entrepreneurs. Marshall was a promoter.

Halas is the crusty patriarch of pro football. He brought it off the sand lots when he signed Red Grange out of Illinois, and he built a dynasty with Bronco Nagurski, Bulldog Turner, Sid Luckman, George McAfee and others. Undaunted by winning just one of the six championships in the last twenty-five years, he still uses his prerogative as owner to send in plays now and then.

That is one, or six, more championships than the Steelers have won though. The Steelers do not even have a division title to their name. Unfortunately Art Rooney, one of the beautiful people of sports, squeezed most of his luck into a legendary three-day spree in the '30s when he won about $250,000 at the track. He had Johnny Unitas and Sid Luckman, and neither played a game for him before they were traded. He also once ran for a minor political office on the platform that he didn't know what the duties were but he would find out if elected; the New York *Times* hailed him as a Diogenes but he was defeated.

The Cardinals won their only championship in 1947. Jimmy Conzleman, coach of that team, is in the legend class too. In addition to playing and coaching and briefly owning a team, he wrote songs, published a newspaper, boxed, was a radio commentator and an advertising executive. Supreme Court Justice William O. Douglas spoke in his behalf when he was inducted into the Hall of Fame.

Curley Lambeau talked a packing house into investing $500 in the Packers in 1919, the year the old original NFL began. They won three championships in the early days, three more with Don Hutson and five with Lombardi. Today the Packers are publicly owned by fans who bought stock to keep them in Green Bay.

George Preston Marshall was bombastic, innovative and self-destructively bigoted. Two out of three ain't bad, but the third spoiled a good thing and Washington teams for a long time. Marshall conceived rules changes that opened up the game—most notably permitting passing anywhere behind the line of scrimmage (instead of at least five yards behind it) and slimming down the ball so it could be passed easily—and then he got Sammy Baugh. Pretty good thinking, and the Redskins won their two championships with it, the last in 1942. But Marshall's refusal to sign a black player until 1962 led to a decline and fall that hasn't become a rise and climb yet.

With Halas and Marshall, Bert Bell was a third dynamic force in the growth of the NFL. Remembered now primarily as a strong commissioner who made the home-television blackout policy stick in the courts, it was Bell who conceived the player draft in 1936. Unbeknownst to him, it would mark a prenatal reference for the schizo-phrenia of the Eagles. The first collegian drafted in the first draft was Jay Berwanger, an All-American halfback from the University of Chicago. The Eagles drafted him and he was stillborn, refusing to go pro. A prophetic development. Or, as Casey Stengel would say, the future of the Eagles was ahead of them.

The Eagles won championships in 1948 and 1949, with Greasy Neale coaching players like Steven Van Buren, Chuck Bednarik and Pete Pihos. A syndicate of a hundred businessmen put up $3000 apiece to buy the team, and in 1950 the head of the syndicate, a powerful politician, reamed out the players like so many ward heelers after a losing game. Neale told him to get out of his dressing room, and the politician fired him when the season was over. Nothing failed like success or succeeded like failure for the Eagles, as events would continue to prove.

In 1958 they got Norm Van Brocklin from the Rams in a trade. With Bob Waterfield and ends Tom Fears and Elroy Hirsch, Van Brocklin had helped make the Rams a devastating offensive team. In one game he passed for 550 yards, in another he threw five touchdown passes in one quarter. He would become the only quarterback to win championships in two cities and the only player in modern times to a) retire after being named the most valuable player in the league, and b) get a job as a head coach right after retiring. He was special.

When the Eagles did poorly in his first season with them, Van Brocklin decided they were a dead end and he wasn't going to die with them and, at age thirty-three, he would quit. The Eagles changed his mind with the promise, suggested by Commissioner Bell, that he would be named coach after the next season. The Eagles tied for second place that next season, but Bell died and the Eagles told Van Brocklin that coach Buck Shaw would like to take one last shot at a championship. Van Brocklin went along with it.

The Eagles then won the championship in 1960 as Van Brocklin had what many of his peers consider the one best season a quarterback ever had. And they don't know the half of it. What Van Brocklin did for all to see was win eight games in the last quarter and then beat the Packers in the playoff—nobody did that again to a Lombardi team—with a collection of culls, castoffs, old pros and a few young lions. What they didn't see was Van Brocklin being consulted by management on key trades, Van Brocklin tutoring backs Tommy McDonald and Pete Retzlaff as they converted to all-pro receivers, Van Brocklin virtually coaching the offense, Van Brocklin walking on the Schuylkill River.

With his soles still wet, Van Brocklin was asked by the Eagles what he wanted as head coach. He said he wanted to name his assistants, which is standard procedure, and that the organization should upgrade its college scouting system by investing $50,000 in it. They said no, and they said no. The first no was all Van Brocklin had to hear. It meant they were reneging on their promise. It meant he was as dead as Bell as far as they were concerned. He took the head coaching job with the brand new Minnesota Vikings.

Van Brocklin had perceived that pro football was changing and that the Eagles weren't changing with it. You could see the change at the draft meetings that were held then in Philadelphia. Cleveland's Paul Brown, who had revolutionized the game with total organization and intensive scouting, would be seated at a table laden with fat notebooks and fatter files and telephones, surrounded by seven or eight assistants. They might have been planning the production of Chevrolets for five years. The Eagles' table would have a half-filled three-by-five-inch card file as a centerpiece, period. It would be surrounded by a general manager and one assistant; their only scout might be out calling on a public telephone. They might have been bill collectors. Like as not, the president of the team, who was the fire commissioner of Philadelphia, would mosey over to the table, finger the three-by-five-inch cards, fish one out and say, ''Here's a kid from Idaho, 6-5 and 245. Why don't we try him?''

There was a certain down-home logic to drafting from the Look All-America in those days, even if it was like fighting General Motors with a covered wagon. Until 1960, when expansion and the AFL intruded on the established order, there was a surplus of talent. Such a surplus that you might get a Van Brocklin in a trade and win a championship that way once in a great while, so why go to all the expense of a college scouting network? The Browns collected so many studs that they traded away Doug Atkins, Willie Davis and Henry Jordan. The Rams, first of the older NFL teams to go heavily into scouting college talent, gave Andy Robustelli and Del Shofner to the Giants. All-pros all.

The danger in the practice of depending on rejects and trades was in the delusion that it could go on forever. Then, when it became necessary to compete with organization and cash for talent, the pioneer owners who had been paying linemen a couple hundred dollars a game twenty years before simply couldn't bring themselves to do it, despite soaring income from attendance and television. The Baltimore Colts, one of the more enlightened franchises, won championships in 1958 and 1959, were making an estimated million-dollar profit a year, and lost their No. 1 pick in 1960 to the AFL because they offered him $8500: he was Ron Mix, who became an all-AFL tackle for ten years. The Eagles didn't sign a No. 1 for the first four years of the war with the AFL, leading both leagues.

The penury of the Eagles inspired the first serious incident in labor-management relations in the NFL, known in labor history as The Great Quarterback Sneak of 1963. Ten days before the first game of the season, Sonny Jurgensen and King Hill left camp because management, as was its custom, negotiated by not negotiating; if a player didn't like the terms offered him he could wait until he did like them. While Jurgensen and Hill were condemned by managements and apologists from coast to coast for leaving their teammates in the lurch, the fact was that their teammates celebrated them as their Debs and Gompers. They gave them a roaring send-off when they departed and two days later, after their demands were met, they gave them heroes' welcomes.

At the end of that season the Eagles were sold for five and a half million dollars, netting a $52,000 profit per share in fourteen years. Had the stockholders waited two months they could have made another $20,000 or so per share because of a $400,000-per-team raise in the league's television contract. Had they waited until 1968 they could have made $160,000 per share, because the team was then sold for $16 million and change.

Between sales there were five seasons of Katzenjammer madness. The new owner after the 1963 season was Jerry Wollman, a construction tycoon whose net worth, according to an NFL investigation, was $25 million. His choice as coach was Joe Kuharich, who turned out to be the costliest football dummy in the annals of block and tackle.

Jerry Wollman, thirty-seven, bright and ebullient, had bought himself the ultimate toy and he was going to have some fun with it. He did, while the money lasted. He spent money like he had terminal cancer. He gave a Rolls-Royce to a stockholder who showed him around town to set up the purchase of the team. He took a gang of friends and relatives to Puerto Rico for a few weeks. He paid the mortgages of some assistant coaches. He rented a fire engine to pick up friends for a party. He bought Connie Mack Stadium. He picked up an expansion hockey franchise and financed a 15,000-seat arena. He was a flamboyant doer and he was jolting Philadelphia out of its conservative sloth.

But he screwed up the Eagles worse than they had been, which was no small achievement. He started by giving Joe Kuharich the gaudiest contract the mind of man could imagine—fifteen years at about $50,000 per. ''I never made a mistake,'' Wollman replied.

In two years a building he was putting up in Chicago began to sink into Lake Michigan and he began to go down with it. He brought an Arabian sheik to one game, and a German prince to another, trying to arrange loans that would salvage his construction empire, his struggling team and his strange coach. He couldn't. Money was tight. He was declared bankrupt and ordered to put the team on the market. Every once in awhile a wind would blow off the roof of his arena, the Spectrum, which he had to sell too, to remind people of his whirl-wind fate.

The inescapable conclusion about this bizarre period was the Joe Kuharich magic had done the job again. His record preceded him to Philadelphia: he had been the only losing coach in Notre Dame history, he had coached six years in the NFL (five with the Redskins, one with the Cardinals) and he had had one winner. He had always inherited losing situations and had always been equal to them. Wollman's infatuation with him seemed hypnotic. Perhaps it was explained by the time he caught a pass in practice and Kuharich told him he would have been a hotdamn flanker.

Kuharich went to work on the team and the fans soon after he took over. He traded Tommy McDonald, the wonderful little end, and Sonny Jurgensen, who had backed up Van Brocklin. There's nothing wrong with trading stars to build a better mousetrap or end run or defense, but a pattern began to emerge from those early moves that suggested self-destructive impulses. In return for McDonald the Eagles got Sam Baker, a kicker, and two ruptured steers, for Jurgensen they got Norm Snead. Kuharich went on to turn star halfback Tim Brown into a jangle of confusion, force the premature retirement of Pete Retzlaff and trade off four more solid players for about a thousand yards of ace bandages. And in an especially acute fit of paranoia he fired his public relations director because he couldn't control criticism of him in the press.

Another pattern emerged. Whatever his talent for doodling with Xs and Os, Kuharich had a lot of trouble when they became people. He couldn't or wouldn't communicate. Asked once what Kuharich said to him after an hour-long meeting, Sonny Jurgensen replied, "You've talked to him. Who knows?" After Jerry Wollman saw the doubletalk comedian Al Kelly perform at a banquet, he shook his head and said, "He sounded like my coach."

Kuharich spoke a private tongue made up of equal parts evasion, malaprop, Stengelese and crooked thinking. These are some of his classics:

"The charge on that blocked kick came either from the inside or the outside."

"Trading quarterbacks is rare but not unusual."

"I'm not vacillating you. I can only answer a question about a conclusive."

"We were three points behind, but that's not the same as being even."

"A missed block here, a missed assignment there, it adds up [after a 56–7 defeat]."

The farewell season of Kuharich and Wollman proved to be a dramatic tour de force. They showed that losing wasn't everything, it was the only thing. The Eagles lost their first ten games. "They say you can't win them

all," said Kuharich. "I say sometimes you can't win one." But with perfection in his grasp—and with the fabulous O. J. (Orange Juice) Simpson theirs in the draft for the losing—they won their next two games and blew it. Kuharich refined the art of losing to its finite limit—losing while winning.

The NFL remains heavily in debt to him for that because it created a comic theater of the absurd. Fans today watch the anti-heroes on the bottom with almost as much zeal as they watch the heroes on top. The race for the poorest record in the league and thus the top draft choice is a game-within-the-game that can be more fun than all the other names of the game, like watching film run backward. The Eagles played the Steelers in what was called the Orange Juice Bowl in 1968, and it was a classic. The score was 3–3 going into the last minute, the teams as futile as the law allows. Then Kuharich ordered the Eagles to try for a first down on fourth down from their own 10-yard line. No dummy he. The Steelers held, kicked a field goal to win and the nation cheered the winless Eagles wildly.

By that time people were even cheering in Philadelphia. A group of fans tried to organize a boycott to demonstrate their disgust over what they branded a civic disgrace, but it was doomed. Philadelphia fans had long been conditioned to watching games out of morbid curiosity. Besides, the sale of the Eagles was assured, to trucking magnate Len Tose, who had already promised to fire Kuharich as his first official act. The goofy saga of Jerry Wollman and Joe Kuharich came to an end with the fans still cheering, disproving the canard, first uttered by Bo Belinsky, that Philadelphians boo funerals.

Kuharich had one winning season in five with the Eagles, giving him two winners in his last fifteen years as a head coach, and his contract does not expire until 1979. He left a mark they will be shooting at for a long time.

Until a few years ago, oddly coinciding with the Wollman-Kuharich capers, the Giants had never experienced such turbulence. They were one of the cornerstone franchises in the league, formed in 1925, winning a championship of the old NFL two years later and winning three championships and ten division titles after that. There were smooth transitions of both family front-office control and field leadership. Steve Owens, who had been an outstanding tackle with the Giants, coached them for twenty-four years; Jim Lee Howell, an outstanding end with the Giants, coached for seven years; Allie Sherman, a brainy assistant with the Giants, was head coach for eight. They had headline players in every era, including Ken Strong, Mel Hein, Tuffy Leemans, Charley Conerly, Frank Gifford, Y. A. Tittle and many more. The Maras were well-liked by other owners—the official

NFL ball used today is called the "Duke" for Wellington Mara—and that never hurt when they wanted to trade. There were no messy labor disputes because players enjoyed the bright lights and commercial potential of the big city. In football, the Giants owned New York.

This was getting to be a bigger and bigger thing and it reached a crescendo in the overtime championship game of 1958, won by the Colts. The game ended dramatically under the lights, electrified the country—and alerted television to football's impact. The football boom was on.

Sam Huff, a very good linebacker playing behind an outstanding line, was deified nationally by the New York-based media (a *Time* cover, a television special) as the hub of the Giants. With an extraordinary series of drafts and trades, and a coaching staff that had Vince Lombardi, Tom Landry and Sherman as assistants, the Giants had broken the stranglehold of the Browns in the Eastern Division. Starting in 1956, they won a championship and five division titles in eight years. The last three were won under Sherman, who replaced Howell in 1961 after the team slipped to third.

Trades for Y. A. Tittle and Del Shofner were instrumental in the rejuvenation under Sherman, but there were signs that the Giant wave was cresting. They were winning with experience and finesse; the flow of talent through the draft had dried up as the opposition's edge in organization began to tell. When the experience and finesse played itself out, which could be any minute, the team could be beached. Recognizing that, the Giants boldly traded tackle Rosey Grier and Huff, who were approaching thirty, for two younger linemen, one of whom had a good season before retiring with an injury while the other was a flop. In 1964 the Giants won two games.

After that disaster the Giants signed Tucker Fredrickson, a big fast fullback, the kind of player teams build around and win championships with. He was the first such superstud they had drafted in nine years—the fire commissioner of Philadelphia could have done better than that. The Giants also picked up Earl Morrall in a trade to replace Tittle, and they made a credible comeback to a 7–7 season in 1965. But Frederickson and Morrall both were injured in 1966 and the Giants won one game.

Desperate, they made a deal with the Vikings for quarterback Fran Tarkenton, giving up their top choices in the next two drafts in exchange for instant excitement and respectability. Some critics thought they had mortgaged their future for a very modest present, but Tarkenton was just twenty-six, he could be around for a decade, and quarterbacks like that do not grow in Central Park. The Giants finished 7–7 in his first two seasons, and they were giving every indication of moving on to brighter tomorrows. In the fifth year of rebuilding,

1968, they beat the Cowboys in Dallas and played the Rams to a near standstill in Los Angeles, playing tough with the big boys again. Then they drafted their first superstud lineman in thirteen years, Fred Dryer. He would never play a regular season game for Allie Sherman.

Most teams, when they fall off the top, teams like the Eagles, Redskins, Cardinals, Bears, Lions, Rams, stay down so long that they think they're up when they get respectable. Sherman was bringing the Giants back from nowhere after two losing and three break-even seasons. But Wellington Mara and Giant fans had been up for so long though that they thought respectability was down. With Joe Namath doing his thing in another part of town, it seemed downer. The Giants fired Sherman.

Coaches come and coaches go and, as Mara put it, "Few die on the job." But the ritual sacrifice did serve the useful purpose of showing just how unstuck everyone in the Giants community had become—a parable of collective insanity that has a blood relative in any given NFL city.

The Giants were victims of the same pioneer frugality that did in the Eagles, plus some good old *hubris*. They didn't keep pace with the competition for talent in their own league, depending on their wits to match expanding scouting systems, and when the AFL entered the competition without a license the Giants took the attitude that any college prospect who chose Kansas City over them probably had a bad upbringing and would lay down in the clutch. This was a widespread conviction in the pre-merger NFL, it never occurring to the established teams that some collegians might have the same pioneering spirit they once had, or that a few of them had attended classes long enough to figure out that fifty cents in Kansas City would buy as much fun as ten cents in New York.

There was every reason for Mara not to take the AFL too seriously in the early days. From Yankee Stadium, where the Giants play, he could look across the Harlem River to the Polo Grounds—where the Giants used to play and where the New York Titans were hiding from the public—and count the house. And Harry Wismer hardly was a threatening eminence. Wismer's greatest moment in sports had come years earlier, telecasting an NFL game, when he described a runner streaking across the 40, the 45, the 50, the 55-yard line, Wismer hired Sammy Baugh as his coach and then wismered around the countryside boosting the AFL, greeting perfect strangers like so, "Congratulations, I'm Harry Wismer," and concocting wild fictions for newspapermen. He was some piece of work. But the league had to pay his payroll a few times and he was forced out of bounds on the 75-yard line.

A syndicate headed by Sonny Werblin bought the

Titans, rechristened them Jets, put them in Shea Stadium, hired Weeb Ewbank, and commenced to move in on the Giants, block by block. Werblin outbid Mara for fullback Matt Snell and guard Dave Herman in 1963, and for Joe Namath a year later. Big-time spenders in Buffalo, Houston, Kansas City and San Diego, supported by television money, were signing good ones too. With the financial pressure mounting after the 1965 season, the AFL pinned the commissioner's badge on Al Davis, a successful coach in Oakland and the league's most aggressive recruiter, to fight the NFL to the finish. It was, thanks to Wellington Mara, a quick finish.

Mara bitterly opposed AFL merger proposals, as did the San Francisco 49ers, because they had the territories that the AFL invaded (with Oakland and the Jets). Mara opposed them ideologically as well as geographically, as the old rich vs. the new rich. He actually forbid his players to fraternize with Jets. But such social gamesmanship couldn't stave off the inevitable. The Jets, and Oakland, were recruiting and drawing well.

It came as a shock then when in the spring of 1966 Mara broke an unwritten tampering rule between the warring leagues by signing place kicker Pete Gogolak, who had played out his option in Buffalo. This was an instant replay of the stuffy gentleman reaching across class lines for an irresistible sweet. And that tore it.

Al Davis had been a central character in the cutthroat Keystone Kops chase for college talent, spiriting the youth of America in and out of motels, airports and banks. He had used cunning, brass knuckles and/or money, as the situation warranted. Mara's provocative act even upset his fellow NFL owners, many of whom, bled by the six-figure bonuses, wanted a settlement. But all of their own stars were signed and they couldn't imagine any immediate retaliation by the AFL.

It took Davis three seconds to arrange that. The AFL signed several NFL stars (e.g., John Brodie, Mike Ditka) to huge contracts to go into effect after their current contracts expired. That meant key people on several teams would have divided loyalties. Knowing Davis, the NFL knew he was only starting. In a few days there was peace.

For Mara, it was wonderful. The AFL agreed to pay $25 million to the NFL over a twenty-year period in return for a common draft, realignment, a Super Bowl, inter-league exhibitions and an equal share of TV revenue. The Giants got $10 of the $25 million, the 49ers $8 million. If Mara had his druthers, he'd druther own New York himself—at least he did until he was tempted in 1971 to abandon the city where he got rich for a proposed new stadium in Hackensack, New Jersey. Still, ten million dollars would buy a lot of other druthers.

It wouldn't buy a defense and that's what Mara needed most. Meanwhile the Jets had their first winning season in 1967 and then went on to win everything in 1968. And Mara began to unravel. He regarded Joe Namath as original sin—sideburns were banned in the Giant dressing room; colorful language still is—and he felt betrayed by newspapers that treated Namath and the Jets seriously. He wrote a letter to the New York *Times* complaining that the Jets were getting preferential treatment. The *Times*, leaving nothing to chance, assigned a man to count the wordage for the season and informed Mara that the Giants still led (2,432,987 to 2,399,106?). Nor did Mara suffer criticism graciously. Elinor Kaine delighted in twitting the Giants in her newsletter, so the Giants vetoed her when she had an opportunity to do her act on the radio station that broadcasts their games. The following summer she sued the Giants (and the Jets and Yale University) when they refused to give her press credentials for the first Giants-Jets exhibition game, at Yale. The suit was settled for one dollar and, with Giant gallantry, a seat in a sexually isolated auxiliary section.

Mara saw the exhibition as an opportunity to put the Jets in their place, prove that their Super Bowl victory over the Colts was a fraud and restore the Giants and the NFL to their rightful place in the Milky Way. All the Giants had to do was win. Namath completed fifteen of seventeen passes and the Jets romped.

A few weeks later, after the Giants lost their fifth exhibition in a row, Mara fired Sherman, who had five years left on a ten-year contract. He hired Alex Webster, an assistant coach who had been an outstanding and popular running back in the '50s and early '60s. The only way to explain this move is in terms of human chemistry, illusion and the supernatural. That's football.

There is no law, of course, that a coach has to stay in office longer than a two-term president. After all only two coaches in the NFL today, Tom Landry of the Cowboys and Hank Stram of the Chiefs, both of whom started with the franchise, have had their jobs longer than eight years. (Witch doctors for soccer teams in Kenya are fired unceremoniously after four straight defeats.) But when there is a changing of the guard by management it should at least hold the promise that the new poor slob is an improvement over the old one. Thus the species may continue its climb from the ooze.

One justified exception to this Darwinian theory of coaching took place last season. Dan Reeves, the owner of the Rams, fired George Allen after he had produced five straight winners. Allen, Reeves felt, had virtually stolen the team away from him. He had moved his office and practice setup thirty miles from Los Angeles, had little communication with Reeves and made him feel he was fortunate to be getting free tickets to the games. Reeves, who once fired and then rehired Allen after the players threatened a rebellion, decided that it was his team, that it wasn't fun any more and that he wanted it back. This was reasonable as long as he didn't name Elliot Gould to succeed Allen, just for laughs. Reeves chose Tommy Prothro of UCLA, an inspiration that may provide a championship, but it came too late for fun. Reeves died a few months later.

Wellington Mara wasn't having fun either. The Maras had a splendid tradition, and Wellington Mara, for all the rashes breaking out on him now, had been an enlightened owner in many respects—e.g., he had given tryouts to black quarterbacks years before that became an issue, and he has held the price line to a nine dollar top (compared to thirteen dollars in Denver). But now he couldn't show his face in town without fans snarling at him. The Jets, good grief, were champions. The status of Giant fans, like Mara's, had been devalued. And it would hit the players too. Second is last in the midtown hangouts where their glasses had been filled before with the grapes of laugh.

The fans had been on Sherman for several years, bursting into song to the good-natured if acid strains of "Good-by Allie" late in losing games. It was a message that Sherman himself could appreciate, to a point; a listener, he once took an idea from an equipment manager and the Giants scored a touchdown with it. His children broke him up by singing "Good-by Allie" one night as they went off to bed. But with the passage of seasons the chorus got uglier at Yankee Stadium, until it sounded like a Fred Waring lynch mob. Elinor Kaine brooded that one of those darlings in the stands might really assassinate Sherman.

Losing is all the chemistry that fans need to elect to punt a coach into a vat of sulphuric acid. In addition Giant fans, spoiled by success, had a feeling of manifest destiny, that the normal cycle of ups and downs shouldn't apply to them. They came to believe that Sherman did nothing but inherit a championship team in 1961 and then, for obscure and perhaps psychotic reasons, jettison their heroes one by one. The Huff trade loomed larger than half a dozen good ones Sherman made (for Tittle, Shofner, Tarkenton, Erich Barnes, Aaron Thomas, Homer Jones, Pete Case and others). Every ten-year-old in the Bronx knew that the Yankees fell from grace because they hadn't competed in the bonus market years before. Every twenty-year-old in Brooklyn knew that the Knickerbockers had spent a lifetime in purgatory because of their front office. But the thirty- and forty-year-old Giant fans made no connection between those barren player drafts and these hard times. "At least," said one, "Webster looks like a coach."

So there was dancing in the streets when Sherman was purged. You would have thought that the Giants sent him to the Rams for Deacon Jones and Merlin Olsen. But no, they did something better. They traded him for an illusion, a potent image of the Great Giant of yesteryear as drawn by Willard Mullin. An all-powerful all-dwarfing all-pro Giant. Alex Webster was the embodiment of that Giant and that time—Big Red, as he was affectionately known, slashing off tackle. Alex Webster, an illusionary time machine, an admitted, somewhat overwhelmed primitive as a coach, was coming off the bench for one of the best coaches in the whole crazy business.

Wellington Mara knew what he was doing. He was guaranteeing himself a comfortable season. It would be more comfortable, and fun, with Webster winning, say, seven games than Sherman winning eight. Who could get mad at Alex Webster? Who could get mad at an owner exercising his constitutional right to have fun?

Two days before the opening game Mara's fun season of 1969 got under way. Webster was given a standing ovation at a pep-rally luncheon and he said, "We're shooting for the Super Bowl, and believe it or not, we're going to be there." Mara said, "The Giants' organization was never more closely unified than it is now. The old magic isn't gone." Magic and illusion. Wake the echoes of the past and march down the field.

The players loved it. In the recorded history of sports, players have been disappointed by a change in coaches three, maybe four times. A new coach is new hope, a chance to show that the old coach didn't know what he was doing when he failed to recognize their extraordinary ability. It means they won't have to listen to the same old spiel, the same threats and pleas—they'll get exciting new ones. Players eagerly welcome a new style in a coach too. When tough Don Shula left the Colts they expressed relief in Don McCafferty's understated approach. When Vince Lombardi succeeded Otto Graham in Washington the Redskins agreed that they needed someone who was tougher on them. For the Giant players, Sherman was cerebral, Webster emotional.

Sherman had run what he called a "total commitment" camp, driving the players hard. But he forgot to totally commit Mara and that was his biggest mistake since the Huff trade. When the Giants lost that last exhibition the players were so irritable that they held a meeting without the coaches, one of those let's-clear-the-air-because-we're-better-than-that-so-buckle-down-Winsocki meetings. Meetings like that can be good or bad, volatile or vaporish, inspiring or depressing. A few hours later Mara made the decision to bring in Webster. One year later Fran Tarkenton stormed out of the dressing room in anger over a move by Webster that resulted in an exhibition defeat, and nothing came of it.

The Giants undeniably were happier with Webster

than with Sherman. But the romantic notion that happy players play better than miserable players would soon be dispelled again. The basic fact about professional football players is that they don't care what you do to them if you win. Rub hot coals on their bellies, impugn their masculinity, get down to the nitty-gritty philosophy of Joe Schmidt of the Lions that "Life is a shit sandwich and every day you take another bite." It doesn't matter. Just win.

A fallout of critical hindsight on Sherman billowed through the press. There was, it was said, a generation gap between him and the players, and a motivational gap, and other gaps too numerous to mention. Affectations and neuroses that would be overlooked or deemed colorful in a winner were transformed into fatal shortcomings. Two-four-six-eight, could Sherman motivate? There is one test of whether a coach is motivating his players as individuals: what happens to the players under other coaches. In eight years no players traded or cut by Sherman blossomed elsewhere (although the Colts would make Earl Morrall a star) and many were as useless as a worn-out ball bag. In the year to come under Webster not a single player would be motivated to unsuspected heights. The veteran players who performed were the veteran players who had always performed.

The Giants won their first game under Webster, beating the Vikings with a fourth quarter rally. They carried Webster off the field and trumpeted his earthy virtues. A Giant coach hadn't been carried off the field in such homage since the previous November. Allie Sherman was his name. "He's one of us," said Tucker Fredrickson of Webster. "He turned us loose," said tackle Bob Lurtsema.

The inmates were running the asylum and they ran it beautifully—for four weeks. There was an assistant in charge of offense, an assistant in charge of defense, and Webster in charge of patting fannies. "They're doing 99.9 per cent of the work," the very open and likable Webster said of his staff; he was getting on-the-job training. Then the Giants lost seven games in a row. Lurtsema was benched for three of them.

More important to Mara and other music lovers, no one was singing "Good-by Alex." Instead the appeased fans went after Tarkenton. Get-the-quarterback is another name of the game, and it applies to fans as much as defensive linemen. The Giants won their last three games and that appeased the fans further. The season was a success. The Giants won six games.

Think about that for a moment. The Giants went from seven to six victories and the season was a success. It's like cutting welfare payments and convincing people on welfare that their diets have improved. Wellington Mara got exactly what it figured he would get when he substituted Webster for Sherman: poorer results and fans

thinking they got better results. A man who can make six seem more than seven is a man to be reckoned with.

Webster accomplished what he was supposed to accomplish. In September he talked about the Super Bowl. He was cheered. In October he talked about Giant spirit. He was cheered. In November he talked about the lack of talent on the team. He was cheered. In December he talked about next year. He was cheered. He could have recited the rules of parliamentary debate and he would have been cheered.

The players went through the emotional bends with Webster. When they won they won for Alex. When they lost they had let Alex down. And behind his back they whispered that nobody knew what the hell was going on around there.

The NFL came to the Giants' rescue in 1970. The schedule was so soft that you could stick a hand in it right up to the elbow; three teams on it wound up with winning records. And the Browns traded Ron Johnson to the Giants. A superior halfback, Johnson added a dimension of speed that would open up the offense for Fran Tarkenton to maneuver. It was no longer Sherman's team: there were eleven new starters on it since he departed (three ends, three linebackers, three defensive linemen, an offensive tackle, Johnson). They won nine games.

It was an amazing season, a season that made you wonder just how important this coaching is anyway. Fran Tarkenton, like Van Brocklin with the Eagles, took control of offense after some peculiar things happened.

The Giants lost three of their first four games. After one of the defeats Tarkenton complained that he was getting advice from too many hysterical assistant coaches during the games. In a second defeat the Giants went for a field goal when they had the ball on their opponents' three-inch line; Webster said he didn't realize the ball was that close. The trouble was that nobody on the staff knew more than Tarkenton did. So he took over, improvising game plans and even plays as he went along. He threw five touchdown passes in one game. He brought the team from three touchdowns behind in the fourth quarter to another victory. He did it all, and the Giants won six games in a row. The season was Tarkenton's best, Johnson gained over 1000 yards, Fred Dryer and the top 1970 draft choice, middle linebacker Jim Files, muscled up the defense. And Wellington Mara explained it as though the schedule and Johnson were innocent bystanders. "Alex Webster," he said, "knows how to motivate people."

Which is the end of this tale of two cities, moral being that it could be a tale of every NFL city. In Oakland, Al Davis plots mad schemes while his team is divided over its two quarterbacks, Daryle Lamonica and George Blanda. In Los Angeles and St. Louis winning coaches were fired last season; the brothers Bidwell who run the Cardinals couldn't agree on firing Charley Winner when he was a loser in 1969 but they could agree on firing him when he won in 1970. George Allen went to Washington and immediately traded the Jefferson Memorial, the Department of Commerce and thirty-four draft picks for a handful of aging Rams. The Saints were going through a shakeup that suggested they were studying the history of the Eagles.

City by city the evidence mounts that touchdowns rather than fumbles are accidents. Joe Schmidt is a profound fellow.

The humor of Jim Murray, his way with words, and ideas about sports, in general and in particular, and his characterizations of those who perform in and around the games grown men play, is legendary. The longtime sports columnist for the *Los Angeles Times* in this piece takes on the role of movie critic; unlike the motion pictures reviewed by Siskel and Ebert or Rex Reed, however, the movie under scrutiny here is a Los Angeles Rams game film. The article also appeared in the anthology *The Sporting World of Jim Murray*.

Love Him, Hated Her

JIM MURRAY

IT WAS Jack Teele, of the Rams, on the phone. "How," he asked, "would you like to come over and see some movies?"

"Oh, boy!" I said. *"Tom Jones?* Peter Sellers? Adults Only?"

"No," he said reluctantly, "not exactly."

"Wait a minute!" I said. "Don't tell me! Doris Day with fudge on her nose? Frank Sinatra pulling a cannon across Spain? I know! A Walt Disney movie called *Some Day My Prince Will Come!"*

"Nope," said Jack.

"Well, what?" I got sharp with him. " 'Girl of the Limberlost,' for heaven's sake?"

"I'll give you a hint," he said. "It's a horror picture."

"Ah!" I said. "Love THOSE. *Frankenstein Meets Godzilla*, eh?"

"No," he said, *"The Rams Meet the Cleveland Browns."*

There was a pause.

"Now," he said. "I have another conundrum for you: who is the world's greatest movie critic and why is it Harland Svare?"

I gave up and went to the Rams office with him. Sure enough, there was coach Harland Svare and his staff in shirtsleeves with scratch paper in a darkened room. A Cinemascope image flickered on screen.

"Some critic," I whispered to Jack. "Bosley Crowther would at least wear a tie—even to an Italian film."

"Just wait," whispered Jack. "You think *The New Yorker* critic is tough on performers? Wait till George Jean Svare gets going."

On screen, two guys bumped into each other. One of them got a nosebleed.

"That's the way to hit!" roared Svare. "Run that again!" He turned to me: "That's what we call a 'Cross 29—Give,' " he explained needlessly. I tried to look interested.

"Do you prefer The Method in your acting or are you a John Wayne Man?" I asked. Harland ignored me. "We grade as we go along," he explained. "We're using a new grading system. It used to be the 0, 1, 2, 3 system. It didn't give us the full story."

"I know," I murmured. "They had the same trouble with the '4-star,' '3-star' system." Harland looked at me funny.

"Anyway," he said, "now we use the 'Good play,' 'Bad play,' 'Average play,' 'Hustle' or "Loaf' scoring system. Lookit, here. Here's Roosevelt Grier vs. the 'Skins—Washington. Rosie had five bad plays. Rosie kind of stunk up the joint in that game."

I demurred. "What you must say, Harland," I cautioned him, "is 'Miscast as a tackle.' Or you might say,

'This Roosevelt was an Unhappy Warrior.' That's the way a critic has to handle it. Or, you might say, 'Loved Them, Hated Him.' It's a question of delicacy, don't you see? You have, after all, your box office to consider. You might leave it ambiguous and say 'R. Grier, a promising newcomer at left tackle, is a sleeper.' ''

Harland paid no attention. ''On the other hand,'' he said, ''look here. In the Cleveland game and the Green Bay game, Rosie played tremendously. He knocked the blank out of everybody.''

I clucked disapprovingly. ''He 'lighted the screen' is what you must say,'' I warned him. ''Or he was 'luminous.' You could even say 'As left tackle, R. Grier gave a moving performance which brought tears to the eyes of the audience.' ''

''It was the 'Skins' game where he brought tears to our eyes,'' corrected Svare. ''By not giving a moving performance. He didn't move an inch all day. It was a terrible bore.''

''There!'' I told him triumphantly. ''You see! There's your mistake right there! A critic must always give the producers an out. Instead of saying, 'A terrible bore,' the compassionate critic should say 'A colossal bore.' Then the company can take out ads and leave the last word out and say 'Colossal!—*Time* Mag.' The way you do it, Dan Reeves would have to advertise 'Terrible!—Coach Svare.' Get it?''

On the screen, Harland's quarterback was being thrown on the seat of his pants. ''Can't we get a block?'' he complained.

I sighed. ''Harland,'' I admitted, ''you're incorrigible. The least you can say is 'Our blocking is unbelievable.' The ad man can then say, 'See for yourself! The film they're calling 'Unbelievable!' '' After all, even in Sinatra's cannon film, some guys had the decency to say 'Audiences will be glad when it's over.' That enabled the ads to say 'Audiences will be glad . . . *The Times*.' ''

''Teele,'' Svare said evenly, ''will you get this George Bernard Shaw out of here?''

In a special *Life* essay on members of the NFC champion Baltimore Colts of 1968, Ogden Nash versified this to describe the mountainous Bubba Smith.

Bubba Smith

OGDEN NASH

When hearing tales of Bubba Smith
You wonder is he man or myth.
He's like a hoodoo, like a hex,
He's like Tyrannosaurus Rex.
Few manage to topple in a tussle
Three hundred pounds of hustle and muscle.
He won't complain if double-teamed;
It isn't Bubba who gets creamed.
What gained this pair of underminers?
Only four Forty-niner shiners.

George Plimpton turned a fan's fantasizing into joyful if terrifying reality by putting down his pen for a while and putting on the pads to play quarterback for the Detroit Lions in the 1960s. The result, of course, was one of football's most memorable books, *Paper Lion,* and the bonding of the author forever to the team of his dreams. Of that latter predicament, so afflictive to so many others as well, Plimpton observed, "When allegiance calls, the archaficionado of pro football sheds the trappings of normal life and, caped in the bliss of his daydreams, flies forth to worship Sunday's sweaty demigods," and then dished up this wonderful article for *Sports Illustrated.*

The Celestial Hell of the Superfan

GEORGE PLIMPTON

IN *HAMLET* there is a fine, tempestuous moment when Laertes comes home to court to find his father, Polonius, skewered and deceased, and his sister, Ophelia, out of her mind and mumbling that owls are bakers' daughters—and, outraged, Laertes cries out: "To hell, allegiance! vows, to the blackest devil!" etc. and we know the young nobleman has had a change of heart toward the court and does not feel as he did.

I've had allegiance on my mind recently in regard to the Detroit Lions football club—which may seem a matter apart, but the history of my concern, the suffering and strain I've undergone on behalf of the team, is not far from being, to use another phrase of Laertes', "a document in madness." The difficulty is that, unlike Laertes, I am unable to rid myself of my enthrallment. The autumn now approaches, and once again I can feel the stirrings, knowing that the fever will break out in a few more days and that as usual my commitment to the Lions will be absolute and agonizing.

I don't even live in Detroit. My condition stems from an experience a couple of years ago when I played briefly with the Lions as an amateur quarterback during their training (SI, Sept. 7 and 14, 1964). From then on, the fortunes of the team became my own. I suffered from afar that season as injuries crippled the Lions and the team had an inconsequential record. Once that autumn, sitting in a waterside café in Bellagio on Italy's Lake Como, I came across the weekend scores in a copy of the Paris *Herald,* and when I read that the Lions had lost a game I rose in anguish out of my chair absolutely stiff with grief, my knee catching the edge of the table as I came up and toppling it over in a fine cascade of Perrier bottles. Last year—though I vaguely hoped the passage of time might ease the frenzy of autumn Sundays—I found that my emotional concern had not been tempered at all. The team had another difficult season (7–5–2), and Sundays were hardly bearable.

The Detroit players themselves are aware of my commitment, and I suspect it amuses them. They put it to the test from time to time. I see the team play when I can, and last year I dropped into their locker room at Franklin Field, Philadelphia—traveling down from New York to watch them play the Eagles in a preseason exhibition game—and when I walked in, already worried about the

— 219 —

game, holding up a hand, calling out, "Hello, hello, hello," glad to see everyone, George Wilson, who was then the coach, spotted me and, grinning, said: "Get that man into uniform, quick." Any citizen with his wits about him would have replied that he was sitting up in section 24 with an attractive girl and friends waiting for him, and beer was going to be sipped from paper cups while the players pushed and heaved in the heat (the temperature was in the high 90s). But I presented a pleased, vacuous grin, willing to do anything they told me to do and, what's more, they *did* outfit me, Friday Macklem, the equipment manager, scrabbling around in the big team trunks and coming up with a uniform of sorts. He didn't have a jersey with zero on it, which is what I wore during my participation with the Lions the year before, but he had a spare with the number 30. This was George Wilson's number when he played on the great Chicago Bear teams with Sid Luckman and Bronko Nagurski. Wilson ran alongside me as we trotted out onto the field, and he warned me not to dishonor it. I never knew what Wilson had in mind—the Lions were likely to do anything, being pranksters of a high order— and I sat nervously on the bench during the game, knowing that if they ran up the score the temptation would be to run me in as quarterback for one or two plays (I knew three or four, and Wilson kept asking me if I had them straight). My sense of allegiance being what it was, I *would* have trotted in, mumbling perhaps but shuffling out toward them, seeing the helmets turn to watch me come, and I would have done what I could. As it was, they put me at the quarterback's table with the phones to the coaches on the rim of the stadium, and they would tell me whom they wanted to talk to, and I would motion to the player and he'd come to the table. The game was close, and since I thought the girl must be wondering what had become of me, I showered at half time and returned to my seat in the stands.

"Where have you been?" my friends asked.

"I've been down there on the bench—suited up," I said, just right, the voice absolutely perfect. "You didn't see me?"

"G'wan," they said.

"Whataya mean?" I cried out. "I was No. 30."

"Ah, g'wan," they said.

"Whataya mean, 'g'wan'? I *was* down there." I was furious. "You didn't see me on the *phones*?"

The people in neighboring seats were craned in toward us, listening, with quizzical looks, as if they thought perhaps the heat had fetched me. I said in a low voice: "Well, never mind."

" 'S been in the bar," I heard one of my friends say to the girl. "Absolutely blotto."

My behavior is perhaps not as odd as I believe; obviously, many millions torment themselves supporting teams of their choice. But there are times when it strikes me as symptomatic of the conduct of—well, what would one call them?—archaficionados, or perhaps more simply, superfans, people absolutely enveloped by their passion. The range is infinite, from the very wealthy— Jerry Wolman, for example, who (it has often been said) bought the Philadelphia Eagles so he could shag footballs with his players on the sidelines—to the crowds in the long overcoats outside the locker room corridors stamping their feet in the cold, waiting for the players so they can crowd forward to aim an affectionate swipe at their shoulder blades as they pass and call out, "Hey, great game, baby!"

Ever since my involvement with the Lions I have kept at a mild study of these superfans—searching, often worriedly since I have felt myself close to their fraternity, for reflections of my own conduct and finding them too often. The superfan has a primary need for identification with the football team: sitting on the bench, hanging around the locker room, calling the football stars by their first names—these are all wish-fulfillments. The position of the team water boy, for example, offers a fine opportunity for the superfan (if he can get the job) since it requires that he run out with his tray of paper cups and mingle with the players on the field. The Philadelphia Eagles have a 68-year-old ex-millionaire named Frank Keegan who has this happy chore. Keegan is now a construction inspector for the state highway commission, which leaves his Sundays free for the water-boy job. His water bucket is the object of more attention than one might think. The big defensive tackle, Eddie Khayat, has an odd fixation about the ladles (there are four of them) being crossed in the buckets, and he is forever looming over the bucket, getting in Keegan's way, to straighten them out.

The Green Bay Packers' water boy is also a superfan—Harvey Raatz, a nightshift worker in the Jos. Schlitz Brewing Company's bottle house. He and a friend, John Loh, a Milwaukee truck driver, have served since 1956, when they happened to overhear that G. E. (Dad) Braisher, the Packer equipment manager, needed volunteer labor. Assisting the equipment manager is not the most edifying or pleasant of jobs—no one but a superfan would apply—being essentially picking up after each player in the locker room, collecting and separating a dozen or so different items from a sweat-sodden heap and cleaning mud from football cleats and helmets. But the two are on a first-name basis with the players, which is important, and then eventually the game days roll around. While Raatz tends to his water bucket Loh works the sidelines, a new ball in hand to toss in on out-of-bounds pass plays. Both have a close view of the game, and they intend to keep at it, they say—adopting the athlete's aphorism—"as long as the legs hold out."

The Cleveland Browns have a number of auxiliaries, all superfans (last year they had a successful radio producer, John Wellman, working for their equipment manager), with perhaps the oddest of them being a Cleveland cigar-store operator named Abraham Abraham. A general handyman to the Browns, Abraham's specific duty during the game is to try to retrieve the football on field-goal and extra-point attempts. A familiar figure behind the end zone, he dresses in a garish brown-orange business suit which he believes lucky and has worn to games for 19 years. He stares into the sky for the ball, his arms stretched out as if waiting for a bundle of laundry to be tossed from an upstairs window. He usually retrieves successfully but he has been engulfed a number of times by mobs of spectators after the ball, and often of late, something of a showman, he has taken to capering around the periphery of the melee calling penalties on the spectators struggling for the ball, throwing his handkerchief down and signaling the infraction with the appropriate arm signals to the crowd. The majority of the penalties are, as might be expected, personal fouls.

The most original of the opportunists that my research turned up was a Chicago Bear supporter, George Motyka, a window washer who works a five-foot-wide squeegee across the plate-glass windows of O'Hare International Airport. For some years he had suffered his Sundays at Wrigley Field in a miserable seat under the scoreboard, so poor a location that he finally wrote a plaintive letter to the Bears' office. To what must have been his surprise, he received a letter back offering him a better, if somewhat ambulatory, view of the game—cavorting up and down the sidelines outfitted in a bear costume as the team mascot. For seven years, thus costumed, in the vicinity of the 50-yard line, Motyka has been watching games through the eye apertures of a reinforced-cardboard bear head. His suit, heavily furred, is stifling hot in the early part of the season and exudes the odor of melting glue. In the winter the snowballs thud up against him (he is a favorite target of people in the stands), but Motyka pays little heed. He considers his move from under the scoreboard into the bear suit as "the greatest thing that ever happened to me." It gives him a fine view of the game, and furthermore he enjoys a certain rapport with the team. He has said: "I give 'em a whack on the butt with my paw when they come off the field from doing something good." A sense of disillusionment set in the year of the Bears' championship, when Motyka felt that for all his cavorting and boosting he should have been voted a piece of the team's winnings. "All they give me," he said, "was a lousy tiepin."

If the superfan can't get close to the field and the players, it appears (from my research) that he gets into a profession where the football players come to *him*—usually he runs a restaurant or a saloon. In Pittsburgh there is Dante Sartorio, a fervent Steeler supporter, who operates Dante's, which Bobby Layne, the Steeler ex-quarterback, refers to in his book *Always on Sunday* as a hangout for "suffering mothers, relaxing athletes and swinging losers."

In Philadelphia there is John Taxin, the impresario of the Old Original Bookbinders Restaurant, a notable establishment, who supports the Eagles with such ardor that he usually picks up the check for any player who eats in the place.

California has John Sproatt, a restaurateur famous for his fog-horn voice and his place, which he calls The Bat Rack. He is an oddity among superfans in that his frenzied admiration is for an individual rather than a team—Norm Van Brocklin, once with the Rams (where Sproatt got to know him), then the Eagles and now the Minnesota Vikings' head coach. When Van Brocklin was quarterbacking the Eagles, Sproatt was certainly the most far-traveled of the superfans, almost invariably having to make a transcontinental trip for each game to watch his idol play.

Sproatt's voice baying encouragement is memorable, but it is rivaled in California, if not eclipsed, by that of a San Francisco superfan named Les Boatwright, another restaurateur, who is popularly known as Lovely. He is a familiar figure at 49er games—such a ferocious rooter that he forms an eddy of discontented spectators around him. Twelve years ago his voice sagged half an octave during a game and never recovered. Though it was still awesomely powerful, Boatwright saw fit to back it up with an air horn. Recently Boatwright has conceded that the air horn is for rooters without class, and he has lowered his decibel potential to that which emits from an old Model T horn squeezed when the mood strikes him, which is often. Visually Boatwright presents as startling a figure as he does vocally, often wearing oversized overalls and a Harpo Marx wig. He usually carries a homemade sign or two (JAM THE RAMS would be a typical banner for a Los Angeles game) that he unfurls at appropriate moments, blocking the view of the people behind him. San Franciscans who arrive at Kezar Stadium to find themselves in a seat near Boatwright often pack up and go home.

"How was the game?" they're asked.

"Never saw it. Went home just before the kickoff."

"What on earth for?"

"Found myself sitting next to Lovely Boatwright."

"Oh well, then, naturally."

When the 49ers play away, Boatwright's neighbors have been known to take umbrage, and they lead Boatwright a lively life. His banners are in shreds by the end of a game, his Harpo Marx wig is askew and his voice begins to flag as he shouts back jibes across the wall of debris that has grown up around him. But even in the enemy camp Boatwright prefers to be up in the stands. Some years ago, in Detroit, the late Vic Morabito, the 49er owner, ran into Boatwright in the hotel elevator and invited him to sit in the owner's box.

Boatwright was flattered, but he said: "Vic, I've come more than 2,000 miles with my air horn, this big sign and two jugs, and I don't think the owner's box is the place to put them to use."

In New York a number of superfans own restaurants—Toots Shor, of course, Joe Allen of Allen's, Danny Lavezzo of P. J. Clarke's and Mike Manuche, who owns a restaurant in the West 50s. Manuche's case is interesting. Four years ago he acquired the status of a talisman. He had turned up at a Giants' practice on Thursday afternoon, then the following Thursday and the Thursday after, and someone noted that on each of the following weekends the Giants won their game. The winning streak was equated with his appearance at practice, and the Giants, who like so many athletes are a superstitious lot, began to expect Manuche to turn up on Thursday to help insure victory the Sunday following.

Manuche performed his role rigorously: he was on hand every Thursday, he often went to team meetings, he traveled with the team, and as time passed and the winning streaks went on through the championship years he evolved a carefully worked-out system of custom and procedure that he adhered to in order to keep the winning streaks alive. He wore certain clothes (on one occasion a battered though lucky pair of underpants got thrown out by his mother-in-law and was retrieved from a garbage pail just as a disposal truck was coming up his Scarsdale, N.Y. street) and ate certain foods during the week.

On the day of the game the complexities were staggering. Leaving for the game, Manuche would get his car going at such-and-such a minute, follow the same route to the stadium, park the car at the same lot, and so on, with fanatical exactitude, down to the manner in which he approached and left his seat. The importance of ritual was felt not only by Manuche, but many of the Giant players as well. Before the game Y. A. Tittle, perhaps the most superstitious of them, and two or three others would go to a special food shop to consume one or two meatball sandwiches apiece, not because anyone enjoyed them but for their good-luck value, which was sufficient to keep the players returning week after week until, as the successful seasons continued, the trip to the eatery took on the solemnity of a pilgrimage.

With the fall of the Giants' fortunes last season, Manuche was hardly of easy mind. I called him up after the season was over and asked him about it. Apparently, as the losses continued, he had tried to establish new patterns of behavior. "We tried all sorts of things—new routes to the stadium, different cars," he told me sorrowfully. "We thought we had something when we won the St. Louis game—but it was no good, of course."

"How about those meatball sandwiches?" I asked.

"Well, when the defeats started they thought perhaps the meatballs were not being *cooked* properly. They had the counterman cook the meatballs just a little longer, then a little less, but nothing helped, and finally they gave up the place entirely. Crazy it all was," Manuche went on. "I mean, you'd think there was a screw loose somewhere the way we behaved."

I said that considering my own behavior over the Lions his was perfectly natural.

"You have the trouble, too?" he asked. "If you get hooked, you're lost—eat some awful meatball sandwich, 50 or 60 of them, if you think it'll do your team any good."

Was there any cure for this state? I asked Manuche.

He was very mournful. He didn't think so; "hooked" was the word he kept repeating.

But then last winter the Lions put me through an experience that almost cured me. They telephoned from Detroit and asked if I would represent them at the National Football League draft at New York's Summit Hotel. Nothing much to it, they told me—sit at a phone and give the Detroit office the names of the players drafted by the other teams, and announce the Lions' choice (which they would phone me from Detroit) when their turn came up. It might take some time, they said, and perhaps I should plan to keep that weekend free (the draft was scheduled to start on a Saturday morning). Would I do it, they wanted to know. Absolutely! I shouted into the phone. I had a full weekend planned, but I would cancel it. A tremendous honor. I only wanted assurances that in my official capacity I could not damage the Detroit organization. Would it be possible for me to draft a 132-pound fullback from Ypsilanti High School?

No, they said coldly, that would be impossible.

On the appointed day I arrived at 8 o'clock in the morning, on schedule, at the Summit Hotel. The league had set aside two large adjoining conference rooms. One of them was equipped with a bar, a buffet table and two television sets that were tuned to different channels so that a burble of sound rose from them, with an occasional scream or sob from a grade-B movie. From the other room it sounded as though things were very lively in there.

The main room, decorated with a deep-red wall-to-wall carpet, was devoted to the business at hand—half the room assigned for television equipment and interviews and the other set up with 14 small tables, one for each team in the NFL (the name designated on a placard) arranged in two long rows of seven each. A speaker's table with its podium from which the draft selections would be announced stood at the head of the room. Each table was decorated with a small, fat football-player doll, a painted brown football tucked under one arm, the appropriate team name painted on its jersey and topped with an oversize helmeted head fixed by a spring so it bounced and turned at the slightest touch for a painfully long period. One sees such dolls bobbing on the back-window shelves of automobiles. When a draft choice was announced and the representatives reached for their phones to call the home offices these dolls, set off by the vibration, would bounce and bob in a little lunatic show of approbation, their faces fixed with the thin half-moon signs of kindergarten portraiture. I don't know why one of us—in the latter stages of the session particularly—did not reach out to crumble his doll. Perhaps it was in the air, because toward the end someone came by and the dolls were packed carefully away in a valise.

When I arrived the room was beginning to fill. Team officials with briefcases sat down at their assigned tables and spread out colored charts and a clutch of sharpened pencils; NFL officials appeared, Commissioner Rozelle among them, who seemed to know everyone, big hellos and handshakes. There were big, wide-shouldered men from the scouting pools, ex-players most of them, who sat at tables at the rear of the room, shucking their coats first thing, wearing short-sleeved shirts so the heft of their bare arms was displayed. There were others—and I was among them—who seemed slightly bewildered among these people: superfans for sure, I decided, who had given up their weekends as I had to help their teams. I introduced myself to some of them "—from Detroit," I said, "the Lions," finding it a difficult thing to say with conviction.

I went to my table with the Detroit placard on it and sat down. The chair was bright leather, the color of a new pocketbook, and air-cushioned so it whistled slightly as I settled into it. I picked up the phone and called the Detroit office. The football doll bobbed in front of me. The brassy, friendly voice of George Wilson, the head coach, now with the Redskins, came on the wire sounding as though he were speaking up through a long pipe.

"I'm ready," I said. "The Giants have first draft choice, and they should be selecting very shortly."

"Good," he said. "Bill Ford will be on the phone for us at this end. Call him when the news comes through."

William Ford bought control of the Lions two years ago for $6 million—a high-order superfan. When I was training with Detroit he would appear on the sidelines to watch the scrimmaging, perched on a shooting stick, his small, blonde daughters flanking him. As the ball moved on the field he would pick up his stick, trail it up and down the sidelines after him, set it again and sit, staring out at his players. He took particular interest in my own eccentric flailings in the Detroit backfield as the last-string quarterback—he was not aware of my privileged position—and I was told later he often described me to his wife over the dinner table. "There's this one fellow," he'd say, shaking his head, "who just isn't going to make it. They keep him on, though. I can't understand it."

I knew what Ford was going to say when he got on the phone. "Hello, Bill," he was going to say. "Hello, is that Bill Ford?" and I would laugh, if somewhat hollowly, and say, "Sure, it sure is."

He calls me Bill Ford because last autumn I made the mistake of using his name to make a reservation in a small, fashionable Beverly Hills restaurant named La Scala on an evening when Ford himself happened to be dining there. The team had come into Los Angeles earlier that day, and in the evening a few of us began to telephone around, trying for a good place to eat. La Scala was not accepting reservations, they told me over the phone.

"This is Mr. Ford," I had said suddenly (it's amazing to what lengths the superfan will go on behalf of the team), "Mr. William Ford in town with the Detroit Lions for the Rams game. A few of us . . . ."

"Yes, indeed, Mr. Ford," said the voice on the other end.

"Right," I said. "We'll be along presently."

We turned up at La Scala not much later, a group of us, with Nick Pietrosante, the Lion fullback, John Gordy, the All-League offensive guard, and Bill Quinlan, the veteran defensive end now with the Redskins—all of us striding up, hungry, under the little marquee into the restaurant, and as soon as we were in there I knew something had gone wrong. The owner was waiting for us, eying us sharply.

"The Ford table," I asked.

"Which of you gentlemen is Mr. Ford?"

"I'm Bill Ford," I said weakly.

"Isn't that interesting," the owner said. "Someone wants to meet you." He put his hand somewhat more firmly than was pleasant on my shoulder and led us to a corner alcove. "Mr. Ford," he said, "may I present Mr. Ford?"

Ford merely grinned, the others taking it up on cue, so it was all right, I suppose. His party had turned up, just by chance, without making a reservation. Naturally, they had been given the "Ford" table and, curious, had remarked at the restaurant's prescience. They were told someone had phoned for reservations. Their eyebrows went up, and, fat cats, they waited to see who the impostors were. They have never allowed me to forget the incident. "Hey, Bill," they all call out when I see them.

Sure enough, when I got on the phone from the Summit to announce the first draft choice, Mr. Ford at the other end said, "Hello, Bill, that you?"

"Absolutely," I said. "Nobody but Bill Ford." I waited for his chuckling to die down, and then I said: "The Giants just picked Tucker Frederickson."

"O.K.," he said. I could tell from the way he drawled it out softly that the big Auburn back had been high on their own list. Detroit was looking for a heavy, hard-running back.

Detroit's position was 11th in the first round and, with each team allowed an hour to make its choice, it was long past noon, and 10 good players later, when our turn came and the phone rang on my desk with Detroit's pick.

"Tim Nowatzke," Bill Ford said. "We're picking Tom Nowatzke." The connection was poor and the name arrived as a blur.

"Once again," I said. "How do you spell it?"

There was a humming of laughter at the other tables, and I had to cover an ear to get the swatch of consonants in the name straight. I wrote it down and took my slip up to the podium, and he was announced by Commissioner Rozelle.

Not long after, Nowatzke himself came in with a Detroit official. He was in New York to receive an award. I looked at him carefully. If he had been a draft choice for another team I would have been impressed enough—a personable-looking athlete with the power indicated along the width and line of his shoulders—but a first draft choice for Detroit, I thought, *my* team, should have been a titanic figure, carrying away the door in his hand as he entered the room, just by accident ripping it off the hinges, apologizing then, bobbing his head not only to apologize but to clear the ceiling, and when he got to the lights, the interviewer looking up at him nervously, he would take the stick microphone to say into it, "Well, gosh, folks," and it would snap in his hands like a twig.

But then not long after Nowatzke's departure my enthusiasm for all things Detroit began to flag. The hours stretched on endlessly. The rounds in the draft (20 altogether) moved slowly, each team using its allotted time to the limit to make sure through its network of representatives and "hand-holders" that its choice would sign his contract. It was apparent the session was going to last long into the next day. Football itself began to seem distasteful, epitomized by the ex-players from the scouting pools wandering about the room in their shirtsleeves. The long hours seemed to have no effect on them. The superfans, slouched wearily at their tables, all seemed scraggly, a sheen of beard appearing on their faces as the night went on, and the dawn came finally, and the sound of traffic began to drift up from the streets. One of the representatives gave a slight groan, and stretching out on the floor next to his table, he slept with his phone on his chest. The scouts grinned and pointed at him. They were from the New York-Green Bay-St. Louis-Cleveland-Baltimore scouting combine (there are three such pools in the NFL), and every once in a while one of them would be called to a team table to advise the home office—Baltimore, say—at the table just in front of me, and the scout would amble up, humming, with a stiff loose-leaf notebook with colored tabs along the side, and when he sat down the air cushion would whistle shrilly under him. He would say to the coach on the other end of the phone:

"Hey, baby. Who? Bailey Gimbel?" He would refer to his book. "A real fine kid, this boy. Big! Oh, run to 260, still growing, quick as a cat—oh, he'll do the 50 in under six, for sure, in gear. And attitude, he's got an attitude you don't have to worry about, real beautiful attitude. Hard-nose."

That was the gist of it—longer, of course, the patois rich, with the emphasis always on speed ("in gear" had nothing to do with a shift of speed but with racing in football togs), "hands" came into it always ("he's got a great pair of hands") and always height and weight. In the early hours of Sunday morning, my attitude sour and indifferent, with nothing to do, even the television sets with their soap operas dead in the next room, the place quiet, I found myself working up a plot to call the home office, whispering sharply into the phone as follows: "Bill, this is . . . ah, Bill. The scout group here has been talking about a real good kid—not drafted yet . . ."

"What's that? What?"

"He's a tackle from Highland Cream Teachers."

"What's that again? The connection . . ."

"Courtney Caroline's his name—everybody's agog in here."

"Everybody's *what*?"

"Agog. Everybody's agog. Bill, the kid's big—a real *fat* kid, run up oh maybe five, *six* hundred pounds, big as a mountain, and big on speed, too, Bill, no hands to speak of, but he can knock you down with those feet, great big cat-quick feet, and as for attitude, he's got a real beautiful attitude; he doesn't *smoke*."

I never called such a thing in. I hadn't the nerve. But when the 12th round came along, about 6 in the morning, a player's name came up, San Francisco's choice, which caught my fancy and gave me a small chance to indicate my new-found attitude of irreverence. When I picked up the phone to report, I said: "Bill, San Francisco has just taken a halfback from Fresno State named Dave Plump."

— 224 —

"Yes, Plump," said Ford. I heard him repeat the name to the others. They kept charts in the home office, crossing off names as I called in the other teams' choices.

"I think we missed a bet there, a great bet," I said. "You could have worked him into the Detroit backfield with Milt Plum, your regular quarterback."

"What's that?" asked Ford. "Speak up. The connection's gone sour."

"Plump!" I shouted into the phone. "You could have had Plump in there for Plum's hand-offs—Plum to Plump!"

I could hear him murmuring distantly at the other end of the line, but then I heard the rustling in nearby seats, the superfans looking over and some of the others, so I said: "Never mind, Bill. Just an idea," and put up the receiver.

Later on, an even livelier parlay of names turned up. The Green Bay Packers on their seventh round had picked up a tackle from Wisconsin, Roger Jacobazzi. On the 20th round, the last one of the draft, Minnesota picked up Cosmo Iacavazzi, the Princeton fullback, and 10 minutes later St. Louis drafted Tony Giacobazzi—a fine welter of azzis, and outrageous, I thought in my gentle state of lunacy, that some team in the NFL had not made the quixotic decision to pick all three. But I did not have time to brood about it, because in that 20th round something happened that returned me irretrievably to the Detroit fold.

Ten minutes before Detroit's choice was due, Aldo Forte, the line coach, called in. He had taken over from Bill Ford, who had finally packed up and gone home. It was one o'clock Sunday afternoon. We had been going for 29 hours.

Forte said: "You all set for our last choice?"

"Sure," I said.

"We got a surprise choice coming up," Forte said. "Big surprise."

"What's that?" I asked.

"Well," Forte said, "we've decided to draft *you!*"

"Come on," I said.

"Sure," he said.

I guessed he was fooling around, but the Detroit coaches were full of pranks, and it would be just like them to do such a thing.

"Honest, Aldo," I whispered shrilly into the phone, "you can't do that. The commissioner'll have a fit if he has to read off my name. He'll start suspending people and slapping fines around."

"Let him," said Forte. "You've hung around long enough to know how we do things out here. You learned five plays when you were training with us. That puts you ahead of someone else we might pick."

"Honest, Aldo . . ." I said.

"The big thing," Forte said, "is that we don't lose you to the Kansas City Chiefs or the Oilers, those guys in the other league." He hung up the phone.

I sat there for 10 minutes, waiting. *Drafted,* I thought. What a great gesture, the epitome of the superfan's dream—his allegiance recognized by being picked in the draft, even if it was the last round.

It was a prank. When the time came they picked someone else. Their last choice was George Wilson Jr., the head coach's son, a tall young quarterback from Xavier, a natural, they all said of him.

I suppose I was relieved that I didn't have to face down Commissioner Rozelle with a slip of paper with my own name on it. But not really. I was put out somewhat. What a shame they had to think of George Wilson Jr. Why him? They had some perfectly decent quarterbacks. Rank nepotism! Walking home in the bright sunlight that Sunday afternoon, I found myself kicking sulkily at the pavement. And then in the pangs of absurd self-pity it occurred to me—with a groan of dismay—that as a superfan I was still as hooked as I ever was; while there might be a brief respite from time to time—a week or two during the off season, perhaps in the early dog days of August—the disease had me thoroughly in its throes. Absolutely hooked.

For 40 years, Shirley Povich covered the sporting world for the *Washington Post,* and he never shunned controversy. George Preston Marshall, founder and colorful owner of the Boston and Washington Redskins was not merely known as a master showman who introduced a marching band and halftime entertainment to pro football. He was also a major innovator in the game itself who was responsible for many progressive rules changes and introduced divisional football with a title playoff. He also had a darker side, however, not the most minor part of which was his attitude regarding blacks playing on his football team. Povich probes in the Marshall shadows with this piece, which is taken from the famous columnist's book *All These Mornings.*

Marshall Was Easy to Dislike

SHIRLEY POVICH

GEORGE PRESTON Marshall paraded into our midst in 1937, the Big Chief of the Washington Redskins. Marshall was bringing his tribe here from Boston, where the natives still didn't cotton much to the red men. He struck it rich in Washington, gave the fans a winner and provided me with a meal ticket—himself. I punched that meal ticket for years, and he punched back—with everything from trying to get me fired to a libel suit against me for two hundred thousand dollars. Franklin Roosevelt was openly feuding with the Supreme Court and Congress during those years. But the Povich-Marshall dispute seemed just as big a topic of Washington conversation.

Marshall was easy to dislike. He bullied many people. He bragged about being big-league, but he deprived his players of travel comforts to save expenses while reaping huge profits. He refused to let Negroes play for the Redskins and thus watched other teams pass him by while he presented the fans of later years with all-white losers.

I was on a train with the Redskins coming home from Chicago. Marshall was bragging to one and all that the Skins had left Chicago with the biggest check ever taken out of that town by a visiting team. When that train reached Harrisburg, Pennsylvania, at six o'clock the next morning, Marshall routed his players out of their beds and herded them into the coach car—saving a few bucks during the rest of the trip.

Once a Redskin lineman broke a leg against the Giants in New York. Marshall sent him home in a freight car, so help me.

He barred me from the dressing room early in his years in Washington, and I found this flattering and ineffective. I could still write, and did, about the man and his team. His squads in the early years were great championship clubs with Sammy Baugh, Cliff Battles, Dick Todd, Wilbur Moore, Charlie Malone, Wayne Milner and Turk Edwards. They were winning championships and the fans were packing Griffith Stadium on Sundays in the Fall. But their enthusiasm, like mine, was limited to the team. They loved Marshall about as much as I did.

The Redskins themselves were exciting the town in those years, though, even when losing. In the late Thirties they lost a game to the Giants in New York under conditions sufficient to make a pro cry.

The Skins tried a field goal late in the game which would have won it for them. Everybody in the stadium thought it was good except the guy who had the final say—Official Bill Halloran. The team and the fans complained bitterly for days about the atrocious call, and feelings were expressed in countless ways.

The guy who said it best was a fan who wrote me a letter saying, "I was loaded at the time, but I saw two balls and two sets of goal posts, and I know damn well one of those balls went through one set of those goal posts."

Marshall tried to get me fired for my written reviews. Our managing editor at the *Post,* Casey Jones, told him: "You run your Goddamn Redskins and I'll run *The Washington Post.*"

There was widespread objection in Washington to Marshall's insistence on doing the coaching himself, leaving his poor—and more intelligent—coaches helpless while he called plays down to the bench via telephone from his box seat. He wasn't even reluctant to join the scene on the sidelines and actually make substitutions while the coaches observed the Marshall Plan at work.

I was watching a Redskin game in Pittsburgh one Sunday and writing tongue-in-cheek observations for my Monday column. Marshall was on the field, pacing up and down the sidelines making substitutions. His pacing kept inching him nearer the sideline stripe. I was moved to write in my column:

If Marshall takes one more step, the Redskins will be penalized for having eleven and a half men on the field.

After the war, with Jackie Robinson leading the way, pro sports integrated their teams, but not the Redskins. It is no mere coincidence of history that the Redskins' last championship was in 1945, just one year before the recognition of the Negro in professional athletics. In addition to its injustices, Marshall's refusal to progress succeeded only in denying to the Redskins this great source of talent which was rapidly being tapped by the other pro football teams.

I struck a sensitive chord every time I threw needles at Marshall in my column on this subject. Once I wrote: "The Redskins' colors are burgundy, gold and caucasian."

After a game in which they were clobbered by the Cleveland Browns, I could write:

Jim Brown, born ineligible to play for the Redskins, integrated their end zone three times yesterday.

Marshall's stubborn refusal over fifteen years to hire a Negro player came to a forceful halt in 1961. That was when Stewart Udall, President Kennedy's Secretary of the Interior, ordered Marshall to stop discriminating in his employment practices or he would bar him from the new government-owned D. C. Stadium, for which Marshall had just signed a long-term contract.

Marshall got the message, all right. He even went to Adam Clayton Powell, then a powerful Negro Congressman, to tell him about plans he had to sign Ernie Davis, the Negro All-American back from Syracuse. They had dinner together, while Marshall tried to blunt Powell's criticism of the Redskins with this encouraging news about his plans for Davis. In a conversation which has not been reported until now, the Marshall strategy was related to Powell. During the entire exchange, Marshall kept referring to Powell, a minister, as "parson."

Toward the end of this summit meeting, Powell, that champion of racial equality, said calmly: "You know, George, I've been thinking. One nigger won't be enough. You need more than one. Three or four niggers would be better."

Marshall, the instant libertarian, replied: "Oh, Parson, you mean a matched set."

The Redskins were integrated anyhow, no thanks to Marshall or Powell. Today they can be damn glad of it. They'd be in pretty sorry shape without Charlie Taylor, Bobby Mitchell, and a lot of others.

Marshall wasn't the only legitimate target connected with the Redskins. He had two others, his wife and his announcer.

His wife—they have since divorced—was the former actress Corinne Griffith. I used to describe her in print as "that veteran star of the silent screen."

She published a book in the early Forties, and I was moved to write a review of that literary masterpiece in my column. The book was called "My Life With the Redskins." In it, Miss Griffith claimed credit for moving the Redskins from Boston to Washington, and she wrote movingly of her trials with Marshall and what she went through with the Redskins.

I said: "I know what she went through. She went through two hundred and eighty-five pages during a wartime paper shortage."

I said the best part of the book was the appendix, showing the Redskin playing records and Sammy Baugh's passing marks. My review said: "This was one operation in which they should have thrown away the body and preserved the appendix."

In 1984, Mike Rathet, sports editor of the *Philadelphia Daily News,* and Don R. Smith, public relations VP of the Pro Football Hall of Fame, joined forces to write a book to honor the Hall and celebrate the game of pro football and those who had earned the ultimate honor of being enshrined there. The result was *Their Deeds and Dogged Faith,* and one of the most enlightening parts of the book was the section devoted to the story of the troubles encountered in the league by black athletes in the earlier days of the NFL's existence. From the end/singer/actor Paul Robeson of the 1920s to the color-barrier-breaking halfback Kenny Washington of the 1940s, the stories of their struggles and eventual triumphs are inspiring ones.

We're Here to Play Football

—— MIKE RATHET AND DON R. SMITH ——

IT WAS fewer than six months after Kenny Washington died in 1971 that Jackie Robinson revealed his thoughts about his UCLA teammate in a national publication. Washington and Robinson had played in the same backfield for the 1939 Bruins, but, while Robinson had gone on to secure an exalted place in history, Washington had been overlooked.

"I'm sure," wrote Robinson, "that he had a deep hurt over the fact that he never had become a national figure in professional sports. Many blacks who were great athletes years ago grow old with this hurt. . . . It would be a shame if he were to be forgotten. I know I never will forget him."

Everyone knows that Robinson broke baseball's color line and serves as a role model for black children aspiring to play professional baseball, but few know that Kenny Washington broke pro football's racial barriers—and did it one year earlier.

Books on blacks in professional sports usually focus on Jackie Robinson. Even books on professional football rarely mention the role of Washington or any of the other black pioneers in the National Football League. The Pro Football Hall of Fame, however, has painstakingly researched the subject and amassed the evidence required for the presentation now in place in the Hall's fourth wing, in a room dedicated to The Pro Football Adventure.

The room contains displays on the Super Bowl, the Miami Dolphins' 1972 perfect season, the formation of the American Football Leagues, and the top twenty lifetime statistical leaders. And it spotlights the usual collection of memorabilia—from a vertical striped stocking saved from the Great Sock Barbecue held by the Denver Broncos to the world's largest trophy, the 22-foot 10-inch monster of polished wood and gleaming brass that is a tribute to the pass-catching streak put together by Harold Carmichael of the Philadelphia Eagles. But nothing seems quite as significant as the research resulting in the display about the 21 black players who in different periods of pro football's history opened doors so that the Jim Browns, O. J. Simpsons, and Earl Campbells would later walk into an arena that would accept them for what they are—football players.

It was not that way when Kenny Washington left UCLA after his senior season in 1939, having displayed exceptional abilities by leading the nation's college players in total yardage with 1,370. That brought him to Chicago for the College All-Star Game, against the Green Bay Packers, and ultimately led to a meeting with George Halas. "I remember George Halas of the Bears asking me to stay around Chicago to see what he could do," Washington said in recalling that period of his career. Halas apparently was trying to see what he could do about an agreement that supposedly existed among the owners not to sign black players, a pact that reportedly had been in force since the end of the 1933 season. "I waited about a week," Washington remembered, "and then I was told that he couldn't use me." Barred from playing in the NFL, Washington joined the Hollywood Bears of the Pacific Coast League and, from 1940 to 1945, played with the minor league team for $50 to $100 a game.

It has to be emphasized that Kenny Washington, like Jackie Robinson, was no ordinary player. Both were exceptional athletes—and there are those (including Washington and Robinson) who felt that Washington might have been the better of the two, even at baseball. "Next to me, Jackie was the best competitor I ever saw," Washington said, "but when he became a baseball star it kind of shook me. I outhit him by at least two hundred points at UCLA." Said Robinson, "Kenny's future in baseball seemed much brighter after his brief exposure to the college game than did mine. In 1937, Kenny batted four fifty-four."

But it was as a football player that Washington made headlines, beginning in 1937, when he took over as the tailback for a team that was to become the best in UCLA history up to that time. Washington set university records for rushing (1,915 yards) and passing (1,300 yards) during his career, many of his passes winding up in the arms of Robinson when he joined the team in 1939 as a junior after two years at Pasadena City College. Robinson played right halfback that season.

In an article he wrote for *Gridiron,* Robinson pointed out:

I took over Kenny's tailback position my senior season of 1940, but there wasn't much to work with. We finished one and nine. But that 1939 season was something special, and it was all because of Kenny Washington. To start off, let me say that Kenny Washington was the greatest football player I have ever seen. He had everything needed for greatness— size, speed, and tremendous strength. Kenny was probably the greatest long passer ever. [There are any number of stories about the exceptional distances Washington could throw a football.] He could throw sixty yards on the fly consistently. . . . On the long

ones, nobody could ever touch him. The Montana game was probably the best I saw Kenny play in 1939. We won twenty to six, and Kenny scored all three of our touchdowns. He ran for a hundred sixty-four yards in eleven carries, a fourteen point seven average, and completely dominated play. Over the years, people downgraded Kenny's speed, but he could run a hundred yards in ten seconds flat—in full uniform. For that era, and for his size—six-foot-one, a hundred ninety-five pounds—that was good running."

Kenny Washington, however, remained on the outside looking in until 1946—and he might not have crossed the line even then if it hadn't been for Dan Reeves. Reeves owned the Cleveland Rams, but wasn't driven by the same motives that inspired Branch Rickey, the owner of the Brooklyn Dodgers who signed Robinson. Reeves, however, was a pioneer in his own fashion, and sensed that the West Coast presented opportunities for the NFL that most owners still were reluctant to explore. His decision to move his Rams to Los Angeles for the 1946 season—and the circumstances surrounding the franchise shift—led to the signing of Washington.

The key to moving West as far as Reeves was concerned was the acquisition of the Los Angeles Coliseum as a playing site. But the rival All-America Football Conference also was trying to lease the stadium. "The AAFC people said we shouldn't be dealing with the NFL—they had an unwritten rule of no colored," recalls Bill Nicholas, at the time the general manager of the Coliseum. Nicholas doesn't volunteer much more, but it appears the Coliseum commission insisted Washington be given a tryout if the commission were to offer the Rams a lease. "One of the conditions definitely was Washington trying out for the team," says Bob Snyder, the Rams' backfield coach who actually signed Washington. "They put it in such a way, when you're battling for your life, you say sure."

While the Coliseum people first initiated the subject of the Rams signing Washington, Snyder believes it likely that the team would have tried to sign him anyway. "If the commission hadn't asked us, we would have tried to get Kenny," Snyder says. "We would have wanted him because of the publicity he would have brought us for being from UCLA." On the other hand, Snyder frankly admits that the Rams would not have signed Washington if the team had remained in Cleveland. "We were looking for names," Snyder says. "I doubt we would have been interested in Washington if we had stayed in Cleveland." It's also important to note that, while Reeves' mission was securing the Coliseum for the Rams, as opposed to breaking the NFL's color line, he did have a battle on his hands before he actually signed Washington.

"All hell broke loose [among NFL owners when word got around that Reeves intended to sign Washington]," Snyder recalls. "There was objection to it—you can bet your butt on that. Quite a bit of objection. But despite the objections, Reeves did it."

"Reeves had the league over a barrel," Washington said. "The Coliseum people warned the Rams that if they practiced discrimination, they couldn't use the stadium. When those NFL people began thinking about all those seats and the money they could make filling 'em, they decided my kind wasn't so bad after all."

When Washington actually signed on March 21, 1946, that made him the first black athlete to sign with a major league professional team in modern-day sports history. Robinson also was signed in 1946, but by the minor league Montreal Royals. He didn't join the major league Dodgers until 1947. Almost immediately after signing with the Dodgers, Robinson phoned Washington. "I asked Jackie if he was afraid," Washington recalled. "He said, 'About as afraid as you were when you became the first last year.' We both laughed."

There wasn't too much laughter for Kenny Washington during his NFL career, however. He already was 28 when he joined the Rams, and both his knees were in terrible shape, the result of injuries first sustained in college and the additional damage he suffered playing in semipro. And opposing players soon discovered his weakness. "When he first began to play, they'd tee off on him," Snyder says. "They'd drop knees on him." On one road trip, Washington scored three touchdowns against an eastern team, but was seriously injured on one play when he was hit by a swarm of players after the referee had blown the whistle. As he trudged off the field, he turned to teammate Jim Hardy and said, "It's hell to be a Negro." Hardy could never get that moment out of his mind. "I'll never forget the hurt in his eyes," Hardy said in revealing the incident. "But his statement wasn't one of self-pity by any means. It was simply a social comment. He was alone, and there wasn't any way to comfort him."

Socially, the Rams tried to ease the pressure on Washington by providing him with a black teammate, signing Woodrow Wilson Strode, who today is a motion picture actor of considerable note. Strode, a receiver at UCLA during the Washington years, signed with the Rams on May 7, 1946, becoming the second black in modern-day NFL history. Snyder admits there was considerable apprehension about reaction to the signings from the players on the Rams, but insists "there was not one incident." For that, he gives much of the credit to quarterback Bob Waterfield, with whom Washington had maintained a friendship for several years. "Three weeks before camp opened, Waterfield and Kenny worked out together by themselves," said Snyder. "That broke the ice. Soon [the players] were all playing cards together. But you had to love Kenny—he was a great, great fellow."

Life on the road, however, was different, or as Snyder puts it, "There was trouble in some hotels." Often, Washington would not stay with the team, even when he would have been permitted to live in the same hotel. Asked why, he once told Snyder he was uncomfortable in an all-white environment. "How would you feel if you were the only white in a room of blacks?" he asked. So, the Rams would ask the home team to find a place for Washington to stay, and they usually would locate a black family to take him in. Tex Schramm, currently the Dallas Cowboys' general manager who was the public relations director for the Rams at the time, never felt that Washington resented being apart from his teammates. "He'd always laugh about it," says Schramm, "because that meant he didn't have curfew. I never sensed any type of resentment on his part. But black people didn't show resentment in those days."

Washington played only two seasons with the Rams before his knees finally gave out, but he proved in that short period that he could play with the best of the era. He gained 859 yards in his 2 seasons, rushing for a team record average of 6.14 yards a carry. "If Kenny could have endured it," says Snyder, "he would have played longer. His knees were so bad when we got him, I don't know how he even walked. We used to drain them every week. He was knock-kneed, a funny runner. But he had great takeoff . . . acceleration . . . and was a great open-field runner. He also had the strongest arm I've ever seen. If he hadn't missed those six years [when he couldn't play in the NFL], he would have been a superstar, one of the premier backs of all time. While I was with the Rams, we had three Heisman Trophy winners—Les Horvath, Tom Harmon, and Glenn Davis. He was better than all three. There's no comparison."

If he hadn't chosen to sign with the Rams, Washington might have joined Robinson in baseball's major leagues. As soon as Robinson signed with the Montreal Royals, major league scouts began to recruit Washington. But Washington already had signed with the Rams for the 1946 season and felt there were compelling reasons for him to set a precedent in the NFL while Robinson cracked baseball's color line. "I feel it was just as important for a colored player to break into pro football as it was in baseball," he said. But, when he was through with football, he did give baseball a whirl, trying out in 1950 with the New York Giants under Leo Durocher. "I could hit the ball a long way," Washington said, "but Durocher told me that all those years of football tightened me up. I was thirty-two and that's no time to be trying to start a baseball career."

A baseball career might have brought Washington the

acclaim he never has been accorded, the status that Robinson wrote he must have longed for as he grew older. Robinson, of course, had it, primarily because baseball was a far more popular sport than pro football at the time both color lines were broken. It also is important to remember that Washington, because of injuries, was nearing the end of his career when he joined the Rams, while Robinson was at his peak when he joined the Dodgers. That, naturally, left Robinson onstage much longer, making *him* the symbol for black youths struggling to knock down racial barriers. Ironically, both athletes died young, little more than a year apart, Washington at age 52, Robinson at age 53. Washington died on June 24, 1971, of polyarteritis (inflammation of the body's arteries) and heart and respiratory problems. His death occasioned no more than several paragraphs in many newspapers. Robinson died on October 24, 1972, of diabetes-caused heart trouble. His death precipitated headline coverage throughout the country.

While Washington never seems to be treated by sports fans and/or sports historians with the same reverence as Robinson, Bob Snyder is among those who feel Washington may have been instrumental in helping to break baseball's color line as well as actually breaking the NFL's. "I have no proof of this," Snyder acknowledges, "but it's always been my feeling that Washington's signing finally tipped Rickey over to do what he did with Robinson—that Washington's signing took the pressure off."

There are also those who believe that Rickey might initially have been influenced in his desire to break baseball's color line by having played football some 40 years earlier on the same team with Charles W. Follis, a halfback honored in the Hall of Fame's display as the first black ever to be paid for playing. Rickey and Follis were teammates with the Shelby (Ohio) Athletic Club in 1902 and 1903, and Rickey was impressed enough to say, "Follis . . . he is a wonder."

Nicknamed the Black Cyclone, Follis was a Virginian by birth, but spent most of his short life of just 31 years in Ohio. Equally skilled at football and baseball (he played three years of professional baseball with the Cuban Giants), Follis began his football career in 1899 when he helped Wooster High School organize a varsity program. He was the team's first captain and right halfback. After high school, Follis played for the Wooster Athletic Association, where he was spotted by Frank Schiffer, the manager of the Shelby Athletic Club. Schiffer lured Follis to Shelby by securing him a job at Seltzer's hardware store, selling bolts of cloth and kegs of nails. He made no waves in the white community and became something of a curiosity for the people in the town, particularly when the Shelby *Globe* began to publicize his exploits and dubbed him "Follis the Speedy."

Follis played for Shelby in 1902 and 1903 without a salary, but the next season Schiffer apparently felt it necessary to legally bind Follis to his team and signed him to a contract on September 15, 1904. The signing was reported in the *Globe:* "The Shelby Athletic Association has secured the services of Charles Follis for this season. The contract has been signed up, and football enthusiasts will be pleased to know that Follis will be on the local team again this year. Follis plays halfback and there is no finer in the state."

Follis led Shelby to a 9–1 record that season. The more Follis succeeded, however, the more bitter his opponents became. Words. Knuckles. Knees. Follis was the target of them all. In a game against Toledo in 1905, the Toledo captain, Jack Tattersoll, became so incensed at the abuse aimed at Follis, that he stopped the game and told the fans, "Don't call Follis a nigger. He is a gentleman and a clean player, and please don't call him that." By 1906, however, ridicule and injuries had taken so large a toll that Follis was forced to quit.

The Hall of Fame history of the black pioneers records only three players besides Follis who were paid for their services in the years prior to the formation of the NFL. The year after Follis left Shelby, the Akron Indians signed a halfback named Charles "Doc" Baker. Baker also played in 1908, 1909, and 1911. The third pro was another halfback, Henry McDonald, who signed with the Rochester Jeffersons in 1911 and played through the 1917 season. The last member of the pre-NFL quartet also was the first lineman, tackle Gideon "Charles" Smith. A star with the Michigan Aggies, Smith was signed by the Canton Bulldogs to play in one of their two annual battles against Massillon, November 28, 1915. It was Smith's only pro game—and he recovered a controversial fumble that preserved a 6–0 victory for Canton.

Of the first four trailblazers, McDonald left the most vivid record of what it was like to play in the early days of the sport. Born in Haiti in 1890, McDonald came to the United States five years later when his natural parents consented to his adoption by an American coconut-banana importer. "He was my father's boss," McDonald explained, "and he just took a liking to me. My natural parents realized it was a great opportunity for me to go to America. I didn't see my mother again for over fifty-five years."

McDonald grew up in Canandaigua and Rochester in New York State, became a schoolboy star in football and baseball, then joined the Jeffersons in 1911. He weighed only 145 pounds, but created quite a stir with his speed and was nicknamed Motorcycle. "Most of the guys were bigger than me," he said, "but I was too quick for them to catch. I could run a hundred yards in ten point two seconds. The world record was ten flat in those days.'' The Jeffs' owner, Leo Lyons, reveled in McDonald's footwork. ''You can't hit or hurt what you can't see,'' he said. ''If you blinked your eyes, McDonald was on his way.''

The financial rewards, however, were extremely limited. ''I played pro ball for nearly fifteen years, and in all that time I never once took home more than fifteen dollars for one day of football,'' McDonald said. ''And I had to play two games to get that much.'' He accomplished that by playing a morning game in Rochester for the Jeffs, then hopping a trolley to Canandaigua and playing for the town team in the afternoon. But he gloried in it, particularly because of his role as a running back—for the players who ran with the ball, not the passers, were the stars of that era. ''Our football was soft and shaped like a watermelon,'' he explained. ''We threw a couple of passes every game, but they were usually a last resort. The ball was made to be carried, not thrown all over the field.'' And when the spectators passed the hat to pay the players, McDonald emphasized, it was the running backs who got the most money, followed by the linemen, and then the passers. If the nature of the game was different from what it is today, so were the spectators. ''The city folks took trolleys to Cobbs Hill and then walked to Twelve Corners [site of Sheehan's Field],'' McDonald remembered. ''I can still see those yellow straw hats and pretty flowered bonnets bouncing up and down as the people hiked to the field.''

Only once was the idyllic setting shattered by a racial incident. That occurred in 1917, when the Jeffs traveled to Canton to play Jim Thorpe's Bulldogs. At one point in the game, Canton's Greasy Neale shoved McDonald out of bounds, cocked his fists, and said, ''Black is black and white is white, and where I come from they don't mix.'' ''But,'' said McDonald, ''Jim Thorpe prevented a real donnybrook. He jumped between us and said, 'We're here to play football.' I never had any trouble after that. Thorpe's word was law on the field.'' And his ability, according to McDonald, sent waves of fear through those who had to tangle with him when he ran with the ball. ''Thorpe hurt you just thinking about trying to stop him,'' McDonald said. ''You were bruised before you ran into him. He scared you with his stare and he rattled your back teeth with his tactics. He was like a runaway horse. You called every collision a gift from God when you were able to rise, breathe regularly, and move on your own power.''

The Hall of Fame's display proceeds from the 4 pre-NFL blacks to trace the history of the 13 who played from the time the NFL was formed in 1920 through 1933, when, suddenly and inexplicably, for the next 12 seasons the league signed no black players. Halfback Fritz Pollard and end Paul Robeson of the Akron Pros and tackle Fred ''Duke'' Slater of the Chicago Cardinals, whose jersey is the only piece of equipment from any of the early blacks on display at the Hall, played as well as any players competing at the time. Pollard and Robeson made unofficial all-league teams in 1921. But Slater, who played his college ball at Iowa, may have been the best of all—he played longer (ten years) and with more success (all-NFL in 1926, 1928, and 1929) than any other early-day black player. A clipping from a 1926 Philadelphia newspaper quoted Red Grange as singling out Slater ''as the greatest tackle of all time.''

Robeson is one of the most unusual players represented in the Hall of Fame. The son of a runaway slave, Robeson gained worldwide fame as a singer and actor and worldwide notoriety for his political beliefs. He played in the NFL with Hammond in 1920, Akron in 1921, and Milwaukee in 1922, but he was best remembered as a football player for his collegiate exploits at Rutgers. A 6-foot 3-inch, 217-pound end, Robeson was the first black ever to attend Rutgers. He also seemed to conquer it, winning Phi Beta Kappa honors as well as 15 varsity letters in 4 sports. In 1917 and 1918, Walter Camp, the father of all-America teams, named Robeson to a spot on his mythical 11. When he did, he paid this written tribute to Robeson: ''There never had been a more serviceable end in football, both on offense and defense. The game of college football will never know a greater end.''

While little is known about Robeson's professional football career, that is not the case with Pollard. Like McDonald, a slight running back—5-feet 8 inches, 155 pounds—Pollard was placed in an all-time ''Dream Backfield'' by Grantland Rice, the dean of American sportswriters at the time. The other members of Rice's mythical backfield were Jim Thorpe, Red Grange, and Ernie Nevers. But while Pollard undoubtedly was one of the best backs in the NFL, it was as a coach that he established his singular place in history. For Fritz Pollard was the first black head coach in the NFL and—with the exception of Willie Wood of the Philadelphia Bell of the World Football League—the only one ever in American professional football. Pollard, however, never considered himself unique because of that. In an interview conducted in 1977 when he was 83, Pollard commented on his coaching career: ''It was no big thing then. I was just another coach and happened to be a colored man.''

Born in 1894, Pollard was named Frederick Douglass after the famous abolitionist, but it wasn't long before he was being called Fritz. It was as Fritz Pollard that he went off to college at Brown, and his freshman season led the team into the first modern Rose Bowl ever played, January 1, 1916, against Washington State. He was even better the following season when in successive games he produced 307 of Brown's 431 total yards against Yale, then amassed 254 of 461 total yards against Harvard.

Pollard put together those amazing figures, it should be emphasized, at a time when Harvard and Yale annually fielded teams ranked among the best in the country. Pollard began his pro career in 1919 with the Akron Pros and later helped recruit Robeson. "We were good friends," Pollard said. "I used to play the piano for Paul and he would sing. Sometimes I would sing, too. I had a pretty good voice then. We even formed an act and performed together."

There is some question when Pollard first began coaching, primarily because there is considerable debate about just what the role of a coach was in the early years of the sport. There is no doubt that Pollard was the coach of the Milwaukee Badgers in 1922, the Hammond Pros in 1923 and 1924, and the Akron Pros in 1925 and 1926. Pollard, however, insists he first coached with Akron in 1920 and 1921. The 1920 season wound up in a dispute over which of three teams actually won the league championship—the first in NFL history—and most record books do not list a champion for that season. But Pollard claims Akron, with a 10-0 record, was the champion. "I remember that real well," he said. "We were given a little gold football [as a trophy for winning]. I found out they didn't want to give the title to my team because I was black."

Relying on an excellent sense of humor, Pollard always tried to fence with those who questioned him about what it was like to be a black player in those days. Invariably, however, he would level with the interviewer. Here's the way it went in one conversation:

All the time I played, which was through 1926, there were always a few colored players. I don't think we were targets or anything. There weren't any real bad situations. About the worst thing that would happen was sometimes when we played an away game the local fans would start to sing "Bye, Bye, Blackbird." But I guess other players were subjected to taunts like that regardless of color. Other times they would have me wait until right before the kickoff to come out on the field. That way I'd just run out and the game would start right away and there wouldn't be any time to raise a ruckus. Once in a while they'd throw stones at me in some of the towns. Now that I think about it, maybe there was a little more prejudice than I first recalled.

Akron was a factory town and they had some prejudiced people there. I had to get dressed for the game in [owner] Frank Neid's cigar factory, and they'd send a car over for me before the game. The fans booed me and called me all kinds of names because they had a lot of southerners up there working. You couldn't eat in the restaurants or stay in the hotels. Hammond and Milwaukee were bad then, too, but never as bad as Akron was. Sometimes it would get a little rough [on the field], but I never tried to mix up with the other team. I'd just grin if they called me names and jump up and try to run through 'em again. One habit I did develop was rolling over on my back as soon as I hit the ground. That way I could get my feet up and in a position to deal with anyone who might think about piling on.

Not much is known about many of the other blacks who played before the curtain came down following the 1933 season, but Pollard offers us a picture of one— Robert "Rube" Marshall, who played for the Rock Island Independents in 1919 and 1920. "He was quite a man," Pollard recalled. "He was over forty years old when he played. He'd been an all-America at Minnesota in 1905 and 1906 and was still playing when the NFL was formed. He was a great one for making his own pads. He would make shin guards by rolling up magazines and taping them to his legs. He'd do the same thing to make forearm pads, only use small magazines. I remember one time he used the corrugated metal from a washboard to fashion rib protectors." Pollard, however, was at a loss to gauge the ability of Marshall, and that's the case with six others who played at the same time— Jay "Inky" Williams, Edward "Sol" Butler, John Shelbourne, Harold Bradley, James Turner and Richard Hudson.

Somewhat more is known about the last two blacks who played in that era—Joe Lillard, a runner and passer who came out of Oregon State, joined the Chicago Cardinals for 1932 and 1933 and was said to have excellent ability, and Raymond Kemp, a Duquesne tackle who played for the 1933 Pittsburgh Pirates. Kemp later became athletic director and football and track coach at Tennessee State, where one of his pupils was Ralph Boston, the Olympic long-jump champion in 1960. In an interview conducted at the Hall of Fame in 1980, Kemp was asked directly why there were no black players in the NFL between 1933 and 1945. He left no doubt about his opinion. "It was my understanding that there was a gentleman's agreement in the league that there would be no more blacks," he said. Was it possible that black players with sufficient ability didn't surface during that period? "I would have to assume," he replied, "that because of the numerous black athletes appearing on the sports scene, some of them would have qualified to play professional football. George Preston Marshall [owner of the Washington Redskins] made a public declaration he wouldn't have a black on his team."

Public declarations are one thing. Gentlemen's agreements made behind closed doors are another if, indeed, they ever were concluded. No one can verify that such an agreement did exist. Tex Schramm, meanwhile, doesn't believe a gentlemen's agreement was in force.

"I don't think there was anything that was a gentlemen's agreement." he says. "You just didn't do it [sign blacks]—it wasn't the thing that was done."

Schramm, however, can't tell us why, beginning in 1934, there were suddenly no black players in the NFL. But maybe that's something that never will be known. What is known is that Kenny Washington was the first black in the NFL since 1933; Woody Strode was the second, and it was just months later in August that Paul Brown of the Cleveland Browns provided the other two trailblazers of 1946 when he signed Ohio State guard Bill Willis and Nevada fullback Marion Motley to AAFC contracts. Willis' first contract, on display at the Hall, called for him to be paid $4,000 a year plus $100 for signing. The bonus provision in the standard AAFC contract form was written in long hand, initialed by Brown, and signed by Willis.

While there is no question that Washington and Strode were the first two blacks to break the post-1945 color line, there also is no question that Brown's signing of Willis and Motley had far more lasting significance. Washington and Strode were soon gone; Willis and Motley not only played for a number of years— Willis for eight and Motley for nine—but played with far greater distinction. Both are Hall of Famers. And, according to his autobiography, Brown's decision to sign Willis and Motley was made before Rickey signed Jackie Robinson. "I had made up my mind before Rickey's action that I wanted both Willis and Motley to play for us," Brown wrote. "I never considered football players black or white, nor did I keep or cut a player just because of his color. . . . I didn't care about a man's color or his ancestry; I just wanted to win football games with the best people possible." By signing Willis and Motley, Brown precluded the possibility of a color line forming in the new AAFC. Nevertheless, he did get some heat for his decision. "Some people in our league resented this action and tossed a few intemperate barbs at me," he wrote, "but I felt those better answered by the players themselves when they played against those teams."

It wasn't always easy to find answers, because Willis and Motley felt they had to maintain restraint in the face of overt antagonism. According to Motley in the book *The Game That Was:*

Paul warned Willis and me. He said, "Now you know that you're going to be in many scrapes. People are going to be calling you names. They're going to be nasty. But you're going to stick it out." It was rough all right. If Willis and I had been anywhere near being hotheads, it would have been another ten years till black men got accepted in pro ball. We'd have set 'em back ten years. I still got many a cleat mark on the backs of my hands from when I would be getting up from a play and a guy would just walk over and step on my hand. I couldn't do anything about it. I'd want to kill those guys, but Paul had warned us. The referees would stand right there and see those men stepping on us, and they would turn their backs. The opposing players called us nigger and all kind of names like that. This went on for about two or three years, until they found out that Willis and I were ballplayers. Then they stopped. They found out that while they were calling us names, I was running by 'em and Willis was knocking the (bleep) out of them. So they stopped calling us names and started trying to catch up with us.

Obviously, that had to be difficult. Both Willis and Motley were outstanding. One of the Browns' smallest linemen at 6 feet 2 inches and 210 pounds, Willis was exceptionally quick and in a class by himself at the defensive middle guard position. "He became the real pioneer of what is now the middle linebacker," Brown says. "Sometimes we'd put him up as the center of a five-man line but quite often, to take advantage of his speed and agility, we'd drop him back and allow him to go to the play. He had no peers through much of his professional career." That is reflected by the fact that in seven of his eight seasons, from 1946 to 1953, he was named all-league, three times in the AAFC and four in the NFL.

Motley, a 6-foot 1-inch, 238-pounder, became the prototype fullback of the era while providing the blocking protection many credit with helping make Otto Graham such an effective passer. Much of his rushing yardage was made on the Browns' famous draw play in which Graham dropped back as if he were going to pass, then handed off to Motley up the middle. "It came about accidentally in one game," Brown says. "Otto got such a hard pass rush he handed the ball to Motley in desperation. The defense had overrun Motley in their desire to get to the quarterback, and Motley swept right through them for a big gain. We looked at the play again and decided it couldn't help but work. In a short time, it became Motley's most dangerous weapon."

Motley was the AAFC's top career rusher with 3,024 yards in four seasons, including his rookie year when he averaged an astonishing 8.2 yards a carry. In 1950, when the Browns moved into the NFL, Motley won the league's rushing title with 810 yards, thus ending Steve Van Buren's three-year domination. He finished his career with 4,720 yards, a 5.7 average, and 39 touchdowns.

The final section of the Hall's tribute to black players lists a number of "firsts," including the first black player on each NFL and AAFC team. That list shows that it wasn't until 1962—16 years after Kenny Washington broke the modern-day color line—that every team finally had at least one black player on its roster. The last team to integrate was Washington, with running backs Ron Hatcher and Bobby Mitchell. Some other firsts of more than passing interest:

- First black drafted by an NFL team—halfback George Taliaferro (Indiana), selected by the Chicago Bears in the thirteenth round of the 1949 draft. Taliaferro, however, signed with the AAFC's Los Angeles Dons.
- First black draftee to play in the NFL—halfback Wally Triplett (Penn State), picked by the Detroit Lions in round 19 of the 1949 draft.
- First "name" star from a predominantly black college—fullback Tank Younger (Grambling), Los Angeles Rams, 1949.
- First black quarterback in the NFL—Willie Thrower (Michigan State), Chicago Bears, 1953.
- First black official—field judge Burl Toler (San Francisco), 1965.
- First black in the Hall of Fame—defensive back Emlen Tunnell, New York Giants and Green Bay Packers, elected in 1967.

There is only one *town* that can lay claim to an NFL football team, all the rest are cities, big cities. Green Bay, Wisconsin, population maybe 88,000 today, about 30,000 when it first sent a team into the league in 1921 is, however, as Quentin Reynolds noted in the introduction to this article for *Colliers* magazine, "... in the football business. Not for profit but for fame. Every citizen considers himself part owner of the club. And every player feels responsible to the town. That's the formula that has produced championship teams." Not just title-takers: the Packers, over the years, have produced some certified dynasties. One of them was just getting started in 1937 when Reynolds, one of the foremost sportwriters of his time, profiled the team and the town and their unique relationship.

Football Town

QUENTIN REYNOLDS

Now SOMEDAY you may be motoring through the northeastern section of Wisconsin on your way to the city of Green Bay. It is a section of wild and unspoiled beauty and you'll find it hard to keep your eyes from the green hillsides which are miraculously dotted with anemones, bloodroots and fawn lilies. Brooks which ripple just off the road will be framed by marsh marigolds and early meadow violets and then you'll come into Indian country, the land of the Oneida tribe transported from New York some hundred years ago. And then suddenly you are lost. You know that Green Bay is only ten miles or so away but in which direction? You stop, and there, sitting contentedly by the roadside, staring at you with wide-open brown eyes, is the cutest little Indian kid you ever saw. So you ask him the way to town.

He points a chubby arm straight ahead and then smiles shyly and you just have to pause and ask him his name.

He says, "LaVerne Lewellen Dilweg Webster."

You're a bit startled at that but that's only because you've never heard of Verne Lewellen or of Lavvie Dilweg or of the Green Bay Packers who belong to the Indians west of Green Bay just as much as they belong to the curbstone quarterbacks of the city. It is of course something that could happen nowhere else in this country.

Levi Webster, a full-blooded Oneida, has always been a great Packers fan. When his first-born arrived six years ago it seemed perfectly natural that he name him for his two great heroes. Lewellen and Dilweg. In Green Bay they'll tell you that Lewellen was the greatest punter ever to curl a toe under a pigskin and they'll add that Dilweg was without any doubt the only end who ever lived. Hence little six-year-old LaVerne Lewellen Dilweg Webster.

Over a period of years the Green Bay Packers have been the best football team in the country and before we go any farther let me add that we are proceeding on the assumption that a good professional team is as much superior to a good college team as a good professional fighter is superior to a good amateur. This assumption is always greeted with loud impolite noises by my friends among the college coaching fraternity but it is my story and I'll stick to it until evidence to the contrary is brought in. Now without any more argument let us go back to the phenomenon that is Green Bay.

Green Bay since 1919, when it entered organized professional football, has won four championships, the only team in the league to achieve that record.

Nearly always the team has been one-two-three in league standing. During that time Green Bay has been consistently the biggest drawing card in pro football and the team has always used a dazzling, colorful and effective attack, usually being one jump ahead of the other teams. Man power in the professional league is pretty evenly divided. Curley Lambeau, of whom more anon, has, I think, provided that extra something or other which has given Green Bay the edge it has enjoyed. But the record of Green Bay is not the sole reason for this article. Green Bay is not an ordinary pro team run by a professional promoter in a rented ball park. The Green Bay Packers are a municipal institution owned and operated by the municipality of Green Bay, as much a part of the city as is the police or fire department, and each of the 40,000 citizens of Green Bay considers himself to be a part owner of the club. That's what makes the Packers different.

Green Bay is a typical American community which has great pride in itself. It is proud of the fact that it is the biggest cheese-packing community in the world; that it is 303 years old; that Eleazer Williams, missionary to the Oneidas and claimant to the title of the "Lost Dauphin," found refuge there in 1642; that there is, and even during the depression there was, practically no poverty in the city; that during prohibition more than a hundred places which dispensed liquid refreshment kept wide open at all times; that the Green Bay Packers are the greatest football team ever assembled. Of these things the 40,000 citizens of Green Bay are proud.

STRICTLY MUNICIPAL

Any youngster at school in Green Bay will tell you that Jean Nicolet founded Green Bay in 1634 and that Curley Lambeau founded the Packers in 1919.

Earl Lambeau was a fine halfback laboring at Notre Dame for Knute Rockne. It was during the war years and Green Bay was buzzing with activity. Wartime plants had hurriedly been thrown up and Lambeau, who had been born and raised in the city, quit college to work for one of them, the Acme Packing Company. But when the green hillsides turned to brown and gold and when the

breeze coming from the bay was tinged with crispness, Curley Lambeau's feet began to get restless. Before Notre Dame he had played in Green Bay's East High School and this was the first autumn that his feet were not encased in heavy, cleated shoes. He just had to play football.

He gathered a few of the boys who worked in the plant and recruited a few others from town and under the name of the Acme Packers the team played a schedule. The Packers would play anyone. Sometimes they won, more often they lost but they loved football and to play it was enough. They played the next year too. By now the Acme Packing Company had served its purpose and had departed, so the team called itself the Green Bay team but the name Packers had become so much a part of it that finally it was generally accepted and so the team remained the Green Bay Packers.

In 1919 the team first played as the Green Bay Packers and in 1921 the team was admitted to the National Football League. The citizens of Green Bay were delighted. "Now Curley and his boys will show those city slickers something," they chortled. Well, the Packers won seven and lost two league games that year and played themselves right into the heart of Green Bay.

Things weren't very good financially with the team. When they'd play home games they wouldn't charge admission; they'd pass a hat and if they collected enough to buy their uniforms they thought themselves lucky.

A group of prominent businessmen in Green Bay began talking it over. Everyone liked this team. Everyone was proud of Curley Lambeau and the way he and his men were pinning back the ears of those teams from the big cities. Why not give them a hand? Well, they sat around the Rotary Club at luncheons and around Oliver's Ice Cream Parlor and around the Chamber of Commerce and they talked. Finally they stopped talking and acted. Men like Andrew Turnball, publisher of the Press-Gazette; Dr. Webber Kelly, Ray Evrard, Leland Joannes, George Calhoun and others organized the Green Bay Football Corporation and from now on Curley Lambeau was to worry only about playing and managing; the corporation would worry about finances. Within two years the city had built a stadium seating 10,000 for the use of the team. Since then the stadium has been enlarged to seat 18,000.

The corporation is strictly a municipal affair. There are hundreds of stockholders, yet the stock pays no dividends and it is impossible under the articles of incorporation for anyone connected with it to make any money. Stock is sold in units of $25, $15 and $5. A box seat for the season goes with a $25 share; a reserved season seat goes with a $15 share and a stock certificate which could be hung nicely on the wall goes with the $5 share. Before the season opens there is usually $12,000 worth of "stock" sold. A very good year will net the corporation a profit of $15,000. This will immediately go for the improvement of the field, the building of new stands and purchase of new equipment, and what is left goes to the American Legion, Green Bay Post.

Only the players, trainers and coaches are salaried. Even the ushers and parking-ground attendants at home games receive no salary. They are legionnaires who do this in return for the profits given to the Legion each year. The directors and officers of the corporation cannot make a penny out of the season no matter how much money the team takes in. They have the same spirit that undergraduates have at a university: this is their team and they'll work their heads off to support it. It is the only team in the professional league which is municipally owned.

From the Camp of the Beaten

——— GRANTLAND RICE ———

I have learned something well worth while
That victory could not bring—
To wipe the blood from my mouth and smile
Where none can see the sting;
I can walk, head up, while my heart is down
From the beating that brought its goad,
And that means more than the champion's crown
Who is taking the easier road.

I have learned something worth far more
Than victory brings to men;
Battered and beaten, bruised and sore,
I can still come back again;
Crowded back in the hard, tough race,
I've found that I have the heart
To look raw failure in the face
And train for another start.

Winners who wear the victor's wreath,
Looking for softer ways,
Watch for my blade as it leaves the sheath.
Sharpened on rougher days;
Trained upon pain and punishment,
I've groped my way through the night,
But the flag still flies from my battle tent
And I've only begun to fight.

B ob St. John of the *Dallas Morning News* provided this pro football update to a classic verse:

> *When the One Great Scorer comes*
> *to write against your name—*
> *He marks—not that you won or lost*
> *—but how you played the game.*
>
> *—Grantland Rice, 1880–1954*
>
> *Bull.*
>
> *—Tex Schramm (Dallas Cowboys president), 1921—*

The New York Giants and their quarterback Fran Tarkenton could not come to terms after the 1971 season and so the discontented scrambler asked to be traded and the team's front office obliged. They returned him to Minnesota where his pro career had begun back in 1961. There he led the Vikings to three Super Bowls and added stats that would earn him NFL career records for passes thrown, passes completed, most yards gained passing, and most touchdown passes. Dick Schaap wrote this tribute to the talented Tarkenton in 1972, his first season back with the Vikes, and it was featured in an anthology of his articles entitled simply *Sport,* published in 1975.

Tarkenton, The Second Coming of Saint Francis

DICK SCHAAP

Fran Tarkenton had flat run out of plays to call. He had already gone through every play on his ready list— the three dozen or so considered most likely to succeed against the Washington Redskins' defense. Tarkenton had called most of the plays at least twice, some three and four times. Now the Minnesota Vikings were getting ready for their 79th offensive play of the game—fourth down on the Washington four-yard line, three and a half yards to go for a first down. Tarkenton wanted to try something the Redskins hadn't seen. He leaned into the Viking huddle and called, "Sixty-four . . . three . . . screen right . . . on two. . . ."

IN THE year 1972, the Minnesota Vikings cheerfully gave up quarterback Norm Snead, wide receiver Bob Grim, running back Vinnie Clements and two high draft choices to get Fran Tarkenton from the New York Giants. The Vikings brought Tarkenton back to the Twin Cities, the place where he had begun his pro football career 11 years earlier, for one reason: To put power in their offense—or, more precisely, to put points on the scoreboard.

For four straight years, from 1968 through 1971, the Vikings—without Tarkenton—had won their divisional championship. For three straight years, from 1969 through 1971, the Vikings—without Tarkenton—had led all 26 pro football teams in fewest points allowed. But only once had the Vikings traveled to the Super Bowl, and that one time, to face Kansas City in January, 1970, the trip was a waste. The Vikings were outclassed to the brink of embarrassment. The Chiefs beat them, 23–7.

The trouble with the Vikings—particularly in the 1970 and 1971 seasons, after Joe Kapp elected to carry his *machismo* to a ridiculous extreme—was that they had a champagne defense and a waterlogged offense. The futility of the offense became so evident, during the 1971 season, Minnesota fans began to suspect, quite seriously, that their team's best chances for scoring came when the other team had the ball. Alan Page might scoop up a fumble. Carl Eller might toss the enemy quarterback for a safety. Paul Krause might pick off a pass. Faced with Minnesota's Purple Gang of defenders, an opposing quarterback—out of sheer fright, like a prisoner of war inventing and revealing military secrets to escape inhuman torture—might give the Vikings anything they wanted: The ball, six points, anything, just to get off the field alive.

The Minnesota offense was frightening, too—but only to its supporters. In 1971, Gary Cuozzo, Norm Snead and Bob Lee took turns at directing the Viking attack, each with some degree of failure. Raquel Welch could have been as effective, and a lot more fun to watch. Not once, in 14 games, did the Vikings score as many as 30 points. Not once, in 14 games, did the Vikings accumulate as many as 25 first downs. Not once, in 14 games, did the Vikings score as many as four touchdowns. And not once, in 14 games, did the Vikings gain as many as 350 yards, running *and* passing. Minnesota's frustration reached a peak in the play-off game against Dallas, the winner favored to go all the way to the Super Bowl title. Dallas won, 20–12, but the game wasn't that close; Dallas led, 20–3, entering the final quarter.

Then Dallas went on to the championship—and Minnesota went on to get Tarkenton. In the first exhibition game of 1972, on the opening kickoff, Clint Jones of the Vikings caught the ball on his own one-yard line and raced 99 yards for a touchdown. As Jones reached the end zone, Tarkenton turned on the sidelines to Viking coach Bud Grant. "See," said Tarkenton, "I told you I'd help your offense."

When the season began, with the official opener against Washington, Tarkenton stopped joking—and started proving his point. By the time Minnesota huddled before its fourth-down play on the four-yard line, the Vikings had already collected 26 first downs and 378 yards against the Redskin defense, one of the finest in football. The Vikings had already run off 78 offensive plays, about 20 above the average. No one could recall the Vikings ever running that many plays; Tarkenton could not recall any team he ever quarterbacked running so many plays. It was an incredible display of offensive strength, of offensive domination.

"Sixty-four . . . three . . . screen right . . . on two. . . ." A screen pass. On fourth down. On the four-yard line. Tarkenton had never in his 12-year career called a screen pass inside the five-yard line. None of the Vikings could remember any quarterback ever calling a screen pass inside the five-yard line. Even the ABC trio up in the television booth—armed with the trio's collective memory and collective vocabulary— could draw no parallel. But nobody argued with Tarkenton in the huddle. No one said a word.

The beauty of Francis Asbury Tarkenton as a quarterback, beyond his natural gifts, is his unpredictability. No quarterback, not even the ones with far stronger arms, not even the one with far weaker knees, has ever done so much to drive opponents to the edge of psychoanalysis. When the Green Bay Packers were the greatest team in football, and Henry Jordan one of the greatest defensive tackles, Jordan used to have nightmares about Tarkenton. The nightmares were endless: Jordan endlessly chasing Tarkenton, endlessly trying to grab him, to punish him, endlessly failing.

When the Vikings regained Tarkenton in 1972, they brought to the drabbest offense in football the most imaginative quarterback. Tarkenton will do anything short of a felony to gain yardage. He loves the short pass; he enjoys using his backs and tight ends as receivers. He doesn't mind the long pass, either; he is capable, by his own measurement, of throwing a football 61½ yards. Tarkenton's passes don't always look pretty—he fluctuates between the spiral and the lob—but they are effective, so effective that he now ranks fifth among all the passers in pro football history. Only Jurgensen, Dawson, Unitas and Starr—all of whom have put in at least 16 seasons—rate higher.

But his passing is not the quality that makes Fran Tarkenton special. It is his running, his scrambling, his logic-defying ability to avoid tacklers that separates Tarkenton from other professional quarterbacks, that gives him his unique crowd appeal. Tarkenton does not have the piston-power of a Greg Landry or even of a Roger Staubach. He does not run hard; he runs slippery. He squirms, he ducks, he darts, he escapes.

A 190-pound six-footer who looks smaller, Tarkenton is about as far from a picture runner as possible. He will never be asked to pose for the Heisman Trophy, yet, in at least one measurable sense, he is the greatest runner in the history of pro football. Of all the thousands who have played the game in the past half a century, Tarkenton is the only man who has averaged six yards or better per rushing attempt for more than 500 carries. And that puts Tarkenton ahead of Jimmy Brown, ahead of Gale Sayers, ahead of everybody.

If Tarkenton's rushing record is improbable, his health record is impossible. In 20 years of playing organized football—four years in high school, four in college and 12 as a pro—Tarkenton has never missed a game because of an injury. He has never even pulled a muscle.

"That," says Tarkenton, "is because I don't have one."

"Sixty-four . . . three . . . screen right . . . on two. . . ." The Vikings broke from their huddle and moved to the line of scrimmage. Tarkenton positioned himself behind the center and scanned the Washington defense. Mick Tinglehoff, the Minnesota center, leaned over the ball. Milt Sunde and Ed White, the guards, flanked Tinglehoff. Ron Yary and Grady Alderman were at the tackles, John Beasley at tight end. Gene Wash-

ington and John Gilliam were the wide receivers, Bill Brown and Dave Osborn the running backs. Tarkenton barked the signals, "Hut . . . hut. . . ." On the second "hut," Tinglehoff slapped the ball into Tarkenton's hands.

In the year 1972, Fran Tarkenton cheerfully gave up a reasonably secure job as quarterback of the New York Giants, the fringe financial and publicity benefits New York City offers a talented athlete, and a comfortable rented suburban home—complete with private waterfall and natural pool—to return to the playing fields of Minnesota, a state he had fled five years earlier. Tarkenton was delighted with the trade; more than anything else in the world, he wanted to play—for the first time in his career—on a team that stood a chance of winning a Super Bowl.

It didn't require a quarterback of Tarkenton's intelligence to realize that the Giants were not that team—and were not likely to become that team before Tarkenton became eligible for Medicaid. Even a defensive lineman could figure that out. (As a matter of fact, one did. His name was Fred Dryer, and mostly because he thought—sometimes out loud—that the Giant lineup was miserable, he got his wish and was traded, eventually landing with the Los Angeles Rams.)

Tarkenton was on better than speaking terms with adversity by the time he joined the Giants in 1967. He had already served six seasons in Minnesota, starting with the year the team was born. In Tarkenton's six seasons, the team won more than half its games only once. In Tarkenton's six seasons, the team was never seriously in contention after the first month of official competition.

When Tarkenton became a Giant in 1967, he took over the leadership of a team that had won only one game in 1966, a team that had plummeted from first place to last in three seasons. Under Tarkenton, the Giants improved 700 percent; they won seven games in 1967. But still, in Fran's five years in New York, the Giants won more than half their games only once, in 1970, when they went into their final regular-season game, against Los Angeles, fighting for a playoff berth. The Rams won the game, and in 1971, the Giants fell apart. They won only four games and lost ten.

Tarkenton, like Dryer, made no secret of his unhappiness with the 1971 Giants. In fact, he made a poll. Each time he bumped into an old friend, who happened to be playing against the Giants, Fran asked the old friend which pro team was the worst he had seen all year. Invariably, the answer was the same, confirming Tarkenton's fears.

He had nothing personal against his Giant teammates (although he did wonder what in the world made the team's management think that Rocky Thompson, as good as any kickoff-return man alive, would ever become a skilled receiver). He lavished praise on Dryer, on tight end Bob Tucker and on running back Ron Johnson, who missed the 1971 season with an injury. Frequently, he invited the Giant offensive line to dinner at his home, partly to promote team spirit, partly to review strategy and partly in the hope that his wife's cooking would make the linemen strong enough to protect his outwardly frail body. (Tarkenton was sacked more often than any other passer in his conference in 1971; the fault, presumably, lay with Fran's blockers, Fran's scrambling and Fran's wife's cooking.)

Tarkenton did have something personal against defeat. He was no longer in football for the money, if he ever was; he was a walking business conglomerate and, more important, a successful one. But at the age of 32, he wanted a championship, and when the Giants dealt him to Minnesota, a team that seemed to lack only a quarterback for a championship mix, naturally Tarkenton was ecstatic.

No one doubted the worth of the Minnesota defense, and Tarkenton himself had no complaints with the offense. "As far as having people around me," said Tarkenton, "I couldn't ask for more."

He ticked off the Viking lineup with enthusiasm. "Ron Yary. Awesome. He manhandles people. Milt Sunde. A nine-year veteran. A Dave Herman-type. Mick Tinglehoff. None better. Ed White. Very likely the strongest man in pro football. Before our exhibition game in Miami, he tore the Yellow Pages book of Miami *in half. Miami.* That's a big city. During training camp, we were coming out of a parking lot and there was a big pillar blocking the driveway. Bill Brown, Paul Krause and I tried to move it, and we couldn't. All together. White lifted it himself. Nobody'll arm-wrestle him. Grady Alderman. Probably better than any offensive tackle in the game."

Tarkenton felt equally pleased with his receivers. "Gene Washington. Enormous talent. Holds the Big Ten hurdles record. Learning something new every day. John Gilliam. A polished receiver. Quick-footed. Great patterns. John Beasley. A good blocker, rough and tough. Not great speed, but he'll catch anything."

The Minnesota running backs, too, left nothing for Tarkenton to desire. "Clint Jones. Not Ron Johnson yet, but he has Ron Johnson-type of ability. Oscar Reed. The quickest fullback I've ever played with. Dave Osborn. Solid. The best No. 4 running back in football. Bill Brown. He's 34, and he doesn't know it."

Tarkenton smiled. "If we don't win," he said, "there's only one place to lay the blame—and that's with me."

As soon as he took the snap from center, Tarkenton moved straight back, drawing the defensive linemen toward him. Tinglehoff, Sunde and White pulled out, sliding to the right, setting up a wall of blockers. Bill Brown, the 12-year veteran with the rookie body, feigned a blocking stance, then moved to his right, four, maybe five yards behind the line of scrimmage. Tarkenton drifted back beyond the ten-yard line and as Ron McDole, the Redskin end, lunged toward him, Fran lobbed the ball over McDole. Bill Brown grabbed it, his fifth reception of the game.

Tarkenton and Brown entered the NFL the same year. After one season in Chicago, Brown went to Minnesota, and for five years the two men were teammates and friends. Brown hadn't been used much in 1971, either as a runner or a pass receiver. He had caught only ten passes all season, his lowest total since his first year with the Vikings. But Tarkenton intended to use Brown fully. In 1964, a year when Brown caught 48 passes, Tarkenton hit him nine times for touchdowns—a record for running backs.

The Tarkenton who teamed with Brown in 1972 bore only a passing resemblance to the Tarkenton who had teamed with Brown in 1964. During his first tour in Minnesota, Tarkenton looked—and acted—the All-American boy. He was, as everyone said, the son of a preacher man from Georgia—the fact that he spent most of his pre-teen childhood in Washington, D.C., was immaterial—and he lived the role. He was very active in the Fellowship of Christian Athletes, and he was not above implying that when he danced away from a tackler, he wasn't doing it by himself; he was being helped by the Great Blocker in the Sky. Tarkenton wore his hair short, not crew-cut, but definitely collegiate and he wore his clothes to match. He wore white shirts and rep ties, and suits so square they would have embarrassed Lawrence Welk. "When I left Minnesota," Tarkenton now recalls, "I didn't even know what Gucci shoes were."

Then he came to New York, arriving a year after a rookie quarterback named Joe Namath assaulted the town, and the contrast between the hell-raising son of a mill worker and the God-fearing son of a preacher man was just too tempting for the press and public to pass up. The two quarterbacks were billed as the saint and the sinner, and it made no difference that neither label fit snug. Broadway Joe, it was assumed, divided his evenings between bar stools and bed; St. Francis split his nights, reportedly, between Bible reading and milk shakes. Actually, without any disrespect to either, Namath and Tarkenton probably would have enjoyed each other's company.

In New York, Tarkenton discovered Gucci shoes with their dazzling patent-leather shine. He discovered Cardin suits, and Bill Blass slacks, and he learned that a hair stylist was a lot more than just a barber. Tarkenton discovered discotheques, and "21," where two could eat for the price of 20 in Minneapolis, and he found out that Coke wasn't the only good-tasting drink on the market. Tarkenton didn't challenge Namath's hours, appetites and habits, but his chances for beatification dimmed. He drifted away from the Fellowship of Christian Athletes, closer to the fellowship of P.J. Clarke's, a celebrity saloon. In Minnesota, Tarkenton was called Francis; in New York, Fran.

For the Second Coming of St. Francis to Minnesota, Tarkenton's clothes were New York sharp—and his hair, sideburns and all, was modishly long. At 34, Bill Brown still had a crewcut. And he wore pink sports jackets which he paired with blue slacks. "Godawful," laughed Tarkenton.

Bill Brown tucked the ball under his arm and followed his blockers inside the five-yard line. Then he veered to the inside—he would have had a clear field to the outside—and just short of the goal line, ran into a tribe of Redskins. Brown powered, drove and burrowed his way into the end zone. The Vikings had a touchdown, and after Fred Cox kicked the extra point, the score was Minnesota 21, Washington 24. With only 70 seconds to play.

From the day the Giants traded him, Fran Tarkenton had been waiting for Minnesota's opening game of the 1972 season. For more than seven months, he had been looking forward to showing what he could do with a real football team. "I never worked harder getting ready for a season," Tarkenton said.

The night before and the day of the game, Tarkenton and all the Vikings stayed in the Holiday Inn near the Minneapolis-St. Paul airport, not far from Metropolitan Stadium. "It was," said Tarkenton, "the longest day of my life." He wandered from room to room, restless, impatient. "Sure, I felt scared," he said. "I had a fear of losing. I wanted to win so badly."

In the first quarter, Bill Malinchak, a member of the Redskins' specialty teams, promoted from the taxi squad only a few days earlier, burst in on the Viking punter Mike Eischeid, threw himself through the air and blocked a kick. Malinchak scooped up the ball and ran for a touchdown. It was the first time a Minnesota punt had been blocked since the year the team was founded. Since 1961, the Vikings had punted 681 times without once being blocked.

Still, with Tarkenton in command, the Vikings struck back and took a 14–10 lead into the final period. Then, the Redskins scored two touchdowns in a minute and a half, and even after the Tarkenton-to-Brown screen pass, Minnesota trailed by three points.

But the Vikings' fans were not quite ready to surrender, to quit on Tarkenton. Most of them remembered the heroics he had provided the first time the Minnesota Vikings played an official football game. The game was played in Minnesota, against the Chicago Bears, and no one expected the Vikings, who had lost five straight exhibitions, to threaten the Bears. But Fran Tarkenton, a 21-year-old rookie, a third-round draft choice from the University of Georgia, came off the bench, threw four touchdown passes, ran for a fifth and beat the Bears, 37–13.

Minnesota lined up for the kickoff, and everyone in Metropolitan Stadium knew that the Vikings were going to attempt an on-sides kick. Fred Cox moved up to the ball and toed it gently over the midfield stripe. Eleven Vikings raced toward the ball. A Redskin fell on it.

"Right then," said Tarkenton, "I knew we had lost. Up until the moment the on-sides kick failed, I thought we had a chance to pull it out."

Tarkenton walked off the field, each step showing his disappointment. He entered the dressing room and flopped down in front of his locker. Only a couple of Minnesota sportswriters interrupted his thoughts, and they quickly left him alone.

"It's funny," Tarkenton said afterward. "In New York, there would've been 20 or 30 writers around me, all of them wanting to know what I did wrong, how I felt, what happened. Out here, the writers stay away. It's like they're suffering with you."

Tarkenton showered and dressed, and as he emerged from the dressing room, Phyllis Tinglehoff, the center's wife, walked up to him. "Francis," she said, "I feel so sorry for you."

Tarkenton, personally, needed no pity. He had turned in a glittering performance. He had completed 18 of 31 passes for 233 yards. He had passed for two touchdowns. He had not surrendered a single interception. He had run with the ball three times and he had gained 35 yards, an average of almost 12 yards a carry. Nobody could blame him for the defeat.

Almost nobody.

In the press box, two Minnesota writers were working on their stories for the next day's papers. One pointed out to the other how Minnesota had dominated Washington statistically. The Vikings earned 26 first downs, Washington 11. The Vikings gained 382 yards, Washington 203. The Vikings ran 79 plays, Washington 48.

The other writer nodded. "It's just like I figured," he said. "Last year, we used to lose the statistics and win the ballgame. Now, we'll win the statistics and lose the ballgame. I told you that's what Tarkenton does for you."

After 12 years in professional football, Fran Tarkenton remains a target for critical assaults upon his manhood and his winning zeal, upon his ability and his leadership. The anti-Tarkenton party line can be traced directly to the man who coached Tarkenton during his first Minnesota stay, Norm Van Brocklin. The gospel, according to Van Brocklin, was this: "Fran Tarkenton will win games he should lose, and he'll lose games he should win, but he'll never win games he has to win."

That theory explains, quite clearly, why Tarkenton concluded after Minnesota's 1966 season that either he or Van Brocklin had to go. (Ironically, both went.)

Tarkenton wrote letters to each of the Vikings' directors, telling them of his desire to be traded, to be shipped as far as possible from Norm Van Brocklin. Tarkenton said he would never play for Van Brocklin; he would sooner retire from football.

Faced with that ultimatum, Jim Finks, the Vikings' general manager, traded Tarkenton to the New York Giants for four draft choices. (The four draft choices turned out to be Clint Jones, Bob Grim, Ron Yary and Ed White. Because of Jones' promise, the Vikings then dealt Tommy Mason to Los Angeles for a draft choice, who turned out to be Alan Page, and for Marlin McKeever, who was traded to Washington for Paul Krause. Because the Vikings had so many high draft choices, they traded one to New Orleans for Gary Cuozzo, who was later sent to St. Louis for John Gilliam. In other words, as a direct or indirect result of that 1967 Tarkenton trade, the Vikings picked up six current starters—Jones, Yary, White, Page, Krause and Gilliam—plus Bob Grim, the key man in the 1972 trade that brought Tarkenton back to Minnesota.)

Tarkenton scrambled away from Van Brocklin—who lost the Viking job to Bud Grant in 1967—but he did not escape Van Brocklin's label. The knock on Tarkenton was modified slightly; what it came down to, essentially, was that Fran Tarkenton was a fine quarterback for a losing team, colorful and exciting, great as a gate attraction, but that he couldn't quarterback a winning team, he wasn't a winner himself, he wouldn't win the big games. It didn't seem a terribly fair judgment—considering the quality of the Minnesota and Giant teams Tarkenton guided in his first 11 seasons—but still it stuck.

The anti-Tarkenton line altered perceptibly as a result of his final season in New York. During the exhibition season, Tarkenton quit the team before a game in Texas, arguing that he would not play without a signed contract and that the Giants were unwilling to negotiate a fair contract with him. Tarkenton said he would rather retire than accept an unfair offer.

Wellington Mara, the Giant owner, did not bend one inch. He did not say, "Come back, Francis." He said,

"Lots of luck in your new career." After a brief holdout in his Atlanta home—he did about as well as the Confederates did against Sherman—Tarkenton came back to New York and accepted essentially the same contract he had labeled unfair a few days earlier. Tarkenton not only lost his demands; he lost face. This did not make Wellington Mara his favorite person.

And then when the season began, and the Giants staggered, and Tarkenton hardly bothered to disguise his unhappiness, Wellington Mara decided that Fran Tarkenton, despite his fine moral upbringing, was not his hero, either.

Tarkenton was shipped back to Minnesota—coach Bud Grant definitely wanted him; general manager Jim Finks, who had felt slighted when Tarkenton wrote to the board of directors instead of turning to him in 1967, went along with Grant—and the Giant organization immediately began to bad-mouth Tarkenton. The new party line was that Tarkenton was a divisive force on the Giants, that he drove a wedge between head coach Alex Webster and the players, that he tried to assume Webster's job, that his ego and his mouth were far larger than his talents. Besides, his passes were hard to catch. Judging from reports filtering out of the Giant office, Tarkenton was being blamed for about eight of the team's defeats in 1971 and Fred Dryer for the other two.

Tarkenton, who is as self-controlled as he is self-confident, accepts the criticism without outward bitterness. The charge that he is not a winner, that he can't win big games, he dismisses as ridiculous. "I've won a lot of games," he says. "In high school. In college. In the NFL. Some of them had to be big ones."

The charge that Tarkenton hurt the Giants, with his attitude and with his play, he accepts as ill-founded but understandable. "Maybe it's the best thing," he says. "When you make a trade, you have to rationalize. You can't make a trade and say it's for the bad of the club. If I were a general manager and I made a trade, I wouldn't praise the guy I was giving away. How could I? How could anyone? You have to say the trade is going to improve your team, and you hope that if you keep saying it enough, maybe the rest of the players will believe it and benefit from it. Don't take it too seriously when people say how bad you are—or how good you are. Only you know."

Tarkenton is very serious, very sincere when he says these things. He knows he sounds mature, and Tarkenton is proud of his maturity.

The morning after the Washington game, the Minneapolis Tribune *came out with a headline: TARKENTON CRUSHED BY LOSS TO REDSKINS. The story underneath began, "Fran Tarkenton probably never has taken a defeat harder. . . ."*

Fran Tarkenton was in a perfectly amiable mood the day after Washington beat the Vikings. If some deep depression was gnawing at him, Tarkenton was a terrific actor. In the afternoon, he went shopping for a motorcycle, he viewed the movies of the Redskin game and he turned down an offer from Sargent Shriver to appear with Shriver at a rally at the Twin Cities airport. Tarkenton and Shriver are friends; they socialize together. But Tarkenton's main business interest—Behavioral Systems, Inc., a company that trains the disadvantaged to enter the working force—has a multi-million dollar contract with the Nixon Administration. Tarkenton did not feel compelled to take a strong stand in the 1972 election.

In the evening, Tarkenton went to dinner at a restaurant called The Jolly Green Giant, a family-type place, large and busy. No one in the restaurant said, "Hello, Francis," no one asked him how he felt, no one asked him about the game, no one asked for an autograph. In P.J. Clarke's, he wouldn't have escaped so easily.

Tarkenton talked about the defeat, and about its impact on him. "I wanted to win," he said. "I wanted to win very much. But not any more than anyone else. This team expects to win. This team should win."

Tarkenton sipped a gin and tonic. "You know, I feel funny playing a children's game in my 30s, but I do it for one reason. I love it. Nothing in my life compares to the ecstasies I get from this game. And nothing compares to the horrible things. But everybody has enormous setbacks in every field. People want to put finality into sports, and it's ridiculous. Look at Jerry West. He went through all those years without winning a championship, and everybody worried about how he suffered, and now he's finally won one, and what has it done to him? Nothing. It hasn't affected him. He's still the same man.

"If I can win a championship, it won't change me one way or the other. I want to win a championship. I want to win one desperately. It's probably what I want right now more than anything else in the world. But if I don't, I'm not going to kill myself. And if I do win a championship, it will probably make me happier than anything else could—right now. But in a few years, it won't make much difference."

Tarkenton finished dinner and left the restaurant. If anyone recognized him, they didn't show it. "In a few years," he said, "I'll be out of football, and not that many people will really care whether I ever won a championship or not. I'll be thinking about other things myself—other goals, other challenges." Tarkenton paused. "I feel bad about losing last night," he said. "But it ain't gonna shake the world."

The Raving

BLACKIE SHERROD

Once upon an interview, while I searched for something new,
From an old and canny coach of football men
While I questioned, rather neatly, suddenly and so completely,
He became so indiscreetly, indiscreetly and even more.
He must be kidding, I muttered, thinking I'm a sophomore,
      Thinking I don't know the score.

Yes, distinctly I remember, it was in the cold November
When the coach brought honesty to the fore.
"Why yes, I know we'll beat them, we'll cook them and we'll eat them,
And if we have to cheat them, well, we'll cheat them," he swore.
"To hell with building character, that's something I ignore.
      You got to win, and nothing more."

"Our boys are much, much stronger; our wind is even longer
They got guys who train at the package store.
Our ends are tall and quicker; theirs couldn't be sicker.
Their coach is full of likker, a bum that I abhor.
If we can win by 100 points, then that'll be the score.
      That much and maybe more."

"They have a soft spot on the right, their guard's a neophyte,
We'll run through that hole for 90 yards or more.
This ain't scuttlebutt, he hasn't got a gut.
Won't bother with that nut, not a blocker on that chore.
Our trap play should work, from here to Singapore.
      Better than ever before."

"Their feller at right half, he's lovesick like a calf
All that he can think of is his blond paramour
You should see his pass defense, it would even make you wince
We'll tear him up like chintz, his zone's an open door.
That pass alone should make three touchdowns or four
      At least that, and maybe more."

"They have a favorite play, when the left half comes this way
On which they've made their yardage heretofore.
They don't know we know it, but he will always show it
Just before they blow it, he might as well yell 'Fore.'
We'll be there to meet him, like Marines upon the shore.
      We'll flatten him on the floor."

"Don't give their team a glance, they haven't got a chance,"
The coach spoke frankly, like a knight of yore.
While he talked, eyes a-snapping, suddenly there came a rapping
As of some one loudly rapping, rapping like a maddened boar.
Two men in white, they entered, and took the old coach o'er
    And led him out the door.

Red Smith is admired as one of the greatest sportswriters in American history, if not *the* greatest; in the words of John Leonard, writing in *The New York Times,* "Red Smith was to sports what Homer was to war." He won a Pulitzer Prize in 1976 and has had his articles collected in various volumes over the more than 50 years during which he entertained and educated sports fans throughout the United States. This wonderfully droll piece originally appeared in *The New York Times* in 1976 and was later included in the anthology *The Red Smith Reader,* published in the year of his death, 1982.

The N.F.L. in American History

RED SMITH

I*N A hot flush of patriotism, the National Football League has jumped aboard the Bicentennial band-wagon and is sponsoring an essay contest for high school students from fourteen to eighteen years of age. For the best paper on "The Role of the N.F.L. in American History," first prize is a $10,000 college scholarship and second is a $5,000 scholarship. There are ten scholarships worth $1,000 each. In addition, the winner gets an all-expense-paid trip to Super Bowl X in Miami next January with his, her or its parents. The following is submitted in the hope of helping young minds to think along productive lines.*

N.F.L. Bicentennial Essay Contest
Box 867
Winona, Minn.

I think pro football is boss and quite historic. I like to read books about pro football, like *Semi-Tough* and *North Dallas Forty.* My little sister likes them, too, and is learning most of the words.

The N.F.L. has made contributions to legal history, medical history and pharmaceutical history. In fact, the Houston Ridge Case was a milestone in all three areas.

Houston Ridge was a defensive end with the San Diego Chargers who got hurt and sued the club, the team doctor and the league. He said they gave him pep pills to kill the pain so he could keep playing after he was hurt. He said he did keep on playing and got hurt worse. He was on crutches a long time.

There was testimony that the Chargers' trainer made phys-ed history by leaving a package of "bennies" or "greenies" or "uppers" in each locker before each game. After the game if a player was afraid he wouldn't sleep that night, they gave him "downers" to settle his nerves.

A druggist testified that he sold 10,000 amphetamines to Irv Kaze, the business manager of the Chargers. "Did you expect Mr. Kaze to ingest 10,000 pills himself?" the druggist was asked. He didn't answer. This is a whole chapter in the history of pharmacology.

Houston Ridge was paid more than $300,000 to settle this suit. That was pretty historic. Later Pete Rozelle, commissioner of the N.F.L., put eight of the Chargers' players on probation for using drugs and fined them different amounts. He fined the club $20,000 and Har-land Svare, the general manager, $5,000.

This year the Chargers have played eight games and

lost them all. Historians think they ought to go back on greenies.

George Burman, who was a reserve center on the Washington Redskins, is one of the most historic Americans since George Washington. In his Farewell Address, President Washington said: "I hold the maxim no less applicable to public than to private affairs, that honesty is always the best policy."

So when somebody asked George Burman about taking dope he said sure, lots of Redskin players smoked grass and ate bennies. This made a lot of people in pro football sore, but today George Burman is a professor of economics at Carnegie-Mellon University, which used to be Carnegie Tech. He tells it like it is about laissez-faire and gross national product.

Our teacher says Samuel Gompers and Eugene V. Debs were great Americans because they did a lot for the labor movement in this country. She also says David Dubinsky, John L. Lewis and Walter Reuther made contributions.

So did Norm Van Brocklin of the National Football League. He was coach of the Atlanta Falcons and when the players went on strike in the summer of 1974 he called up the team representative, Ken Reaves.

"You and your picket sign are going to New Orleans," Norm Van Brocklin told Ken Reaves.

About the same time the Chicago Bears traded away three players including their player representative, Mac Percival. Their owner, George Halas, made a statement that has gone down in history. "This is the greatest thing that's happened to the Bears in five years," he said. "We got rid of those malcontents. It's a great day, a great day!" Since then the Bears have had no malcontents and very few football players.

On November 22, 1963, an opera was having its premiere in a brand-new opera house in Munich. After the first act, word came that President John F. Kennedy had been assassinated in Dallas 6,000 miles away. The theater closed and the people went home. In Rome, Italian taxi drivers draped a cab in black and parked it in front of the United States Embassy. In Israel, every shop closed in every town and kibbutz. In the United States while mourners filed past a flag-draped coffin in the Capitol Rotunda, the National Football League played a full program of games.

That didn't prove the N.F.L. callous or insensitive to history, though. They always play "The Star-Spangled Banner" at N.F.L. games, and the pièce de résistance between halves at Super Bowl IV was a re-enactment of the Battle of New Orleans. The British won.

"I would rather be right than President," said Henry Clay, statesman.

"I don't care what others think, so long as I satisfy myself," say Al Davis, managing general partner of the Oakland Raiders.

The T-formation is taken for granted in modern professional football, but the man most responsible for infusing it back into the game, Clark Shaughnessy, often goes unrecognized for his contribution. The T had not been used for many years when he revived it while coaching at Stanford University in 1939. The following year Papa Bear George Halas brought Shaughnessy out to Chicago to help install the revitalized formation in the Bears' scheme of things. It must have been a good idea because in the championship game of 1940 quarterback Sid Luckman, working from the T, led the Bears to a 73–0 devastation of the Redskins with tailback Sammy Baugh still working out of the single wing. Red Smith pays a little homage here to Mr. Shaughnessy, who may be gone but should not be forgotten. The article first appeared in *Women's Wear Daily* in 1970, and was later featured in the collection *To Absent Friends from Red Smith.*

Clark Daniel Shaughnessy

RED SMITH

THE OBITUARIES identified Clark Daniel Shaughnessy as the coach who revived the T-formation in football, and that's more-or-less accurate. He was the man whose example taught college coaches the possibilities of the T, and he played a part in the explosive events of December 8, 1940, the day professional football entered a new era that has not yet passed.

The one true prophet of the T-formation is George Halas, owner of the Chicago Bears. In 1920 when Halas organized the Decatur Staleys as the prototype of the Bears, he put in the T-formation because that was what he knew; they had used it during World War I at Great Lakes where he and Jimmy Conzelman, Paddy Driscoll, Hugh Blacklock, and other gobs made up a team that won the Rose Bowl game of 1919.

Though he flirted briefly with the single-wing in the early years, Halas never abandoned the T. His Bears were employing it during the 1930s when Shaughnessy was coaching the University of Chicago, and Halas says Shaughnessy was the first college coach to recognize its possibilities.

At any rate, when Chicago abandoned football after the 1939 season and Shaughnessy was hired by Stanford, he installed the T-formation at Palo Alto. He knew what he was doing: Stanford had a mediocre tailback named Frankie Albert who became a great left-handed quarterback, a beast at fullback named Norm Standlee, and a pair of running fools named Hugh Gallerneau and Pete Kmetovic.

Running from the T, the Stanfords blew through

Shaughnessy's first session without defeat and whipped Nebraska in the Rose Bowl. Suddenly Clark Shaughnessy was in demand as an afterdinner speaker. On the banquet circuit he explained that where the single-wing formation stressed power, the T relied on speed and deception. He said that kids who had got lumps on their heads running the single-wing power plays really enjoyed fooling the opposition.

"And the secret of the T-formation's success," Clark Shaughnessy would say, "is simple: get a quarterback like Albert, a fullback like Standlee, and halfbacks like Gallerneau and Kmetovic."

Shaughnessy was no green hand at this stage. After graduation from Minnesota in 1914, he had been head coach at Tulane, at Loyola of the South, and at Chicago. He had been teaching football more than a quarter of a century when he hit the jackpot at Stanford.

It is inconceivable today that a coach whose team was going into the Rose Bowl could leave the campus a month before that game, but Shaughnessy did. At the start of December in 1940 he returned to Chicago as a specialist to polish the Bears' offense. Halas had clung to the T-formation over the years but it was Shaughnessy and Ralph Jones, a bald little man who had been with Halas since the 1920s, who introduced refinements like shuttling linemen and the back-in-motion.

The Bears had finished first in the Western Division of the National Football League and were about to play the Washington Redskins for the world championship. Just a few weeks earlier, they had lost to the Redskins, 7-3.

In Howie Robert's book, *The Story of Pro Football,* a Chicago demigod named Bulldog Taylor tells how it was:

"We were a pretty tense bunch: It was Shaughnessy who relieved the tension. He made the pregame talk and you've never seen anyone so calm. 'You can beat these Redskins,' he said, 'and here's how.' He outlined a play we had charted as our second of the game. 'It might go for a touchdown the first time,' he said. Somehow, we believed him."

The Bears' second play from scrimmage was the one Shaughnessy had diagramed. It didn't work exactly as it had worked on the blackboard.

Bill Osmanski slanted to his left on a dive-tackle plunge, saw his way blocked and swung wide around end. Straightening out, he found Ed Justice and Jimmy Johnston in his way, but all of a sudden here came George Wilson, the Bears' right end, galumphing across the field in search of trouble.

A horse player would say George Wilson put over a parlay. He hit Johnston with a block that flung the victim bodily into Justice and as both defenders went down Osmanski raced on alone for a 68-yard touchdown.

As Shaughnessy had promised, the play worked. It produced the first touchdown in a game the Bears won, 73-0. That game converted virtually every football coach in creation to the T-formation faith. It set off a boom in pro football that still shows no sign of leveling off. Clark Shaughnessy was considered something of a visionary, but not even he could have foreseen it all.

Professional football training camps, those summer hells designed to
sweat into shape veterans and enable the coaches to determine which
rookies are worthy of the big-time, are home to shenanigans as varied as
the personalities of the players who perpetrate them. Kenny Stabler, who
played for the Raiders when the team resided in Oakland, was one of the
most unshackled of free spirits in his heyday, while remaining one of the
best quarterbacks in the game. Along with writer Berry Stainback, he
wrote about his world of football—ribald, intemperate maybe, unorthodox probably—in a book which takes its title from Stabler's nickname,
Snake. This excerpt from it deals with those weeks of hellish summers
that overtured his seasons as a Raider.

The Santa Rosa Five Go to Camp

—— KENNY STABLER (WITH BERRY STAINBACK) ——

SOME OF MY most vivid memories are of training
camps. Although many players have compared life
in a National Football League training camp to being in
a Turkish prison, I loved it.

The Oakland Raiders of my day trained in the long-
sucking heat of Santa Rosa, California, where the sweat
poured like rain for eight weeks. The workouts were
scheduled for ninety minutes in the morning and ninety
minutes in the afternoon. But I'd like to have an Al
Davis pinkie ring for every workout that lasted over two
hours. We got so much conditioning in during practice,
we didn't have to do the extra running that other teams
did. Which was fine—we weren't entering any mara-
thons.

But we worked like hell in practice and tried to keep
from snoring like hell in meetings: ninety minutes in the
afternoon, ninety more in the evening. The meetings
were so boring they made leaf-raking seem like an exciting occupation. I can understand why so many players
hated training camp.

But, as I said, I loved camp. First, because with the

Raiders we went in knowing we were going to win every
year; and second, because we also knew we were going
to have fun. In fact, we expended almost as much energy
devising and executing good times as we did getting
ready for the season. But then the two disciplines went
together like victory and celebration.

The monotony of camp was so oppressive that without
the diversions of whiskey and women, those of us who
were wired for activity and no more than six hours' sleep
a night might have gone berserk. I was fortunate to have
four let's-party-hearty roommates to pal with most of my
years in Oakland. The roomies were halfback Pete Banaszak, wide receiver Freddy Biletnikoff, defensive end
Tony Cline, and middle linebacker Dan Conners. We
lived for the weekly football games and the football-
player nights in between. I liked to think of us as "The
Santa Rosa Five."

We stayed at the El Rancho Motel in Santa Rosa,
about sixty miles north of Oakland, a one-story quadran-
gular building of some sixty rooms. Most of them ac-
commodated two players, but we shared one of the five

two-room suites. Tony, Freddy, and myself had the large main room, with Pete and Dan in the adjoining one. We needed space to socialize.

At a used-appliances store we bought three ancient refrigerators for $10 apiece and installed them in the suite. Those machines whined and groaned twenty-four hours a day, probably costing the motel a fortune in electricity charges. We kept the fridges full of beer, soft drinks, candy bars, and fruit. Mostly beer.

Pete had a girl one year who baked us a pie every week. The pies were also stored in the fridge. The girl was strange. Given all the female "players" who moved through our abode, it was inevitable that the girl would be replaced by new talent, and she was. Yet she kept bringing pies.

"Why don't you ease her out gently?" I asked Pete.

"I like pie," he said.

"She's a tad weird."

"Her pies ain't."

The final week of camp, on her last pie delivery, the girl heaved it at Pete, who ducked. The gooey concoction hit me right in the chest and dribbled down my shirt.

"You're right, Snake," Pete said. "She's weird."

After you've played a few years and have the offense down pat, meetings are the most boring aspect of training camp. Freddy Biletnikoff taught me how to deal with that. Freddy had already played eight years when I took over at quarterback and he had perfected a neat meeting trick.

We always sat together in the back of the room. One night I leaned over and whispered something to him and got no response. I nudged him with an elbow and whispered, "What the hell's wrong with you?" He had been staring straight ahead with the lifeless expression in his eyes that veterans get at meetings, but now he shook his head like a dog coming out of water and said, "I was asleep." "Goddamn," I said to myself, "he's been sleeping with his eyes open!" Well, it took some practice to get that one down, copping z's with your lids up and a semiattentive look on your face. I guess that's when I decided that a determined man can do about anything.

Most of the veterans brought playthings or projects to camp to help them break the boredom. In 1968, my first year in camp, defensive tackle Dan Birdwell brought a junk car to work on. It appeared to me to be well beyond repair. But a teammate explained, "Dan'll fix it or kill it with his bare hands."

I kept hearing stories about how tough Birdwell was, how he liked to not just beat opponents but punish them. "Dan's not happy when he comes off the field after a series," Dan Conners told me, "unless he's got blood and bits of flesh under his fingernails."

Birdwell soon showed me how tough he was. One day he was working on the exhaust manifold of his junker while it was hot. Someone told him he was going to get burned. "Fuck it," he said. "Gotta get this heap together."

The following morning he showed up at practice with great big blisters on his fingers. Guys saw them and told him to see the trainer, take a day off. "These don't bother me," Birdwell said. Then he started popping the blisters and squirting the juice at people.

After working on the car's brakes, Birdwell decided to try them out in the driveway that circled the motel. There was a wooden fence on the side where the dressing room and two playing fields were situated. Birdwell drove around the driveway until he built up speed. As he approached the turn by the fence, he slammed on the brakes. They apparently needed a bit more adjusting. The car hopped off the driveway and crashed right through the fence.

Center Dave Dalby brought the first money-making toys to camp. He hauled in two coin-operated pinball machines and set them up in his room. It cost 25¢ per game, and there was usually a line waiting to play that stretched out of Dave's room and all the way down the hall. You don't know the meaning of the word "tilt" until you've seen a defensive lineman get mad at a pinball machine. But those two machines paid for all of Dalby's preseason bar bills, which about equaled the national debt of Chad.

One rookie came into one camp with a huge jigsaw puzzle. That guy might as well have posted a sign that read: I AM NOT RAIDER MATERIAL. He began assembling the puzzle on two card tables he'd pushed together in his room. As we passed his open door going to and from practice every day, we would check his steady progress. On Friday of the third week, the rookie had about 75 percent of the puzzle together and he said, "By Monday I'll be finished."

"No way," Tony Cline said as we walked on.

"He's pretty fast with that thing," I said.

"Not fast enough," Tony said.

On Monday the kid was cut and the puzzle was still there, incomplete. Of course, he couldn't have finished it anyway. Tony explained, "I stole three pieces."

Another young player who didn't make it with us that season may have sealed his fate with one pass. Don Milan was a quarterback from Cal Poly—San Luis Obispo with a real strong arm. Al Davis, the managing general partner and self-proclaimed genius of the Raiders, liked to stand in the end zone behind the secondary at practice and watch the pass routes and coverage when the ball was delivered. Al seldom misses anything, but even geniuses get distracted on occasion. Somehow Al looked away as Milan released a pass. It went high and sailed over everyone except Al. The ball peeled his head like an onion.

After practice I hurried to Milan's locker and collected the pair of football shoes I'd lent him. Freddy was right behind me asking for repayment of a $5 loan and someone else asked that Don return the jacket he had borrowed. We all knew that the odds on Milan's being in camp very long were not good. He became a backup in Green Bay that season.

George Buehler, a six-four, 285-pound guard, inevitably brought the most interesting toys to camp, intricate models that he would assemble. Once he brought a remote-controlled model airplane that cost about $700. He spent every free moment in camp working on that plane. We'd watch him in his room, his thick, gnarled lineman's fingers fastening tiny parts. Finally, after weeks of labor, he took his plane out for its maiden flight.

Naturally, we all went out on the field to see if his slick-looking craft would actually fly and if George could control it. The plane was terrific and so was George. He had it doing loops, diving, climbing, banking, all kinds of maneuvers. A group of us stood there watching with admiration as George put his plane through its paces like a prized hunting dog. We let out cheers and he was rightly proud.

Then, as he brought the plane down low for some lazy circles and figure eights, Dave Casper came walking by. Casper didn't know what was going on, which in itself was not that unusual; I never knew what was going on with Dave Casper either. He was a very intelligent individual, able to hold two or three conversations at the same time. One-on-one, though, he was sometimes a tad hazy.

The plane dived once right over Casper, a six-four, 245-pound tight end, and he sort of waved it away, like King Kong swatting at the bothersome planes that dove at him in the movie. When Buehler's plane made a second pass, Casper was ready. He grabbed a handful of lava rocks from the path and threw them at the plane—hitting the engine. The plane pitched straight down and crashed, pieces flying in every direction.

Casper just kept walking, without a word to anyone.

I went to George, who stood there dumbfounded. "Maybe you're just too big to play with model airplanes," I said.

I'd usually bring firecrackers to camp. Hundreds of firecrackers. My roommates and I would periodically toss them behind unsuspecting victims, scaring the shit out of guys. We got Casper so many times one week that whenever he saw us coming he'd change directions and give us the finger.

The year after his plane crashed, Buehler constructed a high-dollar remote-controlled tank. This machine was virtually indestructible. Just to make sure it stayed that way, though, George told Casper that if he so much as looked at the tank he was going to bite Dave's face off.

Inside the quadrangle of rooms at the motel was a sidewalk that skirted a courtyard of flowers, bushes, grass, and rocks. The courtyard was about fifty feet by fifty feet, and George ran his tank all over it, over rocks, around flowers, through bushes. I saw that, remembered my firecrackers, and decided they would make a great combination. Especially when Coach John Madden was in his office.

One afternoon between practice and dinner Pete Banaszak and I requisitioned Buehler's tank. I left a note in his box: DON'T WORRY. THE SNAKE WILL RETURN. We went to our rooms, which were directly across from the coaches' offices, and timed running the tank over to them. We taped a handful of firecrackers to the tank and attached a long fuse that we calculated would be just the right length to set off the fireworks as the tank rolled into the coaches' offices. Our calculations proved to be accurate.

Seconds after the bombs burst, a frantic Coach Madden came running out of the office, jabbing index fingers into his ears and screaming, "Who the hell did that? Where'd you go?" Meanwhile we turned the tank around. And while John stood there hollering and turning pink and pulling at his hair as he tended to do whenever he got excited, we ran that little tank between his spread legs and brought it on home.

After that we blew up the coaches' room maybe once a week. Good old John never got after us. At first I thought he just got used to the explosions. Then I noticed that whenever he entered his office he stuffed wads of cotton in his ears.

You never knew what oddity a placekicker might bring to camp. Placekickers are a breed apart, and I don't mean George Blanda, a placekicker who was also a football player. I mean the guys who make a living using no other part of their bodies but their feet, like grape stompers. I have never known a placekicker who wasn't more than a little strange, if not a full-time Twilight Zoner.

Errol Mann, the veteran placekicker from the Lions, signed on with us for the last years of his career. Mann had only two interests: horses and airplanes. So one year he came to camp with a six-foot-high stack of horse magazines and airplane magazines. The next year he brought a horse to camp. The following year he brought an airplane to camp.

"How'd you get the plane here?" I asked him.

"I flew it," he said. "Just got my license this spring. I'll take you up for a spin this afternoon after practice."

"No you won't," I said.

"Why not?"

"I have one rule in life I will not break," I said. "I

will not get into an airplane with a placekicker in the pilot's seat.''

''That's ridiculous.''

''Errol, no offense,'' I said. ''But all of your skills lie in your feet. You really shoulda took up tap-dancing.''

None of the players would fly with Mann. In fact, Errol Mann just may be the only pilot ever to have to fly solo for his entire life.

John Madden knew he was coaching a gang of distinctive individuals. Characters, some called us. Others called us ruffians, mavericks, renegades, oddballs, intimidators . . . and there's no point in mentioning the curse words. But all the labels were fair enough. And I think John decided with the type of people we had that it was necessary to give us a certain amount of room to roam. We had more characters than any other team and John realized that we didn't care for a lot of restrictions, were happier without them, and as a result played better. John handled individuals very well, and I feel that was a prime reason why the Raiders had the best won-lost record in pro football while he was coaching the team.

Al Davis liked to pick up so-called misfits from other teams. He obviously figured that, while they may not have fit in elsewhere, they sure as hell could fit in with us. And those of us who were already Raiders welcomed anyone who could help the ball club, and maybe even add another dimension to our festive occasions.

In August 1975 Al grabbed veteran linebacker Ted Hendricks from Green Bay, where he had not meshed in the Packers' defensive system. His nickname was ''Kick 'em in the Head Ted'' because he had no qualms about applying his feet to opponents when the urge seized him. Hendricks had no qualms about anything.

The day he reported at Santa Rosa he didn't turn out with the rest of us for practice, and we wondered where he was. Then we saw him coming over the hill that rose just beyond the field. He was riding a horse, in uniform. Except on his head was a spike-topped World War I German helmet that he'd painted silver and black, and on the sides were Raider-symbol patch-eyed pirate decals. Everyone cheered. Hendricks rode right up to John Madden and said, ''Okay, Coach, I'm ready to play some football.''

Early in the next season, when the Washington Redskins released John Matuszak, it didn't bother Al Davis that this was the third team to dump ''The Tooz.'' Al snapped him right up. George Allen was the Redskins' coach at the time and writers could not understand why a man who loved veterans the way Allen did would cut one who was six-eight, 280 pounds, and under thirty years of age. ''Vodka and Valium,'' was George's explanation. ''The breakfast of champions.''

I didn't believe that for a minute. Anytime I celebrated with The Tooz, all he ever drank was Crown Royal and the only pills he popped were occasional Quaaludes. ''Crown and ludes, the late supper of champions,'' The Tooz might say.

The day Matuszak arrived at practice he suited up with us, but also delayed joining us on the field. Then he came running at full speed and let out a god-awful scream that made spectators cringe and the rest of us laugh like hell. Al Davis was not amused. He was standing next to Hendricks and Al, kind of thinking out loud, said, ''I wonder if John's worth the gamble?''

Hendricks gave him a you've-got-to-be-kidding look and said, ''Al, what difference will one more make?''

What was most interesting was how many of the outcasts we acquired played better football for us than they ever had with other clubs. Even Hendricks, who'd had excellent years with the Baltimore Colts before his brief decline in Green Bay, had his finest years with the Raiders. Matuszak was much more effective than he had been at Houston or Kansas City. Errol Mann led the AFC in field goals and scoring in 1977. Willie Hall, Warren Bankston, Dave Rowe, Mike McCoy, Pat Toomay . . . the list goes on and on of players whose performance improved in the Raider environment. They became fond of our life-style and our game-style. Al Davis's ''Pride and Poise'' theme for the Raiders was dead right. For all the fun, Raiders got serious on Sunday. Real Serious.

When Toomay joined us he was ecstatic, after playing with the Dallas Cowboys, the Buffalo Bills, and the Tampa Bay Bucks. ''All my life,'' he said, ''I knew that somewhere in the league there must be a club like this.''

Most of the Raider players who were not married drank hard and chased women harder. It relieved the monotony of training camp and the pressure of games. And, goddamn, it was fun.

I was married twice while a Raider, but I never felt like a husband. Perhaps because both of the women I married were more like sparring partners than wives. Obviously, the fault was not all theirs. But I was never deterred from the endless game of prowl-and-party.

My roommates and I had a pact. We all took seats by the door at the 8:00 P.M. meeting and the moment it broke up—around 9:30—we sprinted to our rooms. We'd comb our hair, slap on face juice, and dash to the biggest car we had, usually a Banaszak Buick. We only had ninety minutes to complete what we called ''The Circuit.'' That consisted of hitting at least five bars before we had to be back for the 11:00 P.M. curfew.

The Circuit started each night at Melendy's, the nearest bar, and we never missed stopping at The Music Box. It had a large dance floor, the best live music in Santa Rosa, and The Box was also where the best-looking women usually hung out. No minor consideration.

Every year during training camp the women of Santa Rosa turned out in droves to greet the Raiders, many bearing dance cards that just had to be filled in. Some of the women were beautiful, a great many were attractive, and the balance ranged from plain to ugly as a mud fence. We tried to be selective.

We usually played Boss dice on The Circuit to see who would pay for the drinks. All the while, at each stop, we'd check out the women who appeared to be what we called "players." As we had to be in by curfew, all cars parked, dates would be set for eleven-thirty. The experienced female players knew the routine; others were quick learners. They would drive to the El Rancho, pick you up, and haul you to their place or to another motel. Those players not familiar with the word "shy" would join you in your room, uninhibited by the witnesses to the performance. There were a few tireless spirits who would attend to all five of us. They were known as "60-Minute Players," or "The OT Girls."

When one of the roomies came in real late with a girl, those of us who appeared to be (but were not quite) asleep would peek at the action. Freddy liked to crawl on the floor and get right up close. I bought a kid's plastic periscope to peek around the door frame into the inner room. But the damn thing didn't work unless all the lights in there were on.

One night, when Freddy was between marriages, he was going at it with a girl in his bed for about forty minutes. Pete was under the covers in the next bed, seemingly asleep. When Freddy finished, he whispered to the girl, "You know, Pete Banaszak over there has one of the biggest dongs in camp."

"No kidding!" the girl said, sitting up and eyeing Pete in the semi-darkness. He was lying on his back, his closed eyes facing her, his chest rhythmically rising and falling.

"I'm serious. Pete's hung. Go on over there and pull back the covers. You can see he's out cold."

Pete, of course, had been watching the show slit-eyed. The girl bent down for a good look and when she flipped back the covers, a blue-diamond boner popped up and quivered in her face. The girl let out a muffled cry and hopped back to Freddy. Seeing that Pete's eyes were still shut, Freddy said, "You should see that thing when he's *awake!*"

"Maybe I'll have to come back," the girl whispered, giggling.

Pete's eyes opened and he smiled.

Many nights we'd go right back out after curfew, and many times I didn't return until just before breakfast. We left and returned the same way—through a back door and a hedgerow of bushes rimming the driveway. If I had a midnight date, she would pull in, turn off the

headlights, then slowly circle the driveway. Meanwhile I'd creep through the bushes in a crouch and look up the driveway for her—and usually see about fifteen other veterans hunched down waiting for pickups.

We had a teammate who kept professing how religious he was. He enjoyed chiding some of us for our womanizing. Then one night I went through the hedgerow and who was right beside me but that God-spouting hypocrite. A woman stopped her car and he made for it as if she had the keys to the pearly gates. "Caught, caught!" I half hollered. The next day he denied that it was him I'd seen. For the next week, though, whenever I saw him I'd yell, "Caught, caught!" and watch him turn red.

Then there was the night a car pulled up by me and I slipped in and kept my head down on the seat as usual. The young woman pulled up to the exit under the lighted EL RANCHO MOTEL sign and I looked up. I couldn't believe it. The driver was gorgeous, a girl I'd never seen before—not my date.

She glanced at me as she pulled away and I sat up. "Oh, I thought you were Tony!" she said.

"Well, I thought you were Sue," I said. "But the coaches are on patrol," I lied. "We can't turn back."

"Tony will be upset."

It had to be Tony Cline, who was getting all spiffed up when I hurried out. "He'll be fine," I said. "He's used to disappointment."

"What about you?"

"I've always relied on the kindness of strangers," I said, and she laughed.

All of the surprises during our night forays were not so pleasant. One precurfew evening all of The Santa Rosa Five made connections at The Music Box and later went back there to party with our dates. We were dancing and drinking and having a great time. My girl was a sexy little blonde who danced real close, applying more pelvic action than Tina Turner. I began to get anxious to press on her in private. So I invited her to step out of the smoke-filled bar for a few minutes of fresh air. Then I started trying to sell her on going to her place or a motel.

She was leaning back against the door of a car and I was standing in front of her, a hand on either side of her on the car, just sweet-talking away. All of a sudden, I felt someone else's hand on my shoulder from behind. I turned my head and saw that the person attached to that hand was my second wife.

"I hope she's worth it!" my wife said and stormed away.

She was. I had already been busted for the crime, so I figured I might as well go ahead and do the crime.

Of course, I had to tell the girl that my wife and I were separated (which was true, as long as I was in camp and she stayed home) and going to get a divorce (in a year or so, but why be picky?). I had heard about a couple of other Raider wives who had driven the sixty miles from Oakland to search the bars of Santa Rosa for their husbands, but this was the first trip for my wife. I felt kind of bad that the very first time she had driven up she'd caught me. But then I said to myself, "Almost any night she came she would have caught me." I felt better.

I never got caught with a woman in the El Rancho, though roughly half of our partying occurred right there. But every year in camp a few guys would get nabbed by coaches. They knew the program. The coaches had been around longer than us and periodically they would run a spot check after curfew, around 1 A.M. Invariably, it was a veteran who was found with a girl in his sack.

John Madden did this just to maintain some kind of control. He was not a guy to lay down rules and try to stop the fun completely, as most coaches did, because he knew that football players needed some relaxation. He drew a line, and it was a long one, beyond which you were not to tread. We just rubberized that line and stretched the hell out if it.

If Kenny Stabler and his coach John Madden were at one end of the pro football spectrum of animation, the least subdued one, Roger Staubach and his coach Tom Landry occupied the other end. Staubach's predecessor as quarterback in Dallas, Dandy Don Meredith, said of Roger, "We're going to have to do something about this guy. He's going to ruin the image of an NFL quarterback if he doesn't start smoking, drinking, cussing, or something." And Bob St. John, writing for the *Dallas Morning News*, quipped: "His idea of breaking training is putting whipped cream on his pie." Despite his lack of rowdyism and off-field roistering, Staubach managed to become one of the game's finest quarterbacks ever, good enough for the Pro Football Hall of Fame. In his book, *Time Enough to Win*, Staubach profiles his only professional football coach, the inscrutable Tom Landry, who becomes much more scrutable as a result of Roger's reminiscences.

The Man in the Funny Hat

ROGER STAUBACH (WITH FRANK LUKSA)

I USED TO sit by my home telephone the night before every Cowboy game at Texas Stadium, game plan spread at the desk. At 8 P.M. the phone would ring, and it would be Landry, calling to make a final review of offensive strategy. Funny, the way he'd do it. I'd pick up the phone and say, "Hello." The next thing I would hear was his voice saying, "Now, you know on that Slant 24, we are going to run it from. . . ." He wouldn't say, "Hello, Roger, this is Coach Landry," or anything else before starting right in on the game plan. It was as if I were in the room with him.

Next day when I got to the locker room Dan Reeves, our offensive coordinator who helped call plays from the press box, would sidle up and grin. "Make any changes last night?" he'd ask.

Everyone connected with play-calling knew this was the way Coach Landry operated. He's an amazing man. All week long he'd be involved with various areas of defense and offense so that he really didn't have a chance to study films in depth. We'd see him leaving the practice field on Friday with a load of film cans under his arm and think, "Oh, boy, here we go." He was taking them home to analyze.

During Saturday morning practice he might make some changes. He was good about trying not to change too much. He probably had a lot of things in mind to switch around but he knew he couldn't do it that late. Then he'd watch film again Saturday night and call me to correlate what he'd seen with what we planned to do.

He'd go over everything and ask my reaction to the plays. "On third down, how do you feel about these plays?" he'd say. Or, "What do you feel good with? Are there some you don't like? Which ones do you prefer? What play-action passes do you like best?" I really appreciated that. Then he might make a minor adjustment. Sometimes it would be significant, such as adding a play. I would have all night to think about it, get it set in my mind. On Sunday before the game he would give it to the team as a last-second addition. . . . No, he's not always unflappable. I'd see his jitters in the locker room when he'd walk around and talk to more players than usual. He would be tense, excited, but really have no way to work off his energy. That's when he'd get something in his mind about a certain play. He would come over to me and talk about a technical point. Then off he'd go, but soon he'd be back again. He's talked to me about the same point on the same play as many as *three* times.

After he would leave I'd tell the other quarterbacks, Danny White or Glenn Carano, "Tom's going a mile a minute today. We've been over that play a bunch of times and probably won't even use it." It wasn't a big deal. It was Landry's way of biting his fingernails.

Some of what we'd go over *was* pertinent, but other times I could tell Tom was just going through the motions of trying to occupy himself. He'd try to cover every little point. To be honest, there were times when I tuned him out unless it was something that represented a definite change. But to keep going over something we'd covered all week . . . I didn't need that.

Now if he said, "Instead of 83 Pass from a Red Formation, run it from Red Flip," *that* was significant. The way our system worked was that he would send in the play and I would determine the formation, whether we'd use a man in motion and, of course, the snap count. If he sent that play in and I called Red instead of Red Flip he would brace me and say, "What were you doing in the locker room when we went over this?" . . .

Tom always had a feeling for going back to New York. That trip brought back all the old memories because New York was where he played his NFL career and began coaching on the Giants staff which included Vince Lombardi. Landry was the defensive coordinator there when Cowboys owner Clint Murchison hired him for the Dallas job. New York was The Big Apple to Landry. He even gave us a talk in my early years that if you wanted to make All-Pro you had to do well in The Big Apple. New York was an emotional game for him, and still is even though the Giants haven't been division contenders for years. I could sense that going back was a special occasion for him and his vivacious wife, Alicia.

There was an extra dimension to the Redskins games because of the rivalry. Washington was a consistent reference point to Tom as early as training camp. We started working against Washington-type defenses that soon. When Landry put examples on the blackboard they would always be of the Redskins. "The Redskins play like so, therefore this play has to work in this type situation against them," he'd say. There was no reason to refer to a particular team. He could just diagram a defense. But the references to Washington would come out. I hear it's the same in Washington, that the Redskins are always referring to the Cowboys and what we're doing.

Tom and George Allen, the former Redskins coach, had a thing going between them. You could never tell that about a coach of any other team we played. I'd say George got Tom's goat pretty good because sometimes he talked about Allen in less than the fondest terms. I understand they fell out in the late '60s when Allen coached at Los Angeles and the Cowboys accused the Rams of spying on their practices. Allen came back and said he discovered a Cowboys spy up a tree outside the LA practice field. He claimed it was then Dallas scout Bucko Kilroy, which was a laugh. Kilroy weighed about 300 pounds in those days and had enough trouble climbing into his shoes much less a tree.

Despite their differences I think Landry and Allen could sit down in the offseason and get along fine. They're both fierce competitors. I didn't like Allen when I was playing because he always seemed to start a psychological campaign against me before every game. I've come to understand Allen better and now think he did it because he respected me as a player. The guy's dedicated—football is his whole life—and he got the job done, which is what it's all about.

But he used to get under everybody's skin, mine and Tom's included. Landry didn't like the way the Redskins talked about us through the media. He's really big the other way. He doesn't believe in saying anything about the other team. Landry would get mad if someone on our team did.

"Keep your comments to yourself when you're talking to the press," he'd tell us. "Teams are just going to use what you say against you. There's no point in mouthing off against anybody." Before a game against Washington Landry would say, "The Redskins are talking again," or "George has really got them talking this week."

One thing was different about what the Redskins said. It wound up on our bulletin board, something the Cowboys don't normally use. There are exceptions but Dallas is not a bulletin board team. There always was a lot of material available because teams liked to beat us and didn't mind saying so. Through the '70s Washington led the verbal attack by far.

There were a couple of years, around '74 and '75, when St. Louis got into the act. When those guys beat Dallas it seemed they held a press conference in the locker room to start mouthing off. Really incredible the way the Cardinals went at it.

Not only did Tom object to knocking the other team, he fairly sizzled when something said privately in a team meeting wound up in the next day's newspaper. I always talked to the press but never told anything confidential. Some players did leak things to the papers. If a confidential subject came up in a meeting, they'd leave the meeting and it was like Watergate all over again. Landry would just go crazy over that. He'd come to a meeting the next day and say, "When we're in this room we're like family. We are a team and what's said here is not supposed to leave this room." Sure enough, there it would be in the next day's paper. Someone would have a scoop.

Reporters who followed the Cowboys for years tell me that Tom is tops among NFL head coaches as a cooperative, accessible subject for interview. They say he's unfailingly polite, thoughtful of their job pressures and tolerant of even the dumbest question. But he also seems to view their work in curious fashion.

For instance, he would tell us not to worry about what we read. Then a few weeks later he was saying, "You know what they're writing about us. They say we're finished, that we're down." He'd use *that* to get us motivated. I suspect Coach reads every line of newspaper type relating to the Cowboys. Either he was reading it or somebody was telling him because he sure knew what had been written. Of course, he was on safe ground when he reminded the team we were being written off. The Cowboys in '70 and '71 were buried in the newspapers at midseason and wound up in Super Bowls. The '75 team got there, too, after being written off before the season even began.

It is this relationship with Tom—and more—I left behind. I'll miss the personal glimpses, those uncommon moments when the curtain lifted for a peek at the man behind the sideline mask. Thinking back I suppose the happiest I ever saw him—when he let it show—was after we beat Miami in Super Bowl VI. Players lifted him on their shoulders and carried him off the field. Tom wore a smile as wide as a rainbow that day. You could see the load lifted from his shoulders for all the past playoff disappointments.

To me, Landry's low point was after a playoff loss to Cleveland my rookie year in 1969. We were getting ready to board a flight to Miami for the Playoff Bowl. People were crying for his scalp and he looked like a beaten man that day. We had a meeting at Love Field before taking off and he was the lowest I've ever seen him. He was ashen. He'd had it and he was down.

I'll also remember his stubbornness or conviction, whatever you want to call it. As an illustration, he still believes the ultimate play-calling system is to shuttle quarterbacks on alternate downs. Craig Morton and I were the last NFL quarterbacks to be used that way in a 1971 game against Chicago, which we lost 23-19. Statistically you couldn't entirely blame the system because we had more than 400 yards total offense.

Yet I believe Coach revealed much of himself that day, with his conviction that at least in theory a quarterback shuttle is the premier system. I think he used it with me and Morton because neither of us was the dominant quarterback at the time and he felt *he* was the dominant figure. We were just there to exercise his will. Deep down I feel he likes to be the quarterback on the sideline with the ability to tell the player everything he's supposed to do. He sends in a play and says, "We will run an 88 pass. Look to the post. Watch the weak safety. Keep your eye on this . . ." and goes over the whole thing like we do in a meeting. Then we have it fresh on our minds as we walk on the field—like machines.

What that showed was he had more confidence in himself than his quarterbacks. Landry probably still does but he realizes the quarterback shuttle isn't practical. He still thinks of that concept mainly because he knows if you do it his way it's going to be the right way.

Like a lot of successful people Tom Landry has an ego. His isn't overbearing but it's large and strong. He believes in *his* system and *his* way. It doesn't always matter who the person might be to carry out the system's function—as long as you do it *his* way.

Back when Craig and I shuttled, I think he was saying to himself, "They are just two people. They can pass and hand off. The system is fine." He didn't consider that our styles were different, or that the team needed one player to look to, or how we felt about it. He just looked at it and said, "I have two human beings here and they can throw and do what I tell them and that's it. The job is done." And if you had two robots, yes, it *would* work.

Tom settled for a single quarterback and since then has used guards, tight ends, wide receivers and running backs as play messengers. This is what he feels better about than anything—knowing what the play will be so he and other coaches can concentrate on the point of attack. If the play fails then they determine whether the breakdown was our fault or the defense made a great play. As long as Landry coaches I doubt the play-calling system ever will change. . . .

The Cowboys were successful under Landry's system as he operated it while I was playing. If there had been a losing season or the offense was off, then circumstances might warrant a change. But I'll bet our offense in the last three or four years, probably in all our years together, gained more yards and scored more points than anybody. I couldn't say that the system was hurting for a different approach. And had I, I would have been saying in effect that I could do better. . . .

I knew the play-calling format was something that Tom believed in deeply. It had nothing to do with my ability to call plays. He *liked* it. I believe no matter what he said about strategy and everything else involved, he just liked to call them. If that's what he believed and preferred so strongly I didn't think it was right to put pressure on him to change.

I used to needle Landry from the banquet podium but whether he ever heard or read about it I never knew. I'd start out by saying when I learned Tom was going to call all the plays I didn't care because I was just happy to start.

"I didn't worry about it until one of Landry's neighbors called and told me Tom had been working out in his backyard—throwing the football," my story went on. "That was too much. I realized he didn't like rookie quarterbacks," I'd say and pause. "But a comeback?"

When we were together, however, I picked my spots carefully. I was never insubordinate. But there were what you might call maverick moments.

One of them took place during a sideline conference. A time out was called with only a few seconds left to play. We had the game won so there was no pressure.

As usual I trotted over and stood beside Landry to receive the next play. He was looking at the sky. I stood and waited. He kept looking upwards. On and on we went—me waiting, him transfixed with the heavens.

Finally, Tom turned his gaze on me. Before he could speak I told him, "I always wondered where you got those plays."

Ernie Stautner, our defensive coordinator, and some of the other coaches were there and started laughing like crazy. Tom just looked at me, gave me a play and off I went. He doesn't take to those little jokes out there on the field.

Another time we were on the practice field working on a new goal line play. I faked a handoff and rolled out to the right. The first time I ran it he said, "No, no, no. You have to fake longer." He normally doesn't do this but to emphasize the point Landry got under center like a quarterback. He took the snap, executed a fake to the halfback and rolled out—limping all the way. Coach has a hitch in his stride, a noticeable gimp from an old football knee injury.

Now it was time for me to run the play again. The whole team was watching as I got under center, made the fake and rolled out . . . limping, just like he did. Well, everybody cracked up on the spot. Landry smiled . . . sort of. As I said, he doesn't have a great sense of humor on the field.

Reminiscing about Tom gave me the only choke-up moment during the retirement press conference. I had to force out the words when I spoke of "the nuts and bolts of the Cowboys . . . the man who wears the funny hat on the sideline." The "funny hat" reference wasn't planned and later I wondered whether he appreciated it. Landry *does* take great pride in his hats.

I understood why to the very last this man stirred my deepest emotion and made my voice wobble. Others didn't. Even a few teammates questioned whether it was coincidence or genuine feeling for the coach which almost caused me to lose composure. At first I found their reaction curious, even a bit discouraging in that Landry remained such a distant figure to them.

Then it came to me that Tom and I had been on unique terms. Ours was a relationship like no other on the team. By necessity of a system built around coach-who-calls-plays and quarterback-who-executes-plays, I had observed him close-up longer and more often than any other player. The system put us in almost daily contact, whereas most of my teammates had little personal contact with the head man.

With us it was different. Our dialogue was almost constant. I listened to him during quarterback meetings. He listened to me and other team captains during captains' meetings. We talked on the practice field . . . every Saturday night before home games when he called to review the game plan . . . in pregame locker rooms when he decided on a last-second play change . . . during timeouts as we selected the next play . . . on plane flights outward bound or returning to Dallas.

In this manner I listened to him and learned from him for 11 years. I never totally agreed with everything I heard or was told but still . . . Tom was *the* authority figure to me longer than anyone except my parents. Father, mother and wife aside, he was the person I was most emotionally involved with during my lifetime. As such he moved me through the entire range of human feeling over the years—anger, love, frustration, pride, disgust, awe, loyalty, respect.

In composite I remember him as a towering figure. To me he was, is and always will be special—a man apart from other men. What made him so beyond his brilliant technical grasp of football were two bedrock Landry characteristics: enormous self-discipline and consistency. Landry is the rock against which we all lean, often without realizing it, at some point during our careers.

What is he *really* like? I don't think any of us will ever know or completely understand the man inside. Either purposely or through a naturally aloof personality he will remain hidden to insiders and outsiders alike.

Yet I think my insight of Landry is more balanced than Don Meredith's, who quarterbacked the Cowboys for nine years during the 1960s. Meredith has what I'd describe as a love-hate relationship with the coach. We've never gone into great psychological depth on the subject but this is what I gathered from conversations with Don recently.

One of those sessions took place during the 1979 season. Don and his wife Susan came to our home prior to an ABC-TV Monday night telecast which brought Meredith to Dallas. I believe that through the years Don has mellowed and come to appreciate Landry more. Meredith, who I thought was a great quarterback, went through a tough time building this team, taking unjustified abuse from the fans and feeling the dominance of Landry. All those things were harder to handle in the '60s because things were going wrong on the field. You might have a tendency to blame the system or Tom when it could have been teammates who let Don down. Or maybe he was having a rough time. He just went through a lot building the team and was very close to the point where it was a success when he quit.

When Meredith talks about Landry it's not the same man I know. He has a different feeling about Tom. Some of those feelings I recognize, such as Landry being somewhat aloof and dominant to the point of what he says goes, and what you have to say really doesn't mean much. I've felt that in passing but because I've seen the other sides of Tom I understand him better. The things you say *do* have meaning to him. He just doesn't let it show.

Landry has this sternness about him with everybody. It's not personal. It wasn't anything personal when he cut me short in a meeting. He's done that to his coaches. He doesn't even know he's doing it sometimes. I believe Don took a lot of those situations on a personal basis. . . .

In a different manner and with a different purpose in mind Landry has touched every player who ever suited up for the Cowboys. Each can tell the story behind his mental bruise. . . .

Dandy Don Meredith, Tom Landry's quarterback before he left the field for the broadcast booth, described his coach this way: "Tom Landry is a perfectionist. If he was married to Raquel Welch, he'd expect her to cook."

Tom has a feel for players and you can't get away from that. He has a sense for how far he can push certain guys, what their tolerance is and whether it's worthwhile to push them any further. If he feels he has to push them

further and they don't like it, then he gets rid of them. Thomas Henderson, the linebacker he kicked off the team last season, fell into the latter category.

Only once did I hear a player talking back to Tom. Of all people it was Toni Fritsch, the place kicker from Austria. Toni came to practice one day and probably had had a couple of beers. He was out there kicking when Landry came up to him and started talking about techniques. Fritsch said, "You get away from me! Get away from me!" I don't know if he even realized it was Landry. But he looked around and it *was* Landry. Then Tom realized Toni had tipped a few, fined him $500 and almost kicked him off the team.

For reasons less obvious than Fritsch's indiscretion, I'm sure Tom has been displeased at some point with every player he's ever coached. But that never meant he didn't care about us. He does have a personal concern and I would point to the Bob Hayes narcotics trial as an example. Landry testified as a character witness for Hayes. He looked at that from every angle and went to the courthouse despite the case involving drugs, which he is very much against.

Players tell of the old days when he was less flexible in relating to players. They said when George Andrie's wife was pregnant Tom wouldn't let him go home from training camp when the baby was born. Yet in recent years he's been receptive to personal situations like that. Last year a couple of players went home when their wives were having babies. I believe what most of us didn't realize is that we needed to go to him and explain the problem because he's so engrossed in what he's doing and there are so many players.

Landry wouldn't come around and say, "Hey, Roger, what's wrong today? Feeling OK? Everything all right at home?" But if I went to him and said, "Coach, I have a problem at home, something is wrong and I need some time off," he would know it's important to me. He also understood that problem would affect me on the field if it was left unresolved.

Landry doesn't go in for small talk but he can be a very warm person. He does a lot of things, particularly dealing with kids who are sick, very privately. He goes out of his way to help people. He gives his time, which shows the warmth of the man. Tom probably gets more done quietly behind that cold image than anybody. . . .

Only one aspect of my association with Tom bothered me through the years—that people believed he and I were personally close because of our Christian faith. That always disturbed me because I've never been given anything in athletics. I always earned it. When I joined the Cowboys I didn't undergo a religious transformation. I'd heard that Landry was a very strong Christian, but I was, too. If I'd been transformed into a Christian after I came to Dallas that would have been a beauty.

I never wanted people to think I was trying to get close to him or to use religion to maintain my stability with the team. So actually I went the other way early in my career. I'd stay away from functions he attended. In the last few years I've been more receptive to appearing with Landry; in fact, one year we co-hosted a Fellowship of Christian Athletes dinner in Dallas.

Even that made me uneasy because I had no fore-knowledge that Landry was on the program. If it had happened when I was fighting with Craig for a job I would have been a basket case. I would have had them send out a retraction. I didn't want anyone to think I was using my Christian faith to be close to Tom.

Landry has said many times the priorities in his life are faith, family and football, in that order. He is a great Christian example. Tom not only talks about his faith but lives it. I can think of no better definition of a devout Christian. Despite this common ground between us I didn't pursue a close relationship and neither did he.

As I pointed out he invited me to his home once. He's never been to my house. Keeping our distance was the best way to maintain a respectful coach-quarterback di-alogue. Socializing together wouldn't work because of the demands each of us faced. He had to tell me about my play, and sometimes what he had to say wasn't favorable. I had to be open with him, even if it meant saying I didn't think the last play he called was so hot.

It's obvious that when Tom quits coaching he will be hailed as one of the giants of his profession. Entering the 1980 season he was the fourth all-time winning coach in NFL history behind George Halas, Curly Lambeau and Don Shula. . . .

If Landry [goes] into politics, I would speculate it'd be on the national level, as a United States Senator. If he went into it statewide I think it would be a position of significance, like governor.

Can't you see Tom giving one of his Monday morning critiques to Congress or the Texas Legislature? I can hear him saying, "Senator So-and-so, I've just graded the bill you proposed and it's the worst in the history of the country." Landry wouldn't mess around. He'd do a great job, as he has for the Cowboys.

Knowing what I know about him, I'd be on his band-wagon.

Art Donovan, son of a famous boxing referee, played a vital role in the
defense of the awesome Baltimore Colts of the 1950s, a tackle savage
and adept enough to earn a plaque in the Pro Football Hall of Fame. At
the same time, he was and still is a storyteller as raunchy and laugh-
provoking as any who ever talked about the game and the people he
consorted with while playing it. John Steadman, the sports editor of the
Baltimore News American, captured the essential Donovan in this article,
which later was included in the anthology *The Best (and Worst) of
Steadman.*

Always Story Time with Art Donovan

JOHN STEADMAN

IT'S ALWAYS "tell a story" time with Arthur Donovan. He likes to talk of his boyhood in the Bronx when every Saturday morning he drilled with the neighborhood crowd in a game of "play soldiers" and they made simulated raids across the roof tops of garages.

Donovan's hero was Alexander Wojciechowicz, the famed center at Fordham University who played on some of the toughest teams the college game has ever known.

It was Donovan's desire to go to Fordham, too, but World War II exploded and, when it was over, there was some debate about the resumption of football and what the program was going to be like.

Dropping the A-Bomb got Donovan and millions of Americans home in one piece in World War II. "We were only weeks away from the invasion of Japan," said Art.

"I was with a Marine Division at Okinawa and we had all our gear stenciled and ready to go. I hate to think how many casualties we would have suffered had we gone through with such a mission."

Donovan ultimately went to Boston College, after a brief visit at Notre Dame, and played on a football team that sent 22 players to the pros but in '49 had only a 4–4–1 record.

When Donovan was drafted by the Baltimore Colts in 1950, they didn't much care whether he reported or not. "My old man said, 'If you go down there those big guys will kill you,' " and Art probably took him at his word because he was two days late for training camp.

The first long road trip the Colts took they had to play the Los Angeles Rams in an exhibition in San Antonio. It was disastrous. The Colts got beat 50–21.

After the night of horror, Donovan and his chum, Sisto Averno, got to drinking beer to drown their sorrows. They also got themselves lost.

At 4 A.M., a Sunday morning, they were out in the country and couldn't get a ride home. They walked down a long, dusty Texas road and found a church.

Art hammered on the door of the rectory. A priest put his head out the door and heard Donovan's plea:

"Father, we are a couple of good Catholic boys and we been drinking beer and got lost."

So the priest invited them in for the night and drove them to San Antonio in the morning so they could rejoin the team. It happened over two decades ago but Donovan tells the details with as much vividness for recall as if it occurred yesterday.

And then there was the time the Colts were staying at

the Beverly Wilshire Hotel in Beverly Hills. Art had never seen stall doors on a shower bath.

So he decided to close them, turned on the water, filled the compartment and went swimming with Y. A. Tittle. The water broke loose and came cascading out of the bathroom, damaging carpeting and furnishings in the floor below.

Between his stay with the Colts of 1950 and his return in 1953 with the re-franchised team, Donovan served with the Cleveland Browns, New York Yanks and Dallas Texans.

They once stayed a week in Hershey, Pa., and training rules were lax because the team didn't have even a remote title chance and was only playing out the string.

The players spent most of their time in Vince's, a friendly tavern. They figured that collectively, as a team, they paid bar bills of over $2,500 in the space of five days at 1952 drinking prices.

The Dallas club won only one game, a momentous upset over the Chicago Bears. "George Halas was so mad he took away some bonus money he had given the Bears the week before," said Art, "because it was a disgrace to lose to us."

Donovan played on two of the worst teams the NFL ever knew—the Colts of 1950 and the Texans of 1952. They could each win only one game.

"We had a 34 man player limit, as opposed to 40 today, and only 12 teams. So the job competition was unbelievable back then," he recalled.

Donovan, even though early in his career he was cast with bad teams, became one of the greatest defensive tackles the game has known.

"What times we had. And how about Bert Rechichar and Buddy Young and Bill Pellington and Don Shula and Tom Finnin and Jim Mutscheller, John Unitas, Lenny Moore and Gino Marchetti. What football players they were."

Art paused a second, shook his head and said, "But that's all gone; the game has changed so much it's unbelievable."

But as long as Art Donovan has breath in him, he's going to be able to relate stories and enjoy them like he's hearing them for the first time. There has never been an audience he couldn't hold.

Donovan enjoys talking about his first coach with the Colts, a quiet man named Clem Crowe.

"He used to scrimmage us for three hours and then make me run around the field until he told me to stop," related Art. "I think he was crazy. He had ten kids at home. Maybe they drove him crazy.

"He went to Notre Dame. That might have been another reason why he had ten kids!" Then he switched to talking about a chicken-eating contest he once watched in training camp. The coaches didn't know

anything about it because it was to be staged on a Sunday afternoon when only the players were around.

Donovan said between $300 and $500 had been put down in bets about whether Marchetti or Don Joyce could eat the most chicken.

"Marchetti was eating only the chicken and got up to 26 pieces," recalled Donovan. "But Joyce was eating peas and mashed potatoes and I think he was even eating the bones of the chicken.

"We called Joyce the 'Champ' because he wrestled one time on the pro circuit. Well, Joyce was eating it all, the chicken, peas and potatoes. You know, the full Maryland dinner. Joyce kept eating and went past Marchetti.

"He ate, and we counted, 36 separate pieces of fried chicken. Then the match was over and he poured himself a glass of iced tea. What do you think happened then? He reached in his pocket, pulled out a saccharin tablet, dropped it in his glass and said, 'I'm on a diet'."

Donovan, reaching back in his storehouse of memories, talked about a visit after a game to a favorite San Francisco spot known as the Paddock Bar, where he and some teammates were enjoying some pleasing refreshment.

"We were having a couple beers before we flew back to Baltimore. This powerful built guy was there and said, 'I can beat anybody in the house in arm wrestling' and I said, 'Maybe you can.'

"But he insisted on testing one of us. The only one interested was L. G. Dupre and he weighed 180 pounds. But what a tough little Frenchman. And what a fighter. He could box and handle himself.

"So Dupre took on this guy who was challenging everybody and put his arm down so fast he almost tore it out of its socket. Finally, the big guy got to arguing with the bar owner and then two other guys got involved and, the next thing we knew, the cops were there locking up four men. But not any of us.

"It was the only time I ever saw anything like that in my life and I've been in a lot of bar rooms. Probably four times as many as anybody you can name."

Donovan told about the time he left his bridge in a glass of water at night and Marchetti, then rooming with him, got up to get a drink and almost swallowed Donovan's false teeth in the dark bathroom.

Artie said he was honored to be named to the Pro Football Hall of Fame, but didn't think there were any supermen in the game.

"I know one fellow who had to be laughing when he read I made the Hall of Fame," brought up Artie. "And that was a guard by the name of Bruno Banducci, who played for the San Francisco 49ers and blocked me all over the field. What a great lineman."

In talking about some of the players on his own team,

he felt Alan (The Horse) Ameche, who Artie said "quit before his time," would have been ranked with the great pro fullbacks if he would have had a longer career.

"Bill Pellington was the most underrated," he went on. "Pellington was one of the toughest linebackers the game ever knew. What a great player. I always said that if they gave him a gun he could have done a cleaner job.

"And just like Pellington, I put Dick Szymanski in the same class. They moved him all around from offense to defense but he could play. A real professional."

Donovan wound up telling again about, when a boy, being a member of Eddie McCarthy's Army in the Bronx. As kids, they'd march with wooden guns and McCarthy was the general and they'd stage maneuvers on Saturday mornings.

"The last time I saw Eddie he was headed for Mexico to look for silver. That was in 1946. He just dropped off the map after that. Maybe he fell in a silver mine," added the beaming Irishman.

The good old days are never far away with Artie around. He makes life worthwhile.

Bill Stern's voice was as familiar to sports fans as any that ever graced the radio airwaves in that seemingly primeval age before television found sports or vice versa. Football was one of his favorites and he was a walking, talking encyclopedia of the sport. One of his favorite stories was this one about how Don Hutson, the fleet, adhesive-handed end known as the "Alabama Antelope," came to be a Green Bay Packer, to the unending pleasure of Curly Lambeau, and not a Brooklyn Dodger, to the ultimate chagrin of Shipwreck Kelly.

Man with the Magnetic Mitts

BILL STERN

THERE'S NEVER been an end with more superb skill at catching forward passes and squirming his way to sensational touchdowns, than Don Hutson. Some of the catches he made on a football field defied belief. In every game a "marked man," yet in almost every game for many years, three at college and ten in pro football, Don Hutson scored one or more touchdowns. And often, he scored more points than all the players on the rival team. No wonder friend and foe alike dubbed the slim man with the magnetic mitts, the guy who could catch a butterfly in a blizzard.

The amazing Don Hutson first started on his road to football fame at the University of Alabama. For three years, he had his pal and teammate, Dixie Howell, pitching footballs while he caught them and went scampering for touchdowns. Those were the years when Alabama ran roughshod over its rivals. In 1935 Alabama went to the Rose Bowl to play mighty Stanford, and Dixie Howell and Don Hutson performed an aerial act that stunned Stanford and dazzled the whole football world, with Don Hutson and his glue-fingers making impossible catches of forward passes and paying off with the winning touchdowns.

But when Don Hutson left the college world, the cynics murmured, "Sure, he was a college All-American wonder-boy. But wait until he gets into the big-time. He'll perform no miracles." However, Don Hutson ignored them, and became a football pro, playing with the Green Bay Packers.

For ten gruelling years, he was with the team. His pal and teammate, Dixie Howell, was no longer with him. Other players came along to fling passes at Don Hutson, and still he went on making impossible catches that often bordered on the miraculous. From the first day to the last day, for ten long years, Don Hutson was tops, the greatest end in football, college or pro. In the pro ranks, he broke every record as a pass receiver, and in every game it was always Hutson against the whole rival team. A slight idea of how dangerous he was may be gained from the record he created in his last three years of football when he scored in every game his team played. That's how good Don Hutson was in big-time!

It was in a most curious way that Hutson first broke into pro ball. It was the afternoon of September 22nd, 1935. The Green Bay Packers were playing the Chicago Bears. The famed Packers were in punt formation on their own 17-yard line on the first play from scrimmage. The ball was snapped back from center to Arnie Herber. The two powerful lines clashed and tangled, as Herber faded back to his own goal line, and then, he fired a pass to a teammate. It was a long pass, sixty yards at least. The crowd groaned, for it seemed impossible for the

Packers' end to get under that ball in time, but the new player who had just joined the team got under the ball and made that difficult play look easy. Then he shot past some Chicago tacklers who tried to catch him, and romped across the goal for the only touchdown of that important game. The Green Bay Packers won and Don Hutson, the amiable soft-spoken boy from Alabama had made his professional debut.

Fortunately Don Hutson became a professional player and the exclusive property of the famed Green Bay Packers of Wisconsin, only by a matter of seventeen minutes and a postmark on a letter.

It was a couple of days before the Rose Bowl game between Alabama and Stanford, that Curly Lambeau, coach of the Packers, first spotted Hutson. To Lambeau, he was the kind of end football coaches dream about. Lambeau lost no time in signing up the collegian, and his contract, as league rules required, was mailed to the president of the National League. Curly Lambeau was just about the happiest man in the sport world.

But in the next hour strange things began to pop. For it seemed that Shipwreck Kelly, then part-owner of the Brooklyn Dodgers football team, had also taken a shine to Don Hutson. And he had promised Hutson to meet any offer of any other bidder, once he was ready to sign to play pro football.

When Curly Lambeau began to park on Hutson's trail, tempting him with juicy offers, the collegian, wanting to be fair to Shipwreck Kelly, wired him about the offer.

He telegraphed Kelly some nine times during that week but no answer came from Kelly. Naturally, Hutson decided that Kelly was no longer interested, and so he signed up with the Green Bay Packers and thought the whole thing closed.

But the same day Curly Lambeau mailed the contract to the offices of the League president, Shipwreck Kelly met the collegian. Hutson explained the situation to him and Kelly understood. It seemed that none of the wires had reached him because he had been away in Florida. However, he was determined not to lose this player without a struggle, so he said to Hutson: "Don, I understand; but in all fairness to me, I think I should be given a crack at your services. You sign this contract with me and we'll mail this one too, to the President of the League. Whichever contract arrives first, that man wins."

Don Hutson, feeling obliged to Kelly, signed his second contract. Lambeau's contract and Kelly's contract arrived on the League president's desk at the same time, in the same mail. There was only one way to decide the matter. The League president looked at the posting time of each letter and saw that Lambeau's letter bore the time of 8:30 A.M. while Kelly's time was 8:47 A.M. And so he decided that Don Hutson belonged to the Green Bay Packers. Thus by a matter of seventeen minutes and a postmark, Don Hutson became a player for the Packers, and went on to imperishable fame as a pro football player.

Even in college Ken Strong was stranded in the Big Apple, playing ball for New York University. After that, it was the Staten Island Stapletons and the New York Giants of the NFL and a pair of years with the New York Yanks of a defunct AFL in the 1930s. But he was a triple-threat of immense talent, a halfback who could run, pass, punt, and place kick with the all-time best, a Hall of Famer who truly left his message in the minds of New York football fans of the 1930s. He reminisced about his life in New York football for Bob Curran, who included it in his book of interviews with the early greats of the game, *Pro Football Rag Days.*

From Staten Island to Manhattan, I Couldn't Get Out of New York

KEN STRONG

THERE IS a belief among sports people that athletes who play for New York teams sometimes gain more stature than they deserve because of the publicity they receive in the communications capital of the United States. They will tell you that if Joe DiMaggio had played in Boston and Ted Williams had been in New York, there would be no argument today about who was the better ballplayer.

They will also say that if Otto Graham or Bob Waterfield had played for New York teams, they would have been even more famous than they are. These same people use as their prime example Sam Huff, the former New York linebacker now with the Redskins, who became nationally famous through a TV show called "The Violent World of Sam Huff." They feel that Sam was the third-best linebacker in the National Football League that year, ranking behind Joe Schmidt of the Detroit Lions and Bill George of the Chicago Bears.

One person who might well be dubious about this New York theory is Ken Strong. Ken Strong played for three years at New York University, then a football power. During his collegiate career—he was the leading

scorer in the country during his senior year—he was compared to Ernie Nevers by Grantland Rice.

There are those who say that Ken Strong might be one of the five best all-around athletes of our time. He was such a good baseball player, the Detroit Tigers bought his contract from the Yankees in 1931 for $40,000 and five players. But Ken hurt his wrist in a game in Buffalo and had to give up baseball.

Despite his record in college and as a pro—he was the outstanding running back and kicker for the Giants, scoring 351 points in nine seasons—he is seldom mentioned today when the talk turns to the great ones. Fortunately, the Hall of Fame recognized his achievements and inducted him in the summer of 1962.

A representative for a liquor house in New York, Ken is a popular figure on the New York scene. Here is what he talked about one day in a hotel room in New York City:

After I graduated from N.Y.U., I signed to play baseball with the Yankees. Myself and Johnny Murphy from Fordham. They sent Johnny to Albany and me to New

Haven. This was a break because I was playing in my own backyard, West Haven, my home town.

The Giants football team had just signed a new coach, a fellow named Leroy Andrews, and also had signed Benny Friedman to play quarterback. Andrews contacted me and asked me about getting together to talk contract. We made a date to meet that Friday in the Hotel Taft in New York.

Friday afternoon—it was some time in late August—two fellows stopped me as I came off the field in New Haven and introduced themselves as Bill Blaine and Doug Wycoff. They said they had just landed a franchise in the National Football League and were going to start a team in Staten Island. They said they needed my name and would pay me $300 a game.

I hadn't heard of Blaine before but I had heard of Wycoff. He had played for Georgia Tech and they had played a game in Yankee Stadium one time when I was at N.Y.U. Later, I learned Blaine owned a few saloons and had sponsored a semi-pro team in Staten Island for many years.

Well, I told them that I had a date with Andrews that night to talk about playing with the Giants. Blaine then said that if things didn't work out I should call them right away in Staten Island.

I met Andrews and he offered me $200 a game. When I said I thought I could get more elsewhere, he gave me a cock-and-bull story about not being able to pay more because Benny Friedman was going to be the big star. Then he said Benny had a two-year contract and when it ran out I would get the big money. He also said that I should grab the chance because Mr. Tim Mara, the owner of the club, would introduce me to a lot of influential people.

Now I wasn't much of a talker in those days but I was cocky enough to say that I had just spent four years playing college ball in New York City and had met a lot of influential people. What I was interested in right then, I told him, was being paid for playing football. He said he'd have to think it over and gave me a number to call the next day at noon. It was the number of Mr. Mara's office—he was in the coal business then—at 23rd Street and Lexington Avenue.

After he left, I phoned Blaine in Staten Island. When he asked me how I made out, I said that Andrews offered me fifty dollars a game more than he had. Blaine then said, "We'll give you $5,000 and a paid apartment for the season."

Right away I said, "I accept those terms."

Then he said, "Is it all right with you if we break it to the papers?"

"I don't care what you do," I told him. "I accept your terms."

After that I didn't see much sense in calling Andrews

again. I figured the Giants would read about my signing with the Staten Island Stapletons in the papers. And they did. It wasn't until four years later that I found that they had told Andrews to start by offering me $5,000 for the season and to go up from there if he had to. He had just tried to make a big shot of himself for the Maras before he even started coaching the team.

Playing for the Stapes was some experience. The kids today are impressed with the difference between college ball and pro ball. So was I—only it was the other way around. We had no training camp and practiced three nights a week. For a clubhouse we had an old shed with a shower in it and a few hooks for our clothes. Wycoff was the player-coach and we had no trainer. On the day of the games, Charley Porter, the trainer from N.Y.U., would come down and tape some ankles. Most of the guys taped themselves.

There was an 18-player limit in those days and we usually carried 16 players. Today when you put in a sub, you don't see a big drop in efficiency. On the Stapes those extra five guys were way below the regulars. They were getting $25 a game. When we had to substitute, the whole team suffered.

We played our home games in Thompson Field and we could sit only 6,000 people in the stands. We had a good hard core of about 3,000 fans who came to all the home games. The only time we filled the park was when we played the Giants. It was a natural rivalry and we beat them as many times as they beat us.

We used to have about 10,000 people go from Staten Island to the Polo Grounds to see us play the Giants. We even had a cheerleader. His name was Benny Bramhall. He showed up every week with a big sweater with the letter "S" on the front and a pair of white duck pants. He'd lead the cheers and the fans would really whoop it up.

If we had the room, we could have drawn about 15,000 when we played the Giants at home. Because we didn't, we had to settle for the 6,000.

I'll give you an idea of what those Stape fans were like. During those years I developed a rivalry with Ray Flaherty, the Giants' captain. One day, when we were playing at Thompson Field, I went around his end and he grabbed me in a head lock. Right near one side of the field we had a small wire fence that was right against the sidelines. Now Flaherty started to force me towards the wire fence. And something was getting him real mad. When the whistle blew, he looked up and saw this little old lady leaning over the fence waving an umbrella. She'd been hitting him on the head while he was pulling me towards the sidelines and he thought that I had been reaching up and punching him.

Another time when we were playing the Giants one of our coaches told me to play closer to the line because he was sure the Giants were going to fake a field goal line buck and go 'round the end. I didn't like the idea, but he insisted. He was half right. It was fake buck. But instead of an end run, they threw the ball to Flaherty, who was right in the spot I'd vacated. He went for a touchdown and when he went over the stripe he turned and thumbed his nose at me and said, "Yaah, yaah."

We had some games to remember. One time, I remember, we punted and Hap Moran ran the ball back 80 yards for a touchdown. They kicked off, and I returned it 99 yards for a TD. In two plays, we covered 179 yards and scored two touchdowns.

Because of games like that, in three of the four years the Stapes were in existence we scheduled an extra game each season with the Giants in the Polo Grounds.

But we were fighting a losing battle all the way. If we brought a team in that needed a guarantee, we had to wait till we played them in their park. Once we brought the Bears with Red Grange to Staten Island and had to give them a guarantee. We held them to a scoreless tie— our proudest moment—but Blaine didn't make any money on the deal until we played them the next year at Chicago.

Two years in a row, we played four games in eight days. We'd play Brooklyn on Sunday and Newark on Wednesday. Then we'd go to Philadelphia to play the Frankford Yellow Jackets on Saturday. The Yellow Jackets would then come to Staten Island on Sunday and play us there.

After the '31 season, the Stapes folded. When this decision was definite, I went back to 23rd and Lexington to see Mr. Mara. Right off, he says, "I don't know if I want to hire you. I hear you're a troublemaker."

I said, "What does that mean?"

He answered, "I understand you bawl the other players out."

"That's right," I told him. "I know I'm paid to run with the ball. I can't run with the ball unless someone does some blocking. So I yell at them when they don't block. I play to win. If you don't want a winner, maybe you better not hire me."

He did hire me for $250 a game, the price Andrews had tried to buy me for three years before.

When I joined the Giants I had my first taste of the big league. We had a training camp at Pompton Lakes, New Jersey, where the fighters used to train a lot, and we had a trainer's table where you could get taken care of.

The year I joined the Giants, Harry Newman also joined the club as quarterback. He had graduated from Michigan, where he was a star. We had a good team— Mel Hein at center and Dale Burnett at wingback and people like that. It was still a 60-minute game for all the regulars and when we substituted we weakened the team, but not to the degree that we did at Staten Island.

That was the year the league was split into two divisions, East and West, for the first time. We won in the East and the Bears won in the West. Then, on a flip of the coin, the West won the right to be the home team, and so we had to play them in Chicago for the championship.

It was a great game. It wound up 23 to 21. The Bears won on a play they used a lot that was tough to stop. Bronko Nagurski would start towards the line as if he were going to hit it, as he did so often. Just before he reached the line of scrimmage, he'd jump up and throw a pass to Bill Hewitt coming across from end. Hewitt would then throw a lateral to a trailer.

On the winning play Dale Burnett, a great player, came up too fast to get Hewitt, and when Karr came in to take the lateral he had a clear field ahead of him.

I believe the lead in that game changed six times. The touchdown that gave us the lead the last time was a beauty. We were on about the 35 and the ball was 15 yards in from the left sideline. Harry Newman called for a reverse. In those days, we used what we called the box formation. He lined up about 5 yards behind center and I'd be right next to him. On this reverse, he handed to me as I came around behind him.

When I got to the short side, I saw that things were all jammed up. So I turned and threw the ball back to Newman. When he got it, he tried to run around the wide part of the field. He found that side was jammed up so he circled around. In the meantime, I'd run down the field and was standing in the end zone waving to him. He saw me and threw the ball. I caught it and that put us ahead 21 to 16.

We'd put in two new plays that we were saving for a last-ditch try. After they scored on the jump pass lateral play to go ahead 23 to 21, we got the kickoff and returned to about our own 40-yard line. Before they kicked off, we alerted the officials about our new plays, so there would be no question about the legality of them.

The first play called for all the linemen to shift to the right side of Mel Hein, our center. Since this put Mel at the end of the scrimmage line, it meant he was eligible for a pass. By this time, of course, the old rule about having to be 5 yards behind the line of scrimmage when you threw a pass had been changed. Now you could pass from any point behind the line.

On this play, Mel handed the ball to Newman, who was bending over him just like a T-formation quarterback would. As he did, all the deep backs ran to the right. Newman came behind us faking as if he had the ball under his arm.

Newman didn't have the ball. After Mel passed it to him, Harry slipped it right back to Mel. Now, while everyone was chasing us, Mel was supposed to sort of stroll down the field and when he was in the clear, make a break for the goal line. But he got excited after he covered about 10 yards and he started to run. Naturally, this attracted attention and someone flattened him.

The second new play started just like the first one. All the linemen would line up on the right side of Hein, making Mel eligible for a forward pass again. But this time Newman took the ball and pitched out to Dale Burnett, who could throw the ball a mile.

When Mel went down the field, nobody paid much attention to him once they saw he didn't have the ball. Next thing he knew, he was standing all alone on the 15-yard line waving his arms. Dale wound up and then— unbelievably—the ball slipped from his fingers and punted into the air. Keith Molesworth intercepted for Chicago, and that was the ball game.

There's no question but that if Dale had got the ball to Mel, and he had caught it, we would have had a chance to win the game with a field goal.

The next year, of course, was the famous sneakers game, with the Bears at the Polo Grounds. That story of how we wore the sneakers in the second half because the ground was so hard has been told and retold. By now, almost everyone believes we won the game because of the sneakers.

Actually, the sneakers weren't that much of a factor. By the end of the third quarter and through the fourth quarter they didn't make much difference. The Bears still led 13 to 3, with eight minutes to play. The Bears had started with new pointed cleats made of bakelite, I believe. By the end of the first half they were nubs. That did make a difference. If they had had new cleats for the second half, they would have walloped us.

I have to say we were lucky in that game because this Bear team was one of the greatest teams ever assembled. In some ways, that game reminds me of the Jets-Colts Super Bowl game of 1969. This will be a surprise— everyone gave us less of a chance to beat the Bears than they gave the Jets to beat the Colts in the Super Bowl.

Like the Jets, we had a lot of breaks. Remember that the score was 13 to 3, with eight minutes to play. Ed Danowski, who was our quarterback, was not a danger- ous long passer because his hands were too small. On the first of our strange plays, he dropped back and threw what for him was a long one—a 25-yarder to Ike Franken. Carl Brumbaugh, who was playing safety for the Bears, came in and intercepted the ball right near the goal line. As he came down with the ball, Franken, without breaking stride, took it out of his hands and went over for a touchdown.

Now we're behind 13 to 10. A little while later, we're on their 42 and I try an off-tackle play. When I hit the hole, I was knocked backwards. I spun around and I saw a bit of daylight and I went through it. For some reason, Brumbaugh and the other defensive backs were nowhere near me. I went all the way for a touchdown.

We missed the conversion but now we're ahead 16 to 13. This doesn't look very good when the Bears come right back and start marching down the field.

Then we get the big break. It's fourth and one on our 35-yard line and we all know that Nagurski will come into the line and there's not much we can do about it. As Bronko gets started, he slips, and Bill Morgan, our left tackle, hit him and threw him for a loss. On that one play, Morgan made the All-Pro team for the year.

We moved the ball again and Danowski hit for an- other touchdown pass. Then I got away for another run and we won the ball game 30 to 13. I still say we had no business winning it.

I was sure that after the good season I'd had, and the ending with all the scoring I did in the Bears game, I'd get a good raise. But Mr. Mara didn't agree with me.

The next time I went to his office I brought a lawyer with me. When Mr. Mara saw him, he said, "I don't want to talk to you when you have a lawyer."

Then my lawyer said, "Why not? You have one with you." He was referring to Tim's son, Jack Mara, who had just passed the bar.

In the end, I got an attendance-type deal. That is, if the attendance went over a certain figure, I'd get extra money. Harry Newman had been given an attendance deal earlier, but it had worked out better for him than the club had expected and they didn't want any repetition of this. So they put a ceiling on it. The most I could make was $6,000 for the season.

If they hadn't done this, I would have picked up some extra money, because when the Bears came to town for the third-from-the-last game, we had a big gate—so big that my $6,000 ceiling was reached that day. As a result, I played the last two games of the season for nothing.

That winter, the league established the common draft. This meant that only one club had the right to negotiate with a player. Naturally this meant the clubs could cut salaries. I was cut almost in half to $3,200 a year.

You can understand why I was interested when Jack McBride decided to start a new league called the Amer- ican Football League. He was going to have a team in New York called the Yankees and he wanted me to play for the Yankees. I worked out an agreement whereby $5,000, the same salary I got in my first year with Staten Island, was put into escrow. Then I joined the Yankees.

That was a disaster—for the usual reason. Jack didn't have enough money. One time we played Pittsburgh in Yankee Stadium and we sold a lot of cut-rate tickets. Jack, always trying to keep the costs down, opened only two gates at the Stadium. We had 40,000 people that day but about 20,000 turned away when they saw the crowds at the two gates.

The trips were something. I'll always remember my last trip with the Yankees by day coach to Cincinnati.

There was nothing to eat and no place to sleep. Everyone played cards all the way and when we stopped, some of the guys would run out and try to buy sandwiches.

The league folded at the end of the season and I was out of football. The National Football League considered my move an act of disloyalty and suspended me for five years.

In 1938 the Giants were sending Bill Owen to their Jersey City farm team in the American Conference. They told me that if I went over with Bill and helped get the club started right, I could come back to the big team the next season. I went over there and had a good season. I kicked 14 field goals in six games and led the club in scoring. We lost only one game and Mr. Mara was happy with the season.

When I rejoined the big team in 1939, Tuffy Leemans was the running back and it was pretty obvious that I wasn't about to take the job away from him. Instead I made the club as a blocking back.

That year we beat Washington for the Eastern championship 9 to 7. I kicked two field goals and Ward Cuff kicked one for our 9 points. In that game, I damaged three transverse processes while throwing a block on someone.

The following summer I picked up an ulcer, and after the '40 season I retired.

In 1943, when I was 37 years old, the Giants asked me to come back. There was a manpower shortage because of the war and they felt they could use me for kickoffs and place kicks.

I didn't really feel old until one day in 1944, when we were playing an exhibition game against the Bears. After I kicked off and started downfield, Bulldog Turner, the Bears' great center, came at me. He was just about to hit me when he stopped and said, "Hell, I can't hit you. You're too damn old." Later, when Bulldog coached for the New York Titans, he and I used to meet at a lot of football affairs and we'd laugh about that.

Near the end of that season, my wife told me that my son, Ken Jr., had said he'd heard about my days as a ball carrier but he'd never seen me do anything but kick the ball.

We were playing in Washington that Sunday and on the way down there I mentioned this to Steve Owen. Late in the fourth quarter, when we were ahead 31 to 0, Steve said, "Okay, Strong. Get in there and run the ball." The play was supposed to be an end run but instead of calling "49," the signal for the end run, the quarterback called "47," which was the off-tackle play.

Well, I was hit on the line. I got a few yards and then about five guys fell on me. I didn't think I was going to be able to get up. But I remembered my son and I decided to give it one more try. There was just one play left and I figured I'd be able to last through it.

On the next play, the quarterback called "49" and I went around end. Now Sammy Baugh and the other guys had decided they'd give me a break and give me some running room and maybe let me go all the way. They dropped aside. But there was one young fellow on the team who hadn't been given the word. He hit me and almost killed me.

Well, I managed to get back up and struggle to the sidelines. By the time I got showered and dressed, I was aching all over. But I kept telling myself it was all worth it because the boy had seen me run with the ball.

When I got outside the dressing room, my wife was waiting for me—alone. I looked around and said, "Where's Ken?"

"Oh, he has a cold," she said, "so I decided to leave him home." That was Ken Jr.'s last chance because I retired after that game.

There were some real superstars in my time. Bronko Nagurski was the best power runner I ever saw. Right behind him was a fellow who could back up the line, and when he carried the ball and you hit him, you knew you'd hit someone. That was Clarke Hinkle. Maybe the best passer I saw was Benny Friedman. Of course, Baugh was equal to anyone and he is the man responsible for opening up the game.

In 1962 I rejoined the Giants once more—this time as a kicking coach. While I worked with Don Chandler, I had the chance to see how the game had changed. It has gone a long way since we played three games a week, 60 minutes a game, with the old Stapletons. It will get even better.

Before the prolific Gay Talese turned his journalistic eye to such things as the crime syndicate and sex, he wrote quite a bit about sports. In this article, which originally appeared in *The New York Times* in 1957, he probes the special relationship between the Modzelewski brothers: Dick, alias "Little Mo," a 260-pound defensive tackle for the New York Giants, and Ed, alias "Big Mo," a 215-pound fullback with the Cleveland Browns. The piece was also honored by inclusion in *Best Sports Stories 1958.*

Alias Little Mo

GAY TALESE

DICK MODZELEWSKI, alias Little Mo, is 260 pounds of tough tenderloin with shoulders so broad that he often has to pass through doors sideways.

When he is not playing tackle for the New York Giants, Modzelewski is a warm-hearted, gentle soul who loves to baby-sit for his 108-pound wife, Dorothy. But when he is playing football, he is thoroughly bellicose. He wants to win more than any man since Machiavelli, Dillinger or Leo Durocher.

Leo Durocher once said that if he were playing shortstop and his mother were rounding second, he'd trip her—accidentally.

"I'd help her up, brush her off and tell her I'm sorry," the ex-baseball manager said, "but she wouldn't get to third."

Modzelewski feels likewise and, whenever he can, he tries to knock his brother down and steal the football.

His brother is Ed (Big Mo) Modzelewski, a fullback on the Cleveland Browns.

"Ed is my brother and I love him," said Dick yesterday at Yankee Stadium, where the Giants will meet the Washington Redskins on Sunday. "But on the field he wears a white shirt and I wear a blue shirt and we don't know each other."

Dick is paid considerable money by the Giants for pushing people around. His contributions have had much to do in giving the Giants a defensive line that is virtually unbeatable, unstoppable and unpronounceable. On the line with Modzelewski are John Martinkovic, Andy Robustelli, Jim Katcavage and Walt Yowarsky.

Dick Modzelewski was born in West Natrona, Pa., a small coal-mining town near Pittsburgh where boys begin to play tackle in the streets at eight and where a majority of the male population have had their noses broken at least once.

He is one of six children in a family that weighs collectively about 1,540 pounds. His father, a muscular miner, weighs 220 pounds; his mother, 235 pounds. His two sisters steadfastly refuse to testify.

Big Mo, who is 28, weighs 215; he is called Big Mo because in high school he was larger than Dick, who is 26. The newest Mo in the family is Eugene, who, at 13, weighs 192 pounds and is called Dyna-Mo.

There is also Joe, a 30-year-old brother who weighs 205 and used to be one of Ezzard Charles's sparring partners. Joe won seventeen out of twenty-one fights, but quit when his jaw was broken. He now works in a glass company in Pittsburgh.

Little Mo and Big Mo played high school and college football together and both were All-Americans at Maryland in 1952. They wish they were professional teammates but since they are not, they are enemies whenever the Giants and Browns play. Last year Little Mo stopped Big Mo with a throttling tackle on the 1-yard line in a successful goal-line stand.

Dick estimates that he gets hit between sixty and seventy times a game. Sometimes he gets hit three times on one play.

When he lines up, his nose is usually a foot from that of the opposing tackle's. But professional linemen, he says, don't talk to each other during the afternoon of crouching.

"Oh, once in a while I talk to my brother," Dick said. "When I tackle him, I say, 'You didn't get too many yards, did you?' Or he'll say, 'Is that the hardest you can hit?' "

Dick has never been knocked out in five years of pro football, though he says the person making the tackle generally suffers more than the person being tackled. He was "fogged up" once when a knee owned by a Cleveland Brown player clobbered Dick. The knee, Dick said, did not belong to Ed Modzelewski.

"If you get the wind knocked out of you," Dick said, "the trainer comes out and says to you, 'What time is it?' 'Where are you?' 'Who are we playing?' If you say, 'We're playing Hawaii,' the trainer leads you off the field."

No matter how excellent the players' conditioning might be, a pro lineman is fatigued before the game is over, Modzelewski said.

"You start feeling the bumps and bruises in the final quarter, but if your team is winning you don't mind. But if you're losing, those bumps and bruises hurt like hell."

Modzelewski stands 5 feet 11½ inches and claims to be the shortest Giant on defense. He has an 18½-inch neck and his shirts, all tailor-made, cost $14 each. His sports jackets are size 48.

He has blue eyes, over which he wears contact lenses. Lenses were recommended when he was in high school on an afternoon when the foe's halfback ran right past him with the football and Little Mo didn't see him.

With his wife and two-year-old son, Mark, Dick lives in a hotel near the Stadium. He would like to sleep late on Mondays because he is usually sore and scratched, but Mark usually falls out at 8 A.M. And Monday is the day that his wife and Mrs. Ken MacAfee often spend eight hours shopping and spend lots of money downtown, and Ken and Dick baby-sit.

"Me and Ken take the kids out for a walk, then give them lunch, then put them to bed," Dick said. "Then Ken and me go back to sleep."

On Dec. 15, when the Browns come to town, Dick will probably entertain Big Mo with dinner and drinks.

"We'll go to the movies the night before the game," Dick said, "and Ed will try to pump me for information and I'll try to pump him for information. After that we'll come home to my place and talk and have a few drinks."

And then, with a smile totally lacking in fraternalism, "Maybe I can slip Ed a couple of quick ones."

Who would have thought *Rolling Stone* magazine would exhibit even the slightest interest in professional football? And who would ever have imagined that they would commission Dr. Hunter S. Thompson, whose insightful, outrageous, unexpurgated observations gave rise to "Gonzo" journalism, to contribute some, well, unique interpretations of the sport and those who are involved with it? It just goes to show that nothing associated with professional football is predictable, except maybe Tom Landry wearing a hat. This piece on Raiders owner Al Davis and his then-Oakland ballclub first appeared as part of an article entitled "Fear and Loathing at the Super Bowl" in *Rolling Stone,* and later was included in an anthology of Thompson's writing under the title *The Great Shark Hunt.*

Mano a Mano with the Oakland Raiders

HUNTER S. THOMPSON

The Raiders kicked you out? For what? Drug rumors? [Laughter] Well, it's nice to know they're starting to give writers the same kind of underhanded chickenshit they've been laying on players for ten years. . . . Yeah, it varies from team to team: Like, for me, getting traded to Pittsburgh after all that time in Oakland was like finally coming up for air. As a matter of general philosophy, though, the National Football League is the last bastion of fascism in America.

—Tom Keating, Defensive tackle for the Pittsburgh Steelers

To REACH the Oakland Raiders' practice field you drive from San Francisco across the Bay Bridge and then south on U.S. 17 to Exit 98 at Hegenberger Road at the south end of Alameda Bay . . . turn right at the off-ramp that leads to the Oakland International Airport; glance back at the Edgewater Inn and the squat-white concrete-block building right next to the Edgewater that says "Oakland Raiders" and then swing north again.

About six miles past the airport entrance, the Oakland Hilton and a speedboat raceway—the road gets narrow and seems to be heading downhill, through a wet desert of stunted jack-pines (or scrub-oaks, or whatever they call those useless little trees that grow on the edge of swamplands all over the country, near places like Pensacola and Portland) . . . but this is Oakland, or at least San Leandro, and when you drive 20 miles out of San Francisco to a lonesome place like this, you want a pretty good reason.

. . . Or at least a decent excuse.

The only people who make this run regularly, in the autumn months between late August and December, are Bay Area sportswriters and people on the payroll of the Oakland Raiders—players, trainers, coaches, owners, etc.—and the only reason they make this grim trip day after day is the nervous fact that the Raiders' practice field and daily headquarters is located, for good or ill, out here on this stinking estuary across the bay from San Francisco.

It is a hard place to find unless you know exactly where to look. The only sure giveaway sign, from the highway, is a sudden rise of thin steel scaffolding looming out of the jack-pines about 200 yards west of the road—and two men in cheap plastic ski jackets on a platform at the top of the tower, aiming big grey movie cameras down at whatever's happening on the other side of that tree-fence.

Turn left just beyond the film-tower, park in a muddy lot full of new Cadillacs and flashy sports cars, and walk up a grassy bank to a one-story concrete-block building that looks like a dog-kennel or a Pepsi-Cola warehouse in St. Louis . . . push through a big metal fire-door & along a naked corridor decorated on both sides with black and grey helmets, sharp-edged footballs, red-white-and-blue NFL stickers . . . and finally around a corner into the weight-room, a maze of fantastically-complicated machinery with signs all around warning "unauthorized persons" to keep their goddamn hands off of *everything*. One of the weight-machines costs $6500 and is designed to do nothing but stretch knots out of trapezius muscles; another, costing $8800, is a maze of steel cables, weights and ankle-hooks that will—if used properly—cure kinks, rips and contusions out of every muscle from the hip to the achilles tendon. There are other machines for problems of the feet, neck and elbows.

I was tempted to get physically involved with every machine in the building—just to know how it felt to get jerked around by all that fantastic machinery. I was also tempted to speak with the trainers and sample whatever medications they had to offer—but pro football locker rooms are no longer the wholesale drug dispensaries that they were in the past. National Football League Commissioner "Pete" Rozelle—along with "President" Nixon and the network TV moguls—have determined that drugs and pro football won't mix; at least not in public.

On my first visit to the locker room—and on all other visits, for that matter—I avoided both the weight machines and the trainers. There was no point, I felt, in compromising the story early on; although if I'd known what kind of shitrain I was heading into I would have sprung every machine in the building and gobbled every pill I could get my hands on.

But I felt a certain obligation, back then, to act in a "professional" manner . . . and, besides, for my first look at the Raider practice field I was accompanied by a friendly little fellow named Al LoCasale, who had told me when I called on the phone that he was "executive assistant" to the Raiders' general manager and would-be owner, Al Davis.

LoCasale led me through the locker room, past the weights and the trainers, and out through another small door that opened onto a long green pasture enclosing two football fields, four goal posts, many blocking sleds and tackling dummies, and about 60 men moving around very actively, gathered in four separate groups on both fields.

I recognized John Madden, the head coach, running the offensive unit through short-pass drills on the field to my right . . . and on the other field, about 50 yards to my left, another coach was running the defensive unit through some kind of drill I couldn't recognize.

Far down at the other end of the field where the defensive unit was working, I could see George Blanda, the Raiders' 46-year-old reserve quarterback and premier place-kicker, working with his own set of handlers and banging one kick after another "through the uprights"—from the 30 or 35 yard line. Blanda and his small crew were paying no attention to what was happening on the offensive and defensive fields. Their job was to keep George sharp on field-goals, and during the two hours I was there, that afternoon, he kicked at least 40 or 50, and I never saw him miss one.

There were two other solitary figures moving around on the field(s) beyond the small enclosure near the locker-room door where LoCasale and several assistants made sure the half-dozen local sportswriters stayed. One was Ray Guy, the rookie punter and number one draft choice from Mississippi, who spent all afternoon kicking one ball after another in tall spiraling arcs above the offensive unit to a brace of ballboys just in front of the sportswriters' huddle . . . and the other was a small wiry man in a tan golf jacket with a greasy duck-tail haircut who paced along the sidelines of both fields with a speedy kind of intensity that I never really noticed until he suddenly appeared very close to me and I heard him ask a sportswriter from the *San Francisco Chronicle* who I was and what I was doing there. . . .

The conversation took place within 10 yards of me, and I heard most of it.

"Who's the big guy over there with the ball in his hand?" asked the man with the DA.

"His name's Thompson," replied Chronicle sportswriter Jack Smith. "He's a writer for *Rolling Stone*."

"The Rolling Stones? Jesus Christ! What's he *doing* here? Did *you* bring him?"

"No, he's writing a big article. *Rolling Stone* is a magazine, Al. It's different from the Rolling Stones; they're a rock music group. . . . Thompson's a buddy of George Plimpton's, I think . . . and he's also a friend of Dave Burgin's—you remember Burgin?"

"Holy shit! Burgin! We ran him out of here with a cattle prod!"

I saw Smith laugh at that point, then he was talking again: "Don't worry, Al. Thompson's okay. He wrote a good book about Las Vegas."

Good god! I thought. That's it. . . . If they read that book I'm finished. By this time I'd realized that this strange-looking bugger named "Al," who looked like a pimp or a track-tout, was in fact the infamous Al Davis—general manager and de facto owner (pending settlement of a nasty lawsuit scheduled for court-action early this year) of the whole Oakland Raider operation.

Davis glanced over his shoulder at me, then spoke back to Smith: "Get the bastard out of here. I don't trust him."

I heard that very clearly—and if I'd had any sense I'd have abandoned the whole story right then, for reasons of extreme and unnatural prejudice; call the office and say I couldn't handle the bad vibes, then jump the next plane to Colorado. . . . I was watching Davis very closely now, and it occurred to me that the fiendish intensity of his speech and mannerisms reminded me very strongly of another Oakland badass I'd spent some time with, several years earlier—ex-Hell's Angels president Ralph "Sonny" Barger, who had just beaten a multiple-murder rap and then copped out, they said, to some kind of minor charge like "Aggravated Assault with Intent to Commit Murder," or "Possession of Automatic Weapons" (submachine-guns), "Possession of Heroin (four pounds) with Intent to Sell, and Sexual Assault on Two Minors with Intent to Commit Forcible Sodomy" . . .

I had read these things in the *Chronicle* . . . but . . . What the hell? Why compound these libels? Any society that will put Barger in jail and make Al Davis a respectable millionaire at the same time is not a society to be trifled with.

In any case, the story of my strange and officially ugly relationship with Al Davis is too complicated for any long explanations at this point. I spent several days pacing the sidelines of the Raider practice field with him—prior to the Pittsburgh, Cleveland and Kansas City games—and the only thing I remember him talking about is "Environmental Determinism." He spoke at considerable length on that subject, as I recall, but there is nothing in my notes to indicate precisely what he said about it.

Shortly after I heard him tell Smith to get rid of me on that first afternoon, I walked over to him and somehow got wound up in a conversation about how he was having trouble buying property in Aspen because "some people out there," thought his money was "dirty" because of his known connections in Las Vegas. "Hell, that's no problem," I told him. "I once ran for sheriff in

Aspen; I know the place pretty well, and I can tell you for sure that at least half the money out there is dirtier than any you're likely to come up with."

He stopped and eyed me curiously. "You ran for sheriff?" he said. "In Aspen, Colorado?"

I nodded. "Yeah, but I'd rather not talk about it. We didn't lose by much, but losing in politics is like losing in football, right? One vote, one point—"

He smiled crookedly, then began pacing again. "I don't give a damn about politics," he said as I hurried along the white-lime sideline to keep up with him. "The only things that interest me are economics and foreign affairs."

Jesus Christ! I thought. Economics, foreign affairs, environmental determinism—this bastard is sand-bagging me.

We paced back and forth a while longer, then he suddenly turned on me: "What are you after?" he snapped. "Why are you out here?"

"Well . . ." I said. "It would take me a while to explain it. Why don't we have a beer after practice tomorrow and I'll—"

"Not tomorrow," he said quickly. "I only come out here on Wednesdays and Thursdays. They get nervous when I'm around, so I try to stay away most of the time."

I nodded—but I didn't really understand what he meant until an hour or so later, when Coach Madden signaled the end of that day's practice and Davis suddenly rushed onto the field and grabbed the quarterback, Ken Stabler, along with a receiver and a defensive back I didn't recognize, and made them run the same pass pattern—a quick shot from about 45 yards out with the receiver getting the ball *precisely* at the corner of the goal line and the out-of-bounds line—at least twelve consecutive times until they had it down exactly the way he wanted it.

That is my last real memory of Al Davis: It was getting dark in Oakland, the rest of the team had already gone into the showers, the coach was inside speaking sagely with a gaggle of local sportswriters, somewhere beyond the field-fence a big jet was cranking up its afterburners on the airport runway . . . and here was the *owner* of the flakiest team in pro football, running around on a half-dark practice field like a king-hell speed freak with his quarterback and two other key players, insisting that they run the same goddamn play over and over again until they had it *right*.

That was the only time I ever felt I really understood Davis. . . . We talked on other days, sort of loosely and usually about football, whenever I would show up at the practice field and pace around the sidelines with him . . . and it was somewhere around the third week of my random appearances, as I recall, that he began to act very nervous whenever he saw me.

I never asked why, but it was clear that something had changed, if only back to normal . . . . After one of the mid-week practices I was sitting with one of the Raider players in the tavern down the road from the fieldhouse and he said: "Jesus, you know I was walking back to the huddle and I looked over and, god damn, I almost flipped when I saw you and Davis standing together on the sideline. I thought, man, the world really *is* changing when you see a thing like that—Hunter Thompson and Al Davis—Christ, you know that's the first time I ever saw *anybody* with Davis during practice; the bastard's always *alone* out there, just pacing back and forth like a goddamn beast. . . ."

Bulldog Turner, the Chicago Bears' great center and linebacker of the 1940s, sure is some kind of raconteur. He proved it beyond a reasonable doubt to author Myron Cope who interviewed him for his book *The Game That Was*. The flavor of the man was captured by Cope in his introduction to the interview: "It was mid-March, a crisp, sunny day in the rolling, green countryside of central Texas. Out by the stable, Clyde (Bulldog) Turner asked if I cared for a beer. Then he went behind the stable and plucked two cans of beer from the cool ground under a shade tree. . . . Owing to a touch of sugar that afflicts him, Bulldog has been warned by his doctor to abstain from alcohol, and so in order to escape recriminations from his wife, he has found it convenient to store an occasional libation in the outdoors. He recalled a few years before, a newspaperman had come down from Dallas to interview him, and . . . Bulldog plunged his arm into a large bin of oats and fetched up a bottle of vodka. 'I'll be damned!' said the newspaperman." Turner warned his interviewer that maybe he was not worth an interview after all. Myron Cope did not agree. "I knew, of course, that I had wandered into the presence of a master storyteller." Indeed he had.

The Raconteur of Cowhouse Creek

CLYDE "BULLDOG" TURNER

I'LL TELL you how I come to be called Bulldog, but along that line I'll have to explain a few things. First of all, I come from Yoakum County 'way out in West Texas, where my dad was a cowboy. He worked for big ranches. Hell, they had to be big to make a living, because that wasn't too good a country up there. No trees or nothing. I was born in a little cabin on a ranch, in 1919, and when I was three or four, we moved into a town called Plains. That was the only town in the county at that time, so naturally the courthouse was there. Two fillin' stations and two stores and a post office and the courthouse is all I remember being in Plains. There wasn't even any town square. There wasn't enough town to go around.

Up there in Plains, you went all the way from the first grade to graduation in the same school building, and of course there was no such thing as a football team. The only football I ever saw there was in the Sears Roebuck catalog. To me, it was an odd-shaped ball, and that was all. I didn't know anything about football till after we moved to Sweetwater. In 1932 my dad came over there and traded for some property and started buying and selling cattle, and then he came back and got us.

It was my junior year when I first went to Sweetwater High. I noticed that some of the boys there had a big "S" on a knit sweater they wore, and that those boys got all the attention. In the fall there'd be pep rallies, and people would go down to the station to see those boys off on the train. So I decided that maybe I ought to get me one of those knit sweaters. Finally I learned that the boys wearin' 'em were football players.

But I didn't go out for football right away, because in the fall of the year people started to gather cotton, and that's what I did the first fall. We lived in town but it wasn't but a couple of blocks till we went into the country. Out there—oh, maybe a mile—was a cotton farm. So I used to run home from school and change my clothes and grab a cotton sack and run out there. I'd throw a few rocks in the sack to make it weigh a little heavier, and between school and dark I'd make about thirty-five cents. Of course, I'd give my dad part of it. The Depression was getting real tough then, and as I look back now, I can't see how my dad was making a living. Yet we were living good. We were eating simple things, but all them things are still my favorite foods. We were probably poor, but I didn't know it.

I picked cotton all that fall, and then I told my dad, "I'm going to quit picking cotton. I'm going out for football." He asked why, and I said, "I want to get me a sweater." That's all I wanted was that ol' slip-on knit sweater with a big ol' "S" on it.

Well, man, I went through many a rough hour to get that sweater. The first day I went on the field was the roughest day I ever spent on a football field. That includes college through pro. I had cleat marks all over my shins. Right then I was nothing, and that season I was just a shock trooper. They'd use me anywhere. There were fourteen on the squad, the Sweetwater Mustangs, and I was number-one substitute. I played every position except quarterback, I guess. Sammy Baugh was two years ahead of me at Sweetwater High, so that makes two of us from one school that made the Pro Football Hall of Fame. But Sammy had already gone when I started.

That year we had a lousy team. We won maybe a game or two out of the whole season, but I got my sweater and in getting it I developed something that I didn't anticipate. I found that I loved to play football. I found I loved any kind of competition. So I was real fired up and looking forward to the next football season,

but then they said I couldn't play anymore for the high school.

I was fifteen then, see, and I was supposed to graduate. My older brother Jay actually was fourteen when he graduated. A lot of boys down here in Texas graduated young. Why, I don't know. Nobody ever asked me before. Maybe the schools were letting them jump grades or something. Anyway, I was supposed to graduate, but the move from Plains to Sweetwater was such a big jump that I failed my first year at Sweetwater and when I was supposed to graduate at fifteen, I didn't. I had to go another year. But they said I was ineligible for football, because I'd already had eight semesters of high school. So at fifteen I was ineligible for high-school competition.

That nearly run me crazy. I said, "Heck, I can't stand this." So I ran off from home. I ran off to see if I could get me a place on a college team. And now I'm getting to why I'm called Bulldog.

At that time I had an old cow, as I recall, and cows brang about eight dollars. I sold that cow and bought me some new gloves and a new coat, and I think I still had a good bit of money before I left. I hitchhiked around for a while and then I went to Fort Worth and checked into a hotel. In those days you could get a room for $1.50 a week, so I stayed there and went around to more colleges within hitchhikin' distance and told them, "I want to be an athlete." Every damn one of them turned me down. They said, "Well, we're all filled up." See, I had no reputation as a football player.

After a while my whiskers started to grow a little bit, but I'd forgotten to take a razor with me because at home I had been using my brother's razor. Yet I do remember shaving at Fort Worth, and what I did, I pulled out an old dresser drawer in that hotel room and found old razor blades in there, and I'd soap up my face with the regular hotel soap and hold an old razor blade against my comb, and then shave.

I was getting along all right in Fort Worth, but after I had been turned down by about seven or eight colleges around the countryside, I was pretty near out of money, and then I remembered I was a musician. I had played stringed instruments. Banjo and guitar. So I went down to this big theater, although as I looked back on it now it was a little ol' burlesque striptease place, and asked to see the manager. I told him I played the banjo. He said, "Well, we don't use the banjo." I said, "I think it would add something to the show, to have a banjo with the piano." So he said, "Well, it might work out all right at that. You got a banjo?" I said. "No," so he said, "Then we can't use you," and I didn't get the job.

So I headed for Lawton, Oklahoma—for Cameron State Agricultural College at Lawton, Oklahoma. I had heard they kind of took tramp athletes, so I said, "I'll make it to there.'' I had a dime and a candy bar in my pocket when I got out on the highway.

A guy came by in a great big ol' yellow roadster-type car, and said, "You got any money to help me buy some gas?" I said, "No, sir, I got ten cents is all I've got left." He said, "Oh, well, I'll give you a ride anyway." So we didn't drive but about forty or fifty miles till he pulled in a gas station and says, "Well, if you ain't got any money for gas, I believe I'll let you buy me a cigar." I thought, "You dirty son of a bitch." I told him, "I ain't got but that one dime, and if you want it I'll buy that much worth of gas." Then he said, "No. I believe I will let you buy me a cigar." And he spent my last dime for a cigar, and that candy bar was the last bite I had to eat for five days and five nights.

I'll tell you how country I was at that time. I got up to Lawton, Oklahoma, and I went in there and met the athletic director and the coach and all. I had been better than two days getting there. It was wintertime, and I was half frozen. The coach looked me over and said, "Son, why don't you come over to the cafeteria with us and have lunch?"

Well, that word *cafeteria* scared me to death. Never heard of it. Didn't know what the hell a cafeteria was. So rather than expose my ignorance, I said, "No, thank you. I just ate before I came in." Which was a damn lie, because I hadn't eaten in two days by this time.

So I waited there in that room and sat down on a cane-bottomed chair, and I was so tired that I went to sleep and fell into a big ol' stove and burned myself. I didn't burn myself bad, but I'm telling you how tired I was. The coach and the athletic director came back and asked me to stay the night, but by then I was feeling so ignorant that I said no and got back on the road.

Wichita Falls is not too far down from Lawton, yet it took me a couple of days to get there. See, I noticed these Mexicans coming by me on the highway in big new cars, and I said, "I'll be damned! Down there where I live, the Mexicans don't many of them drive cars like these." But directly one of them came by without a hat on, with just a band around his head, and finally it dawned on me—"Goddammit, these are Indians up here!" They had struck oil and they was all driving these big ol' cars, but the difficulty was, they wouldn't pick you up. So I was two days getting to Wichita Falls, and then I spent the night there, which made five days and five nights without a meal.

In the morning I hitchhiked down as far as Throckmorton, not far south of Wichita Falls, and I was starving to death. I walked into a filling station, which also was kind of a grocery store, and I asked, "How much them apples?" The man had some green apples there, and as I told you, I had bought me some new gloves when I left home and I wanted to find out what I could

get most of for my gloves. I said, "I want to trade my gloves for something to eat."

The man said, "I'll trade you a sack of them apples for your gloves. They're twenty-five cents a sack."

That was a big old sack—I'd say half a bushel in there. But I was so hungry I needed that. So I traded him them gloves, and I tied into them apples. But I ate only about half a apple and I'm full. My stomach starts cramping. I hadn't had anything to eat in so long, my stomach just drawed up. I ate about half a apple and I'm plumb full, and here I got the whole sack. So I was out there hitchhiking and carrying that sack of apples with me, and I thought, "I could have traded for something a hell of a lot easier to carry."

Finally a guy stopped and said, "Where you trying to go?"

"I'm trying to get to Sweetwater," I said. I wanted to get home.

"Well, I'm going to Sweetwater," this guy told me, "but I'm a salesman and I got to stop several places, so I won't get in there till tonight. You could probably beat me there." But I said, "No, I believe I'll just stay with you, if you don't mind."

So we come into a little ol' town called Rule, Texas, and it's getting about noon. I know it's time to eat. I'm thinking, "If this guy's a nice guy, maybe he'll buy me lunch." He was a pottery salesman. He had a lot of pottery in his car. So he parked at the curb and took some pottery into a store and filled an order or something, and then he pulled down the street and said, "I've got to run in here and see a guy." I watched him go into a café and he was in there an *hour,* and I said, "That dirty son of a bitch. He ain't gonna buy me no lunch." Man, I wanted to get home, 'cause I knew Mama's got something for me to eat if I ever get there. So finally the pottery salesman come back out, and we stop at every little town on the road while he sells a few pottery. Finally about 8:30 or 9 o'clock that night, he got me to Sweetwater. I had been gone three weeks. I walked in the house and Mamma started crying.

I guess I looked real bad. I had lost a lot of weight and my eyes were sunk back. My brother Jay was sitting in there with my dad, and Jay was laughing and slapping his leg. "Oh, you finally decided to come home," he said. My dad laughed and said, "Well, it wasn't so great out there, you seeking your fortune." But I had been out there trying to get myself a scholarship, because I wanted to compete in athletics. And that leads up to the story where I got the nickname Bulldog.

I went back to high school and really knuckled down. Meantime, we had a fullback in Sweetwater High that was a pretty good fullback—a big ol' boy named A. J. Roy. He was a good buddy of mine. Frank Kimbrough, the head coach at Hardin-Simmons, was interested in A. J. Roy. Kimbrough already had turned me down when I was on the road hitchhikin', but he had said to me, kind of off the cuff, "Come on down next season. We'll try you out." So A. J. and I thought we'd both get an invitation down there together when the time came. During the summer we started training. We'd run sixteen miles out to Lake Sweetwater and sixteen miles back. We didn't know anything about getting in shape, but we figured you had to be running.

So while we'd be running along them damn highways we decided that if we got into a scrimmage at Hardin-Simmons and one of us wasn't looking too good, why, here's how we'd handle it. If it was A. J. looking bad, I'd say, "Hey, Tiger! You're not acting as tough as you did back home." And if it was me looking bad, he'd say, "Hey, Bulldog! Get in there and hit 'em like you did at home!" We'd kind of make out like we were just having a bad day. There in 1936 Hardin-Simmons and all them schools had tryouts, just like a pro camp. You made the team, you got a scholarship. If you didn't make the team, you didn't stay. We wanted to stay in school. . . .

In 1939, my senior year, we rode out to play Loyola of Los Angeles in Gilmore Stadium, Los Angeles, and it held about eighteen thousand people. Well, we had a sellout crowd. I mean, I never saw so many people in my life. They were setting on the *walls*. Anyway, I had a super game against those Loyola guys, and, boy, we smoked 'em. I played linebacker on defense, and I was making tackles from one sideline to the other. They had a big star out there and I hit him so hard that he looked up and said, "I don't know your name, but you're the hardest hitting son of a bitch I ever saw in my life." Boy, that impressed me, 'cause he was All-American, see? Can't remember his name, but he was a big star. And his telling me that really fired me up, so when I got another shot at him I hit him good again. I'm telling you, he's laying out there and blood's running out of his ears. I had later on heard that any time blood runs out of your ears, you're gonna die, and I've always wondered if that boy ever got over that. I never did know.

Now at that time, George Richards, who owned the Detroit Lions, had a house out there in Los Angeles, and what happened, a guy phoned him at halftime and said, "George, you better come out here to the game. There's a guy out here you ought to be here watching." So when the game was over, George Richards was right there and he said, "Would you be interested in playing pro football?"

I said, "You bet." By that time, see, I'd already seen a newsreel on the Green Bay Packers on pro football, and I saw how big them ol' boys were and liked it. And so George Richards said, "Well, I'd like to have you on my team, the Detroit Lions." I'd never heard of the Detroit Lions or anybody else, except I had seen that film on the Green Bay Packers. "We're going to see that you get with the Lions," George Richards told me, and later on, after I played in the East-West game in San Francisco, he asked me to come on down to Los Angeles as his guest.

He had a whatever-you'd-call-him—a guy that was working for him named Church. Church picked me up in a big limousine and took me out to George Richards' house to have lunch with him. We went into a big ol' dining room, and there was a great big ol' table. And Richards sits down at one end and I sit at the other, and there's Church kind of in the middle. There's nothin' on the table—nothin'. But servants brang you each course. They brang you the service that you were going to use for each course. Well, back home when I sat down to dinner all the food was on the table. You'd pass this and pass that and everybody's up close and you eat. But here we didn't do it that way. Me and Mr. Church, I think maybe we had pork chops, and George Richards had some kind of game bird—quail or something. They'd get a little ol' dried-up pork chop and set it on a big ol' white plate, you know, and serve it off a big ol' silver service tray. I thought that was a hell of a way to eat, but anyway, that's the way we ate.

Then George Richards asked me, "Would you like to go to the track?" I said, "No, I don't know anything about that." The pros were in town to play what was then the Pro Bowl—the champions played an all-star team made up from the rest of the teams—so I said, "I thought I'd like to go out and maybe watch the pros practice." So George Richards said, "Fine. Mr. Church will drive you." He handed me forty or fifty bucks and said, "Here. If you had gone to the track I'd have bet this for you, so you might as well put it in your pocket." Man, that was the most money I ever saw in my life. And I'm being drove around!

So we watched these big hogs practice, and I said, "They're not bad. They probably come pretty close to me." See, I never was *taught* to play center, but I developed my own style. Most guys would get down over that ball like an ol' hen over a nest o' eggs, their elbows all bent, and you could knock them back if you hit them up high. But I started keepin' my shoulders and head up. And now I noticed that these pros kept their arms straight, which I was the first one to do. And I said, "Well, I'll be derned. Maybe they've been playing a little center."

I was able to meet a few of the people around there, and I was real impressed. I met one of the coaches, ol' Hunk Anderson. We went to the hotel room with Hunk. I remember ol' Hunk had to go back to the hotel about two or three times a day and change shorts. He had a bad case of hemorrhoids or something. He was the line coach for Detroit, and I was pretty impressed with him. See, he'd pull off his clothes there, and, man, he really had muscles in them legs. He said, "We're going to be happy to have you with the Lions. But we got to keep all this quiet till after the draft."

The thing was that George Richards had told his head coach, Gus Henderson, to draft me number one. And he told me that if any of the other teams wrote to me about playing football, I should tell them I'm not interested. So when the draft came up, Detroit was about the third pick, but instead of picking me, Gus Henderson picked some quarterback that nobody ever heard of. Some guy named Doyle Nave from Southern California that never even showed up. Harry Wismer, who was the broadcaster for Detroit games at that time, told me later that he was the guy that ran to the phone right quick and called George Richards and told him, "Gus Henderson didn't pick Bulldog Turner, and the Chicago Bears picked him." So George said, "I can't get anyone to run things the way I want them to," and he fired Gus Henderson.

Meantime, George Richards didn't give up on me. He said, "You're still going to be with the Lions. You just tell the Bears you're not going to play pro football." He said, "I own three radio stations, a glass factory, and a bunch of other things—I don't know what all. I'll make you a coach at a high school out here in California for the first year, and after George Halas gives up on you, you go with the Lions."

So I went along with that, but then Halas invited me to Chicago on an expense-paid trip to fly up. Being the country boy that I was, I had never been on an airplane before, so I couldn't say no. You know, it took all day to fly to Chicago then. I left Abilene in the morning and landed in Oklahoma City and I don't know how many places, and got into Chicago that night. George and his wife met me at the airport, which George Halas don't do normally. But I didn't sign a contract. I was grateful for the trip, but I kind of strung George along, you might say. However, Richards found out I went up there, and he was mad.

He came down to Abilene, Mr. Richards himself did—he and Mr. Church. They came to the hotel there, and they registered incognito. Now as I told you, me and Hershell Schooley were getting along real good, so I told Hershell, "George Richards that owns the Detroit Lions is in town and he wants to talk to me tonight." Well, goddamn, you can't tell a newspaperman secrets. Her-

shell said, "I'm going with you," and carried a pad and pencil.

We went up there to the room and Mr. Richards came out of the shower with a towel wrapped around him and he said, "Who is *this?*" I said, "This is Hershell Schooley, a reporter." Richards said, "A reporter!" And man, he hit the ceiling. He said, "I've come all the way from California incognito, and what are you doing with a goddamn newspaperman here?"

Well, now, ol' Hershell was just about as thick as one of those fireplace pokers over there. He was about six feet tall, and I guarantee you he wouldn't have weighed a hundred pounds. He wore about a twelve collar and it's 'way too big for him. But he jumped up and he drawed back and said, "Why, you old son of a bitch, we think more of this boy here than you *ever* will in your life! We're not going to take this kind of talk!"

I thought they were gonna fight, ol' man Richards with a towel around him and ol' Hershell with a suit and a tie on. They were just drawed back like, and neither one of them could have whupped nobody. But I was proud of ol' Hershell, and that one thing that happened kind of kept me thinkin', "You know, maybe this Richards don't think so much of me." Anyway, Mr. Church and me cooled the smoke down, and I thought, "If he's so hot for me, maybe it's time to see if he means it and cash in." I said to Mr. Church before I left, "I need about fifty or sixty dollars." He said, "Fine. Mr. Richards said to give you whatever you need." So I said, "Say, it's wintertime and I don't even have an overcoat." He said, "Fine. Mr. Richards will buy you one." And the first thing I know, I got to really putting it to him, and finally I worked out a deal, they was going to send me a hundred a month until something happened on the high-school coaching job. But real soon after that, I think maybe I asked them to quit sending me the hundred. Mr. Richards promised me the world and I'm sure he would have kept his promise, but I signed with the Bears. I didn't want to lay out a year.

Then the league found out that George Richards had been trying to get me, and they fined him five thousand dollars for tampering with me after I was drafted by the Bears. They said Mr. Richards had spent five hundred dollars getting my teeth fixed. Well, that wasn't the truth. He never spent a nickel on my teeth. But he must have been a heck of a swell guy, because he never even denied anything. He sold his ball club and got out of football, and it was an injustice, because he had never spent a nickel on my teeth.

Harold "Red" Grange was an authentic sports legend before he even got out of school. The dazzling halfback for the University of Illinois would lure crowds of 60,000 and more into stadia throughout the Big Ten in the early 1920s. His name ranked up there on the same stratum as Babe Ruth and Jack Dempsey. And when he came to professional football, in a most unorthodox way, along with the game's first real agent, C. C. "Cash and Carry" Pyle, he put that sport on the proverbial map, giving it a respectability and a popularity that it had not experienced before. The following, excerpted from *The Chicago Bears, An Illustrated History*, tells the story of how the Galloping Ghost finished his college career on a Saturday and began his pro career the following Thursday and then, under the direction of maestro Pyle, led the Bears on a fabulous barnstorming tour that took them out to New York for a game that saved the Giants' financially faltering franchise, on down the east coast to Florida, across through New Orleans to southern California, and on up the west coast all the way to Seattle.

The Year of the Ghost

RICHARD WHITTINGHAM

ON AN EVENING in early August, 1925, two young men walked into the Virginia Theatre in Champaign, Illinois, a college town about 100 miles south of Chicago. Each flashed one of the free passes that the theater owner, Charles C. Pyle, had handed out to all the players on the University of Illinois football team, and then settled into their seats to watch Harold Lloyd in the silent film comedy *The Freshman*.

They were interrupted, however, when an usher came down the aisle and tapped one of the football players on the shoulder. "Mr. Pyle would like to see you upstairs in his office," he said.

"Probably wants your autograph," said the other player, who was Illinois's starting fullback, Earl Britton.

"Probably wants some free tickets for a game," his friend said as he started to get up. That young man, the one who then followed the usher up the aisle, was Britton's running partner at Illinois, left halfback Harold Grange, better known to millions of sports fans throughout the country as "Red," or the "Galloping Ghost," or the "Wheaton Iceman" (because he had worked summers hauling blocks of ice around that suburb of Chicago), or just "No. 77."

What Pyle wanted from Grange was not an autograph

or free football tickets. C. C. Pyle had an idea, a plan that would irrevocably alter the course of professional football, and what he wanted was to talk it over with Red Grange. And because of their discussion, although neither of them was aware of it at that moment, the 1925 football season was destined to become one of the most important in the evolution of professional football.

The sequence of events actually began in the office of the Chicago Bears a month or two before the season started. With the frustrations and disappointments of three consecutive second-place seasons all too fresh in their minds, owners George Halas and Dutch Sternaman knew that they needed something extra—anything—to push the Bears over into a league championship. Besides wanting a winner, they were troubled by the economics of the game. Costs were rising sharply, but attendance was not. In those early days of pro football, only 5,000 or 6,000 fans could ordinarily be coaxed to invest $1 for a bleacher seat or $2 for a box seat to watch a Sunday Bear game. Maybe 10,000 or 11,000 spectators would show up if the weather was perfect and the opponent was their crosstown rivals, the Cardinals, or a team that could display Jim Thorpe, whom people still wanted to see even though by 1925 he was pretty much past his prime. College football, on the other hand, was the nation's autumn pastime; just 10 miles south of Cubs Park, 40,000 or 50,000 fans would turn out to watch a University of Chicago game at Stagg Field, and other Big Ten games might draw close to 75,000 paying spectators. It was disillusioning for Halas and Sternaman to see filled Sunday after Sunday only about one-fourth of the 30,000 seats of the recently enlarged Cubs Park. It was also becoming economically precarious, they knew. "Something had to be done to bring in customers if we were to continue," George Halas said. "We decided what the Bears needed was a big-name star."

And *the* biggest-name star ever to play the game of football, everyone in 1925 knew, was Red Grange.

Red Grange was a senior at the University of Illinois that year and at 5-feet-11 and 175 pounds the most dazzling running back ever to carry a football on an American gridiron. A breakaway runner with speed and the ability to make the sharpest cuts and the most exciting moves, he was already a legend, at 22 years of age, as revered in his sport as Babe Ruth, Jack Dempsey, Bill Tilden, and Bobby Jones were in theirs. No one drew more fans into a stadium than "No. 77." Everywhere he went, newspaper reporters hounded him for quotes. Newsreel cameramen from *Movietone* and *Pathé* wanted to capture him on film, whether he was playing football or simply walking down a street. Radio broadcasters were forever putting microphones before his face for a few words to be carried over the airwaves to the millions

of people throughout the country who knew his name and his reputation.

But Red Grange was not just a name. He had earned his fame on the football field. Those who questioned his abilities did not do so for long. Fielding ("Hurry-Up") Yost, coach of Michigan in 1924 when his team was considered the best in the nation, for example, said somewhat snidely of Grange before the Michigan-Illinois game: "All Grange can do is run." He quickly learned how dreadfully right he was on one count and how wrong on another. First, Grange could indeed run—for five touchdowns, four in the first quarter, against Yost's team, compiling a phenomenal game total of 402 yards on 21 carries. Second, Grange could in fact do more than run, which he proved when he threw six completed passes, one for a touchdown, as Illinois crushed top-ranked Michigan 39–14. That was only one of his many spectacular games, however. By the end of his college career, he had been named to the All-America team three years in a row, had rushed for a total of 3,637 yards, and scored 31 touchdowns.

Red Grange was "the big name" that George Halas and Dutch Sternaman wanted for the Chicago Bears. And so they wrote several letters to him in the early summer of 1925 regarding the possibility of his becoming a pro—more precisely, a Chicago Bear—at the end of the coming college season. None of the letters were answered. Pro football was just not one of his considerations then.

"I hadn't thought really about turning professional," Grange explains. "Not at first, anyway. I hadn't talked to anybody about it. Not until that night I was sitting in the movie house in Champaign."

One of Grange's reasons for not giving it much thought was that in 1925 professional football was still generally disdained, considered crassly commercial, if not morally destitute, by most people. Professional baseball was well accepted, while football was looked on as so disreputable that many of the pros took to advertising their game as "Post Graduate Football."

C. C. Pyle, whose initials sportswriters would later say stood for "Cash and Carry" or "Cold Cash," was not your ordinary theater owner. In the words of Red Grange: "He was a dapper little guy, sort of a peacock strutting in spats and carrying a cane." Pyle, however, was more than a figure of sartorial elegance; he was also an entrepreneur, a promoter, and an ambitious businessman whose aims were far loftier than simply owning a few movie theaters in places like Kokomo, Indiana, and Champaign. He had always had his eyes open for that one opportunity to break out of the small-town syndrome and into the big time. When Grange walked into his office and sat down across the desk from him, Pyle knew that his opportunity had finally arrived.

"Red, how would you like to make a hundred thousand dollars . . . maybe even a million?"

Grange looked at him suspiciously. That was the kind of money a gambler might talk about. "How?" he asked.

"Playing football, my boy, just playing football," Pyle answered, and went on to explain his plan. Grange would finish up his college season, then join a pro team to finish up their longer-lasting season, and *then* they would take that team on a whirlwind tour of the country. Hundreds of thousands of people would turn out to see the famous Red Grange play in cities where they had never had the chance before. The team would travel to places like New York and Boston, of course, but also down to Florida and out to California. He would arrange everything, Pyle said. He would be Grange's manager.

Grange was overwhelmed with the possibilities and said that he was interested. He also mentioned that the Bears' organization up in Chicago had expressed interest in him. Pyle nodded; he had already suspected that the Bears would be interested in the talents of "No. 77." He, in fact, had thought Chicago would be the ideal place for Grange. The team was good, it needed a Grange to make it great, and he was impressed with the way the team was handled. He would contact the Bears.

Pyle was correct. Halas and Sternaman were definitely still interested in the prospect of Red Grange joining their organization. So Pyle took a train to Chicago and paid a call on Halas and Sternaman. Grange went back to the classrooms and the football field of Illinois, with a warning from Pyle not to discuss with anyone the possibility of his turning pro at the end of the college season.

There was a tenet in the NFL's Code of Ethics, written by President Joe Carr himself, that read:

"Tampering with players on College teams shall not be tolerated by this League."

But what constituted tampering, other than the outright recruiting of a player before he had finished his college playing eligibility, had never been clearly defined. Pyle did not want to take any chances. It was touchy enough to join the pros in 1925, especially for a famous player like Grange, and Pyle wisely wanted nothing to interfere with or tarnish the move once it took place.

In Chicago, three of the shrewdest, most resolute bargainers to be found anywhere in 1925 sat down and agreed in principle as to the football future of Red Grange. Sternaman and Halas had been surprised at the suggestion of a full-scale national tour, but they liked the idea. Details of the financial arrangements, however, would not be settled until *after* Grange's last game of the college season, nor would any money exchange hands in

any form until that time. In that way, there could be no charge of "tampering," they felt. But negotiations would begin immediately after the final gun of Grange's last game, which was scheduled for November 21, when Illinois would play Ohio State at Columbus. Pyle, Halas, and Sternaman agreed to meet in the Morrison Hotel in Chicago that very Saturday and, when the game ended, to work there until every last financial detail was settled.

Despite the secrecy of the behind-the-scenes maneuvering of Pyle and the Bears' owners, rumors began to pop up all over regarding the possibility of Red Grange becoming a pro when his college football days were over. Some people were saying that he had already secretly signed a contract with the Bears, others that the signed contract was in the hands of Tim Mara of the New York Giants. There was also the story that a promoter was putting together a team that included Grange and the Four Horsemen of Notre Dame, who had ended their college careers the season before, to tour the country playing against pro teams. As the season moved along, the rumors grew in number. And so did the criticism. Newswriters, coaches, college officials all spoke out on the subject of Grange possibly playing football for money. "He is a living legend now," one Chicago news reporter wrote. "Why go and sully it."

Even his football coach at Illinois, Bob Zuppke, the same man who had coached Halas and Sternaman and more than a half-dozen other players who in 1925 were on the Chicago Bears' roster, counseled Grange against making any such move. "Football isn't meant to be played for money. Stay away from professionalism," Zuppke urged him.

But Grange could not subscribe to that kind of reasoning. "You get paid for coaching, Zup," he replied. "Why should it be wrong for me to get paid for playing?"

It was a question that Zuppke could not really answer. Still, it did not sway him from his opposition to Grange's becoming a pro. He told Red that if professional football thrived it would turn college football into a mere training ground for the pros. That would destroy college football in the end, he said. "Zuppke was correct," Dutch Sternaman later observed. "College football did become a training ground, but that never adversely affected the game played by collegians. If anything, it strengthened it."

Zuppke also told Red he ought to go back to Wheaton and talk with his father before making any decision about his future. Coach Zuppke felt sure that Lyle Grange would advise his son against joining up to play football for "tainted" money. Red did go to see his father, and Coach Zuppke was right; Lyle Grange voiced the opinion that his son would be better off pursuing some other career. "But when you turned 21, I told you that you would have to make your own decisions,'' he reminded Red. ''And this is one of them. But whatever decision you make, I'll stand behind you.'' The decision had, in fact, already been made. Now it was simply reaffirmed in Red's mind.

By the time the last game of the college season approached, the rumors had it that Grange was already signed up by a pro team, and they were so widespread that serious questions were raised as to whether or not he could play in the game. If he had signed, he was no longer an amateur athlete and would be ineligible to play for Illinois. Both Coach Zuppke and Illinois's athletic director George Huff were forced to confront Grange to see if there was any truth to the rumors. There was not, Grange told them emphatically. Then, hoping to end all the speculation, he went on record with a statement to the working press. ''After the game I'm going to listen to offers. Maybe I'll accept one of them . . . But you can be sure I haven't signed a scrap of paper with anyone, and I haven't told anybody what I'm going to do.''

In Columbus, Ohio, on November 21, Red Grange trotted out onto the field to play his last college game, against Ohio State. More than 70,000 people were on hand—''half of them, it seemed, were newspaper writers and photographers,'' one observer commented. ''No. 77'' led Illinois to a 14–9 win. When the final gun was sounded, his college career over at last, Grange was besieged on the field by reporters. He told them: ''I intend to sign an agreement to play with the Chicago Bears,'' and then he disappeared into the locker room.

And with that, George Halas and Dutch Sternaman sat down in a room in the Morrison Hotel in Chicago with C. C. Pyle and Frank Zambreno, a theatrical agent whom Pyle had enlisted to help in the negotiations. ''Cash and Carry'' Pyle knew what he wanted for his prize property, and he was not going to settle for anything less. The discussions went on through the night. ''We made a tactical error,'' Halas said later. ''Sternaman and I sat together to lend each other moral support through all this haggling. Pyle and Zambreno were smarter. They'd take turns. While one talked the other would sneak off and snatch a few winks of sleep.'' As it turned out, however, no one was really the smarter because the agreement the four men worked out in that Chicago hotel room on that cold November night would prove to benefit not only Grange, Pyle, and the Chicago Bears, but all of professional football as well.

While Pyle, Halas, and Sternaman were arguing the dollars and cents of the situation, Red Grange was trying to elude the literally hundreds of news media people who wanted to talk with him. He managed to get back to his hotel in Columbus, but the lobby was so awash with reporters, well-wishers, and curiosity-seekers that he was forced to make his exit down an old fire escape into an alley. He did not plan to travel back to Champaign with the team; instead, with hat pulled down over his eyes and coat collar turned up, looking more like a henchman of Al Capone than a young college football player, he boarded a train for Chicago. When word somehow leaked out that Halas, Sternaman, and Pyle were meeting in the Morrison Hotel to hash out Grange's contract, the lobby there was quickly carpeted with newsmen. They had also heard the rumor that Grange himself would be arriving at the Morrison to sign the final document, but that was not true. From the train station in Chicago, he took a taxi to the Belmont Hotel, about four miles from the Morrison, registered under a bogus name, and waited there to hear from Pyle.

Finally, in the early morning hours of Sunday, November 22, an agreement was reached. It called for the ''Red Grange/C. C. Pyle Company'' to receive a guarantee of $2,000 per game against a percentage of the gate both for the remaining league games and for the exhibition games in the ''Red Grange/Chicago Bears'' tour of the nation. Grange and Pyle would split their earnings 60/40, with the larger share going to Grange and with Pyle paying any business expenses that they would incur. The actual contract would not be signed until Monday because the two tired Bear owners still had a football game to play and coach that afternoon.

The game was against the Green Bay Packers. About 7,000 fans turned out at Cubs Park to watch it. Fueled perhaps by the adrenalin that came with signing up Grange, the Bears went out and mauled the Packers, who had beaten them earlier in the season, 21–0. And on the bench but in ordinary street clothes—including a raccoon coat—was the newest Chicago Bear, Red Grange. It was announced that on the coming Thursday, Thanksgiving Day, Grange would don a Chicago Bear uniform and play his first professional football game. It was *the* sporting news of the year. But the tone of the news was not necessarily positive. This wire service story, not exactly in the tradition of objective journalism, was one of the milder ones.

Chicago, Nov. 22 (AP)—Harold (Red) Grange today plunged into the business of capitalizing on his gridiron fame by signing to play professional football, against the wishes of his father as well as George Huff, director of athletics of the University of Illinois, Coach Robert Zuppke and others who had hoped he would accept other offers held out to him.

The big question now being asked was: would Red Grange be able to bring out for the pros the tens of thousands of fans that he had when he was playing for Illinois?

That question was answered very shortly. Tickets for

the Thanksgiving Day game against the Chicago Cardinals went on sale Monday at the Spalding Sporting Goods Store on State Street in downtown Chicago. People were lined up for blocks, and within three hours all 20,000 tickets that had been printed were sold. It was promised, however, that a new printing would make more tickets available the following day and that they would also be sold at the ball park on the day of the game; that is, if there were any left. By game time on Thanksgiving Day, a standing-room-only crowd of 36,000 people filled Cubs Park to watch Red Grange play. And all the tickets that had been printed for the game a few days later against a little-known team, the Columbus Tigers, were already sold out. In the words of George Halas: "There had never been such evidence of public interest since our professional league began in 1920. I knew then and there that pro football was destined to be a big-time sport." And, of course, from that moment on, it was.

After the Thanksgiving Day meeting with the Cardinals and the next Sunday's with the Tigers at Cubs Park, the Bears would go on the road. The entire project loomed so large, so complicated, so financially awesome that C. C. Pyle hired an assistant manager to help him handle Red Grange and the tour. Pyle then revealed the logistics of the tour he had arranged. It would actually be two tours, one of eight games and the other of nine. But it quickly became apparent that he had never been a football player himself. The first tour had the Bears playing *eight* games in *eight* different cities in a *12-day* period, a schedule unheard of before in any form of organized football. It would include the last games of the regular season. After the first tour, the team would have a week and a half to rest before the first game of the second tour, which would be played on Christmas Day. The other eight games in the second tour would be played over a more sensible period of one month, but during that time the team would travel by train from Chicago to the tip of Florida, as far west as the California coast, and as far north as Seattle. Nothing, it could be said, stood in the way of "Cash and Carry" Pyle's scheduling.

Before he suited up for his first pro game, Grange was given a crash three-day course on the Bears' plays by Halas and Sternaman. And someone hastily sewed a "77" on a Bear jersey (up to then no other player on the Bears' team had a number higher than 29). But on Thursday, the 36,000 people who postponed their turkey dinners to sit in the damp November cold and watch Red Grange perform in the mud of Cubs Park found little to get excited about. Grange carried the ball from scrimmage 16 times, gaining a total of only 36 yards, and threw six passes, completing one. Nor did he have a chance to exercise one of his most devastating

specialties—returning punts. Paddy Driscoll, the Cardinal's premier back and punter, figured wisely that it would be in his team's best interest not to kick the ball anywhere near Grange. As Driscoll later explained: "It was a question of which of us would look bad—Grange or Driscoll. I decided it wouldn't be Paddy." And Driscoll was a fine enough punter to accomplish just that. But no one played any better than "No. 77" that day, and the game ended in a 0–0 tie. Yet young Red Grange was suddenly a lot wealthier than he had been the week before, when he was rooming in the Zeta Psi fraternity house in Champaign. That afternoon he earned the handsome sum of $12,000, not bad for a few hours' work in that era of minimal income taxes, when you could buy an Auburn Roadster for less than $1,500 or bed down in a first-class hotel, with three meals thrown in, for $6.50.

Three days later, neither Grange's less-than-spectacular debut nor a heavy snowstorm would keep 28,000 fans from gathering again at Cubs Park to watch the Bears play. It was a truly miserable day and if the Bears had not been showcasing "No. 77" they probably would not have drawn more than one or two thousand die-hard fans to watch them play the Columbus Tigers. But pro football, at least in Chicago, had changed— there was no doubt about it. As one Chicago newspaper headlined in its sports section, "A New Era in Pro Football Has Begun."

The snow and cold did not seem to bother Red Grange, however, That afternoon he gained twice as many yards rushing (72) as he had the game before, caught two passes, and returned a kickoff for 28 yards. With a touchdown by Joey Sternaman, another by Laurie Walquist, and two successful extra points kicked by Joey, the Bears were able to squeeze out a 14–13 victory over the Tigers.

After this game, Earl Britton, Grange's running mate from Illinois and seat mate in the Virginia Theatre that fateful night earlier in the year, and a few other players were added to the team for the grueling tour that lay ahead. As it turned out, the Bears would need every able, healthy body they could get in order to field a team, as game after game in such quick succession took a brutal toll on the players.

Tuesday the team left for St. Louis for a Wednesday afternoon game against a team of professional and semi-pro players that had been hastily put together by Francis Donnelly, a St. Louis mortician and sometime promoter. The temperature at game time reached a high for the day of 12 degrees above zero, and only 8,000 spectators were willing to endure the bitter cold on that weekday afternoon to watch a football game. But those who did show up saw Red Grange deliver his finest performance as a pro. He scored four touchdowns, and that, along with touchdowns by Joey Sternaman and Verne Mullen, a second-string end who played behind George Halas, was enough for an impressive 39–6 victory. The only touchdown for the St. Louis team was contributed by Jimmy Conzelman, who had taken a temporary leave of absence from his Detroit Panther team to play in the game. After St. Louis, the Bears luxuriated in a two-day rest, the longest they would have on the first tour, but one day of it was spent traveling by train to Philadelphia.

The tour, with the aid of Pyle's huckstering, was gathering much more publicity than pro football ordinarily would in those days. At one time or another during the tour the nation's most widely read sportswriters—Damon Runyon, Grantland Rice, Westbrook Pegler, even Ford Frick, the future commissioner of major league baseball—would travel with the Bears.

Philadelphia welcomed the Bears with a driving rainstorm for their Saturday afternoon game against the Frankford Yellow Jackets. Under Guy Chamberlin, the Yellow Jackets had a first-rate roster, including Link Lyman, who had come over from Cleveland with Chamberlin, and a cast of lesser-knowns like the Mutt and Jeff combination of Jug Earpe (6-feet-2, 240 pounds) and Two Bits Homan (5-feet-5, 144 pounds). Lyman, however, would join the Bears in two weeks for their second tour and stay around to play seven seasons with them.

Grange again ran the Bears to a victory (14–7) by scoring both touchdowns; the conversions were contributed by Joey Sternaman. As Westbrook Pegler, then traveling with the team, put it in his sports column: "Red Grange, the only football player who ever enjoyed the luxury of a manager and a substitute manager, scored two personal touchdowns and a personal victory over the Frankford Yellow Jackets . . . some 35,000 soggy customers melted away in the early dusk, drenched and satisfied."

The Bears were equally drenched by the downpour in Philadelphia, but after the game they weren't able to melt away into the early dusk. They had to rush to the train station, still in their wet, muddy uniforms, and catch the last train to New York because the schedule called for them to face the Giants at the Polo Grounds the next afternoon. As the players were changing out of their uniforms aboard the train, everyone was painfully aware that the soggy jerseys and mud-splotched pants couldn't be cleaned in time for the game and probably wouldn't even be dry by then. C. C. Pyle, who it seemed was never more than a few feet away from the team or the young man he managed, leaned over to George Halas and said: "This tour will make you so wealthy, Halas, that next year you'll be able to afford two sets of uniforms."

It was a tired and bruised Chicago Bear team that finally checked into the Astor Hotel in Times Square that

Saturday night. But they were also buoyed up by the prospect of what awaited them the next day.

Actually, when all the fence climbers and gate-crashers were added to those who purchased tickets to the game, the crowd was estimated at more than 73,000 (the official seating capacity of the Polo Grounds in 1925 was 65,000). Never in the short history of professional football had a crowd so large been enticed into a sports stadium.

What they saw was a powerful Bears team that easily defeated the Giants, 19–7. They also saw Red Grange play for 35 of the game's 60 minutes, during which time he rushed 11 times for a total of 53 yards, ran back two punts for 13 yards, completed two short forward passes, picked off a pass thrown by Bill Rooney, and ran the interception back 35 yards for a touchdown. Actually Joey Sternaman, who played the full 60 minutes of that game just as he had in the game the day before, outrushed Grange, scored the other two touchdowns, and drop-kicked an extra point for the Bears. But the publicity was reserved for the "Ghost," whether he galloped or not. As sportswriter B. G. FitzGibbon put it in the language of the 1920s: "Red Grange did his stuff . . . he convinced the 70,000-and-odd persons assembled in the Polo Grounds that he was, slangily speaking, 'the berries.'"

Monday was a day off for the Bears, which afforded them the luxury of having their uniforms cleaned and dried and time to nurse the wounds, bruises, and sore muscles they had picked up by playing three football games in the past five days.

Some of the players were content to spend the day resting up; others took in the sights around the island of Manhattan. Still others sought out their own particular pleasures in the sprawling city of speakeasies and sophistication that only the month before had come under the indulgent rule of Mayor Jimmy Walker, sometimes known as "Beau James."

Red Grange, however, spent the day with his manager going over the other ways that his name and his presence could be merchandised—movies, product endorsements, personal appearances, nothing would be overlooked by Pyle. Entrepreneur Pyle felt sure that he and Grange could earn at least as much money from these ventures as they would from Grange's football playing. As it turned out, he was right. The Red Grange/C. C. Pyle Company, it is estimated, grossed about $125,000 from these outside enterprises, about equal to the amount it reaped from gate receipt guarantees and percentages from the two tours.

A visitor also dropped by C. C. Pyle's suite in the Astor Hotel that day. The Sultan of Swat, Babe Ruth of the New York Yankees, decided to stop in and introduce himself to the young man with whom he was now sharing the sports page headlines. Red Grange remembers that the Babe was full of advice, which over the years has been variously reported to include such bits of wisdom as:

"Kid, don't believe anything they write about you."
"Get the dough while the getting is good, but don't break your heart trying to get it."
"Don't pick up too many checks."

Washington, D.C., was the next stop. And it was the beginning of a portion of the trip that made the previous phase of three games in five days seem like a lark. This segment called for three games in three days: Tuesday in Washington, Wednesday in Boston, and Thursday in Pittsburgh.

The exhaustion and the pain of the tour were beginning to show on all the Bear players. But the road show itself was not without its lighter moments. The Washington stopover, in fact, has always prompted one of Red Grange's favorite stories. Whisked to the White House and introduced to President Calvin Coolidge as "Red Grange, who plays with the Bears," he was quickly humbled, when the austere Coolidge nodded and then said, "Young man, I always liked animal acts."

Later that day, the Bears handily defeated a group of eastern pro and semi-pro players who went under the name of the Washington All-Stars, 19–0. But the glorious string of victories ended that afternoon in the Washington stadium. The following day in Boston, the Providence Steam Roller, who had signed up two of the legendary Four Horsemen of Notre Dame—Jim Crowley and Don Miller—beat the Bears 9–6 in an official league game. A tired Red Grange did not play much that day, and he was credited with gaining only 18½ yards in the game. The 25,000 spectators who jammed Boston Braves Field were not happy with the afternoon's entertainment, and at the end of the game, the Bears had to virtually fight their way through a jeering, rioting crowd to get to the locker room.

The loss to the Providence Steam Roller was the first the Bears had suffered since Grange had joined the team. But it was not the last. The fatigued and injury-ridden Bears were slaughtered the next day by a Pittsburgh team of unknowns that had been specially assembled for the game. The score was 24–0. Grange saw action for only one play. On his first run from scrimmage, he tore a muscle in his left arm and had to leave the game.

The injury was severe enough to keep him from playing in the game against Jimmy Conzelman's Detroit Panthers two days later. When it was announced in that city that Grange would be conspicuously absent from the field of play, 10,000 people demanded (and received) refunds on the tickets they had purchased. A meager crowd of just over 4,000 paid to watch the Panthers destroy a battered Bear team 21–0.

How badly were they battered at this stage of their tour? Howard Roberts, a Chicago newsman, chronicled the problems. Besides the injury to Grange, "Laurie Walquist had a broken toe, Milt Romney a twisted ankle, Dutch Sternaman an injured shoulder, Joe Sternaman a lame knee, Ed Healey and George Trafton leg injuries and Halas himself, not to be outdone, developed a boil on his neck." It was so bad that trainer Andy Lotshaw, who had enough on his hands just tending to the injured and tired players, was enlisted to play tackle so that the Bears could field an 11-man team, even though he hadn't played in a game for years.

One day, as the first Bear-Grange tour was coming to an end, "Cash and Carry" Pyle cornered Westbrook Pegler, who was never known to treat anyone gently in his writings. "I don't understand it, Pegler," he said. "Through this whole tour, you drink all my booze and then write all these bad things about me in your column."

"Look, Pyle," Pegler said. "You don't have to worry about anything I write about you until I stop referring to your name in the singular."

The final game of the tour was back at Cubs Park. Tim Mara, who had been on the verge of going out of business until the Bears and Red Grange lured more than 73,000 people into the Polo Grounds a week earlier, now had plenty of money to transport his New York Giants to Chicago for the last league game of the season. The Bears who took the field that day were a decimated team. But Grange was back in uniform, despite his very sore arm, because no one wanted to see a repeat of what had happened in Detroit the day before, when thousands of people rushed to return their tickets. Even so, only about 18,000 fans showed up for the game, far fewer than the record crowds that had jammed Cubs Park for Grange's first two appearances. And for those who did show up that cold Sunday in December, it was a disheartening experience. The Bears lost 9–0, and Grange was able to do little more than protect his arm from further damage.

It had now been 18 days since Red Grange put on his first pro football uniform, and in that 2½-week period, he had played in nine games and earned approximately $50,000.

The game with the Giants officially ended the 1925 season for the Bears. Their record of 9–5–3 included three losses to league teams in the last week of their tour

---

— 297 —

and left them in seventh place in the final NFL standings, the lowest they had ever been in their six seasons of pro ball. The Chicago Cardinals, with an 11–2–1 record, were awarded the championship that year, following another of those contested claims to the title that had to be settled by NFL president Joe Carr.

The name Red Grange in 1925 was not associated merely with the game of football. "Cash and Carry" Pyle saw to it that it was attached to a variety of products. Among the items that carried Grange's name or endorsement that year were:

a candy bar	*ginger ale*
a brand of cigarettes	*sweaters*
yeast foam malted milk	*a cap*
a doll	*shoes*
a fountain pen	*socks*

Grange's fame and the effect of his endorsement in the commercial world would pave the way for later stars to peddle a wide assortment of products, ranging from Fords (by Dick Butkus) and rental cars (O. J. Simpson) to pantyhose (Joe Namath).

Red Grange had brought glamour to the latter part of the season and, of course, he had brought the spectators out to the ball parks where he played. But if a football hero on the team were to be singled out, it would have to be Joey Sternaman, who accounted for 62 points, the third highest total in the NFL (after Charlie Berry of the Pottsville Maroons and Paddy Driscoll of the Cardinals). Sternaman rushed for five touchdowns, caught one touchdown pass, threw passes for three more, and kicked three field goals and 17 extra points.

The NFL season had ended, but the Bears' season was far from over. Their second tour was about to commence. For this one, Pyle arranged for the players to have their own Pullman car and a personal porter so they could travel in appropriate style. He also saw to it that each player was outfitted with a sweater with "Bears" emblazoned on the front, matching knickers, and bright-colored knee socks. With that flourish, the team chugged out of the sleet and ice of Chicago to the midwinter warmth of sunny Florida.

The nine teams the Bears would encounter in the next month would comprise players picked up in each city especially for that particular exhibition game. Some of the players were exceptionally good but most of them were locals of dubious quality, and the teams lacked the advantage of having played together except for a few practice sessions.

The first stop was Coral Gables, just outside Miami, where a temporary stadium had been erected for the game. The Bears defeated the Coral Gables Collegians 7–3, with Grange scoring the game's only touchdown. From there, the Bears began working their way back up the Florida peninsula. In Tampa, on New Year's Day, they faced a team calling themselves the Cardinals, who had recruited a 37-year-old and sadly-out-of-shape Jim Thorpe. To no avail—the Bears trounced Tampa 17–3.

Jacksonville, the next stop, was to be something really special. John S. O'Brien, who would have liked to be the successful promoter that C. C. Pyle had become, was putting together the Jacksonville Stars along with a few other Florida backers. He had succeeded in getting himself named the manager of Stanford's great fullback Ernie Nevers, who, after Grange, was the most famous college football player of the day. O'Brien had grandiose plans, but he was no match for Pyle.

In a February, 1926, issue of *Liberty* magazine, Walter Davenport reported on this exchange between the two promoters:

"It should be the battle of the century, Mr. Pyle," said Mr. O'Brien. "I aim to cover the South with announcements that no red-blooded man should miss the titanic struggle between the Galloping Ghost and the Lion of the Sierras—Red and Ernie. It will be a sell-out with lamentable numbers turned away at the gate."

"I'm glad to hear it," said Mr. Pyle, "because you will now read with less pain our contract, which, I regret to say, has embarrassed other managers. . . ."

Ernie Nevers did show up for the game. So did Red Grange, C. C. Pyle, and the other Bears (with an already-banked $20,000 guarantee for the game and a 65% share of all earnings from it). But the spectators didn't. Inflated ticket prices ranged from $8.50 down to $5.50 (more than four times what was charged in Cubs Park), and a depressed Florida economy obviously contributed to a dismal attendance figure of 6,700 fans. The Jacksonville promoters absorbed a loss of about $12,500. And the collision on the football field of the two college goliaths was less than spectacular. Grange gained 29 yards in five carries and threw one touchdown pass. Nevers rushed for a total of 46 yards and scored one touchdown. The Bears won easily, 19–6.

In the opulence of their private railroad car, the Bears then made their way along the Gulf Coast to New Orleans, where they defeated a team called the All-Stars 14–0. As part of the pre-game fanfare and hype, all the Bears were taken out to Fair Grounds Racetrack to watch the newly named feature race, the Red Grange Handicap. A horse called Prickly Heat won the race, and

Grange himself went to the winner's circle to present the jockey with an emorous pink floral football.

The second tour was turning into more of a barnstorming sideshow with Pyle leading the theatrics and pyrotechnics like a true P. T. Barnum. But no one seemed to mind.

In Los Angeles, the next stop, Pyle had Grange and the other Bears posing with everyone from Mary Pickford to Charlic Chaplin. He even gathered several members of the team on the roof of the Biltmore Hotel, where they were staying, to throw footballs down into a crowd of 5,000 that had gathered for a Pyle-sponsored gimmick. Any person to catch one—no easy feat considering the speed and angle of a football rocketing down 13 stories—would be awarded $25 and get to keep the football. This publicity stunt cost Pyle a total of $100.

The promotion and the pizzazz paid off, at least in Los Angeles. A crowd estimated at more than 75,000 filled the Los Angeles Coliseum to watch the Bears pummel a make-up team called the L. A. Tigers that was headed by George (''Wildcat'') Wilson, an All-American from the University of Washington. The score was 17–7. Playing on the line for the Tigers that day was a large, gravel-voiced young man who would go on to make a name for himself in the movies—Andy Devine.

The Bears then traveled down to San Diego to defeat a team called the Collegians 14–0 and up to San Francisco, where they suffered their only loss of the tour (14–9). From there they went on to Portland, Oregon, for a 60–3 devastation of a predominantly semi-pro aggregate of athletes who called themselves the All-Stars and finally to Seattle for an easy 34–0 win on the last day of January, 1926.

The tour was finally over. Grange and Pyle had pocketed roughly $150,000 from the gate receipts alone, bringing their total for the two tours to $250,000. The Chicago Bears' organization had earned a little more than $100,000 from both tours. In the words of George Halas, it was ''the first financial cushion we'd managed to accumulate.'' For the other Bears players, however, it was not a financial bonanza—they had worked hard to earn the $100 to $200 a game each was paid. But they did have an opportunity to build an incredible scrapbook of memories on a pilgrimage that had taken them from Cubs Park to Times Square, the White House, Miami Beach, New Orleans' French Quarter, Hollywood, the Wrigley mansion on Santa Catalina Island, Tijuana, the palatial estate of William Randolph Hearst at San Simeon, Fisherman's Wharf, and a raft of other interesting and out-of-the-ordinary ports of call.

For the Bears as a team, the official NFL season was disappointing. But what had taken place during and after the regular season, when looked at in proper perspective, was much more important. As George Halas put it some 30 years later, ''I believe that as a result of our Grange tour, pro football for the first time took on true national stature.'' Indeed it did. Professional football was introduced in cities across the country, to people who up to that time had only heard vague rumblings about its existence and the questions regarding its commercialism and alleged lack of ''solid moral fiber.'' Now one of the nation's great sports idols was part of it, and the people came in droves to see him play the game. It would still take many more years before pro football would become the enormously popular spectator sport it is today, but the season of 1925 was the first real step in that direction.

Red Grange/Chicago Bear Tours 1925–26 (All games on the road, except Dec. 13)		Bears	Opponents
Tour 1			
Dec. 2	St. Louis	39	6
Dec. 5	Frankford Yellow Jackets (at Philadelphia)*	14	7
Dec. 6	New York Giants*	19	7
Dec. 8	Washington, D.C.	19	0
Dec. 9	Providence Steam Roller (at Boston)*	6	9
Dec. 10	Pittsburgh	0	24
Dec. 12	Detroit Panthers*	0	21
Dec. 13	New York Giants*	0	9

(cont.)

Tour 2		Bears	Opponents
Dec. 25	Coral Gables	7	3
Jan. 1	Tampa	17	3
Jan. 2	Jacksonville..	19	6
Jan. 10	New Orleans	14	0
Jan. 16	Los Angeles	17	7
Jan. 17	San Diego...	14	0
Jan. 24	San Francisco	9	14
Jan. 30	Portland, Ore...	60	3
Jan. 31	Seattle	34	0

* League games; all others exhibition games

Over the years pro footballers have combined careers. George Halas fooled around with the New York Yankees baseball team while he was trying to start a career in professional football. Almost 70 years later, Bo Jackson was attempting to do the same thing (with the Kansas City Royals) only earning about a million dollars more in each sport than Halas. But certainly one of the most memorable, and humorous, career dichotomies was that of Hall of Fame-bound George Trafton, the best center/linebacker in football during the 1920s, who took to the pugilistic ring to prove that gridiron toughs were tougher than baseball diamond roughnecks. Mike Wilson, a member of the Pro Football Researchers Association, created this chronicle for *Coffin Corner,* the organization's official publication, and described the piece thusly: "How a loudmouthed first baseman, a happy-go-lucky linebacker, a ne'er-do-well boxing promoter, an anonymous lay-down artist, and a gallery of on-looking luminaries created and then destroyed the Non-Boxing Heavyweight Championship of the World."

Raging Bullchips

MIKE WILSON

THINGS WERE different in the Roaring Twenties. Boxers fought at least once a month. Baseball really was the national pastime. Athletes did their talking in newspapers instead of into TV cameras. And sports fans wore their naiveté as proudly as they would any uniform.

Just as that chaotic decade was coming to a close, a series of bizarre prize fights took place in and around Chicago. These fights cast a dark shadow over the National Pastime and nearly destroyed what little dignity existed in the worlds of professional boxing and football.

In 1929, a gangly gust of Texas-bred wind named Arthur Shires was attracting attention in his first full year as first baseman for the Chicago White Sox. He was hitting .312 and was considered a strong defensive player. He also was earning quite a reputation as a fighter.

Early in the season, he was content to punch out opposing players or an occasional spectator. But, when that didn't seem to quench his aggressions, our slugger turned on his own dugout. More specifically, on Sox manager Lena Blackburne.

Shires won the first bout with a decisive TKO over his 42-year-old mentor. Then, unafraid of threats of being traded, he forced a rematch late in the year.

Several club officials tried to stop this second melee, but it was the club's traveling secretary, Lou Barbour, who got caught right smack in the middle. Once he discovered he couldn't stop the fight, he decided to unleash a few of his own frustrations by biting a nearby—and unsuspecting—thumb.

Unfortunately, that thumb was his *own!* And the bite wound required eight stitches.

When the scrap was all over, Shires had recorded his second victory and had dubbed himself Arthur "The Great." . . .

[Meanwhile]

Chicago Bear center-linebacker George Trafton (a member of Pro Football's Hall of Fame) was across town celebrating one of his birthdays. He claimed it was his 28th . . . but friends who recalled his stories of an army hitch in 1917 and '18 *after* graduating from Notre Dame, found 28 a little hard to swallow.

Whatever his age, he and his pals were feeling no pain when the result of the Shires-Daly fight came over the radio. [Shires kayoed Dan Daly in 21 seconds of the first round of a highly-hyped, quasi-legitimate bout in Chicago.]

Trafton's friends all praised Shires; big George (6' 1", 230 lbs.) scoffed at him. Furthermore, the Bear center said he could whip any puny baseball player with just one hand. That crack was more than Garland Grange (George's teammate and Red's brother) could resist.

Grange quickly telephoned Mullen at the roller rink and, before he hung up, he had challenged Art Shires on Trafton's behalf. Everyone at the party laughed and cheered big George . . . then memories of the challenge faded amidst morning headaches.

But Mullen didn't have a headache. He had visions of greenbacks dancing in his head as he phoned George that Tuesday to pin down details of an upcoming fight. However, in the very bright light of day, George Trafton saw no particular reason to battle the ferocious first baseman and he told Mullen so. That's when the promoter mentioned a $1,000 guarantee and a percentage of the gate . . . and when Trafton regained his muddled memory.

Sure, he would fight The Great on Monday, just six-and-a-half days away.

At this point, we need to put things in their proper perspective. Baseball and boxing were the key sports of the period. Professional football, on the other hand, was regarded with all the respectability of an alley fight. In fact, local papers often neglected to post the scores of home team games. But, if any Bear player (other than Red Grange) was known to the average Chicagoan, it was George Trafton.

Trafton's unusual notoriety is best explained by quoting a fellow Chicago Bear: "George is the toughest, meanest, most ornery critter alive." And, in later years, the public would discover this aggressiveness was equalled only by his persistence.

In 1930, the Chicago Bears did not offer him a contract. Instead, they told the press he had retired. Big George squelched that report by releasing the following statement:

"Although the Messrs. Halas and Sternaman did not offer me a contract, I've joined the squad anyway and am going to make them give me back my old job at center."

He played every game in 1930. Then, again in 1931, Halas, planning to build with youth, would tell Trafton he was through. George would vow he would be the Bears' starting center in the season opener . . . and he would be right. The same old problem would pop up again in 1932. The newspapers would carry the coach's lineup for the coming year and George's name would not be on the list. But he would show up uninvited for practice and, at the age of 31-*plus,* beat out all competition.

This was George Trafton, Arthur "The Great" Shires' next ring opponent. And, what had started out as a party gag, was now the prime topic of Chicago conversation. Unfortunately, not all the conversation was favorable.

For example, there was the talk coming from the Benevolent and Protective Brotherhood of Professional Pugilists. This group of assorted fighters and handlers publicly denounced the scheduled bout. Joe Sherman, brotherhood president, instructed his ethics committee to investigate the fight, then issued this stance: "The members of the brotherhood feel their art is being taken too lightly and that the promoters are showing a tendency to pack the premises at the expense of the finer phases of pugilism."

Sherman also made sure Shires and Trafton were aware all *professional* fighters were members of his brotherhood, including any sparring partners they might encounter during the week. This was not a threat, he said. He was merely cautioning both so-called boxers as to the hazards of the sport and didn't want his organization blamed for any injury which might accidentally be inflicted by a "brother."

He should not have opened his mouth . . . because, as soon as he had, the sports writing community was quick to help him put his foot in it.

What about the fight in New York the same night as the Shires-Daly contest, they asked. Wasn't that between two of Sherman's *brothers?* Hadn't the first round gone without one, single blow being landed? Then, in the second round, when the knockout finally came, wasn't it caused by a crushing blow to the *shoulder?* And, hadn't the loser earned the instant moniker, Fainting Phil Scott?

Obviously, all these embarrassing questions ended the brotherhood's threats. But that wasn't the end of all threats.

Just prior to the much-publicized fight, two characters with obvious—but unnatural—bulges under their armpits paid Trafton and his manager, Garland Grange, a visit. They wanted to know who was going to win. Trafton proudly announced he was; they said *wrong*.

The two football players decided their boxing careers were over. They wanted no part of a fixed fight . . . and they didn't want to take up residence in the crowded Chicago River. But, before they could let Mullen know the deal was off, they had another visitor.

They recognized him immediately as the infamous "Machine Gun" Jack McGurn. (McGurn would be killed a few years later in a gangland war.) Now it was his turn to ask who was going to win the fight. When George sheepishly repeated that *he* was, McGurn said *good*. He was glad to hear everything was on the up-and-up, and urged both Trafton and Grange to let him know if anyone was to suggest otherwise.

When they told him about the other two guys, McGurn assured them he would take care of everything. He wished George luck and left. The two thugs, like Sherman's brotherhood, were never heard from again.

So much for Trafton's training program, the brotherhood and gangsters. But what was The Great up to all this time? Surely, he wasn't in training.

Of course not! Instead, he was making plans for his *third* fight. Remember, a football player just wasn't the celebrity a baseball player was in 1929. So, Art went shopping for one of his own kind and he came up with cross-town rival Hack Wilson. The Windy City really went wild with that news and, now, the rest of the country was beginning to take notice.

Up on the north side, Cub slugger Wilson had heard about all the money Shires was getting for putting on gloves, and he was eager to get in on the profit sharing. But money wasn't his only motive. A few months earlier, he had lost a fly ball in the sun during the fourth game of the World Series . . . and second-guessers had been accusing him of blowing the championship ever since. By whipping Shires, thought Wilson, he could be a good guy once again.

Meanwhile, Jim Mullen was ecstatic. Just a few weeks before, he was unable to make ends meet; then the Shires-Daly affair put him in the black; the Shires-Trafton battle was already a sell-out; and, now he was thinking of renting one of Chicago's two baseball parks for the Shires-Wilson confrontation.

By the time December 16 rolled around, the city was in a frenzy. Mullen was counting his chickens. Shires was all scarlet and gold braid. And Trafton was reluctant! In fact, just five minutes before the fight, he wanted to call the whole thing off . . . not from fear, but from pride.

You see, the final phase of his training program had been to play a quarter of the New York Giant game the day before the fight. During that brawl, George made a bone-crushing tackle on the Giants' rugged fullback Tony Plansky . . . and gave himself a handsome black eye.

Now, with the crowd growing impatient, Trafton was concerned with the shiner . . . and his image. He didn't want anyone to think that Shires had done that to him. Instead, he insisted the crowd, the press, and the listening radio audience be told just how he got the black eye, before he would put one foot in the ring.

As the ringmaster was doing that, Trafton had another visitor. This one didn't have a gun, but he did have a snoot full of booze. He staggered up to big George, leaned on the center's shoulder and announced that he—and only he—had the secret to beating The Great. He remembered how Shires had charged across the ring to get to Daly, so, if Trafton just stuck out his big left hand, Shires would surely run smack into it.

And that, said George's unofficial trainer, would be all there was to that. The plan sounded logical to Trafton; finally he was ready.

Shires had been ready. He felt gorgeous and was strutting around in his crimson robe. Trafton, in a Chicago Bear-blue robe, was quite drab in comparison, only his size and three full ringside rows of his teammates seemed in his favor. Most of the cheers were for Art.

Then the bell rang!

Shires started with the same sort of wild burst of energy he had used to put poor Mysterious Dan Daly away so quickly; but big George's long left arm held him off. Art tried again: no success. Everyone in roller arena howled for Trafton to swing, unaware he was content to wait for Shires' suicide plunge into the extended glove.

Art charged again; still nothing.

Maybe Trafton decided his tactic really was impractical, or maybe he just got tired of holding up his heavy glove. Whatever the reason, in the middle of round one, he suddenly dropped his guard and joined The Great toe-to-toe in the center of the ring for a pier-six brawl . . . much to Arthur's chagrin.

A ponderous right hit him smack on the chin. His knees buckled and he grabbed Trafton's legs in desperation. Somehow he managed to regain his footing without a count, just in time to stumble into a thundering right uppercut that could have—and *should* have—ended the match. He went down for a two count, stood halfway up as the bell rang, then wilted without being touched again.

His corner help was able to revive him and he came back in round two filled with determination. But little else. In the first few seconds, he wandered into a wild right hand that finished the fight.

Oh, don't be confused. That right didn't knock Shires out, it was just the last semblance of a punch thrown inside the ring the rest of the night.

From that moment on, the brave gladiators came out of their corners only to loiter and pant in the center of the ring. To offer a little non-violent variety, first one would seem to chase the other around, then they would trade places. Once, if only by accident, they did meet face-to-face, toe-to-toe. Deafening cheers pleaded for a knockout, but both men's arms appeared welded to their sides.

The football player was accustomed to hostile crowds. He laughed and even managed to wave to his fellow Bears. Shires, last week's tough guy, could only muster a weak smile far below his standard fare. Obviously, both were praying for the bell to ring before they fell from exhaustion.

Carroll "Pat" Flanagan, who was describing the fiasco to the radio public, didn't see any humor in Trafton's chatting with his ringside comrades, so, in the best broadcasting tradition, he called it like he saw it. That was a *mistake!*

His microphone was just outside the ring and right in front of Bear guard Bill Fleckenstein. When Fleck heard Flanagan's negative comments about his teammate, he threw the most damaging blow of the night—a stinging right to the announcer's chops. Flanagan's blow-by-blow account signed off ahead of schedule with a strained, "I've been struck!"

The crowd, by now, was aware the fight inside the ring was going nowhere, so it began to create its own amusements. Since camera flashbulbs of that era often made explosive pops when they went off, many startled bystanders instinctively attacked the photographers. Other bystanders then instinctively attacked the attacking bystanders. Confusion took over.

The aisles were jammed with private squabbles and the fans *outside* the roller rink mistook all the noise *inside* as a response to an exciting boxing match—a match they were missing. So, they broke through windows and crashed the gate to see what was happening.

Just as everything was about to get out of hand—and before the police could arrive in force—the Shires-Trafton bout was over and semi-silence awaited the judges' decision. The referee raised George's hand; the crowd cheered; and the apparent silliness of it all squelched the impending riot.

The purse for both men set a new record for previous amateurs boxing in a professional ring. Nevertheless, Hack Wilson lost interest in fighting Shires . . . or Trafton, for that matter. And poor Jim Mullen had to forget about ever hobnobbing with the very rich.

The title of this article is what Amos Alonzo Stagg, University of Chicago coach and grand old mentor of the game, as well as a host of other college football coaches, told everyone in the 1920s: pro football was less than despicable. Or in his own inimitable words: "And now comes along another serious menace, possibly greater than all others, *viz.* Sunday professional football." It was enough to prompt the pros to dub their game "post graduate football." If that was not bad enough, midway through the twentieth century Army coach Earl Blaik came along to tell all listeners that the game was just simply, well, inferior. He told that specifically to *New York Herald Tribune* sports editor Stanley Woodward, who dutifully preserved the thoughts as only a good scribe would. The article was included in the collection *Collier's Greatest Sports Stories.*

The Pro Game Isn't Football

STANLEY WOODWARD

IT HAD BEEN a game to rouse the dead. The supposedly unbeatable Cleveland Football Browns had gone into the second half trailing by 21 points, and 70,000 people had howled a savage éloge to a team that appeared to be at the mercy of the underrated New York Yankees.

But in the second half an exhumation began to shape up and when the iron November twilight closed in on Yankee stadium, the New Yorkers were fighting the clock to hold a 28-all tie.

The Cleveland comeback had been cruelly systematic. Marion Motley, the big fullback, had taken a series of hand-offs from quarterback Otto Graham and riddled the core of the Yankee line. Graham, keyman of a T attack that was suddenly alive, had whipped passes to his buttonhooking halfbacks and had found Dante Lavelli and Mac Speedie, his spectacular ends, with long loopers. The Stadium was in a turmoil as the Browns started for

their fifth touchdown. But time ran out on them before the tie could be broken.

Going downtown I shared a cab with Colonel Earl (Red) Blaik, the Army coach. He sat in his corner silent and apparently unmoved by the recent heroics. Trying to start a conversation, I said, "Great game, eh?"

"Yes," said the Colonel, composedly rubbing his chin, "but it wasn't football."

Not football!

Recently, when Collier's asked me to report the Colonel's views on college versus professional brands of the game, I reminded him of his cryptic remark in the cab after the Cleveland-Yankee hair-raiser three years ago.

He was in his shirt sleeves behind his big desk on the top floor of the West Point gymnasium during an interlude between sessions of clinical football. Down the hall

— 305 —

the movie projector whirred as members of the staff studied the technique of some impending opponent.

"Sure, I remember it," he said, "and that's what I think. Football is a college game. It calls for these things: youth, condition, spirit, plus continuous hard work by coaches as well as players."

What's the matter with professional football?

"Nothing. It's what it aims to be. It's a show. The pros are in the entertainment business."

Subsequent questioning revealed that Earl Henry Blaik, Colonel U.S. Cavalry, Retired, developer of five undefeated Army teams in nine years, doesn't think a pro eleven would stand a chance if it undertook a schedule of eight or nine games against tough college teams.

He admires the individual skills of the professional players, likes to see the games himself. But he doesn't think the pros work at team development like the colleges. He doesn't think the players keep in good condition. He thinks they lack spiritual lift. He thinks they are turning the game into basketball by depending almost wholly on the forward pass. He misses the detailed execution of the college running attack. In pro football he discerns no "second effort," i.e., getting downfield to block the secondary or pursuing a runner who has got away.

His comments are observations rather than criticisms. He says he does not know the problems of pro football and admits the pros may be proceeding in a logical manner for the promulgation of their business—which is show business.

"However," he says, "I don't learn anything from pro football. I know that if I could not develop a team which would play harder, faster and with greater co-ordination than the pros, my career as a college coach would be—shall I say—limited."

That day and other days I listened while Colonel Blaik expounded the revolutionary theory that the best football is not played by the pros and cannot be. His approach was positive—an evaluation of the college game rather than a mere arraignment of the shortcomings among the pros. In an attempt to get at the reasoning behind his conviction I attended meetings of the Army football staff and practice sessions of the squad. I sat in the projection room while the coaches ran movie reels of past games with prospective opponents. I listened to detailed discussions of blocking methods and faking techniques. Ultimately I began to see what the Colonel meant when, albeit without malice, he classified the pros as mere showmen.

The work a collegiate coaching staff puts into football is staggering. Blaik himself hasn't taken a vacation in nine years. Day after day around the calendar, Sundays and holidays often included, he is at work either in the football office or out on the Plains where the cadets practice.

He is not unique among college coaches. Frank Leahy of Notre Dame, Bennie Oosterbaan of Michigan, Bob Neyland of Tennessee, Dutch Meyer of Texas Christian, Lynn Waldorf of California, Bud Wilkinson of Oklahoma and many others apply enough fanatical devotion to their profession to make them millionaires in a more rewarding field. To beat their teams you have to match them in staff work as well as man power.

The Army football office occupies a whole floor in the east tower of the West Point gymnasium. It has cubicles for assistants and scouts, a conference room, a projection room and filing space for hundreds of movie reels and scouting reports on every team and every player Army is scheduled to, or conceivably may, play against.

Blaik's office, a square room in the front of the tower, is dominated by a huge photographic blow-up of General Douglas MacArthur, the Colonel's personal hero. There is also a composite chart of the schedules of all impending Army opponents, leather chairs, a sofa and ash trays strategically aligned for visitors. The Colonel doesn't smoke.

In this room, with occasional shifts to the movie room or practice field, I made Blaik the slightly unwilling victim of an inquisition on pro football.

Do you actually believe, Colonel, that a good pro team could not beat a good college team?

"Wait a minute! I don't say that. I think a good pro team might get itself up to beat a good college team in a single game. But if the pro team were put into a league with good college teams—like Notre Dame, Michigan, Ohio State, Oklahoma, Southern California, Tennessee and Texas (we'll leave West Point out of this)—it would have to learn to play football the way the colleges do or it wouldn't stand a chance. A fiery team like Tennessee would cripple a pro club."

Don't you think the professionals have better man power?

"I do not. Football is a Spartan game in which youth, spirit and condition count heavily. The colleges have the boys in their best years. Few of them ever play as well after they become professionals.

"As they grow older they acquire responsibilities and perspective, also caution. They lose the reckless abandon that marked their play in college. They get bigger and fatter. They may look imposing to the fans, but they are not the same football players. I know, and other college coaches know, that an active, enthusiastic young fellow of 190 pounds can do everything better than an old pro who weighs two-fifty or -sixty."

When Colonel Blaik is thinking things out, he has a habit of whirling his reading glasses round and round by the bows. He whirled them fiercely, as he continued:

"What happens to the leading college players who go into pro football? They take their places in the front line immediately and without exception. They become stars at once. In fact, some who don't quite make it in college become the keymen of their professional clubs. Perhaps they are the best men the pros get because they're still a little hungry.

"Look at George Ratterman (New York Yanks quarterback), for instance. He's a top professional player but he never was better than second string at Notre Dame."

But you say you like to see professional games?

"That's true, and I like to take the Army squad to see them. The players have great individual skills, and a college boy—particularly a quarterback—can learn a lot about playing his position by watching the pros. Take Frankie Albert of the San Francisco 49ers. He's adept at carrying out the fakes which help set up a pass. He holds the defense in place by simulating hand-offs to his backs. He fakes in one direction and passes in another.

"But he didn't learn that in pro football. He had it all when he played for Stanford."

Have you had any players who have benefited from watching the pros?

"Yes, several of them. For instance, Arnold Tucker, who played quarterback here with Blanchard and Davis; and Dan Foldberg, offensive end and captain of our present team. Foldberg got a lot out of watching those Cleveland ends (Speedie and Lavelli). From them he has learned new ways of getting loose to receive passes, how to change direction and pace, how to make the final fast cut which shakes off the defense."

If the pros have such able individuals, why can't they make them into superior football teams?

"There are lots of reasons. One is, they don't work at it. Their main objects are to get hold of the good college players after they are graduated and to get crowds into their ball parks. Everyone connected with a pro club participates in the ballyhoo. Everyone scouts players. They only work on the development of a team for a couple of months in the fall.

"After their preseason work they don't scrimmage, and you can't have a football team unless you go through your repertory over and over again under game conditions.

"Here at West Point we have about 20 basic offensive plays, with variations. In addition we have other plays devised to capitalize special weaknesses or to run against special defenses.

"In spring practice we scrimmage the basic plays more than a hundred times apiece. When the squad turns out in the fall we have to start over, the players are rusty. So we scrimmage the plays a hundred more times or so. Throughout the season we continue to use contact work to keep the players sharp.

"You don't develop good teeth by eating mush. You don't keep a blocker sharp by giving him theory and letting him go through the motions in dummy.

"I don't know whether it would be good sense for the pros to work on plays as we do. When you scrimmage you always run the risk of getting someone hurt and the pros can't afford to have the players the public wants to see on the bench.

"In addition, it may not be feasible to train pros as we train undergraduates. It's an old story to them. They probably don't have the enthusiasm for cracking skulls that you find in young fellows who haven't been overfed on football."

The Colonel whirled his glasses intensely.

"You know, even in college, players sometimes get on the downgrade in their last year. Take Red Cagle. He played here at West Point after four years at Southwestern Louisiana Institute. He was best as a yearling (sophomore). After that his performance was definitely not so good. As a pro he never came close to his early West Point form."

Colonel Blaik came to West Point from Dartmouth where he made a phenomenal record, once going through 22 consecutive games without a defeat. Looking for a better comparison between the potentialities of fiery youth and sated experience, he went back to that era.

"You remember the game between Dartmouth and Cornell in 1940. That was the time the referee made a mistake and gave Cornell five downs at the very end. On the last play of the game Cornell scored on a pass. This made it 7 to 3, but later, after conclusive evidence that the referee had made an error had been produced, Cornell ceded the game to Dartmouth; the score in the record book is Dartmouth 3, Cornell 0. Bob Krieger had kicked a field goal for Dartmouth early in the fourth period.

"What I'm trying to illustrate is that Dartmouth, a young team, beat Cornell, a veteran team, which hadn't lost in two years, strictly on youthful fire and emotional uplift. Our team hadn't any business finishing within 40 points of Cornell."

The accent on youth, the emphasis on strategy, the constant effort to build from the ground are themes from the Colonel's own career. After four years of football at Miami University, Oxford, Ohio, he played his fifth and last year at West Point. He served three years in the cavalry after graduating from the Military Academy with the two-year class of 1920, then resigned and, with his father, went into the house-building business in Dayton, Ohio, his home town.

Blaik didn't decide to become a full-time professional coach until 1934. After years of seasonal assistant coaching at West Point, Ernest Martin Hopkins, president of Dartmouth, persuaded him to come to the Indian campus that year and redeem a hopeless situation. He did that, then moved back to Army as head coach in 1941 to undertake the same kind of job.

Having built up two football teams to formidable status through extraordinary resource and application, he's a little impatient with those who think—as the pros seems to—that football coaching is not a full-time job. As a fifty-two-year-old 190-pounder who can still get into the uniform he wore as a second lieutenant, he's a little intolerant of players who handicap themselves by lugging around excess avoirdupois.

"All the pro teams are full of big fat men, some of them 40 pounds over their most efficient playing weight. I know for certain that a man who wears a rubber tire can't play football with one who is down to hard condition, no matter what the big man's weight advantage may be. The fat man is useless in the attack and he can't move laterally on the defense. He's useful only if the ball carrier runs straight into him.

"What do you find in professional football?" The Colonel pointed an accusing finger at me and went on to answer his own question.

"You find that the average defensive lineman covers the spot he's assigned to and doesn't do one thing more. He thinks he's done his job if he stops all the plays directed at him. He doesn't chase a runner who goes in the opposite direction. Here, let me show you something."

He led us into the movie room and put on a reel of the 1950 practice game between Army and Boston University. He fiddled with the projector, then found what he wanted.

"Watch this," the Colonel said. "This will show you what I think defensive men should do.

"See, Boston has the ball. There's the runner, going around our left end. See, our end is knocked down. The runner is around him. But watch now."

For a second the BU halfback seemed to have a clear path, then from every angle Army players started arriving. The runner was deluged by tacklers just as he turned the corner to go downfield. Even the end who had been knocked down scrambled up and got a hand on him. When the whistle blew, only two Army players were on their feet. The rest, nine of them, were in on the tackle.

"That's pursuit," said Colonel Blaik, shutting off the machine. "The pros don't have it. Sometime they make a good first effort but they don't go through with the job. That's why Steve Van Buren of the Philadelphia Eagles and Charley Trippi of the Chicago Cardinals make so many long runs without any discernible downfield blocking. Nobody chases them. They get by the defenders in a certain sector and they're gone.

"Downfield blocking? The pros don't have that either. The pro lineman may carry out his primary block but he isn't going to chase 50 yards down the field all afternoon to hit the safety man. His nature rebels against it. It takes a young man with untarnished spirit to do that."

You'll admit, Colonel, the pros are wonderful with the forward pass.

"I'll agree with you that they have great passers and great receivers, but I do not concede that an uninterrupted succession of passes is football.

"Recently I saw a pro game in which one team threw 47 passes. Think of it! Forty-seven!

"What did the defensive linemen do when the opposition was throwing 47 passes? They stood there and looked at the ball. Rushing the passer is grueling work. It requires a great outlay of speed, strength, energy and determination. A man must drive himself if he is going to try to break through on every pass play. So the pros stand on the line of scrimmage and hope some secondary-defense man will knock the pass down.

"Now, if you don't rush the passer he will complete a large percentage of his throws. That's why you have such big scores in professional football. By using the pass as the principal weapon and by failing to put pressure on the passer, the pros have cheapened the touchdown and damaged their game, at least for some of us."

Couldn't it be said that Notre Dame, Army, Oklahoma and some of the other powerful college teams have cheapened the game by scoring so frequently?

"Perhaps that's right. But at any rate we don't trade touchdowns every few minutes. And we play balanced football by co-ordinating passing and running.

"The pros have practically given up the running attack. Clark Shaughnessy, who used to coach the Los Angeles Rams, had his team at Bear Mountain (nine miles from West Point) for a week last fall and he and I had several talks. He told me it's useless to run against a pro team because the defensive line is so strong. 'The men are too big,' he said.

"I couldn't let that pass. 'Now wait a minute, Clark. If the pros are so good on the defense they must have something on the offense. Do you mean to tell me your 230-pound guard can't move the other fellow's 230-pound guard at least part of the time?'

"The truth is, the pros won't pay the price to develop a running attack. After their preseason training they don't scrimmage, and I've already told you what my experience has been in the development of running plays. You soften the rugged daily schedule and the plays don't work. The blocking goes off; the timing goes off.

"Some people may argue that certain pro clubs do have a running attack—that the Philadelphia Eagles have one. I say that Steve Van Buren is a great runner and that he is helped enormously by the fact that the defensive men he plays against don't pursue."

Did the Colonel ever see a professional team with a real running attack?

"Yes, one. That was Pittsburgh when it was coached by the late Jock Sutherland. He had a bunch of castoffs from the other National League clubs and he turned them into a football team with a balanced attack in which the forward pass held its proper place.

"How did he do it? The way we do it in college football. He scrimmaged his team throughout the season. He kept the blocking and timing sharp. He wasn't teaching typical professional football. He was teaching college football, the same kind he taught during his years at the University of Pittsburgh. The old pros on his team may have hated him, but he kept them at it by the force of his personality, and he darned near won the championship even though he had inferior man power."

The Colonel was drawing diagrams on his desk pad, describing with X's and O's the single-wing formation which the late Sutherland made famous and which he himself used to teach before he turned to the T.

"It's silly for Clark Shaughnessy to tell me it's impossible to run against a pro defense," he continued. "I've seen it done. A year ago Herman Hickman put together a little All-Star team recruited entirely from graduates of Eastern colleges. It practiced less than three weeks, then played the professional New York Giants and ran all over them.

"Herman did a fine coaching job, but he didn't have much in the way of man power and I'm certain his outfit wouldn't have stayed close to any first-class college team. Yet he humiliated the Giants, who had practiced two months in preparation. How do you account for it?

"My answer is that Herman's team was full of spirit and determination—the things which make the college game what it is. Wanting to win, the boys worked in-tensely hard in practice. When they went on the field they were in condition and they were emotionally ready. The Giants were not."

The Colonel's contention was given additional support last August when the College All-Star football team, coached by Dr. Eddie Anderson, of Iowa and Holy Cross, gave the champion Philadelphia Eagles a severe drubbing at Soldier Field in Chicago.

The score, 17 to 7, does not fully indicate the superiority of the college team. Two or three more All-Star touchdowns barely missed fire. Once Charlie Justice of North Carolina, the running star of the game, was barely nipped by the heels en route to an apparent touchdown. Again, a sure-fire pass was dropped.

The college team was trained at Delafield, Wisconsin, far from the bright lights. It attained good physical condition and high morale. Once it directed its two-platoon power at the Eagles, it was all over. The pros were badly licked, and apparently exhausted when they went off the field at the half.

The two men who carried the burden of offense for the collegians were little fellows. Justice weighs a bare 170 pounds, and Eddie LeBaron, the offensive quarterback who ran the team and did the passing, is 10 pounds lighter. The All-Stars' savage 5-4-2 defense smothered Steve Van Buren, widely considered the greatest runner in professional football.

In summing up his ideas, the Colonel said, "I suppose I sound pretty critical. However, I go to the pro game and I take my squad whenever I can. It's good entertainment, and isn't that what it's supposed to be?"

I thought back to that roaring tie between the Cleveland Browns and the New York Yankees. Yes, I had been entertained.

But was it football?

Since 1979, Paul Zimmerman has been the senior writer for professional football for *Sports Illustrated,* and perhaps one of the most widely read writers on the sport. He played tackle himself for Stanford and Columbia, it is told, wrote earlier for the sports section of the *New York Post,* and he does indeed know the game. Zimmerman penned *The Thinking Man's Guide to Pro Football* in the 1980s, one of the most enjoyed books ever written on the sport, then revised and updated it. From that latter tome, this chapter, dealing with the wonderfully weird, the zanies, the otherwise outrageous, who have participated in the pro experience in their own unique ways, has been gratefully elicited.

A Gallery of Ruffians, Flakes and Oddballs

PAUL ZIMMERMAN

BEST OF ALL, I like the flakes, the loonies, the zanies . . . the throwbacks to a simpler era.

I felt very bad when Jack Rudnay retired after the 1982 season. Rudnay was Old World. He played center for the Chiefs for 13 years. He played with broken fingers and chipped vertebrae and torn muscles. He didn't have much use for people who hadn't paid their dues. Tom Keating, the Raiders' defensive tackle, finished his career with K.C. and he tells this story about Rudnay.

"It was 1974, the strike year. Rudnay was the leader of the strike faction, the pickets. The rookies were working out in camp. One day we read a quote by David Jaynes, the rookie quarterback, the number three draft. He said, 'I can lead this team to victory.' Rudnay just smiled. 'We'll see about that,' he said.

"Now the strike is over, we're back in for our first workout. Rudnay's the center, Jaynes has been the quarterback in camp so he's the first one to take snaps. Hank Stram's up in the tower. In the locker room Rudnay had taken a scissors and cut the crotch out of his football pants. Everything hangs out.

"Rudnay's over the ball. Jaynes looks left, looks right, just like he's been taught. He calls his signals . . . 'Brown right, X left, ready, set . . .' and he reaches down for the ball . . . whooo! The ball goes flying.

"Stram yells, 'What's going on down there?'

" 'He won't take the snap, coach,' Rudnay says.

" 'Let's get another quarterback in there,' says Hank, and that's the beginning of the end of David Jaynes."

Bill Bain is a mournful looking 300-pound tackle for the Rams. He'd bounced around the league for five years before L.A. picked him up, cut him once and then re-signed him.

"I love training camp," he once said, "because that's the only time of the season I get to play."

Last year Irv Pankey, the regular left tackle, tore an Achilles tendon and was through for the season, and Bain was the starter.

"All this means," he said, "is that I make the cut next week. Look, I know they like Irv more than me. I like Irv more than me, too."

One year in camp he decided life wasn't worth living. "Honestly, if I could get a $2 million life insurance policy, I'd hire a hit man to do away with me. We all have to die sometime. I've always loved to sleep, anyway. Why live all your life?''

Special teams is as good a breeding ground as any for flakes. If they didn't start that way, a career of wedge-busting will turn them a bit goofy.

It's October 1982. The NFL players are on strike. Redskin fullback John Riggins has just played two games in two days, the NFLPA All-Star games, and now it was late, and as the car carrying him back to his hotel after game number two was creeping through the deserted streets of Los Angeles, Riggins was suddenly aware that a very small and very crazy person sitting next to him in the back seat was digging him in the ribs with his elbow.

"Shot for shot, waddya say?'' said 5'9" Louie Giammona, who'd spent eight years on the Jets' and Eagles' special teams.

"What?'' Riggins said.

"I'll trade you shot for shot, you hit me, I hit you, waddya say?''

"Louie,'' Riggins said, "this is not the way to win my friendship.''

"OK, then you hit me, hit me!'' Louie said, bouncing up and down in the seat. "I don't mind. I love it.''

"Well, Louie, I'll tell you what we'll do,'' Riggins said, brushing away the sleep for a moment. "When we get back to the hotel room, we'll tape your ankles together, and hang you from the ceiling upside down. Then we'll take turns using you for a heavy bag—if that's what you really want.''

Riggins was the leader of an active little band of zanies on the Jets, before he went to Washington. There was Steve Tannen, the cornerback who wrote poetry, and Lou Piccone, the lowest-paid player in football one year, and Mike Adamle, who'd stand in the locker room slapping Piccone in the face—and vice-versa—before they took the field for special teams duty. When Adamle was traded to Chicago he said, "Football's like that. It's like *Let's Make a Deal*, the idiot's game. Pete Rozelle is Monty Hall, a guy comes in dressed like a radish and a deal is made.''

But Riggins was the king. I remember phoning him at his home in Centralia, Kan., the day he was drafted in 1971. "What was your number one sports thrill?'' I asked. It was late in the day and I was tired.

"Watching the neighbor's pigs being born,'' he said.

Two years later he was a holdout in camp. He grew a Mohawk haircut. He finally signed his contract four days before the season opener.

"Damnedest sight you ever saw,'' Weeb Ewbank said. "He signed that contract sitting at the desk in my office. He had that Mohawk haircut, and he was stripped to the waist and he was wearing leather pants and a

derby hat with a feather in it. It must have been what the sale of Manhattan Island looked like.''

"Sports to me,'' Riggins says, "was always fun. The real me was kind of a jerk . . . kick the basketball around, run around the court trying to pull a guy's pants down, throw the ball at a guy's head and yell 'Catch!' hang around the back of the huddle and chitchat, cause distractions, get my share of belly laughs . . . I'm still that way.

"Don't forget that I'm from Kansas, and Kansas has a rich tradition of outlaws . . . the Younger Brothers, Quantrill's Raiders, Bonnie and Clyde. Meade, Kansas, was the Dalton Gang's hideout, and there are still a lot of flourishing Jesse James fan clubs in the state. I went out for athletics because in Centralia there were three types of kids: the big, fat sissies, the guys with the ducktail haircuts and black leather jackets, and the athletes. My hair was too curly for a ducktail, so I had to go with sports. If I'd had straight hair I might be in prison today.''

Tannen is an actor in L.A. now.

"You know what killed me?'' he said the day after Riggins was named MVP for Super Bowl XVII. "Watching Mike Adamle interviewing Jack Kent Cooke on TV after the game and asking him, 'Is Riggins as crazy now as he was then?' Crazy? With the Jets Adamle used to take off all his clothes on flights back from games and sit there in his underwear. 'Why, Mike?' I'd ask him. 'More comfortable,' he'd say.

The old AFL had more than its share of characters, but one of the most memorable was Larry Eisenhauer, the defensive end for the Patriots. Larry's father, old Dutch, a crew-cut 275-pounder who once upon a time raised hell for the Long Island Aggies in Farmingdale, used to accompany the Patriots on their trips. When the Patriots played San Diego they'd stay at a place called the Stardust Motel. The big feature of the Stardust was the Mermaid Bar, where you'd sip your drink and watch four young water ballerinas performing in front of you in a glass pool. One hot night Larry's dad felt like a swim.

"Where's the pool, Larry?'' old Dutch said, and of course Larry steered him over to the Mermaid.

"Never saw anything like it,'' a writer said. "I was having a drink and all of a sudden this goddam whale in a blue woolen swim suit was swimming right at me.''

"How was your swim, dad?'' Eisenhauer wanted to know after Dutch got through with his show.

"OK, Larry, but I had this strange feeling that there were a whole lot of eyes on me.''

One afternoon a Charger PR man stopped by and handed the Boston players a bunch of Charley Charger coloring books. The Patriots took them over to poolside, and the rumor that night was that Eisenhauer had spent the rest of his day coloring his Charley Charger book.

"It's a goddam lie," he said later. "I wasn't coloring the thing. I was just reading it."

Before games Eisenhauer was one of the noted dressing room maniacs. He'd attack walls, lockers, anything that got in his way. On the field he played with a wild intensity seldom seen today. Boston used to have a daytime kiddie show in those days call *Boom Town*, featuring Rex Trailer and his sidekick, Pablo. One day they decided to film a show at Fenway Park, and the action would center around the Patriots football team. Pablo would grab the ball and run for a TD, with all the Patriots chasing him. Eisenhauer was picked to be one of the chasers.

Once the action started, though, a hidden bell clanged and all the 6'5", 250-pounder saw was an enemy player running for a touchdown, a guy who had to be stopped. So he stopped him.

"I'm kind of ashamed of it now," he said later. "Pablo was only about 5'3", and he was slow, so it wasn't any trick catching him. I didn't really hurt him. I just sort of jumped on his back. But what the hell? Why give the guy a free touchdown?"

Not that the AFL had a monopoly on characters. The NFL in those days had people like Alex Karras and Artie Donovan and Alex Hawkins, who used to tell people, "I went to high school in Charlestown, West Virginia, and I'd get myself ready for the big game by playing solitaire, having a chew of tobacco and listening to Webb Pierce sing, 'I'm in the jailhouse now.' "

And, of course, there was Joe Don Looney.

By the time Joe Don got to the University of Oklahoma he had logged time at Texas, TCU, and Cameron JC in Lawton, Okla. He had been kicked off the team at Oklahoma for slugging a student assistant coach, and then came the pinball trip through the pros—New York to Baltimore to Detroit to Washington to the Army to New Orleans, all within six years.

Before his senior year at Oklahoma, he had spent a summer in a Baton Rouge, La., health studio. He was 6'1", 224, when he left. He could run the hundred in 9.8, lift 290 pounds in a military press, 450 in a squat. He drank a gallon of milk a day and swallowed 20 different kinds of protein pills.

"Have you considered his attitude?" someone asked Wellington Mara after the Giants drafted him number one in December 1963. "I have considered those shoulders, those legs, and those 224 pounds," Mara said.

He lasted with the Giants for 28 days. People remember him punching and flailing at Allie Sherman's recoil-blocking dummies. Trainer Sid Morett remembers that Looney wouldn't throw his used socks and jock into a bin so marked because "no damn sign is going to tell me what to do." He wouldn't talk to reporters because "they just get things fouled up," and when publicist

Don Smith pushed a note under his door, Looney pushed it back out. "And don't you bother me either," he said.

Practices bored him and he preferred playing catch with a nine-year-old boy on the sidelines. In scrimmages he ran the seven-hole when he was supposed to run the five-hole. "Anyone can run where the holes are," he said. "A good football player makes his own holes."

In August he was traded to Baltimore, and after a few workouts the Colt coaches said his attitude was 100 percent improved. He scored a touchdown on a 58-yard run against the Bears and came off the field in tears. Joe Don was ready to blossom.

Then in November he broke down a door and slugged the male member of one of two young married couples cowering in the hallway. It was all a big mix-up, he said at the trial. He and his buddy were looking for the apartment of some nurses, and besides that, he was pretty upset because Barry Goldwater had gotten beaten so badly in the presidential election.

And when Looney's lawyer, William D. MacMillan, suggested probation before the verdict, he gave the world a definitive appraisal of his man: "This verdict would keep the one couple from having a feeling that Looney might develop a 'persecution complex' over the matter, and the other couple would not have a future fear of Looney retaliating against them."

A week later Looney jumped into the ring during a tag-team wrestling bout involving Red Berry and Bruno Sammartino in the Civic Center and helped quell what he figured was a riot. Promoter Phil Zacko thanked Joe Don for protecting his wrestlers. "He should be commended," the promoter said.

Baltimore coach Don Shula couldn't see it that way, and before the next camp opened, Looney was gone— traded to Detroit for Dennis Gaubatz. And while the Lions' coach, Harry Gilmer, was explaining, "I believe that with his rookie year behind him, things will straighten out. I don't believe he will be a problem," the Colts were relating a few Looney stories they had held back until then.

There was, for instance, the time he cut out of a party carrying a blanket. "Where are you going?" someone asked him. "I'm going to sleep in the cemetery," he said. "It's nice and peaceful there."

Next morning a teammate asked him how it was. "I had a good talk with a guy about death down there," Joe Don said.

There were the stories that John Unitas told—about the time Joe Don asked someone to "watch my cheeseburger for me," while a team meeting was going on; about the time the team was gathered in the locker room for the pregame prayer, and someone heard a noise in the equipment room, and there was Looney, listening to the radio and doing the Mashed Potato all by himself;

and the night Shula dispatched his troubleshooter on the team, Hawkins, to baby-sit Joe Don.

"I watched him pace up and down the apartment," Hawkins said. "I listened to him rant and rave. I heard of his grand scheme to buy an island near New Guinea, buy a boat, get some girls and some Texas buddies and go down there and breed a new race. Joe eventually went to sleep. I didn't dare close my eyes."

When Joe Don got to Detroit, Gilmer rubbed his hands and said that the Lions' running attack would center around Looney. The Detroit publicity department predicted that Joe Don could be the first 1000-yard runner in the team's history. But Looney's first real headlines in Detroit involved a fight in the parking lot of the Golden Griddle Pancake House in Royal Oak. There was something about a tab for $3.28 and a misunderstanding over who should pay it, and the scene finally ended with Looney trying to smash a beer bottle and use the jagged end, just like people did in the movies, only the bottle wouldn't break.

Then there were problems with his back, and finally, in one September game in 1966, Gilmer told Looney to carry a message in to quarterback Milt Plum. "If you want a messenger," Joe Don told the coach, "call Western Union." That ended his career in Detroit. Next stop, the Redskins.

"We're walking down Washington Boulevard in Detroit the day after Joe Don got traded by the Lions," said Bob Tate, a Detroit bartender and a friend of Looney's, "and Joe looks up and says, 'You know, Tate, I sure am glad I'm not a building.'

" 'Yeah, Joe,' I said, 'it would be awful hard on you moving from town to town.' "

In Washington he achieved instant stature. He scored a touchdown in his first game ("it was a twin-two-sweep-trap . . . that means as much to me as it does to you"), Coach Otto Graham said he was finally shaping up, the headlines involved the "new" Looney, and the honeymoon lasted right up until he announced he was playing out his option because of a salary squabble.

He wound up in the army for a year, and finally New Orleans picked him up as a free agent. He packed up his mastiff hound, which he had loaded down with barbells ("to build up the dog's leg muscles") and almost converted into a health food addict with a sunflower seed and wheat germ oil diet, and headed south. The last report on the dog was that he had made a raid on a nearby henhouse.

"I might have known," sighed Doug Atkins, the Saints' giant defensive end. "The minute the kid straightens out, the dog goes bad."

He lasted a year with the Saints. He traveled around the world: Hawaii, Hong Kong, Peru. He became a hippie . . . "Long hair, beard, sandals, beads, the whole nine yards," Hawkins says. He met a guru, Swami Muktananda, Baba to his friends, followed him to India, trimmed his weight to 150 pounds, and worked as a common laborer and keeper of the swami's elephant. He shoveled elephant droppings; "Chief of Compost" was the way he described his job. He wrote to a friend and said he had set a world record in the shoveling event, 12 wheelbarrow loads in one hour and 10 minutes, bettering the old mark by two minutes. When Baba died in November 1982, Joe Don came back to Texas and joined Baba's successors, a brother-sister team.

"I might add," Hawkins says, "the sister is not short on looks."

In a story syndicated by News Group Publications, Inc., last year, Hawkins wrote that at last sight, Joe Don, 40 years old now and 195 pounds, had found inner peace through Siddha Meditation and Siddha Yoga. "He has found the answers, he says," Hawkins wrote. "I hope he has, because if he hasn't, you ain't heard the last of Joe Don Looney yet."

In pro football's infant days there were plenty of gamblers and drinkers and roughnecks, but these were mostly poor men, and if not for football they'd be loading trucks and hauling freight and plowing rocky little patches of ground in country towns.

"Jug Earp, Mike Michalske, Cal Hubbard," the Green Bay druggist, John Holzer, once said. "They played their hearts out for $35 or $50 a game. They had a fierce desire, an almost animal desire for contact."

"I remember one time when Bronko Nagurski was horsing around in a second-floor hotel room with a teammate," old referee Ronnie Gibbs said, "and Bronko fell out of the window. A crowd gathered and a policeman came up and said, 'What happened?'

" 'I don't know,' said Nagurski. 'I just got here myself.' "

George Halas used to tell the story about a 1933 Bear game in which Nagurski knocked out Philly linebacker John Bull Lipski.

"Bull had great recuperative powers, and he came back in the game and tried to tackle Bronko again, and he was rendered unconscious again. Two of the Philadelphia substitutes came off the bench and started to drag Bull off the field. Bull came to near the sidelines and started muttering something about getting back in there.

"But play had already resumed, and the Bears were headed in his direction on a sweep with Nagurski leading the interference. Bronko overtook Lipski and the two subs about five yards from the sidelines, and *WHAM*, he threw a block that sent all three of them flying into the Eagles' bench.

"Poor Lipski was knocked out for the third time, a record that should stand until another Nagurski comes along, if one ever does."

When some of these old-timers became coaches, they evaluated their talent in an elemental way. They set their linemen on each other, one-on-one. The guy who survived was the first stringer. The Giants' old coach Steve Owen was saved from the Oklahoma dust bowl by football and he never forgot it. He lived by two mottos: "Football is a game played down in the dirt and always will be" and "Football was invented by a mean son of a bitch, and that's the way the game's supposed to be played."

In 1924, Steve tried out for the Kansas City Cowboys in Old Blues Park, along with a character named Milt Rhenquist of Bethany, Kan.

"The Swede was dressed in overalls and work shoes," Owen wrote in *My Kind of Football*. "He weighed about 240 and had heavily calloused hands. The Swede in scrimmage battered one-half of our regular line. He wasn't scientific, just effective."

They used to say that the Steelers' Ernie Stautner, who played defensive tackle at 230 pounds, could have been transported 40 years back into time, pound by pound, and he would have fit right in with the leather-helmet boys. Ernie knew one move, the straight all-out shot, dead on his man, with every sinew and nerve dedicated to that one killing charge.

Once in camp a rookie lineman challenged him to a fight, so Ernie, a trifle mystified, but no less vicious, beat hell out of the youngster.

"Some damn fool college coach told that kid," Ernie said, "that the best way to make a pro team was to lick the toughest veteran they had. He got some bad information there."

The ruffians of football came in all packages, from the wildly flamboyant Eisenhauer to the cold, tight-lipped Dan Birdwell, ex-defensive tackle of the Oakland Raiders.

"I've got bruises all over my body from bumping into Dan around the kitchen," his wife, Diane, said. "Or taking a gouge from him while he's asleep. He won't even play with our three children for fear of injuring them."

The toughest running back in those old AFL days was Buffalo's 250-pound Cookie Gilchrist.

"The oddest thing about him," said Jet linebacker Larry Grantham, who'd been his teammate in the AFL All-Star game, "was that he would strip and shower at halftime."

"How did he get his pads back on in time for the second half?" someone asked Grantham.

"Pads? Cookie didn't need pads. Just a helmet and enough bennies to fill the palm of one hand."

Collectively the biggest group of flakes ever piled into one roster belonged to the Oakland Raiders. In their old AFL days they had some mean dudes but they weren't the real bullyboys of the league. That honor belonged to Kansas City, with a lineup of towering monsters who liked to grind people into the dust. The Raiders had their share of roughnecks, though—Ben Davidson, Birdwell and Ike Lassiter along the defensive line; and at fullback, Hewritt Dixon, Hughie the Freight, whose running style was to bludgeon prospective tacklers with a forearm. In 1971 they drafted a safetyman from Ohio State, Jack Tatum, reputed to be the hardest hitter in college football, and teamed him with George Atkinson, who'd been converted from a fairly mild-mannered cornerback into a vicious little strong safety.

Raider history is a dark tableau of violence—Davidson breaking Joe Namath's cheekbone with a roundhouse right that began somewhere between Hayward and Alameda, Atkinson clubbing Lynn Swann unconscious with a blow to the back of the head, the collision between Tatum and Darryl Stingley that left Stingley paralyzed for life, an incident underscored by the fact that Tatum showed absolutely no remorse thereafter.

"They're not really bad fellas," Kansas City coach Paul Wiggin said. "They're just trained to kill."

When they made it to the '77 Super Bowl, though, and came under scrutiny of the press, another element surfaced. Mixed in with the hard guys were some genuine eccentrics, some characters Damon Runyan would be proud of . . . Blinky and Tooz and Matzoh Ball and the Commissioner and the Scientist and Kick 'em in the Head Ted.

The Scientist was George Buehler, the 270-pound right guard. His specialty was electronic gadgetry. He had a little remote-controlled tank that would pick up his mail for him in camp. One day in practice he was flying his remote-controlled model plane around the field and it crashed into the goal post.

"I lost radio contact," he explained.

Training camp was in Santa Rosa, the only camp that players actually enjoyed going to. John Madden ran a loose ship. One day 16 of them walked off in the middle of practice. They had a golf tournament to go to. Another afternoon a rookie spotted all the defensive backs heading for the sidelines.

"Where are you going?" he asked.

"On our field trip," one of them said, and they walked through the gate and lay down in an adjoining field.

Blinky was flanker Fred Biletnikoff. On the road he roomed with Pete Banaszak, a halfback.

"Before every game," Banaszak said, "Blinky'd say he had to visit his friend Earl in the bathroom. Earl was the sound of Freddy throwing up."

Once, during a game, the referee called time out and walked Henry Lawrence, the offensive tackle, off the field.

"Why'd you do that?" Madden asked.

"Because he's goofy," the ref said.

"I know that," Madden said. "So what?"

One year the Raiders drafted a 6′9″ defensive end named Charlie Philyaw because he'd looked good in the Senior Bowl practices. I remember interviewing Charlie in Mobile before that game.

"I'm glad they picked me to play here," he said. "I've never played in this game before."

Sometimes in camp Charlie would drift into the wrong meeting room. Once he sat in the offensive room for 15 minutes before someone told him he was in the wrong place. Meanwhile the defensive line coach, Tom Dahms, was carrying on quite well without him.

"Charlie's missing," someone told him.

"Good," said Dahms.

"All my life," said Pat Toomay, the defensive end who bounced around from Dallas to New England to Tampa Bay before Oakland picked him up, "I knew that somewhere in the league there must be a club like this. I just didn't know where it was."

The Raiders became a haven for outcasts. Having trouble? See Al Davis. They picked up Ted Hendricks from Green Bay in '75, Kick 'em in the Head Ted. He fit right in. One day in camp Madden called, "OK, everybody up," and Hendricks came charging onto the field on a horse, in full uniform, with a traffic cone for a lance. Once, on Halloween, he showed up with a hollowed-out pumpkin for a helmet. When everybody started lifting weights he made his own barbell, two empty drums attached to a bar, great mass but no weight. He called it the Hurricane Machine.

"How can you stand it?" Madden asked Hendricks's wife, Jane, one day.

"I'm into bird watching," she said.

Then the Raiders picked up John Matuszak, and that made the act complete. The 6′8″ defensive end had been with three NFL teams and one in the WFL, briefly. A court order kept him out of the WFL after he jumped—and played in one game. At the hearing the Houston Oilers' lawyer, Bill Eckhardt, asked him if he could have signed with the Canadian League, rather than the Oilers, when he was drafted.

"No," Matuszak said.

"Why?"

"Because it's not my country. I love my country, as the land of the free and the home of the brave."

Before camp opened in '74, Tooz invited linebacker Steve Kiner to his apartment for dinner. Talk soon turned to the players' strike.

"I'm staying out," Matuszak said. "You're with us, aren't you?"

Kiner stopped between bites to answer, "No, I'm going to report."

With that Tooz reached across the table and picked up Kiner's plate. End of dinner.

He was violent and erratic and subject to abrupt mood switches. The only one who could control him was his wife, Yvette, who was as tightly wired as he was. When he joined the Chiefs in '74 Tooz snuck Yvette into the dorm at training camp. That was their honeymoon.

"You'd go down to the bathroom in the morning," Rudnay said, "and there were three commodes. In the outer two you'd see football players' feet, big, flat calloused feet. In the middle one there would be this pair of little, dainty feet in sandals. And outside the door Toozie would be standing guard.

"One night Toozie and I were walking back from the dining hall and he said, 'Better be careful. Yvette's on the warpath tonight.' No sooner has he said it but this car comes roaring up, with the headlights blinding us. Toozie yells, 'Run for it!' and we take off across a field, and she pulls off the road, and she's bearing down on us, and he says, 'This way . . . the cemetery.' So we make it to the cemetery, and she's madder than hell because she can't follow us, through all the tombstones, and she leans out the window and yells at him, 'You big pussy!' and he's laughing like hell and giving her the finger, and she's giving him the finger back. . . ."

"The last time I saw Yvette," Jane Hendricks says, "she was going down Union Street in San Francisco on roller skates, in a miniskirt, waving to all the people she passed."

In '76 the George Allen Redskins picked up Matuszak and then cut him in camp. It was unusual for George to cut a veteran defensive lineman. The writers asked him why. "Vodka and Valium," he said. "The breakfast of champions."

So the Raiders picked him up. Before they did Al Davis asked Hendricks if it was worth the gamble.

"Al," Hendricks said, "what difference will one more make?"

Since then the Raiders have added new ones, of course. In 1980 they drafted a 255-pound tackle named Matt Millen and made him an inside linebacker. When Millen was in high school he was troubled by calcium deposits in his right elbow that bent his arm into an L shape. He and his buddy went down to the metal shop and put his elbow in a vice and tried to straighten it.

"Ed grabbed my shoulder and pulled," Millen says. "It was straight out of the Three Stooges . . . Drs. Fine and Howard. But it only traumatized my elbow worse."

In '82 they traded for Lyle Alzado, the flamboyant defensive end who once spent a summer working as a garbage collector in Long Island.

"What was your major in college?" a writer asked him at a pre–Super Bowl press conference when he was with the Broncos.

"Garbiology," Alzado said. "I was a garbiologist."

"Oh, you worked out of the science building," the guy said.

"Yeah," said Alzado. "Inwood Sanitation."

Writers once asked him about his school song. He'd gone to Yankton College in South Dakota. What did he do, for instance, when he was a rookie with the Broncos and they made him stand up in the dining hall and sing the Yankton song? Once, when track man John Carlos was a rookie with the Eagles, they got him up to sing his school song, and he sang "Jingle Bells." A few veterans said that's when he first got in bad with the club—for not showing proper spirit. How about Alzado?

"I'll give you 10 bucks if you can sing one line of the Yankton song, if anyone can," he said. "Listen to this:

Hail Yankton College,
Center of the continent and yooooon-i-verse,
We're the Black and the Gold, fight! fight! fight!
Fight for the Black and Gold. . . .

"Pretty good, huh? I made it up myself, but the guys in the dining room didn't know that. They'd listen for a while, and then they'd throw rolls and tell me to sit down."

When the Raiders met the Cowboys in their 1983 big midseason battle, everyone saw it as a clear clash of ideologies.

"I like our image much better than the Dallas Cowboys' image," Millen said, "because ours is much more appealing to the general public—especially the degenerates."

"It's really a fork in the road," the Cowboys' Drew Pearson said. "You go one way or the other way. There's absolutely no middle ground between these two teams."

Oh, the Cowboys have had their share of flakes through the years. There was Larry Cole and the Zero Club, a group devoted to total inactivity of mind and body. Once, when the Cowboys were playing in St. Louis, Cole's teammates and fellow Zero Club members, Toomay and guard Blaine Nye, decided to drag him down to Harold's Tattoo Parlor and get him tattooed with a plow inscribed with the motto "Born to Raise Wheat," a tribute to his home town of Granite Falls, Minn. The only problem was they couldn't get him out of the bathroom, where he'd fallen asleep. And of course there was Pete Gent, the free-agent wide receiver who wound up writing novels, such as *North Dallas Forty*. Gent enjoyed tweaking Tom Landry.

On one return flight from a game Landry came over to Gent on the plane and said, "Pete, Bob Hayes is hurt; you'll be moving to the other side next week. So be ready."

"You mean," Gent said, "that I'm going to play for Philadelphia?"

Defensive players always have seemed the flakiest. Alex Karras parlayed an NFL career devoted to concerted zaniness into a lucrative acting profession. The story I enjoy hearing him tell the most is the one about his participation in the 1957 Balkan Games in Athens.

"It was open to anyone of Greek or Slavic ancestry, so I signed up and got a free trip out of it," Karras said. "I told them I threw the shot and discus, even though I never tried it in my life. On the boat going over, our coach told me there was no place to throw, but I could practice my form.

"He watched me and then he said, 'Your style is pretty unorthodox. What kind do you use?' I told him, 'Step-over.' I finished last in the shot put with a 32-footer."

Kickers have always been a fine collector's item for flake hunters. One year Garo Yepremian, the little bald-headed kicker, turned down a $10,000 hair transplant offer. "There are already too many Elvis Presley looka-likes," he said.

A writer once asked him where he'd gone to college.

"Bald State," said his New Orleans teammate Barry Bennett.

Once, in Buffalo, Booth Lusteg blew a late field goal that cost the Bills the game. Two fans waited for him in the parking lot and assaulted him. Later the police asked him if he wanted to file a complaint.

"No," Lusteg said. "I deserved it."

Dallas writers were very saddened when Danny Villanueva, the Cowboys' Mexican-American kicker, left after the 1967 season. When he first came to the Cowboys in 1965, he took the regular team psychological exam, and the psychologist reported to club officials that he shouldn't be called Taco, the nickname the Rams had given him. "It saps his confidence," the psychologist explained.

"How about calling him Toro?" said a sportswriter.

"Great," said the psychologist.

Then Villanueva walked over to meet the press.

"Call me Taco," he said.

In 1966 he ran a fake punt 23 yards against the Cards, which started people speculating that perhaps he had been a halfback in college.

"I was a Mexican then, too," said Danny.

When George Blanda set the NFL kicking record, his younger brother, Paul, couldn't understand what all the excitement was about.

"I don't know why everybody's fussing over the records George set," he said. "I've had five fathers-in-law."

Sometimes the coach sets the tone. The old Colts were an incongruous bunch, but as long as they kept winning,

Weeb Ewbank let them go their own way. The country boys used to like to play tricks on their Irish tackle from the Bronx, Artie Donovan. One night at training camp some of them found a dead groundhog, skinned it and buried it under his bed sheets.

"You hillbillies ought to have your mind on football," Artie said when he found it. "Just look at that poor dead fish."

And there was the time the late Gene "Big Daddy" Lipscomb, the Colts' other All-Pro tackle, made his off-season wrestling debut. He scored a pin with his secret hold, a "hammer slam." What, his teammates wanted to know later, was a hammer slam?

"Just squeezin', I guess," said Big Daddy.

"One year Jim Parker had a job selling cemetery lots," Ewbank says. "He kept pestering Big Daddy about them, and finally Big Daddy couldn't stand it any more.

" 'OK,' he said, 'gimme two in the shade.' "

"Old players just seemed to look different," Donovan says. "The Bears especially. Like John Kreamcheck, their defensive tackle. He had hair coming out of his nose, wild, bushy hair coming down over his face, he always needed a shave. Once when we came into Wrigley Field we saw him outside the stadium warming his hands over a garbage can. Weeb said, 'Why, he doesn't look like anything more than a damn derelict. I don't think he looks tough at all.' George Preas, our left guard, said, 'Oh yeah, then you go and play against him.' "

Coaches. The late Norm Van Brocklin once was asked in a magazine interview, "What's your favorite play?"

"*Our Town*," he said, "by Thornton Wilder."

There have been mean players through the years, of course, ferocious hitters. Along with Tatum I'd rate Hardy Brown, a sandy-haired 196-pound linebacker, as the hardest hitter I've ever seen. He had no outstanding attributes as a player except for a knack of popping his right shoulder with killing force and velocity.

"When he hit a guy," said 49er teammate Ed Henke, "it sounded like a rifle going off in the stadium. He missed a lot of tackles, but he just killed 'em when he hit 'em. There were no face guards in those days, and Hardy had a shoulder block that could numb a gorilla. It was a skill nobody could duplicate."

"One year we played against him, when he was with Chicago in the old AAFC," Y. A. Tittle recalls. "We ran a play against him and one of our guys was lying on the ground. Then we ran another play and Hardy stretched another guy. So I called the Bootsie Play—everybody get Hardy Brown. When it was over there were two of our guys lying on the ground. There was a lot of grumbling in our next huddle.

" 'The hell with this,' one guy said. 'Let's go back to the old way. He was only picking us off one at a time then.' "

Sometimes it's just sheer animal instinct that drives them. Mike Curtis, the old Colts' linebacker, was nicknamed the Animal. Even the home fans booed him. Hendricks says he was once standing next to Curtis as they were coming onto the field in Buffalo's old War Memorial Stadium and "a hot dog came out of the stands and hit Mike right on the head, *bonk!* I mean I'd never seen that before. I learned not to stand next to him."

In a game against the Dolphins in Baltimore in 1971 a fan came on the field and grabbed the football as the Dolphins were about to run a play. He had come down from Rochester on a bus and he'd been drinking all the way. Before anyone knew what had happened Curtis was on the guy and had popped him with a forearm that sent him flying one way, the ball the other, and that completely unzipped his jacket.

"Did you see that, did you see those instincts?" Colt center Bill Curry said afterward. "Everybody else was just standing around but Mike reacted purely on instinct. I felt like telling that fan, 'That's what I have to face in practice every day.' "

I remember the week leading up to the 1980 Super Bowl. The Steelers were in a nasty mood. They'd been practicing on a soggy field. Their legs felt sore. One day after practice their middle linebacker, Jack Lambert, sat in the hotel bar, staring darkly into his beer. The teeny-boppers spotted him. They ran over to get his autograph.

"Are you into astrology, Jack?" one of them said.

"Yeah," he grunted.

"What's your sign?"

"Feces," he said.

Index

About the Author

Richard Whittingham is the author of many books, a number of which are about sports, especially pro football. He has also contributed articles to magazines and newspapers on pro football. He has written the now standard *What A Game They Played*, an oral history of pro football in its earliest days through World War II, as well as definitive histories of the Chicago Bears, New York Giants and Dallas Cowboys. He is presently at work on a book about the Washington Redskins.